OSINT TECHNIQUES

RESOURCES FOR UNCOVERING ONLINE INFORMATION

ELEVENTH EDITION

MICHAEL BAZZELL & JASON EDISON

OSINT TECHNIQUES:
RESOURCES FOR UNCOVERING ONLINE INFORMATION
ELEVENTH EDITION

Library of Congress Control Number (LCCN): Application submitted

ISBN: 9798345969250

Revision: 2025.01.02

CONTENTS

ABOUT THE AUTHORS

MICHAEL BAZZELL

Michael Bazzell investigated computer crimes on behalf of the government for over 20 years. During the majority of that time, he was assigned to the FBI's Cyber Crimes Task Force where he focused on various online investigations and Open Source Intelligence (OSINT) collection. As an investigator and sworn federal officer through the U.S. Marshals Service, he was involved in numerous major criminal investigations including online child solicitation, child abduction, kidnapping, cold-case homicide, terrorist threats, and advanced computer intrusions. He has trained thousands of individuals in the use of his investigative techniques and privacy control strategies. After leaving government work, he served as the technical advisor for the first season of the television hacker drama *Mr. Robot*. His books *OSINT Techniques* and *Extreme Privacy* are used by several government and private organizations as training manuals for intelligence gathering and privacy hardening. He now assists individual clients in achieving ultimate privacy, both proactively and as a response to an undesired situation. More details about his services can be found at *IntelTechniques.com*.

JASON EDISON

Jason Edison is a 25-year veteran with a major U.S. metropolitan police department where he serves as the technical lead for the agency's Criminal Intelligence and Cyber-Crime Sections. He instructs internal department teams as well as outside organizations in the areas of Operational Security for Covert Operations, Countering Electronic Surveillance, Cyber-Crime Investigations, and Open-Source Intelligence. Prior to his current assignments, Jason worked as a Federal Task-Force Officer, running under-cover and electronic surveillance operations for long-term organized crime investigations.

ELEVENTH EDITION PREFACE

The previous (tenth) edition of this book was originally written in late 2022. In late 2024, I was asked to update this book, as it is required reading for numerous college courses, university degrees, and government training academies. It had been two years since our last update, which is an eternity in technology. I never want stale or inaccurate information being presented within training programs, so I created this revision. **I estimate that 20% of the content is brand new, 20% has been updated to reflect changes throughout 2024, and the remaining 60% is recycled from the previous edition.** This edition also includes the entirety of the digital supplement guides *The Ultimate Virtual Machine* and *Leaks, Breaches, & Logs*, which replaced all tenth edition content related to those topics. You could say that this edition is a "Complete Works" of all available OSINT material which is relevant for 2025. Much of the remaining tenth edition content was still applicable and only needed minor updates to reflect changes since 2022. If you have read the previous edition, you will find most of those overall strategies within this book. However, I have added many new methods which complement the original text in order to cater to those who always need accurate information. I also removed a lot of outdated content which was no longer applicable. I believe there is much new value within this updated text.

My primary goals with this new edition are two-fold. First, we need to continue our path of self-reliance which was introduced in the previous editions. This edition introduces a completely rebuilt Debian Linux OSINT virtual machine which is simpler to create, full of new features, and easier to operate. It is also much more stable and private than previous Ubuntu builds. I present all required commands to replicate my own system and offer an automated script which allows you to generate your own working environment. Second, I have reworked all of the OSINT techniques throughout all chapters. Many of the search methods targeted toward Facebook, YouTube, X (Twitter), Instagram, and other online services which were presented in the previous editions have begun to fail as these companies change their products. The updated tutorials here offer new solutions.

The biggest change within this edition is the addition of my co-author, Jason Edison. Jason runs the official IntelTechniques online video training program and conducts live training sessions globally. I brought him in for many reasons. This book is a monster, and keeping it updated takes a lot of time. I recruited him to help me make sure we had a book worthy of a new edition. More importantly, I no longer personally conduct OSINT investigations as part of my daily routine. Jason still works for the government in an OSINT capacity and is buried within OSINT investigations every day. I wanted an active investigator to play a large role within this publication, and I am no longer that type of investigator. While we both have a passion for OSINT, Jason lives in that world more than I do now. In order to keep a fluid theme, we will use the first-person of "I" "me", and "my" throughout the book. This is a collective first-person presentation, and we both stand by the entire guide.

Please consider the following technical note in regard to this book. I typically push my self-published titles through five rounds of editing. The fees associated with editing a book of this size (over 300,000 words) are substantial. This edition was put through only two rounds of editing, so I expect a few typos still exist. If you find any, consider reporting them to books@inteltechniques.com. We also want to hear when things break. My staff cannot respond directly to any emails, but we can correct future copies. The decision to restrict editing was mostly due to hard deadlines for courses, but book piracy also played a strong role. We have seen a drastic shift from most readers purchasing the book to the vast majority downloading illegal free PDF copies available a few weeks after the initial release. If you purchased this edition, I sincerely thank you. You represent a shrinking society. If you downloaded this book from a shady site, please consider purchasing a legitimate copy. We now offer both print and digital PDF versions. Details are at **https://inteltechniques.com/books.html**.

Keeping a book up to date about ways to access information on the internet is a difficult task. Websites are constantly changing or disappearing, and the techniques for collecting all possible public information from them are affected. However, new resources appear constantly, and much of this book contains new techniques which were previously not available. This book was accurate as of December 1, 2024. **If, or more likely when, you find techniques which no longer work, use the overall lessons from the entire book to push through the changes and locate your content.** Once you develop an understanding of the strategies, you will be ready to adapt. I am truly excited to introduce a new level of OSINT. ~MB (& JE)

INTRODUCTION

OSINT TECHNIQUES

I taught my first Open Source Intelligence (OSINT) course in 1999 to a small group of local police chiefs in Illinois. I had not heard of the term OSINT at the time and I did not realize there was an official name for the methods I was teaching. I simply thought I was demonstrating a powerful way to use the internet as a part of everyday investigations. Most in the room had little interest in my session, as they had not experienced the internet much. Well, times sure have changed. OSINT is now quite the buzz word within several communities. Hacking conferences proudly host OSINT training sessions; cyber security groups include it within their strategies for hardening customers' systems; law enforcement agencies dedicate entire investigation units to online research into criminals; journalists rely on the methods every day; and even the social engineering crowd has adopted it as part of their playbook. I never anticipated OSINT would become a household name within most technology circles.

As my company continues to provide OSINT training sessions, the audiences seem to grow every year. It is no longer a course reserved for tech-savvy employees. We now see people with minimal online experience being thrown into investigation and analyst positions. We see crowds desperate for the latest investigation techniques, only to see those methods disappear without notice as social networks come and go, or change their search options. Search techniques seem to be more fickle than ever, and I am always concerned about losing online resources.

Open Source Intelligence, often referred to as OSINT, can mean many things to many people. Officially, it is defined as any intelligence produced from publicly available information that is collected, exploited, and disseminated in a timely manner to an appropriate audience for the purpose of addressing a specific intelligence requirement. For the CIA, it may mean information obtained from foreign news broadcasts. For an attorney, it may mean data obtained from official government documents which are available to the public. For most people, it is simply publicly available content obtained from the internet.

Overall, this book includes several hundred sources of free information and software which could identify personal information about anyone you might be investigating. All of the resources are 100% free and open to the public, with a few minor exceptions. Each method is explained, and any creative search techniques involving the resources are detailed. When applicable, actual case examples are provided to demonstrate the possibilities within the methods. The topics in this book can be read in any order and referenced when a specific need arises. It is a guidebook of techniques that I have found successful in my investigations.

Locating this free online information is not the final step of OSINT analysis. Appropriate collection and reporting methods will be detailed and referenced. Whether the data you obtain is for an investigation, a background check, or identifying problem employees, you must document all of your findings. You cannot rely on the information being available online forever. A website may shut down or the data may be removed. You must preserve anything of interest when you find it. The free software solutions presented here will help you with that. OSINT search techniques do not apply only to websites. There are many free programs which automate the search and collection of data. These programs, as well as application programming interfaces, will be explained to assist the advanced investigator of open source intelligence. In summary, this book is to serve as a reference guide to assist you with conducting more accurate and efficient searches of open source intelligence. This is not a debate of the various opinions about online reconnaissance for personal information. It is not a historical look at OSINT or a discussion of your administrative policy. Furthermore, it is not a how-to guide for criminals to steal your identity. Nothing in this book discusses illegal methods.

When I first considered documenting my OSINT techniques, the plan was to post them on my website in a private area for my co-workers. This documentation quickly turned into over 250 pages of content. It had grown too big to place on my site in a manner that was easy to digest. I changed course and began putting together this book as a manual to accompany my multiple-day training sessions. It has grown to a huge textbook which could never include every beneficial resource on the internet.

Many readers work in some form of law enforcement or government agency. Police officers can use these techniques to help locate missing children or investigate human trafficking. Intelligence analysts can apply these methods to a large portion of their daily work as they tackle social media posts. Detectives can use the search techniques to re-investigate cases that have gone unsolved. I embrace these techniques being used to locate facts which can help solve crimes. This book also caters to the private sector, especially security divisions of large corporations. It can help these teams locate more concise and appropriate information relative to their companies. These methods have been proven successful for employees who monitor any type of threat to their company, from physical violence to counterfeit products. I encourage the use of these techniques to institutions which are responsible for finding and eliminating "bad apples". This may be the human resources department, application processing employees, or "head hunters" looking for the best people. The information about a subject found online can provide more intelligence than any interview or reference check.

Parents and teachers are encouraged to use this book as a guide to locating social media content posted by children. In many households, the children know more about the internet than the adults. The children use this to their advantage and often hide content online. They know that it will not be located by their parents and teachers, and often post inappropriate content which can become harmful in the wrong hands. This book can empower adults and assist with identifying important personal information which could pose a threat toward children. A large portion of my intended audience is private investigators. They can use this book to find information without possessing a deep understanding of computers or the internet. Explicit descriptions and occasional screen captures will ensure that the techniques can be recreated on any computer. Several universities have adopted this book as required reading, and I am honored to play a small role in some amazing courses related to network security.

I realize that people who use these techniques for devious purposes will read this book as well. Colleagues have expressed their concern about this possibility. My decision to document these techniques came down to two thoughts. First, anyone that really wants to use this information in malicious ways will do so without this book. There is nothing in here that could not be replicated with some serious searching and time. The second thought is that getting this information out to those who will use it appropriately is worth the risk of a few people using it for the wrong reasons. Please act responsibly with this information.

Finally, a parting thought before you begin your journey through OSINT analysis and collection. This book was written as a reference guide. It does not necessarily need to be read straight-through sequentially, but it was written as a chronological guide for most investigators. I encourage you to skip around when needed or if you feel overwhelmed. The second chapter about Linux may make you want to abandon the teachings before ever utilizing an online resource or website. When you encounter material that seems too technical or not applicable, please move on to the next chapter and consider returning later. The book is suitable for all skill levels, and there is something here for everyone. You can always return to the advanced topics when you are ready.

IMPORTANT! Digital Commands and Files

Throughout this book, I present numerous Terminal commands which must be entered exactly, and I refer to several files which can be downloaded in order to simplify your usage of the various tools, techniques, and scripts. These are all hosted on my website and available free to you. As each file or script is referenced, I provide a download link to simplify the learning process, but you can also access all digital content at any time at **https://inteltechniques.com/osintbook11**. The username is **osint11** and the password for this book is **bk3t7**. Please embrace this online page, and the files and the commands offered within it, as a vital part of this book. They should minimize frustration and save time as you complete the tutorials. Copying and pasting from the online site will be much easier than replicating from this book. This also allows us to update commands as they change. **Always check this site for the latest information, as the book can become outdated.**

SECTION I
OSINT PREPARATION

This entire section explains the essential steps which I believe any online investigator should complete before ever conducting a search online. We should never jump into an investigation without being digitally secure with a clean computer and software which has not been compromised from previous activity. We should begin each investigation with confidence, knowing we are working within an environment without any contamination from previous investigations. It will take a lot of work to create our perfect playground, but replicating a pristine environment for each investigation will be easy. Much like a DNA forensics lab must be configured and ready before an investigation, your OSINT lab should face the same scrutiny.

The first four editions of this book began with search engine techniques. Right away, I offered my methods for collecting online information from various popular and lesser-known search websites. This may have been due to my own impatience and desire to "dive in" and start finding information. This edition will begin much differently. Before you attempt any of the search methods within this book, I believe you should prepare your computing environment. I was motivated to begin with this topic after teaching a multiple-day OSINT class. On day two, several attendees brought laptop computers in order to attempt the techniques I was teaching during the course. During a break, I observed police officers searching Facebook on patrol vehicle laptops; private investigators using old versions of Windows while browsing suspects' blogs; and cyber security professionals looking at hacker websites without possessing any antivirus software, script blockers, or a virtual private network (VPN).

I have also been guilty of all of this. Early in my career of researching OSINT, I did not pay much attention to computer security or proper browsing habits. While I was aware of malicious software, I knew I could reinstall Windows if something really bad happened. This was reactive thinking. I believe that we must all proactively address vulnerabilities in our own privacy and security while conducting online research. This section is not meant to be a complete guide to computer security. Instead, I hope to quickly and efficiently propose the most beneficial strategies which will protect you from the majority of problems. Applying the changes mentioned in this section will provide a valuable layer of security to your online investigations and overall computing habits.

Virtual machines are an important part of our arsenal and we will be referring to "host" and "guest" operating systems throughout the chapters. The "host" is your existing desktop or laptop computer and the "guest" is any operating system which is running virtually. I will explain how to ensure your computer host is secure; configure virtual machines for each investigation; embed Linux applications into Windows and Mac hosts; customize OSINT software which will be available at all times; create your own set of search tools to automate queries; prepare a virtual Android environment for mobile investigations; and easily clone all of your work for immediate replication if anything should become corrupt, damaged, or compromised. Your efforts now will pay off ten-fold in the future.

There is a lot to digest here. Please allow yourself to skip over any technical sections and return to them once you understand the overall intent of the material. Many readers will skip to Section Two and start practicing various online OSINT techniques. Some will navigate directly to Section Three to start exploring breach data. Others might read through the entire book before ever touching a computer. Approach the content in the way which suits you best. Most importantly, do not let the technical aspects deter you from finding areas which will benefit your own investigations the most.

I offer one last vital piece of information before we start. I encourage you to generate your own opinions as you read along. You may disagree with me at times, which is ideal. That means you are really thinking about how all of this applies to you. **If everyone unconditionally agrees with every word I say, then I am probably not saying anything interesting. If this book only presented content which no one could dispute, then there was no need for the text.** Please read with an open mind and willingness to try new things. Let's begin.

CHAPTER ONE
WHY VIRTUAL MACHINES?

What data is on your computer? Is there a virus, malicious software, or spyware hanging around from casual browsing in questionable places? Does your internet cache include tracking cookies from Amazon, Facebook, Google, and others? Is there evidence of your last investigation stored within your bookmarks, documents, or download queue? If the answer is "maybe" or "I don't know" to any of these, you have a contaminated computer. If your investigation enters court testimony, you may have a lot of explaining to do once an expert witness who specializes in computer forensics takes the stand. If your screen captures display evidence unrelated to your investigation, you could compromise the entire case. You may think I am being overly cautious, but we can no longer take any chances when it comes to the purity of our online evidence.

This is where virtual machines (VMs) can eliminate most of our concerns, especially Linux VMs. Linux operating systems have been a part of my OSINT investigations and trainings for many years. They are lightweight, run on practically any hardware, cost nothing, and provide a level of security that cannot be obtained through traditional operating systems such as Microsoft Windows. I can navigate to any malicious website, download every virus possible, and eliminate all traces of my activity by simply deleting the VM and cloning a new machine. Upon reboot, there are no viruses and everything works exactly as intended when the system was created. VMs provide unlimited disposable environments.

Virtual machines conduct virtualization of a particular computer system. They are computer operating systems on top of computer operating systems. Most commonly, a software program is executed within an operating system, and individual operating systems can launch within that program. Each virtual machine is independent from the other and the host operating system. The environment of one virtual machine has no impact on any others. Quite simply, it is a way to have numerous computers within your single computer. You can safely investigate a single target within a secure environment with no contamination from other investigations. You will be able to clone an original VM in minutes and will no longer need to worry about persistent viruses, tracking cookies, or leftover evidence.

Many years ago, this may have been intimidating to non-technical users. Today, implementing a Linux VM into your investigations is relatively easy. Once you start exploring the world of online search techniques, you will likely encounter malicious software or viruses at some point. If you investigate cyber criminals, this will be sooner rather than later. The malicious code will almost always target Windows machines. By choosing Linux as your investigations system, you greatly lessen the concern about infections.

By conducting all of your work in a VM, you protect the host operating system from infection. By isolating each of your investigations into their own VM, you prevent any contamination from one to another. Finally, by generating a new VM for every case, you protect the integrity of all past, current, and future investigations. I cannot stress the importance of isolated VMs enough. If you ever face a motion of discovery for a copy of your investigative environment, your VM will save you many headaches.

During my final year of government work, I testified at the trial of a person who was transporting minors to several states to be sexually abused by paying offenders. The defense asked the judge to grant them full access to my investigative computer for scrutiny of my work. Since I conducted the entire online investigation within a VM, I convinced the judge that the defense should only receive a copy of the VM and not a clone of my entire computer, which had been used for other cases. Handing over a 4 GB file was much easier than allowing my hard drive to be cloned and scrutinized. I hope you see the value of not only conducting investigations within a VM, but saving the state of your work for future inspection. This guide will revisit both of these considerations many times.

I have known the value of VMs for a long time, but I was only scratching the surface of their potential. In 2016, I was contacted by David Westcott. We knew each other through our OSINT work, and he asked if I was interested in creating a custom OSINT virtual machine. I had always considered this, but had concerns about my skills at hardening Linux systems and pushing out finished builds. David had worked on other public Linux releases, and was much more comfortable distributing custom systems. I began designing my dream OSINT build, sending him weekly requests, and he began taking the ideas and executing them within a test product. By 2017, the first public version of our new operating system was released and titled Buscador (Seeker in Spanish). This concept is not new. Many readers are likely familiar with Linux digital security distributions such as Kali. We wanted that same experience for the OSINT community. Buscador was designed from the ground up with considerations for OSINT investigations. The web browsers were pre-configured with custom settings and extensions, and numerous OSINT software applications were already preconfigured to accept search queries.

An important part of Buscador was the applications. On many Linux builds, launching software is not similar to traditional operating systems. While the software is installed, you must still launch a Terminal window and type the specific commands required. This can be very difficult and unforgiving. There are seldom point-and-click icons that launch similar to Windows. This has always created a barrier between the geeks and the norms. Either you know how to issue Linux commands or you do not. If you don't, then you never get to take advantage of the power of Linux and Python. We wanted to eliminate that barrier. We wanted to make powerful Linux programs easily accessible to everyone. My initial thought was to create Bash scripts similar to batch files in Windows, but David came up with a much easier and more appropriate way. Every tool inside Buscador had its own icon in the Dock, executed by clicking with a mouse, which walked the user through the menus. After collecting the required data, each program executed the proper commands behind the scenes and delivered the content directly to the user. We believed this to be unique in our community. Every person, at any skill level, could use Buscador as a Linux virtual machine for immediate OSINT work.

Today, my views of pre-built virtual machines have changed. While I am proud of our work with Buscador, I believe you should no longer rely on systems from third parties. Buscador is no longer updated with new versions, and there is no online repository to apply updates to the many applications within the virtual machine. I no longer offer a direct download link to Buscador from my site because security patches have not been applied since 2019. Anyone using Buscador now receives errors due to outdated applications and most users do not have the training to apply their own updates in order to correct any issues. Creating a virtual machine which was user friendly had many benefits, but also some unintended consequences.

My goal in this book is to help you easily create and maintain your own OSINT Linux virtual machine with all of the easy-to-use features of Buscador. Together we will install and test numerous OSINT applications. We will then build custom scripts to make our daily usage of these applications easy. We will revisit and apply the lessons from my previous books, but then expand our options into many new features. We will easily archive our investigative work when warranted, and have the confidence to present our findings when demanded.

Overall, we should never rely on a single source for our OSINT tools. It is easier than ever to build your own OSINT VM while keeping it updated. By the end of this guide, you will possess a custom OSINT Linux machine which rivals any pre-built options available through various providers. Better yet, you will have built it yourself and can replicate your steps whenever desired, while also being able to explain your actions.

In a perfect world, we would possess a dedicated computer for each online investigation which we conduct. We do not live in that world, so virtual machines are the next best thing. You still conduct all of your actions on a dedicated local machine, and do not need to rely on cloud-based services to access your work.

The next six chapters are divided for macOS, Windows, and Linux users. I encourage you to read through all of them, but I respect anyone who skips to the chapters about their specific host. If you only possess one computer for OSINT work, then you should only apply the two chapters which match the operating system within that host. I present them in order of recommendation (macOS, Linux, then Windows), but everything within the rest of this guide functions the same on any of these options.

CHAPTER TWO
macOS HOST OPTIMIZATION

At risk of sounding hypocritical, I prefer modern macOS machines for most OSINT use over Windows and Linux. Before readers of my book *Extreme Privacy* and listeners of my former podcast scold me, please consider my reasons. I always have at least two computers which are part of my daily office usage. My personal machine is a Linux laptop. It is only for personal activity and is never used as part of any investigations. My OSINT machine is a MacBook Pro with an M-series Apple Silicon chip. It is blazing fast and executes virtual machines better than my Linux host. It is also quite secure by default. I never touch the host operating system, and conduct all investigations within various virtual machines. I rely on a free and open-source application called UTM for VMs, which I find to be superior to the Linux and Windows options explained within the next chapters. Let's tackle macOS.

In a perfect world, you have an unlimited budget and are ready to purchase new hardware which has no association from your true identity to Apple. However, we do not live in that perfect world. Whether you are ready to purchase new equipment or need to recycle current hardware for future use, this chapter will explain all options and considerations. Let's start with new gear.

When Apple computers switched to their own ARM-based processors, instead of using trusted Intel chips, I was bummed. Numerous applications no longer functioned correctly and virtual machines were troublesome. Those days are over. The latest machines which include Apple's M-series processors are blazingly fast with low power consumption and minimal heat. Apps work better than ever. I have yet to hear my internal fans on my MacBook Pro, which was a daily occurrence on older machines. I now recommend the latest hardware available and believe the products with Apple's chips are superior to those with Intel processors. If you are buying new gear, make sure you are taking advantage of these benefits.

Selecting a machine is a very personal choice. Laptop options include the MacBook, MacBook Air, and MacBook Pro while desktops include the Mac mini, Mac Pro, and Mac Studio. I have never owned a Mac desktop, but I have purchased my share of Apple laptops. Today's least expensive small laptops will probably meet the needs for casual users, but the MacBook Pro models are all I will consider. I believe the latest 14" MacBook Pro laptops hit a sweet spot with productivity and value.

As I write this, the latest MacBook Pro's possess the M3, M3 Pro, and M3 Max processors. The previous generations possess the M1/M2, M1/M2 Pro, and M1/M2 Max chips. I am writing this from a 2021 14" MacBook Pro with the M1 Pro processor. What should you choose? Well, there are many conflicting opinions on this, and mine might not match yours. However, here is my advice. If you want the most affordable M-series machine, I believe any M1 or M2 processor on a MacBook Pro will suffice for OSINT work. If you want the latest machine for longevity of the hardware with operating system support, then the M3 series might be best for you. Either way, I recommend the Pro processors for most people. These provide more cores than the standard chips and more overall power. However, the Max processors would be overkill for most readers.

I believe most readers would get by with the minimal number of processor cores available with the latest 14" MacBook Pro, which is currently 11 (CPU) and 14 (GPU). Increasing the number of cores can assist with resource-intensive tasks, but most users would never take advantage of the power. You know if you need the extra boost. Since we will rely heavily on VMs, I recommend 32 GB of RAM. The standard 512 GB of storage may work for some (1 TB is better), and external drives are more affordable than embedded storage upgrades. My machine possesses a 4 TB internal storage drive because I work with large data sets (breach data) and need the fastest possible drive when working with the files. While these are great specs, I overpaid for the luxury.

I firmly believe that the newer M3 2023 models are worth the minimal current price increase from the previous 2021 generation. However, I have seen brand-new previous-generation laptops deeply discounted at various

Apple resellers. If I were buying a new machine today, it would definitely be the newer M-series model. If you already possess an M1 machine which meets your needs, I see no reason to upgrade to the M2 or M3. The real-world comparisons will be negligible. If you upgrade from an Intel processor to an M1/M2/M3, I believe you will be shocked at the difference. My point is that I recommend a machine with newer ARM-based M1, M2, or M3 processors for most readers. While you can use older hardware with Intel chips, and almost all of this guide will still apply, you are missing out on a phenomenal increase in power and battery life.

I will now assume that you possess your desired macOS device if you plan to go that route. Regardless of its condition or previous usage, I believe every reader should now reformat the drive and apply a fresh install of the operating system. This ensures that we are all on the same page for an identical experience. Make sure you have completely backed up all important data before continuing, as **the following processes will erase everything on the drive.**

If you purchased a brand new M1, M2, or later device which does not possess an existing Apple ID account, and has never been turned on, you can skip to the next section. If you are working from an existing device, regardless of the processor type, we should consider several tasks. First, update the operating system to the latest available version. As I write this, my machine possesses Apple's Sonoma version of macOS, specifically 14.0. By the time you read this, that exact number will change. I always recommend the latest stable version available, and avoid any beta (test) builds. **The following assumes you possess macOS Sonoma as your operating system and are able to update to the latest version of macOS Sonoma.** This will require devices made after 2018, but unsupported devices can still take advantage of the rest of this book using previous versions of macOS. You will need to slightly modify the steps for your specific operating system.

Open the "System Settings" application; click the "General" option and then the "Software Update" setting. Allow your machine to download and install all available updates, and then reboot. Once your machine is fully updated, conduct the following within macOS to reinstall a fresh version of the operating system.

- Open the "System Settings" application.
- Click the "General" option and then "Transfer or Reset".
- Click the "Erase All Content and Settings" button.
- Enter your password within the "Erase Assistant".
- Confirm all warnings and allow the process to complete.

Previous versions, such as Ventura, Monterey, or Big Sur, should also provide the option to reset the system through either the "Erase Assistant" or "Recovery" mode. You will need to research options for your non-Sonoma version. Upon reboot, you should possess a clean installation of macOS ready for initial configuration.

I will now assume that you either have a brand-new computer or a recently-reset device. Either way, it should appear as a new installation when turned on for the first time. Regardless of your processor type or history with the machine, the following applies as if you were a new user.

Upon launching macOS for the first time, your experience may be unique from mine. Updates to the operating system from Apple and specific hardware configurations could present minor variations from the steps outlined here. I took the following actions within a new macOS Sonoma installation, which had not been updated to the latest release. It was the original stock Sonoma version 14.0. **Yours may appear slightly different.**

- Select desired language and click the right arrow.
- Select country and click "Continue".
- Click "Customized Settings".
- Confirm preferred language.
- Confirm location.
- Confirm dictation (required).

- Click "Not Now" for Accessibility options.
- If prompted, choose "My computer does not connect to the internet".
- Click "Continue" and "Continue" again if requested to connect to the internet.
- Click "Continue" for Data & Privacy notification.
- Click "Not Now" for the Migration Assistant.
- Click "Set Up Later" to bypass the Apple ID requirement.
- Confirm by clicking "Skip".
- Click "Agree" to the Terms and Conditions.
- Confirm by clicking "Agree".
- Create a local computer account. This should be a generic name, such as "Laptop" or "Computer", and should include a very strong password which you can remember. I never provide any password hint to this screen. Click "Continue" when finished.
- Do not enable "Location Service" and click "Continue".
- Confirm choice by clicking "Don't Use".
- Select your desired time zone and click "Continue".
- Deselect all analytics options and click "Continue".
- Click "Set Up Later" to bypass "Screen Time" settings.
- Disable Siri and click "Continue".
- Choose your desired screen mode and click "Continue".
- Launch "System Settings" from the Dock.
- Select "Wi-Fi" from the left menu and disable it.
- Disable both "Ask to join networks" and "Ask to join hotspots".
- Select Bluetooth from the left menu and disable it.

Next, I want to configure the operating system's firewall. This is much different than the software firewall explained in my macOS privacy guide. This is only responsible for the way the operating system treats incoming connections. The following steps enable the firewall and configure it to block incoming connections unless we specifically allow them when prompted. It also stops the OS from confirming incoming requests for information.

- Select "Network" from the left menu and select "Firewall".
- Enable the Firewall and click "Options".
- Disable "Automatically allow built-in software to receive...".
- Disable "Automatically allow downloaded signed software to receive...".
- Enable "Stealth mode".
- Click "OK".

If you want to truly ensure that Siri is not listening in on your activity, you can conduct the following, which may be redundant.

- Select "Siri & Spotlight" from the left menu.
- Click "Siri Suggestions & Privacy".
- Click each option and disable all toggles, then click "Done".

Let's conduct a few more configurations within System Settings.

- Select "Privacy & Security" from the left menu.
- Select "Analytics & Improvements" and verify all are disabled.
- Select "Privacy & Security" from the left menu.

- Select "Apple Advertising" and disable "Personalized Ads".
- Select "General" from the left menu.
- Select "Software Update".
- Click the "i" in the circle and deselect everything.

Next is likely the most important setting within this chapter. By default, the data stored on your macOS system is not encrypted. Physical access to your computer using sophisticated forensic equipment could extract your data. If you lose your laptop, or it is stolen, there is a chance that the culprit could acquire your sensitive files. The best way to prevent this is to apply full-disk encryption through Apple's FileVault with the following steps.

- Select "Privacy & Security" from the left menu.
- Click "Turn On..." next to "FileVault".
- Enter your system password and click "Unlock".
- Choose "Create a recovery key and do not use my iCloud account".
- Document this recovery key somewhere safe and click "Continue".

Your device will now encrypt the drive, including all data stored within it. This is a vital piece of protection which I believe should be enabled by default.

Your macOS device should now be more private and secure than it was, but I have a few additional settings I like to apply. These are all personal preferences, and you may want to tweak these differently.

- Select "Desktop & Dock" from the left menu.
- Disable "Show suggested and recent apps in Dock".
- Disable "Show recent apps in Stage Manager".
- Select "Wallpaper" from the left menu.
- Choose a solid color instead of the default macOS image.
- Select "Lock Screen" from the left menu.
- Change "Start Screen Saver when inactive" to "Never".
- Change "Turn display off on battery when inactive" to "For 1 hour".
- Change "Turn display off on power adapter when inactive" to "For 1 hour".
- Change "Require password after..." to "Immediately".

These settings prevent the macOS screen saver from kicking in, and instead disable the display after a set amount of time. This also makes sure that your password is required the moment a screen is disabled or the device is placed into standby mode, such as closing the lid of a laptop.

Next, I want to modify the default way in which Apple allows you to see the data stored within your device. Apple is proud of the "simple" features of macOS. Things just work and you are not bombarded with complex options. However, you are also severely restricted. As one example, macOS hides all "hidden files" from view within Finder. While most users do not care about this data, I do. Much of my most important data is within a hidden "Library" folder to which I have no access. Let's fix that.

- Open Finder and select the "Macintosh HD" in the left menu.
- Select "Users", and then your device's username.
- Notice the view of this folder, which should appear similar to the following.

On your keyboard, press and hold shift + command + . (period). Your view should change similar to the following image. You can now see all files determined to be hidden by macOS. This will be vital once we backup our system.

While we are in Finder, let's modify some settings.

- Click Finder in the upper-left menu bar and then select "Settings".
- Choose the "General" tab and consider my choices presented next.
- Choose the "Tags" tab and consider my choices presented next.
- Choose the "Sidebar" tab and consider my choices presented next.
- Choose the "Advanced" tab and consider my choices presented next.

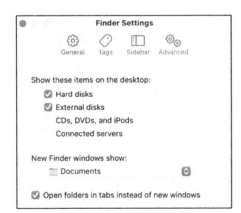

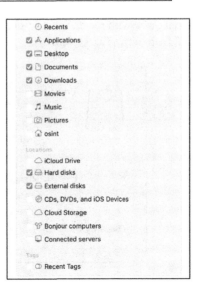

You should now have a stable and protected operating system ready for third-party applications. As a reminder, you have not associated your new machine with an Apple ID, and hopefully you never will do so. Without this connection, Apple has limited capabilities associating the activity occurring on your machine with a specific user or account. By refusing to attach an Apple ID, you are much more private and secure. I have not assigned an Apple ID to my current (or previous) machine, and I never will again in the future.

Encrypted External Drives

In a later chapter, I explain how to export virtual machines onto an external USB SSD, and the importance of encrypting the data within this drive. I believe this applies to any external drive which we connect to our macOS devices **which will not be used to transfer data from our VM**. You should NOT apply the following to a drive you will later want to access within your OSINT Linux VM. This is only for drives which will be connected to your macOS host for the purposes of backing up data. USB drives are often lost or stolen. Therefore, we should always encrypt the data stored on them. This is not always easy. Sometimes, macOS hides the settings we need to protect an external device. As an example, I inserted a small USB drive which was formatted as "FAT32", which is common for universal drive access. I wanted to erase the drive and encrypt it. However, the Disk Utility application (Applications > Utilities) only displayed the following options. Right-clicking the drive in Finder also did not present an option to encrypt the drive.

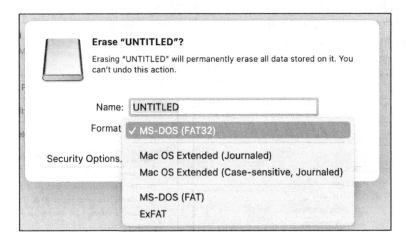

The first step to take within the Disk Utility application is to select "Show All Devices" under the "View" menu. Next, select the device (not the formatted volume) within the left menu and click the "Erase" button. This may still only present volume formats which cannot be encrypted. Be sure to change the "Scheme" to "GUID Partition Map". You should now see an option of "APFS (Encrypted)" under "Format". This option will encrypt the entire external drive with macOS encryption. I believe this is the best option for users who will only need to access this drive from a macOS system.

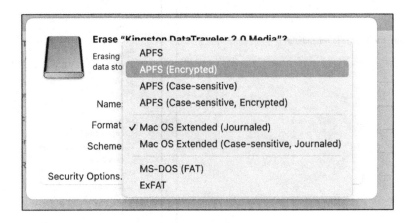

Rosetta

I highly recommend you ensure that Rosetta is installed on your system. This software, which is provided by Apple, helps applications which do not support ARM-based devices run smoothly on new macOS systems. You likely already have it installed, but you can confirm with the following command. You will need internet access enabled for the rest of this chapter.

```
softwareupdate --install-rosetta --agree-to-license
```

Antivirus & Antimalware

Mac users do not have any built-in antivirus protection, and most do not need any. The software architecture of Mac computers is much more secure, and viruses are rare (but they do still occur). I do not recommend free commercial products such as Avast, Kaspersky, and others. They tend to be more of an annoyance than helpful, and their business practices can be questionable. **However, I do believe that it is irresponsible to have absolutely no protection whatsoever on an investigative machine**. I was once asked during testimony of a federal trial to disclose any security software present within my investigation computers. I was glad my response was not "none". This would have likely introduced a defense blaming an infected workspace. I was proud to disclose my open-source solutions.

When I conduct investigations from a Mac computer, I always possess three software applications which can be executed at any time without any of them running full-time in the background of my operating system. However, we must first install Homebrew. Homebrew (often referred to as Brew) is a very beneficial program when there is a need to install macOS software which would usually already be present on a Linux computer. It also happens to have pre-configured versions of the applications I am about to discuss. The easiest way to install Brew is to visit the website brew.sh and copy and paste the following command into the Terminal application ("Applications" > "Utilities" > "Terminal").

```
/bin/bash -c "$(curl -fsSL
https://raw.githubusercontent.com/Homebrew/install/HEAD/install.sh)"
```

After Brew installation is complete, you will likely be presented with one or two commands which need to be manually executed within Terminal. My installation presented the following notice.

```
==> Next steps:
- Run these two commands in your terminal to add Homebrew to your PATH:
    (echo; echo 'eval "$(/opt/homebrew/bin/brew shellenv)"') >> /Users/ventura/.zprofile
    eval "$(/opt/homebrew/bin/brew shellenv)"
```

This is unique to my installation, as my chosen username was "ventura" at the time. Copy any commands presented here and paste them within the same Terminal window, executing each by striking return. Let's test everything with a few commands.

- `brew doctor` - This command confirms that Brew is configured properly and that all paths are set. You should receive a notice that "Your system is ready to brew".
- `brew update` - This command checks for any pending updates to Brew itself. You should receive a response of "Already up to date".
- `brew upgrade` - This command updates any installed programs. You should receive no response since we have not installed anything.
- `brew analytics off` - This command disables Brew's embedded analytics which monitor the number of times an application is installed using Brew. These metrics are only used to understand how users interact with the product, but I prefer to limit my exposure.

You are now ready to use Brew as a software installation repository. Treat this as a replacement for the App Store, but it does not require an Apple ID. Let's use it to install our first three applications.

Task Explorer (objective-see.com/products/taskexplorer.html): This free Mac-only application is simple yet effective. It identifies all running processes and queries them through a service called Virus Total. If it finds a suspicious file, it alerts you with a red flag in the lower-right corner. Clicking the flag allows you to see more details about the potential threat. I execute this program weekly from any Mac machine I am using. If you have picked up a virus on your host, this program should quickly identify it. However, it does not remove any infections. For that, you will need to research any suspicious files. Install this application with the following.

```
brew install --cask taskexplorer
```

KnockKnock (objective-see.com/products/knockknock.html): Similar to the previous option, which is maintained by the same company, this program conducts a scan of your Mac device. However, it is looking for persistent programs which are set to launch upon boot. Since most viruses inject themselves to launch the moment your computer starts, this program may identify threats which were missed by the previous program if they were not running at the time. After opening this application, click the scan button and allow the process to complete. You will receive a notification about any suspicious files. I execute this weekly along with Task Explorer. Please note that it also only notifies you of issues, and does not remove them. Install this application with the following Terminal command.

```
brew install --cask knockknock
```

ClamAV (clamav.net): ClamAV (not to be confused with the unnecessary paid option of ClamXAV) is a community-driven and open-source antivirus database, which is freely available to anyone. It usually does not score very high on "Top 10 Antivirus" websites, which are commonly paid advertisements. However, it is completely free; does not run on your system non-stop; only executes when you desire; and can be completely removed easily. Unfortunately, there is no easy software installation process, and no point-and-click application. You will need to manually update the database through a Terminal command, then scan your system. ClamAV does not remove any viruses by default, it only discloses the presence and location of suspicious files. In my use, ClamAV has never found a virus which impacted a macOS computer. Instead, it has identified numerous malicious files which target Windows machines, but were present on my system (mostly as email attachments). This notification allowed me to manually remove those files, which could prevent future infection of my Windows virtual machines. Remember, you may not NEED antivirus software on your OSINT macOS host, but possessing it will allow you to defend any scrutiny if your investigation should appear in court. The following instructions will configure macOS to be better protected. Enter the following commands, hitting "Return" after each line, into the same Terminal application previously used.

```
brew install clamav
sudo mkdir /usr/local/sbin
sudo chown -R `whoami`:admin /usr/local/sbin
brew link clamav
cd /opt/homebrew/etc/clamav/
cp freshclam.conf.sample freshclam.conf
sed -ie 's/^Example/#Example/g' freshclam.conf
```

These steps will install ClamAV; switch to the installation directory; make a copy of the configuration file; and then modify the configuration file to allow ClamAV to function. You are now ready to update your antivirus database and conduct a scan. Type the following commands into Terminal, striking return on your keyboard after each line.

```
freshclam -v
clamscan -r -i /
```

The first option will download all virus definition updates, and should be executed before each scan. The second option conducts a scan of the entire computer, and will only prompt you with details of found viruses. While it may appear to be dormant, it is working, and will notify you upon completion. All of these commands must be exact. Always copy and paste them instead of manually typing from the book.

ClamAV may occasionally present a false-positive report of a virus. Do not panic. Research the file on the internet and identify the issues. If you receive reports of malicious files within email, simply delete those messages. Note that the above scans only SEARCH for viruses, they do not REMOVE threats. If you would like to conduct a scan and automatically remove suspicious files, you must conduct a different command. Please note this could be dangerous, and could permanently remove necessary files. I always run a scan, research the threats found, and execute the following scan ONLY if I am confident the files should be removed.

```
clamscan -i -r --remove=yes /
```

I confess I do not execute ClamAV often. A full scan can take hours and is unlikely to locate threats not found by the previous two applications. However, Task Explorer and KnockKnock do not protect against malicious applications which target Windows environments. ClamAV may find files which are malicious even if they are not a direct threat to your Mac computer. If you conduct government investigations, especially those which may result in prosecution, I believe you have an obligation to possess and execute some type of traditional antivirus software. ClamAV is a safe and reliable option. If I were still investigating federal crimes, I would conduct a complete scan of my Mac computer with all three of these programs weekly. If nothing else, it allows me to confirm in my report that my machine was clean.

Telemetry

Apple computers collect and send as much, if not more, telemetry as Windows machines. Apple insists this is for your benefit and to help create a fun and efficient computer experience. If you would like to stop Apple from collecting any details about your usage, you will need to install a software firewall application. I use a paid program called Little Snitch, but a free option called LuLu may work just as well for your needs.

First, you should question whether you need this type of protection on an OSINT machine. As I stated previously, I never conduct any investigations within the macOS operating system. I only rely on virtual machines, and my activities within those machines are not seen by Apple. Since these firewall applications cannot intercept data within the VMs we will create later, a firewall might be overkill for this situation. I explain more options in my macOS privacy guide for personal macOS devices. If you do not conduct investigations within the operating system, and rely only on virtual machines as explained throughout this guide, then I do not believe a software firewall is as important.

VPN Configuration

Virtual Private Networks (VPNs) provide a good mix of both security and privacy by routing your internet traffic through a secure tunnel. The tunnel goes to the VPN's server and encrypts all the data between your device and that server. This ensures that anyone monitoring your traffic before it reaches the distant server will not find usable, unencrypted data. Privacy is also afforded through the use of a distant server. Because your traffic appears to be originating from the VPN's server, websites will have a more difficult time tracking you, aggregating data on you, and pinpointing your location. While conducting OSINT research, a VPN prevents websites from knowing your true location or company network details. If you visit your target's personal website, you do not want that person knowing any identifiable information about the connection.

Virtual Private Networks are not a perfect anonymity solution. It is important to note that VPNs offer you privacy, not anonymity. The best VPNs for privacy purposes are paid subscriptions with reputable providers. There are several excellent paid VPN providers out there and I strongly recommend them over free providers. Free providers often monetize through very questionable means, such as data aggregation. Paid VPN providers monetize directly by selling you a service, and reputable providers do not collect or monetize your data. Paid providers also offer a number of options which will increase your overall privacy and security.

I currently use and recommend Proton VPN. I offer further information and the best affiliate purchase links on my site at **inteltechniques.com/vpn.html**. Purchases include unlimited use, connection to multiple devices simultaneously, and fast speeds. I pay for my VPN with Bitcoin in an alias name, but that may be overkill for many readers. For most readers, I recommend sticking with the standard macOS application provided by the VPN company. These branded apps should suffice for most needs. Proton VPN can be downloaded with the following Terminal command.

```
brew install --cask protonvpn
```

Once installed, simply provide your account credentials and launch your VPN connection. Fortunately, Proton VPN has made their applications completely open-source. This makes it much more difficult to hide malicious programming within them.

My VPN policy is quite simple, but my opinions about VPN companies can be complex. Any time that I am connected to the internet from my macOS device, I am connected through my VPN. Any VMs running within this host are also protected with the same VPN IP address. I rely on Proton VPN through their app on my macOS device only while I am traveling. Home devices are protected through a firewall with Proton VPN, as explained in *Extreme Privacy: VPNs & Firewalls*. At home, I never need to launch a VPN within my computer itself due to the VPN firewall.

Password Manager

While you conduct your online investigations, you will likely create and maintain numerous accounts and profiles across various services. Documenting the profile details, including passwords, for these services can be a daunting task. A password manager provides a secure database to store all of the various settings in regard to these profiles. My choice is KeePassXC. I believe we should all have a robust password manager on our OSINT host machine, and not necessarily within a VM. Since we may often delete, rebuild, or export our VMs, storing our passwords within them may be risky. If we store all passwords on the host machine which runs the VMs, we always have access to any account.

KeePassXC is an open-source password manager that does not synchronize content to the internet. There are many convenient online password managers which are secure and keep all of your devices ready for automated logins. Those are great for personal security, and millions of people are safely using them. However, it is not enough for our needs. Since you will be storing data connected to online investigations, you should protect it in an offline solution. KeePassXC is cross-platform and free. It will work identically on Mac, Windows, or Linux. The following installs it on macOS.

```
brew install --cask keepassxc
```

Next, conduct the following as an exercise.

- Launch KeePassXC and select "Database" > "New Database".
- Provide a name to your new password database, such as Passwords, and click "Continue".
- Move the encryptions settings slider completely to the right and click "Continue".
- Assign a secure password which you can remember but is not in use anywhere else.
- Click "Done" and select a safe location to store the database.
- Close the program and verify you can open the database with your password.

You now have a secure password manager and database ready for use on your host machine. Whenever you start using Linux virtual machines, as explained soon, all of your passwords will be available within the host, and the VM will store no credentials. Next, assume you are ready to change the password to your covert Facebook profile. Navigate to the menu which allows change of password. Next, conduct the following within KeePassXC.

- Right-click within the left column and select "New Group".
- Name the group Facebook and click "OK".
- Select the Facebook group on the left menu.
- In the right panel, right-click and select "New Entry".
- Provide the name of your covert account, username, and URL of the site.
- Click the black dice icon to the right of the "Password" field.
- Click the eyeball icon.
- Slide the password length slider to at least 40 characters.
- Copy the generated password and paste into the "Password" and "Repeat" fields.
- Change your Facebook password to this selection within your account.
- Click "OK" and save the database.

You successfully created a new, secure, randomly generated password for your covert profile. You will not remember it, but your password manager will. Allow your password manager to generate a new random password containing letters, numbers, and special characters. If the website you are using allows it, choose a password length of at least 50 characters. When you need to log in, you will copy and paste from the password manager. For each site which you change a password, your password manager will generate a new, unique string. This way, WHEN the site you are using gets breached, the passwords collected will not work anywhere else. More importantly, recycled passwords will not expose your true accounts after the breached data becomes public. There should be only a handful of passwords you memorize, which brings us to the next point.

The password to open your password manager should be unique. It should be something you have never used before. It should also contain letters, numbers, and special characters. It is vital that you never forget this password, as it gives you access to all of the credentials that you do not know. I encourage users to write it down in a safe place until memorized. It is vital to make a backup of your password database. When you created a new database, you chose a name and location for the file. As you update and save this database, make a copy of the file on an encrypted USB drive. Be sure to always have a copy somewhere safe, and not on the internet. If your computer would completely crash, and you lose all of your data, you would also lose all of the new passwords you have created. This would be a huge headache. Prepare for data loss now.

I no longer recommend the KeePassXC browser extension for OSINT investigations. There is nothing insecure about it, but it requires you to copy the master database within any virtual machines unnecessarily, and technically provides some connection from one investigation to another within the VM. This is not a huge deal, but we should always be willing to scrutinize our strategies and become more secure investigators.

By keeping your passwords in an offline database, you eliminate this entire attack surface. By keeping your password manager ready in your host machine, you will have immediate access to it regardless of which virtual machine you are using during an investigation.

Summary

I will assume you now possess a sanitized macOS device ready for your investigations through a VM. Ideally, you will never conduct any personal or investigative tasks within this environment. It will only serve as the host for the many VMs which you will soon create.

CHAPTER THREE
macOS VM SOFTWARE

This is where I deviate heavily from some previous editions. In the past, I relied solely on VirtualBox VM software for all Windows, macOS, and Linux machines. While VirtualBox still works well for Windows and Linux, it is not recommended for Apple devices. There are two reasons, and the first is Apple silicon chips. All modern (and future) macOS machines now use Apple's own processors based on the ARM architecture. VirtualBox does not fully support this, and maybe never will. Second, Apple's operating system security can be a hurdle when installing VirtualBox. With almost every application update, I need to confirm that I want the software installed; modify system security settings; and allow my system to reboot. I present a much simpler and more stable option for Apple devices called **UTM** (mac.getutm.app).

UTM is a free open-source virtualization and emulation program which allows macOS users to launch practically any virtual system within machines which have either Intel or ARM (Apple) processors. This means it will work with any Apple computer, regardless of the hardware. UTM employs Apple's Hypervisor virtualization framework to run ARM operating systems on Apple Silicon at near native speeds. On Intel-based machines, traditional x86/x64 operating systems can be virtualized. In addition, lower performance emulation is available to run x86/x64 on Apple Silicon as well as ARM64 on Intel. This allows us practically any option desired, and is unique to this program. Even the paid alternatives do not offer all of these features. The software relies on QEMU, which has always been otherwise difficult to configure. I now rely solely on UTM for all VMs on my macOS machine, and I find it to be superior to a Windows or Linux host. If you have Homebrew installed, the following Terminal command downloads and installs UTM.

```
brew install --cask utm
```

Upon opening UTM, you have the option to "Create a New Virtual Machine". If this is ever not visible, you can replicate the action by clicking "File" > "New" within the program's menu. Choosing this selection presents options which may be new to readers. You can select to either "Virtualize" or "Emulate" your new VM. We should understand the difference.

Virtualize: This process is accomplished with the help of hardware, typically the hypervisor. It virtually shares the hardware resources of a single physical computer into multiple virtual devices by allocating dedicated resources from the host system to the newly created virtual system. This is typically much faster than emulation and the option we will choose for our new VM. If you have an M1, M2, or newer Apple processor, you cannot virtualize x86/x64 operating systems, you can only virtualize ARM-based systems. Similarly, you cannot virtualize ARM-based systems from a x86/x64 machine. When using virtualization, the operating system must be created for the processor present within the device.

Emulate: This process is much more forgiving, but can be slow. It uses software to emulate specific hardware. This means that the VM needs a software interpreter translating its code into the host system's language. This eats up a lot of resources and can make things drag. Since the VM does not run on the host's physical hardware, emulation is slower when compared to virtualization. By contrast, in virtualization, the guest system gets direct access to the host's allocated resources, resulting in better speed. It is great to have this option, but we will not use it within this chapter.

UTM macOS VM on macOS Host (ARM Processor)

Let's build our first VM within UTM together. If you own an Apple computer with an M1, M2, M3, or later Apple processor, you can easily run multiple macOS virtual machines within UTM. This provides a "test" copy of macOS for any experimentation without modifying your host operating system. I find these macOS VMs to run almost as fast as the native host, which is quite impressive. The following applies only to Apple processors.

First, you must download an "IPSW" file from a legitimate Apple source. I prefer to visit the following website and download the latest "Final" IPSW file, such as UniversalMac_14.2.1_23C71_Restore.ipsw.

https://mrmacintosh.com/apple-silicon-m1-full-macos-restore-ipsw-firmware-files-database/

The full URL source of the file was as follows.

https://updates.cdn-apple.com/2023FallFCS/fullrestores/052-22662/ECE59A41-DACC-4CA5-AB23-FDED1A4567DE/UniversalMac_14.2.1_23C71_Restore.ipsw

Once you have the IPSW file on your machine, you are ready to continue with installation.

- Launch UTM and click "Create a New Virtual Machine".
- Choose "Virtualize" and then "macOS 12+".
- Click "Browse" and select your downloaded IPSW file.
- Modify the RAM to 50 % of your current resources.
- Modify the CPU to half of the "Performance" cores. My 10-core M1 Pro has 8 performance cores, so I chose "4" for this option.
- Click "Continue"; specify the desired size of the drive; click "Continue", then "Save".
- Click the "Settings" icon and click the "Display" menu.
- Choose the display of your device, enabling "HiDPI".
- Click "Save" and exit the settings if necessary.

If you want a shared drive for accessing files across each version of macOS, complete the following.

- From the macOS host, open "System Settings" > "General" > "Sharing".
- Enable "File Sharing" and click the information button.
- Click the "+" and browse to the desired shared folder.
- Click "Add" then "Done".
- In the UTM program, open the settings for the macOS VM.
- Ensure "Network" is set to "Shared Network" and click "Save".
- In the UTM VM settings, click the shared directory menu and select "Browse".
- Select the same folder previously shared and click "Open".
- Launch the macOS VM and open Finder.
- Go to "Finder" > "Settings" > "Sidebar" and enable "Connected Servers".
- Click "Network" within Finder and double-click the host.
- Click "Connect As…" and enter your host OS credentials.
- Enable "Remember this password…" and click "Connect".

If you want to temporarily disable internet connectivity from your host device while you configure your operating system and firewall, conduct the following before the initial boot.

- Right-click the "Network" menu item and select "Remove".

Conduct the following to re-enable internet connectivity from the host machine.

- Select the desired VM within UTM.
- Click the "Settings" icon in the upper-right.
- Click "New" in the left menu and select "Network", then click "Save".

It is important to note that UTM uses Apple's native virtualization framework on Apple Silicon hardware. Therefore, connections within any UTM virtual machine cannot be intercepted by a software firewall, such as Little Snitch. This is why you never see options to block traffic from within UTM VMs. I do not have an issue with this because I am mostly running Linux VMs within UTM which do not possess abusive telemetry. However, you may encounter a scenario where you want to run a VM without any network connectivity to the internet. When this occurs, conduct the previous steps.

Before launching, I recommend modification to the screen resolution. I right-clicked on my machine within UTM and selected the Display menu item. I then changed the resolution to 3840 x 2160 and activated "HiDPI". This substantially increased the VM resolution for my external monitor. You should play with these options until you find the setting appropriate for your machine.

Launch your new macOS VM. You may need to confirm the installation by pressing "OK". Allow the process to complete, which may take some time. Once complete, you have a fully-functioning macOS VM which should be as smooth and responsive as the native host. You have the ability to copy files to and from the VM when needed. It could be used to test software before committing on your macOS host or to conduct sensitive activity which may be inappropriate for your daily host. I conduct many online investigations within both macOS and Linux virtual machines.

Note that the drive for your macOS VM will be 100% full. Whatever size you set will create a file that size for the VM. There is currently no shrinking option for macOS VMs, but we will shrink our Windows and Linux VMs later. Let's take a look at the file we generated by creating this VM. Within UTM, right-click on your new macOS VM and select "Show in Finder". You should be presented the Finder application which has been navigated to the default VM storage folder within macOS, which should be the following.

/Users/[your macOS username]/Library/Containers/UTM/Data/Documents/

In my example, the single file holding all of the data within my macOS VM is called "macOS.utm" and is 68.77 GB in size. This file size will never change regardless of the actual amount of data held within the VM. This only applies to macOS VMs, and I will show the difference with a Windows VM in a moment. Knowing how to open this storage location will be important when I explain VM backups and archives.

UTM Windows VM on macOS Host

UTM can also host Windows VMs, but they must be based on ARM builds if you want them to load in M1 or newer processors. **This section is completely optional**. I respect if some people prefer to avoid Windows altogether. If you would like the practice, you will need an official Windows 11 ARM-based ISO installation file. Microsoft does not make this easy, but downloading a Windows installation file is completely legal. I prefer to use a program called CrystalFetch, which obtains Windows installation media directly from Microsoft and converts it into the proper format. It can be installed within macOS with the following command.

```
brew install --cask crystalfetch
```

After installation, conduct the following.

- Launch the program.
- Select "Windows 11", "Apple Silicon", and your desired language.
- Choose the desired edition (Default is fine).
- Click "Download" and accept the terms.
- Allow the download and conversions process to complete.
- When prompted, select the desired file storage location and click "Move".

You now have a Windows 11 ISO, which can be used to create a VM within UTM with the following steps.

- Within UTM, select "File" then "New".
- Choose "Virtualize" and then "Windows".
- Click "Browse" and select your downloaded ISO file.
- Click "Continue".
- Modify the RAM to 50 % of your current resources.
- Modify the CPU to half of the "Performance" cores. My 10-core M1 Pro has 8 performance cores, so I chose "4" for this option.
- Click "Continue" and specify the desired size of the drive.
- Click "Continue" then "Save".
- Click the "Display" menu item and change the Display Card to "virtio-ramfb".
- Ensure all possible check boxes are selected.
- Click "Save" and exit the settings if necessary.

If you want a shared drive for accessing files across each OS, complete the following.

- In the UTM window, click "Browse" next to "Shared Directory".
- Select the desired shared host folder and click "Open".

Launch the Windows 11 VM and press any button to install Windows 11. You can now go through the installation process and declare you "don't have a product key". When prompted within Windows, install the UTM Guest Tools. Once Windows 11 is successfully installed, shut the VM down and "clear" the installation file from within the VM settings CD-ROM. If you have a Windows 11 license, you can apply it within the VM once fully rebooted. If not, you can either purchase a license online or run this VM in trial mode, which will eventually expire based on the version downloaded. If desired, you could replicate all of these steps to create a new VM after the expiration and continue use of Windows 11 for free. You now have the UTM for macOS basics covered. Later, we will use UTM to create the ultimate Linux OSINT VM for macOS. Next, we should understand some advanced options within UTM.

UTM USB Connection

UTM offers simple USB device access for Windows and Linux VMs. If you are running a macOS VM within macOS, the previous strategy of a shared folder works best. While any USB drive is attached to the host computer, select the "USB Devices" icon in the upper-right of the UTM Windows or Linux VM window. This presents a list of attached USB devices. You can select the USB storage device which will remove it from the host (macOS) and allow access within the VM (Windows or Linux). Note that this transfer will likely generate a macOS warning about removing a drive without ejecting it first, but there should be no harm in this. If you plug in a USB device while the VM is running, it should prompt you to choose where you want it used (host or VM).

By default, UTM uses a generic USB 3.0 driver for access to external USB drives. This should work for most purposes. On occasion, I have had to switch this to the USB 2.0 driver when inserting older USB drives. If you encounter a USB drive which cannot be recognized by the VM, shut down the VM and go to the UTM VM settings. Change "USB 3.0" to "USB 2.0" (or vice versa) within the "Input" tab. You can also disable USB support entirely in this menu, but it is generally not recommended.

UTM Read-Only VM Execution

One of my favorite features of UTM is the ability to launch a VM without saving any changes. This is beneficial when you want to test something but do not want to cause any irreversible damage to the VM. I often launch a pristine Linux VM in a read-only environment to install new software for the first time to identify any potential issues. Once I know I want to commit to the application, I shut down the read-only VM and relaunch it in normal mode. Before launching any Windows or Linux VM, right-click the desired VM and select "Run without saving changes". Any activity conducted during this session will not be preserved within the VM.

UTM VM Exports and Clones

While a VM is shut down and the VM window is closed, you will see options within the main UTM application for the selected VM in the upper-right. Let's focus on the "Clone selected VM" and "Share" menu options. Clicking the clone option simply presents an option to make a full clone. This allows us to preserve our original VM and make copies whenever we want to conduct an investigation. The share option allows us to export an entire VM within a ".utm" file for easy archiving or sharing. The dialogue will prompt you to choose the export location. As a reminder, you can always see the location of all VMs within UTM by navigating to the following directory within the macOS host.

/Users/[your macOS username]/Library/Containers/UTM/Data/Documents/

If this location is not convenient, and I believe it is not, you can move your VM to any folder desired with the "Move selected VM" option within the main windows. I keep all of mine within a dedicated folder on my macOS host. Note that you can only move them once using the button option, and this is likely unnecessary for most users.

UTM Snapshots

UTM offers a Terminal-based snapshot option, but it is not similar to VirtualBox's offering which will be discussed soon. Personally, I never use UTM snapshots and always rely on clones or exports, as previously explained.

UTM Issues

Unlike using VirtualBox within various Windows and Linux machines, UTM within a macOS system has very few issues. The software was designed only for macOS which reduces some of the typical cross-platform bugs. Since it is made for Apple hardware, it seems much more fluid than other software. Once you have experienced UTM on a macOS, you may never want to touch other options again.

UTM VM Size & Shrinking

The hard drive space of your Windows and Linux VMs will keep growing unnecessarily. When you make changes within the VM, all of the data is somewhat preserved, even deleted content. Fortunately, UTM makes the shrinking process easy. While a Windows or Linux VM is shut down, select it within the main UTM window. Go to the Settings for that VM and select the IDE drive of your operating system within the left menu. Click the "Reclaim Space" button and confirm the option. You will see the size decrease if free space was available. I do this after every major update to any Windows or Linux VM.

UTM VPN Issues

Several readers have reported that using the macOS Proton VPN application in "Kill Switch" mode blocks all internet to a VM. I was able to replicate this, and now recommend disabling "Kill Switch" mode in the Proton VPN host application while using a UTM VM.

Summary

I currently rely on a 2021 MacBook Pro (M1) for all of my online investigations. I only use virtual machines within UTM and possess no other virtualization software on my machine. I simply find UTM to be much more stable than the equivalents for other operating systems. I can quickly launch multiple Linux, Windows, and macOS VMs for my OSINT needs. A Linux VM boots in less than 10 seconds; a Windows VM in less than 19 seconds; and macOS VMs somehow boot in only 6 seconds. I can easily test software and customizations without much of a time commitment. We will create our ultimate Linux machine soon.

CHAPTER FOUR
LINUX HOST OPTIMIZATION

I suspect very few readers possess a Linux host machine for their OSINT investigations, but I find it much more reliable than Windows. Of macOS, Linux, and Windows, a Linux host running a Linux VM will present the fewest software errors. Consider some recommendations for Linux machines.

Complete System Wipe

Most Linux systems have an embedded reset function, but I never use them. Whenever I want to reinstall a Linux operating system, I do so from a bootable USB drive which contains Ventoy. Ventoy allows you to place various Linux ISO files at the root of a USB drive and boot to it. After boot, you can select which OS you want to execute or install. The Ventoy downloads page presents options for Windows, Linux, or a live ISO. These likely forward to https://github.com/ventoy/Ventoy/releases. The following will create your own Ventoy bootable USB drive.

- Download the Linux version, titled similarly to "ventoy-1.0.79-linux.tar. gz".
- Decompress the file, which should present a folder similar to "ventoy-1.0.79".
- Open Terminal and navigate to the directory of the folder.
- Execute "./VentoyGUI.x86_64" in Terminal.
- This should present the Ventoy installation application.
- Choose the desired USB device and click "Install", then confirm when prompted.

Note that this will overwrite all data on the device. Your Ventoy boot device is now ready for use, but it does not contain any bootable operating systems. This is where Ventoy excels. Instead of manually configuring multiple systems for boot, you only need to possess the bootable ISO files for any systems desired. The drive has an ExFat formatted partition which can hold any type of data. This means we can use it as a storage drive and multi-boot drive. I downloaded all of the ISO files for the various systems which I may need, such as Debian, and then re-titled the files to match my desired display. I then inserted this new drive within my computer and rebooted. I was sure to select the proper USB boot option within the BIOS (Basic Input / Output System). I could then select any of the downloaded operating systems and each would boot as if I had inserted a dedicated USB boot device. The files will appear exactly as the file names on the drive. The remainder of the drive can be used to store any data desired. Only available bootable Linux and Windows systems will display within the Ventoy boot screen. This makes it easy to install or re-install a Linux operating system.

I use a SanDisk Extreme Portable 1TB USB SSD (https://amzn.to/3BLIHwd). It loads live systems without any delay or stuttering, and installs new systems in a flash. It also allows me to use the remaining 95% of the drive for fast file transfer. Once you are accustomed to the speed of a fast USB SSD for booting and installation of Linux systems, you can never go back to slow flash drives. Today, I keep my multi-boot with me at all times. Often, I forget that booting is the main purpose since I also use it to transfer large files. The best-case scenario is that you will never need it. If you do, you will be glad you made these efforts.

Antivirus & Antimalware

Much like the Apple section, I recommend possessing ClamAV on your Linux OSINT host for the same reasons. If your OSINT work should ever be scrutinized in court, the opposing counsel may raise concern over the lack of antivirus protection. This attorney will know nothing about Linux system security, but neither will the judge or the jury. This is more about "checking the boxes" of a secure machine and less about the protection from Linux-targeted viruses. It is easier to simply testify that you possess security software and confirm that scans are run on a schedule than to explain why your Linux machine does not need antivirus software. You are always more likely to identify viruses which target Windows machines than Linux, but this is the game we play. These could be attachments within email messages which are not a threat to your Linux installation, but should still be removed. The following commands within Terminal installs ClamAV.

```
sudo apt update
sudo apt install -y clamav clamav-daemon
```

You are now ready to update your antivirus database and conduct a scan. Type the following commands into Terminal to stop the service, update the database, and restart the service.

```
sudo systemctl stop clamav-freshclam
sudo freshclam
sudo systemctl start clamav-freshclam
```

These commands download all virus definition updates and should be executed before each scan. We now have two options for a scan of our entire drive. The first scans your data and notifies you of potential viruses. However, it does not remove any files. I always execute this option first. The second command repeats the scan while deleting any infected files.

```
clamscan -r -i /
clamscan -r -i --remove=yes /
```

ClamAV may occasionally present a false-positive report of a virus. Research the file on the internet and identify the issues. If you receive reports of malicious files within email, simply delete those messages.

Telemetry

Most Linux machines collect very little telemetry and allow us to easily prevent data from being sent from our machine. Your Linux host may have telemetry enabled. During installation, Ubuntu presents options to disable common telemetry, but let's assume Ubuntu users did not modify the proper settings. The following commands disable telemetry within Ubuntu, and there is no harm executing these if using another system.

```
sudo apt purge -y apport apport-symptoms ubuntu-report whoopsie
sudo apt autoremove -y
```

System Cleaner

I recommend BleachBit as my weekly Linux system cleaner. Type the following to install the application.

```
sudo apt install bleachbit
```

Clicking the nine dots in the Dock will present two BleachBit applications. The second icon executes the software with administrative privileges and is the option I choose. Upon first launch, click "Close" to accept default configuration. Select every option except the "Free disk space" feature. Click "Preview" to see a report of recommended cleaning. Click "Clean" to execute the process. I run this program weekly.

Full-Disk Encryption

Much like the macOS section, I always recommend full-disk encryption within any Linux host (but not Linux VMs). Some Linux operating systems, such as Pop!_OS, make this easy and the default setting during installation. Other systems, such as Ubuntu, make this option easy during installation, but you must change the default setting. If you plan to re-install Ubuntu as your host operating system, this is a great time to make sure the full disk is encrypted. Again, this only applies to a host computer running Linux, not a Linux VM. Every Linux system is unique, but Ubuntu presents an "Advanced Features" option during the installation process which allows you to "Use LVM with the new Ubuntu installation" and "Encrypt the new Ubuntu installation for security". This then presents an option to generate the password for the disk encryption. Always follow the recommendations for your chosen Linux host.

VPN Configuration

Virtual Private Networks (VPNs) provide a good mix of both security and privacy by routing your internet traffic through a secure tunnel. The tunnel goes to the VPN's server and encrypts all the data between your device and that server. This ensures that anyone monitoring your traffic before it reaches the distant server will not find usable, unencrypted data. Privacy is also afforded through the use of a distant server. Because your traffic appears to be originating from the VPN's server, websites will have a more difficult time tracking you, aggregating data on you, and pinpointing your location. While conducting OSINT research, a VPN prevents websites from knowing your true location or company network details. If you visit your target's personal website, you do not want that person knowing any identifiable information about the connection.

Virtual Private Networks are not a perfect anonymity solution. It is important to note that VPNs offer you privacy, not anonymity. I currently use and recommend Proton VPN. Go to **inteltechniques.com/vpn.html** for further information and the best affiliate purchase links. Purchases include unlimited use, connection to multiple devices simultaneously, and fast speeds. I pay for my VPN with Bitcoin in an alias name, but that may be overkill for many readers. For most readers, I recommend sticking with the standard Linux application provided by the VPN company. These branded apps should suffice for most needs. Proton VPN can be downloaded by following their official instructions online at https://protonvpn.com/support/official-linux-vpn-debian. Once installed, simply provide your account credentials and launch your VPN connection. Fortunately, Proton VPN has made their applications completely open-source. This makes it much more difficult to hide malicious programming within them.

My VPN policy is quite simple, but my opinions about VPN companies can be complex. Any time that I am connected to the internet from my Linux device, I am connected through my VPN. Any VMs running within this host are also protected with the same VPN IP address. I rely on Proton VPN through their app on my Linux device only while I am traveling. Home devices are protected through a firewall with Proton VPN, as explained in *Extreme Privacy: VPNs & Firewalls*. At home, I never need to launch a VPN within my computer itself due to the VPN firewall.

Password Manager

While you conduct your online investigations, you will likely create and maintain numerous accounts and profiles across various services. Documenting the profile details, including passwords, for these services can be a daunting task. A password manager provides a secure database to store all of the various settings in regard to these profiles. My choice is KeePassXC. I believe we should all have a robust password manager on our OSINT host machine, and not necessarily within a VM. Since we may often delete, rebuild, or export our VMs, storing our passwords within them may be risky. If we store all passwords on the host machine which runs the VMs, we always have access to any account.

KeePassXC is an open-source password manager that does not synchronize content to the internet. There are many convenient online password managers which are secure and keep all of your devices ready for automated logins. Those are great for personal security, and millions of people are safely using them. However, it is not enough for our needs. Since you will be storing data connected to online investigations, you should protect it in an offline solution. KeePassXC is cross-platform and free. It will work identically on Mac, Windows, or Linux. If you are running any Debian-based distribution, the following commands will install it.

```
sudo add-apt-repository ppa:phoerious/keepassxc
sudo apt update && sudo apt install keepassxc
```

Next, conduct the following as an exercise.

- Launch KeePassXC and select "Database" > "New Database".
- Provide a name to your new password database, such as Passwords, and click "Continue".
- Move the encryption settings slider completely to the right and click "Continue".
- Assign a secure password which you can remember but is not in use anywhere else.
- Click "Done" and select a safe location to store the database.
- Close the program and verify you can open the database with your password.

You now have a secure password manager and database ready for use on your host machine. Whenever you start using Linux virtual machines, as explained soon, all of your passwords will be available within the host, and the VM will store no credentials. Next, assume you are ready to change the password to your covert Facebook profile. Navigate to the menu which allows change of password. Next, conduct the following within KeePassXC.

- Right-click within the left column and select "New Group".
- Name the group Facebook and click "OK".
- Select the Facebook group on the left menu.
- In the right panel, right-click and select "New Entry".
- Provide the name of your covert account, username, and URL of the site.
- Click the black dice icon to the right of the "Password" field.
- Click the eyeball icon underneath the black dice icon.
- Slide the password length slider to at least 40 characters.
- Apply the generated password.
- Change your Facebook password to this selection within your account.
- Click "OK" and save the database.

You successfully created a new, secure, randomly generated password for your covert profile. You will not remember it, but your password manager will. Allow your password manager to generate a new random password containing letters, numbers, and special characters. If the website you are using allows it, choose a password length of at least 50 characters. When you need to log in, you will copy and paste from the password manager. For each site which you change a password, your password manager will generate a new, unique string. This way, WHEN the site you are using gets breached, the passwords collected will not work anywhere else. More importantly, recycled passwords will not expose your true accounts after the breached data becomes public. There should be only a handful of passwords you memorize, which brings us to the next point.

The password to open your password manager should be unique. It should be something you have never used before. It should also contain letters, numbers, and special characters. It is vital that you never forget this password, as it gives you access to all of the credentials that you do not know. I encourage users to write it down in a safe place until memorized. It is vital to make a backup of your password database. When you created a new database, you chose a name and location for the file. As you update and save this database, make a copy of the file on an encrypted USB drive. Be sure to always have a copy somewhere safe, and not on the internet. If your computer would completely crash, and you lose all of your data, you would also lose all of the new passwords you have created. This would be a huge headache. Prepare for data loss now.

I no longer recommend the KeePassXC browser extension for OSINT investigations. There is nothing insecure about it, but it requires you to copy the master database within any virtual machines unnecessarily, and technically provides some connection from one investigation to another within the VM. This is not a huge deal, but we should always be willing to scrutinize our strategies and become more secure investigators.

By keeping your passwords in an offline database, you eliminate this entire attack surface. By keeping your password manager ready in your host machine, you will have immediate access to it regardless of which virtual machine you are using during an investigation.

CHAPTER FIVE
LINUX VM SOFTWARE

For Linux hosts, I still recommend **VirtualBox** (virtualbox.org) for VM creation and execution. I will first explain how to install the application and then ways to configure a virtual machine. VirtualBox installation instructions can be found at virtualbox.org but are not usually straightforward. The default steps will install an outdated version on most machines. At the time of this writing, the following Terminal commands installed VirtualBox 7 on a Linux host.

```
wget -O- https://www.virtualbox.org/download/oracle_vbox_2016.asc |
sudo gpg --dearmor --yes --output /usr/share/keyrings/oracle-
virtualbox-2016.gpg

echo "deb [arch=amd64 signed-by=/usr/share/keyrings/oracle-virtualbox-
2016.gpg] http://download.virtualbox.org/virtualbox/debian
$(lsb_release -cs) contrib" | sudo tee
/etc/apt/sources.list.d/virtualbox.list

sudo apt update
sudo apt install virtualbox-7.0
sudo apt upgrade
```

Install the VirtualBox Extension Pack with the following steps.

- Download "Extension Pack" at https://www.virtualbox.org/wiki/Downloads.
- Launch VirtualBox and select "File" > "Tools" > "Extension Pack Manager".
- Click "Install" and select the downloaded file.

VirtualBox should update through your standard Linux update processes whenever a new version is available. You should be prompted to download a new Extension Pack after an updated version is launched. If you ever receive an error about a mismatch in software, repeat the above steps to install the latest Extension Pack. While VirtualBox is free for personal use, make sure you or your organization meets the requirements for usage of the software, especially the free Extension Pack license. You will receive a notice within Terminal asking you to verify that you have read the requirements. Striking "Tab" then "Enter" on the keyboard acknowledges the first screen, and striking the left arrow then "Enter" completes the second.

The only requirement for VirtualBox to function is a computer that supports virtualization. Any modern Windows or Linux host should work without any modification. Most mid-range and high-end computers made within the past five years should have no problem, but may require you to enable virtualization support in the BIOS during startup. Netbooks, older machines, and cheap low-end computers will likely give you problems. If you are in doubt about meeting this requirement, search for your model of computer followed by "virtualization" and you should find the answers. The rest of this section will assume that your Linux host computer meets this requirement and now possesses VirtualBox.

VirtualBox Windows VM on Linux Host

This section is completely optional. I respect if some people prefer to avoid Windows altogether. If you would like the practice, begin by installing Windows 11 within VirtualBox on a Linux host computer. We will not use this for OSINT investigations, but it is a good primer on the process. This will help when we create our ultimate Linux OSINT VM later. It can also be a good idea to maintain a Windows VM on a Linux host if you need to run Windows software. Conduct the following to download the installation file.

- Navigate to https://www.microsoft.com/software-download/windows11.
- Choose "Windows 11..." under the "Download Windows 11 Disk Image(ISO)" section.
- Click "Download Now", select the desired language when presented, and click "Confirm".
- Click the "64-bit Download" button.

Microsoft often blocks VPN connections from this process. I had to use a dedicated VPN IP address to complete the download (as explained in *Extreme Privacy: VPNs & Firewalls*). You could also download it from public Wi-Fi if your home connection is behind a VPN. Once you have the file downloaded, conduct the following within VirtualBox. **Some versions of VirtualBox may present these options in a different order with slight changes to the wording.**

- Click "Machine" then "New" in the menu.
- Enter a name, such as "Windows11".
- Click the drop-down under "ISO Image"; click "Other"; and select the Windows ISO file.
- Choose the "Edition" as "Windows 11 Pro" (if not already selected).
- Choose the "Type" of "Microsoft Windows" (if not already selected).
- Choose the "Version" of "Windows 11 64-bit" (if not already selected).
- Select the "Skip Unattended Installation" and click "Next".
- Choose a memory size of half of your system's memory.
- Change the "Processor(s)" to half of the available CPUs.
- Deselect "Enable EFI" and click "Next".
- Choose the maximum desired size of your VM (150GB) and click "Next" then "Finish".
- Click "Settings" for this new VM.
- Click the "Advanced" tab and enable "Bidirectional", "Shared Clipboard" and "Drag n' Drop".
- Click "Shared Folders" in the left menu and click the "Plus" icon to the right.
- Under "Folder Path", click the drop-down and select "Other".
- Choose the Downloads folder and click "Open".
- Enable the "Auto-mount" option and click "OK".
- Click "OK" to save all changes and close the settings.
- Click the "Start" option and press any key if prompted.
- If presented, click the white icon next to any VirtualBox pop-ups to eliminate them.
- If the screen is too small, click "View" in the VirtualBox menu and select "Virtual Screen 1" > "Scale to 200%". Most users will not need to do this.
- In the Windows installation screen, click "Next".
- When you see "Install Now", press Shift and F10 simultaneously (FN+Shift+F10 on Apple).
- Enter "regedit" and strike Enter.
- Navigate to Computer\HKEY_LOCAL_MACHINE\SYSTEM\Setup.
- Right-click on the Setup folder, click "New" then "Key".
- Name the new key "LabConfig" and press Enter (Right-click and Edit is necessary).
- In the right frame, right-click, select "New" then "DWORD (32-bit) Value".
- Name the new value "BypassSecureBootCheck" and press "Enter".
- Double-click this new entry and change the value to "1", then click "OK".
- In the right frame, right-click, select "New" then "DWORD (32-bit) Value".
- Name the new value "BypassTPMCheck" and press "Enter".
- Double-click this new entry and change the value to "1", then click "OK".
- In the right frame, right-click, select "New" then "DWORD (32-bit) Value".
- Name the new value "BypassCPUCheck" and press "Enter".
- Double-click this new entry and change the value to "1", then click "OK".
- In the right frame, right-click, select "New" then "DWORD (32-bit) Value".
- Name the new value "BypassRAMCheck" and press "Enter".

- Double-click this new entry and change the value to "1", then click "OK".
- Close the Registry Editor and Command Prompt, then click "Install Now".
- When prompted, choose "I don't have a product key".
- Select the "Windows 11 Pro" version of Windows 11 and click "Next".
- Accept any license terms and then choose the custom installation option.
- Select the default drive and click "Next".
- Allow the installation to finish and restart.
- Choose the desired location and keyboard layout, skipping additional layouts.
- Skip the naming option and choose the option for use with work or school.
- Choose "Sign-in Options".
- Choose the option to connect to a "Domain".
- Provide a username and password, then confirm the password.
- Choose three security questions and provide your desired answers.
- Disable all options in the privacy settings, then click "Next" and "Accept".
- Allow the final process to complete.
- Click "Devices" in the VirtualBox menu and select "Insert Guest Additions CD Image".
- If required, click "Download" and "Insert".
- Open Windows Explorer and select the "CD Drive".
- Double-click "VBoxWindowsAdditions", click "Yes", "Next", "Next", then "Install".
- Click "Finish" and allow a reboot (end any hung applications if necessary).
- Enter your password to log into Windows (ignore any errors).
- Shut down the VM and enter the Settings menu.
- Select the Storage option and click VBoxGuestAdditions "CD".
- Click the blue CD icon to the right, remove the disc, and click "OK".
- Within Terminal in Linux, execute "`sudo gpasswd -a $USER vboxusers`".

This may have seemed exhausting for a simple Windows installation. Many of these steps were required because Windows 11 now conducts numerous checks to see if your computer should have the privilege of possessing its software. The registry modifications eliminate these checks since Microsoft would otherwise block the VM installation without these settings. We also had to choose specific options to avoid a mandatory Microsoft online account. These are yet more reasons I avoid Microsoft Windows. When we build our ultimate OSINT Linux VM, this process will be much simpler.

You now have a fully functioning and legal Windows 11 VM at your disposal. You can resize the window as desired and install any Windows applications. This is a trial, and the trial will eventually expire. When it does, you could replicate these steps to generate a new machine. Surprisingly, this is allowed and encouraged from Microsoft. You may notice branding within the desktop advising it is a trial. If that bothers you, you must acquire a license and install from traditional media. This method is the easiest option to possess a legal copy of Windows within a VM at no cost.

VirtualBox USB Connection

VirtualBox offers USB device access for Windows and Linux VMs, but this requires some configuration. Navigate to the settings for your desired VM and select the "USB" option in the left menu. Click the first blue icon to the right to create a new filter, and click "OK". Start the VM and allow it to completely boot. While any USB drive is attached to the Linux host computer, select the "Devices" VirtualBox menu item and highlight "USB". This will allow you to select the USB drive within the host to access within the VM.

By default, VirtualBox uses a generic USB 3.0 driver for access to external USB drives. This should work for most purposes. On occasion, I have had to switch this to the USB 2.0 driver when inserting older USB drives. If you encounter a USB drive which cannot be recognized by the VM, shut down the VM and go to the

VirtualBox VM settings. Change "USB 3.0" to "USB 2.0" (or vice versa) within the "USB" tab. You can also disable USB support entirely in this menu, but it is generally not recommended.

VirtualBox Exports

If you ever want to preserve a specific state of a VM within VirtualBox, you can export an entire session. This may be important if you are preserving your work environment for court purposes. When I am conducting an investigation that may go to trial, or discovery of evidence will be required, I make an exact copy of the operating system used during the investigation. This can be completed a couple of different ways.

The simplest route is to copy the entire folder of a desired VM. You can right-click on any VM while it is shut down and select "Show in File Manager". You could then copy this folder to an external drive or other location. This does not require any export or creation of a new file. You could also export the entire VM into a single file. This is the method I prefer. While the VM is shut down, select "File" > "Export Appliance" within VirtualBox. Select your VM and click "Next", "Next", then "Finish". This will create a new file within your Documents folder which can later be imported into any instance of VirtualBox.

At the end of my OSINT work on a case, I shut down the machine and export it to a file. This file can be imported later and examined by anyone else who has a copy. The exported file is added to my digital evidence on an external drive. I now know that I can defend any scrutiny by recreating the exact environment during the original examination.

VirtualBox Clones

Once you have a VM configured and ready for use, you may want to clone it and work from the copy. This way, the original VM stays uncontaminated. We will discuss this much more later when we build our ultimate OSINT VM. For now, let's conduct an example with the Windows 11 VM we just built. Conduct the following.

- Right-click on the Windows VM and select "Clone".
- Provide a name such as "Windows11Clone", click "Next", and click "Clone".

You now have two identical VMs, each in their own data folders. If you were to work within the cloned copy and do any damage, you still have the original VM in a perfect state. For clarity, consider my routine for every OSINT investigation I conduct, which takes advantage of the "Clone" option within VirtualBox.

- Launch the Original VM weekly to apply updates or global changes, then close the VM.
- In the VirtualBox menu, right-click on the Original VM and select "Clone".
- Create a new name such as Case #19-87445 and click "Continue" (or "Next") then "Finish".

This creates an identical copy of the VM ready for your investigation. You have no worries of contaminating your original VM. You can keep this clone available for as long as needed while you continue to work within several investigations. You can export the clone in order to preserve evidence, or delete it when finished. Neither action touches the original copy. It is similar to possessing a new computer for every case and having all of them at your disposal whenever you want to jump back into an investigation.

VirtualBox Snapshots

A great feature of virtual machines is the use of Snapshots. These "frozen" moments in time allow you to revert to an original configuration or preserve an optimal setup. Most users install the virtual machine as previously detailed, and then immediately create a snapshot of the unused environment. When your virtual machine eventually becomes contaminated with remnants of other investigations, or you accidentally remove or break a feature, you can simply revert to the previously created snapshot and eliminate the need to ever reinstall. Consider how you might use snapshots, as detailed in the following example.

- After creation of your new virtual machine, apply all updates.
- Completely shut down the machine.
- Click the three lines menu next to the VM and select Snapshots.
- Click the "Take" button and name the Snapshot, such as today's date, and click "OK".

You could now start this machine and download every virus known. You could then shut it down and return to the Snapshots menu. Clicking on the Snapshot and selecting "Restore" would wipe out all of the activity which had occurred since the snapshot was taken, and would allow you to boot to your original clean environment. Clicking "Delete" would remove the Snapshot and prevent you from ever going back to the pristine state (not recommended). Today, I rarely use snapshots, as I believe they are prone to user error. I much prefer cloned machines or exports. Clones require more overall disk space, but provide a greater level of usability between investigations. Snapshots will also generate more wasted space, especially if you create many within one VM.

VirtualBox VM Size & Shrinking

The hard drive space of your Windows and Linux VMs will keep growing unnecessarily. When you make changes within the VM, all of the data is somewhat preserved, even deleted content. Unfortunately, VirtualBox does not make the shrinking process as easy as UTM for macOS. To replicate, we will take a few steps within the Windows VM (Linux VMs will be explained later).

- Remove any undesired files and empty the trash.
- Search within Windows for "Defrag" and open the Drive Optimization program.
- Choose your C Drive and click "Optimize".
- Search for, and execute "Command Prompt".
- Execute the following command:
  `curl https://download.sysinternals.com/files/SDelete.zip -o SDelete.zip`
- Execute the following command: `tar -xf SDelete.zip`
- Execute the following command: `sdelete64.exe c: -z`
- Accept any terms and shut down the Windows VM when process is complete.

This procedure technically filled your VM completely with blank space, which may not sound ideal. With the VM turned off, open Terminal within the Linux host and navigate to the folder containing the VM file you want to shrink. For my test machine, this was the following (replace "osint" with your host name).

```
cd '/home/osint/VirtualBox VMs/Windows11'
```

You must then execute a Terminal command which compacts the "vdi" file within the VM folder. For me, the command was the following.

```
VBoxManage modifymedium disk Windows11.vdi --compact
```

You will see the size decrease if free space was available. I do this after every major update to any Windows or Linux VM, but this will become more important once we have created our ultimate OSINT VM later.

VirtualBox Issues

I wish I could say that every reader will be able to easily build virtual machines on any computer. This is simply not the case. While most computers are capable of virtual machine usage, many demand slight modifications in order to allow virtualization. Let's take a look at one of the most common errors presented by VirtualBox.

VT-x is Disabled: Any version of this error is the most common reason your VMs will not start. This indicates that the processor of your computer either does not support virtualization or the feature is not enabled. The fix for this varies by brand of machine and processor. Immediately after the computer is turned on, before the operating system starts, enter the BIOS of the machine. This is usually accomplished by pressing delete, F2, F10, or another designated key right away until a BIOS menu appears. Once in the BIOS, you can navigate through the menu via keyboard. With many Intel processors, you can open the "Advanced" tab and set the "Virtualization (VT-x)" to "Enable". For AMD processors, open the "M.I.T." tab, "Advanced Frequency" settings, "Advanced Core" settings, and then set the "SVM Mode" to "Enable". If none of these options appear, conduct an online search of the model of your computer followed by "virtualization" for instructions.

VirtualBox Displays: Some users have reported the inability to resize VM windows within VirtualBox and see the "Auto-resize Guest Display" menu option greyed out. The following commands within Terminal of the Linux VM should repair this issue. There is no harm running these if you are unsure.

```
sudo apt update
sudo apt install -y build-essential dkms gcc make perl
sudo rcvboxadd setup
reboot
```

VMWare Workstation Pro Windows VM on Linux Host

The previous tutorials all rely on VirtualBox as our VM software. VirtualBox is not without flaws. Many users become frustrated and seek other VM clients. While I prefer VirtualBox due to its open-source nature, I respect that others may want something a bit more polished. I recommend most readers also possess VMWare Workstation Pro. VMWare now offers the fully-functioning Workstation Pro software for personal use, but requires corporations and other entities to obtain a commercial license. Make sure you understand your own requirements. **This section is also completely optional**. I respect if some people prefer to avoid Windows altogether. If you would like the practice, consider the following.

First, determine if you already have the required software. If you possess the deprecated VMWare Workstation Player, launch it and see if it prompts you to upgrade to the full Workstation Pro version. If so, allow this to complete. If there are errors, which is common, uninstall the deprecated Player version with the following Terminal command then install from scratch.

```
vmware-installer -u vmware-player
```

VMWare Workstation Pro can be installed with the following steps, which bypass the need to create an online account with them.

- Navigate to https://www.techspot.com/downloads/189-vmware-workstation-for-windows.html.
- Click "Workstation Linux" and download the file.
- Within Terminal, navigate to your downloads with `cd Downloads`.
- Type "`chmod +X VM`" and then strike the tab key, then Enter.
- Type "`sudo ./VM`" and then strike the tab key, then Enter.
- Launch VMWare Workstation Pro; accept the terms and license; accept updates on startup; decline the "Customer Experience"; and choose the personal use option (if you qualify).

Some report errors about module installation when executing the program. The following should resolve.

```
git clone https://github.com/mkubecek/vmware-host-modules
cd vmware-host-modules
git checkout workstation-17.5.1
sudo make ; sudo make install
```

Let's replicate the previous tutorial from installing Windows 11 into VirtualBox, with modifications which are appropriate to VMWare Workstation Pro.

- Click "File", then "New Virtual Machine" in the menu.
- Select the "Typical" option.
- Select "Installer disc image file (ISO)" and select the installation file previously downloaded.
- Click "Next" and enter a name, such as "Windows11", then click "Next".
- Enter and confirm a "TPM" password to bypass Windows restrictions and click "Next".
- Choose the maximum size of your drive and select "Store Virtual Disk as a single file".
- Click "Next" and then the "Customize Hardware" button.
- Choose a memory size of half of your system's memory.
- Change the "Processor(s)" to half of the available CPUs.
- Click "Close" then "Finish".
- Click within the VM and press any key when prompted. You may need to click several times after a few restarts until the process is more streamlined.
- In the Windows installation screen, click "Next" then "Install Now".
- When prompted, choose "I don't have a product key".
- Select the "Windows 11 Pro" version of Windows 11 and click "Next".
- Accept any license terms and choose the custom installation option.
- Select the default drive and click "Next".
- Allow the installation to finish and restart.
- Choose the desired location and keyboard layout, skipping additional layouts.
- Skip the naming option and choose the option for use with work or school.
- Choose "Sign-in Options".
- Choose the option to connect to a "Domain".
- Provide a username and password, then confirm the password.
- Choose three security questions and provide your desired answers.
- Disable all options in the privacy settings, then click "Next" and "Accept".
- Allow the final process to complete.
- Click "Virtual Machine" in the VMWare menu and select "Install VMWare Tools".
- Click "Install", select the notification of a new drive in Windows, and click "Run Setup.exe".
- If you are not prompted to run the setup file, launch it from the CD Drive.
- Accept the default options and install the software.
- Click "Finish" and allow a reboot (end any hung applications if necessary).
- Enter your password to log into Windows (ignore any errors).

That was quite simpler than the VirtualBox tutorial. VMWare allowed us to bypass some of the Windows restrictions without registry modification and the overall configuration was more straight-forward. So, what is the catch? File sharing within VMWare Workstation Pro is difficult and often fails. Overall, I believe you should have both programs installed within your Windows or Linux host. Only you can decide which client is better for your needs.

VirtualBox & VMWare Workstation Pro VPN Issues

Several readers have reported that using the Linux Proton VPN application in "Kill Switch" mode blocks all internet to a VM. I was able to replicate this, and now recommend disabling "Kill Switch" mode in the Proton VPN host application while using a VirtualBox or VMWare Workstation Pro VM.

Summary

Hopefully, you now have VirtualBox and VMWare Workstation Pro installed and configured within your Linux host. We will rely on these later when we build our ultimate OSINT VM.

CHAPTER SIX
WINDOWS HOST OPTIMIZATION

Most readers will possess a Windows-based computer. This is my least favorite option for this type of work, but we must all deal with any limitations presented by our employers or our own comfort within an operating system. I was a dedicated Windows user from 3.11 to 7, but transitioned away when 10 hit the scene. If your host computer has a Windows operating system, there are several things to consider. First, which version do you have and does it receive vital system security patches? As I write this, I still believe Windows 10 is the best version to possess, but its days are numbered. It will be supported with updates throughout October of 2025. At that time, one will be forced to move to Windows 11 or whatever Windows 12 will look like in the future. Currently, Windows 11 is the most recent version and the option likely included with a new computer. Therefore, I will assume it is the version Windows users will possess. Let's start with an optional complete wipe of the system.

Complete System Wipe

First and foremost, backup any important data. Connect an external drive via USB and copy any documents, configuration files, and media which will be removed when you reformat the machine. Common locations include the Desktop, Downloads, and Documents folders within the home folder of the current user. Double check that you have everything you need, because the next step is to remove all data from the drive. Most modern Windows computers possess a hidden "restore" partition. To factory reset Windows 11, search "reset" and then select the option to go to "Reset this PC". If desired, choose the option to remove everything and follow the prompts. The result will be a new operating system free of any previous contamination. If you do not have this option, or possess an older Windows operating system, you will need the original installation media or a restore CD from the manufacturer. Upon boot, refuse any requests to create a Microsoft account, and only provide the necessary information to log in to Windows, such as a vague username and password. I prefer to eliminate any internet connection to this machine before I conduct this activity. This usually prevents Microsoft from demanding an online account. You may want to visit the previous tutorial for installing Windows 11 to a VM within Linux for tips to avoid creating an account. You may want to revisit the tutorial in the previous chapter for installing Windows 11 to a VM within Linux for more tips.

Antivirus & Antimalware

There are a dozen popular antivirus companies that will provide a free Windows antivirus solution. For most Windows users, I simply recommend to use Microsoft's products. Users of Windows 10 and 11 should use the default Windows Defender included with their installation. Privacy enthusiasts will disagree with this advice, and I understand their stance. Microsoft products tend to collect your computer usage history and analyze the data. Unfortunately, their core operating systems also do this, and it is difficult to disable long term. Therefore, I believe that Windows users are already disclosing sensitive information to Microsoft. Using their antivirus solutions will not likely enhance the data being collected. I believe that a Windows OSINT host machine should only be used to execute Linux VMs. If that is the scenario for you, then the default Microsoft Defender is sufficient. I no longer recommend additional security software. Let's make sure you have the latest security patches with the following steps.

- Click the task bar and search "defender", then open the "Windows Security" application.
- Click the shield tab and select "Protection Updates", then click "Check for Updates".
- Apply any pending updates.
- Click the task bar and search "updates", then open the "Check for Updates" application.
- Apply any pending updates.

Telemetry

Microsoft's Telemetry service continuously collects the following data, plus numerous additional details, sending it to their corporate servers in Seattle.

- Typed text on keyboard and microphone transmissions
- Index of all media files on your computer
- Webcam data and browsing history
- Search history and location activity
- Health activity collected by HealthVault, Microsoft Band, and other trackers
- Privacy settings across Microsoft application ecosystem

This data would make it very easy to identify you, your location, and all online activity. Microsoft claims this collection of data is only to enhance your experience. I find this invasive, and I will present options to disable much of the data collection. I strongly advise users to attempt to minimize the amount of data Microsoft collects about your computer usage. I already explained a few options during the installation process, but there is much more content which needs blocked. There are many free utilities which assist with this, but I have found **O&O Shut Up 10++** to be the most effective and current. Download the latest version at https://www.oo-software.com/en/shutup10 then install and launch the software. You will see many individual options which can be enabled or disabled. A red icon indicates that feature is disabled while green indicates enabled. The wording can be murky. In general, anything red indicates that data about that topic is being sent to Microsoft while green indicates the service is blocked.

As an example, one option states "Disable suggestions in the timeline". The default option is disabled (red). Switching to green tells us that this threat is disabled, and we are protected. You can ignore any warnings about restore points. Some may want to play with each individual setting. Most choose a pre-determined level of privacy. In the "Actions" option at the top, you will see three categories of "Recommended", "Recommended and somewhat recommended", and "Apply all settings". The first option is very safe and applies normal blocking such as disabling advertisement IDs. The second option is a bit stricter and blocks everything except automatic Windows updates, Windows Defender, and OneDrive. The last option blocks everything possible.

My preference is to select the "Recommended and somewhat recommended" option, and then enable the "Disable sending URLs from apps to Windows Store" (Current User) and "Disable Microsoft OneDrive" (Local Machine) options. This leaves updates and Defender running, which are vital to the overall security of your machine. After you have made your selections, close the program and allow Windows to reboot. Open the application again to make sure your desired settings were maintained. Every time you update the Windows operating system, take a look to see if you need to re-enable your choices here. If you ever have troubles because of your level of protection, you can reverse these changes any time from within the application.

System Cleaner

In some previous books, I recommended a cleaning application called CCleaner. I no longer use this product because of some unethical practices of its owner Piriform. Some versions of CCleaner contain Ad-ware which has been accused of collecting user metrics. My preference today is to use **BleachBit** (bleachbit.org). BleachBit is very similar to CCleaner, but can be a bit more aggressive. I select all available options with the exception of "Wipe Free Space". Choosing this would overwrite all free space on the hard drive which is time consuming. BleachBit removes leftover internet history content, temporary files, and many other types of unwanted data. I execute this program weekly on any Windows or Linux host I use.

VPN Configuration

Virtual Private Networks (VPNs) provide a good mix of both security and privacy by routing your internet traffic through a secure tunnel. The tunnel goes to the VPN's server and encrypts all the data between your device and that server. This ensures that anyone monitoring your traffic before it reaches the distant server will not find usable, unencrypted data. Privacy is also afforded through the use of a distant server. Because your traffic appears to be originating from the VPN's server, websites will have a more difficult time tracking you, aggregating data on you, and pinpointing your location. While conducting OSINT research, a VPN prevents websites from knowing your true location or company network details. If you visit your target's personal website, you do not want that person knowing any identifiable information about the connection.

Virtual Private Networks are not a perfect anonymity solution. It is important to note that VPNs offer you privacy, not anonymity. I currently use and recommend Proton VPN. Go to **inteltechniques.com/vpn.html** for further information and the best affiliate purchase links. Purchases include unlimited use, connection to multiple devices simultaneously, and fast speeds. I pay for my VPN with Bitcoin in an alias name, but that may be overkill for many readers.

For most readers, I recommend sticking with the standard Windows application provided by the VPN company. These branded apps should suffice for most needs. Proton VPN can be downloaded by following the instructions at https://protonvpn.com/download-windows. Once installed, simply provide your account credentials and launch your VPN connection. Fortunately, Proton VPN has made their applications completely open-source. This makes it much more difficult to hide malicious programming within them.

My VPN policy is quite simple, but my opinions about VPN companies can be complex. Any time that I am connected to the internet from my device, I am connected through my VPN. Any VMs running within this host are also protected with the same VPN IP address. I rely on Proton VPN through their app on my device only while I am traveling. Home devices are protected through a firewall with Proton VPN, as explained in *Extreme Privacy: VPNs & Firewalls*. At home, I never need to launch a VPN within my computer due to the firewall.

Password Manager

While you conduct your online investigations, you will likely create and maintain numerous accounts and profiles across various services. Documenting the profile details, including passwords, for these services can be a daunting task. A password manager provides a secure database to store all of the various settings in regard to these profiles. My choice is KeePassXC or Bitwarden. I believe we should all have a robust password manager on our OSINT host machine, and not necessarily within a VM. Since we may often delete, rebuild, or export our VMs, storing our passwords within them may be risky. If we store all passwords on the host machine which runs the VMs, we always have access to any account.

KeePassXC is an open-source password manager that does not synchronize content to the internet. There are many convenient online password managers which are secure and keep all of your devices ready for automated logins. Those are great for personal security, and millions of people are safely using them. However, it is not enough for our needs. Since you will be storing data connected to online investigations, you should protect it in an offline solution. KeePassXC is cross-platform and free. It works the same on Mac, Windows, or Linux. Visit https://keepassxc.org/download/#windows to download KeePassXC for Windows.
Next, conduct the following as an exercise.

- Launch KeePassXC and select "Database" > "New Database".
- Provide a name to your new password database, such as Passwords.
- Move the encryptions settings slider completely to the right and click "Continue".
- Assign a secure password which you can remember but is not in use anywhere else.
- Click "Done" and select a safe location to store the database.
- Close the program and verify you can open the database with your password.

You now have a secure password manager and database ready for use on your host machine. Whenever you start using Linux virtual machines, as explained soon, all of your passwords will be available within the host, and the VM will store no credentials. Next, assume you are ready to change the password to your covert Facebook profile. Navigate to the menu which allows change of password. Next, conduct the following within KeePassXC.

- Right-click within the left column and select "New Group".
- Name the group Facebook and click "OK".
- Select the Facebook group on the left menu.
- In the right panel, right-click and select "New Entry".
- Provide the name of your covert account, username, and URL of the site.
- Click the black dice icon to the right of the "Password" field.
- Click the eyeball icon next to the black dice icon.
- Slide the password length slider to at least 40 characters.
- Change your Facebook password to this selection within your account.
- Click "OK" and save the database.

You successfully created a new, secure, randomly generated password for your covert profile. You will not remember it, but your password manager will. Allow your password manager to generate a new random password containing letters, numbers, and special characters. If the website you are using allows it, choose a password length of at least 50 characters. When you need to log in, you will copy and paste from the password manager. For each site which you change a password, your password manager will generate a new, unique string. This way, WHEN the site you are using gets breached, the passwords collected will not work anywhere else. More importantly, recycled passwords will not expose your true accounts after the breached data becomes public. There should be only a handful of passwords you memorize, which brings us to the next point.

The password to open your password manager should be unique. It should be something you have never used before. It should also contain letters, numbers, and special characters. It is vital that you never forget this password, as it gives you access to all of the credentials that you do not know. I encourage users to write it down in a safe place until memorized. It is vital to make a backup of your password database. When you created a new database, you chose a name and location for the file. As you update and save this database, make a copy of the file on an encrypted USB drive. Be sure to always have a copy somewhere safe, and not on the internet. If your computer would completely crash, and you lose all of your data, you would also lose all of the new passwords you have created. This would be a huge headache. Prepare for data loss now.

I no longer recommend the KeePassXC browser extension for OSINT investigations. There is nothing insecure about it, but it requires you to copy the master database within any virtual machines unnecessarily, and technically provides some connection from one investigation to another within the VM. This is not a huge deal, but we should always be willing to scrutinize our strategies and become more secure investigators.

By keeping your passwords in an offline database, you eliminate this entire attack surface. By keeping your password manager ready in your host machine, you will have immediate access to it regardless of which virtual machine you are using during an investigation.

Hopefully, you now have a newly-refreshed Windows machine with many protections against the threats you will face while conducting online investigations. Your system is ready for virtual machines to be built and executed, and you will be ready to defend the security of your strategies if ever questioned in court or by a client.

CHAPTER SEVEN
WINDOWS VM SOFTWARE

For Windows hosts, I still recommend **VirtualBox** (virtualbox.org). I will first explain how to install the application and then ways to configure a virtual machine. VirtualBox installation instructions can be found at virtualbox.org. At the time of this writing, VirtualBox could be downloaded from https://www.virtualbox.org/wiki/Downloads by selecting the "Windows Hosts" and "Extension Pack" download options (two files). Install VirtualBox by double-clicking the first downloaded file. Accept all default options except the "VirtualBox Python Support". Disable that option in the "Custom Setup" screen. After installation has completed, allow the program to launch. Then, double-click the second Extension Pack file to install it into VirtualBox. While VirtualBox is free for personal use, make sure you or your organization meets the requirements for usage of the software, especially the free Extension Pack license.

The only requirement for VirtualBox to function is a computer that supports virtualization. Any modern Windows or Linux host should work without any modification. Most mid-range and high-end computers made within the past ten years should have no problem, but may require you to enable virtualization support in the BIOS during startup. Netbooks, older machines, and cheap low-end computers will likely give you problems. If you are in doubt about meeting this requirement, search for your model of computer followed by "virtualization" and you should find the answers. The rest of this section will assume that your Windows host computer meets this requirement and now possesses VirtualBox.

I must issue an ironic warning. While my team and I were testing everything here, creating Windows VMs on top of Windows hosts presented the most problems, errors, and frustrations. We also found countless other people online complaining of the same issues. If you can avoid Windows hosts in favor of macOS and Linux machines, please do. If you cannot, we will work through it together. **This section is completely optional**. I respect if some people prefer to avoid Windows VMs altogether. If you would like the practice, continue. If not, wait until the Linux VM chapter.

VirtualBox Windows VM on Windows Host

Let's begin by installing Windows 11 within VirtualBox on a Windows host computer. We will not use this for OSINT investigations, but it is a good primer on the process. This will help when we create our ultimate Linux OSINT VM later. It can also be a good idea to maintain a second copy of Windows on a Windows host in the event you need to test Windows software without impact to your host. Conduct the following to download the necessary installation file.

- Navigate to https://www.microsoft.com/software-download/windows11.
- Choose "Windows 11..." under the "Download Windows 11 Disk Image(ISO)" section.
- Click "Download Now", select the desired language when presented, and click "Confirm".
- Click the "64-bit Download" button.

Microsoft often blocks VPN connections from this process. You could also download it from public Wi-Fi if your home connection is behind a VPN. Once you have the file downloaded, conduct the following within VirtualBox.

- Click "Machine" then "New" in the menu.
- Enter a name, such as "Windows11".
- Click the drop-down under "ISO Image"; choose "Other"; and select the Windows ISO file.
- Choose the "Edition" as "Windows 11 Pro".
- Choose the "Type" of "Microsoft Windows".
- Choose the "Version" of "Windows 11 64-bit"

- Select the "Skip Unattended Installation" and click "Next".
- Choose a memory size of half of your system's memory.
- Change the "Processor(s)" to half of the available CPUs.
- Deselect "Enable EFI" and click "Next".
- Choose the maximum desired size of your VM (150GB) and click "Next" then "Finish".
- Click "Settings" for this new VM.
- Click the "Advanced" tab and enable "Bidirectional", "Shared Clipboard" and "Drag n' Drop".
- Click "Shared Folders" in the left menu and click the "Plus" icon to the right.
- Under "Folder Path", click the drop-down and select "Other".
- Choose the Downloads folder and click "Open".
- Enable the "Auto-mount" option and click "OK".
- Click "OK" to save all changes and close the settings.
- Click the "Start" option and press any key when prompted.
- If presented, click the white icon next to any VirtualBox pop-ups to eliminate them.
- If the screen is too small, click "View" in the VirtualBox menu and select "Virtual Screen 1" > "Scale to 200%". Most users will not need to do this.
- In the Windows installation screen, click "Next".
- When you see "Install Now", press Shift and F10 simultaneously (FN+Shift+F10 on Apple).
- Enter "regedit" and strike Enter.
- Navigate to Computer\HKEY_LOCAL_MACHINE\SYSTEM\Setup.
- Right-click on the Setup folder, click "New" then "Key".
- Name the new key "LabConfig" and press Enter (Right-click and Edit is necessary).
- In the right frame, right-click, select "New" then "DWORD (32-bit) Value".
- Name the new value "BypassSecureBootCheck" and press "Enter".
- Double-click this new entry and change the value to "1", then click "OK".
- In the right frame, right-click, select "New" then "DWORD (32-bit) Value".
- Name the new value "BypassTPMCheck" and press "Enter".
- Double-click this new entry and change the value to "1", then click "OK".
- In the right frame, right-click, select "New" then "DWORD (32-bit) Value".
- Name the new value "BypassCPUCheck" and press "Enter".
- Double-click this new entry and change the value to "1", then click "OK".
- In the right frame, right-click, select "New" then "DWORD (32-bit) Value".
- Name the new value "BypassRAMCheck" and press "Enter".
- Double-click this new entry and change the value to "1", then click "OK".
- Close the Registry Editor and Command Prompt, then click "Install Now".
- When prompted, choose "I don't have a product key".
- Select the "Windows 11 Pro" version of Windows 11 and click "Next".
- Accept any license terms and choose the custom installation option.
- Select the default drive and click "Next", then allow the installation to finish and restart.
- Choose the desired location and keyboard layout, skipping additional layouts.
- Skip the naming option and choose the option for use with work or school.
- Choose "Sign-in Options".
- Choose the option to connect to a "Domain".
- Provide a username and password, then confirm the password.
- Choose three security questions and provide your desired answers.
- Disable all options in the privacy settings, then click "Next" and "Accept".
- Allow the final process to complete and provide your password when prompted.
- Click "Devices" in the VirtualBox menu and select "Insert Guest Additions CD Image".
- If required, click "Download" and "Insert".
- Open Windows Explorer and select the "CD Drive".
- Double-click "VBoxWindowsAdditions", click "Yes", "Next", "Next", then "Install".

- Click "Finish" and allow a reboot (end any hung applications if necessary).
- Enter your password to log into Windows (ignore any errors).
- Shut down the VM and enter the Settings menu.
- Select the Storage option and click the "VBoxGuestAdditions.iso" CD.
- Click the blue CD icon to the right, remove the disc, and click "OK".

This may have seemed exhausting for a simple Windows installation. Many of these steps were required because Windows 11 now conducts numerous checks to see if your computer should have the privilege of possessing its software. The registry modifications eliminate these checks since Microsoft would otherwise block the VM installation without these settings. We also had to choose specific options to avoid a mandatory Microsoft online account. These are yet more reasons I avoid Microsoft Windows. When we build our ultimate OSINT Linux VM, this process will be much simpler.

You now have a fully functioning and legal Windows 11 VM at your disposal. You can resize the window as desired and install any Windows applications. This is a trial, and the trial will eventually expire. When it does, you could replicate these steps to generate a new machine. Surprisingly, this is allowed and encouraged from Microsoft. You may notice branding within the desktop advising it is a trial. If that bothers you, you must acquire a license and install from traditional media. This method is the easiest option to possess a legal copy of Windows within a VM at no cost.

VirtualBox USB Connection

VirtualBox offers USB device access for Windows and Linux VMs, but this requires some configuration. Navigate to the settings for your desired VM and select the "USB" option in the left menu. Click the first blue icon to the right to create a new filter, and click "OK". Start the VM and allow it to completely boot. While any USB drive is attached to the Windows host computer, select the "Devices" VirtualBox menu item and highlight "USB". This will allow you to select the USB drive within the host to access within the VM.

By default, VirtualBox uses a generic USB 3.0 driver for access to external USB drives. This should work for most purposes. On occasion, I have had to switch this to the USB 2.0 driver when inserting older USB drives. If you encounter a USB drive which cannot be recognized by the VM, shut down the VM and go to the VirtualBox VM settings. Change "USB 3.0" to "USB 2.0" (or vice versa) within the "USB" tab. You can also disable USB support entirely in this menu, but it is generally not recommended.

VirtualBox Exports

If you ever want to preserve a specific state of a VM within VirtualBox, you can export an entire session. This may be important if you are preserving your work environment for court purposes. When I am conducting an investigation that may go to trial, or discovery of evidence will be required, I make an exact copy of the operating system used during the investigation. This can be completed a couple of different ways.

The simplest route is to copy the entire folder of a desired VM. You can right-click on any VM while it is shut down and select "Show in File Manager". You could then copy this folder to an external drive or other location. This does not require any export or creation of a new file. You could also export the entire VM into a single file. This is the method I prefer. While the VM is shut down, select "File" > "Export Appliance" within VirtualBox. Select your VM and click "Next", "Next", then "Finish" or "Export". This will create a new file within your Documents folder which can later be imported into any instance of VirtualBox.

At the end of my OSINT work on a case, I shut down the machine and export it to a file. This file can be imported later and examined by anyone else who has a copy. The exported file is added to my digital evidence on an external drive. I now know that I can defend any scrutiny by recreating the exact environment during the original examination.

VirtualBox Clones

Once you have a VM configured and ready for use, you may want to clone it and work from the copy. This way, the original VM stays uncontaminated. We will discuss this much more later when we build our ultimate OSINT VM. For now, let's conduct an example with the Windows 11 VM we just built. Conduct the following.

- Right-click on the Windows VM and select "Clone".
- Provide a name such as "Windows11Clone", click "Next", and click "Finish".

You now have two identical VMs, each in their own data folders. If you were to work within the cloned copy and do any damage, you still have the original VM in a perfect state. For clarity, consider my routine for every OSINT investigation I conduct, which takes advantage of the "Clone" option within VirtualBox.

- Launch the Original VM weekly to apply updates or global changes, then close the VM.
- In the VirtualBox menu, right-click on the Original VM and select "Clone".
- Create a new name such as Case #19-87445 and click "Continue" (or "Next") then "Clone".

This creates an identical copy of the VM ready for your investigation. You have no worries of contaminating your original VM. You can keep this clone available for as long as needed while you continue to work within several investigations. You can export the clone in order to preserve evidence, or delete it when finished. Neither action touches the original copy. It is similar to possessing a new computer for every case and having all of them at your disposal whenever you want to jump back into an investigation.

VirtualBox Snapshots

A great feature of virtual machines is the use of Snapshots. These "frozen" moments in time allow you to revert to an original configuration or preserve an optimal setup. Most users install the virtual machine as previously detailed, and then immediately create a snapshot of the unused environment. When your virtual machine eventually becomes contaminated with remnants of other investigations, or you accidentally remove or break a feature, you can simply revert to the previously created snapshot and eliminate the need to ever reinstall. Consider how you might use snapshots, as detailed in the following example.

- After creation of your new virtual machine, apply all updates.
- Completely shut down the machine.
- Click the three lines menu next to the VM and select Snapshots.
- Click the "Take" button and name the Snapshot, such as today's date, and click "OK".

You could now start this machine and download every virus known. You could then shut it down and return to the Snapshots menu. Clicking on the Snapshot and selecting "Restore" would wipe out all of the activity which had occurred since the snapshot was taken, and would allow you to boot to your original clean environment. Clicking "Delete" would remove the Snapshot and prevent you from ever going back to the pristine state (not recommended).

Today, I rarely use snapshots, as I believe they are prone to user error. I much prefer cloned machines or exports. These require more disk overall space, but provide a greater level of usability between investigations. Snapshots will also generate more wasted space, especially if you create many within one VM.

VirtualBox VM Size & Shrinking

The hard drive space of your Windows and Linux VMs will keep growing unnecessarily. When you make changes within the VM, all of the data is somewhat preserved, even deleted content. Unfortunately, VirtualBox does not make the shrinking process as easy as UTM for macOS. To replicate, we will take a few steps within the Windows VM (Linux VMs will be explained later).

- Remove any undesired files and empty the trash.
- Search within Windows for "Defrag" and open "Drive Optimization".
- Choose your C Drive and click "Optimize".
- Search for, and execute Command Prompt.
- Execute the following command:
  ```
  curl      https://download.sysinternals.com/files/SDelete.zip      -o
  SDelete.zip
  ```
- Execute the following command:
  ```
  tar -xf SDelete.zip
  ```
- Execute the following command:
  ```
  sdelete64.exe c: -z
  ```
- Accept any terms and shut down the Windows VM when process is complete.

This procedure technically filled your VM completely with blank space, which may not sound ideal. With the VM turned off, open Command Prompt within the Windows host and navigate to the folder containing the VM file you want to shrink. For me, this was the following.

```
cd "C:\Users\OSINT\VirtualBox VMs/Windows11"
```

Next, we must add the program to our path with the following command.

```
PATH "C:\Program Files\Oracle\VirtualBox"
```

You must then execute a command which compacts the "vdi" file within the VM folder. For me, the command was the following.

```
VBoxManage modifymedium disk Windows11.vdi --compact
```
You will see the size decrease if free space was available. I do this after every major update to any Windows or Linux VM, but this will become more important once we have created our ultimate OSINT VM later.

VirtualBox Issues

I wish I could say that every reader will be able to easily build virtual machines on any computer. This is simply not the case. While most computers are capable of virtual machine usage, many demand slight modifications in order to allow virtualization. Let's take a look at one of the most common errors presented by VirtualBox.

VT-x is Disabled: Any version of this error is the most common reason your VMs will not start. This indicates that the processor of your computer either does not support virtualization or the feature is not enabled. The fix for this varies by brand of machine and processor. Immediately after the computer is turned on, before the operating system starts, enter the BIOS of the machine. This is usually accomplished by pressing delete, F2, F10, or another designated key right away until a BIOS menu appears. Once in the BIOS, you can navigate through the menu via keyboard. With many Intel processors, you can open the "Advanced" tab and set the "Virtualization (VT-x)" to "Enable". For AMD processors, open the "M.I.T." tab, "Advanced Frequency" Settings, "Advanced Core" settings, and then set the "SVM Mode" to "Enable". If none of these options appear, conduct an online search of the model of your computer followed by "virtualization" for instructions.

VT-x is not available: This is usually isolated to Windows 10 machines. Navigate to the Windows Control Panel and open "Programs and Features". Click "Turn Windows features on or off" and uncheck all "Hyper-V" features. Click "OK" and reboot. If the Hyper-V option is not enabled, enable Hyper-V, restart the computer, disable Hyper-V, and reboot again. Attempt to start your VM with these new settings. This may seem backwards, but it makes sense. Previous versions of VirtualBox cannot run if you are using "Hyper-V" in Windows. Basically, both systems try to get exclusive access to the virtualization capabilities of the processor. Hyper-V within Windows receives the access first and impedes VirtualBox from the capabilities. The latest version of VirtualBox attempts to correct this. If the previous setting did not help, try to re-enable all of the Hyper-V options within Windows, reboot, and try to boot your VM again. If you are still experiencing problems, read the troubleshooting chapter of the VirtualBox manual on their website. Expand any errors received and search the provided error codes to identify further solutions.

VirtualBox Displays: Some users have reported the inability to resize VM windows within VirtualBox and see the "Auto-resize Guest Display" menu option greyed out. The following commands within Terminal of the Linux VM should repair this issue. There is no harm running these if you are unsure.

```
sudo apt update
sudo apt install -y build-essential dkms gcc make perl
sudo rcvboxadd setup && reboot
```

VMWare Workstation Pro Windows VM on Windows Host

The previous tutorials all rely on VirtualBox as our VM software. VirtualBox is not without flaws. Many users become frustrated and seek other VM clients. While I prefer VirtualBox due to its open-source nature, I respect that others may want something a bit more polished. I recommend most readers also possess VMWare Workstation Pro. VMWare now offers the fully-functioning Workstation Pro software for personal use, but requires corporations and other entities to obtain a commercial license. Make sure you understand your own requirements. **This section is also completely optional**. I respect it if some people prefer to avoid Windows altogether. If you would like the practice, consider the following.

First, determine if you already have the required software. If you possess the deprecated VMWare Workstation Player, launch it and see if it prompts you to upgrade to the full VMWare Workstation Pro version. If so, allow this to complete. If there are errors, which is common, or you are not presented an option to upgrade, uninstall the deprecated Player version. VMWare Workstation Pro can be manually installed with the following steps, which bypass the need to create an online account with them.

- Navigate to https://www.techspot.com/downloads/189-vmware-workstation-for-windows.html.
- Click "Workstation Windows" and download the file.
- Double-click the downloaded file and allow all default options for installation, except be sure to disable "Join the VMWare Customer Experience".
- Launch the program and choose the personal use option (if you qualify).

Let's replicate the previous tutorial from installing Windows 11 into VirtualBox, with modifications which are appropriate to VMWare Workstation Pro.

- Click "File" then "New Virtual Machine" in the menu.
- Choose the "Typical" option and click "Next".
- Select "Installer disc image file" and select the Windows installation file previously downloaded.
- Click "Next" and enter a name, such as "Windows11", then click "Next".
- Enter and confirm an encryption password to bypass Windows restrictions and click "Next".
- Choose the maximum size of your drive (64 GB) and select "Store Virtual Disk as a single file".
- Click the "Customize Hardware" button.
- Choose a memory size of half of your system's memory.
- Change the "Processor(s)" to half of the available CPUs.
- Click "Close" then "Finish".
- Click within the VM and press any key when prompted (this disappears quickly).

- In the Windows installation screen, click "Next" then "Install Now".
- When prompted, choose "I don't have a product key".
- Select the "Windows 11 Pro" version of Windows 11 and click "Next".
- Accept any license terms and choose the custom installation option.
- Select the default drive and click "Next".
- Allow the installation to finish and restart.
- Choose the desired location and keyboard layout, skipping additional layouts.
- Skip the naming option.
- Choose the option for use with work or school.
- Choose "Sign-in Options".
- Choose the option to connect to a "Domain".
- Provide a username and password, then confirm the password.
- Choose three security questions and provide your desired answers.
- Disable all options in the privacy settings, then click "Next" and "Accept".
- Allow the final process to complete.
- When prompted, click "Install VMWare Tools".
- If required, choose this option from the "VM" menu.
- Click "Install", select the notification of a new drive in Windows, and click "Run Setup.exe".
- Accept the default options and install the software.
- Click "Finish" and allow a reboot (end any hung applications if necessary).
- Enter your password to log into Windows (ignore any errors).

That was quite simpler than the VirtualBox tutorial. VMWare allowed us to bypass some of the Windows restrictions without registry modification and the overall configuration was more straight-forward. So, what is the catch? VMWare Workstation Pro has some limitations. The most vital is that file sharing within VMWare Workstation Pro is difficult and often fails.

Overall, I believe you should have both programs installed within your Windows or Linux host. Only you can decide which client is better for your needs.

VMWare Workstation Pro Issues

- Windows VMs on top of Windows hosts often display an "EFI" warning which may prevent a machine from booting. If you see this error, click within the VM as quickly as you can and press any key.
- If you get your cursor stuck within a VM window, pressing the "alt" and "ctrl" keys simultaneously should release it.
- If you encounter other errors, you are not alone. Running any Windows VM on top of a Windows 10 or 11 host is frustrating to say the least. Search your errors online and research the issues and remedies.
- If you are unable to install a Windows 11 VM on top of a Windows host, don't worry. We should have much better success installing our Linux VM later.

VirtualBox & VMWare Workstation Pro VPN Issues

Several readers have reported that using the Windows Proton VPN application in "Kill Switch" mode blocks all internet to a VM. I was able to replicate this, and now recommend disabling "Kill Switch" mode in the Proton VPN host application while using a VirtualBox or VMWare Workstation Pro VM.

Summary

Hopefully, you now have VirtualBox and VMWare Workstation Pro installed and configured within your Windows host. We will rely on these later when we build our ultimate OSINT VM.

CHAPTER EIGHT
OSINT VM OPERATING SYSTEMS

Finally, we can begin creating our ultimate OSINT VM. Until now, we have focused on preparing our host machines; configuring virtual machine software clients; and generating non-Linux VMs to understand the virtualization process. Next, we will create a Linux VM which will be the foundation for our OSINT investigative VM. We will use all of the principles explained previously, but apply everything toward Linux instead of macOS or Windows. First, we must pick a version of Linux for our needs.

This may be quite controversial to some Linux enthusiasts, but I now recommend Debian as an ideal Linux operating system for our OSINT machine. While I use Pop!_OS for my personal host machine due to the privacy, security, and overall convenience of that operating system on my hardware, pure Debian is more appropriate for a wider audience on VMs.

Unlike Ubuntu, Debian offers an official ARM-based build for Apple machines; presents no default telemetry; does not force premium features such as Ubuntu Pro on us; and does not follow a release schedule based on specific dates and years. While Debian has been known to present hardware driver issues on some host machines, it will work well inside our VM software. If you are comfortable with Pop!_OS or any other Debian flavor of Linux such as Ubuntu, and insist on using it versus Debian, go for it. For those who want an easier option, **I will only explain the OSINT VM process using Debian**. If you are new to Linux, I highly recommend that you replicate my steps presented here verbatim until you find a specific need to deviate to another operating system. Overall Debian is more minimal than popular options such as Ubuntu or Pop!_OS.

You may be surprised I no longer recommend Ubuntu. It is one of the most popular Linux distributions, and it is based on Debian as its backbone. Ubuntu is the product of a corporation called Canonical. Some still criticize Ubuntu for including Amazon software in the default downloads, which provided affiliate funding to Ubuntu when you made an online purchase, but this has been removed in current versions. Many people dislike the forced usage of their proprietary Snap software, but that is also going away soon. Most of the steps within the rest of this guide could be replicated with Ubuntu and even other non-Debian flavors of Linux if desired, with minimal differences within installation menus, but you would encounter some errors. The general functions should all remain the same.

As I write this, the current official release of Debian is 12.5 stable, and my entire build is based on that release. This version will receive updates and security patches for at least three years while it is the current release, plus two additional years of long-term support after the next major version is released. This means that we should have support patches for Debian 12 until at least mid 2027, and likely into 2028. By then, we will have migrated to Debian 13. I will update this guide once a new major revision to Debian is available. **Always use the most current stable release**.

Previous versions of this content presented a combination of instructions for various operating systems. This was mostly due to limited printed page space. With this digital guide, I present isolated detailed instructions for each host operating system (macOS, Linux, and Windows). This should prevent any confusion about the steps required for your specific host operating system. As you go through this chapter, you should choose the appropriate path for your host, and ignore instructions for other operating systems. I present obvious paths and subsequent steps as we go along. I promise this will all make sense once we start. Let's go in order, and start with macOS hosts. If you have a Linux or Windows host, you should skip to the relevant section.

UTM Linux OSINT VM on macOS Host (ARM Processor)

In a previous chapter, we used UTM to create a Windows 11 VM on a macOS device with an Apple processor. This required us to find an ARM version of Windows for use with newer macOS machines. This brings us to our need to choose the proper Linux path based on our hardware. You must choose the appropriate version of Debian for your processor. If you have an M1, M2, M3, or later processor, you need the ARM version of Debian. You can click the Apple logo in the upper-left of your device and select "About This Mac" to identify your version. Below is the current download link for ARM builds. Once you are on the page for your hardware, download the current ISO file, similar to "debian-12.5.0-arm64-netinst.iso".

Debian arm64: https://cdimage.debian.org/debian-cd/current/arm64/iso-cd/

If choosing the ARM version, make sure you do not accidentally select the AMD version, and vice versa. Let's work through the entire Debian installation process for macOS hosts together. Launch UTM and conduct the following.

- Click "File", then "New".
- Choose the "Virtualize" option and then select "Linux".
- Click the "Browse" button, select the Debian ISO file, click "Open", then click "Continue".
- Choose half of your system's memory and CPU cores. If you had 16 GB of RAM and an eight-core processor, you would change the RAM to "8192" and the CPU Cores to "4". Never leave the cores as "Default", as it can confuse the operating system. Click "Continue" when complete.
- The size of the drive should be set to the maximum you will ever need. This is not the size of the VM as it grows, it is only the max. I set mine to "150" GB. Click "Continue".
- I prefer to enable file sharing, as it makes it easier to extract evidence from your investigation onto your host. Browse to your desired shared folder (I chose Downloads) and click "Open" then "Continue".
- Provide a name for your new VM, such as "Debian Stock" and click "Save".
- Click the arrow icon to start your new Linux VM. The screen may appear black for a while.

You are now ready to install Debian. Upon initial boot of your new VM within UTM, conduct the following steps. The traditional and ARM versions will have differences, but the idea is to work through any installation screens. Consider the following.

- Select "Install" and strike the Enter or Return key.
- Strike the Enter or Return key to select the default language, location, and keyboard.
- If desired, use the arrow keys to select a more appropriate option on each screen.
- Strike the Enter or Return key to accept a hostname of "debian".
- Strike the Enter or Return key to decline a domain name.
- Do not provide any "root" password! Since this is a VM, we will allow the primary user to have root privileges. Simply strike Enter or Return twice.
- Enter "osint" (lowercase and without quotes) as the user account, username, full name, and user password. **This is a mandatory step as part of the tutorials and scripts presented in this book.** While any other usernames and passwords could work at first, you will face issues as you proceed. Make sure **all usernames, computer names, and passwords are "osint".**
- Choose your desired time zone and strike the Enter or Return key.
- Choose the "Guided - use entire disk" option.
- Choose the "Virtual disk" option and "All files in one partition".
- Strike Enter or Return to "Finish"; then left arrow key to select "Yes"; then Enter or Return.
- When prompted, strike Enter or Return to skip any other media.
- Strike the Enter or Return key to accept the default package manger and archive mirror.
- Strike the Enter or Return key to bypass any proxy.
- Strike the Enter or Return key to bypass anonymous statistics.

- Press the spacebar to select "Debian desktop environment"; strike the down arrow key to highlight "GNOME"; press the spacebar to select it; ensure "standard system utilities" are selected; then strike Enter or Return. This is the default desktop environment I will use during my tutorials. If you have a strong opinion that another environment is better, choose your preference.
- Allow Debian to complete the installation. Once you see "Installation complete", click the "CD" icon in the upper-right of the UTM VM window; highlight the CD/DVD option, and click "Eject".
- Strike Enter or Return to "Continue" and restart.
- If you only see a black screen for too long, press the "left triangle" within UTM to restart.

Your device should boot to the operating system. I have occasionally encountered the following issues.

- If it boots into the installation ISO again, shut the machine down. In the main UTM window, select your new machine and click the settings icon in the upper-right. Under "Drives", identify the CD/DVD drive and change "Image Type" to "None". Reboot the VM and boot into the Debian Desktop.
- If receiving a pop-up about errors, I prefer to enable "Remember this in future" and "Ignore future problems", then click "Don't Send". We will apply updates soon which should correct any pending issues.
- Click "Install Now" if prompted for updates, and let them finish.

The following will finish the default configuration upon initial boot.

- Log in to your VM and select "Next" twice; disable "Location Services"; click "Next"; then "Skip"; then "Start Using Debian GNU/Linux".

Some desired capabilities, such as clipboard and file sharing, require the installation of UTM's Spice daemon. Click the "Activities" menu (upper-left) within the VM; click the nine dots (Show Applications) within the lower-right; click "Terminal"; and execute the following.

```
sudo apt install spice-vdagent spice-webdavd -y
```

Copy and paste capabilities should be working after a reboot, but you may not see your shared folder within Files on Debian. The following should fix this.

- Shut down the VM (upper-right menu > power button) and close the UTM VM window.
- Within the main UTM window, click the "Settings" icon in the upper-right for your VM.
- Select "Sharing" on the left.
- Change "Directory Share Mode" to "Spice WebDAV" and click "Save".
- Reboot the VM.
- Click the "Shared folder" icon in the upper right of the UTM Debian VM window.
- Confirm your desired shared folder location.
- Open the "Files" icon within Debian and click the "Other Locations" option in the left menu.
- You should see a folder titled "Spice client".
- Single click that folder and wait for your system to recognize the share.
- Confirm you can access the shared folder within the left menu of Files.

Sometimes, it can take several minutes for the share to become available to Debian. Once it does, it should appear until the VM reboots. Whenever you need to access the shared folder, simply click the Spice folder under "Other Locations" for that session. You can now copy files from your VM directly to your macOS host and vice versa. I typically only do this after the VM has been booted for a while and I need the shared folder.

While the machine is shut down, I like to confirm the following options within the settings menu by right-clicking and choosing "Edit" (or click the Settings icon).

- Input > USB Support > USB 3.0
- Sharing > Directory Share Mode > Spice WebDAV
- Display > Emulated Display card > virtio-ramfb
- Display > Retina Mode > Enabled

You can now shut down the VM and continue to the section titled "Preserve Stock Debian".

UTM Linux OSINT VM on macOS Host (Intel Processor)

If you possess an older macOS device with an Intel processor, you should not use the ARM version of Debian for your VM. Instead, you can use the default Debian amd64 ISO available on the Debian website. You can click the Apple logo in the upper-left of your device and select "About This Mac" to identify your version. Below is the current download link. Once you are on the page for your hardware, download the current ISO file, similar to "debian-12.5.0-amd64-netinst.iso".

Debian amd64: https://cdimage.debian.org/debian-cd/current/amd64/iso-cd/

If choosing the AMD version, make sure you do not accidentally select the ARM version, and vice versa. Let's work through the entire Debian installation process for macOS hosts together. Launch UTM and conduct the following.

- Click "File", then "New".
- Choose the "Virtualize" option and then select "Linux".
- Click the "Browse" button, select the Debian ISO file, click "Open", then click "Continue".
- Choose half of your system's memory and CPU cores. If you had 16 GB of RAM and an eight-core processor, you would change the RAM to "8192" and the CPU Cores to "4". Never leave the cores as "Default", as it can confuse the operating system. Click "Continue" when complete.
- The size of the drive should be set to the maximum you will ever need. This is not the size of the VM as it grows, it is only the max. I set mine to "150" GB. Click "Continue".
- I prefer to enable file sharing, as it makes it easier to extract evidence from your investigation onto your host. Browse to your desired shared folder (I chose Downloads) and click "Open" then "Continue".
- Provide a name for your new VM, such as "Debian Stock" and click "Save".
- Click the arrow icon to start your new Linux VM. The screen may appear black for a while.

You are now ready to install Debian. Upon initial boot of your new VM within UTM, conduct the following steps. This traditional AMD and the ARM versions have some differences, but the idea is to work through any installation screens. Consider the following.

- Select "Graphical Install" or allow it to load as default.
- Choose your Language and select "Continue".
- Choose your Location and select "Continue".
- Choose your Keyboard and select "Continue".
- Leave the name as "debian" and click "Continue"; then click "Continue" again.
- Do not set a Root password, and simply click "Continue".
- Provide a user account name as "osint" (lowercase and without quotes); a username of "osint"; and a password of "osint". **This is a mandatory step as part of the tutorials and scripts presented in this book.** While any other username could work at first, you will face issues as you proceed. Please make sure **all entries are "osint"**. Since this is a virtual machine inside a secure computer, minimal security is acceptable.

- Choose your Time Zone and click "Continue".
- Choose the "Guided - use entire disk" option and click "Continue".
- Choose "QEMU HARDDISK" and "All files in one partition", clicking "Continue" after each.
- Click "Continue"; select "Yes"; and click "Continue" to begin the installation.
- When prompted, confirm "No" to bypass local media and click "Continue".
- Choose the default package manager and click "Continue" three times.
- Select "No" and click "Continue" to disable statistics.
- Select "GNOME"; ensure "Debian desktop environment" and "standard system utilities" are also enabled; and click "Continue" to accept the desktop environment I will use during my tutorials. If you have a strong opinion that another environment is better, choose your preference.
- If prompted, click "Continue" to install GRUB; choose "QEMU HARDDISK" and click "Continue".
- Allow Debian to complete the installation. Once you see "Installation complete", click the "CD" icon in the upper-right of the UTM VM window; highlight the CD/DVD option; click "Eject"; then click "Continue" within Debian.
- After reboot, log in and click "Next" twice; disable "Location Services"; click "Next" then "Done"; then "Start Using Debian...".

Your device should boot to the operating system. I have occasionally encountered the following issues.

- If it boots into the installation ISO again, shut the machine down. In the main UTM window, select your new machine and click the settings icon in the upper-right. Under "Drives", identify the CD/DVD drive and change "Image Type" to "None". Reboot the VM and boot into the Debian Desktop.
- If receiving a pop-up about errors, I prefer to enable "Remember this in future" and "Ignore future problems", then click "Don't Send". We will apply updates soon which should correct any pending issues.
- Click "Install Now" if prompted for updates, and let them finish.

Some desired capabilities, such as clipboard and file sharing, require the installation of UTM's Spice daemon. Click the "Activities" menu (upper-left) within the VM; click the nine dots (Show Applications) within the lower-right; click "Terminal"; and execute the following.

```
sudo apt install spice-vdagent spice-webdavd -y
```

Copy and paste capabilities should be working after a reboot, but you may not see your shared folder within Files on Debian. The following should fix this.

- Shut down the VM (upper-right menu > power button) and close the UTM VM window.
- Within the main UTM window, click the "Settings" icon in the upper-right for your VM.
- Select "Sharing" on the left.
- Change "Directory Share Mode" to "Spice WebDAV" and click "Save".
- Reboot the VM.
- Click the "Shared folder" icon in the upper right of the UTM Debian VM window.
- Confirm your desired shared folder location.
- Open the "Files" icon within Debian and click the "Other Locations" option in the left menu.
- You should see a folder titled "Spice client".
- Single click that folder and wait for your system to recognize the share.
- Confirm you can access the shared folder within the left menu of Files.

Sometimes, it can take several minutes for the share to become available to Debian. Once it does, it should appear until the VM reboots. Whenever you need to access the shared folder, simply click the Spice folder under "Other Locations" for that session. You can now copy files from your VM directly to your macOS host and vice versa. I typically only do this after the VM has been booted for a while and I need the shared folder.

While the machine is shut down, I like to confirm the following options within the settings menu by right-clicking and choosing "Edit" (or click the Settings icon).

- Input > USB Support > USB 3.0
- Sharing > Directory Share Mode > Spice WebDAV
- Display > Emulated Display card > virtio-ramfb
- Display > Retina Mode > Enabled

You can now shut down the VM (if booted) and continue to the section titled "Preserve Stock Debian".

VirtualBox Linux OSINT VM on Linux Host

If you tested both VirtualBox and VMWare Workstation Pro during previous chapters, you may now have a preference for a VM client. I prefer VirtualBox over VMWare when using new powerful hardware, but VMWare tends to be faster on older hardware. Ideally, you will use both throughout this chapter and make a decision once you experience real-world results. Download the latest Debian ISO at https://cdimage.debian.org/debian-cd/current/amd64/iso-cd/. Always download the proper file, similar to "debian-12.5.0-amd64-netinst.iso". Next, let's work through the entire Debian installation process for Linux hosts together. Some versions of VirtualBox may present these options in a different order with slight changes to the wording. Launch VirtualBox and conduct the following.

- Click "Machine" then "New" in the menu.
- Enter a name of "Debian Stock".
- Click the drop-down in the "ISO Image" section; select "Other"; and choose the ISO file.
- Enable the "Skip Unattended Installation" option and click "Next".
- Choose a memory size of half of your system's memory.
- Change the "Processor(s)" to half of the available CPUs.
- Deselect "Enable EFI" and click "Next".
- Choose the maximum desired size of your VM as 150 GB, and click "Next" then "Finish".
- Click "Settings" for this new VM.
- Click the "Advanced" tab and enable "Bidirectional", "Shared Clipboard" and "Drag n' Drop".
- Click "Shared Folders" in the left menu and click the "Plus" icon to the right.
- Under "Folder Path", click the drop-down and select "Other".
- Choose the Downloads folder and click "Open".
- Enable the "Auto-mount" option and click "OK".
- Click "OK" to save all changes and close the settings.
- Click the "Start" option and boot the VM.
- If presented, click the white icon next to any VirtualBox pop-ups to eliminate them.
- If the screen is too small, click "View" in the VirtualBox menu and select "Virtual Screen 1" > "Scale to 200%". Most users will NOT need to do this.
- Select "Graphical Install" or allow it to load as default.
- Choose your Language and select "Continue".
- Choose your Location and select "Continue".
- Choose your Keyboard and select "Continue".
- Leave the name as "debian" and click "Continue"; then click "Continue" again.
- Do not set a Root password, and simply click "Continue".
- Provide a user account name as "osint" (lowercase and without quotes); a username of "osint"; and a password of "osint". **This is a mandatory step as part of the tutorials and scripts presented in this book.** While any other username could work at first, you will face issues as you proceed. Please make

sure **all entries are "osint".** Since this is a virtual machine inside a secure computer, minimal security is acceptable.

- Choose your Time Zone and click "Continue".
- Choose the "Guided - use entire disk" option and click "Continue".
- Choose "VBOX HARDDISK" and "All files in one partition", clicking "Continue" after each.
- Click "Continue"; select "Yes"; and click "Continue" to begin the installation.
- When prompted, confirm "No" to bypass local media and click "Continue".
- Choose the default package manager and click "Continue" three times.
- Select "No" and click "Continue" to disable statistics.
- Select "GNOME"; ensure "Debian desktop environment" and "standard system utilities" are also enabled; and click "Continue" to accept the desktop environment I will use during my tutorials. If you have a strong opinion that another environment is better, choose your preference.
- If prompted, click "Continue" to install GRUB; choose "VBOX..." and click "Continue".
- Allow Debian to complete the installation. Once you see "Installation complete", click "Continue" to allow a reboot.
- After reboot, log in and click "Next" twice; disable "Location Services"; click "Next" then "Done"; then "Start Using Debian...".
- Shut down the VM.

Currently, the automated option to download and install Guest Additions does not work properly within Debian. Therefore, we will manually download the file and install within the VM.

- Within your VirtualBox client software, click "Help" and "About" to identify the exact version of your software. Mine was 7.0.10.
- Navigate to https://download.virtualbox.org/virtualbox within your Linux host; select your exact version of VirtualBox; download the VBoxGuestAdditions ISO file; open the VirtualBox settings for the VM; click "Storage"; click the "Empty" CD icon; click the CD icon to the far right; select "Choose a Disk File"; select your Guest Additions ISO; select "Open" and "OK".
- Start the OSINT VM and click "Activities" in the upper-left once booted.
- Click the Files icon in the center of the lower Dock.
- Navigate to the "VBox..." option in the left menu and click "Run Software" to the right.
- Confirm to "Run" the software; enter your password when prompted; and restart the VM.
- Click "Activities", the nine dots, then "Terminal", and execute the following to enable sharing.

```
sudo groupadd vboxusers
sudo usermod -aG vboxusers osint
sudo groupadd vboxsf
sudo usermod -aG vboxsf osint
```

- Shut down the VM.
- Within the VirtualBox program, click the Settings for the VM.
- Under "Storage", right-click VBoxGuestAdditions and choose "Remove Attachment".
- Confirm with "Remove", click "OK", and restart the VM.

You should now have VirtualBox Guest Additions installed. You can test this by resizing the screen. If you make the VM full screen, you should see the overall screen resolution change with it. If you previously changed the scaling of the window in VirtualBox, you may want to change it back to 100%. If it looks good, do not make the change. If the screen is still too small, right-click the Debian VM desktop and choose "Display Settings". If the option is present, choose a "scale" of 200% and see if that works better for you. **Overall, I like the VM to possess maximum resolution possible within the VM client, in full screen mode, with a choice of the higher scale within the VM if needed.** Every computer (and user) is unique, so use these settings to make it look best for your eyes.

Your device should now boot to the operating system with the ability to resize the screen as desired. You should also be able to access the Downloads folder of the host machine from within the VM through the "sf_downloads" mounted disk. After any pending updates are installed, shut down the VM and continue to the section titled "Preserve Stock Debian".

VMWare Workstation Pro Linux OSINT VM on Linux Host

If you tested both VirtualBox and VMWare Workstation Pro during previous chapters, you may now have a preference for a VM client. I prefer VirtualBox over VMWare when using new powerful hardware, but VMWare tends to be faster on older hardware. Ideally, you will use both throughout this chapter and make a decision once you experience real-world results. Download the latest Debian ISO at https://cdimage.debian.org/debian-cd/current/amd64/iso-cd/. Always download the proper file, similar to "debian-12.5.0-amd64-netinst.iso". Next, launch VMWare Workstation Pro and conduct the following.

- Click "File" then "New Virtual Machine" in the VMWare menu.
- Choose the "Typical" option and click "Next".
- Select "Use ISO image"; select the Debian file previously downloaded; and click "Next".
- Provide a name of "Debian Stock" and click "Next".
- Choose the max size of your drive as 150 GB and select "Store Virtual Disk as a single file".
- Click "Next" then click the "Customize Hardware" button.
- Choose a memory size of half of your system's memory.
- Change the "Processor(s)" to half of the available CPUs.
- Click "Close"; deselect "Automatically power on..."; and click "Finish".
- Launch the machine and if prompted, click "OK" on any windows about hardware.
- Select "Graphical Install" or allow it to load as default.
- Choose your Language and select "Continue".
- Choose your Location and select "Continue".
- Choose your Keyboard and select "Continue".
- Leave the name as "debian" and click "Continue"; then click "Continue" again.
- Do not set a Root password, and simply click "Continue".
- Provide a user account name as "osint" (lowercase and without quotes); a username of "osint"; and a password of "osint". **This is a mandatory step as part of the tutorials and scripts presented in this book.** While any other username could work at first, you will face issues as you proceed. Please make sure **all entries are "osint"**. Since this is a virtual machine inside a secure computer, minimal security is acceptable.
- Choose your Time Zone and click "Continue".
- Choose the "Guided - use entire disk" option and click "Continue".
- Choose "VMWare" and "All files in one partition", clicking "Continue" after each.
- Click "Continue"; select "Yes"; and click "Continue" to begin the installation.
- When prompted, confirm "No" to bypass local media and click "Continue".
- Choose the default package manager and click "Continue" three times.
- Select "No" and click "Continue" to disable statistics.
- Select "GNOME"; ensure "Debian desktop environment" and "standard system utilities" are also enabled; and click "Continue" to accept the desktop environment I will use during my tutorials. If you have a strong opinion that another environment is better, choose your preference.
- If prompted, click "Continue" to install GRUB; choose "/dev/sda"; and click "Continue".
- Allow Debian to complete the installation. Once you see "Installation complete", click "Continue" to allow a reboot.
- After reboot, log in and click "Next" twice; disable "Location Services"; click "Next" then "Done"; then "Start Using Debian...".
- Reboot the VM.

Your device should now boot to the operating system with the ability to resize the screen as desired. I have occasionally encountered the following issues.

- Click "Install Now" if prompted for updates.
- If you do not see your VM within the VMWare home screen, make sure you have enabled "File History" under the host's "Settings" > "Privacy" > "File History & Trash" menu.
- If your cursor is not available within the VM, or you cannot select anything, restart it.
- The shared folder within the VM will likely not function. VMWare requires several commands specific to your installation to temporarily share a folder with the host. At the time of this writing, a known bug was preventing this. I currently recommend using a USB device connected to the VM to transfer files, which we will do together later.

After any pending updates are installed, shut down the VM and continue to the section titled "Preserve Stock Debian".

VirtualBox Linux OSINT VM on Windows Host

If you tested both VirtualBox and VMWare Workstation Pro during previous chapters, you may now have a preference for a VM client. I prefer VirtualBox over VMWare when using new powerful hardware, but VMWare tends to be faster on older hardware. Ideally, you will use both throughout this chapter and make a decision once you experience real-world results. Download the latest Debian ISO at https://cdimage.debian.org/debian-cd/current/amd64/iso-cd/. Always download the proper file, similar to "debian-12.5.0-amd64-netinst.iso". Next, let's work through the entire Debian installation process for Windows hosts together. Launch VirtualBox and conduct the following.

- Click "Machine" then "New" in the menu.
- Enter a name of "Debian Stock".
- Click the drop-down in the "ISO Image" section; select "Other"; and choose the ISO file.
- Enable the "Skip Unattended Installation" option and click "Next".
- Choose a memory size of half of your system's memory.
- Change the "Processor(s)" to half of the available CPUs.
- Deselect "Enable EFI" and click "Next".
- Choose the maximum desired size of your VM as 150 GB, and click "Next" then "Finish".
- Click "Settings" for this new VM.
- Click the "Advanced" tab and enable "Bidirectional", "Shared Clipboard" and "Drag n' Drop".
- Click "Shared Folders" in the left menu and click the "Plus" icon to the right.
- Under "Folder Path", click the drop-down and select "Other".
- Choose the Downloads folder and click "Select Folder".
- Enable the "Auto-mount" option and click "OK".
- Click "OK" to save all changes and close the settings.
- Click the "Start" option and boot the VM.
- If presented, click the white icon next to any VirtualBox pop-ups to eliminate them.
- If the screen is too small, click "View" in the VirtualBox menu and select "Virtual Screen 1" > "Scale to 200%". Most users will NOT need to do this.
- Select "Graphical Install" or allow it to load as default.
- Choose your Language and select "Continue".
- Choose your Location and select "Continue".
- Choose your Keyboard and select "Continue".
- Leave the name as "debian" and click "Continue"; then click "Continue" again.
- Do not set a Root password, and simply click "Continue".
- Provide a user account name as "osint" (lowercase and without quotes); a username of "osint"; and a password of "osint". **This is a mandatory step as part of the tutorials and scripts presented in this**

book. While any other username could work at first, you will face issues as you proceed. Please make sure **all entries are "osint".** Since this is a virtual machine inside a secure computer, minimal security is acceptable.

- Choose your Time Zone and click "Continue".
- Choose the "Guided - use entire disk" option and click "Continue".
- Choose "VBOX HARDDISK" and "All files in one partition", clicking "Continue" after each.
- Click "Continue"; select "Yes"; and click "Continue" to begin the installation.
- When prompted, confirm "No" to bypass local media and click "Continue".
- Choose the default package manager and click "Continue" three times.
- Select "No" and click "Continue" to disable statistics.
- Select "GNOME"; ensure "Debian desktop environment" and "standard system utilities" are also enabled; and click "Continue" to accept the desktop environment I will use during my tutorials. If you have a strong opinion that another environment is better, choose your preference.
- If prompted, click "Continue" to install GRUB; choose "VBOX..." and click "Continue".
- Allow Debian to complete the installation. Once you see "Installation complete", click "Continue" to allow a reboot.
- After reboot, log in and click "Next" twice; disable "Location Services"; click "Next", "Skip", and "Done"; then "Start Using Debian...".
- Within the VirtualBox top menu, click "Devices"; click "Insert Guest Additions..."; click "Activities" in the upper-left of Debian; open the Files application; click the "VBox" option in the left; click "Run Software in the upper-right; confirm with "Run"; enter your password when prompted; allow the installation to complete; and press Enter to close the window when prompted.
- Click "Activities", the nine dots, then "Terminal", and execute the following to enable sharing.

```
sudo groupadd vboxusers
sudo usermod -aG vboxusers osint
sudo groupadd vboxsf
sudo usermod -aG vboxsf osint
```

- Shut down the VM.
- Within the VirtualBox program, click the Settings for the VM.
- Under "Storage", right-click VBoxGuestAdditions and choose "Remove Attachment".
- Confirm with "Remove", click "OK", and restart the VM.

You should now have VirtualBox Guest Additions installed. You can test this by resizing the screen. If you make the Debian VM full screen, you should see the overall screen resolution change with it. If you previously changed the scaling of the window in VirtualBox, you may want to change it back to 100%. If it looks good, do not make the change. If the screen is still too small, right-click the Debian VM desktop and choose "Display Settings". If the option is present, choose a "scale" of 200% and see if that works better for you. **Overall, I like the Debian VM to possess maximum resolution possible within the VM client, in full screen mode, with a choice of the higher scale within the Debian VM if needed.** Every computer (and user) is unique, so use these settings to make it look best for your eyes.

You should also be able to access the Downloads folder of the host machine from within the VM through the "sf_downloads" mounted disk. Notice that it boots to a view of the Dock at the bottom and a windowed Desktop above. Clicking within this Desktop navigates to it and hides the Dock. We will change this soon. After any pending updates are installed, shut down the VM and continue to the section titled "Preserve Stock Debian".

VMWare Workstation Pro Linux OSINT VM on Windows Host

If you tested both VirtualBox and VMWare Workstation Pro during previous chapters, you may now have a preference for a VM client. I prefer VirtualBox over VMWare when using new powerful hardware, but VMWare tends to be faster on older hardware. Ideally, you will use both throughout this chapter and make a decision once you experience real-world results. Download the latest Debian ISO at https://cdimage.debian.org/debian-cd/current/amd64/iso-cd/. Always download the proper file, similar to "debian-12.5.0-amd64-netinst.iso". Next, launch VMWare Workstation Pro and conduct the following.

- Click "File" then "New Virtual Machine" in the VMWare menu.
- Choose the "Typical" option and click "Next".
- Select "Installer disc image file"; select the Debian ISO file; and click "Next".
- Provide a name of "Debian Stock" and click "Next".
- Choose the max size of your drive as 150 GB and select "Store Virtual Disk as a single file".
- Click "Next" then click the "Customize Hardware" button.
- Choose a memory size of half of your system's memory.
- Change the "Processor(s)" to half of the available CPUs.
- Click "Close"; deselect "Power on..."; and click "Finish".
- Launch the machine and if prompted, click "OK" on any windows about hardware.
- Select "Graphical Install" or allow it to load as default.
- Choose your Language and select "Continue".
- Choose your Location and select "Continue".
- Choose your Keyboard and select "Continue".
- Leave the name as "debian" and click "Continue"; then click "Continue" again.
- Do not set a Root password, and simply click "Continue".
- Provide a user account name as "osint" (lowercase and without quotes); a username of "osint"; and a password of "osint". **This is a mandatory step as part of the tutorials and scripts presented in this book.** While any other username could work at first, you will face issues as you proceed. Please make sure **all entries are "osint".** Since this is a virtual machine inside a secure computer, minimal security is acceptable.
- Choose your Time Zone and click "Continue".
- Choose the "Guided - use entire disk" option and click "Continue".
- Choose "VMWare" and "All files in one partition", clicking "Continue" after each.
- Click "Continue"; select "Yes"; and click "Continue" to begin the installation.
- When prompted, confirm "No" to bypass local media and click "Continue".
- Choose the default package manager and click "Continue" three times.
- Select "No" and click "Continue" to disable statistics.
- Select "GNOME"; ensure "Debian desktop environment" and "standard system utilities" are also enabled; and click "Continue" to accept the desktop environment I will use during my tutorials. If you have a strong opinion that another environment is better, choose your preference.
- If prompted, click "Continue" to install GRUB; choose "/dev/sda"; and click "Continue".
- Allow Debian to complete the installation. Once you see "Installation complete", click "Continue" to allow a reboot.
- After reboot, log in and click "Next" twice; disable "Location Services"; click "Next", "Skip" and "Done"; then "Start Using Debian...".
- Click "Install Tools" from the bar at the bottom of the screen; click "Activities" within the Debian VM; and select the "Files" application visible in the lower Dock.
- Select "VMWare Tools" within the left menu; right-click the "VMWareTools...gz" file and select "Copy"; select "Downloads" and click within the empty area to the right; right-click and select "Paste"; right-click the "VMWareTools...gz" file; and choose "Extract".

- Click through the VMWare folders within Downloads until you see a file called "vmware-install.pl". Right-click this file and choose "Run as program". If you receive a warning, type "n" and press Enter. You should now have VMWare Tools installed.
- Reboot the VM.

Your device should now boot to the operating system with the ability to resize the screen as desired. I have occasionally encountered the following issues.

- Click "Install Now" if prompted for updates.
- If your cursor is not available within the VM, or you cannot select anything, restart it.
- The shared folder within the VM will likely not function. VMWare requires several commands specific to your installation to temporarily share a folder with the host. At the time of this writing, a known bug was preventing this. I currently recommend using a USB device connected to the VM to transfer files, which we will do together later.

After all updates are installed, shut down the VM and continue to the section titled "Preserve Stock Debian".

Preserve Stock Debian

Regardless of your host operating system (macOS, Linux, or Windows) or VM client (UTM, VirtualBox, or VMWare Workstation Pro), you should now possess a VM with a clean version of stock Debian. You could launch this VM and start configuring your OSINT investigative environment, but I encourage you to first create a clone of this machine while it is in such a pristine state. This way, you can always return to an untouched version of Debian which has not been modified if needed. I often need to do this when I mess something up while testing new software. This prevents me from creating a new Debian VM from scratch every week. Shut down all VMs and consider the following.

UTM (macOS): You can right-click on any VM within UTM and choose the option of "Clone" to create an identical copy. You can then right-click the new version and select "Edit" to change the name. In the following image, I created a clone titled "OSINT VM", which can be customized without impacting my "Debian Stock" VM.

VirtualBox (Linux and Windows): You can right-click on any VM within VirtualBox and choose the option of "Clone" to create an identical copy. You can provide a unique name during this process and accept the default options. I created a clone titled "OSINT VM", which can be customized without impacting my "Debian Stock" VM. The image below displays my software.

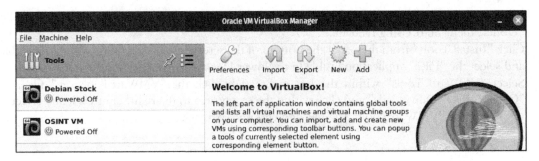

VMWare Workstation Pro (Linux and Windows): You can right-click on any VM within VirtualBox and choose the option of "Manage" then "Clone" to create an identical copy. You can provide a unique name during this process and accept the default options. I created a clone titled "OSINT VM", which can be customized without impacting my "Debian Stock" VM. The following image displays my software.

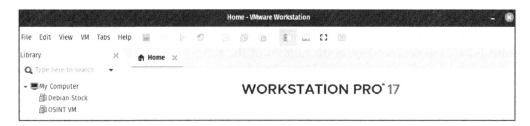

You should now have at least two VMs. One is untouched Debian Stock which we will preserve for future clones if needed. I launch this VM once monthly to apply all updates and keep it ready to go. The OSINT VM is the option we will use to create our ultimate OSINT VM in the next chapter. Once our VM is finished, we will use these same methods to make a clone before each online investigation.

Remove VMs

We can remove VMs with the following steps.

- UTM (macOS): Right-click any VM and select "Delete". This will remove the entry from the menu and delete any files associated with the VM.
- VirtualBox (Linux and Windows): Right-click any VM and select "Remove". This presents an option to remove the entry from the menu or remove the entry and delete any associated files.
- VMWare Workstation Pro (Linux and Windows): Right-click any VM and select "Remove". This provides options to remove from the library or delete completely.

Display Settings

You should be able to adjust your VM window as desired, or make it full screen for best view. However, the resolution is likely still low. Consider the following.

- Right-click on the Debian desktop and choose "Display Settings".
- Change the resolution to the maximum for your screen's ratio and click "Apply" then "Keep Changes".
- If the text is now too small, select the "200% Scale" and click "Apply" then "Keep Changes".

Play with these settings until you find the perfect fit. Remember to always use the highest resolution available within the VM client and then choose the 100%, 200%, or additional options present within the Debian display preferences.

Debian Desktop Interaction

The following image displays my Debian UTM installation at this point. Notice that it boots to a view of the Dock at the bottom and a windowed Desktop above. Clicking within this Desktop navigates to it and hides the Dock. We will change this soon.

Debian Customization

From this point forward, only use the "OSINT VM" for any customization. The only exception should be to occasionally open the "Stock Debian" VM to apply any updates.

Persistent Dock

When Debian boots, you see the dock at the bottom of the screen, but it disappears once you click on the workspace. I prefer a static Dock within my VM, on the left of the screen, which is always visible. If you do too, conduct the following.

- Open your web browser by clicking the Firefox icon after entering the "Activities" menu.
- Navigate to https://extensions.gnome.org/extension/307/dash-to-dock.
- Click "Install" and confirm twice.
- Click the Activities menu; search "Extensions"; and open the Extensions application.
- Under Dash to Dock, click "Settings".
- Select "Left", disable "Intelligent Autohide"; enable "Panel mode"; and adjust the icon size as desired (I prefer 32). You should see a much better environment for launching applications.

Terminal in Dock

We will use Terminal more than any other application throughout this guide. While we will use an automated script to rebuild our Dock icons later, we should go ahead and add Terminal to it now.

- Click the nine dots in the lower-left of Debian.
- Hover over the Terminal application.
- Right-click and select "Pin to Dash".

Terminal Appearance

Unlike Ubuntu, the default Gnome Terminal in Debian has a white background. Many of the Linux applications which we will use force white text which would not be visible within this window. Therefore, consider changing the appearance of Debian's Terminal with the following steps.

- From within Terminal, select the three bars menu and choose "Preferences".
- Change the "Theme Variant" from "Light" to "Dark" and close the settings.

Debian Background and Windows

Personally, I do not like the default colors and wallpaper of Debian, and prefer something more professional. Debian removed the ability to easily change wallpaper to a solid color, so we will do it all through Terminal. I conducted the following on my new VM. The fourth and final command adds maximize, minimize, and full-screen buttons to all windows.

```
gsettings set org.gnome.desktop.background picture-uri ''
gsettings set org.gnome.desktop.background picture-uri-dark ''
gsettings set org.gnome.desktop.background primary-color 'rgb(66, 81, 100)'
gsettings set org.gnome.desktop.wm.preferences button-layout ":minimize,maximize,close"
```

The remaining steps within Debian create a better OSINT investigations environment.

- Launch "Settings" from the "Show Applications" Menu.
- Click "Notifications" and disable both options.
- Click "Privacy", then click "Screen Lock" and disable all options.
- Click "File History & Trash", then disable all options.
- Click the back arrow, "Power", then disable "Automatic Suspend".
- If desired, click "Mouse & Touchpad" then enable "Natural Scrolling".
- Close all Settings windows.

Debian Centered Windows

By default, Debian opens all new windows to the left of the screen. I prefer them to be centered, especially when launching the custom scripts, which we will download later. You can modify this setting with the following steps.

- Click the nine dots in the lower-right of Debian.
- Search "Tweaks" and open the application.
- Click "Windows" and enable "Center New Windows".
- Close the Tweaks application.

Debian Desktop Icons

By default, Debian does not display icons on the Desktop. There is much debate about whether this is a benefit or a nuisance. I prefer to see files within the Desktop folder display on the Desktop itself. We can enable this with the following steps, but we will use Terminal commands to replicate this in Chapter Fourteen.

- Open your web browser by clicking the Firefox icon after entering the "Activities" menu.
- Navigate to https://extensions.gnome.org/extension/2087/desktop-icons-ng-ding.
- Click "Install" and confirm twice.
- Within Terminal, execute `cd ~/Desktop && rm *.desktop` to eliminate the unnecessary icons.

Debian Updates

It is important to keep the software on this original VM updated. There are different ways to do this, but I will only focus on the direct Terminal method. Execute the following commands.

```
sudo apt update && sudo apt upgrade -y
```

I typically check for updates weekly. Later, I present a script which does this for us. You should now have at least one Debian VM titled "OSINT VM" which we will customize for our OSINT investigations. Once we have finished, we will use the previous tutorials to clone this VM for each investigation.

CHAPTER NINE
OSINT VM WEB BROWSERS

Your internet browser is likely the most vital application within your ultimate OSINT VM. If you are a Windows user, your default web browser is either Internet Explorer or Microsoft Edge. Apple users are presented Safari by default. Many computers now rely on Google's Chrome browser for internet access. I believe OSINT professionals should avoid all of these if possible. All are inferior in my opinion, and you will encounter difficulties with some of the websites you visit. Therefore, we need a better browser.

Firefox (mozilla.org)

The Firefox browser is my primary window into the internet on all of my machines, including my OSINT VMs. It has enhanced security and a feature called "Add-ons" or "Extensions". These are small applications which work within the browser that perform a specific function. They will make searching and documentation much easier. I occasionally use a Chromium-based web browser when absolutely necessary, and will explain an option later. However, many of the extensions that I need are more compatible with Firefox.

For the purposes of this chapter, I will assume you are configuring the Firefox application included in your new Debian VM. However, all of the methods explained here could be replicated within your host or any other computer. If you will be using your host computer for any web browsing, Firefox is highly recommended as the default browser. Regardless of where you will be conducting your online investigations, have a properly configured Firefox application.

Throughout this chapter, we will build an ideal configuration of Firefox for OSINT investigations. At the end of the chapter, I offer a pre-configured profile which you can download into your VM for a turn-key approach. However, I encourage you to replicate my steps manually to understand each feature before relying on the downloadable profile. Whenever you need to quickly build a new VM for investigative use, you can import my configuration to bypass all the labor.

Firefox Security

Before identifying Firefox resources which will aid in our OSINT research, we must first secure our browser to the best of our ability. While the default Firefox installation is much more private and secure than most other browsers, we should still consider some modifications. I personally use Firefox for all of my OSINT investigations in my VMs, and as my default web browser on my personal laptop. I no longer possess multiple browsers for various tasks. I believe that Firefox is the most robust, secure, and appropriate option for almost any scenario. However, I recommend changing the following settings within Firefox.

- Click on the menu in the upper right and select "Settings".
- In the "General" options, uncheck "Recommend extensions as you browse" and "Recommend features as you browse", which prevents some usage information from being sent to Firefox.
- In the "Home" options, change "Homepage and new windows" and "New tabs" to "Blank page". This prevents Firefox from loading their default page.
- Disable all Firefox "Home Content" options.
- Uncheck everything in the "Address Bar" menu.
- Click the "Privacy & Security" menu option and select "Strict" protection.
- Check boxes "Tell websites not to sell or share my data" and "Do Not Track".
- Check the box titled "Delete cookies and site data when Firefox is closed".
- Uncheck the box titled "Show alerts about passwords for breached websites".
- Uncheck the box titled "Suggest Firefox Relay...".

- Uncheck the box titled "Suggest strong passwords".
- Uncheck the box titled "Fill usernames and passwords".
- Uncheck the box titled "Ask to save passwords".
- Uncheck the box titled "Save and fill addresses".
- Uncheck the box titled "Save and fill payment methods".
- Change the History setting to "Firefox will use custom settings for history".
- Uncheck "Remember browsing and download history" and "Remember search and form history".
- Check the box titled "Clear history when Firefox closes". Do not check the box titled "Always use private browsing mode", as this breaks Containers.
- In the Permissions menu, click "Settings" next to Location, Camera, Notifications, and Virtual Reality. Check the box titled "Block new requests…" on each of these options. If you will never need audio communications within this browser, you could do the same for Microphone.
- Uncheck all options under "Firefox Data Collection and Use" and "Website Advertising Preferences".
- Uncheck all options under "Deceptive Content and Dangerous Software Protection". This will prevent Firefox from sharing potential malicious site visits with third-party services.
- Select "Enable HTTPS-Only Mode in all windows".
- Enable "Max Protection" under "DNS over HTTPS" and select "NextDNS".

This is where I again deviate from previous editions. I often walk a fine line between OSINT and privacy. In my book *Extreme Privacy*, I took many actions in order to protect every facet of our online privacy and security. This included a complete hardening of the Firefox browser which I use as a daily driver on my personal machine. In previous editions of that book, I carried over many advanced Firefox settings into the recommended OSINT machine. Today, I no longer feel these actions are appropriate. Over the past year, many of the Firefox "about:config" modifications which I had previously presented began causing minor issues within investigations. Some invasive sites, which needed documented as part of an investigation, could not be viewed due to overprotective settings. I have had to remind myself of the scope of this book. It is designed to assist with investigations and collection of digital evidence.

Several readers have asked if I recommend the latest "Global Privacy Control" and "Do Not Track" settings within Firefox for OSINT investigations. While I encourage people to activate these options within their personal machines, I do not recommend them for our OSINT browsers. These two settings can modify the way a target website interacts with your browser. If you are trying to capture the way a site delivers data to the end user, but you are preventing the site from exchanging information with your browser, you may be altering the content which would have been delivered to a normal user. While we want to practice good digital hygiene while we conduct investigations, we do not want to strictly prohibit all intrusive data from reaching our screens.

Our OSINT machine is not designed for personal internet usage and simply does not need the same security through modifications which I believe are appropriate for a personal computer. Therefore, I have removed all advanced Firefox settings from this book. Doing so eliminates the likelihood that problems will occur, and enables the browser to be seen as another common configuration ready to view any website.

Firefox natively respects your privacy and security more than other browsers. These recommendations are for those that want to tweak additional settings that may provide a new layer of protection, even if minimal.

I want to stress that the enhanced Firefox privacy and security settings presented within *Extreme Privacy* are still very appropriate for personal machines. I just don't believe they are necessary here. For those who follow both sides of my work (OSINT and privacy), please continue to use the advanced strategies within your personal machines. With this book I want to strive harder to isolate these two worlds. While OSINT and privacy complement each other, they should not be lumped into one bucket when it comes to our digital strategies.

Default Search Engine

In the previous configurations, I left Google as the default search engine whenever text is typed into the URL bar. This was because Google typically brings us the best results. This may be appropriate for your investigations, but you may be missing out on results from Bing and other engines. I prefer to use SearXNG for all initial queries, and then migrate to Google or Bing if I need to dig deeper into a result.

SearXNG is a metasearch engine which aggregates the results of multiple search engines, such as Google, Bing, and others, but does not share information about users to the engines queried. It is also open source and can be self-hosted. The easiest way to get started is to visit https://searx.space/ and test a few public instances. If you want to make one of them your default search engine within Firefox, conduct the following.

- Navigate to your chosen public server and conduct any search.
- Right-click on the URL and select "Add" next to the magnifying glass icon.
- Navigate to Firefox's Settings menu and click the "Search" option.
- Change your default search engine to the new option.

From any search result, I prefer to click the "Preferences" option on the far right and make a few modifications. I disable any auto-complete options; disable SafeSearch; switch to a light theme; enable results in new tabs; and enable additional search engines throughout all topics.

If you want to store these changes so they will be preserved after you restart Firefox, you must conduct the following.

- Navigate to Firefox's Settings menu and click the "Privacy & Security" option.
- Click "Manage Exceptions" next to "Delete cookies...".
- Enter the domain of your SearXNG instance, such as "https://baresearch.org".
- Click "Allow" and "Save Changes".

If you do not trust a public instance of SearXNG, you can host your own, as explained next. I currently have a self-hosted SearXNG instance running in my VM, which allows me to query dozens of search engines simultaneously from my browser without trusting any third-party middle man. You may have a policy which prohibits you from conducting investigations through untrusted online third-party search engine aggregators. If you decide to use SearXNG as part of your routine, consider running your own instance locally. If you have played with any of the public instances of SearXNG, you may now see the benefits of an aggregated search service. You may also be considering the risks associated with this behavior. Let's start with the benefits of a public instance.

- All queries are submitted to search engines from a third-party server.
- The IP addresses collected from engines are those of the server, not yours.
- Your queries cannot easily be associated to one user by the engines.

That may sound great, but there are risks with public instances. Consider the following.

- The host of the instance could monitor your queries.
- If the host is popular, some engines may block access.
- If the host has an outage, you are without service.

Overall, I believe it would be very unusual for a SearXNG host to monitor queries. This cannot be done with the SearXNG software, and they would have to go out of their way to collect data about users. I just do not see the motive of that. However, anything is possible. Personally, I prefer to self-host my own instance of SearXNG. Consider the following benefits.

- All queries are submitted from your machine directly to the engines.
- The tracking code on engine websites is removed from the SearXNG pages.
- Minimal usage ensures that all options function reliably.
- Does not rely on the uptime of an online instance for my queries.

As always, there are also risks. My IP address is submitted with every query I make, but I am always behind a VPN so I am not bothered by that. The ability to host my own code and know that no one else is intercepting that data is more important to me. You can never hide the queries from the search engines themselves, but you can limit the information loaded into your browser by not visiting their sites directly. Receiving results from multiple search engines simultaneously is very advantageous. Take some time to determine whether you are better served with a public instance or your own. I took the following steps on my Linux VM to configure my own host locally. If you decide to replicate these steps, you should copy and paste this in its entirety.

```
sudo -H apt-get install -y \
    python3-dev python3-babel python3-venv \
    uwsgi uwsgi-plugin-python3 \
    git build-essential libxslt-dev zlib1g-dev \
    libffi-dev libssl-dev
mkdir ~/Documents/searxng
cd ~/Documents/searxng
git clone "https://github.com/searxng/searxng"
python3 -m venv searxngEnvironment
source searxngEnvironment/bin/activate
pip install -U pip
pip install -U setuptools
pip install -U wheel
pip install -U pyyaml
cd searxng
pip install -e .
sudo -H mkdir -p "/etc/searxng"
sed -i "s|ultrasecretkey|$(openssl rand -hex 32)|g" searx/settings.yml
sudo -H cp searx/settings.yml /etc/searxng/settings.yml
export SEARXNG_SETTINGS_PATH="/etc/searxng/settings.yml"
deactivate
```

My machine was now configured to run the SearXNG software. The following commands execute the program.

```
cd ~/Documents/searxng
source searxngEnvironment/bin/activate
cd searxng
python searx/webapp.py
```

The software is now running in the background. You can minimize this Terminal window. As long as it is not closed completely, the service is running. You can launch Firefox and navigate to http://127.0.0.1:8888 to load your own instance. Any modifications you make to this will be stored within your software, regardless of cookies. You can execute the following to fetch any updates.

```
cd ~/Documents/venv/searxng/searxng
git pull "https://github.com/searxng/searxng"
```

If desired, you can add these two commands to the Linux update script, which is explained later. You could also add the launch commands to the maintenance scripts we will build later in this guide.

Firefox Add-ons (Extensions)

There are thousands of extensions available for Firefox. Some are helpful, some are worthless, and some are just fun. This chapter will discuss several of them. The Firefox Add-ons, sometimes called extensions, detailed here will include a website for each option. You can either visit the website and download the add-on, or search for it from within Firefox. The latter is usually the easiest way. While Firefox is open, click on the menu in the upper right and then "Add-ons and Themes". This will present a page with a search field in the upper right corner. Enter the name of the extension and install from there. The following are my recommendations, in order of importance.

Firefox Containers: Isolate specific sites within tabs.
uBlock Origin: Block undesired scripts from loading.
DownThemAll: Download bulk media automatically.
Bulk Media Downloader: Download bulk media automatically.
FireShot: Generate screenshots of partial and entire web pages.
Nimbus: Alternative screen capture for large web pages.
SingleFile: New alternative screen capture option for HTML files.
Exif Viewer: Identify metadata embedded inside a photograph.
User-Agent Switcher and Manager: Emulate various browsers and devices.
Image Search Options: Conduct automatic reverse image searches.
Search By Image: An alternative tool for reverse image search.
Web Archives: Search archived versions of the current website.
Copy Selected Links: Quickly copy all hyperlinks from a website.
OneTab: Collapse or expand tabs into a single resource.
Stream Detector: Identify embedded video streams for archiving.

The following pages provide explicit instructions for installing and configuring each of these Add-ons. At the end, I will explain how you can export your settings and replicate your work across practically any Firefox installation. This will preserve your work and allow you to receive an identical experience if conducting investigations across multiple computers. I will also present an option to run a few commands to replicate the setup explained within this chapter. This will also benefit your virtual machines. Ideally, you would complete all browser configurations within your original VM before cloning, exporting, or use of snapshots.

Firefox Containers (https://addons.mozilla.org/addon/multi-account-containers)

The first Firefox Add-on which I use daily is the Multi-Account Containers option from Mozilla. Multi-Account Containers allows you to separate your various types of browsing without needing to clear your history, log in and out, or use multiple browsers. These container tabs are like normal tabs, except the sites you visit will have access to a separate slice of the browser's storage. This means your site preferences, logged-in sessions, and advertising tracking data will not carry over to the new container. Likewise, any browsing you do within the new container will not affect your logged in sessions, or tracking data of your other containers.

OSINT investigators can use this technique in many ways. With a traditional browser, you can only be logged in to one instance of a social network. If you are logged in to a covert Facebook account, then open a new tab and navigate to Facebook, you will be presented with the same logged-in account used in the previous tab. With containers, we can isolate this activity.

You can log in to one Facebook account in one container, another Facebook account in a second container, and any additional accounts in their own containers. This applies to any service, such as X (Twitter), Reddit, or others. This allows us to simultaneously access multiple accounts within the same service without logging out or opening a different browser. Let's configure it.

Once installed, you might see a new icon in the upper right in your Firefox browser which appears as three squares and a "+" character. Many readers may not see this icon because it is in the "Extensions" menu item in the upper-right which appears similar to a puzzle piece. Click this icon; right-click "Firefox Multi-Account Containers"; and select "Pin to Toolbar". This will place our new extension icon directly within the browser toolbar.

Click on this new icon and click your way through the introduction windows. Choose "Not Now" for any Firefox features. You can now select the container you want to open. Default options include choices such as Personal and Shopping, but you can modify these any way you desire. You can create, delete, and edit containers from the main menu. When you click the "Manage Containers" option, you can change the color or icon associated with a container or change the container name. The following tutorial replicates my configuration.

- Open the Multi-Account Containers menu.
- Click "Manage Containers".
- Delete all containers by selecting each and clicking "Delete This Container".
- In the "Manage Containers" menu, click the + in the upper left.
- Enter the name of your new container, such as "Alias 01".
- Choose a desired color and icon.
- Repeat this process to create the number of containers desired.

At a bare minimum, I recommend containers labeled "Alias 01", "Alias 02", "Alias 03", and "Alias 04". You can now either open a new container as a blank page or open links in a new or different container. The following are a few of my usage examples.

Multiple Logins: While in Firefox, I want to open Facebook inside a unique container. I click on the containers menu and select Alias 01. This opens a new blank tab within this container. I navigate to Facebook and log in to an alias account. I then want to log in to a second Facebook account, so I click on the containers menu and select Alias 02. This opens a new tab in that container. I then navigate to Facebook and receive a login prompt. I log in to my second account and can switch back and forth between tabs. You should note that Facebook can see you have the same IP address for each login, but they cannot see your cookies from one session to the other. You could replicate this process for any other service. You could also have numerous Gmail accounts open within one browser.

Safety: While I am viewing my target's X (Twitter) profile, I see a link to an external website from his page. I am logged in to a X (Twitter) account within this container and I do not know what this linked website will try to load. I do not want to jeopardize my investigation. I right-click on the link and choose "Open link in New Container", and then select the desired container tab. The page I open cannot see any cookies stored within my container associated with my X (Twitter) login.

Dedicated Container: I assign specific websites to a container so they will always open in that container. I use this for Google because I do not want my search history associated with other investigation activities. If I ever visit Google as part of an investigation, the site will open in a new container tab which I designated "Google". This is regardless of which tab I try to use. The following steps configure this option.

- Create a Containers tab titled "Google".
- Click on the Containers menu.
- Open a new Google tab.
- Connect to google.com and click the Containers menu.
- Select "Always open This Site in…".
- Select the desired container.
- Navigate to google.com from a standard tab.
- Select "Remember my decision…".
- Click "Open in…" the desired container.

When complete, you have created a rule within Firefox. Any time you connect to google.com, regardless of the container you are in, or if you have Google set as your default search from within the URL field, Firefox will open a new "Google" tab to complete your connection. This isolates your Google traffic from any other tab, and applies to any Google sites, such as Google Voice, Gmail, etc.

If you regret making this type of rule, you can either delete the entire container or just the policy for that site. In this example, I can go to the Containers menu; click the "Manage Containers" option; then select the Google container; then click the delete option.

When I first installed this add-on, I went a bit too far with customized containers. I wanted all Facebook pages to load in their own container, which prevented the ability to log in to multiple accounts. I removed this option and established the rule mentioned previously which allowed me to have multiple logins, but lost the isolation from Facebook to other websites. I created containers for most of the sites I visited, which was overkill.

There is no perfect solution. Evaluate your needs and create the most appropriate set of containers vital to your investigation. If you want to isolate a container to only open designated sites, click "Manage Containers"; select the desired container; and enable the "Limit to Designated Sites" option. This prevents accidental openings of undesired sites within a secure container.

uBlock Origin (addons.mozilla.org/firefox/addon/ublock-origin/)

I have previously recommended NoScript, Adblock Plus, Privacy Badger, and Disconnect as privacy Add-ons that would help stop unwanted ads, tracking, and analytics. These are no longer present on any of my systems. I now only use uBlock Origin, as it replaces all of these options. This section may seem a bit overwhelming, but experimenting with the advanced settings should help you understand the functionality. Install uBlock Origin from the Firefox Add-ons page or directly at the previous URL. You are now protected on a basic level. By default, most known advertisements, tracking code, and malicious content is blocked. This step alone would provide much needed protection from the internet. However, we can take it further.

Click on the uBlock Origin icon in the Firefox toolbar and select the "Dashboard" icon to the right, which appears as a settings option. This will open a new tab with the program's configuration page. On the "Settings" tab, click the option of "I am an advanced user". This will present an expanded menu from the uBlock Origin icon from now forward. Click on the "Filter lists" tab and consider enabling additional data sets that may protect your computer. I find the default lists sufficient, however I enable "Block outsider intrusion into LAN" under "Privacy" and "EasyList/uBO-Cookie Notices" under "Annoyances". Click "Apply Changes" and Update Now" after these selections. You now have extended protection that will be applied to all visited websites without any interaction from you. When you encounter a web page with a lot of advertisements, such as a news media website, it should load much faster. It will block many of the pop-ups and auto-play media that can be quite annoying when conducting research. This protection will suffice for most users, but dedicated OSINT analysts may choose to take a more advanced approach.

After you have enabled the Advanced settings as explained above, clicking on the uBlock Origin icon should now present an expanded menu which will change as you visit different sites. In order to explain the function of this menu, I will conduct a demonstration using the website cnn.com as it appeared in late 2022. Figure 9.01 displays the default view of uBlock Origin with the site loaded. Scrolling down this list of scripts that have either been loaded or blocked, you can see several questionable scripts such as X (Twitter), Amazon, and Turner. These scripts allow tracking across multiple websites and are the technology responsible for monitoring your interests, web history, and shopping habits.

This menu is split into three columns. The first simply identifies the type of code or domain name of the script. The second column is global settings. Anything changed here will apply to all website visits. The third column contains settings for the current website. A single plus sign (+) indicates that less than ten scripts were allowed from that specific option. Two plus signs indicate that between ten and one hundred scripts were allowed. The single minus sign (-) indicates that between one and nine scripts were blocked from that domain, while the dual minus signs tell us that ten to one hundred scripts were blocked. In Figure 9.01, we see that over ten scripts were allowed from cnn.com, and at least one script was blocked from sending data to X (Twitter). This is all default behavior and provides a balance of functionality and security. uBlock Origin decides which content should be allowed and which should be blocked.

Using this same page, let's modify the options. In Figure 9.02 (left), I have clicked on the far-right portion of the first cell in the third column. This turned the entire third column red in color. This action activated an option to refresh the page (arrows) and an option to save the change (padlock). Clicking the padlock and then refreshing the page presented me with the example in Figure 9.02 (right). Since I blocked every script, the page would not fully execute. It could not load images, design scripts, or any JavaScript. This is not useful at all, so I disabled my actions by clicking on the left (grey) section of the top cell in the third column, which turned the entire column back to grey in color. Saving these changes and refreshing the page brought me back to the example in Figure 9.01.

Figure 9.01: An advanced view of uBlock Origin.

We can also take this to the opposite extreme. In Figure 9.03 (left), I clicked on the "power button" in the upper-right. This turned the entire left edge green in color, and allowed all scripts to load on cnn.com. This includes the dozens of intrusive scripts that could load advertisements on the page. You can also see that small plus signs confirm that scripts were allowed to run while the minus signs in Figure 9.03 (right) state the opposite. For most users, this allowance would seem irresponsible. However, there is a specific reason that we want the ability to allow all scripts. If you are collecting evidence, especially in criminal cases, you may want to archive a page exactly as it was meant to be seen. When we block scripts, we are technically modifying the page (evidence). By intentionally allowing all scripts before the collection of the screen capture, we know that we are viewing the page in an unmodified format. This may be overkill for many investigators, but you should know your options.

Next, we will modify the second (middle) column, which will apply settings globally. By default, all options are grey in color, which is desired by most users. This indicates that the default block list is applicable, and only invasive scripts will be blocked everywhere. For demonstration, I clicked on the right (red) portion of the top cell in the second column. This turned the entire column red, and indicates that all scripts across all websites will be blocked. After I saved my changes, every website will only load the most basic text content. This will prohibit much of our research.

Loading a page such as a X (Twitter) profile resulted in no usable content. By clicking on the uBlock Origin icon and clicking the left (grey) sections of specific cells within the third column, I enabled those scripts without allowing everything on the page. While you may not be able to see the colors in Figure 9.03 (right), you can see the difference in shading. In this example, the entire second column is red. This indicates that all scripts are blocked globally. The third column is mostly red, but the options for twitter.com and twimg.com are grey. Those scripts will be allowed, if approved by uBlock Origin's rules, only for that domain. If I load a blog that has scripts from X (Twitter), they would still be ignored.

These are extreme examples. Let's bring this back to some sanity. The following is how I recommend using uBlock Origin. Install, enable advanced options, and proceed with your work. When you arrive at a website that is blocking something you want to see, open the menu and click on the left (grey) section of the top cell in the third column. That will allow everything to load on that page, and that page only. When you are about to navigate to a questionable site that may try to install malicious code on your machine, click on the right (red) section of the top cell in the second column. That will block all scripts on all pages. Conduct your research and reverse the change when you are finished. Remember to click the save button (padlock) after each change and refresh the page.

Hopefully, you are practicing these settings and learning how this program functions. It is an amazing option that has protected me many times. If you are doing things right, you have likely completely messed-up your settings and are now blocking things you want while allowing things you do not. Don't worry, we can reverse all of our mistakes by first changing the global (second column) settings back to grey (left section of top cell). Next, return to the dashboard settings of the add-on, and click on the "My Rules" tab. In the second column (Temporary Rules), select all of the text and press the delete key on your keyboard. Click the "Save" button in this same column and then the "Commit" button to apply these settings everywhere. This resets our extension and brings us back to default usage regardless of your modifications. This is important in the event you go too far with settings in the future. Removing and reinstalling the extension does not always wipe this data out of your system.

The primary benefit of uBlock Origin over other options is the simple ability to block malicious scripts without customization, while having an option to allow or block any or all scripts at our disposal. This is a rarity in these types of Add-ons. Another benefit is the ability to bypass website restrictions, such as a news site blocking articles unless the visitor has a subscription service. Consider the following example with the Los Angeles Times. Visiting the page allows you to view three articles for free, but you must have a paid subscription in order to continue using the site. If I click on the uBlock Origin menu while on this page, select the right (red) option on the right (third) column under the setting for "3rd party scripts", then the padlock icon, and reload the page, I see a different result. I am now allowed to see the article. This is because this website relies on a third-party script to identify whether a visitor is logged in to the service. This modification presents unlimited views of articles without registration on this and thousands of other websites.

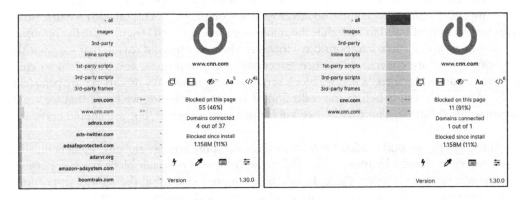

Figure 9.02: Disabled scripts within uBlock Origin.

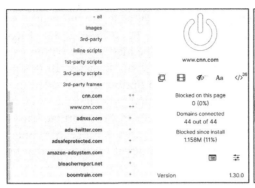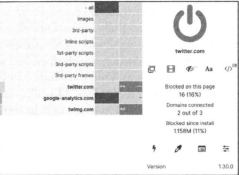

Figure 9.03: Fully and partially enabled scripts with uBlock Origin.

The final example of uBlock Origin within this chapter, which I rely on with my daily browsing, is the Inline Scripts blocker. For this demonstration, I will navigate to cnn.com. Clicking on almost any article presents a new page, including new annoyances. An undesired video begins playing while scrolling down the page, multiple images from unrelated articles populate over some of the article text, a pop-up advertisement interrupts my view, and over 56 scripts attempt to monitor your activity. uBlock Origin blocks the malicious scripts, but not all of the annoyances. We could block each script individually, but that is time consuming. Instead, consider a simple modification of the inline scripts setting.

Click on the uBlock Origin menu while on the desired page, select the right (red) option on the right (third) column under the setting for "inline scripts", then the padlock icon, and reload the page. The site should load much faster and block all of the inline scripts being pushed to you by the provider. You should notice that all pages on cnn.com load immediately, and without all of the undesired media interfering with your research. Clicking the grey area in this same box reverses the action. I apply this feature to practically every news website I visit. It blocks vital information if your desire is to obtain a screen capture as evidence, but provides a much more pleasing environment if you simply want to read the articles.

DownThemAll (addons.mozilla.org/firefox/addon/downthemall)

DownThemAll simplifies the process of extracting bulk data from a web page. It attempts to identify linked video, audio, images, documents, or any other type of media within a site. It then allows you to easily download everything at once. Consider the following example. Archive.org possesses a copy of a website which once offered several gigabytes of marketing data containing millions of records on Americans, including full names, addresses, telephone numbers, and interests. The archive can be found at the following URL.

https://web.archive.org/web/20151110195654/http://www.updates4news.com:80/kyledata/

This URL presents hundreds of large CSV and TXT files. Later in this book, I discuss how to properly parse through this content and create your own searchable file with this example. For now, I simply need to download each file. While on the page, click on the DownThemAll toolbar menu and select "DownThemAll". In the new window, you should see all of the data links present on this site. Clicking the "All Files" box near the bottom selects each of the files. Clicking "Download" in the lower right begins the process of downloading all of the data from the page (which may take hours), and places each file in the default download location for your operating system. Please do not download this data set yet, as it will fill your disk space in your VM. We will discuss external storage methods later. This add-on is a requirement for any browser I use. I find it to work better than the next option, but consider all alternatives for your own needs.

Bulk Media Downloader (addons.mozilla.org/firefox/addon/bulk-media-downloader)

Similar to DownThemAll, this add-on can make downloading a large number of media files easy. It should serve as a backup in the event you find a page which DownThemAll will not function properly. If you locate a page of several audio or video files, it can be time consuming to save them all manually. Additionally, you run the risk of accidentally skipping a file. Bulk Media Downloader provides a solution. As an example, I navigated to X (Twitter) and searched the word Video. This presented hundreds of embedded videos within a single page. I launched Bulk Media Downloader, which displayed a pop-up option over my browser. In this pop-up, I can select specific file types such as Video or Audio. I chose only the Video option and reloaded the X (Twitter) page in the background. The Bulk Media Downloader tool began populating video links as I scrolled down the X (Twitter) page. Clicking the Download button retrieved all of the videos in MP4 format. This utility works well on sites that have a large number of embedded audio or video files, as well as those that contain numerous documents. You can select or deselect entries individually, or select categories at the bottom that fit your needs.

Fireshot (addons.mozilla.org/en-us/firefox/addon/fireshot/)

Documenting and archiving your progress with an OSINT investigation is as important as the intelligence discovered. The general rule is that if you do not have proof of your findings, then they never existed. Full Web Page Screenshots, also known as FireShot, provides you with an easy solution to capturing all of your results. When enabled, this extension is a button in the upper right portion of your browser. It appears as a blue square containing the letter "S". Clicking the icon presents a menu with options. The best option is to select "Capture entire page" and then "Save to PDF". This will create a PDF document of the entire page exactly as it appears in your browser and then save it to anywhere you choose. The file can later be archived to a removable storage device. The title of the document will match the title of the web page and it will include the URL of the page.

This method is preferred over a standard screen capture for several reasons. A typical screen capture only captures the visible area and not the entire page. You must then open a program into which you "paste" the data and then save the file. This extension automates this and saves it in a format that is difficult to edit. This can be beneficial during testimony.

By accessing the "Options" area of the menu, you can assign customized naming features. Click "Show filename template settings" in the options page and change the default value to the following.

%n-%u-%t-%y-%m-%d-%H-%M-%S

This setting will change the default name of each page capture. Each file will be named a numerical value, followed by the website URL, followed by title, and followed by the date and time of capture. Changing the %n value to 0 and the Pad option to 3 will ensure that your captures always start with a numerical value of 0 and ascend chronologically. This can help determine the order of evidence you retrieved. Be sure to "Apply" and then "Save" after you have made your desired changes. Notice that you can quickly see the order captured (first three digits), target website, description, and date & time.

Nimbus (addons.mozilla.org/firefox/addon/nimbus-screenshot)

While FireShot is my preferred screen capture utility within Firefox, there are some instances where it does not perform well. If you have a target's Facebook page that has a lot of activity present, this may create a screen capture too large for FireShot. The rendering process will likely expend all of the computer's video memory and fail to create the file. When this happens, I use Nimbus as my first backup.

Nimbus allows you to specify whether you want to capture only the visible portion of the page, the entire page, or a custom selection from the page. The drop-down menu presents these choices and the result is saved as a PNG file. This is not optimal for online investigations, but is better than no capture at all. Another feature of Nimbus is the ability to manipulate captures. I believe that this is bad practice as we usually want to provide the most authentic and accurate evidence as possible. I do not want to manipulate any potential evidence. Therefore, I recommend the following configurations.

- Click on the Nimbus icon and choose the "gear" icon in the lower-right.

- In the "File name pattern" field, insert {url}-{title}-{date}-{time}. This will name every capture with the URL and title of the target website along with date and time of capture.
- Check "Enable Quick Screenshot" and select the "Entire Page" option in the first row and "Download" option in the second row.

After these changes, clicking the Nimbus icon in the menu bar will no longer present a menu with options. Instead, it will automatically select the entire page, apply the proper file naming, and download the capture as a maximum quality PNG file to your Desktop. While a PDF file created with FireShot is the preferred file format, a PNG file has other advantages. The PNG file is more universal and does not require PDF viewing software such as Acrobat Reader. However, PNG files are easy to edit, and establishing the integrity of the file may be difficult. I believe that Nimbus should be used as a supplement to FireShot.

One common failure of both FireShot and Nimbus is the capture of extremely large Social Network pages. While this is rare on computers that have ample resources such as processing power and RAM, it can be quite common on older machines with low specifications. Surprisingly, I have found FireShot to work better on large X (Twitter) profiles and Nimbus to be best for large Facebook pages. I have no logic to offer for this discovery. Again, having both at our disposal will make us better prepared for online evidence collection. When both fail, consider Firefox's own solution, displayed next.

Firefox Screenshot

You may not like either FireShot or Nimbus. In general, you get what you pay for with these (they are free). When I have an extremely long Facebook or X (Twitter) page, I find both of those options mediocre at best. Lately, I find myself using the embedded Firefox Screenshot utility more than anything else. Consider the following example. I loaded my own X (Twitter) profile and scrolled back to posts from a year prior. This generated quite a long page and my computer fans increased speed due to the heat generated from my processor. I attempted a screen capture with both FireShot and Nimbus, and each failed. I then executed the following with Firefox.

- Right-click within the page and select "Take Screenshot".
- Choose "Save full page" and click "Download".

The process ran for about three minutes and saved an image .png file to my default downloads directory. It was several megabytes in size. The default filename includes the word Screenshot, date, and title from the webpage.

SingleFile (addons.mozilla.org/en-US/firefox/addon/single-file/)

The previous options have always been the standard way of saving content. However, we should always embrace new services. In late 2022, I was struggling to archive a large page, which led me to seeking alternative capture Add-ons. SingleFile saves any page as a HTML file, which can bypass many resource restrictions while generating a PDF. Before we test it, let's modify several settings. After right-clicking the SingleFile icon in the menu bar and choosing "Manage Extension", I conducted the following.

- Click the "Preferences" tab.
- Expand "User Interface" and enable "Open saved pages in a new tab".
- Expand "HTML Content" and disable "Remove hidden elements".
- Enable "Save original URLs of embedded resources".

You can now load any page and click the SingleFile icon to begin the process. The add-on will collect all of the content from the page and embed it into a single HTML file within the Downloads folder of your VM or host. You can open this file within your web browser to see the archive. Our changes simply apply settings which try to save an archive close to the original. By opening the result in a new tab after completion, we will know that everything worked.

We can also save multiple tabs all at once within the SingleFile menu. Executing this feature archived each page as a separate file and also opened each archive for immediate viewing. You should notice the file names now include the title of the page and full timestamp. The sizes assure us that all of the data is embedded into the file. Since this utility is embedding Base64 images directly into the HTML file, we only have one file to archive or export. Lately, this tool has been much more reliable than PDF export options, and the source of the HTML captures additional pieces of data for our investigation.

Exif Viewer (addons.mozilla.org/en-us/firefox/addon/exif-viewer)

This extension provides right-click access to the Exif data embedded into images. Later chapters explain what Exif data is and how it can be useful. With this extension enabled, you can right-click on any full-size image located on a web page. The menu option is "View Image Exif Data" and a new window will open when selected. This window will identify any available metadata about the image. Figure 9.05 (left) displays the right-click menu with a new option to View Image Exif Data. Overall, most photos on social networks do not contain any metadata. They have been "scrubbed" in order to protect the privacy of users. However, many blogs and personal websites display images that still contain metadata. While Chapter Twenty will explain online websites that display this metadata, a browser add-on is much more efficient. In my experience, this extension will increase the number of times that you will search for this hidden content.

User-Agent Switcher (addons.mozilla.org/firefox/addon/user-agent-string-switcher)

Occasionally, you may visit a website that does not want to cooperate with Firefox. Browsers notify websites of their identity and websites can alter or refuse content to certain products. One example is that some older websites require Microsoft's Internet Explorer to view the content. Even though Firefox is capable of displaying the information, a website can refuse the data to the browser. Another example is mobile websites that display different content if viewing from an iPhone instead of a computer. This can now all be controlled with User-Agent Switcher and Manager. Note that this is a different application than the recommendation within the previous edition of this book (User-Agent Switcher). User-Agent Switcher and Manager offers many new features, one of which we will discuss in the Instagram chapter.

When installed, you have a new option in your browser. The menu allows you to choose a mobile operating system, such as iOS or Android, or a desktop browser such as Internet Explorer or Chrome. It will also allow you to specify your operating system such as Mac or Windows. Whatever you choose, this data will be sent to any site that you visit. If you visit a website of a tech-savvy target, he or she may know that you were looking around. You may also be revealing that you are using a specific browser, such as Firefox, and a Windows computer (common in government). You could now change your agent to that of a mobile device or Google Chromebook which may not look as suspicious.

To do so, you would click on the menu bar icon; select the desired browser to emulate (such as Edge), select the desired operating system (such as Windows); choose exact offering (such as Edge 92.0.1 Windows 10); and click "Apply (container on window)". Click the "Test UA" button to visit a page which will confirm your new active user-agent. To return to the default Firefox option in your native operating system, click on the "Restart" button and refresh the page. Figure 9.04 displays an example where a mobile version of Yahoo was delivered to a desktop computer. Figure 9.05 displays the same page without any user-agent spoofing.

I have used this on several occasions to bypass poor security protocols. During one investigation, I had encountered a web forum of a hacking group that always appeared blank upon visit. Google had indexed it, but I could not see any content. By changing my default agent to Firefox on a Linux machine, I was allowed to see the content. The group had enabled a script that would only allow the page to be viewed on Linux computers.

In another situation, while still employed by the government, various mandated online training needed to be completed in order to maintain specific certifications. This government-hosted training was poorly designed and required users to access via Internet Explorer. Since I used an Apple computer, I could not connect until I changed my agent to Internet Explorer within my Firefox browser.

Please note that user-agent spoofing will not fool every website. If the target site includes JavaScript which scans for additional identifiers, such as touch points and video cards, the real details may be presented. I host a demonstration page at **https://inteltechniques.com/logger** which you can use to see how some sites may bypass your trickery. While this level of scrutiny is rare, it is a possibility. Always know what websites may be able to see about your computer and connection before any sensitive investigation. Refresh my test page as you make changes to this extension.

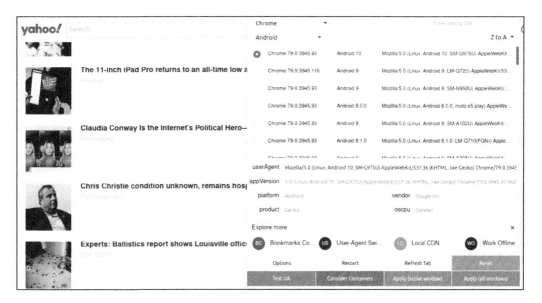

Figure 9.04: User-Agent Switcher and Manager disguising a desktop system as a mobile device.

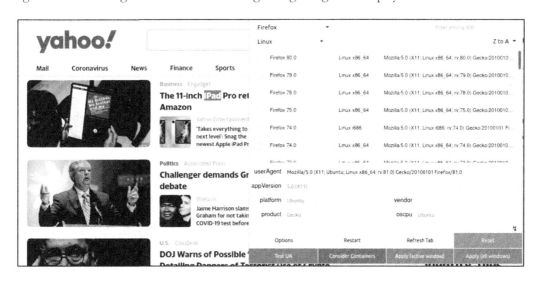

Figure 9.05: A page without user-agent spoofing.

Image Search Options (addons.mozilla.org/firefox/addon/image-search-options/)

A later chapter explains reverse image search engines and how they can identify more target photographs. Popular options include Google Images and TinEye. This extension automates the reverse search when an image is right-clicked. When installed, "Image Search Options" is present when you right-click on an image. Highlighting this option presents several reverse image search services including Google, Bing, TinEye, Yandex,

Baidu, and others. You will later learn how my online search tool will execute an image search across all of those services at once. However, this tool can be beneficial due to the convenience and obscure services such as Karma Decay, which looks for copies of images on Reddit. This add-on removes any excuse to not always check reverse images on target websites. With this add-on enabled, you will be ready to enhance your searches during that investigation.

Search By Image (addons.mozilla.org/en-US/firefox/addon/search_by_image)

The previous option has been present in my OSINT VMs for a long time. Recently I added Search By Image as an alternative add-on. While it seems to be updated more often and has additional options, Image Search Options also has unique services missing from this one. I plan to keep them both available in case one should ever become blocked by a specific service. However, Search By Image has one huge advantage. It allows you to capture an image from a page without knowing the source URL or being able to right-click an image file. Consider the following scenario.

Assume you are on a website which has either restricted right-click access or has embedded images in a way which makes them inaccessible. This is very common within newer social networks. Search By Image allows you to crop any visible part of a page and then conduct a reverse image search analysis across multiple services. The following steps walk through the process.

- Left-click the Search By Image icon in the upper-right of the browser.
- Change the "Select URL" drop-down menu to "Capture".
- Select the desired service, such as Bing.
- Use your cursor to draw a rectangle around the target image.
- Click "Search" in the lower popup menu.

A new tab should open with your reverse image search results. This can be a vital utility when you encounter sites which strive to prevent unauthorized copying of content. I have also used this on protected PDF files which contain images but do not allow right-click access or ability to extract images. You could even open a locally-stored PDF within Firefox in order to take advantage of this tool.

Web Archives (addons.mozilla.org/en-US/firefox/addon/view-page-archive)

This extension provides a link to archived versions of websites whenever a page has been modified, is unavailable, or has been deleted. Let's change a few settings before we tackle usage. I clicked the Web Archives icon in the menu bar; expanded the three dots to see the menu; selected "Options"; and enable all search engines. We can now click the Web Archives icon and choose from multiple services. Each will query the current tab for archives from previous dates. We also have the "All" option which opens a new tab for each activated service, which can be fairly resource intensive.

Copy Selected Links (addons.mozilla.org/firefox/addon/copy-selected-links/)

This simple add-on will identify any hyperlinks within the selected text of an individual web page. It will store the links within your operating system's clipboard, which allows you to paste them into any application of your choice. While only a small utility, it can quickly turn a large project into an easily completed task.

Using the utility is fairly straightforward. While on any website, select any or all text, right-click anywhere in the page, and select the "Copy selected links" option in the menu. The links will be stored in your clipboard and you can paste them into Notepad, Excel, or any other productivity application. There are unlimited uses for Copy Selected Links, and below are a few of my favorite.

- **Facebook**: When I am on my target's list of Facebook friends, I will select all text and use Copy Selected Links to quickly record each hyperlink to an individual's profile. I will then paste these into Excel for later analysis. Comparison with previous captures identifies those that were "unfriended".
- **X (X (Twitter))**: When I am viewing a X (Twitter) profile, I will use this utility to capture all links to external websites and photos.
- **YouTube**: When viewing a person's YouTube videos page, Copy Selected Links allows me to paste the entire collection of linked videos into a report.
- **eBay**: While viewing results from a search for a specific fraudulent product, I can quickly copy the active hyperlinks to each auction and paste them directly into a report in seconds.
- **Human Trafficking**: While viewing ad results for suspected human trafficking victims, I can copy all active hyperlinks and paste directly into a report, email, or memo for other investigators.
- **PDFs**: Since I can open PDF files within Firefox, I can also use this tool to extract all hyperlinks from within the file.

Performing screenshots during my investigation in these examples would never identify the direct links to the visible content. A combination of screen captures and links provides a more comprehensive report. I always press "ctrl-a" to select all of the content; right-click within the page; and choose "Copy selected links". I can then paste all hyperlinks from that page within any text editor.

OneTab (addons.mozilla.org/en-US/firefox/addon/onetab/)

This extension provides simple and effective management of browser tabs by allowing you to collapse any open pages into a list of bookmarks. Once installed, it is activated by clicking on the blue funnel icon on your toolbar. Doing so will close any open tabs and open the OneTab management page. The collapsed tabs are displayed on this page as a group of bookmarks. Each individual bookmark is made up of a page title, with the respective URL embedded as a link. Any previously saved tab groups are stored further down the page in reverse chronological order.

Interacting with the management page is straight forward. At the top of each tab set is an editable title which defaults to the number of tabs in that group. Left-click on the title to change it to something logical for that set of links, such as "Username Subject X". To the right of the title is a date and timestamp indicating when the list was saved. You can drag and drop individual bookmarks to change the order in each group or to move links from one group to another. Clicking on "Restore all" will re-open each of the bookmarks into its own tab.

The bookmarks are links, not saved pages, so you will be reloading any non-cached page content from the remote host. Selecting "Delete all" will destroy the bookmarks in that group. Selecting "More…" gives options to rename, lock, or star the tab group. "Star this tab group" pins that group to the top of your management page, independent of the date and time created.

Using "Share as web page" is not recommended as it creates an html page of your tab group on the OneTab servers. The preferred method for transferring OneTab bookmarks is to use the export feature, which is found in the upper right menu. This will allow you to copy links as plain text and paste them into a secure platform.

OneTab defaults to deleting the bookmarks from a group if you select "Restore all". To change this behavior, select "Options" and select "Keep them in your OneTab list". Right-clicking on a web page will bring up the OneTab context menu which allows for more granular tab selection. OneTab collects no user data unless you intentionally click on the "Share as web page" feature. Barring that feature, all data is stored locally.

Stream Detector (addons.mozilla.org/en-US/firefox/addon/hls-stream-detector)

This extension has become vital during my daily OSINT routines due to the prevalence of streaming video within my daily investigations. Whether pre-recorded or live, many websites now deliver video via embedded streams rather than traditional files. While we could once easily right-click an online video and download the file as an MP4, that is rare today. We must now be prepared to encounter video stream protocols such as playlists (M3U8) and transport stream (TS).

Let's take for example videos posted on X (X (Twitter)) by CNN. When presented with a video on CNN's X (Twitter) feed right-clicking this video provided an option to copy the video address, but nothing to download it. Monitoring the network activity of the page through "Inspect Element" presented numerous small files, none of which were the entire video. However, clicking on the Stream Detector extension and refreshing the page presented the options visible in Figure 9.06. These M3U8 URLs represent streaming videos available on the current page. If there is a M3U8 listed as "master" that is typically the video of interest but often I will need to test each M3U8 link and locate the specific video of interest by process of elimination. Clicking this link copies it to the clipboard so that it may be pasted into VLC for playback or conversion.

Downloading and opening this link within VLC media player, which is explained in the next chapter, plays the entire video within the software. The Linux-based Python tools which we create in the next chapter help us download the entire video for offline use. While this extension may seem complicated now, it will simplify archiving of online video streams in the next chapter. For now, the power of this utility is the ability to document our evidence. I can now disclose the exact digital source of the video stream. This can be extremely valuable when a website is later removed or altered, but the media remains untouched on the media hosting server. We will explore online video streams much more later.

HLS	3_d6SLLXqIDdUIZB.m3u8	-	(1) CNN on X: "JUST IN: Three ...	8/2/2024 10:27:28 AM	✕
HLS	5hPRILYO5O1eGewP.m3u8	-	(1) CNN on X: "JUST IN: Three ...	8/2/2024 10:27:28 AM	✕
HLS	yoItjduVBfWbHKSD.m3u8	-	(1) CNN on X: "JUST IN: Three ...	8/2/2024 10:27:28 AM	✕
HLS	TQaOwnCWDyUcuLzj.m3u8	-	(1) CNN on X: "JUST IN: Three ...	8/2/2024 10:27:27 AM	✕
HLS	uPpFdNYF3B4ckKc2.m3u8	-	(1) CNN on X: "JUST IN: Three ...	8/2/2024 10:27:27 AM	✕
HLS	pedhP0LL9IQ3i11O.m3u8	-	(1) CNN on X: "JUST IN: Three ...	8/2/2024 10:27:27 AM	✕
☐ Disable detection	Copy all visible URLs		Clear this URL list		Options

Figure 9.06: The Stream Detector extension displaying embedded video streams.

If this extension provides value to your investigations, but you find some sites which do not function, consider adding another Firefox extension titled **The m3u8 Stream Detector** (addons.mozilla.org/firefox/addon/the-m3u8-stream-detector). It may pick up missing streams. This add-on will be vital during the Broadcast Stream chapter much later in the book. We will use it to immediately identify files which stream live news coverage from all over the world, and that file will be used to populate our custom search tool. This is a great example of how one OSINT resource works in tandem with others.

Firefox Toolbar Customization

Remember that many Firefox extensions will be embedded into the "puzzle" icon, which I do not like. I want them available to me instantly, and I want them in my preferred order. I conduct the following.

- Right-click any empty spot on the toolbar and select "Customize Toolbar".
- Drag any undesired icons, such as "Pocket" and "Account" down to remove.
- Drag remaining items into the order desired and click "Done" when finished.

Exporting and Importing a Pre-Configured Profile

At this point, it may seem overwhelming when thinking about the abundance of Add-ons and their proper configurations. I currently use several Windows, Apple, and Linux virtual machines and must keep my Firefox browser updated on all of them. I no longer manually update each browser. Instead, I maintain a single Firefox browser that includes all customizations that I desire. I then import these settings into any other browsers in order to replicate the experience across every computer I use. In a moment, I share my profile for easy import.

The following instructions allow you to export your final settings and import the same customizations into other investigative computers. Only execute this tutorial on a new install of Firefox that has no saved settings, or within a version of Firefox that you want to be overwritten. Do not overwrite your current version if you have bookmarks, extensions, or other data that you want to keep. You should backup any settings if proceeding on an older install. As a final warning, the following steps will overwrite any custom options applied to your target Firefox installations.

- Open your CONFIGURED version of Firefox; click the menu button (three horizontal lines); click "Help"; then "More Troubleshooting Information".
- Under the "Application Basics" section, click on "Open Directory". A window with your profile files will open. Close Firefox, but leave this window open.
- Copy these files into a new folder on a removable drive.
- Open your NEW version of Firefox; click the menu button (three horizontal lines); click "Help"; then "More Troubleshooting Information".
- Under the "Application Basics" section, click on Open (or Show) Folder (or Directory). A file window will open. Close Firefox, but leave the window open.
- Paste the content of the new folder on your removable drive into this folder. Overwrite any files when prompted. Restart Firefox.

The result should be a copy of Firefox which contains every add-on you configured from this chapter. This profile could be copied to an unlimited number of computers, as long as the versions of Firefox were identical.

Custom Firefox Profile

While I prefer readers create their own Firefox configuration, I respect that a lot of effort is required to replicate these steps within multiple machines. Therefore, I have created a custom file which includes every configuration explained within this chapter. It can be used within a new Debian VM with an untouched Firefox installation. The following will only work within Debian. First, launch Firefox then close it. Open Terminal and copy and paste the following commands all at once.

```
sudo apt update
sudo apt install -y curl
cd ~/Desktop
curl -O https://inteltechniques.com/data/osintvm/ff-template.zip
unzip ff-template.zip -d ~/.mozilla/firefox/
cd ~/.mozilla/firefox/ff-template/
cp -R * ~/.mozilla/firefox/*.default-esr*
cd ~/Desktop && rm ff-template.zip
```

Future chapters explain more about these types of commands, but let's digest these for future use. The first command installs curl, which we will use to download a file via Terminal. The second command changes the path within Terminal to our desktop. The next command downloads my custom Firefox template to the desktop. The fourth command decompresses the file and extracts all data. The next command changes our directory to the downloaded decompressed files and the final commands copy our Firefox template file into the appropriate folder and delete the downloaded file. Re-launching Firefox should now present the following customizations.

Firefox Custom Profile Issues

As I was preparing to publish this edition, I noticed that Firefox occasionally resets the profile within the browser. If you are missing the extensions, you can conduct the following at any time to restore them. First, close Firefox and execute the following within Terminal to delete the current profile and create a new build. Enter "A" if prompted to overwrite files. This can also be done if you simply want to rebuild your Firefox installation to the default settings from this chapter.

```
cd ~/.mozilla/firefox/*.default-esr*
rm -r *
cd ~/Desktop
curl -O https://inteltechniques.com/data/osintvm/ff-template.zip
unzip ff-template.zip -d ~/.mozilla/firefox/
cd ~/.mozilla/firefox/ff-template/
cp -R * ~/.mozilla/firefox/*.default-esr*
cd ~/Desktop && rm ff-template.zip
```

NOTE: The default version of Firefox within Debian is the Extended Support Release (ESR) build. While I would not use this on my personal host machine, it works well for an OSINT VM. It receives updates less frequently than the traditional version, but offers better stability for usage within our VM.

Chromium-Based Browser

I always prefer the previous custom Firefox configuration for my daily investigations. However, I also want the availability of an untouched Chromium-based browser when needed. This might be to appear as a more standard user to whatever website I am accessing or in the event I have tweaked my Firefox browser to the point of blocking some online content. It could also be to take advantage of a Chromium-based extension which is not available within Firefox. Sometimes, I want an untouched browser to document the exact way an intrusive website appears to the average user without any modification extensions. I believe every good OSINT machine should have a secondary browser option.

Google Chrome is an excellent browser that is known for being very fast and responsive, and it is also very secure by nature, but compromises privacy since Google receives a lot of data about your internet usage. Chrome is based on open-source Chromium, but Chromium can be tricky to install and keep updated, especially for ARM-based machines. Both Firefox and Chromium "sandbox" each tab. Sandboxing restricts the content in that tab to that tab only, preventing it from "touching" other tabs in the browser, or the computer's hardware. This is a very important feature in preventing malware from being installed when you visit a malicious website.

This is where I deviate again from previous editions. I believe our best Chromium-based browser within an OSINT VM is Brave. This is for two reasons. First, Brave has removed most of the connections to Google which helps prevent sharing of usage details. Second, Brave works the same on traditional and ARM-based systems. We can install it with the following commands.

```
sudo curl -fsSLo /usr/share/keyrings/brave-browser-archive-keyring.gpg
https://brave-browser-apt-release.s3.brave.com/brave-browser-archive-
keyring.gpg

echo "deb [signed-by=/usr/share/keyrings/brave-browser-archive-
keyring.gpg] https://brave-browser-apt-release.s3.brave.com/ stable
main"|sudo tee /etc/apt/sources.list.d/brave-browser-release.list

sudo apt update && sudo apt install brave-browser -y
```

After installation, launch Brave and skip all onboarding options. Disable any options to "make Brave better" which sends diagnostic data to their servers. You are now ready to use the browser.

If you do not need a Chromium-based browser, and can complete all of your investigations within Firefox, Brave can be omitted from your VM. However, possessing this option can be beneficial when needed. You can also use it to access Tor network sites, as explained next. I keep Brave ready on my VM, but rarely open it.

Tor Browser (torproject.org)

Tor is an acronym for The Onion Router. Basically, it allows you to mask your IP address and appear to be browsing the internet from a false location. It also allows you to access sites hosted on the Tor network, which is the reason we need it within our VM. If you ever encounter a URL which ends in ".onion", you should open that link in the Tor Browser. Installing Tor Browser into Linux is no longer an easy task. Most Terminal commands floating around the internet no longer work and the official Tor website recommends manual steps which require launching via Terminal every time. This is a good opportunity to install the application manager Flatpak onto our system, which will make the Tor Browser installation and execution easy. It will also provide a graphical software repository for future application installation. Conduct the following, and reboot after full installation and configuration.

```
sudo apt update && sudo apt install flatpak -y
flatpak remote-add --if-not-exists flathub
https://dl.flathub.org/repo/flathub.flatpakrepo
flatpak install flathub org.torproject.torbrowser-launcher -y
flatpak run org.torproject.torbrowser-launcher
```

This will configure the Tor Browser and present two new applications on your device. After reboot, launch the option titled "Tor Browser". The next task that Tor will complete is to create a connection to a Tor server. This connects you to a server and routes all of your internet traffic through that server. After the connection is successful, it will load a custom version of the Firefox browser. Now, every website that you visit through this browser will assume you are connecting through this new IP address instead of your own. This provides a layer of privacy to stay hidden from a suspect and allow access to the Tor network.

Tor Browser may be overkill for most investigations. If you are only searching and monitoring common services such as Facebook, X (Twitter), or YouTube, this service is not needed. If you are visiting personal websites and blogs of a tech savvy hacker, you should rely on your VPN. I only use this to access sites on the Tor network. When using Tor, you may notice a drastic decrease in the speed of your internet. This is normal and unavoidable. This often improves the longer you are connected. To stop the service, simply close the browser. This will disconnect the Tor network and stop all services. Any activity conducted through the Tor browser is not associated with your real internet connection or VPN. You can update Tor Browser, and all other Flatpak applications, with the following command.

```
flatpak update
```

If you are attempting this through UTM on a newer macOS device, expect problems. Tor Browser currently does not support ARM-based hardware. There are a few unofficial projects supplying ARM-based builds, but I avoid them for now. I will monitor the situation and update this guide once we have a reliable solution. Until then, you can launch Brave and choose the "New Private Window with Tor" option within the far-right menu. This will allow you to access Tor network websites.

Hard Page Refresh

I close this chapter with one last important tip. Internet cache can be a hurdle within your investigations. Any time you visit a website, files are downloaded to your computer. Many sites have instructions embedded into them which tell your browser how it should behave. It may instruct it to load images from your local cache from your computer instead of fetching them again from the web server in order to decrease demand on the network. You can click the refresh button all day, but it might only renew the page with previously downloaded content. If images on your target website have changed, you may never know. This is where a hard refresh can assist.

The following steps force your browser to reload an entire page from the online resources instead of any locally-stored cache files. I make a habit of doing this often to make sure I am viewing the most recent content.

- Brave or Firefox (Linux and Windows): Press Shift+CTRL+R.
- Brave or Firefox (macOS): Press Shift+Command+R.
- **Most browsers: Hold Shift while clicking the reload icon.**

Summary

Your browser might be the most vital piece of your OSINT investigations. Make sure you spend some time customizing it the way you need it.

CHAPTER TEN
OSINT VM APPLICATIONS

Hopefully, you now have a functioning Linux Debian OSINT VM ready for further customization. That alone provides a very secure environment for your online research. However, possessing customized software applications within your VM would greatly enhance your investigations. Debian provides some basic applications in the default installation, but I want to take that to the next level. In this chapter, we are going to customize your Debian VM with numerous OSINT applications which will provide many new investigative aids. Until now, much of this guide has been similar to my previous tutorials, while providing much more extensive details. In my book *OSINT Techniques, 10th Edition*, this portion of the content combined Linux-based applications with custom scripts which automated many tasks. This is where I deviate from the previous book. In this chapter, I will only focus on manual installation and execution of several OSINT applications, without explaining any of the automated scripts. This is for two reasons.

First, I want you to be able to articulate the behind-the-scenes manual processes. If you ever need to testify or explain your actions, I don't want a response to be "I just pushed the button". Second, I want you to be able to troubleshoot problems which may arise as commands change. Knowing how to manipulate the commands to execute Linux-based apps will take you much further than waiting on me to update a script. Don't worry, I will still provide automation to every task within this chapter through the use of bash scripts, including completely-configured files which can be downloaded from my website, but you will have to wait until Chapter Eleven for that. Until then, please allow yourself to absorb the boring manual processes and their results. While this chapter may seem dry and tedious at times, I promise the future benefits will be worth the effort.

Consider this chapter to be the manual approach in order to understand every detail of our ultimate OSINT VM, and Chapter Eleven to be the "easy" way. Later, in Chapter Fourteen, my automated installation script will allow you to create our entire machine, including all scripts, with only one command and almost no effort. Please do not jump to that chapter, we still have a lot to learn. This is a long chapter.

Debian possesses a software "store" in which you can point and click through various Linux applications and install them with ease. However, I discourage users from this method. Your choices are minimal and there are likely better alternatives available. Instead, we will use the Terminal for almost all of our application installations. If you followed the previous tutorials, you may already have the Terminal application in your software Dock within your Debian VM created earlier. If not, you can always find the Terminal application by clicking the "Activities" menu and then the nine dots within the Dock on the left of your screen. Open the Terminal application and leave it open while we install some required software. I present this chapter in sections according to the type of OSINT data being retrieved. Let's ease into things slowly and cover some basics surrounding online videos.

Videos: VLC Media Player (https://www.videolan.org/)

By default, your Windows and Mac operating systems include media players which allow execution of audio and video files. Your default Debian virtual machine may not have this luxury. However, this is easy to correct. VLC is an application which can play practically any media files you throw at it. You could find VLC within the Debian Software application, but I prefer to manually install it. This also provides our first explanation of installation commands in Linux. Within Terminal, type the following commands, pressing return after each.

```
sudo apt update
sudo apt install vlc -y
```

Let's break this down, as you will see similar instructions throughout this chapter.

sudo: This command executes any following text with elevated privileges. It is similar to running a program in Windows or Mac as the administrator. When using this command, you will be required to enter your password. Note that passwords entered within Terminal do not appear as you type them, but they are there. Simply press enter when finished typing. Any additional sudo commands in the same terminal session should not ask for the password again until enough time passes in which Debian wants to make sure you still want these elevated privileges.

apt update: This command updates the Debian lists of available upgrades to packages which need upgrading, as well as new packages that have just come to the repositories. It basically fetches information about updates from the repositories previously mentioned.

apt install: This tells Debian to install a specific software application, such as VLC. Since we added "-y" to the command, we do not need to confirm installation during the process.

After you have executed these commands, you should see VLC installed within the "Applications" menu by clicking the nine dots icon in the Dock to the left. You can launch the application within this menu and it should be set as the default option for opening most downloaded media files. Upon first launch, disable the "Allow metadata network access" option and click "Continue", as seen below.

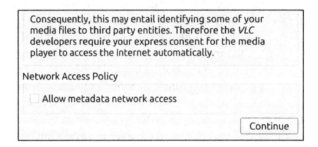

Videos: FFmpeg (https://ffmpeg.org/)

This is another set of media tools, but these only work within Terminal. We will need them when we start adding utilities to manipulate and download videos. Enter the following into Terminal and press enter.

```
sudo apt install ffmpeg -y
```

Later, we will create scripts which will automate the following functions. For now, let's understand the manual process. Assume that you possess a video file named evidence.mpg in your Downloads folder, and you have already navigated to that folder within Terminal with "cd Downloads".

Play Video: This option will force FFmpeg to attempt to play any video file with multiple video codecs. This will often play videos that would not otherwise play using standard media players such as Windows Media Player and VLC. This will also play many surveillance videos without the need for third-party programs. I once used this technique to play a corrupt video file which captured a homicide, but standard video players could not understand the data.

```
ffplay evidence.mpg
```

Convert Video to MP4: This option simply converts any target video to a standard MP4 format. This is beneficial when the target video possesses a unique codec that prohibits playing universally. If the above option can play the video, this option can convert it so that any computer should be able to play it natively. I often used this to send copies of videos to prosecutors forced to use Windows computers. this is especially important when dealing with ".webm" videos from YouTube. Not everyone will have the software for playing these videos, but an MP4 should play on any system.

```
ffmpeg -i evidence.mpg evidence.mp4
```

Extract All Video Frames: This is likely the most used utility within this set of applications. After supplying a target video, this tool will extract the still images from the video. The result is a folder of uncompressed bitmap (bmp) image files depicting practically every frame of the video. This is beneficial when close examination of frames is necessary. I include this every time a crucial video will be used during prosecution of a crime.

```
ffmpeg -y -i evidence.mpg %04d.png
```

Extract Video Frames Every Second: The previous example may download way more images than you desire. If you have a video five minutes in length at a high frame-rate, you may generate thousands of images. The following command extracts only one image per second.

```
ffmpeg -i input.mp4 -vf fps=1 %04d.png
```

Extract Audio: This option extracts the raw audio file out of any video, converts it to a 320k MP3 file, and saves the file. I have used this to extract audio from video confessions and interviews, and it works well on any online videos downloaded from the internet.

```
ffmpeg -i evidence.mpg -f mp3 -ab 320000 -vn music.mp3
```

Rotate Video: You may encounter a video which has been captured from a mobile device and is rotated 90 degrees clockwise. This option allows us to rotate the video counterclockwise to a traditional view, and flips the video vertically to generate a traditional view of a cellular video. This is beneficial during courtroom presentation, especially when a jury is involved. this also converted to a universal MP4 file.

```
ffmpeg -i evidence.mpg -vf transpose=0 evidence.mp4
```

Merge Videos: You might have multiple video segments from the same original video which need combined into one file. The following command assumes that I have a file called "video1.mp4" which needs another file titled "video2.mp4" added to the end of it. After the execution, one file called "output.mp4" will possess both videos as one.

```
ffmpeg -i video1.mp4 -i video2.mp4 -filter_complex
"[0:v][0:a][1:v][1:a]concat=n=2:v=1:a=1" -vsync vfr output.mp4
```

Remove Redundant Frames: This option removes single frames of a video that appear extremely similar to the frame preceding it. In other words, it takes out all of the frames which are the same (no action) and only leaves desired activity. This is great for surveillance video which contains hours of one scene without motion detection.

```
ffmpeg -i evidence.mpg -strict -2 -vf
"select=gt(scene\,0.005),setpts=N/(25*TB)" evidence.mp4
```

As you can see, these commands can be lengthy and technical. We will later create one single custom script which will allow us to easily choose which service we want to execute. The following image displays a folder of generated screen captures with one file opened.

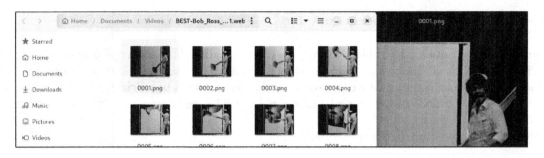

Important Python Information

I present a vital warning before we continue installing numerous applications via Terminal. Some will fail to install completely on the first attempt. This is often due to a broken or missing dependency which is required by the application. Sometimes, repeating the steps solves the issue, while other scenarios require us to wait until the program is updated by the developer. There is no harm in repeating the steps presented here if you run into complications.

You will see some Pip errors or warnings displayed while you install some apps. These are often dependency version conflicts, and typically do not impact the functions of the program. Since we will install most programs within isolated virtual environments, these errors will not actually break any programs as they claim. While we will take steps to eliminate as many errors as possible, yellow warning and red error text within Terminal is common, especially warning about executing commands as Root. Please ignore these warnings on our OSINT VM.

Python Virtual Environments

The installation of the previous applications using Apt were very basic. However, many applications will require installation through the Package Installer for Python (pip), which will also install multiple dependencies which are required for each program. Some programs only want specific versions of these dependencies and may not work if newer versions are installed. In past editions, I lumped all Python applications within the root operating system, which began to cause dependency conflicts. I no longer configure all applications and dependencies within the root operating system. Today, I place Python programs within their own virtual environment using either Python venv or pipx, each of which creates an isolated environment for the installation. This prevents conflicts from one PIP program to another and keeps our system clean. Enter the following into Terminal, which will provide the necessary configuration for both venv and pipx in Debian.

```
sudo apt update
sudo apt install python3-pip -y
sudo apt install python3-venv -y
sudo apt install pipx -y
```

We could now install applications via pipx by entering the following commands (**Please do not replicate these steps yet**).

```
pipx install streamlink
pipx ensurepath
```

After closing and reopening Terminal, we would have full access to the Python application Streamlink (explained soon). The installation and all dependencies were performed in an isolated environment which will not impact any current or future Python applications. This is much easier than the venv option, but will not work on all installations. We could have conducted the following to achieve the same result with venv (**Please do not replicate these steps yet**).

```
mkdir ~/Downloads/Programs
mkdir ~/Downloads/Programs/Streamlink
cd ~/Downloads/Programs/Streamlink
python3 -m venv streamlinkEnvironment
source streamlinkEnvironment/bin/activate
sudo pip install streamlink
deactivate
```

Now, let's walk through each of these commands to better understand the strategy.

mkdir: Makes new directories for our software.
cd: Changes the directory to our Programs folder.
python3 -m venv streamlinkEnvironment: Creates environment.
source streamlinkEnvironment/bin/activate: Activates it.
sudo pip install streamlink: Installs the application.
deactivate: Stops listening for instructions.

Basically, we created a new isolated folder which will contain the pip installation and all supporting files. We activated the environment before we started installing our software, and the installation was performed in a folder isolated from the other applications within our operating system. Once we were finished, we stopped the environment so nothing else would be placed within it. This prevents many software conflicts, and is especially important as we continue to pour more Python applications. Overall, I prefer pipx whenever I have an option to install a Python application which supports pip. Whenever I have a Python application which requires the installation of several dependencies, I prefer venv. I will offer many more examples of each throughout this chapter.

Software Dependencies

Before we proceed into the next sections, we need to apply two configurations to our OSINT VM. The first installs Git, which will be heavily used in upcoming tutorials. Execute the following within Terminal.

```
sudo apt install git -y
```

Next, we must disable an annoyance which has presented itself within some Debian-based systems. Anytime we install anything with pip, we receive an error about installing dependencies globally, even though we are installing them within isolated virtual environments. We should disable this warning with the following Terminal commands.

```
cd /usr/lib/python3.11
sudo rm EXTERNALLY-MANAGED
```

Videos: YT-DLP (https://github.com/yt-dlp/yt-dlp)

This may be my most-used Linux utility. The original Python script called YouTube-DL was the backbone which helped us download bulk videos from YouTube and other sources. In recent years, a fork of this script called YT-DLP has taken over as a more reliable option. Install with the following.

```
pipx install yt-dlp && pipx ensurepath
```

After we close and reopen Terminal, we will now have the necessary utilities installed for our media needs. This process is not too exciting, and you will not immediately see anything useful after these actions. However, you are laying the groundwork for the upcoming scripts. The YT-DLP script is ready to use, but only through the

Terminal application. Let's conduct an example in order to understand the features, and then discuss a way to automate queries.

Assume that we are looking for videos of Bob Ross teaching viewers how to paint with oils. You found the Bob Ross video channel located at https://www.youtube.com/user/BobRossInc. Clicking on the "Videos" option on that page presents https://www.youtube.com/user/BobRossInc/videos. This page displays over 600 full episodes of his television program, along with other recent related videos. Clicking one of these videos presents the following URL.

https://www.youtube.com/watch?v=lLWEXRAnQd0

You want to download the video from this page in the best quality possible in order to attach it to your case. The default YT-DLP command to do this is as follows.

```
yt-dlp "https://www.youtube.com/watch?v=lLWEXRAnQd0"
```

This will download the video to whichever directory you are in within Terminal. By default, you are likely in your home folder, but that is not a great place to save a video. Therefore, let's change the saved location to your desktop with the following commands.

```
cd ~/Desktop
yt-dlp "https://www.youtube.com/watch?v=lLWEXRAnQd0"
```

You should now see the video file on your Desktop in Debian. Playback will likely appear poor within the VM, but you could copy that file out to your host for proper playback through the shared folder on your Desktop. When you retrieved this video, you may have noticed that two files actually downloaded (one video and one audio). This is because YT-DLP has detected that you have FFmpeg installed, and it chose to download the highest quality option for you. If you had not possessed FFmpeg, you would have been given a lower quality version. This is because YouTube presents separate audio and video files to the viewer when a high-quality output is chosen. YT-DLP works in tandem with FFmpeg to download the best quality option and merge the result into a playable file. This is the best way to extract a single video from YouTube and other video sources. However, the true power is on bulk downloads.

Assume you downloaded the previous file in reference to your investigation. You then see that your target possesses hundreds of videos on his YouTube "Videos" page. You want all of these videos, located at https://www.youtube.com/user/BobRossInc/
videos. YT-DLP can download these with the following.

```
yt-dlp "https://www.youtube.com/user/BobRossInc/videos"
```

This will take some time to download everything, especially if the videos are long. If you want to cancel this command, press "Ctrl" and "C" on your keyboard at any time. This terminates any process within Terminal and may be beneficial throughout this chapter.

YT-DLP now includes features to download other data associated with a YouTube video, including comments, subtitles, and description. We can modify our first download command to download all data associated with the video as follows.

```
yt-dlp "https://www.youtube.com/watch?v=lLWEXRAnQd0" --write-comments
yt-dlp "https://www.youtube.com/watch?v=lLWEXRAnQd0" --write-subs
yt-dlp "https://www.youtube.com/watch?v=lLWEXRAnQd0" --write-
description
```

These commands target the desired video page; load all of the data requested; export it to a JSON text file; then download the video file wherever your current Terminal path is set. If you want to download the data without the entire video, you can add "--skip-download" to your command, as follows.

```
yt-dlp "https://www.youtube.com/watch?v=1LWEXRAnQd0" --write-subs --skip-download
```

In this example, the subtitle file appeared on my Desktop, as that was the last place I had navigated within Terminal. This produced a text file with a .vtt file extension. Below are the first two lines of it.

```
00:00:29.988 --> 00:00:32.108
- Hello, I'm Bob Ross and I'd like to welcome
```

This generated the default language of English for the file. However, there may be more languages within this data. The following command repeats the process and downloads all languages.

```
yt-dlp "https://www.youtube.com/watch?v=1LWEXRAnQd0" --write-subs --sub-langs all --skip-download
```

The following is the first two lines of the file containing Spanish subtitles

```
00:00:29.988 --> 00:00:32.108
- Hola, soy Bob Ross
```

Imagine the following scenario. You have a suspect on YouTube with hundreds of videos. You have been tasked to download every video and identify the exact files and timestamps of every time he said the word "kill". One command within YT-DLP would provide all of the data you need to conduct a search within all text files, and the corresponding video evidence. We can also combine all of this into one command to download the video, all comments, all subtitles, and description with the following command.

```
yt-dlp "https://www.youtube.com/watch?v=1LWEXRAnQd0" --write-comments --write-subs --sub-langs all --write-description
```

If you wanted the text-based information without downloading the video (or entire channel of videos), you would conduct the following.

```
yt-dlp "https://www.youtube.com/watch?v=1LWEXRAnQd0" --write-comments --write-subs --sub-langs all --write-description --skip-download
```

We can also use YT-DLP to embed the default subtitles into the video, which will appear when played back, with the following command.

```
yt-dlp "https://www.youtube.com/watch?v=1LWEXRAnQd0" --embed-subs
```

Note that all text files downloaded will be in JSON format. While the files can be opened within any text editor, the format will be difficult to digest. **I always recommend opening these JSON files within Firefox for the best view.**

While named YT-DLP, this utility works on most popular video websites. You should have no issues downloading individual or bulk videos from YouTube, Vimeo, and many others. The bulk download option has saved me numerous hours of manually downloading videos individually. I have yet to find any size or file number limitations. This utility is likely my most used program within Linux, aside from browsers.

In 2019, I discovered a potential issue with this command. Since many video websites are now offering "Ultra-HD" 4K resolution videos, the file size can be quite large. Downloading an entire channel can take hours and the files may contain over a terabyte of data. While I appreciate that YT-DLP always defaults to the highest resolution video available, I may want to choose a lower resolution when downloading hundreds of files. The following commands execute YT-DLP; queries a new high-definition target video; downloads the best quality video up to a resolution of 1440p, 1080p, 720p, or 480p respectively; downloads the best quality audio available; merges the two streams into one media file; and saves the video for archiving. Note that you would need to delete each video if you wanted to test another resolution.

```
yt-dlp "https://www.youtube.com/watch?v=h6XCQUuZQU4" -f
'bestvideo[height<=1440]+bestaudio'
```

```
yt-dlp "https://www.youtube.com/watch?v=h6XCQUuZQU4" -f
'bestvideo[height<=1080]+bestaudio'
```

```
yt-dlp "https://www.youtube.com/watch?v=h6XCQUuZQU4" -f
'bestvideo[height<=720]+bestaudio'
```

```
yt-dlp "https://www.youtube.com/watch?v=h6XCQUuZQU4" -f
'bestvideo[height<=480]+bestaudio'
```

In the previous section about FFmpeg, I explained how you could extract the audio from a video file and save it as an MP3. We can do the same thing with YT-DLP with even more features. Assume you want to extract the audio from an online video which you do not possess on your device. The following extracts the native audio in the best quality available.

```
yt-dlp "https://www.youtube.com/watch?v=h6XCQUuZQU4" -x
```

The result was a file with an extension of ".opus", which is common for YouTube. The following command extracts that same audio, but saves it a s universal MP3 with high 320 kbps encoding.

```
yt-dlp "https://www.youtube.com/watch?v=h6XCQUuZQU4" -x --audio-format
mp3 --audio-quality 320k
```

Most videos you download from YouTube will be in their own ".webm" format, which not play on many computers. You could use FFmpeg to convert downloaded videos to MP4, or just use the following YT-DLP command which does this for you.

```
yt-dlp "https://www.youtube.com/watch?v=1LWEXRAnQd0" --recode-video mp4
```

If this seems overwhelming, please don't worry. Once we get to our video download script, you will click a couple of buttons to replicate everything here.

Videos: Fragmented Videos

It is very common for websites to present embedded videos which consist of hundreds of small pieces of streaming video frames. These files load seamlessly while viewing a video, but this delivery method can make the download process difficult. Some sites do this to prevent copying of proprietary content, while others eliminate unnecessary download of large single files if the video is stopped before the end. While YT-DLP is a great program, it is not perfect. Submitting a URL which contains a fragmented video is likely to fail. Therefore, we need to understand a manual way to approach this issue. Consider the video at the following URL

https://www.dailymotion.com/video/x42bdc7

Submitting this type of URL to YT-DLP often results in an error because it cannot properly detect the video.

Before playing the video, right-click within your Firefox or Chrome browser and select "Inspect". Click the "Network" tab within the new window at the bottom of your browser, then click the play button within the video. You should see numerous connections, similar to those in the following image.

245754439_mp4_h264_aac.m3u8	200	xhr	dmp.quality switch mse.5b77.
245754439_mp4_h264_aac_hd_hfr.m3u8	200	xhr	dmp.quality switch mse.5b77.
x42bdc7.m3u8?auth=1722807809-2562-ozbxlnyw-06f1f12...id_dm=b...	(blocked:other)	xhr	dmp.photon vendor.2d4c686.
x42bdc7.m3u8?auth=1722807809-2562-ozbxlnyw-06f1f12...id_dm=b...	(blocked:other)	xhr	dmp.photon vendor.2d4c686.
x42bdc7.m3u8?auth=1722807809-2688-hm29y4dy-f557fd8...tps%3A...	(blocked:other)	script	dmp.advertising.06d4761...js.
x42bdc7.m3u8?auth=1722807809-2688-lhypn0pf-655e7ab...png%2Ci...	(blocked:other)	xhr	dmp.photon vendor.2d4c686.
x42bdc7.m3u8?sec=cvhBxtFekt3Vjd6jmr0hOUQ-oowviCOfR...02770&...	200	xhr	dmp.quality switch mse.5b77.

Any ".ts" files are small video fragments which are being streamed to your browser. This target video URL contains hundreds of these files. Instead of targeting the video fragments, we want the "m3u8" file which acts as a playlist for all of the video pieces. An example is displayed above in the second row. Right-click on this option; highlight "Copy"; and select "Copy URL". Paste this URL into your video download tool. I prefer the yt-dlp option. In this example, my URL is as follows.

https://vod.cf.dmcdn.net/sec2(Ssb3Z4xaO2eyCTqKmR8svWl6x777TzWc4q1-MZbefmErwTwS9w fE3wMrlFkfXT-xJ3p81ftUrViKBXwYfQCXzeKYC_gyQep0C-jTum0FvhL9p1Lqj1vWrUfFRSfItglzNz Gnhi6w69stLQ1k6mvL6w)/video/934/457/245754439_mp4_h264_aac.m3u8

Since you are providing a playlist of these video fragments to the download tool, the software can identify the list of videos and reconstruct them into a single video file. The previous URL resulted in a one-hour single video in MP4 format without any sign of spilt files. I rely on this technique weekly. It works for 99% of streaming videos, but I occasionally find a difficult target. I can usually bypass most download restrictions with the next technique.

Videos: Blocked Downloads

Some services generate much effort toward prevention of video downloads from their sites. If the previous download tactics resulted in errors, you may have encountered a blocked file or stream. In most scenarios, you can bypass this with a modified "referer". Consider the following example and modify for your own usage. In 2021, I was contacted by a former colleague who had a unique request. He was trying to download an old episode of the television show "Live PD" as part of an investigation. The episode originally aired in 2016 and pirated copies on torrent sites had all disappeared. It was the 56th episode of the first season and he had exhausted his search. A query of "live pd" "s01e56" "watch" on Google displayed several sites which claimed to possess the video. The first page of results loaded a video player but encountered an error when the stream was attempted. Basically, the video file no longer existed so it could not be streamed within the browser. I finally found the following website which would play a video stream of the target episode.

https://ww1.123watchmovies.co/episode/forensic-files-ii-season-4-episode-1/

I could watch the video, but submitting this URL to YT-DLP resulted in an error. The Firefox plugin previously explained could not detect the actual video stream URL because this site embeds the video within a custom player which intentionally makes the download process difficult. I right-clicked the page while the video was streaming; selected the "Inspector" option; clicked the "Network" tab; and sorted the results by "Transferred" size. I immediately saw the following file streaming through the browser and becoming a large file.

https://or245qq.cloudatacdn.com/u5kj2vhwwtelsdgge5wtopkhjl7tagkowrpl3m35xkwqxdinp6aynmbmyjaa/y1 b18peb5s~67XyWB6C5D

I submitted this new URL to YT-DLP, but the result was a small empty video file without any content. This is because the target website includes a strict policy which prevents download of content from any source besides an approved URL. While this site is allowed to stream the video, I would be blocked if I tried to stream it on my own site. Therefore, our video download attempt appears to be an unauthorized source. This is becoming more common. I clicked on the "v.mp4" file within the Inspector menu in my browser and looked for the "Referer" field. It appeared as "Referer: https://gomoplayer.com/". This instruction tells the target website that gomoplayer.com is referring its own content into its embedded player software and the video should be allowed to play on this site. We now know the required referer and can emulate this within our own computer. The following command was entered.

```
cd ~/Downloads && yt-dlp
https://or245qq.cloudatacdn.com/u5kj2vhwwtelsdgge5wtopkhjl7tagkowrpl3m3
5xkwqxdinp6aynmbmyjaa/y1b18peb5s~67XyWB6C5D?token=2t191sedw3sid3llafayx
j68 --referer https://dood.la/
```

This changes our working directory to the Downloads folder; launches the yt-dlp software; provides the direct URL of the target video; and informs the service that the original referer is the same option as required (even though this is not true).

Videos: Streamlink (https://streamlink.github.io/)

YT-DLP presented an option to download an online video file. This can be useful if you know the exact location of the data. This is great, but it can be unforgiving. If you do not know the exact stream URL, you are out of luck. This is where Streamlink can assist. This powerful software can identify, play, and archive many live or pre-recorded video streams by simply providing the URL of the website in which it can be viewed. We will need to install it with the following commands.

```
pipx install streamlink
```

We can now restart Terminal and use the tool. The following command played the best quality version of a live stream from a Twitch user conducting a cooking lesson, through VLC. If there is no live stream at this URL, you can find another stream on Twitch to replicate.

```
streamlink https://www.twitch.tv/happycheftv best
```

Pressing ctrl+c on the keyboard kills the execution. Instead of watching the stream, we can capture it to a file named "happycheftv" within our default directory with the following command.

```
streamlink https://www.twitch.tv/happycheftv best -o happycheftv
```

If we wanted to watch and archive the data in real-time, we can use the following command.

```
streamlink https://www.twitch.tv/happycheftv best -r happycheftv
```

Finally, when the live stream is over, I can convert the archived data into a standard video file within my Documents folder titled happycheftv.mp4 with the following command.

```
ffmpeg -i happycheftv -c copy ~/Documents/happycheftv.mp4
```

This utility works well with most live and pre-recorded video streams within popular platforms such as Twitch and Vimeo. However, some sites cause errors. I prefer to use this tool in tandem with the Stream Detector extension mentioned in the next chapter. After entering the live news video stream from KTLA into Streamlink, I was notified "No plugin can handle URL". However, when I loaded this site within my custom Firefox build, as explained in the next chapter, I could see that the Stream Detector extension captured the M3U8 stream from this live broadcast. I copied the link and then executed it within Streamlink. Streamlink immediately began playing and archiving the video since I had provided the direct stream. No video capture utility is perfect, and do not expect this option to work every time. However, it is one of the best options we have.

Videos: Custom Scripts Teaser

By now, you may feel overwhelmed at the commands which must be executed every time you need to capture online evidence. I will warn you that it gets worse throughout this chapter. However, as I have said several times now, the custom scripts explained within Chapter Eleven make all of this easy. I want to pause here for a moment to show you how these scripts appear. The following image (left) displays the selection menu of the Videos script which you will download soon. The image (right) displays a prompt for a target URL which will be executed on your behalf. This script covers everything we have discussed in this chapter up to this point. When using this script in your ultimate OSINT VM, you will never need to memorize a Terminal command. The hard work will happen behind the scenes so you can focus on the investigation. This will be the last time I mention the scripts until we install them. I simply want you to see what is coming up so you do not abandon this chapter completely.

Usernames: Sherlock (github.com/sherlock-project)

Sherlock queries a username and tries to identify online accounts which might be associated with the target. While I prefer newer options, it is one of the first Linux tools to search username data and is a staple in any OSINT VM. However, any username tool will occasionally display false positives, including Sherlock. This is why we will install multiple options. Sherlock is installed with the following command.

```
pipx install sherlock-project
```

We must now construct a proper execution of the command, as follows, with an explanation after.

```
sherlock inteltechniques --csv -o ~/Documents/Report.csv
```

`sherlock`: This is the application.
`inteltechniques`: This is the target username.
`--csv`: This creates a CSV spreadsheet file as the output.
`-o ~/Documents/Report.csv`: This specifies the output save location.

The results follow, and provide numerous leads for our target.

[+] AllMyLinks: https://allmylinks.com/inteltechniques
[+] CGTrader: https://www.cgtrader.com/inteltechniques
[+] Contently: https://inteltechniques.contently.com/
[+] GitHub: https://www.github.com/inteltechniques
[+] Kik: https://kik.me/inteltechniques
[+] Linktree: https://linktr.ee/inteltechniques
[+] Reddit: https://www.reddit.com/user/inteltechniques
[+] Snapchat: https://www.snapchat.com/add/inteltechniques
[+] SteamGroup: https://steamcommunity.com/groups/inteltechniques
[+] Telegram: https://t.me/inteltechniques
[+] Twitch: https://www.twitch.tv/inteltechniques
[+] WordPress: https://inteltechniques.wordpress.com/

Usernames: SocialScan (github.com/iojw/socialscan).

SocialScan is very similar to Sherlock, but the execution is much simpler. It can be installed with the following Terminal commands.

```
pipx install socialscan
```

Within Terminal, you can now execute queries of usernames as follows.

```
socialscan inteltechniques
```

It currently only queries a few services, but the on-screen results are reliable. The first query above confirmed that I have accounts on GitHub, Reddit, and X (Twitter), as seen below.

```
osint@osint:~/Downloads/Programs/socialscan$ socialscan inteltechniques
---------------------------------------------
          inteltechniques
---------------------------------------------
GitLab
Tumblr
GitHub
Reddit
Twitter
Instagram: Please wait a few minutes before trying again.

Available, Taken/Reserved, Invalid, Error
Completed 8 queries in 1.07s
```

While we are searching usernames, we can also query an email address through SocialScan, as previously explained, with the following command. Since this program relies on color-coding the results in Terminal, we will force a JSON file with the following command.

```
socialscan test@gmail.com --json ~/Documents/test@gmail.com-ss.txt
```

The following partial result tells us that the email address of test@gmail.com is not available on Pinterest, which indicates someone with that email address created an account there.

```
"platform": "Pinterest",
"query": "test@gmail.com",
"available": "False",
"valid": "True",
"success": "True",
"message": "Unavailable"
```

Usernames: Blackbird (github.com/p1ngul1n0/blackbird)

While the previous two options were fairly basic, Blackbird is quite thorough. It checks over 500 sites. We can install it with the following.

```
cd ~/Downloads/Programs
git clone https://github.com/p1ngul1n0/blackbird
cd blackbird
python3 -m venv blackbirdEnvironment
source blackbirdEnvironment/bin/activate
sudo pip install -r requirements.txt
deactivate
```

We can submit a query with the following command.

```
python3 blackbird.py -u inteltechniques --pdf
```

This presents the results on the screen, but also creates a file called inteltechniques.pdf in the "results" folder within the Blackbird package (~/Downloads/Programs). The following is a partial display of results, which identifies many new leads and also displays content associated with some of the accounts.

[!] Searching 'inteltechniques' across 582 social networks
[+] - #10 Reddit account found - https://www.reddit.com/user/inteltechniques/about.json
[+] - #1 Facebook account found - https://www.facebook.com/inteltechniques [200 OK]
[+] - #14 Linktree account found - https://linktr.ee/inteltechniques [200 OK]

|--Name: @inteltechniques
|--Description: Linktree. Make your link do more.
|--picture: https://assets.production.linktr.ee/profiles/_next/static/logo-assets/default-image.png
[+] - #19 Xhamster account found - https://xhamster.com/users/inteltechniques [200 OK]
[+] - #16 Twitter Archived account-
http://archive.org/wayback/available?url=https://twitter.com/inteltechniques
[+] - #12 Github account found - https://github.com/inteltechniques [200 OK]
|--picture: https://avatars.githubusercontent.com/u/64741023?v=4?s=400
[+] - #25 WordPress Site account found - https://inteltechniques.wordpress.com/ [200 OK]
[+] - #43 Kik account found - https://ws2.kik.com/user/inteltechniques [200 OK]
[+] - #83 TryHackMe account found - https://tryhackme.com/p/inteltechniques [200 OK]
[+] - #99 Snapchat Stories account found - https://story.snapchat.com/s/inteltechniques [200 OK]
[+] - #312 GitHub account found - https://github.com/inteltechniques [200 OK]

Usernames: Maigret (github.com/soxoj/maigret)

This is a fork of Sherlock, which was previously explained, but currently scans over 2800 sites. This makes it the most thorough of all options. It also includes text, CSV, HTML, JSON, and PDF reporting, which is a great benefit to this utility over the others. Install with the following.

```
cd ~/Downloads/Programs
git clone https://github.com/soxoj/maigret
cd maigret
python3 -m venv maigretEnvironment
source maigretEnvironment/bin/activate
sudo pip3 install .
deactivate
```

We can submit a query with the following command, which forces all modules to be used, and outputs data to both a text file and PDF file within the "reports" folder for the program. The text file only contains links to profiles associated with the target. The PDF contains more information including URLs, follower counts, account creation dates, and additional details. The following image (left) displays a partial result of a Reddit account, as exported to a PDF. Compare that with the generic account details presented in the text file in right image. Of all username tools available in this chapter, I believe Maigret is the most robust.

```
maigret -a -P -T inteltechniques
```

Reddit	
Tags: discussion, news	
https://www.reddit.com/user/inteltechniques	
Details	
Reddit id	t5_j7tzj
Reddit username	IntelTechniques
Fullname	IntelTechniques
Is employee	False
Is nsfw	False
Is mod	False
Is following	True
Has user profile	True
Hide from robots	False
Created at	2018-05-15 15:24:04 UTC
Total karma	171
Post karma	28
Comments karma	123
Awards given karma	0
Awards got karma	20

```
https://ebay.com/usr/inteltechniques
https://www.reddit.com/user/inteltechniques
https://zen.yandex.ru/inteltechniques
https://community.waveapps.com/profile/inteltechniques
http://en.gravatar.com/inteltechniques
https://gramho.com/explore-hashtag/inteltechniques
https://tjournal.ru/search/v2/subsite/relevant?query=inteltechniques
https://www.influenster.com/inteltechniques
https://account.protonmail.com/api/users/available?Name=inteltechniqu
https://www.hoobly.com/u/inteltechniques
https://vkfaces.com/vk/user/inteltechniques
https://dota2.ru/forum/search?type=user&keywords=inteltechniques&sort
http://forum.arjlover.net/member.php?username=inteltechniques
https://rpggeek.com/user/inteltechniques
https://githubplus.com/inteltechniques
https://www.hipforums.com/members/?username=inteltechniques
https://videogamegeek.com/user/inteltechniques
https://ws2.kik.com/user/inteltechniques
https://askvoprosy.com/polzovateli/inteltechniques
http://player.ru/member.php?username=inteltechniques
https://coder.social/inteltechniques
http://www.chevrolet-cruze-club.ru/forum/member.php?username=inteltec
http://archive.org/wayback/available?url=https://twitter.com/inteltec
http://archive.org/wayback/available?url=https://twitter.com/inteltec
https://forum.cockroachlabs.com/u/inteltechniques
https://discussion.dreamhost.com/u/inteltechniques
Total Websites Username Detected On : 33
```

Usernames: WhatsMyName-Python (github.com/C3n7ral051nt4g3ncy)

This is a fork of WhatsMyName, which no longer functions as an application. This version relies on the last-known working code, and can provide value if the previous options did not. This program is very slow, but very thorough. Let's install it with the following.

```
cd ~/Downloads/Programs
git clone https://github.com/C3n7ral051nt4g3ncy/WhatsMyName-Python.git
cd WhatsMyName-Python
python3 -m venv wmnpythonEnvironment
source wmnpythonEnvironment/bin/activate
sudo pip3 install -r requirements.txt
deactivate
```

We can now execute a query with the following commands.

```
cd ~/Downloads/Programs/WhatsMyName-Python
python3 whatsmyname.py -u inteltechniques
```

This test required several minutes to complete, but I did receive a few results which I did not see previously. The image below displays a partial sample of the results. Instead of only displaying potential accounts, it also tells you which services did not possess an account.

We see a lot of redundancy within these username options. This is never a bad thing. Sometimes, one or more of these lookup services fails or blocks my VPN. When that happens, I move on to another option. While I prefer Blackbird over the others, you may have a different favorite. I like Blackbird because of the JSON output and easy readability within Firefox. You may prefer a tool which compresses the data right into Terminal. Please be familiar with each and never expect them all to work well on any given day. Having multiple options allows us to raise or lower our confidence with the displayed results.

Usernames: BDFR (https://github.com/aliparlakci/bulk-downloader-for-reddit)

I have found Reddit to become a common source for online evidence within my investigations. If you have discovered a target Reddit username with the previous tools, you should consider archiving all posts made by the target. BDFR can be installed with the following commands.

```
pipx install bdfr
```

The following command downloads all "submissions" from a specific user on Reddit into a designated folder in the Documents directory. These are also referred to as "posts" (but not comments to a post).

```
mkdir ~/Documents/inteltechniques/
bdfr archive ~/Documents/inteltechniques/ --user inteltechniques --
submitted
```

The following command downloads all comments from a specific user on any post.

```
bdfr archive ~/Documents/inteltechniques/ --user inteltechniques --all-
comments
```

The results will be saved into .json files within folders labeled for each Subreddit name. These files are best viewed within Firefox. While BDFR also allows download options for entire Subreddits, I find it too slow and unreliable. Archiving a user's data is also slow, but will typically complete with good results. The following displays a downloaded post as opened within Firefox.

Email: Holehe (github.com/megadose/holehe)

This program is similar to the previous username options, but only allows input of an email address. It queries dozens of services using several identification strategies such as registered users and password recovery prompts. Installation is completed with the following commands.

```
pipx install holehe
```

The following command within Terminal queries an email address through all services and outputs the results to a text file titled as the target email address.

```
holehe test@gmail.com > ~/Documents/test@gmail.com-Holehe.txt
```

A partial result follows. Anything with a "+" indicates a positive presence of the target email address within a website; a "-" indicates that the address is not associated with an account; and an "x" indicates that no result was found either way due to an automated block.

[-] wattpad.com
[+] wordpress.com
[-] xing.com
[x] yahoo.com
[+] zoho.com
[+] Email used, [-] Email not used, [x] Rate limit

You can eliminate the ">" and everything after to force the results to populate the screen, but I would rather output my results to a file for later viewing.

Email: Eyes (https://github.com/N0rz3/Eyes)

This program is similar to Holehe, but with different options. It provides an easy passive way to determine if an email address on a custom domain is hosted at Proton Mail, and then attempts to associate it with accounts on X (Twitter) and GitHub. Let's install it together.

```
mkdir ~/Downloads/Programs/eyes
cd ~/Downloads/Programs/eyes
git clone https://github.com/N0rz3/Eyes.git
cd Eyes
python3 -m venv eyesEnvironment
source eyesEnvironment/bin/activate
sudo pip install -r requirements.txt
deactivate
```

We can now query an email address with the following commands.

```
cd ~/Downloads/Programs/eyes/Eyes
python3 eyes.py test@gmail.com
```

Email: GHunt (github.com/mxrch/Ghunt)

This Terminal-based program requires some work to configure it properly, but the rewards justify the efforts. Expect some frustration as you configure your VM for future use of GHunt. First, let's install everything with the following commands.

```
pipx install ghunt
```

Next is the hard part. You must possess valid login cookies from an active Google account. This is because the Google API, which you will use to find information about various accounts, requires you to be logged in to an account in order to access these details. Therefore, you must acquire several pieces of data from your own Google account.

I recommend using an account which you rarely access. As long as you do not log in to this account from a web browser AFTER you obtain these cookies, they should stay valid for long-term usage. Conduct the following.

- Navigate to mail.google.com within your VM version of Firefox
- Make sure you are logged in to your desired account.
- Right-click within Firefox and select "Inspect"
- Select the "Network" tab.
- Refresh the page.
- Click the small magnifying glass in the center.
- Search for "oauth2_4/" and "aas_et/".
- Copy the characters immediately following these entries.
- Execute ghunt login from Terminal.
- Choose the option to enter the oauth_token and provide the "oauth2_4/" value.
- Choose the option to enter the master token and provide the "aas_et/" value.

If this fails, and it often does, you can also use the GHunt Firefox browser extension to gather the required data. Details for this can be found at https://github.com/mxrch/GHunt. GHunt will attempt to populate your

Google identifiers from a logged-in account without manual access. This is much easier, and only requires the extension to be active while you are generating the data required for configuration. You can remove the extension once GHunt is functioning. I prefer the manual method in order to document the data and its location, but I respect the easy route.

The exact protocol for applying login details to GHunt changes often. I suspect many readers will have issues with this, due to no fault of their own. Visit the GitHub page for the project to see which method is currently working the best. Once you have the required data stored within GHunt, we can conduct the following queries through GHunt.

```
ghunt email larry@google.com
```

The result is as follows.

```
[+] 1 account found !
Name : Larry Page
[+] Custom profile picture !
=> https://lh3.googleusercontent.com/a-
/AOh14GiUjlWnt4MNgr7Wmeyb3PzXlka4E8PFEIlF27oIxIA
Profile picture saved !
Last profile edit : 2021/11/27 10:01:21 (UTC)
Email : larry@google.com
Gaia ID : 111627209495762463002
Hangouts Bot : No
[+] Activated Google services :
- Hangouts - Photos - Maps
[+] YouTube channel (confidence => 37.5%) :
- [Larry Page] https://youtube.com/channel/UCmpDzlgzPdbzShSzH48mCHg
- [Larry Page] https://youtube.com/channel/UCJuR7fG13KEpEPr8EH7bsgw
- [Larry Page] https://youtube.com/channel/UCNXk_sA4Kv3rDIYo8vI-gLQ
- [Larry Page] https://youtube.com/channel/UCefpKs_q0UsJV5_1n5_H13A
Google Maps :
https://www.google.com/maps/contrib/111627209495762463002/reviews
[-] No reviews
Google Calendar :
https://calendar.google.com/calendar/u/0/embed?src=larry@google.com
[-] No public Google Calendar.
```

Let's dissect our findings. We now know the name of the user and his profile photo has been saved within the "profile_pics" folder inside the GHunt installation directory. We are provided a date and time of his last profile update; his Google Accounts and ID Administration ID (GAIA); his four YouTube channels; and confirmation that he uses Hangouts, Photos, and Maps. We also know that he has not written any map reviews. This summary was provided almost instantaneously.

The following Terminal command would search a Google Drive ID, and a fictitious result follows.

```
ghunt drive BxiMVs0XRA5nFMdKvBdBZjgmUUqptlbs74OgvE2upms
```

```
Drive ID : BxiMVs0XRA5nFMdKvBdBZjgmUUqptlbs74OgvE2upms
[+] Creation date : 2011/05/12 18:29:28 (UTC)
[+] Last edit date : 2011/05/12 18:29:28 (UTC)
Public permissions :
- reader
```

```
[+] Owner found !
Name : A Googler
Email : gdocsteam@gmail.com
Google ID : 02845897149113753960
[+] Custom profile picture !
=> https://lh3.googleusercontent.com/a-
/AOh14GhXaVAhS8Ci08Xito5iVJVsooEhsgUIGhZ45NjTfQ=s64
Profile picture saved !
```

We now know the document creation date/time; the last modified date/time; owner name; owner email; owner Google ID; and owner Google profile image. The automated version of this can also be found in your "Username/Email" tool within your OSINT VM.

Next, we can query a Google Accounts and ID Administration ID (GAIA) with the following command.

```
ghunt gaia 105144584335156066992
```

The result follows.

```
Name : Thrice
Gaia ID : 105144584335156066992
[+] YouTube channel (confidence => 50.0%) :
- [Thrice] https://youtube.com/channel/UC_gH-AQqoOUZ4ykZBCLdvww
Google Maps :
https://www.google.com/maps/contrib/105144584335156066992/reviews
```

Any time I encounter a Google email address, Google Drive account, or GAIA, I launch this tool. However, it can be quite finnicky. It commonly fails and requires me to enter fresh Google account identifiers. I often refer to this as an advanced tool, but wanted to include it here because of its presence within the custom tools.

Email: H8Mail (https://github.com/khast3x/h8mail)

This program queries email addresses against breach data search services. We can install with the following.

```
pipx install h8mail
```

The program is now installed, but will not function because we have not created a configuration file. The following must be done only once.

```
cd ~/Downloads
h8mail -g
```

The program is now installed and the configuration file has been generated, but it will still not function because we have specified any services which should be queried. The following must also be done only once, and will enable queries through the free Leak Lookup engine.

```
sed -i 's/\;leak\-lookup\_pub/leak\-lookup\_pub/g' h8mail_config.ini
```

The program is now ready to be used. The following command queries an email address against all enabled services. Notice that we must specify the location of the configuration file within the command.

```
h8mail -t test@gmail.com -c ~/Downloads/h8mail_config.ini
```

We can also force a username query option with the following.

```
h8mail -t test -q username -c ~/Downloads/h8mail_config.ini
```

The results appear similar to the following, which present several new OSINT leads. We now know that our target is present within several specific data breaches. Several other services are available within the configuration file, but they demand a premium API key. Leak Lookup is the only valuable free option, but you may wish to explore the other opportunities by visiting the H8Mail website.

```
LEAKLOOKUP_PUB |      lorangb@gmail.com > collection-1
LEAKLOOKUP_PUB |      lorangb@gmail.com > collection-4-u
LEAKLOOKUP_PUB |      lorangb@gmail.com > zeeroq.com
LEAKLOOKUP_PUB |      lorangb@gmail.com > cointracker.io
LEAKLOOKUP_PUB |      lorangb@gmail.com > collection-4-eu
LEAKLOOKUP_PUB |      lorangb@gmail.com > dropbox.com
LEAKLOOKUP_PUB |      lorangb@gmail.com > ledger.com
LEAKLOOKUP_PUB |      lorangb@gmail.com > myfitnesspal.com
LEAKLOOKUP_PUB |      lorangb@gmail.com > myheritage.com
```

Email: Hash Tools

If you search any breach data about your target's email address or username, you are likely to encounter hashed passwords. Most websites store passwords in "hashed" form. This guards against the possibility that someone who gains unauthorized access to the database can retrieve the plain-text passwords of every user in the system. Hashing performs a one-way transformation on a password, turning the password into another string, called the hashed password. "One-way" means that it was practically impossible to go the other way and turn the hashed password back into the original password. This was true many years ago, but not so much today. There are several mathematically complex hashing algorithms that fulfill these needs. Some are very insecure and others are nearly impossible to crack.

I recommend **Name That Hash** and **Search That Hash** (github.com/HashPals/) for identification of hash types and the passwords behind them. You can install each within your OSINT virtual machine with the following commands.

```
pipx install search-that-hash
pipx install name-that-hash
```

Within Terminal, you can now execute the following to search a hash within multiple online services.

```
nth --text "5f4dcc3b5aa765d61d8327deb882cf99"
```

The result appears as follows.

```
Most Likely MD5, HC: 0 JtR: raw-md5 Summary: Used for Linux Shadow files.
```

You can also conduct the following with Search That Hash.

```
sth --text "5f4dcc3b5aa765d61d8327deb882cf99"
```

The result appears as follows.

```
5f4dcc3b5aa765d61d8327deb882cf99
Text : password      Type : MD5
```

We now know that the hash value is a MD5 representation of the password "password".

Images: Gallery-DL (https://github.com/mikf/gallery-dl)

I previously explained YT-DLP as an all-in-one bulk online video download solution. **Gallery-DL** (github.com/mikf/gallery-dl) is a similar option for image collections. You can easily install this within Terminal by entering the following commands, which also provide an isolated Python environment.

```
pipx install gallery-dl
```

Let's conduct a demonstration. Assume you have located a target's online Flickr account at flickr.com/photos/henrik_lindberg and you want to archive all of the images within a specific album. The following command would download the data to the current folder within Terminal (command is entered as one line).

```
gallery-dl
https://www.flickr.com/photos/henrik_lindberg/albums/72157630549692722
```

The result is all 187 images from the photo gallery. This is a very valuable and efficient resource. Gallery-DL currently supports over 150 services including Tumblr, 4chan, Flickr, Imgur, Reddit, and numerous "adult" websites. The following displays the program in action (left) and downloaded files (right).

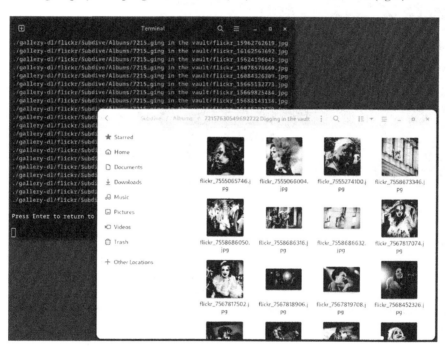

Images: RipMe (github.com/RipMeApp/ripme)

Next, you might want a graphical solution for your investigation when you encounter a situation which presents a large number of photos. I previously mentioned browser extensions which help automate this process, but they have limits. My preference is always the Gallery-DL, but it may not function on the site which you have targeted. We should always consider other automated options. I have had great success with RipMe. This application requires Java to be installed on your machine. I refuse to install Java on any Windows or Mac host due to security concerns, as it adds an additional layer of vulnerability. However, I have no objection to installing it within a Linux virtual machine. Enter the following within Terminal.

```
cd ~/Downloads
sudo apt install wget
sudo apt install default-jre -y
wget
https://github.com/ripmeapp/ripme/releases/latest/download/ripme.jar
chmod +x ripme.jar
```

Debian has made the process to open Java files difficult, but you can enter the following Terminal commands to launch RipMe. Fortunately, our custom scripts will bypass this entire requirement later.

```
cd ~/Downloads
java -jar ripme.jar
```

Once you have the program open, enter any target URL and click "Rip". This application supports image downloads from Imgur, X (Twitter), Tumblr, Instagram, Flickr, Photobucket, and Reddit. The following displays Terminal (left) and the program (right).

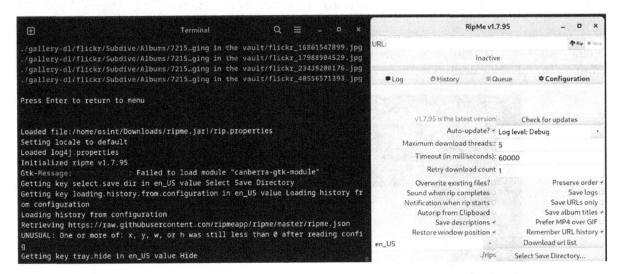

Images: Instagram

There are several independent programs which assist with bulk-download of Instagram data. The first is **Instaloader**, which has been a staple within Buscador since the beginning. Since it occasionally stops working, pending an updated release, we also want **Toutatis** and **Osintgram** available at all times. The results of each are very similar, but it is good to have redundant options. **Since Instagram aggressively tries to break these programs, expect problems with any or all of them at some point.** Let's install the first two applications within our new pipx environment.

```
pipx install instaloader && pipx install toutatis
```

Let's install Osintgram with the following venv environment.

```
cd ~/Downloads/Programs
git clone https://github.com/Datalux/Osintgram.git
cd Osintgram
python3 -m venv OsintgramEnvironment
source OsintgramEnvironment/bin/activate
sudo pip install -r requirements.txt
deactivate
```

Next, you should open Firefox within your VM and sign into the Instagram account you will use for OSINT investigations. This tells Instagram that you are intentionally logging into your account from your current IP address, and is required before the next steps will work. We must now sign into this same account within the programs. Begin with Instaloader by executing the following.

```
instaloader --login=username
```

Make sure you replace username with your Instagram username and supply the password for that account when prompted. This only needs to be supplied once during configuration, and the application will store the credentials. Next, let's discuss Toutatis. This application provides Instagram account details, often including full email addresses and partial telephone numbers. This extra level of disclosure requires a unique piece of information from our account. Each time you run the command, you are required to enter your Instagram "Session ID". The following steps will identify this information.

- Log in to an Instagram account from your Firefox browser.
- Right-click an empty area of the page and choose "Inspect".
- Click the "Network" tab in the new menu at the bottom.
- Navigate to any user's Instagram page.
- In the Inspector menu, click on an entry similar to "200 GET www.instagram.com" and click the "Cookies" tab in the menu to the right.
- Scroll down this list and find "sessionid:".
- Copy the alphanumeric entry.

Keep this Session ID somewhere which is easy to access. Next, execute the following from within ~/Download/Programs/Osintgram to replicate this login credential storage for Osintgram.

```
make setup
```

Now that you have all programs installed and configured with credentials, we can test them. Start with the following commands for Instaloader within Terminal. Please note this is not my account but serves as a good demonstration with minimal content.

```
cd ~/Desktop && instaloader user mikeb
```

Instaloader should have created a new folder titled mikeb on your Desktop containing the user's images. The following command would execute Toutatis for the target of "mikeb" with your Session ID of 24316:Lh59ygrmY4N:4.

```
toutatis -u mikeb -s 24316:Lh59ygrmY4N:4
```

The result is similar to the following, which I have partially redacted.

```
Full Name: Mike Brandon | userID : 1144153003
Is business Account : False
Is private Account: False
Follower: 70 Following : 31
Number of posts: 18
Number of tag in posts : 0
Obfuscated phone       : +44 **** ****77
```

I find this information extremely valuable, and the process only takes a few seconds to complete. You could easily copy and paste these details into your report. Next, let's look at Osintgram. First, navigate to the software folder with the following command.

```
cd ~/Downloads/Programs/Osintgram/
```

We can conduct numerous types of queries on "mikeb". The following would display this user's photos, stories, comments, captions, followers, followers' telephone numbers, followings, followings' telephone numbers, and general account information.

```
python3 main.py -c photos mikeb
python3 main.py -c stories mikeb
python3 main.py -c comments mikeb
python3 main.py -c captions mikeb
python3 main.py -c followers mikeb
python3 main.py -c fwersnumber mikeb
python3 main.py -c followings mikeb
python3 main.py -c fwingsnumber mikeb
python3 main.py -c info mikeb
```

I would be shocked if all three Instagram programs worked for you. This is because Instagram likes to block access to these types of applications. If you received any "challenge" errors, that means Instagram has found your activity to be suspicious. You would need to log in to your Instagram account again through Firefox and confirm the activity as non-malicious. If you execute any of these tools and receive no results, it may also be because of this error. I am intentionally leaving extra room on this page for future modifications to these utilities.

Domains: EyeWitness (https://github.com/ChrisTruncer/EyeWitness)

This Python script automates the collection of screen captures from websites. Imagine the following scenario. You are investigating a long list of website addresses that was provided to you as a lead. Maybe they were websites visited from a suspect's computer; a list of social network profiles discovered during your previous X (Twitter) scrapes; or just a self-created list of URLs associated to your investigation. Manually visiting each site and using a screen capture tool can be overwhelming. Instead, let's automate the task. Install EyeWitness to your VM with the following official commands within a new instance of Terminal.

```
cd ~/Downloads/Programs
git clone https://github.com/ChrisTruncer/EyeWitness.git
cd EyeWitness/Python/setup
sudo ./setup.sh
```

We need to add a few commands to our installation process, and you should copy and paste all of these at once into Terminal.

```
wget
https://github.com/mozilla/geckodriver/releases/download/v0.34.0/geckod
river-v0.34.0-linux-aarch64.tar.gz
tar -xvzf geckodriver*
chmod +x geckodriver
sudo mv geckodriver /usr/local/bin
```

You can now execute EyeWitness, but you must first navigate to the folder where the Python script is located. We will correct this with a custom script in a moment, but let's first test the application within Terminal with the following two commands.

```
cd ~/Downloads/Programs/EyeWitness/Python
```

```
./EyeWitness.py --single https://inteltechniques.com -d
~/Documents/EyeWitness/
```

When finished, you should have a new file within your Documents/EyeWitness folder titled Report.html. Double-clicking this file opens it within Firefox. You can submit a list of URLs with the following commands, assuming you have a file on your Desktop called sites.txt, with one URL per line.

```
./EyeWitness.py -f ~/Desktop/sites.txt --web -d ~/Documents/EyeWitness/
```

The following image displays the first result from my "sites.txt" file which contained exactly the following data.

```
https://inteltechniques.com
https://unredactedmagazine.com
```

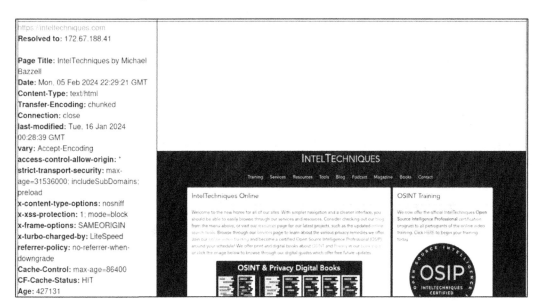

The results include screen captures of each target website and detailed information including the server IP address, page title, modification date, and full source code of the page. This is very beneficial in two ways. First, it automates the task of researching multiple target websites. Second, it saves each page as it existed at a specific moment in time. If your suspect deletes or modifies a website after you have captured it, you possess evidence of a previous state. The annoyances of this method include the requirement to create a text file and need to articulate the location of the data within Terminal. We can make this easier with a custom script.

This utility can be very beneficial when you have dozens, hundreds, or even thousands of domains of interest. I once converted a list of over 300 suspect URLs into a folder of screen captures of each. This allowed me to quickly identify which accounts were truly valuable to my investigation by simply viewing the evidence similar to photos in an album. The report was several hundred pages but was generated in only a few minutes.

Domains: HTTrack (httrack.com)

There are several ways to make an exact copy of a static website and this software will walk you through the process. You may want to do this when you locate a target website and are concerned the site could be taken down. Any time that you find any content that will be used in court, you should archive the entire site. This application automates the process. The result is a locally stored copy in which you can navigate as if it were live. This is beneficial in court when internet access is not appropriate, or a website has been taken offline. The following command within a new Terminal session will download the software and configure it within your operating system.

```
sudo apt update && sudo apt install httrack webhttrack -y
```

You can now type `webhttrack` at any Terminal prompt and the graphical version of the software will execute within your default browser. Typing `httrack` will load the Terminal version. You should also have the Domains Tool (domains.desktop) available in your Applications menu. When the application loads, you can select either option. The Terminal version presents text prompts to enter your target data. The browser version does the same thing, but it is point-and-click instead of text entry. Note that the browser version will likely require you to "try again" upon launch and select the option to load a non-secure website. This is not a risk, but it is an annoyance.

Clicking the "next" button in the browser version will bring you to the project screen. Give your project a title, preferably the website name, and choose a location to save all of the data. Click next and then "add URL". Enter the exact website that you want to archive. Do not enter any login or password. Click "next", then "finished", and you are done. The application will begin extracting all public information from the site. This can take a while, depending on the size of the site. When complete, you will have an exact copy in which you can navigate and search offline. Archiving to an external drive creates a replica that can be held for future analysis. This program only works on smaller static websites, and cannot archive large dynamic sites such as social networks.

HTTrack is a very old program, and was never intended to function within today's latest technology. However, it still works surprisingly well on small business websites. It can also extract a surprising amount of content from large sites such as Wikipedia. I once used this service to extract several gigabytes of scraped LinkedIn data from a questionable website before it disappeared, which included profiles, names, email addresses, user IDs and employment history. This tool should always be ready in your arsenal. The following image displays the dated entry screen.

Domains: Waybackpy (https://github.com/akamhy/waybackpy)

Most readers are probably already aware of the power of the Internet Archive while searching for online content which has since been removed. Browsing a target domain on the Wayback Machine website can be very fruitful, but automating the collection of that data can be more beneficial. Install Waybackpy with the following command.

```
pipx install waybackpy
```

Let's execute the script to conduct a few tasks, using pretendradio.org as a target. First, we will make a directory in the Documents folder for data and then enter it.

```
mkdir ~/Documents/waybackpy
mkdir ~/Documents/waybackpy/pretendradio.org
cd ~/Documents/waybackpy/pretendradio.org
```

Next, let's generate all known URLs indexed by Internet Archive into a text file with the following.

```
waybackpy --url "https://pretendradio.org" --known_urls > 1.txt
```

This creates a text file in the current directory which displays every URL being monitored and archived by Archive.org, but does not present the content of each page. This file will likely have many duplicates within it, so let's remove them with the following.

```
sort -u -i 1.txt -o 2.txt
```

The file labeled 2.txt only contains one URL for each option instead of mostly redundant addresses.

If desired, the following would tell you the oldest version of the website they have collected. Replacing "oldest" with "newest" would identify the opposite.

```
waybackpy --url "https://pretendradio.org" --oldest
```
The following result tells us the first copy they possess is from April 24, 2017.

https://web.archive.org/web/20170424221444/http://pretendradio.org:80/

Overall, this tool only provides information about Archive.org's collection of a domain, but not the actual content of each URL. For that, we will rely on the next tool.

Domains: Waybackpack (https://github.com/jsvine/waybackpack)

This program will extract the data behind Archive.org's cached websites. Install with the following.

```
pipx install waybackpack
```

We can now execute the program and have it extract the HTML data behind every archive associated with a URL. The following command will generate several folders within our target directory, each labeled as the date of the Archive.org acquisition. Notice that there is a trailing "/" at the end of the URL in the command. For some reason, this program will **not work without it**.

```
waybackpack https://pretendradio.org/ -d
~/Documents/waybackpy/pretendradio.org
```

Each folder should possess an HTML file which can be opened within Firefox. Consider the following two examples. The first displays the website as it appeared the first time it was captured. The second displays the site as it appeared many months later, possessing actual content.

Imagine you have a target URL which has hundreds of archives throughout the past decade. This is a quick way to see annual changes to the site and document the evidence. Each of these is an archived home page of the target website from a different date. Double-clicking them will load the pages within a web browser which should display the target site similar to the way it previously appeared. However, a keyword search can also be beneficial. You can use the embedded search function within the Files application which is presented after successful completion of the script. The following image displays my search of these files for the word "prison". The results identify files of interest.

Domains: Amass (https://github.com/owasp-amass/amass)

Amass is a very powerful program, but we will only focus on one area. This option can take a long time to run, but it is very thorough. I only run it when I have a specific need for the data. It attempts to determine any possible subdomains of a target domain, among many other recon features. Installation is a very manual process, but we can automate it with a few steps. Per their GitHub page, you can navigate to either URL to download the official latest releases.

https://github.com/owasp-amass/amass/releases/latest/download/amass_Linux_arm64.zip
https://github.com/owasp-amass/amass/releases/latest/download/amass_Linux_amd64.zip

However, I find this cumbersome if you want universal instructions which would apply to any architecture (AMD vs ARM). Therefore, let's conduct the following.

```
cd ~/Downloads
ver=$(dpkg --print-architecture)
wget https://github.com/owasp-
amass/amass/releases/latest/download/amass_Linux_"$ver".zip
mkdir ~/Downloads/Programs/Amass
unzip amass_Linux_"$ver".zip -d ~/Downloads/Programs/Amass/
cd Programs/Amass/amass_Linux_"$ver"/
mv * ~/Downloads/Programs/Amass
rm -r ~/Downloads/Programs/Amass/amass_Linux_"$ver"/
rm '/home/osint/Downloads/amass_Linux_arm64.zip'
```

These commands navigated to our Downloads folder; stored the version of our processor (AMD vs ARM); conducted a Wget command to download the appropriate version for our VM; made a new directory for the program; unzipped the files in the compressed archive; moved the files to a standard location; deleted the unnecessary file and folder. The following commands allow us to execute the software with the optimal selections.

```
cd ~/Downloads/Programs/Amass
./amass intel -o ~/Documents/cnn1.txt -active -ip -whois -d cnn.com
```

This creates a report located in the Documents folder. In my test with my own website, it immediately identified several other domains hosted on my shared server, a few of which were associated with me. The following image displays results for domains related to cnn.com.

```
cnn-traveller.com
cnnarabic.com
cnncenterretail.com
cnnmoney.com
cnnmoneycontrol.com
cnnpolitics.com
cnntech.com
cnntraveler.com
```

Domains: Photon (https://github.com/s0md3v/Photon)

This option does not attempt to find subdomains. Instead, it searches for internal pages within a target website. It creates a report located in the Downloads/Programs/Photon folder. Install with the following.

```
cd ~/Downloads/Programs
git clone https://github.com/s0md3v/Photon.git
cd Photon
python3 -m venv PhotonEnvironment
source PhotonEnvironment/bin/activate
sudo pip install -r requirements.txt
deactivate
```

We can now execute with the following commands.

```
cd ~/Downloads/Programs/Photon
python3 photon.py -u inteltechniques.com -l 3 -t 100
```

The results are quick and impressive. The "external" file lists outgoing hyperlinks from the target URL to other websites; the "files" text file lists files stored within the URL, such as PDFs and other documents; and the "internal" file lists URLs hyperlinked from the target to other pages on the same site. When targeting my own website, Photon identified all of the xml configuration files for pfSense and all issues of UNREDACTED Magazine in PDF. The following was extracted directly from the files.txt report generated by the program.

```
https://inteltechniques.com/issues/001.pdf
https://inteltechniques.com/issues/002.pdf
https://inteltechniques.com/issues/003.pdf
https://inteltechniques.com/issues/004.pdf
https://inteltechniques.com/issues/005.pdf
https://inteltechniques.com/issues/006.pdf
2022.FW4B-PIA-US-Netflix.xml
2-port-ProtonVPN-US-DNS-No-VPNPassword-admin1234.xml
2023/FW2B.xml
2022.FW6B-PIA-US-Netflix.xml
6-port-ProtonVPN-west-DNS-No-VPNPassword-admin1234.xml
```

Domains: Sublist3r (https://github.com/aboul3la/Sublist3r)

This program scans much faster than Amass, but will only find common subdomains. This may be sufficient for most tasks. It creates a report located in the Documents folder. In my test, it found 808 subdomains of cnn.com. Install with the following.

```
cd ~/Downloads/Programs
git clone https://github.com/aboul3la/Sublist3r.git
cd Sublist3r
```

```
python3 -m venv Sublist3rEnvironment
source Sublist3rEnvironment/bin/activate
sudo pip install -r requirements.txt
deactivate
```

We can now execute with the following.

```
cd ~/Downloads/Programs/Sublist3r
python3 sublist3r.py -d cnn.com -o ~/Documents/Sublist3r-cnn.txt
```

Partial results follow.

```
alerts.cnn.com
dev.alerts.cnn.com
www.dev.alerts.cnn.com
qa.alerts.cnn.com
56m.qa.alerts.cnn.com
admin.qa.alerts.cnn.com
56m.admin.qa.alerts.cnn.com
ec2.admin.qa.alerts.cnn.com
ec2.qa.alerts.cnn.com
alertshub.cnn.com
admin.alertshub.cnn.com
dev.alertshub.cnn.com
www.dev.alertshub.cnn.com
```

We now have new targets to research.

Domains: TheHarvester (https://github.com/laramies/theHarvester)

This program searches a supplied domain with the intent of providing subdomains, hosts and, occasionally email addresses associated to the target. It creates a report located in the Documents folder. During my search of cnn.com, it located 72 hosts and 16 email addresses. Further investigation into these results may reveal new sources of information. Install with the following.

```
cd ~/Downloads/Programs
git clone https://github.com/laramies/theHarvester.git
cd theHarvester
python3 -m venv theHarvesterEnvironment
source theHarvesterEnvironment/bin/activate
sudo pip install -r requirements.txt
deactivate
```

We can now execute with the following.

```
cd ~/Downloads/Programs/theHarvester
python3 theHarvester.py -d cnn.com -f ~/Documents/cnn.json -b
duckduckgo
```

We can open the generated JSON file within Firefox to see the data, as follows.

```
 6:        "agility.cnn.com"
 7:        "amp.cnn.com"
 8:        "arabic.cnn.com"
 9:        "archives.cnn.com"
10:        "audience.cnn.com"
11:        "audience.qa.cnn.com"
12:        "cdn.cnn.com"
13:        "center.cnn.com"
14:        "chat.cnn.com"
15:        "cms.cnn.com"
16:        "cnnespanol.cnn.com"
17:        "cnnpressroom.blogs.cnn.com"
18:        "content.api.cnn.com"
```

Domains: Carbon14 (https://github.com/Lazza/Carbon14)

This application helped an investigation as I was writing this. I was investigating an anonymous blog, with the intent of learning more about the age of the site. It was a brand-new WordPress installation, and every post had the same recent date and time. It had obviously been created recently, but then received an import from an older blog. I wanted to know more about the true dates of the original posts. This is the perfect scenario for Carbon14. It searches for any images hosted within the page and analyzes the metadata for creation dates. A query of my own site indicates that the static page was last modified on January 16, 2024, but one of the images was created in 2022. If this were my target, I would now have suspicion that the original blog posts were from an earlier date. These dates can be intentionally or unintentionally altered, so this is not a forensically sound method. It is simply an additional piece to the puzzle which may warrant further investigation. I find that Carbon14 works best on static websites and blogs. I have also had surprising success when targeting social network profiles. Install with the following

```
cd ~/Downloads/Programs
git clone https://github.com/Lazza/Carbon14
cd Carbon14
python3 -m venv Carbon14Environment
source Carbon14Environment/bin/activate
sudo pip install -r requirements.txt
deactivate
```

Execute with the following.

```
cd ~/Downloads/Programs/Carbon14
python3 carbon14.py https://inteltechniques.com
```

Below is an example of the output on the screen.

```
Date (UTC)            Date (US/Mountain)   URL
-------------------   ------------------   ----------------------------------------
2022-03-25 14:01:23   2022-03-25 08:01:23  <https://inteltechniques.com/img/cert.png>

2023-12-10 18:17:33   2023-12-10 11:17:33  <https://inteltechniques.com/img/AD-ALL.png>
```

Domains: Change Detection (github.com/dgtlmoon/changedetection.io)

In the chapter about domains, I explained several online services which would monitor a URL for changes. These are beneficial, but there are some scenarios where they might be inappropriate. You might have a sensitive URL which you do not want to share with an online service, or a site with very minor changes which is not being picked up by the free services. This is where Change Detection can help. It is locally installed and available only to you. The following configures the application.

```
pipx install changedetection.io
```

We can now test with the following entries into Terminal, copied and pasted all at once.

```
mkdir ~/Documents/ChangeDetection
changedetection.io -d ~/Documents/ChangeDetection -p 5000 &
sleep 3
firefox http://127.0.0.1:5000
```

The first command makes sure we have a directory created for results and the second command launches the server and Firefox simultaneously. The following image displays an example. The first option was created for my home page. I can click the "Recheck" button to fetch a new live copy. Clicking the "Diff" button shows me any changes. The image below it identifies two paragraphs which were modified between visits. This tool provides the same service as the online options, if not better, but gives you full control within your Linux machine.

Domains: Archive Box (github.com/ArchiveBox/ArchiveBox)

I previously explained how we could use online services to document the current state of a website; see previous versions through archived sources; and be notified of changes when they occur. In 2022, I began using Archive Box as an all-in-one solution. We can install and initialize the application with the following, which you may have already accomplished in Chapter Five.

```
pipx install archivebox

mkdir ~/Documents/archivebox
cd ~/Documents/archivebox
archivebox init
```

Once installed, change into our directory; add our target website; launch the server; and open the database within our browser. Note that you must enter the full URL, including "https://".

```
cd ~/Documents/archivebox
archivebox add 'https://notla.com'
archivebox server 0.0.0.0:8000 & firefox http://0.0.0.0:8000/
```

The following image displays results as they are being fetched. Archive Box captured the target with SingleFile through Chrome; generated a PDF and screenshot; performed a WGET of the live page; extracted the page from Archive.org; fetched all HTML code; and downloaded any media files. This is an impressive tool. Combined with the automated script in your Linux VM, this service should be used often. Knowing the manual approach is important, but automated tools allow us to work faster and more efficiently.

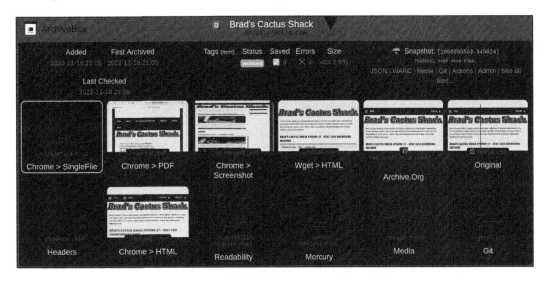

Metadata: Exiftool (https://exiftool.org/)

Image metadata, also called Exif data, will be explained later in more detail. It can include the make, model, and serial number of a camera or location data of the capture. Third-party applications to view this data are no longer necessary because Debian has this feature embedded in the default image viewer. Simply open any image, click the three horizonal lines, and select Properties. The Metadata and Details tabs display all available details such as camera information, location, and dates. However, this does not help much in regard to bulk images. We can easily install a Terminal-based utility which allows for automated export called Exiftool. The following command in Terminal will complete the process.

```
sudo apt update && sudo apt install libimage-exiftool-perl -y
```

You can now view the metadata from a single image as follows.

```
exiftool evidence.jpg
```

If you had multiple images, you could analyze all of them at once and export your results into a spreadsheet. Consider the following example where I possess a folder of images on my Desktop titled "Evidence". I want a spreadsheet of all available Exif data in reference to these images. The following command in Terminal will create a report on my Desktop titled Report.csv.

```
cd ~/Desktop/Evidence && exiftool * -csv > ~/Desktop/Report.csv
```

This command launches ExifTool (exiftool); reads all files in the current folder (*); specifies creation of a CSV file (-csv); and saves the file output to the Desktop titled as Report.csv (> ~/Desktop/Report.csv). I do not use this feature often, but it has saved me a lot of work when needed. I once possessed a folder of 200 images retrieved from a directory on my target's blog. This command created a spreadsheet with all metadata from the images, which identified GPS locations valuable to the investigation.

The following is a partial example of the type of valuable data you may find within digital images. In this example, I identified the date, time, and exact location of the device when the image was captured.

```
GPS Altitude          : 217 m Above Sea Level
GPS Date/Time         : 2010:11:08 15:37:18Z
GPS Latitude          : 40 deg 27' 32.00" N
GPS Longitude         : 90 deg 40' 23.00" W
```

Metadata: Metagoofil (https://github.com/opsdisk/metagoofil)

Metagoofil is a Linux option designed to locate and download documents. It does not always work perfectly, as you are at the mercy of search engines to provide the data. When Google decides to block Metagoofil, its usefulness ceases until the software receives an update. Install with the following steps.

```
cd ~/Downloads/Programs
git clone https://github.com/opsdisk/metagoofil.git
cd metagoofil
python3 -m venv metagoofilEnvironment
source metagoofilEnvironment/local/bin/activate
sudo pip install -r requirements.txt
deactivate
```

The following Terminal commands in your Linux VM switches to the proper directory (cd); launches Python 3 (python3); loads the script (metagoofil.py); sets the target domain (-d cisco.com); sets the file type as pdf (-t pdf); and saves the output to the Desktop (-o ~/Desktop/). This could be repeated for different file types.

```
cd ~/Downloads/Programs/metagoofil
python3 metagoofil.py -d cisco.com -t pdf -o ~/Desktop/
```

This automatically downloads any found documents. We could now analyze these documents with ExifTool as mentioned previously with the following commands within Terminal. The following commands navigate you and then creates a report.

```
cd ~/Desktop/ && exiftool * -csv > ~/Desktop/Report.csv
```

I always prefer to download and analyze document metadata within Linux. In my experience, this utility works fairly well when NOT using a VPN, but Google may block your VPN connection. My protocol in regard to document metadata collection and analysis is as follows.

- If I already possess numerous documents on my computer, I create a metadata CSV spreadsheet using ExifTool. I then analyze this document.
- If my target website possesses few documents, I download them manually through Google or Bing within a web browser.
- If my target website possesses hundreds of documents, I use Metagoofil, but only download one file type at a time. If my target were cisco.com, I would execute the following commands in Terminal.

```
python3 metagoofil.py -d cisco.com -t pdf -wo ~/Desktop/cisco/
python3 metagoofil.py -d cisco.com -t doc -wo ~/Desktop/cisco/
python3 metagoofil.py -d cisco.com -t xls -wo ~/Desktop/cisco/
python3 metagoofil.py -d cisco.com -t ppt -wo ~/Desktop/cisco/
python3 metagoofil.py -d cisco.com -t docx -wo ~/Desktop/cisco/
python3 metagoofil.py -d cisco.com -t xlsx -wo ~/Desktop/cisco/
python3 metagoofil.py -d cisco.com -t pptx -wo ~/Desktop/cisco/
```

Metadata: MediaInfo (https://mediaarea.net/en/MediaInfo)

This is a utility for displaying hidden metadata within a media file. The most common example is the metadata within a video obtained directly from the original source. First, open Terminal and type the following to install the application within the Activities menu of Debian.

```
sudo apt update && sudo apt install mediainfo-gui -y
```
You can now click on the MediaInfo icon in the Activities menu to launch the program. Click on the "File" option in the menu and then open either a file or folder. The default view offers little data, so click on "View" and then "Text" from the menu. This presents all metadata available within the file. In my test, I received the (partial) output visible in the following image from a video sent to me via email directly from a mobile device. It identified the make, model, and operating system version of the device, along with GPS information about the location during capture. Note that this type of data is usually not available from videos downloaded from the internet. The ideal scenario is that you possess a video file sent directly from a device.

```
Format                       : MPEG-4
Format profile               : QuickTime
File size                    : 545 KiB
Duration                     : 5 s 488 ms
Overall bit rate             : 813 kb/s
Recorded date                : 2013-05-30T10:51:14+0100
Make                         : Apple
xyz                          : +55.4062-002.6372+123.982/
Model                        : iPhone 5
com.apple.quicktime.software : 6.1.4
```

Metadata: mat2 (https://0xacab.org/jvoisin/mat2)

While you may want to VIEW metadata within images with the previous command, it is just as likely you will want to REMOVE data from your own media. Maybe you want to upload an image as part of a covert investigation. That image could have metadata such as dates, times, locations, and camera details. This is where MAT2 (Metadata Anonymisation Toolkit 2) can assist. First, we must install it with the following.

```
sudo apt update && sudo apt install mat2 -y
```

Next, we can issue a command to clean a file. Assume I have an image on my Desktop titled dirty.jpg. The following command would change to the Desktop directory and create a new file called "dirty.cleaned.jpg".

```
cd ~/Desktop && mat2 dirty.jpg
```

Metadata: xeuledoc (https://github.com/Malfrats/xeuledoc)

This application extracts metadata hidden within Google Documents, including the documents owner's name, email address, and Google identifiers. This is a great way to determine who is behind an online Google document which is part of your investigation. The following commands install the program.

```
pipx install xeuledoc
```

We can now execute the application toward a Google document. Consider the spreadsheet located at the following location.

https://docs.google.com/spreadsheets/d/1KXksB1vj7fXPNS4OYL0idQne3HXVnamtUP1h0ut3xwk

This page provides a link to a third-party piracy website claiming to offer one of my books for download. There is nothing within this spreadsheet which identifies the creator of this document. However, xeuledoc can assist. The following command queries the tool with the document link.

```
xeuledoc
https://docs.google.com/spreadsheets/d/1KXksB1vj7fXPNS4OYL0idQne3HXVnam
tUP1h0ut3xwk
```

The result appears in the following image.

We now have a name and email address to research.

Metadata: Sherloq (https://github.com/GuidoBartoli/sherloq)

Sherloq is a standalone application which can help identify modified areas of photographs. The advanced capabilities to alter images within Photoshop can easily fool our eyes. Computers are more difficult to convince. Let's install the application first, then discuss the usage. Conduct the following within Terminal. Note that ARM-based processors may not be able to use this program.

```
cd ~/Downloads/Programs
sudo apt install python3-testresources subversion -y
git clone https://github.com/GuidoBartoli/sherloq.git
cd sherloq/gui
python3 -m venv sherloqEnvironment
source sherloqEnvironment/bin/activate
sudo pip install -r requirements.txt
deactivate
```

You can now launch this application manually with the following command within Terminal.

```
python3 ~/Downloads/Programs/sherloq/gui/sherloq.py
```

Sherloq replicates many of the online image metadata and manipulation detection methods which were explained in my other books. The benefit here is the ability to conduct an examination offline. If you have a sensitive photo, you may not want to upload it into one of the many online metadata websites. Instead, you may want to keep it restricted to your local machine. Click the "Load Image" button and select a photo. There are numerous options present within the left menu.

Consider the following image. The upper-right image displays the "Principal Component Analysis" which highlights the lips of the subjects for potential digital manipulation. If you investigate online images often, I encourage you to understand all of the options available within this software application. The author's website at github.com/GuidoBartoli/sherloq should assist.

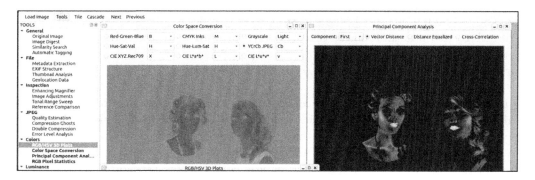

Frameworks: Spiderfoot (https://github.com/smicallef/spiderfoot.git)

This program introduces more valuable utilities than any other single resource within this book. This will take some effort to install and configure, but the benefits justify the work. I installed the application into the custom Linux VM with the following steps.

```
cd ~/Downloads/Programs
git clone https://github.com/smicallef/spiderfoot.git
cd spiderfoot
python3 -m venv spiderfootEnvironment
source spiderfootEnvironment/bin/activate
sudo pip install -r requirements.txt
pip install pyopenssl --upgrade
deactivate
```

If we are inside the Spiderfoot directory (~/Downloads/Programs/spiderfoot), we can launch the Spiderfoot service with the following command.

```
python3 ./sf.py -l 127.0.0.1:5001
```

If executing manually, you would need to launch the service and then tell Firefox and connect to http://127.0.0.1:5001. We can replicate both with the following.

```
python3 ./sf.py -l 127.0.0.1:5001 & firefox http://127.0.0.1:5001
```

Let's take a look at the interface and conduct an example query. After launching the Spiderfoot program within Firefox, click the "New Scan" option. Provide a name for your session (IntelTechniques) and a domain (inteltechniques.com). Choose your desired "Use case" and click "Run scan". I chose "All" in order to test the features, but this can be intrusive toward your target site. Choose the level of access appropriate for your investigation. The scan will launch and may take a while to complete, possibly hours. The amount of data acquired will be substantial, and I will only focus on a few areas of interest. The default screen displays the current progress and a log file. The "Browse" button in the upper left allows you to start peering into the data found about your target. Below are the sections of interest to my own site.

- Account on external site (Four online profiles connected to my brand)
- Human Name (Identification of my full name and three associates)
- Leak site content (56 Pastebin files referencing my domain)
- Similar domain (Two domains with similar spelling)
- Web technology (Pages on my site which rely on PHP, and my version)

The "Graph" button displayed a detailed chart of connections from my domain to external sources. This application scours a domain, IP address, or email address for hundreds of data points which may provide value. Clicking the "Scans" button provides options to stop, re-run, or delete a scan result. It also provides a status summary of each current scan, and you can execute numerous scans simultaneously.

Frameworks: Recon-ng (https://github.com/lanmaster53/recon-ng)

Recon-ng is a full-featured web reconnaissance framework written in Python. Complete with independent modules, database interaction, built-in convenience functions, interactive help, and command completion, Recon-ng provides a powerful environment in which OSINT research can be conducted quickly and thoroughly. This utility provides automation to many of the redundant tasks that OSINT examiners find themselves performing on a daily basis. I offer a warning before proceeding. This is a technically complicated portion of this book. Please don't let that scare you off, we will approach each step slowly. First, we need to install Recon-ng into our OSINT Original virtual machine. Type the following into Terminal.

```
cd ~/Downloads/Programs
git clone https://github.com/lanmaster53/recon-ng.git
cd recon-ng
python3 -m venv recon-ngEnvironment
source recon-ngEnvironment/bin/activate
sudo pip install -r REQUIREMENTS
deactivate
```

This should install Recon-ng, and typing `./recon-ng` from within this directory launches the application. This screen will display the current version, and I am writing this based on version 5.1.2. The following command would be used to update your version of Recon-ng.

```
cd ~/Downloads/Programs/recon-ng
git pull https://github.com/lanmaster53/recon-ng.git
```

Recon-ng does not possess many online tutorials. The guides that I have found are mostly an index of commands with little explanation. Instead of trying to summarize how the program functions, I will walk you through actual usage and explain as we go. I will start with the basics and then conduct numerous actual searches. In lieu of screen captures, I will include all text input and output in `10 pt Courier New font`. Upon executing Recon-ng, you will be notified that no modules are installed. This is normal, and we will add them as we need them. At this prompt, let's begin with the help command. Typing `help` reveals the following commands and explanations.

```
back            Exits the current context
dashboard       Displays a summary of activity
db              Interfaces with the workspace's database
exit            Exits the framework
help            Displays this menu
index           Creates a module index (dev only)
```

```
keys              Manages third party resource credentials
marketplace       Interfaces with the module marketplace
modules           Interfaces with installed modules
options           Manages the current context options
pdb               Starts a Python Debugger session (dev only)
script            Records and executes command scripts
shell             Executes shell commands
show              Shows various framework items
snapshots         Manages workspace snapshots
spool             Spools output to a file
workspaces        Manages workspaces
```

Typing `marketplace search` will reveal the current functions available. Think of the marketplace similar to a list of utilities within Recon-ng, and each option as a "resource". Just like Bing is a website resource that we can use through a web browser, "bing_domain_web" is a specific resource that we can use in Recon-ng. At any time, you can type `marketplace info` into Recon-ng to receive details about a specific item. As an example, typing `marketplace info virustotal` displays the following description.

```
path          | recon/netblocks-hosts/virustotal
name          | Virustotal domains extractor
author        | USSC (thanks @jevalenciap)
version       | 1.0
last_updated  | 2019-06-24
description   | Harvests domains from the Virustotal by using the
report API.
required_keys | ['virustotal_api']
dependencies  | []
files         | []
status        | not installed
```

This provides the detailed description, and whether the utility requires an API key or other dependencies. It also confirms we have not installed the module. We will execute this option later in the chapter. For now, we must set up our first investigation. Before we can conduct any research within this program, we must create a workspace. A workspace is a container that will isolate your work from one investigation to another. Think of a workspace as a case file. You may have a stack of cases on your desk, each with its own folder. All of your work on a case stays within the associated folder. Workspaces are similar. You should create a new workspace for each investigation. They can be deleted later or preserved for additional work. You can type `workspaces list` at any time to see the currently used workspaces. For now, we will create a new workspace titled OSINT by executing the command of `workspaces create OSINT`.

After creation, you will automatically begin using the new workspace. If you have created more than one workspace, such as one titled OSINT2, you can switch to it by typing `workspaces load OSINT2`. You might have a workspace for every target suspect or a single workspace for an entire case. Each situation will be unique. Now that you have a space created, we can begin. Let's start with a very simple yet powerful query, using the Profiler module. First, we must install the module with the following command within Recon-ng.

```
marketplace install profiler
```

The module is now installed, but is not loaded. The following loads the module.

```
modules load profiler
```

Now that the module is loaded, we can add any input desired. Since this module queries usernames, we will add our target of "inteltechniques" with the following command. Note that SOURCE is uppercase, which is required.

```
options set SOURCE inteltechniques
```

We should test our input with the following command.

```
input
```

The response should now be the following.

```
+-----------------+
|  Module Inputs  |
+-----------------+
|  inteltechniques |
+-----------------+
```

Finally, we can launch the module with the following command.

```
run
```

This script should query the username of inteltechniques against numerous online services. It does not present any results when complete, but did locate and store valuable data. To view the results, type the following.

```
show profiles
```

The results appear similar to the following.

```
-----------------------------------------------------------------+
1|inteltechniques|Gravatar|http://gravatar.com/inteltechniques| images
2|inteltechniques|reddit|https://www.reddit.com/user/inteltechniques|news
3|inteltechniques|Twitter|https://twitter.com/inteltechniques|social
```

In just a few seconds, we queried dozens of online services and immediately received only the three which contained the presence of our target username. This demonstrates the ability to save a substantial amount of time by using Recon-ng. If you were tasked to locate online profiles of ten suspects, this could be completed in a few minutes. Let's repeat the process, but with another username, with the following commands.

```
options set SOURCE humanhacker
run
show profiles
```

The following result displays the additional online profiles collected during this second query. Recon-ng will continue to store target data as you receive it. This is one of the more powerful features of the application.

```
1|inteltechniques|Gravatar|http://gravatar.com/profiles/inteltechniques|images
2|inteltechniques|reddit| https://www.reddit.com/user/inteltechniques | news
3|inteltechniques|Twitter | https://twitter.com/inteltechniques | social |
4|humanhacker|Blogspot| http://humanhacker.blogspot.com | blog |
5|humanhacker|Disqus| https://disqus.com/by/humanhacker/| discussion |
6|humanhacker|Flipboard | https://flipboard.com/@humanhacker| tech |
7|humanhacker|GitHub| https://api.github.com/users/humanhacker| coding |
8|humanhacker|Instagram | https://www.instagram.com/humanhacker/| social |
```

```
 9|humanhacker|Kongregate|http://www.kongregate.com/accounts/humanhacker|gaming
10|humanhacker|Kik | https://kik.me/humanhacker| social |
11|humanhacker|Medium| https://medium.com/@humanhacker/latest| news |
12|humanhacker|Technet|https://social.technet.microsoft.com/humanhacker|tech
13|humanhacker|Minecraft|https://namemc.com/name/humanhacker gaming
14|humanhacker|Pornhub|https://www.pornhub.com/users/humanhacker|XXX PORN   |
15|humanhacker|scratch|https://scratch.mit.edu/users/humanhacker/| coding
16|humanhacker|reddit|https://www.reddit.com/user/humanhacker          | news
17|humanhacker|Twitch.tv|https://twitch.tv/usernames/humanhacker|gaming
18|humanhacker|Twitter    | https://twitter.com/humanhacker| social     |
19|humanhacker|Xbox| https://www.xboxgamertag.com/search/humanhacker/| gaming
```

Let's conduct another example within a different module. First, we must leave our current module by typing back. This returns us to our workspace. Next, install four additional modules with the following commands.

```
marketplace install bing_domain_web
marketplace install google_site_web
marketplace install brute_suffix
marketplace install pgp_search
```

We will use these in order and target the website cnn.com. First, we will load the bing_domain_web option with the command of modules load bing_domain_web. Next, we will set our source with options set SOURCE cnn.com and execute the script with run. This command queries the Bing search engine for hosts connected to the domain cnn.com. The result identified over 70 unique hosts, including the following.

```
[*] [host] internationaldesk.blogs.cnn.com (<blank>)
[*] [host] crossfire.blogs.cnn.com (<blank>)
[*] [host] reliablesources.blogs.cnn.com (<blank>)
[*] [host] lightyears.blogs.cnn.com (<blank>)
[*] [host] commercial.cnn.com (<blank>)
[*] [host] collection.cnn.com (<blank>)
```

We can replicate this type of search on Google to make sure we are not missing any hosts that could be valuable by typing back, then modules load google_site_web, then options set SOURCE cnn.com, and finally run. This notifies us 38 total (15 new) hosts found, which indicates that Bing found more hosts than Google, and Google found 15 hosts that we did not have in our collection from Bing. Since Recon-ng can parse out duplicates, we should have a list of unique hosts with a combined effort from both Google and Bing. Typing show hosts will display all of them. Below is a small portion.

```
news.blogs.cnn.com
m.cnn.com
buzz.money.cnn.com
thechart.blogs.cnn.com
globalpublicsquare.blogs.cnn.com
tech.fortune.cnn.com
```

Next, let's type back to leave the current module and then modules load brute_suffix to load our next demo. Since there is no domain set as our source for this module, we will add one with options set SOURCE social-engineer.org. There are many top-level domains (TLDs) aside from .com and .org. Executing run will scour the various TLDs such as .net, .tv, and others. After completion, typing show domains will display our updated set of target addresses ready for further searching. In this example, I was notified that additional domains were located, including the following.

```
social-engineer.be          social-engineer.dev
social-engineer.ch          social-engineer.info
social-engineer.com         social-engineer.me
social-engineer.de          social-engineer.us
```

These are all new leads that should be analyzed later. We could now repeat our previous module execution of `bing_domain_web` and `google_site_web` to likely grow our list of hosts substantially. This is a good time to pause and consider what is happening here. As we find data, Recon-ng stores it within our workspace. Every time we conduct a new search, or repeat a previous search, all of the new data is appended. This prevents us from documenting everything that we locate because Recon-ng is keeping good notes for us. This can allow us to collect an amount of data otherwise impossible to manage manually. Let's move on to individual contacts.

Typing `show contacts` will display any contacts stored within the current workspace. You likely do not have any, so let's add some. First, type `back` to make sure you are out of the previous module. Next, load another module with `modules load pgp_search`. This will scan all of the stored domains that we have located and search for any email addresses associated with public PGP keys within those domains. We have not set a source for this module, but you likely already have some ready for you. In a previous example, you searched social-engineer.org within other top-level domains and received numerous results. If you type `input` within this module, you should see those same domains listed. This is because Recon-ng is constantly storing found data and making it available for future use. If we type **run**, this list will be searched, but no results will be found. Note that this list does not possess our target domain of social-engineer.org, and only the additional names previously found. You may wish to remove these sources, and then add a fresh new source, with the following.

```
options unset SOURCE
options set SOURCE cnn.com
```

Typing **run** and striking enter executes the process, while submitting `show contacts` afterward displays the results. The following is the partial output with new email addresses identified. Each of these addresses are now stored in your workspace, ready for the next round of research.

```
| 2      | barsuk    |   |          | barsuk@cnn.com
| 3      | Tristan   |   | Helmich  | tristan.helmich@cnn.com
| 4      | Paul      | P | Murphy   | paul.p.murphy@cnn.com
```

Let's reflect on how this can be beneficial. Assume that you are investigating numerous websites. Recon-ng provides dozens of utilities which automate queries and provides immediate information. Magnify this by tens or hundreds of domains, profiles, or other target data, and you have an easy way to replicate several hours of work. In another scenario, you are investigating a list of potential email addresses connected to a case. Entering these into Recon-ng allows you to execute your searches across all accounts. The effort to check one address is the same to check thousands. This impressive capability is only a small fraction of what can be done with this application.

This seems like a good time to back away, create a report, and start a new set of actions. The following commands will back out of our current module; install the reporting feature; instruct Recon-ng that we want to use the reporting tool; mandate a graphical html (web) template be used; set the "Customer" as IntelTechniques; set the "Creator" as M.Bazzell; and execute the process.

```
back
marketplace install html
modules load html
options set CUSTOMER IntelTechniques
options set CREATOR M.Bazzell
run
```

Note the output after the final command. It identifies that the report is complete, and provides the storage location. Since I am running Recon-ng from my OSINT virtual machine, the default location is ~/.recon-ng/workspaces/OSINT/results.html. Therefore, I can open the home folder on my desktop; double-click the ".recon-ng" folder; double-click the "workspaces" folder; double-click the "OSINT" folder; and then open the "results" file. Please note you must have "Show Hidden Files" option enabled from within the preferences menu of the Files application. Note that the Domains, Hosts, and Contacts sections are not expanded, but contain a lot of information. At the bottom of this file, the "Created by", date, and time clearly identify these report details.

Hopefully this demonstration explained the usage of Recon-ng. Executing `exit` in the window closes everything, but removes nothing. Before our next example, let's delete our previous work and start fresh. Note that deleting a workspace removes all associated data and reports. Make sure you have exported your evidence if needed. First, relaunch Recon-ng. The following commands display the current workspaces; delete the OSINT workspace; and create a new workspace titled location.

```
workspaces list
workspaces remove OSINT
workspaces create location
```

This chapter explains only a small portion of the capabilities of Recon-ng. Please consider revisiting the modules listed at the beginning and experiment with the execution of each. Overall, it would be very difficult to break the application, and any errors received are harmless. You will receive best results by requesting API keys from the services which require them. The "Info" screen of each Recon-ng module displays any requirements within the "Required Keys" field. Many API keys are free and open new possibilities. Overall, an entire book could be written about this application alone. The goal of this section was simply to familiarize you with the program and demonstrate the power of automated queries.

If you would like more information about Recon-ng, please visit the official Github page at https://github.com/lanmaster53/recon-ng. From there, you can join a dedicated group in order to participate in discussions about errors, features, and overall usage. While Recon-ng has not been updated in some time, and many believe the project has been abandoned, the tools still perform well for specific tasks.

Frameworks: Mr. Holmes (https://github.com/Lucksi/Mr.Holmes)

I started using this program in late 2023 and have found great value in it. Install with the following.

```
cd ~/Downloads/Programs
git clone https://github.com/Lucksi/Mr.Holmes
cd Mr.Holmes
sudo apt update
sudo chmod +x install.sh
sudo bash install.sh
```

Execute "1" when prompted to begin and "2" when prompted for auto-installation. This will configure everything for you. When finished, you can execute the software with the following.

```
cd ~/Downloads/Programs/Mr.Holmes && python3 MrHolmes.py
```

Upon the first execution, you will need to enter "Y" to accept the terms of the software, but should not be reminded after that. You will see a menu similar to the following.

```
(1)SOCIAL-ACCOUNT-OSINT
(2)PHONE-NUMBER-OSINT
(3)DOMAIN/IP-OSINT
```

```
(4)CONFIGURATION
(5)DATABASE(GUI)
(6)UPDATE
(7)PORT-SCANNER
(8)E-MAIL
(9)DORKS-GENERATOR
(10)PEOPLE-OSINT
(11)ENCODING/DECODING
(12)PDF-GRAPH CONVERTER
(13)FILE-TRANSFER
(14)SESSION-OPTIONS
(15)EXIT
```

I chose the first option which prompted for a username. After confirming that I did not want to use a proxy, I could choose to check this username or "scrape" it. The latter takes more time but may identify services skipped with the other option. While testing this, I learned that someone is using my username on Chess.com, as follows.

```
[+]TRYING ON: Chess.com
[v]USERNAME inteltechniques FOUND
[v]LINK: https://www.chess.com/member/inteltechniques
[I]TAGS:[Chess,Chess.com]
```

Next, I tested the phone number option, and was impressed. You must enter the full number including country code, but not the "+" before it. The program then queries public sites and offers to reformat the number in various ways to see if it is present within major search engines. It then exports a report into the ~/Downloads/Programs/Mr.Holmes folder. The following is only a partial result.

```
SCANNING EXECUTED ON: Date: 09/02/2024 10:13:04
INTERNATIONAL NUMBER: +1 618-462-8000
LOCAL NUMBER: 6184628000
COUNTRY PREFIX: +1
COUNTRY CODE: US
COUNTRY: United States
AREA/ZONE Alton, IL
CARRIER/ISP: AT&T
TIMEZONE: America/Chicago
NAME: Public Library
LOCATION: "Latitude": "30.8124247", "Longitude": "34.8594762"
```

The program then generated hundreds of search engine "Dorks" which may reveal more details, such as the following, which could be expected within a browser.

```
GOOGLE-DORKS:
https://www.google.com/search?q=inurl:%226182166453%22
https://www.google.com/search?q=intext:(%226182166453%22)
https://www.google.com/search?q=intext:(%226182166453%22)filetype:txt
https://www.google.com/search?q=intext:(%226182166453%22)filetype:csv
https://www.google.com/search?q=intext:(%226182166453%22)filetype:pdf
https://www.google.com/search?q=intext:(%226182166453%22)filetype:doc
https://www.google.com/search?q=intext:(%226182166453%22)filetype:docx
YANDEX-DORKS:
https://yandex.com/search/?text=6182166453
https://yandex.com/search/?text=(6182166453)mime:txt
```

```
https://yandex.com/search/?text=(6182166453)mime:pdf
https://yandex.com/search/?text=(6182166453)mime:csv
https://yandex.com/search/?text=(6182166453)mime:doc
https://yandex.com/search/?text=(6182166453)mime:log
https://yandex.com/search/?text=(6182166453)mime:docx
```

The actual list would have filled five pages. The email option was also beneficial. Overall, this program automates a lot of the manual steps which I explain in *OSINT Techniques, 10th Edition.* I encourage you to explore all of the options and become familiar with the layout. The automated scripts presented within the next chapter will launch the program and open any reports when complete. If you want to maually access a report, navigate to ~/Downloads/Programs/Mr.Holmes/GUI/Reports. Also, never "click" on "OK" when the function is complete, only press the Enter or Return key on the keyboard. For some reason, clicking "OK" kills the application.

Frameworks: sn0int (https://github.com/kpcyrd/sn0int)

This is another framework which I started using in late 2023. At the time of this writing, it did not function within ARM-based processors such as Apple's M-series, but that may be fixed by now. We can install with the following, which should be copied and pasted all at once.

```
cd ~/Downloads/Programs
sudo apt install curl sq
curl -sSf https://apt.vulns.sexy/kpcyrd.pgp | sq dearmor | sudo tee
/etc/apt/trusted.gpg.d/apt-vulns-sexy.gpg
echo deb http://apt.vulns.sexy stable main | sudo tee
/etc/apt/sources.list.d/apt-vulns-sexy.list
sudo apt update && sudo apt install sn0int
```

This program is very similar to Recon-ng. We can launch it with the following.

```
sn0int
```

You should be prompted to install the basic packages with the following command.

```
pkg quickstart
```

You are now ready to experiment with sn0int. Start by executing the following command.

```
help
```

This will display the main modules, which should appear similar to Recon-ng.

```
add            Add new entities to the database
autonoscope    Manage rules to remove entities from scope
autoscope      Manage rules to automatically add entities to scope
delete         Delete entities from the database
keyring        Manage saved credentials
pkg            Manage installed modules
noscope        Exclude entities from scope
run            Run the currently selected module
scope          Include entities in the scope again
select         Select entities from the database
stats          Show statistics about your current workspace
```

```
target          Preview targeted entities or narrow them down
use             Select a module
workspace       Switch to a different workspace
```

Let's create our case workspace with the following

```
workspace 2024-001
```
We can now add data. Let's start with adding a domain to the investigation.

```
add domain
```

You should be prompted to provide a domain, similar to the following.

```
inteltechniques.com
```
We have now added a piece of evidence to our case. The following lists all packages.

```
pkg list
```

The result should be similar to the following partial options.

```
kpcyrd/ctlogs 0.7.0: Query certificate transparency logs to discover subdomains
kpcyrd/dns-mx-domains 0.1.1: Discover mail server from MX records for domain
kpcyrd/dns-mx-emails 0.1.0: Discover mail server from MX records for emails
kpcyrd/dns-ns 0.1.0: Add a domains NS records to scope
kpcyrd/dns-ptr 0.2.0: Run reverse dns lookups
kpcyrd/exif 0.1.1: Extract exif data from images
kpcyrd/geoip 0.1.0: Run a geoip lookup for an ip address
kpcyrd/irc-monitor 0.3.0: Monitor an irc network for users
kpcyrd/keybase 0.2.0: Collect accounts and emails from keybase accounts
kpcyrd/keybase-domains 0.1.0: Find keybase proofs for domains
kpcyrd/keybase-profiles 0.1.0: Find keybase proofs for online accounts
```

Let's load the ctlogs option with the following.

```
use ctlogs
```

We can now execute the query as follows.

```
run
```

The result should be similar to the following.

```
"inteltechniques.com": Adding subdomain "www.inteltechniques.com"
"inteltechniques.com": Adding subdomain "blog.inteltechniques.com"
```

We have now added new evidence to our case which can be used for future queries. The overall function of the sn0int modules works very similar to Recon-ng. This has only been one basic query. If you believe this framework can be valuable to your investigations, and I believe it can, please visit https://sn0int.readthedocs.io and become familiar with all of the commands.

Frameworks: Internet Archive (https://archive.org/developers/internetarchive)

This utility may not technically be a "framework", but I felt it fit best within this category. This tool allows you to explore and download large data sets with minimal effort. An example should help explain the benefits. Install with the following.

```
pipx install internetarchive
```

Now consider the content located at https://archive.org/details/hackercons. This is a "collection" of hacker conference videos which consists of almost 15,000 items. One of these is another "collection" located at https://archive.org/details/notacon_2006. I am quoting collection because that is how the Internet Archive identifies a set of data available within a group. The Notacon collection contains the 39 videos from that conference in 2006. We could manually download them from the website, but that is tedious. If there were 1,000 videos, it would take way too long. Instead, we will acquire the content with our new Internet Archive utility.

We could execute `ia download notacon_2006`, which would download every file within the collection, but that would download multiple versions of each video and all of the metadata associated with each entry. Since each video possesses a MP4 version, we should use the following.

```
ia download --search 'collection:notacon_2006' --glob="*.mp4"
```

This launched the utility (ia); specifies we want to download data (download); instructs the program to query data (--search); specifies the collection we want ('collection:notacon_2006'); and skips any file which is not an MP4 (--glob="*.mp4"). The following image displays a Terminal progress (top) and Files location (bottom).

Applications: Screen Capture

I previously mentioned multiple unique methods of capturing website evidence within your browser. However, you may need a more robust solution for capturing your entire screen. This can be approached from two specific avenues. First, you could record either a still or video capture of your entire computer from your host. In other words, you could use the default capturing software within your Windows or Mac machine to record video or save a screenshot of your Linux VM. I do not recommend this. Recording from your host displays evidence of your other operating system. While it would likely never be an issue, it exposes you unnecessarily. Consider the following.

You are a detective investigating a homicide. You find evidence online implicating your suspect. You are on a Windows computer, but all of your investigation was conducted within a Linux VM. You launch recording software on the Windows computer and record a video of your work. This video was submitted to the defense. For a brief moment, the video captured a file on your Windows desktop titled Accounts.xlsx. It is a spreadsheet containing all of your covert online accounts, has no connection to the investigation, and was not intended to be exposed. The defense makes a motion to analyze this file, as they believe it could be associated with the investigation. The judge approves, and you must share all of your covert accounts with the other side. Does this sound far-fetched? It happened to a colleague of mine in 2014.

I have become more paranoid of digital mistakes than necessary, but I believe we should never take chances. Therefore, I recommend that all of your screen captures be executed within your VM. Fortunately, Linux has many options. First, let's consider the default Debian screenshot utilities. The following keyboard keys and key combinations create high-resolution exact screenshots of your VM.

- PrtSc: Save a screenshot of the entire screen to the "Pictures" directory.
- Shift + PrtSc: Select and save a screenshot of a specific region.
- Alt + PrtSc: Save a screenshot of the active window to the "Pictures" directory.

The PrtSc key on your keyboard should also launch the print screen dialogue menu. If you do not have a keyboard capable of this, you can also search "screen" in the Activities menu to open the "Take a Screenshot" utility. Within it, you can switch between a still capture and video recording, then select the desired area. Whenever I need to record a video of all actions taken within an investigation, this is the utility I rely on. It is native to the operating system and always works. If it does not work best for you, consider the next application called Kazam.

Applications: Kazam (https://github.com/henrywoo/kazam)

This is a minimal tool for screen recording. It also includes screenshot support, but I find the native Debian option easier and faster. Kazam is most suitable for getting the task done quickly without providing many options. The following steps will install and execute a Kazam capture.

- In Terminal, execute the following:

```
sudo apt update && sudo apt install kazam -y
```

- Launch Kazam from the Applications menu (make a shortcut if desired).
- Click "Capture" within the application.
- After the countdown, your entire screen is being captured.
- When finished, click the icon in the upper right and choose "Finish Recording".
- Choose "Save for later"; click "Continue"; choose a location; and click "Save".

You now possess a high-resolution video of your entire session. This can be very beneficial in many scenarios. I have used this to document a specific portion of my investigation when a simple still capture would not suffice. It could also be used to explain a search technique through video, which can be easily replicated by the person receiving a copy. I appreciate the simplicity of this application, and the lack of any branding or logos within the videos. I have found it to be buggy within ARM-based versions of Debian, but others work well.

Applications: BleachBit (https://www.bleachbit.org/)

I explained BleachBit in previous chapters. Type the following into Terminal to install the application.

```
sudo apt update && sudo apt install bleachbit -y
```

Clicking the nine dots in the lower left will present two BleachBit applications. The second icon executes the software with administrative privileges and is the option I choose. Upon first launch, click "Close" to accept default configuration. Select every option except the "Free disk space" feature. Click "Preview" to see a report of recommended cleaning. Click "Clean" to execute the process. I run this program within my primary OSINT VM after every major update to keep it clean and minimal. I ran it at this point of the guide after testing several applications and received the following result, removing 1.5 GB of unnecessary data.

Applications: Google Earth Pro (google.com/earth)

Google Earth Pro is a standalone application that takes the Google Maps data to another level. With this application, we have access to many mapping tools. These tools can import data from spreadsheets and help you visualize the content. In order to maintain the scope of open source intelligence, I will focus on only a few specific tools. First, we need to enter the following commands within Terminal to install the software. Note that Google Earth Pro does not currently support ARM-based systems.

```
wget http://dl.google.com/dl/earth/client/current/google-earth-
stable_current_amd64.deb
sudo apt install -y ./google-earth-stable_current_amd64.deb
sudo rm google-earth-stable_current_amd64.deb
```

Within the application, the first step is to display your location of interest. This can be accomplished by typing the address or GPS coordinates in the upper left search field. When you see your target location and have set the zoom to an appropriate level, you are ready to start adding layers. By default, you will only see the satellite imagery of the location. The menu on the left possesses options for adding new content to this view. The last box in this menu is titled "Layers". Inside this menu are several data sets that can be enabled and disabled by the checkbox next to each. I recommend disabling all layers and then enabling one at a time to analyze the data that is added to your map view. The following details will explain the layers of interest.

- Photos - Digital images uploaded through social networking sites
- Roads - Text layer of road names
- 3D Building - Alternative 3D view of some locations
- Gallery - User submitted content including YouTube videos

Another Google Earth feature available that is often overlooked is the Historical Imagery option. This can be activated by selecting the "clock" icon in the upper menu bar of the application. This will open a slider menu directly below the icon. This slider can be moved and the result will be various satellite images of the target location taken at different times.

Usually, the quality of the images will decline as you navigate further back in time. This can be useful in identifying changes in the target location such as building modifications, additional vehicles, and land changes. Drug enforcement agents often use this tool to monitor suspected drug growth at a target location. While the Google Earth program is not updated often, the imagery content within is pulled directly from the Google archives. It is vital within our arsenal of tools and I find it more pleasant to navigate than the official Google Maps website. This resource has assisted many of my investigations over the past decade by providing historic satellite imagery which was unavailable from any other online source. Note that Google Earth Pro will not currently install within Apple ARM-based virtual machines or hosts. Hopefully, Google will create an ARM version in the near future.

Updates

Once you have your new VM created, be sure to apply all updates with the following commands. After all updates are applied, you should reboot the VM.

```
sudo apt update && sudo apt upgrade -y
```

Miscellaneous Repairs

We have installed a lot of software and should clean up a bit. The following attempts to fix any issues we cause within all of our installations.

```
sudo apt update --fix-missing
sudo apt --fix-broken install
sudo apt autoremove -y
```

Troubleshooting

I do not expect everything presented here to work flawlessly for every reader. I wish it were that simple. You may encounter issues. My best advice is to restart the process with which you are having the trouble, and follow all instructions exactly as written. Even then, you may experience frustration. The following are some tips which have helped members of my online video training.

• When typing in Terminal, you can hit the tab key and it will suggest all the possible options that start with the string you have typed so far. It will also autocomplete your command if only one option exists. For example, if you are trying to navigate to your Downloads/Programs folder, you can just type "cd ~/Dow" [tab], then "Pro" [tab] to complete the command. Typing cd ~/D [tab][tab] would list all folders starting with D.
• Use the "up" arrow key to navigate through previous commands.
• "Ctrl" + "C" kills any running process, and typing "ls" displays the directory contents.
• You can copy and paste to/from Terminal, but only with right-click (not "Ctrl" + "V").
• Keyboard arrows will move you through a Terminal command, but mouse clicks do not.
• You can modify the size of your Dock icons in "Settings" > "Dock".

Hidden Files

By default, Debian hides system files which should not normally be manipulated. You may need to see these within the Files application. The following steps allow you to see all files on the system, and the change is persistent between reboots.

• Open the "Files" program in either your Dock or Applications menu.
• Click on the three horizontal lines in the upper right area.
• Select "Show Hidden Files".
• Close the "Files" program.

Large File Transfer

We have configured our VM to possess a shared folder. This is an avenue to transfer files from within the VM to the host and vice versa. This can be used to copy evidence from within the VM to your host for preservation to external media. I have experienced limitations with this method. If I have hundreds of large videos, I often receive errors when I try to copy all of them to my host through the shared folder. This is much more prominent in VirtualBox versus UTM. The best solution I have found is to transfer evidence directly to a USB drive within the VM. If desired, you could choose this method and eliminate any shared folder on the VM.

When you insert a USB drive into your host computer, it is immediately read by your primary operating system. Your running VM does not see the device. Within the VirtualBox menu, you can choose "Devices", then "USB", and try to click on the USB drive, if found. The issue you may face is that your host has the drive locked and will not allow the VM to take over. You can usually resolve this by ejecting the USB drive within your host. On both Windows and Mac, you should see an eject icon next to the drive or by right-clicking the device. After ejecting, attempt to load the USB device again through the VirtualBox menu. This may present another issue. If your USB device is formatted specifically for Mac or Windows, it may not be readable by Linux. I suggest specifying a USB device solely for use within this VM and formatting it in a way so that it can be read universally by any operating system.

- Insert the USB device into your computer while the VM is running.
- Eject the device from your host OS if necessary.
- In the VirtualBox VM window, click on "Devices", "USB", and the device name.
- In Debian, launch the Activities menu.
- Type "Disks" into the search field.
- Click on the USB drive listed in the left column.
- Click on any boxes within the "Volumes" section.
- Click the minus (-) icon and "Delete" when prompted.
- Repeat until there are no volumes present.
- Click the "+" icon, click "Next", provide a name, choose "Fat", and click "Create".

This will create a USB drive on which files can be read and written within any file system. You cannot possess files larger than 4 GB in size, but I have never had an issue with that during investigations. When you insert the USB device into your computer, you can choose to allow your primary OS see it, or load it into your VM. I have found this method to be much more reliable than transferring large files through the shared folder. You should practice both techniques and pursue the most appropriate option for your investigations.

Summary

You should now have an understanding of the many benefits of a Linux OSINT VM. We have installed and configured numerous Linux applications which are ready for use. The chances of every application mentioned here installing without any issue is slim. Programs break, updates cause issues, and the countless variables on your system can be problematic. When something fails, keep moving on to the other options. Next, let's automate much of the work within these Terminal-based programs with custom bash scripts. I promise we are close to locking our settings in for all future investigations.

CHAPTER ELEVEN
OSINT VM SCRIPTS

I believe this chapter presents the most valuable portion of this entire guide. Until now, we have executed all terminal commands manually. We had to know all of the proper commands, switches, inputs, outputs, and queries. In this chapter, we will automate all of this and only need to supply the target online data we are seeking after clicking an icon. This is not a new revelation. In Buscador, David and I provided all applications pre-configured for use since 2018. Buscador included desktop shortcuts with icons to launch programs and scripts to help execute specific queries. As previously stated, we should not rely on third parties to create and maintain these VM configurations (even my own public resources). The goal here is to teach you how to replicate that work and easily generate your own custom VM with pre-built scripts, and possess the ability to modify them as needed. If conducting the following tutorials to your original VM, you will only need to take these steps once. Each clone you create will maintain all your hard work, as explained later.

Some of this chapter may seem complicated at first. I promise everything becomes easier as you practice. This will be a crash course in Linux bash scripts, but the lessons learned now will pay off in future usage. Chapter 14 automates this entire process which creates a 100% functioning OSINT VM within a few minutes. For now, let's download my custom bash scripts into your new VM so we can open, view, and modify them, with the following Terminal commands, which can be copied and executed all at once.

```
mkdir ~/Documents/scripts
cd ~/Documents/scripts
curl -O https://uvm:317@inteltechniques.com/osintvm/api.sh
curl -O https://uvm:317@inteltechniques.com/osintvm/domain.sh
curl -O https://uvm:317@inteltechniques.com/osintvm/framework.sh
curl -O https://uvm:317@inteltechniques.com/osintvm/image.sh
curl -O https://uvm:317@inteltechniques.com/osintvm/metadata.sh
curl -O https://uvm:317@inteltechniques.com/osintvm/update.sh
curl -O https://uvm:317@inteltechniques.com/osintvm/user.sh
curl -O https://uvm:317@inteltechniques.com/osintvm/video.sh
```

Important: If you downloaded the files but they all consist only of "401 Unauthorized" within them, then you are probably trying to download outdated files. Always make sure you are operating from the latest revision of this guide, which can be identified on the third page of this PDF and confirmed online at https://inteltechniques.com/book1b.html. Any time we heavily modify or update these files, we will purge old versions in order to prevent accidental download of outdated content. As long as you are executing the previous commands from the latest version of this guide, you will always receive the most recent updates.

Your VM now possesses the bash scripts, but they cannot be executed yet. Execute the following to make each script able to run as a program.

```
cd ~/Documents/scripts
chmod +x api.sh
chmod +x domain.sh
chmod +x framework.sh
chmod +x image.sh
chmod +x metadata.sh
chmod +x update.sh
chmod +x user.sh
chmod +x video.sh
```

You can now execute a script as follows within Terminal (we will create shortcuts for these soon).

```
cd ~/Documents/scripts && ./video.sh
```

Let's take another look at the options in the video script which was presented in the previous chapter, as seen below. Next, let's take a look at some actual text within the video.sh script. This will provide a good opportunity to explain each element of the file and the impact on functions. After that, I will only demonstrate the functions of the other scripts without explaining the code within them, but you can open any script to see the text. You can now open the video.sh script within your text editor or simply follow along in the next few pages. We will begin with the header of the file.

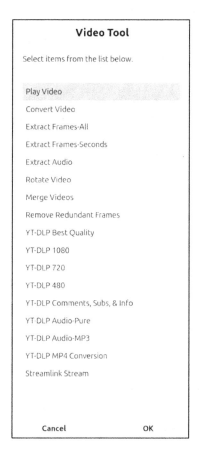

The following identifies itself as a bash script. This allows us to execute the file within Terminal.

```
#!/usr/bin/env bash
```

The following are headers which will not be executed because they have "##" before each line. This tells Terminal to ignore the text, but it can still be seen within a text editor. This serves as a way to present information about the file which has no function.

```
## Updated: December 1, 2024, specifically tweaked for Debian
## Please report any issues to errors@inteltechniques.com
## Copyright 2024 Michael Bazzell
## These instructions are provided 'as is' without warranty of any kind
## License information:
https://inteltechniques.com/data/osintvm/license.txt
```

The following builds the menu which is presented upon launch. The two occurrences of "menu" provides an identifier for the menu itself and then later designates that the menu functions begin. Zenity is the software we will use to build the menu and present a graphical option; "--list" identifies the type of menu; "--column" specifies only one column to display; each entry is presented in quotes; and the "--height" and "width" settings make sure the items are visible in the menu.

```
menu=$(zenity --list --title "Video Tool" --column "" "Play Video"
"Convert Video" "Extract Frames-All" "Extract Frames-Seconds" "Extract
Audio" "Rotate Video" "Merge Videos" "Remove Redundant Frames" "YT-DLP
Best Quality" "YT-DLP 1080" "YT-DLP 720" "YT-DLP Comments, Subs, &
Info" "YT-DLP Audio-Pure" "YT-DLP Audio-MP3" "YT-DLP MP4 Conversion"
"Streamlink Stream" --height="800" --width="300")
case $menu in
```

The following is our first menu function and the script to play a video. The first line must match the same title which was in the first menu. The presence of "file=$" is used to prompt the user for input. In this example, it launches Zenity; prompts the user to select a file from a file manager; and then stores that file location for a future function. The third line tells Terminal to execute "ffplay" and then supply the file which was previously selected. The script then presents a dialogue to press enter to return to the menu and then executes the script again for another function.

```
"Play Video")
file=$(zenity --file-selection --title "Video Tool")
ffplay "$file"
echo
echo "Press Enter to return to menu"
read data
exec /home/osint/Documents/scripts/video.sh
```

The following is similar to the previous example, but has added a new feature. The second line prompts the user to select a file as it did in the previous example, which stores the entire path of the file, such as "/Home/osint/Documents/file.mp4". I now want to only capture the file name itself without the path, so I added the "file2" option. That tells Terminal to remember only the file name at the end of the captured file path. The script then makes sure that a folder called Videos exists within the Documents folder; launches FFmpeg to open the path of the file originally selected; save the converted file as the selected file name (not path) with an MP4 extension; opens the Videos folder on the Desktop; and continues the same end process as the previous example.

```
"Convert Video")
file=$(zenity --file-selection --title "Video Tool")
file2=$(basename "$file")
mkdir ~/Documents/Videos/
ffmpeg -i "$file" ~/Documents/Videos/"$file2".mp4
open ~/Documents/Videos/
echo "Press Enter to return to menu"
read data
exec /home/osint/Documents/scripts/video.sh
```

The following function is quite different than the previous two examples. In those, we selected a local file from our system. With this function, we want to provide a URL. It confirms our directory exists and then prompts the user to supply a URL within a Zenity dialogue. It then launches YT-DLP and specifies the output format and location. The downloaded file will be named similar to "BEST-Bob Ross.webm" and will be saved in the Videos folder.

```
"YT-DLP Best Quality")
mkdir ~/Documents/Videos/
url=$(zenity --entry --title "Video Tool" --text "Enter Target URL")
yt-dlp -o ~/Documents/Videos/BEST-"%(title)s.%(ext)s" "$url" --
restrict-filenames
open ~/Documents/Videos/
echo
echo "Press Enter to return to menu"
read data
exec /home/osint/Documents/scripts/video.sh
```

The following is very similar to the previous option, but only downloads the data associated with a video, and not the video itself. For this utility, the script navigates directly to the Videos folder (cd) so that all data is preserved there.

```
"YT-DLP Comments, Subs, & Info")
mkdir ~/Documents/Videos/
cd ~/Documents/Videos/
url=$(zenity --entry --title "Video Tool" --text "Enter Target URL")
yt-dlp "$url" --write-comments --write-subs --sub-langs all --write-
description --skip-download
open ~/Documents/Videos/
echo
echo "Press Enter to return to menu"
read data
exec /home/osint/Documents/scripts/video.sh
```

The following makes use of a timestamp. This ensures that the file which is generated possesses a unique name which includes the current date and time. This prevents accidental overwriting of data in the event you capture the same live stream twice. The second line tells Terminal to capture the current date and time and store it within memory. The sixth line launches Streamlink; captures the URL previously entered; saves the best quality; and saves the file as the current date and time, similar to "2024-01-01-12-04", in the Videos folder. This file can be renamed later if desired.

```
"Streamlink Stream")
timestamp=$(date +%Y-%m-%d_%H_%M)
mkdir ~/Documents/Videos/
cd ~/Documents/Videos/
url=$(zenity --entry --title "Video Tool" --text "Enter Target URL")
streamlink "$url" best -r $timestamp
open ~/Documents/Videos/
echo
echo "Press Enter to return to menu"
```

```
read data
exec /home/osint/Documents/scripts/video.sh
```

The following is "case" backwards and ends the script.

```
esac
```

You can now launch these scripts from within Terminal, but that is a pain. Instead, we will download shortcuts to each script; apply an icon to each shortcut; and move the files to their proper location. Download each file with the following commands.

```
cd ~/Documents/scripts
curl -O https://uvm:317@inteltechniques.com/osintvm/api.desktop
curl -O https://uvm:317@inteltechniques.com/osintvm/domain.desktop
curl -O https://uvm:317@inteltechniques.com/osintvm/framework.desktop
curl -O https://uvm:317@inteltechniques.com/osintvm/image.desktop
curl -O https://uvm:317@inteltechniques.com/osintvm/metadata.desktop
curl -O https://uvm:317@inteltechniques.com/osintvm/search.desktop
curl -O https://uvm:317@inteltechniques.com/osintvm/update.desktop
curl -O https://uvm:317@inteltechniques.com/osintvm/user.desktop
curl -O https://uvm:317@inteltechniques.com/osintvm/video.desktop
curl -O https://uvm:317@inteltechniques.com/osintvm/api.png
curl -O https://uvm:317@inteltechniques.com/osintvm/domain.png
curl -O https://uvm:317@inteltechniques.com/osintvm/framework.png
curl -O https://uvm:317@inteltechniques.com/osintvm/image.png
curl -O https://uvm:317@inteltechniques.com/osintvm/metadata.png
curl -O https://uvm:317@inteltechniques.com/osintvm/search.png
curl -O https://uvm:317@inteltechniques.com/osintvm/update.png
curl -O https://uvm:317@inteltechniques.com/osintvm/user.png
curl -O https://uvm:317@inteltechniques.com/osintvm/video.png
```

We must now move the .desktop shortcuts into a location where the operating system can see them to present them within our applications menu.

```
cd ~/Documents/scripts
sudo mv *.desktop /usr/share/applications/
```

Let's take a look at one of these files, specifically video.desktop. The following identifies the name of the shortcut (Video Tool); the location of the script (.sh); and the location of the icon (.png).

```
[Desktop Entry]
Type=Application
Name=Video Tool
Categories=Application;OSINT
Exec=/home/osint/Documents/scripts/video.sh
Icon=/home/osint/Documents/scripts/video.png
Terminal=true
```

You should now be able to see these script shortcuts within your applications menu. Sometimes, a reboot is required. You can now launch any of these shortcuts to immediately see the script menu dialogue. However, I prefer to place them within my Dock for easy access. The following Terminal commands remove all current icons within the Dock; add our most vital OSINT tools to the Dock; and resize the icons to fit the desktop better. You could tweak the size (32) to match your own preference, and omit any applications desired.

```
gsettings set org.gnome.shell favorite-apps []
gsettings set org.gnome.shell favorite-apps "['firefox-esr.desktop',
'org.torproject.torbrowser-launcher.desktop',
'org.gnome.Nautilus.desktop', 'org.gnome.Terminal.desktop',
'update.desktop', 'search.desktop', 'video.desktop', 'user.desktop',
'image.desktop', 'domain.desktop', 'metadata.desktop',
'framework.desktop', 'api.desktop', 'google-earth-pro.desktop',
'kazam.desktop', 'org.gnome.Settings.desktop']"
gsettings set org.gnome.shell.extensions.dash-to-dock dash-max-icon-
size 32
```

You can now launch these scripts from your Dock, which should appear similar to the image below, but vertical on the left instead of horizontal at the bottom. Take some time to play with them and understand their functions. Overall, they should replicate every example I have presented within the previous chapter, often in the same order previously displayed. Whenever these files are updated, you will receive a notification to the email address used for the purchase of this guide. You would then execute the previous steps to update the files on your VM.

While you can view any of these scripts at any time within a text editor, I will not waste pages here displaying all of the code (which will change over time anyway). Instead, I will focus on each script and the functions of each option. I will start with the Update Tool and work through the rest in order of appearance in the Dock. The API Tool will be explained in the next chapter.

Update Tool

This may be the most vital custom script within the dock. There is an official Debian software updates application within the Activities menu, but I never use it. It only updates system software, and would never apply pending updates to most of our programs. Instead, we can apply all system and application updates with one script, which you previously downloaded. Launch the "Updates" shortcut from your Dock or the Activities menu and let it go to work. It will likely require your password and can take some time to finish. If you prefer to manually update everything, copy and paste the code into Terminal. This can be beneficial when you want to catch any errors which may be hidden from the script. The following displays the text within the script.

```
#!/usr/bin/env bash
sudo apt update
sudo apt upgrade -y
sudo apt update --fix-missing
sudo apt --fix-broken install
sudo apt autoremove -y
pipx upgrade-all
flatpak update
cd ~/Downloads/Programs/sherlock
git pull https://github.com/sherlock-project/sherlock.git
source SherlockEnvironment/bin/activate
sudo pip install -r requirements.txt 2>/dev/null
deactivate
cd ~/Downloads/Programs/blackbird
git pull https://github.com/p1ngul1n0/blackbird
source blackbirdEnvironment/bin/activate
sudo pip install -r requirements.txt 2>/dev/null
```

```
deactivate
cd ~/Downloads/Programs/WhatsMyName-Python
git pull https://github.com/C3n7ral051nt4g3ncy/WhatsMyName-Python.git
source wmnpythonEnvironment/bin/activate
sudo pip install -r requirements.txt 2>/dev/null
deactivate
cd ~/Downloads/Programs/eyes
git pull https://github.com/N0rz3/Eyes.git
cd Eyes
source eyesEnvironment/bin/activate
sudo pip install -r requirements.txt 2>/dev/null
deactivate
cd ~/Downloads
wget -N
https://github.com/ripmeapp/ripme/releases/latest/download/ripme.jar
chmod +x ripme.jar
cd ~/Downloads/Programs/Osintgram
git pull https://github.com/Datalux/Osintgram.git
source OsintgramEnvironment/bin/activate
sudo pip install -r requirements.txt 2>/dev/null
deactivate
cd ~/Downloads/Programs/EyeWitness
git pull https://github.com/ChrisTruncer/EyeWitness.git
cd Python/setup
sudo ./setup.sh
cd ~/Downloads
ver=$(dpkg --print-architecture)
wget https://github.com/owasp-
amass/amass/releases/latest/download/amass_Linux_"$ver".zip
mkdir ~/Downloads/Programs/Amass
unzip amass_Linux_"$ver".zip -d ~/Downloads/Programs/Amass/
cd Programs/Amass/amass_Linux_"$ver"/
mv * ~/Downloads/Programs/Amass
rm -r ~/Downloads/Programs/Amass/amass_Linux_"$ver"/
rm '/home/osint/Downloads/amass_Linux_arm64.zip'
cd ~/Downloads/Programs/Photon
git pull https://github.com/s0md3v/Photon.git
source PhotonEnvironment/bin/activate
sudo pip install -r requirements.txt 2>/dev/null
deactivate
cd ~/Downloads/Programs/Sublist3r
git pull https://github.com/aboul3la/Sublist3r.git
source Sublist3rEnvironment/bin/activate
sudo pip install -r requirements.txt 2>/dev/null
deactivate
cd ~/Downloads/Programs/theHarvester
git pull https://github.com/laramies/theHarvester.git
source theHarvesterEnvironment/bin/activate
sudo pip install -r requirements.txt 2>/dev/null
```

```
deactivate
cd ~/Downloads/Programs/Carbon14
git pull https://github.com/Lazza/Carbon14
source Carbon14Environment/bin/activate
sudo pip install -r requirements.txt 2>/dev/null
deactivate
cd ~/Downloads/Programs/metagoofil
git pull https://github.com/opsdisk/metagoofil.git
source metagoofilEnvironment/bin/activate
sudo pip install -r requirements.txt 2>/dev/null
deactivate
cd ~/Downloads/Programs/sherloq
git pull https://github.com/GuidoBartoli/sherloq.git
cd gui
source sherloqEnvironment/bin/activate
sudo pip install -r requirements.txt 2>/dev/null
deactivate
cd ~/Downloads/Programs/spiderfoot
git pull https://github.com/smicallef/spiderfoot.git
source spiderfootEnvironment/bin/activate
sudo pip install -r requirements.txt 2>/dev/null
deactivate
cd ~/Downloads/Programs/recon-ng
git pull https://github.com/lanmaster53/recon-ng.git
source recon-ngEnvironment/bin/activate
sudo pip install -r REQUIREMENTS 2>/dev/null
deactivate
cd ~/Downloads/Programs/Mr.Holmes
git pull https://github.com/Lucksi/Mr.Holmes
wget http://dl.google.com/dl/earth/client/current/google-earth-
stable_current_amd64.deb
sudo apt install -y ./google-earth-stable_current_amd64.deb
sudo rm google-earth-stable_current_amd64.deb
echo
read -rsp $'Press enter to continue. \n'
echo
```

Search Tool

This shortcut simply launches Firefox and navigates directly to the IntelTechniques online search tools. These are updated often and ready to simplify many of your online queries. More information about these search options is available later within this book. The following image displays the result upon launch.

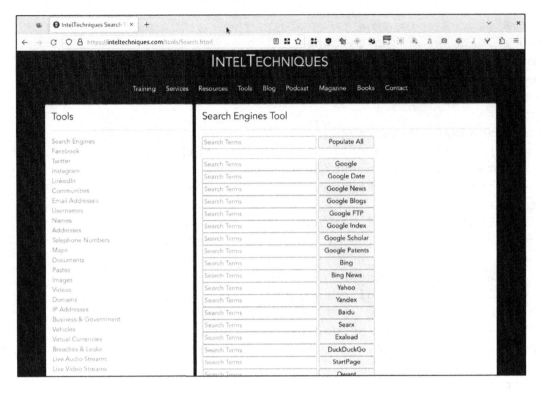

Video Tool:

Play Video: This selection prompts you to select a file on your device and plays it.

Convert Video: This converts a file to MP4 and opens the storage location of the file.

Extract Frames-All: This selection extracts every frame of a video as a PNG file and then displays the storage location of the new files.

Extract Frames-Seconds: This selection extracts one frame every second of a video as a PNG file and then displays the storage location of the new files.

Extract Audio: This selection extracts the audio file of a video; converts it to MP3; and then displays the storage location of the new file.

Rotate Video: This selection rotates a video counter-clockwise 90 degrees and then displays the storage location of the new file.

Merge Videos: This selection prompts you for two videos; merges them together; and then displays the storage location of the new file.

Remove Redundant Frames: This selection attempts to remove any frames identical to each previous frame and then displays the storage location of the new file.

YT-DLP Best Quality: This selection downloads the best quality video from a URL and then displays the storage location of the new file.

YT-DLP 1080: This selection downloads the best quality video from a URL, up to 1080p, and then displays the storage location of the new file.

YT-DLP 720: This selection downloads the best quality video from a URL, up to 720p and then displays the storage location of the new file.

YT-DLP 480: This selection downloads the best quality video from a URL, up to 480p and then displays the storage location of the new file.

YT-DLP Comments, Subs, & Info: Downloads comments, subtitles, and info.

YT-DLP Audio-Pure: This selection extracts the raw audio of a video from a URL480p and then displays the storage location of the new file.

YT-DLP Audio-MP3: This selection extracts the audio of a video from a URL; converts to MP3; and then displays the storage location of the new file.

YT-DLP MP4 Conversion: This selection downloads a video from a URL; converts it to MP4; and then displays the storage location of the new file.

Streamlink Stream: This opens a live stream; records the content; and displays it.

User Tool

Username-Sherlock: This selection prompts you for a username; queries it through Sherlock; and then displays the report.

Username-SocialScan: This selection prompts you for a username; queries it through SocialScan; and then displays the report.

Username-Blackbird: This selection prompts you for a username; queries it through Blackbird; and then displays the report.

Username-Maigret: This selection prompts you for a username; queries it through Maigret; and then displays the report.

Username-WhatsMyName: This selection prompts you for a username; queries it through WhatsMyName; and then displays the report.

Username-BDFR: This selection prompts you for a username; queries it through BDFR; and then displays the report.

Username-H8Mail: This selection prompts you for a username; queries it through H8Mail; and then displays the report.

Email-Holehe: This selection prompts you for an email address; queries it through Holehe; and then displays the report.

Email-SocialScan: This selection prompts you for an email address; queries it through SocialScan; and then displays the report.

Email-Eyes: This selection prompts you for an email address; queries it through Eyes; and then displays the results.

Email-GHunt: This selection prompts you for an email address; queries it through GHunt; and then displays the report.

Email-H8Mail: This selection prompts you for an email address; queries it through H8Mail; and then displays the report.

Hash-NameThatHash: This selection prompts you for a password hash; queries it through NameThatHash; and then displays the result.

Hash-SearchThatHash: This selection prompts you for a password hash; queries it through SearchThatHash; and then displays the result.

Image Tool

Gallery-DL: This selection prompts you for a URL; executes Gallery-DL; and displays the results.

RipMe: This selection launches the RipMe application.

Instaloader: This selection prompts you for an Instagram username; executes Instaloader against it; and displays the results folder.

Toutatis: This selection prompts you for an Instagram username; executes Toutatis against it; and displays the results file.

OsintGram: This selection is unique in our scripts. It prompts you for an Instagram username; then prompts you to select the type of data of interest; executes OsintGram against it; and displays the results folder.

Domain Tool

EyeWitness Single URL: This selection prompts you for a URL; executes EyeWitness; and displays the results storage folder.

EyeWitness Multiple URL: This selection prompts you for a list of URLs; executes EyeWitness on each; and displays the results storage folder.

HTTrack-Terminal: This selection launches HTTrack within Terminal.

HTTrack-Browser: This selection launches HTTrack within Firefox.

Waybackpy: This selection prompts you for a URL; executes Waybackpy; and displays the results file.

Waybackpack: This selection prompts you for a URL; executes Waybackpack; and displays the results storage folder.

Amass: This selection prompts you for a URL; executes Amass; and displays the results file.

Photon: This selection prompts you for a URL; executes Photon; and displays the results storage folder.

Sublist3r: This selection prompts you for a URL; executes Sublist3r; and displays the results file.

TheHarvester: This selection prompts you for a URL; executes TheHarvester; and displays the results within Firefox.

Carbon14: This selection prompts you for a URL; executes Carbon14; and displays the results file.

ChangeDetection: This selection prompts you for a URL; executes the ChangeDetection server; launches Firefox; and displays the frontend.

ArchiveBox: This selection prompts you for a URL; executes the ArchiveBox server; launches Firefox; and displays the frontend.

Metadata Tool

Exiftool File: This option prompts you to select a file; executes Exiftool to generate the metadata associated with the file; then displays a report of the result.

Exiftool Folder: This option prompts you to select a folder; executes Exiftool to generate the metadata associated with all files within the folder; then displays a report of all results.

Metagoofil: This option prompts you for a domain; executes Metagoofil against the domain; acquires any associated documents within the domain; and displays the folder containing the results. You could execute the previous option to extract all metadata from the found files.

mat2: This option prompts you to select a file; removes all metadata within the file; and saves a clean copy next to the original.

xeuledoc: This option prompts you for the entire URL of a Google document; executes xeuledoc against the URL; and displays the results.

Launch Sherloq: This option launches Sherloq.

Launch Mediainfo: This option launches Mediainfo.

Framework Tool

Launch Spiderfoot: This option launches the Spiderfoot server and the frontend through Firefox.

Launch Recon-ng: This option launches Recon-ng via Terminal.

Configure Mr. Holmes: This option launches the Mr. Holmes installation script. This is needed if you use the automated script presented later, or need to update the program.

Launch Mr. Holmes: This option launches Mr. Holmes via Terminal.

Launch sn0int: This option launches sn0int via Terminal.

Internet Archive Collection: This option prompts you for a collection name within the Internet Archive; downloads all content within that collection into a new folder; then displays the content of the folder.

Internet Archive Collection Filetype: This option prompts you for a collection name within the Internet Archive; prompts you for a file extension; downloads all content within that collection matching the file extension into a new folder; then displays the content of the folder.

Summary

You should now possess updated custom scripts which replicate much of the manual process presented throughout this guide. While these make it easy to conduct research using Linux applications, you should always understand all processes executing within the background.

CHAPTER TWELVE
OSINT VM APIs

An application programming interface (API) enables companies to offer their data and functionality to external third-party developers and within their own products. This allows customers (you) to communicate directly with a company's data without navigating to a web page, logging in, and clicking buttons. It also allows companies to deliver fancy content without the user needing to understand how databases and other technology works. When you are on Facebook and click a person's profile, Facebook is acquiring that data through a series of internal APIs and servers. This is true for most online services which have a search function. Think of the API as the protocol which delivers the text which gets turned into pretty pages in your browser. This is a very basic explanation, but enough to get us to some demonstrations.

Everything within this chapter will require an API key, which is similar to a password issued only to you. You will need to provide that key every time you request data from a service. At the end of this chapter, I will explain a custom script which can be modified to include your own API keys. Afterward, you will only need to supply the target data you are researching, and never enter the API key again. First, let's work through the process manually. We will start with People Data Labs.

People Data Labs (peopledatalabs.com)

I am a bit hesitant to present this resource because it seems too good to be true. This "people data" collection company offers 1,000 free queries of their premium data sets to anyone. We have seen other similar companies offer the same type of deal, such as Full Contact and Pipl, only to convert to a paid model without any type of trial. People Data Labs may be planning the same marketing strategy, but let's take advantage of the resource while it is available. You must create a free trial account at the website under the option of "Get API Key". I recommend providing an email address associated with a personal domain for best results. You want to appear as legitimate as possible. Your new account will provide a unique API key for your usage within the "Dashboard" of the page. Mine appeared similar to the following.

```
5c0ck097aa376bb7741a1022pl2222e3d45chs
```

Since this service does not provide a traditional search option, we must create URLs for our queries. This URL can be entered into a web browser or script. We will keep things simple for now. The following URL submits a query for "sean@peopledatalabs.com" in any browser.

```
https://api.peopledatalabs.com/v5/person/enrich?pretty=true&api_key=5c0
ck097aa376bb7741a1022pl2222e3d45chs&email=sean@peopledatalabs.com
```

The results are presented as text in JSON format. The following is a partial summary. The full result included four pages of details. I found the following most beneficial.

```
"full_name": "sean thorne",
"birth_year": "1990",
"linkedin_url": "linkedin.com/in/seanthorne",
"facebook_url": "facebook.com/deseanthorne",
"twitter_url": "twitter.com/seanthorne5",
"work_email": "sean@peopledatalabs.com",
"mobile_phone": "+14155688415",
"email address": "sthorne@uoregon.edu",
"email address": "sean@hallspot.com",
"education": "university of oregon",
```

While this is an obviously staged demo, the results are impressive. I have been able to convert a personal email address of a target into a full resume with social network profiles and cellular telephone number. We can also use that same API key to query by a telephone number. The following queries a U.S. number of 222-555-1212 with my test API key.

```
https://api.peopledatalabs.com/v5/person/enrich?pretty=true&api_key=5c0
ck097aa376bb7741a1022p12222e3d45chs&phone=+12225551212
```

The results are once again impressive. As an example, I provided a private direct office number of a previous government colleague. The full result would fill many pages, but I have provided a partial summary of the best parts below. I replaced any sensitive details with "REDACTED".

```
"full_name": "emily REDACTED", "female",
"linkedin_url": "linkedin.com/in/REDACTED",
"linkedin_username": "REDACTED",
"linkedin_id": "REDACTED",
"facebook_url": "REDACTED",
"personal_emails": "REDACTED@charter.net"
"industry": "law enforcement",
"job_title": "police officer",
"job_last_updated": "2022-08-29",
"location_metro": "st. louis, missouri",
"location_street_address": "REDACTED drive",
"location_postal_code": "REDACTED",
"location_geo": "REDACTED",
"location_last_updated": "2022-08-31",
"company": "illinois law enforcement board",
"school": "southern illinois university",
```

Within seconds, I identified the name, gender, LinkedIn profile, Facebook profile, personal email, profession, location, home address, secondary employment, and education details associated with my target telephone number. I even know when she last updated these details. I cannot overstate the value of this free trial. We can also query by social network profile, such as a X (Twitter), Facebook, or LinkedIn username. The following URL structure should be used with your own API key.

X (Twitter):
```
https://api.peopledatalabs.com/v5/person/enrich?pretty=true&api_key=5
c0ck097aa376bb7741a1022p12222e3d45chs&profile=www.twitter.com/inteltech
niques
```

Facebook:
```
https://api.peopledatalabs.com/v5/person/enrich?pretty=true&api_key=5
c0ck097aa376bb7741a1022p12222e3d45chs&profile=www.facebook.com/inteltec
hniques
```

LinkedIn:
```
https://api.peopledatalabs.com/v5/person/enrich?pretty=true&api_key=5
c0ck097aa376bb7741a1022p12222e3d45chs&profile=www.linkedin.com/inteltec
hniques
```

Let's take a look at the X (Twitter) result for my own name. It immediately identified the three locations which have been present within my X (Twitter) profile over the past decade, as follows. I am not aware of any other service which could replicate this data going back to 2009.

```
"st. louis, missouri, united states",
"washington, district of columbia, united states",
"new york, new york, united states"
```

I submitted a query for a Facebook target (facebook.com/zuck) and received the following partial result.

```
"full_name": "mark zuckerberg",
"birth_year": "1984",
"linkedin_url": "linkedin.com/in/mark-zuckerberg",
"facebook_url": "facebook.com/zuck",
"mobile_phone": "+16506447386",
"emails": "mzuckerb@fas.harvard.edu",
```

This is powerful data, especially considering a social network profile was the starting point. All of these queries can be completed within your web browser, but I hope you will consider the script which I will explain momentarily. Let's move on to reverse caller ID options.

Twilio (twilio.com)

I previously explained my usage of the Twilio Lookup service in other books as my favorite telephone number query option. However, it has one annoyance. Every time I want to search a number, I must log in to Twilio; confirm my 2FA; navigate to the Lookup option; and receive my results embedded into their web portal. That is not extremely difficult, but it does slow me down. That is why I only rely on their API for my everyday queries. Assuming my Twilio Account SID was 11111; my Twilio token was 22222; and my target U.S. number was 202-555-1212, the following command copied and pasted into Terminal would conduct my query.

```
curl -X GET 'https://lookups.twilio.com/v1/PhoneNumbers/+12025551212?
Type=caller-name&Type=carrier' \
-u 11111:22222 | python3 -mjson.tool
```

There is a lot to unpack here. Let's first understand where we get the information required. Once you have a Twilio trial established, the home page of your portal should display your "Account SID" and "Auth Token". The Auth Token is the same as an API key for our purposes. Next, let's work through that command, which is actually two lines, but prints as four for the book formatting.

`curl`: This is our command which will download data from a URL.
`-X`: This specifies a request method for communication with the server.
`GET`: This is the method we want to use (GET).
`'https://lookups.twilio.com/v1/PhoneNumbers/`: The URL.
`+12025551212`: This is our target telephone number.
`?Type=caller-name&Type=carrier'`: This requests name and carrier.
`\`: This inserts a new line without executing just yet.
`-u 11111:22222`: This is our Twilio Account SID and Auth Token.
`| python3 -mjson.tool`: This displays the data in an easier format to read.

The following is a redacted result when I searched one of my Google Voice numbers which has been leaked throughout various services.

```
"caller_name": "MICHAEL BAZZELL",
"caller_type": "CONSUMER",
"country_code": "US",
"carrier": {"mobile_country_code": "311", mobile_network_code":
"910","name": "Google (Grand Central) - Level3","type": "voip",
```

I find this impressive. Not only did Twilio identify the name of the VOIP account owner, it also identified the carrier (Google). I use this lookup tool every day. Twilio also offers additional Lookup services through third-party databases, but I no longer recommend them. These each withdraw an additional small fee from your trial balance, and some require a verified or "upgraded" account to function. I rarely receive any valuable data which was not already provided from the Twilio Lookup API.

Telnyx (https://refer.telnyx.com/refer/zrfmo)

If I could only search two telephone number services, this would be my second pick after Twilio. I found this service in late 2020 and I am impressed. The URL above offers a trial account with $10.00 in free queries. However, they are extremely scrutinous of new accounts. They will likely ask you how you will be using their service, and I encourage you to consider my Twilio registration tactics within the VoIP sections of my mobile or desktop guides. Once you do obtain a trial, it could last several years with minimal usage. Unfortunately, there is no way to submit a single URL as a query within a web browser. You must submit a request within Terminal, similar to Twilio, which includes several pieces of data. The following is the submission structure.

```
curl -X GET \
     --header "Content-Type: application/json" \
     --header "Accept: application/json" \
     --header "Authorization: Bearer XXXX" \
     "https://api.telnyx.com/v2/number_lookup/+12025551212?type=carrie
r&type=caller-name"
```

You could do this manually, replacing "XXXX" with your Telnyx API key (visible within your portal) and "2025551212" with your target number, but that is complicated. Instead, consider using my custom script, as explained at the end of this chapter. The following displays the redacted results of querying my Google Voice number through Telnyx.

```
    "country_code": "US",
    "national_format": "(618) xxx-xxxx",
    "phone_number": "+1618xxxxxxx",
    "fraud": null,
    "carrier": {
        "mobile_country_code": "",
        "mobile_network_code": "",
        "name": "Level 3/1",
        "type": "fixed line",
        "error_code": null,
        "normalized_carrier": ""
    "caller_name": "caller_name": Michael Bazzell,
    "nnid_override": null,
    "portability": {
        "lrn": "618xxxXXXX",
        "ported_status": "",
        "ported_date": "",
        "ocn": "6115",
        "line_type": "fixed line",
        "spid": "",
        "spid_carrier_name": "LEVEL 3 COMMUNICATIONS
        "spid_carrier_type": "",
        "city": "BELLEVILLE",
        "state": "Illinois"
    "valid_number": true,
```

CID Name (cidname.com)

Similar to Twilio and Telnyx, you must create a free trial account in order to use this service. You must provide an email address and telephone number, and I have used temporary addresses and Google Voice to bypass this restriction. Navigate to this website and register for a free account. Upon completion, you should receive an email with an API license key that is valid for approximately 100 free successful searches. You will not be charged for empty results. If you do not receive the API key via email, log in to your account and retrieve it from the portal. You are now ready to submit requests for caller ID information. To do this, you must formulate an API request in your browser which includes your authentication key and target number to search, as follows.

```
https://dip.cidname.com/2025551212/XX&output=raw&reply=none
```

This queries the domain (cidname.com), our authentication key (XX) and our target number (2025551212). I recommend saving the address of your first query as a bookmark or favorite if you plan to use this through a browser instead of our automated script presented in a moment. I currently only recommend CID Name if you are unable to create a Twilio or Telnyx account, or if you simply want another service to verify the confidence in a previous result. A search of my Google Voice number simply revealed "Michael Bazzell".

Caller ID Summary

Before reverse caller ID lookups, this information would have required a subpoena. In one recent scenario, a cellular telephone number searched on one of these services revealed the name "Jennifer S" in the result. During an interview with this subject, she disclosed that "Jennifer S" is how she identifies her account on the telephone bill that she shares with other family members. She was unaware that this data was sent to the receiving number. On many searches, the full name will be present. This should explain why you may be noticing a caller's name on your caller ID display when he or she is calling from a cellular number. There are many caller ID options available on the internet. Most services offer a free trial, even if it is not advertised. Adding a few dollars to each service may provide more queries than you will ever need. Take advantage of the free trials to determine which services work best in your investigations. Overall, reverse caller ID services can tell us more about a target telephone number than the standard people search engines. In many cases, you can immediately obtain data that would have required a subpoena just a few years prior. Always utilize all of the services in order to gauge the confidence in the results. If this is overkill for your needs, there are other web-based search engines that are easier to use.

Breach Directory (breachdirectory.org)

This service allows query of email address, username, password, domain, or hash value against popular known data breaches. I dedicate an entire guide with multiple chapters toward breach data, but let's focus only on publicly available content within this API here. First, you will need to obtain a free API key from Beach Directory's Rapid API repository located online at https://rapidapi.com/rohan-patra/api/breachdirectory. Once you have that, you would replace "XXXXX" in the following examples with your own key. The results for each are using the test data within each query. After the examples, I will offer some OSINT considerations and further investigation.

Breach Directory Email Search (Identifies Partial Passwords and Full Password Hashes):

```
wget --quiet \
     --method GET \
     --header 'X-RapidAPI-Key: XXXXX' \
     --header 'X-RapidAPI-Host: breachdirectory.p.rapidapi.com' \
     --output-document \
     -
'https://breachdirectory.p.rapidapi.com/?func=auto&term=123@gmail.com'
```

Breach Directory Email Result:

```
"success": true,
"has_password": false,
"sources": "Ledger.com"
"has_password": true,
   "password": "bart****",
   "sha1": "4a161083c434dd9aa89c0ba91ec37143a47662fd",
   "hash": "jMgujSG0GO4Gtu3gnM2KIfuVMphiLznm",
 "sources":
   "MyHeritage.com",
   "Paxful.com"
"has_password": true,
   "password": "pala*****",
   "sha1": "2234e9ff8c40dc43cd2ab13c4fc7efca12baf0bb",
   "hash": "sUi6A0IvcpETYOOJnFCAWOmVLI1ifjnz7Q==",
 "sources":
   "MyFitnessPal.com",
   "Dropbox.com",
   "Collection 1",
   "Myspace.com"
```

Breach Directory Username Search (Identifies Partial Passwords and Full Password Hashes):

```
"Username")
echo "Username: "
read data
wget --quiet \
    --method GET \
    --header 'X-RapidAPI-Key: XXXXX' \
    --header 'X-RapidAPI-Host: breachdirectory.p.rapidapi.com' \
    --output-document \
        - \
'https://breachdirectory.p.rapidapi.com/?func=auto&term=badguy143'
```

Breach Directory Username Result:

```
"success": true,
"found": 2,
"has_password": true,
  "password": "pala*****",
  "sha1": "2234e9ff8c40dc43cd2ab13c4fc7efca12baf0bb",
  "hash": "sUi6A0IvcpETYOOJnFCAWOmVLI1ifjnz7Q==",
"sources": "MyFitnessPal.com"
"has_password": true,
  "password": "p0ba**",
  "sha1": "f0b261eb28eb14fb9a493c9857eb4d107a1ad0a9",
  "hash": "zSR\/X0xA4lioFowltKCVw+nEIo1yOg==",
"sources": "Collection 1"
```

Breach Directory Password Search (Identifies Number of Identical Passwords Found):

```
wget --quiet \
```

```
    --method GET \
    --header 'X-RapidAPI-Key: XXXXX' \
    --header 'X-RapidAPI-Host: breachdirectory.p.rapidapi.com' \
    --output-document \
    -
'https://breachdirectory.p.rapidapi.com/?func=password&term=password1'
```

Breach Directory Password Result:

```
    "found": 587
```

Breach Directory Domain Search:

```
wget --quiet \
    --method GET \
    --header 'X-RapidAPI-Key: XXXXX' \
    --header 'X-RapidAPI-Host: breachdirectory.p.rapidapi.com' \
    --output-document \
    -
'https://breachdirectory.p.rapidapi.com/?func=domain&term=cnn.com'
```

Breach Directory Domain Result:

(This option was not working at the time of writing, but is expected to return.)

Breach Directory Hash Search:

```
wget --quiet \
    --method GET \
    --header 'X-RapidAPI-Key: XXXXX' \
    --header 'X-RapidAPI-Host: breachdirectory.p.rapidapi.com' \
    --output-document \
    -
'https://breachdirectory.p.rapidapi.com/?func=dehash&term=482C811DA5D5B
4BC6D497FFA98491E38'
```

Breach Directory Hash Result:

```
    "found": true
    "password": password123
```

Let's dig deeper into these results. In the first example with an email address, you saw the following.

```
    "password": "pala*****",
    "sha1": "2234e9ff8c40dc43cd2ab13c4fc7efca12baf0bb",
```

This service masks the password, but includes a SHA1 hash of it. This is a good opportunity to expose the entire password. If you were to enter an identified hash of "2234e9ff8c40dc43cd2ab13c4fc7efca12baf0bb" into the hash tool which was added to your VM during the previous chapters, the result would display the full unredacted password. If we were to enter that password into the "Password" option above, the service would tell us the total number of accounts which include that compromised password. For obvious reasons, I will not display all of that here. We also see the "sources" of this data. We now know that our target possessed accounts at Myspace, MyHeritage, and others.

Historical Whois Information

People who currently hide their identity behind "whoisguard" protections may not have always done so. If you want to dive deeper, an API can disclose details unavailable anywhere else. I present options for two services, one of which offers a free trial.

WhoisXMLAPI (whois.whoisxmlapi.com)

In order to use this service, you must first sign up for a free account and confirm your email address. Sign in to the new account and click your profile in the upper-right corner. Select the "My Products" option and make note of your API key. Mine was similar to "at_0vPfsSUdf1ZpiCxc5". You should now have 500 credits toward historical domain registration queries. The command is as follows.

```
curl 'https://whois-
history.whoisxmlapi.com/api/v1?apiKey=at_0vPfsSUdf1ZpiCxc5
&domainName=inteltechniques.com&mode=purchase' | python3 -mjson.tool
```

You could also access the URL directly within a browser at the following.

```
https://whois-
history.whoisxmlapi.com/api/v1?apiKey=at_0vPfsSUdf1ZpiCxc5
&domainName=inteltechniques.com&mode=purchase
```

This command queries the service; identifies the API key to be charged; provides the domain name to query (inteltechniques.com); and outputs the data in JSON format for easy reading. When conducted against my site, I received several pages worth of details. Most were notifications that I use a whois masking service, and that my true details were unavailable. However, the following was of most interest. In 2013, I did not immediately pay for the whois protection, and WhoisXMLAPI grabbed the following copy of my registration details.

```
"registrantContact": {
    "name": "Michael Bazzell",
    "street": "1700 E Broadway",
    "city": "Alton",
    "state": "Illinois",
    "postalCode": "62002",
    "email": "info@inteltechniques.com",
    "telephone": "16184628253",
```

Fortunately, that is not a sensitive physical address, the email does not forward to me, and the telephone number is not mine. However, you would have uncovered the true owner of my site if I were doing something bad. This service provides free credits to numerous additional domain-related services, but I find them to be no more valuable than the free web-based options previously discussed. The historical API is the only option I access.

Whoxy (whoxy.com)

Whoxy allows a free demo at https://www.whoxy.com/whois-history/demo.php, but you will be rate-limited if it detects abuse. They do not offer a free trial of their API, but the fees are minimal. The current price is $2.00 for 400 queries. The following is the URL structure.

```
https://api.whoxy.com/?key=XXXX&history=inteltechniques.com | python3 -
mjson.tool
```

The following response is very similar to the previous service.

```
"registrant_contact": {
      "full_name": "Michael Bazzell",
      "mailing_address": "1700 E Broadway",
      "city_name": "Alton",
      "state_name": "Illinois",
      "zip_code": "62002",
      "country_name": "United States",
      "email_address": "info@inteltechniques.com",
      "phone_number": "16184626666"
```

RapidAPI Telephone Search (rapidapi.com)

Since the original publication of this guide, several readers have expressed frustration at the difficulties obtaining free trial accounts from Twilio or Telnyx for telephone number lookups. I can relate. I have had my own issues with both companies, but currently possess funded accounts which are vital to my investigations. If you are unable (or unwilling) to acquire these services, there are still other options which may be almost as valuable. RapidAPI offers numerous API connections, many of which query caller ID databases.

The first step is to create an account at rapidapi.com. I was able to provide a burner email address and was not required to enter any payment information. I selected the free "Basic" plan. Next, we must subscribe to some beneficial API services through the site. I navigated to the following links; clicked the "Subscribe to Test" button at each; and chose the free tier for each. Once you have subscribed to any service, make note of your "X-RapidAPI-Key" visible within the testing area. You will need that to replicate my queries.

https://rapidapi.com/trestle-solutions-inc-trestle-solutions-inc-default/api/reverse-phone-api
https://rapidapi.com/trestle-solutions-inc-trestle-solutions-inc-default/api/smart-cnam-api
https://rapidapi.com/DataCrawler/api/eyecon
https://rapidapi.com/DataCrawler/api/phone-number-caller-id-lookup
https://rapidapi.com/DataCrawler/api/viewcaller
https://rapidapi.com/DataCrawler/api/truecaller4

Once you are subscribed to the free tier of an API service, you can formulate queries within Terminal to access the data. The following Terminal commands execute queries at each of the previous six services in the same order. Make sure to replace "2025551212" with your target telephone number and "XXX" with your own RapidAPI key. While all of these are configured for numbers within North America, many of these services offer queries through other countries. When present, change the "Code" from "1" (North America), to your targeted country code. Some services present a two-character "Country Code" within the command, such as "US", which can be modified. All of these services restrict your queries. Some restrict to 3 free lookups each month while others allow up to 100 (per free RapidAPI account).

```
curl --request GET --url 'https://reverse-phone-
api.p.rapidapi.com/3.1/phone?phone=2025551212' --header 'X-RapidAPI-
Host: reverse-phone-api.p.rapidapi.com'    --header 'X-RapidAPI-Key:
XXX'  | python3 -mjson.tool

curl --request GET --url 'https://smart-cnam-
api.p.rapidapi.com/3.1/cnam?phone=2025551212' --header 'X-RapidAPI-
Host: smart-cnam-api.p.rapidapi.com' --header 'X-RapidAPI-Key: XXX' |
python3 -mjson.tool

curl --request GET --url
'https://eyecon.p.rapidapi.com/api/v1/search?code=1&number=2025551212'
```

```
--header 'X-RapidAPI-Host: eyecon.p.rapidapi.com' --header 'X-RapidAPI-
Key: XXX' | python3 -mjson.tool

curl --request GET --url 'https://phone-number-caller-id-
lookup.p.rapidapi.com/api/v1/search?code=1&number=2025551212' --header
'X-RapidAPI-Host: phone-number-caller-id-lookup.p.rapidapi.com' --
header 'X-RapidAPI-Key: XXX' | python3 -mjson.tool

curl --request GET --url
'https://viewcaller.p.rapidapi.com/api/v1/search?code=1&number=20255512
12' --header 'X-RapidAPI-Host: viewcaller.p.rapidapi.com' --header 'X-
RapidAPI-Key: XXX' | python3 -mjson.tool

curl --request GET --url
'https://truecaller4.p.rapidapi.com/api/v1/getDetails?phone=2025551212&
countryCode=US' --header 'X-RapidAPI-Host: truecaller4.p.rapidapi.com'
--header 'X-RapidAPI-Key: XXX' | python3 -mjson.tool
```

The results will vary from each provider. The following is a redacted example from the first option. I queried a Google Voice number associated with my name.

```
"carrier": "Google (Grand Central) - Level3 - SVR",
    "is_prepaid": false,
    "is_commercial": false,
    "belongs_to": {"name": "Michael John Bazzell",
        "gender": "M",
        "type": "Person",
    "current_addresses": [
            "location_type": "Address",
            "street_line_1": "[REDACTED PREVIOUS ADDRESS]",
            "city": "[REDACTED]",
            "postal_code": ""[REDACTED]",
            "state_code": "CA",
            "country_code": "US",
            "is_active": false,
            "delivery_point": "SingleUnit",
    "historical_addresses": "[REDACTED PREVIOUS ADDRESS]",
```

I have added these search options to the API script which you may have previously downloaded. If you are using an older version of the script, which was created before adding this new section, it can be updated with the following Terminal commands within your OSINT VM. Make sure to modify the API keys within the script, as explained next.

```
cd ~/Documents/scripts
curl -O https://uvm:317@inteltechniques.com/osintvm/api.sh
chmod +x api.sh
```

If any of these services are no longer functioning, search through RapidAPI for a replacement. There are hundreds of additional OSINT-related APIs to choose from. Querying "OSINT", "Caller ID", "Telephone", and "Email" should get you started. Once you find an option of interest, change the drop-down menu in the right portion of the "playground" to "Shell" > "cURL" and copy the command presented. You can then modify this as needed to execute within Terminal or place within your script. I will also update this section and the corresponding script as I find new useful services.

API Script

You may feel overwhelmed with these options. I can relate. For many years, I stored bookmarks of all URLs and APIs within my browser, then modified the content of each URL with my new target telephone number or other data. This always felt sloppy and often wasted credits. In 2022, I finally created my own search script which can be executed from within our Linux OSINT VM. As long as you followed the steps in the previous chapter, you should already possess the API script in your VM, along with a shortcut within either your Activities menu or the Dock.

You can launch the API Tool script, but it will not function yet. Instead, locate the api.sh file within your Documents/scripts folder and open it within your text editor. You must provide your own API keys issued by any services which you wish to search. Replace any instance of "XXX" within the script with your own API keys, as previously explained. The following is a sample for the first two entries, displaying placeholder text of "XXX" for each API key which needs to be entered. Some entries, such as Twilio, require an account identifier, and those are represented with "YYY".

```
$opt1 )
data=$(zenity --entry --title "PDL Email" --text "Email Address")
mkdir ~/Documents/API/
cd ~/Documents/API/
curl
'https://api.peopledatalabs.com/v5/person/enrich?pretty=true&api_key=XX
XX&email='$data'' > $data-PDL.txt
open ~/Documents/API/
exit;;
$opt2 )
data=$(zenity --entry --title "PDL Phone" --text "Phone Number")
mkdir ~/Documents/API/
cd ~/Documents/API/
curl
'https://api.peopledatalabs.com/v5/person/enrich?pretty=true&api_key=XX
XX&phone='$data'' > $data-PDL.txt
open ~/Documents/API/
exit;;
```

Once you have added your own API keys, you can execute the script, which is labeled as "API Tool". Select the service you desire, then enter the target data when prompted. The results will be saved to a text file which will be placed in the "API" folder within your "Documents" folder. The folder should open upon completion. As a final reminder, you must replace each occurrence of "XXX" and "YYY" within my script with your actual license keys or credentials if you want to use this technique. There are unlimited API services out there which provide valuable data unavailable within any web browser. When you find the next amazing API, hopefully you now have the ability to add it to your custom scripts.

CHAPTER THIRTEEN
OSINT VM MAINTENANCE

Once you have your custom OSINT Linux VM created and configured, you must maintain it. This includes applying frequent updates, shrinking to avoid data bloat, and proper clones or exports. I will assume that you have applied all of the previous chapters and now possess at least two VMs within your VM client software. One should be titled "Debian Stock" which only contains a pure Debian install, and the other should be titled "OSINT VM" which possess all of the configuration up to this point in the guide.

Updates

I prefer to launch the "OSINT VM" machine weekly and execute the Updates Tool script from the Dock. This applies all system and application updates. I then close this VM so it is ready to be shrunk and cloned for the next investigation. I launch the "Debian Stock" VM once monthly and then open Terminal to execute "`sudo apt update && sudo apt upgrade`" to keep it updated. This keeps my stock VM current in the event I want to rebuild my OSINT VM or make a new copy for another task. Once all of my VMs are updated, I can shrink, clone, and export them however desired for my investigations.

I present the next several pages of tutorials for each VM client in order of UTM, VirtualBox, and then VMWare Workstation Pro. Within each set, I explain the proper steps for shrinking, cloning, and then exporting your new OSINT VM. Much of this content will be redundant to the techniques within previous chapters, but these will all apply directly to our OSINT VM instead of other operating systems. While your OSINT VM is shut down, consider the following.

UTM OSINT VM Shrinking

The hard drive space of your UTM Debian OSINT VM will keep growing unnecessarily. When you apply updates within the VM, all of the original data is somewhat preserved, even deleted content. Fortunately, UTM makes the shrinking process easy. While your OSINT VM is shut down, select it within the main UTM window. Go to the Settings for that VM and select the VirtIO drive of your operating system within the left menu. Click the "Reclaim Space" button, confirm the option, and click "Save" when complete. You will see the size decrease if free space was available. I do this after every update to my OSINT VM.

UTM OSINT VM Clones

While your OSINT VM is shut down and the VM window is closed, you will see options within the main UTM application for the selected VM in the upper-right. Let's focus on the "Clone selected VM" option, which appears similar to an icon with two documents. Clicking this presents an option to make a full clone. This allows us to preserve our original OSINT VM and make copies whenever we want to conduct an investigation. I selected my "OSINT VM" machine; clicked the icon; confirmed the operation; right-clicked the new clone; selected "Edit"; renamed it to "OSINT VM 2024.02.01"; and clicked "Save". The result can be seen in the image below.

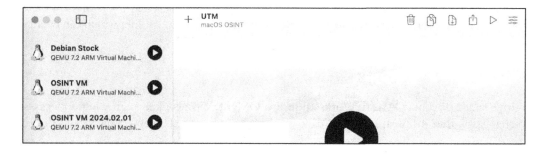

UTM OSINT VM Exports

The "Share Selected VM" option allows us to export an entire VM within a ".utm" file for easy archiving or sharing. The dialogue will prompt you to choose the export location. You can now provide this file as part of the discovery process, or save it off-site as a backup of your Stock Debian and OSINT VM machines. I selected my "OSINT VM" machine; clicked the Share button; selected my Downloads folder; and clicked "Save".

VirtualBox OSINT VM Shrinking

The hard drive space of your VirtualBox OSINT VM also keeps growing unnecessarily. When you make changes within the VM, all of the data is somewhat preserved, even outdated and deleted content. Unfortunately, VirtualBox does not make the shrinking process as easy as UTM for macOS. To replicate, we will take a few steps within the OSINT VM. First, apply any pending updates; remove any undesired files; and empty the trash. Then, execute the following within Terminal.

```
dd if=/dev/zero of=zerofillfile bs=1M
```

This procedure technically filled your VM completely with blank space, which may not sound ideal. With the VM turned off, open Terminal within the Linux host (or Command Prompt within a Windows host) and navigate to the folder containing the VM file you want to shrink. For me, this was the following.

```
cd ~/VirtualBox\ VMs/OSINT\ VM/
```

You must then execute a Terminal command which compacts the "vdi" file within the VM folder. For me, the command was the following.

```
VBoxManage modifymedium disk OSINT\ VM.vdi --compact
```

You will see the size decrease if free space was available.

VirtualBox OSINT VM Clones

Once you have your OSINT VM configured and ready for use, you should clone it and work from the copy. This way, the original VM stays uncontaminated. Within the VirtualBox client, while the VM is shut down, right-click on the OSINT VM; select "Clone"; provide a name such as "OSINT VM 2024.02.01"; click "Next"; and click "Clone". You now have two identical VMs, each in their own data folders. If you were to work within the cloned copy during your investigation and do damage, you still have the original OSINT VM in a perfect state.

VirtualBox OSINT VM Exports

You can preserve a specific state of a VM within VirtualBox by exporting the entire session. You can now provide this file as part of the discovery process, or save it off-site as a backup of your Stock Debian and OSINT VM machines. You have two options. I selected my "OSINT VM" machine; right-clicked on the OSINT VM while it was shut down; and selected "Show in File Manager". I then copied this folder to an external drive. This does not require any export or creation of a new file. You could also export the entire VM into a single file. While the VM was shut down, I selected "File" > "Export Appliance"; selected my OSINT VM; and clicked "Next", "Next", then "Export". This created a new file within my Documents folder which can later be imported into any instance of VirtualBox.

VMWare Workstation Pro Shrinking

The hard drive space of your VMWare Workstation Pro OSINT VM also keeps growing unnecessarily. When you make changes within the VM, all of the data is somewhat preserved, even outdated and deleted content.

Surprisingly, VMWare makes the shrinking option within their software quite easy. While the VM is shut down, select it within the VMWare Workstation Pro menu and click "VM" in the upper menu, then "Settings". Select the hard disk option in the left and click the "Compact Disk" button to the right. This will shrink the VM and you will see the size decrease if free space was available. I do this after every update to my OSINT VM.

VMWare Workstation Pro Clones

Once you have your OSINT VM configured and ready for use, you should clone it and work from the copy. This way, the original VM stays uncontaminated. Within the VMWare client, while the VM is shut down, right-click on the OSINT VM; select "Manage" then "Clone"; click "Next" three times; provide a name such as "OSINT VM 2024.02.01"; click "Next"; and click "Finish". You now have two identical VMs, each in their own data folders. If you were to work within the cloned copy during your investigation and do any damage, you still have the original OSINT VM in a perfect state.

VMWare Workstation Pro Exports

You can preserve a specific state of a VM within VMWare Workstation Pro by making a copy of the entire VM folder while a VM is shut down. Right-click the desired VM within VMWare Workstation Pro and select "Open VM Directory". Copy this folder to any other directory. You can now provide this VM as part of the discovery process, or save it off-site as a backup of your VMs.

Desktop Environments

In an earlier chapter, we installed Debian and selected Gnome as our desktop environment. This is always my preference, but it may not be yours. It appears very similar to Ubuntu and Pop!_OS, and has a very clean (and minimal) feel. Even if you did not select additional desktop environments during the initial installation, you can always add them later through Terminal with the following.

Cinnamon: `sudo apt install task-cinnamon-desktop -y`
KDE (Plasma): `sudo apt install task-kde-desktop -y` (press Enter twice during installation)
LXDE: `sudo apt install task-lxde-desktop -y`
LXQt: `sudo apt install task-lxqt-desktop -y`
MATE: `sudo apt install task-mate-desktop -y`

After installation, log out, and then click your username. Before entering your password, click the settings icon in the lower right area. It will present a new menu of options. You can select any desktop environment, then continue the login process. Unless you change any selection, Debian will always default to the last chosen option. I should state again that I prefer Gnome for our purposes, and all tutorials within this guide have been specifically tweaked for that desktop. I do not install any of these additional options. There is no harm in experimenting with the alternative desktop environments. You may find one which works better for you than me. Some mimic Microsoft Windows more than traditional Unix-style desktops, and vice-versa. Your ultimate OSINT VM should fit best to your needs.

Summary

Hopefully, you now have three Linux VMs in pristine condition. One is your stock Debian instance which can always be used to clone when trying new things or rebuilding a VM. The OSINT VM contains all of your configurations which should never be used for investigations. The third is a clone of the OSINT VM which is ready for an active investigation. Keep your originals clean and only use them for updates. Make clones of it for each investigation, but be sure to shrink them before cloning. Also, make sure you have a safe backup copy stored outside your primary device. Most importantly, understand the steps you have taken. Expect problems! However, most of the time, a future update will fix things which currently do not work. When something is not functioning properly, move on to the next tool.

CHAPTER FOURTEEN
OSINT VM AUTOMATED BUILD

While this guide has provided the steps to build your own OSINT VM, you may still feel overwhelmed with the effort. Therefore, the following command might be the most valuable text within this book for some readers.

```
wget https://uvm:317@inteltechniques.com/osintvm/install.sh && chmod +x
install.sh && ./install.sh
```

This command downloads a custom script called install.sh; makes the file executable; and then launches it. This script includes every Linux configuration, installation, download, and customization mentioned throughout this book, beginning at "Debian Customization" in Chapter Eight. After you build your Debian VM by manually conducting the steps previously explained, create a new clone of your Debian Stock VM and launch this command from within Terminal. You will be prompted to enter your password and confirm a dialogue, but the rest happens behind the scenes. After completion, you possess the same VM which was built during this entire book. Note that Firefox and Tor Browser will launch and close on their own during this process.

You may feel frustrated with me. You may wonder why I did not start the book with this script. While I rely on this single script often, it is cheating. Running a single command and achieving a complete VM is convenient and time-saving, but it also eliminates any need to understand the processes. I believe the education received while manually building an OSINT VM is more valuable than the final product itself. However, this automated script simplifies the process when we need to quickly create another OSINT VM. It also allows me to apply updates as needed from my end. You could launch this script a year after reading this book and immediately apply all updates and changes which have occurred since publication.

An ideal scenario would be that you are already familiar with the VM creation and configuration process, but you do not have an updated OSINT VM from which to clone. You have a Debian Stock VM, but no OSINT applications. Entering this command within the Terminal of a cloned VM should build your OSINT VM in about 15 minutes.

If you look at the script after download, which should be available within your "Home" folder inside your Debian install, you will see that it appears very similar to the commands entered throughout this book. This new script is simply executing each line as we did manually. While it can be a valuable time saver, you also risk missing any errors which occur during execution. I encourage you to ignore this script until you have confidence in your ability to create your virtual machine manually. I find it more satisfying to use a VM which I created myself instead of one generated by an automated script, but I want you to have options. If this script should fail on your VM, revert to the manual methods in order to identify the issue.

I hope I have sparked your interest for proper OSINT investigative environments and Linux applications.

CHAPTER FIFTEEN
ANDROID VIRTUALIZATION

For several years, online researchers have been navigating through various social networking websites for information about individuals. Whether it was older sites such as Friendster and Myspace, or current networks such as X (Twitter) and Facebook, we have always flocked to our web browsers to begin extracting data. Times have changed. Today, an entire generation of social network users rarely touch a traditional computer. They operate completely from a cellular telephone or tablet. Many of the networks through which individuals engage will only operate on a mobile device. Services such as Snapchat, Tinder, and TikTok do not allow a user to access content from a traditional web browser. As this shift occurs, investigators must transition with it. Our preparation is not complete until we have disposable Android environments in place.

This chapter will focus on the huge amount of information available through mobile platforms that is not accessible through a web browser. I will explain a method of emulating a portable device within a traditional computer. Before we dive into the nuts and bolts of making things work, we should discuss why this is the way to go. In my investigations, documentation is my primary reason for launching a simulated mobile device within my computer operating system. If I conducted my investigation on an actual smartphone, documenting my findings can be difficult. Mobile screen captures only cover a small amount of visible content. Extracting any captured images can be a hassle. Referencing my findings within a final report can become very tedious. When using Android emulation within my traditional computer, I can easily create numerous screen captures, record a video of my entire investigation, and paste my results directly into the report.

Privacy and security are also important reasons to consider emulation versus directly investigating from a portable device. I have seen many law enforcement investigators conduct a search or use an app directly from their personal or work phones. This opens that device to scrutiny and discovery. An attorney could rightfully request a copy of the investigator's phone in order to conduct an independent forensic analysis. That would make most people nervous. Additionally, if I encounter malicious software or a virus from my portable device, it could affect all future investigations using that hardware. Emulation will remedy both of these situations.

The idea of Android emulation (or virtualization) is to recreate the mobile operating experience within an application on your computer. This application will execute in the same manner that your web browser, word processor, or email client would open. It will have the exact same appearance as if you were staring at a telephone or tablet. Any actions that you take within this emulated device will not affect anything else on your computer. Think of it as an encapsulated box, and nothing comes in or gets out, very similar to our Linux VM previously explained. A great feature of emulation is that you can create unlimited virtual devices. You could have one for every investigation in order to prevent any contamination.

Some readers will question why I chose to explain Android emulation instead of iPhone. The most obvious reason is the number of options. I will explain software solutions for recreating the Android environment on your computer. An iPhone simulator will only function on Apple computers and has very limited features. The Android techniques will work on any major operating system. Additionally, we can create Android virtual machines that possess all original functionality. An iPhone simulator will not connect to most applications and features, and provides almost no value to the OSINT investigator.

The following pages differ greatly from previous editions of this book. Even if you have previous Android machines functioning for your investigations, please read through this chapter. I believe you will find alternative ways of Android virtualization which could benefit your investigations. Also, the software used throughout this chapter will display different wording within various operating systems. The menus and windows referenced here were all tested on macOS, and will have slight variations on Windows and Linux hosts. Use the overall methods to your advantage instead of scouring for an exact replica of my configuration. By the time you read this, new versions of all applications will display slight modifications from my examples.

The previous editions of this book focused heavily on Genymotion and VirtualBox for Android virtualization. These cross-platform applications allowed us to easily create virtual Android environments which appeared as magical mobile devices on our screens. **I no longer recommend Genymotion or VirtualBox as our best options.** I have several reasons, as outlined in the following.

- Genymotion requires a user account in order to access your Android virtual machine. This requires an email address and includes tracking of your activity.
- Genymotion has limited their free option for personal use. Relying on their software during professional investigations may violate their terms of service.
- Genymotion continues to make the free version difficult to locate and download.
- Genymotion relies on VirtualBox for all virtualization. This introduces additional layers of complexity, troubleshooting, and limitations.
- VirtualBox does not currently support Apple M1 or later processors, and runs poorly on Apple Intel machines. This prevents Genymotion from running on newer Apple hardware.
- Both Genymotion and VirtualBox only support x86 virtual machines, which prevents native ARM virtualization for those with machines which support ARM builds.
- Both options are inferior to native Android virtualization.
- Many mobile applications specifically block Genymotion, VirtualBox, or other x86 builds.

Instead, we will build our Android devices without the need for an account through Genymotion or Google. We can stay fairly anonymous and rely on cross-platform software provided by the creator of Android.

Android Studio (developer.android.com/studio)

This software was created and is maintained by Google, the maker of Android. It is designed for Android developers who need to create and test mobile applications within a desktop environment before applying them to actual mobile devices. While this software has way more features than we need as online investigators, I believe it has the best Android virtualization option. It can be installed with the following commands (assuming macOS users have Brew installed and Windows users configured Chocolatey, as previously explained).

- Linux: `sudo snap install android-studio`
- macOS: `brew install --cask android-studio`
- Windows: `choco install androidstudio`

Once you have it installed, you must launch and configure the applications. This will appear slightly different on each operating system and within each major software revision. However, the following steps which I took on my macOS OSINT machine should assist.

- Launch Android Studio.
- Do not import any settings but allow any default downloads.
- Choose "Don't Send" for analytics, then click "Next" in the Welcome Wizard.
- Choose the "Standard" option and click "Next".
- Select your desired appearance, click "Next", accept both agreements, and click "Finish".

Android Studio will download numerous items, which may take some time. If you receive any download errors, choose the "Retry" option. Once everything has been successfully downloaded, click "Finish". This should launch the new application window, and the following should be performed.

- Click "New Project", then "Next" to confirm "Empty Activity".
- Provide a name for your application (I chose "OSINT"), and click "Finish".
- Allow all additional default downloads and click "Finish".

The application will navigate to the main developer panel, and you should see several downloads continue in the lower right. Allow everything to complete before proceeding. You should then see a vertical bar on the right titled "Device Manager". Clicking this should present a virtual device, which may be titled similar to "Pixel_3a". This will likely contain the latest version of Android, but we should also explore other options. Click the "Create device" button, as seen in Figure 15.01. This allows you to select from many virtual Android options. I chose to add a Pixel 6 Pro to my available devices, and selected the most recent API level, which can also be seen in Figure 15.01.

Figure 15.01: The Android Studio Device Manager.

Before we launch our first device, we should consider an important adjustment. Since Android Studio is targeted toward developers, virtual Android devices launch within the developer portal. I prefer my devices to launch within their own window, so I make the following configuration change in the "Preferences" or "Settings" menu within Android Studio.

- Click on "Tools" then "Emulator".
- Disable "Launch in a tool window" and click "OK".

Now choose your desired device and click the arrow button to launch. You should see a device similar to that in Figure 15.02 (left). You are now running a virtual version of Android within your desktop environment. Next, let's configure the device for future OSINT usage.

- Remove any desired applications from the home screen by clicking, holding, and dragging up.
- Launch the Chrome browser and deny any features.
- Search for F-Droid and visit the F-Droid site.
- Click "Download F-Droid" and confirm request.
- When finished, click the "Open" option and then "Settings" when prompted.
- Enable "Allow from this source" and click "Install" then "Open". Allow notifications.
- Within F-Droid, search for "Aurora Store" and select it.
- Click "Install" then "Settings"; enable "Allow from this source"; and click "Install".
- Click the circle "Home" button within the floating sidebar.

You should now see two additional applications within your home screen. Let's open Aurora Store and make the following configuration changes.

- When prompted, select the Terms of Service box and click "Accept".
- Click "Next" four times to navigate through the settings.
- Click "Grant" next to each option and "Allow" when prompted.
- Enable any access menu and use the back button until all options show "Granted".
- Click "Finish" then "Anonymous".

Aurora Store should now connect you to their proxy for the Google Play Store. You should be able to download any applications as you would on any other device. If you are on a VPN, you may be blocked from this connection. During my own configuration, I had to connect to a dedicated VPN IP address to complete the connection. Once you are within Aurora, install an application. I searched "Facebook"; chose the first option; clicked "Install"; then confirmed my choice. I can now open the Facebook mobile application within a secure virtual environment from my desktop computer.

Let's digest these steps. You installed F-Droid which is an open-source package installer for Android. It allowed us to install Aurora Store which is an anonymous replacement for the Google Play Store. Through Aurora Store, you installed Facebook to ensure the ability to add apps. You authorized all applications to install additional apps on your device, which should only be a one-time requirement. You can now launch Aurora Store and install practically any app desired. During this writing, I installed the following apps and moved them to my home screen, as visible in Figure 15.02 (right).

Facebook	Messenger	WhatsApp	Instagram	X (Twitter)	Snapchat	Kik
TikTok	TextNow	Truecaller	Bumble	Telegram	YouTube	Tinder

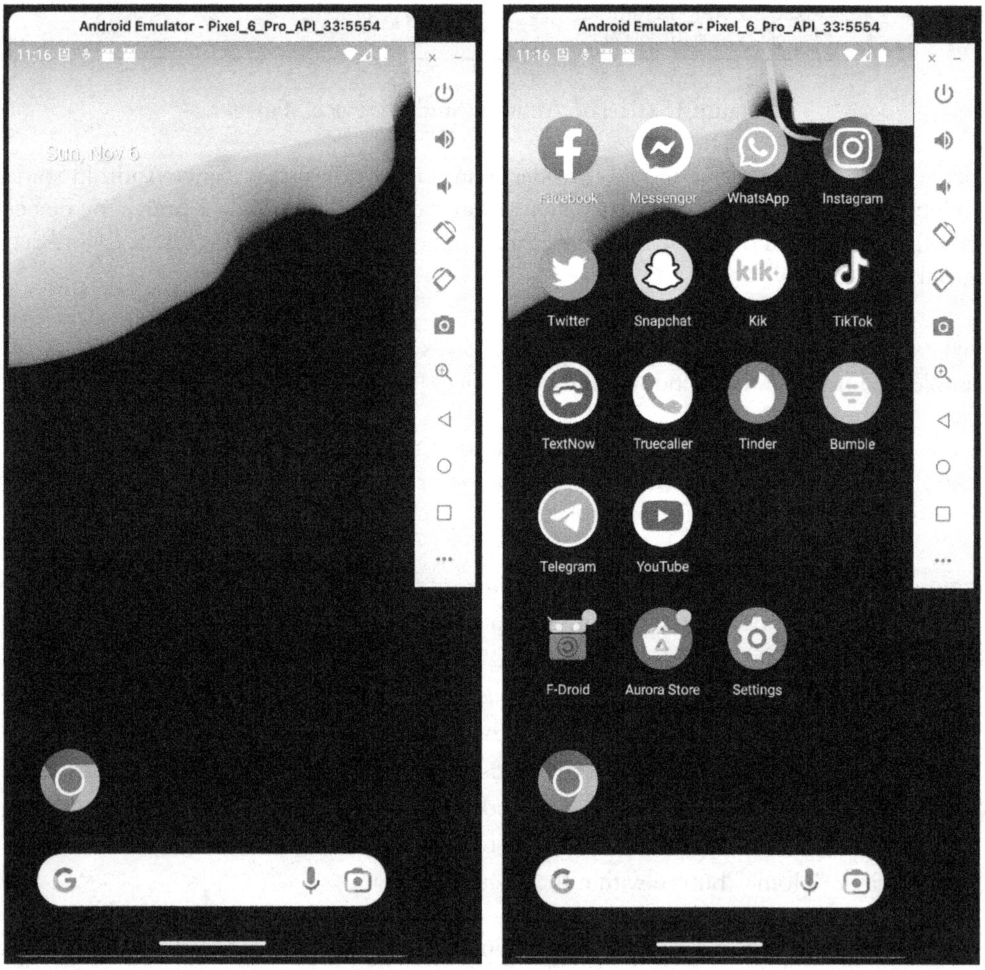

Figure 15.02: Virtual device screens within Android Studio.

Navigating these screens is identical to a physical device. However, controlling them from a mouse and keyboard may take some practice. You can click the circle on the floating bar to return to your home screen at any time. The square button allows you to browse through open apps and swipe them up to close them. The left arrow takes you back one step within an app. Always click and hold an app before moving it, and dragging the screen right or left navigates between home spaces.

Since we are working with a virtual device on a computer screen, there are a few nuances which should be discussed. By default, internet access is gained through your host computer. If you ever find that applications seem to stop communicating, check and be sure that "Wi-Fi" is enabled. I have experienced unexplained internet outages which were corrected by re-enabling Wi-Fi under "Settings". The easiest way to turn the device off is to click the power button on the top of the floating bar. Go ahead and turn the device off so we can explore cloning options. Once the screen is black, click the "X" in the floating bar and return to the Android Studio application.

Click the three dots next to your device, as seen in Figure 15.01. Click "Duplicate" and call the device "OSINT Primary". Click "Finish" and launch the device. You can now make any changes to this virtual Android device without impacting your original OSINT copy. You can create a new Android device for every investigation, as explained within Chapter Two about virtual machines. Once you have a device with all desired apps, you can clone it without the need to replicate your work. You can also delete devices from within this menu. Clicking "Show on disk" allows you to locate the machine on your drive and archive the folder for later use.

Relaunch a device and click the three horizontal dots at the bottom of the floating bar. This opens the extended controls for your Android device. The Location tab allows you set a location which will be announced to any application which wants to know it. This allows you to spoof your location to apps which only provide nearby content, such as dating apps. Figure 15.03 (left) displays this menu while Figure 15.03 (right) shows the Maps app as it confirmed my spoofed location.

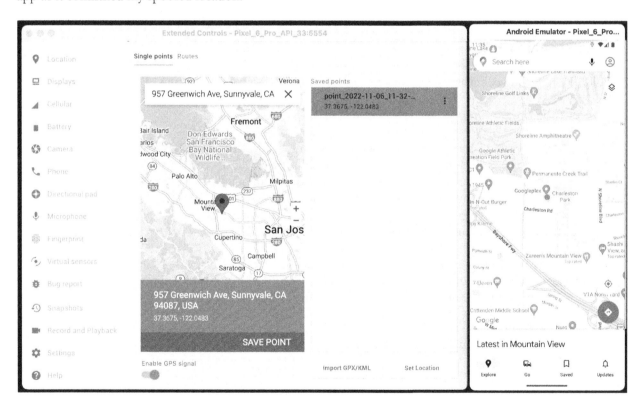

Figure 15.03 Location settings and confirmation.

Once you have your Android device configured exactly as desired, you can make a clone via the Android Studio application. While powered down, select your device from the Device Manager; click the three dots to expand the menu, and choose "Duplicate". You can also delete any unneeded devices on this screen.

Finally, once you have your desired Android virtual machine configured, you may want to launch it without the need to open Android Studio; select the device; execute the environment, power-on the operating system, and close the main application. Fortunately, we can do all of this within Terminal, and launch ONLY the Android devices without any other clutter. The following commands are based on my macOS M1 OSINT host, but it should be easy to modify the paths and executable names using the overall lessons from Chapter Six. The following switch to the Android Studio directory and list all configured Android machines.

- `cd ~/Library/Android/sdk/emulator/`
- `./emulator -list-avds`

The result appears similar to the following.

`Pixel_6_Pro_API_33`

We can now launch that machine with the following quick-boot command, which will also save any changes.

- `./emulator -avd Pixel_6_Pro_API_33`

The following will cold-boot the machine as if it were fully rebooted from an off state, and save changes.

- `./emulator -avd Pixel_6_Pro_API_33 -no-snapshot-load`

We can modify this command to launch the machine, but not save any changes, with the following command.

- `./emulator -avd Pixel_6_Pro_API_33 -no-snapshot-save`

Finally, the following command will launch the device as it was on first boot, erasing all custom data.

- `./emulator -avd Pixel_6_Pro_API_33 -wipe-data`

What do I do? I created a script with these desired options and devices. However, I mostly execute machines with "`./emulator -avd Pixel_6_Pro_API_33`". This preserves my current state and loads the quickest. When I want to erase a machine and start over, I can do so without the GUI interface, or researching any commands. The text from my script is located at the following URL on my website.

https://inteltechniques.com/data/osintbook11/android.txt

Use the lessons from Chapters Four and Six to make this script executable within Linux or macOS. Use the batch file demonstration from Chapter Six to make this data work for Windows. Launching this script presents the following, and will only work if you also created a Pixel 6 Pro with API 33.

```
1) List Devices
2) Launch Pixel 6 (Quick-Changes Saved)
3) Launch Pixel 6 (Quick-Changes Not Saved)
4) Launch Pixel 6 (Cold-Changes Saved)
5) Launch and Wipe Pixel 6
Selection:
```

After you have your desired location configured and you have confirmed accuracy, you can start to put this feature to work. The following tutorials explain how I use various mobile applications within my OSINT investigations, especially location-aware applications. This could never be a complete documentation. Any time you encounter a target using a service which possesses a mobile application, you should consider installing that app to see what further details you can obtain about the target's profile.

Facebook/Messenger/Instagram: The Facebook app on Android will appear similar to a compressed view of a standard profile page. The benefit of the mobile app is the ability to check into places. After launching the app and logging in for the first time, allow Facebook to access your location (which is spoofed). When you click the "Check In" option, Facebook will present businesses near your current spoofed location. If you choose a location, and create a post on your timeline, Facebook will verify that you were there. I have used this when I needed to portray that I was somewhere I was not. This method can help you establish credibility within your pseudo profile. I also once helped a victim confuse her ex-husband with this technique. I posted from her Facebook account leaving my spoofed location enabled. After wasting his time going to random places trying to find her, he began doubting the information that he uncovered about her whereabouts.

WhatsApp: WhatsApp Messenger is an instant messaging app for smartphones that operates under a subscription business model. In addition to text messaging, WhatsApp can be used to send images, videos, and audio media messages to other users. Locations can also be shared through the use of integrated mapping features. You will need to create an account and provide a telephone number for verification. This number can be a cellular, landline, or VOIP number. After you have an account, you can communicate directly with any target using the service. I have found that several of my targets refuse to converse over traditional text messaging, but freely text over WhatsApp. If you conduct any covert operations, you should have this set up ahead of time.

X (Twitter): The first time that you use X (Twitter) within your Android environment, you might be asked if you want to share your location. While I usually discourage this type of activity, sharing your spoofed location can have many benefits. Similar to Facebook, you can make yourself appear to be somewhere which you are not. You may want to confuse your target. If you know that he or she will be monitoring your social networks using the techniques in later chapters, this method should throw them off and be misleading.

Snapchat: Much of the content within Snapchat is only visible within a mobile environment. Having access to the mobile app is vital. If you simply want to search public posts, we will tackle that via a traditional browser later in the book.

TikTok: While I will explain investigation techniques for this network much later in the book, having the mobile app ready is important. The TikTok website does not currently allow native keyword search, but the mobile app does. Preparation now will provide great benefit later.

TextNow: If you conduct online investigations and communicate with a suspect, it is very possible that you may be asked to send or receive a standard SMS text message. Since your virtual device does not possess a cellular connection, and it is not assigned a telephone number, there are no native opportunities for this activity. However, you can install TextNow, which allows you to send and receive SMS text messages. With this setup, you can conduct all of your communications through the virtual device, and preserve the evidence within a single archive.

Truecaller: A later chapter explains reverse caller ID services and how they can identify subscriber information associated with telephone numbers. There are several additional services that only support mobile use. Truecaller is a powerful service which allows search of unlimited cellular and landline numbers in order to identify the owners. Other options include Mr. Number and Showcaller.

Tinder: This dating app relies on your location in order to recommend people in your area that want to "hook up". It can use your Facebook account associated with your device or a VOIP telephone number for the login credentials. The preferences menu will allow you to specify the gender, age range, and distance of the targeted individuals. Most people use this to identify members of their sexual preference within one mile of their current location. The users can then chat within the app. I have used this to identify whether a target was at home or another location. During one investigation, I set my GPS in my Android emulator to my target's residence. I then searched for men his age within one mile and confirmed he was at home. If I did not get his profile as a result, I could change my GPS to his work address or favorite bar. When I received his profile in the results, I knew that he was near the spoofed location. I could do all of this from anywhere in the world.

Contact Exploitation: Many applications allow (and encourage) you to locate your friends' profiles within the service by their email address or telephone number. This is one of the most reliable ways which apps can keep you within their ecosystem. As investigators, we can use this to our advantage. Apps such as CashApp allow you to enter your friends' telephone numbers and it will display their complete profile. You could replicate this with any online target. Sometimes, the only way I can identify a telephone number's owner is to search it via mobile applications. I have found that adding my unknown target's cellular telephone number to the Android phone's address book will often obtain the following information relative to the target.

- Associated Facebook accounts (name) from the "Find Friends" feature.
- Google Play purchases and reviews (interests) from the Google Play Store.
- Associated X (Twitter) accounts (name) from the "Find Friends" feature.
- WhatsApp usernames and numbers (contact) registered to the cell number.

Basically, entering a target's phone numbers and email addresses into your address book on an Android emulator forces many apps to believe that you are friends with the person. It overrides many authority protocols that would otherwise block you from seeing the connection from the real details to the connected profiles. Figure 15.04 displays a redacted result of one attempt. I launched "Contacts" from within the Android applications and added a cellular number of a target with any name desired. I then launched Facebook and clicked the "Find Friends" option. Facebook immediately identified an account associated with the number entered.

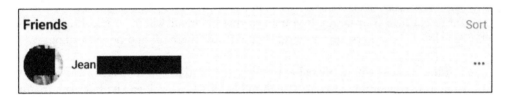

Figure 15.04: A Facebook "friend" disclosure after adding a cellular number to Contacts.

Let's consider another example using the popular secure messaging program Signal. When I downloaded the Signal app, it wanted me to register a telephone number. I chose a Google Voice number and configured the app. I then added my target's cellular number into my Android contact list and asked Signal to search for friends. Signal immediately confirmed that my target was active on Signal. This alone is valuable in regard to behavior, but not very helpful to establish identity. If I launch a new window to send a message to the number, even if I do not send the data, I may see a name associated with the account. This would need to be a deliberate act by the target, but this behavior is common.

Secure Communications Apps: If you plan to communicate directly with targets of your investigation, you should be familiar with the popular secure communication preferences. Asking a suspect of a sex trafficking investigation to text you via cellular telephone number will not be well received. If you possess a secure Proton Mail email address or Wire encrypted communications username, your request may be honored. Possessing these apps within your Android environment allows you to contain the evidence within a VM and protect your host machine. You could also possess multiple accounts through these providers and log in only after cloning your machine, as explained later.

There are many other beneficial apps. Now that you have an idea of how to integrate mobile applications into your investigations, you can apply the same techniques to the next future wave of popular apps. Many social network apps have no association with location. This content can still have value to an investigation. Some apps, such as Kik, only function within a portable device. You cannot load a web browser on a traditional computer and participate with these networks. However, you can access them from within your Android virtual machine. The goal within this chapter is simply preparation. While we have not yet discussed specific investigation methods within these services, having a virtual Android device ready now will ease the explanations later.

Genymotion (genymotion.com)

I previously mentioned that Android devices created directly within Android Studio are preferred over those provided through third parties. I stand by those statements, but I also respect readers who may prefer other options. Genymotion may have undesired issues in regard to privacy and licensing, but the product can also be beneficial to those who have issues with the previous example. Many readers report that Genymotion Android VMs load faster, feel smoother, and seem more intuitive on Windows machines, but I have yet to experience that. This application-based Android solution is extremely easy to use. It works with Windows, macOS, and Linux operating systems, but not devices with newer Apple processors.

First, you must create a free account online at genymotion.com. This can be all alias information, and the login will be required in order to fully use the application. After you have created the account and successfully logged in to the site, navigate to genymotion.com/download and click on the "Download Genymotion Personal Edition" link. This presents the standard download page for Windows, Mac, and Linux. If prompted, choose the version without VirtualBox, as you should already have that program installed. Executing the download and accepting all default installation options will install all of the required files. When the setup process has completed, you will have a new icon on your desktop titled Genymotion. This entire process should occur on your HOST operating system, and not within a virtual machine.

Execute this application and note that an Android virtual machine may already be pre-installed and ready for launch. Instead of accepting this default option, consider creating your own machine in order to learn the process for future investigations. I recommend deleting this machine by clicking the menu icon to the right of the device and choosing "Delete". Perform the following instructions in order to create your first custom Android devices.

- In the left menu, expand the "Android API" menu and select the highest number. My option was 10.0 at the time of this writing. On the right, choose the device. I chose "Google Pixel XL" since I have a high-resolution screen, and then clicked "Add custom device". You may want to choose a device with a smaller screen for your hardware.
- Rename this device similar to Android 10.0 Original. Change the "Android Version" to the highest option and click "Install". This will download and configure the device for immediate use, and can take several minutes.
- Launch the new device by double-clicking the new machine present in the Genymotion software. The machine will load in a new window which should appear similar to the screen of an Android telephone. Click "OK" to any feature notifications. Figure 15.05 (left) displays the default view of my home screen.
- Navigate within the Android emulator by single-clicking on icons and using the "Back" icon in the lower left that appears similar to a left facing arrow.
- Consider the following customizations to improve the look and feel of the device. Figure 15.05 (right) displays the view of the home screen after these configurations.
- Drag any app icons up and drop them in the "Remove" option.
- Click and hold the bottom of the screen and drag up to view installed applications.
- Drag the Settings icon to your home screen and open the app.
- Choose "Display", then "Sleep", and select "30 Minutes".
- Choose "Security", then "Screen Lock", and choose "None".
- Press and hold the main window, select "Wallpaper", and change if desired.
- Shut down the device and open VirtualBox.
- Similar to the VM settings, change the Video Memory to the maximum.
- Change the Memory size to half of the system resources.
- Relaunch your device from within the Genymotion application.

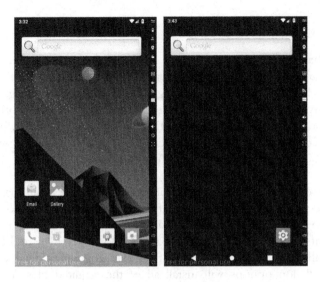

Figure 15.05: A default Android screen (left) and the custom version free of clutter (right).

You should now have a functioning replica of a standard Android device. However, you are missing several features. The biggest void is the absence of key applications such as Google Play and Gmail. Without core Google services, you cannot download apps to your device as part of your investigation tools. This has been the biggest hurdle with emulation. Consequently, there is finally an official fix, and an alternative option for advanced users. First, let's try the easy way by using the Genymotion built-in Google features.

- While inside our virtual Android device, click the "Open GAPPS" icon in the upper right corner. Accept the agreement and allow Google Apps to install. Select the option to restart the devices.
- Your browser should open to https://opengapps.org/?source=genymotion. Select "ARM64", the version of the device that you created (10.0.0), and "Stock". Click the red download option in the lower right and save the large file to your Desktop. Do NOT open the downloaded zip file.
- Drag and drop the downloaded zip file into your running Android device. Accept any warnings. You may receive errors. When complete, close and restart the device.

You should now have the Google Play Store in your applications menu. Launching it should prompt you to connect to an existing or new Google account. Consider using an anonymous account that is not used for anything else. I do not recommend creating a new account from within this virtual machine because Google will likely demand a cellular telephone number for verification. I prefer to create Google accounts from a traditional computer before connecting to the virtual Android device. After syncing with an active Google account on your new device, you should now be able to enter the Google Play Store. You should also now see all core Google services in your applications menu.

You can now install any apps within the Play Store. If any apps refuse to install because of an incompatible device, you could replicate the F-Droid and Aurora Store technique explained in the previous tutorial. The addition of Google Play will allow you to natively install Android applications as if you were holding a real telephone or tablet. Launch Google Play and you will be able to search, install, and execute most apps to your new virtual device. After you install a new program, click on the applications menu. Click and hold the new app and you will be able to drag it to your home screen. Figure 15.06 (left) displays the screen of my default investigation emulator. Next, you should understand the features embedded into the Genymotion software.

When you launch an Android virtual machine, you will see a column on the right side of the window and a row of icons horizontally on the bottom. The bottom icons are part of the emulated Android system. Clicking the first icon will navigate you backward one screen from your current location. If you are within an app, this would take you back one step each time that you press it. The second icon represents the "Home" option and will always return you to the home screen. The third button is the "Recent Apps" option and it will load a view of recently opened applications. The icons on the right of the emulator are features of Genymotion and allow you to control aspects of the Android machine from outside of the emulator. These replicate the features discussed with Android Studio. Note that many options are not available in the free version, but I have never found that to be a hindrance to my investigations. Genymotion is quite clear that if you plan on making money by designing an app through their product, you should pay for a license. Non-commercial usage allows unlimited use of the free personal version.

The GPS option within Genymotion is the most beneficial feature of their toolset. Clicking this icon and clicking the Off/On switch will execute the location spoofing service. You can either supply the exact coordinates directly or click on the "Map" button to select a location via an interactive Google map. Figure 15.06 (middle) displays the default GPS menu in the disabled state. Figure 15.06 (right) displays coordinates entered. I recommend changing the altitude, accuracy, and bearing settings to "0". Close this window and you will see a green check mark in the GPS button to confirm that your location settings are enabled.

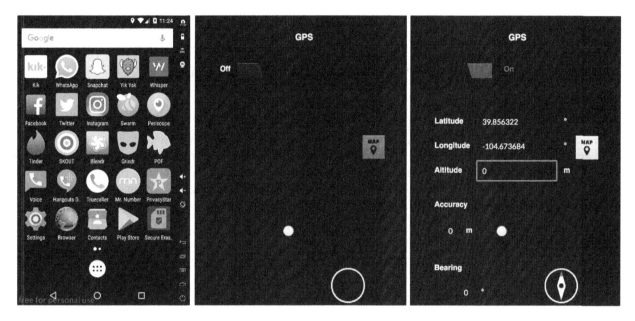

Figure 15.06: An Android screen with apps (left), disabled GPS menu (middle) and spoofed GPS (right).

Virtual Device Cloning

Similar to the tutorials for cloning Linux virtual machines, we can apply the same process toward our new Genymotion Android VM. You should consider a new Android virtual device every time to research a target. The following instructions will clone the exact state of any virtual Android device within VirtualBox, including devices created within Genymotion.

- Create and customize an Android virtual device as desired. Configure all apps that you want present in all cloned copies. Optionally, execute the app "Secure Eraser" to eliminate unnecessary hard drive space. Shut down the machine completely.
- Open VirtualBox from your Applications folder (Mac) or Start menu (Windows). Right-click the machine that you want to duplicate and select "Clone". Figure 15.07 displays this program with a right-click menu option from an active machine.
- Provide a name for your new machine. This could be "Investigation Original Copy" or "2021-1234". Choose the options of "Full Clone" and "Current Machine State" and click the "Clone" button. VirtualBox will create an exact duplicate of the chosen machine in the default folder for VirtualBox machines. You can identify this folder by right-clicking your new machine and choosing "Show in Finder" (Mac) or "Show in Explorer" (Windows).

You can now use this cloned device to conduct your investigation. Any changes made within it will have no impact on the original device. In fact, I titled my original investigation device "Android Original 9.0", as seen in Figure 15.07. This way, I know to only open it to apply updates, and never for active investigations. Every time I need to use a device to research a target, I quickly clone the original and keep all of my cases isolated.

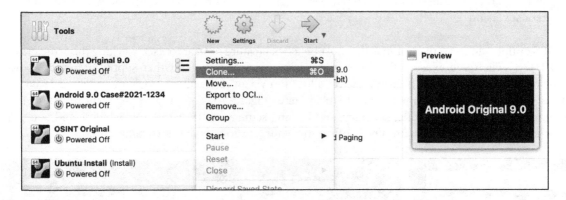

Figure 15.07: A VirtualBox menu with a clone option in the menu.

Virtual Device Export

You may be asked to provide all digital evidence from your investigation as a matter of discovery. This could happen to a forensic examiner hired in a civil case or law enforcement prosecuting a criminal case. This is the precise reason that I create a new virtual device for all my investigations. Not only is it a clean and fair environment, it is easy to archive and distribute when complete. The following instructions will generate a large single file that contains the entire virtual operating system and apps from your investigation.

- Open VirtualBox in the same manner as previously mentioned.
- Select the target virtual device, click on "File" in the menu bar, and select "Export Appliance". Select the device again and provide the save location and name of the file.
- Click "Export" and allow the process to complete. The final result will consist of a single file that can be archived to DVD or flash media.
- This file can be imported into VirtualBox by choosing the "Import Appliance" option in the File menu. This would allow another investigator to view the exact investigation environment as you.

Android within Android Studio and Genymotion are not your only options. Third-party applications such as **BlueStacks** (bluestacks.com) and **Andy** (andyroid.net) offer the same basic functionality with added overhead and requirements. After installation, most of these programs work the same way as VirtualBox. In fact, most of them rely on VirtualBox on the back end. **I choose Android Studio over these because it is the most native way to present Android.** It is also quite fast.

I encourage you to experiment with all of the options, and choose any that work best for you. I always keep a version of Android Studio and Genymotion available and updated at all times. At the time of this writing, my Android Studio machine seemed more responsive and functional, but my Genymotion devices were more isolated. Only you can decide the best path for your investigations, but I encourage you to explore both options.

Overall, I believe the future of OSINT collection will become more focused on mobile apps that have no website search option. In order to conduct thorough online investigations, mobile environment emulation is required. I highly recommend practicing these techniques with non-essential apps and data. This will better prepare you for an actual investigation with proper evidence control. Expect frustration as apps block access from within virtual devices due to fraud. However, the occasional investigation success through virtual Android environments justifies all of the headaches encountered along the way.

CHAPTER SIXTEEN
CUSTOM SEARCH TOOLS

From 2010 through 2019, I offered a set of public free interactive online investigations tools. In June of 2019, I was forced to remove these tools due to abuse and legal demands. They returned to my website in 2022, exactly three years later. In the previous edition of this book, I offered an offline version of these tools which could be self-hosted and immune from vague takedown requests. This chapter revisits these tools and offers several enhancements. The goal of this chapter is to help you create and maintain your own custom search tools which can automate queries for any investigation. First, let's talk about why this is so important.

I assumed my search tools would be around as long as I maintained my site. I learned the hard way that nothing lasts forever. We can no longer rely on third-party tools, a theme which I have overly-emphasized throughout this entire book. Any online search tool outside of your control could disappear any day. While mine have returned, they could go away again at any time.

That is not the worst possible outcome. We never truly know what information various online search tools are storing about our searches and activity. Many aggregated search sites possess numerous tracking cookies and practically all "link collections" force embedded analytics capturing data about every visitor. Creating and hosting your own tools eliminate these issues. We still must query sensitive data to a final repository of information, but let's eliminate the middle-man. All of the tools presented in this chapter, and referenced throughout the book, do not need to be placed online within a website. You can store them on your computer and launch them without fear of questionable connections. Let's get started.

First, download a copy of all search tool templates used within the entire book. This can be found at **https://inteltechniques.com/data/osintbook11/tools.zip**. Unzip this archive to a destination of your choice. If using the Linux, Mac, or Windows OSINT builds which were previously explained, you should already have the necessary files on your Desktop. I always suggest saving them to the Desktop for easy access. However, anywhere should suffice. Be sure to extract all of the files within the zip file.

This collection reveals a folder titled "Tools" consisting of multiple files within it. Technically, you have everything you need to replicate my public search tools locally on your own machine. However, it is up to you to modify these as needed. You will eventually want to remove dead sources, add new features, and modify the structures due to changes at third-party websites. I will use my Email Tool as a demonstration. Figure 16.01 displays the current view of the Email tool. As you can see, there are several individual search options and a "Submit All" feature at the bottom. Inserting an email address into any of these fields will query that address through the designated option, or the final field executes a search through all of them.

Let's pick apart one of these queries from within the code. By default, double-clicking on any of the files within the search tool folder opens the selected option within your default web browser. This is required for any of them to function. In order to edit the files, we must open them within an HTML editing tool or any text processing application. If you are on a Mac, that could be TextEdit, Windows users have Notepad, and Linux users have Text Edit. All work fine for our needs. Lately, I prefer **VSCodium** (vscodium.com), which is a cross-platform free text editor.

If you open the file titled email.search.html within a text editor ("File" > "Open"), you will see the code which makes this document function within a web browser. The following explains each section. Complete understanding of each term is not required to use and modify your own tools, but these pages may serve as a reference if you ever want to make substantial changes.

<!DOCTYPE html><html>

This informs a web browser that this is a web page, even if offline, and begins the page.

```
<style>
ul {list-style-type: none;margin: 0;padding: 0;width: 200px;background-color: #f1f1f1;}
li a {display: block;color: #000;padding: 8px 16px;text-decoration: none;}
li a:hover {background-color: #555;color: white;}
li a.active {background-color: #303942;color: white;}
li a.grey {background-color: #cdcdcd;color: black;}
li a.blue {background-color: #b4c8da;color: black;}
table td, table td * {vertical-align: top;}</style>
```

This sets the style requirements such as colors and sizes of the content within the page. You can experiment with these settings without risking the function of the tools.

<head>

This informs your browser that the "head" or "header" portion of the page begins now.

<title>Email Search Tool</title>

This represents the title of the page, visible in the browser tab.

</head>

This discloses the end of the "head" or "header" section.

<body>

This informs your browser that the "body" portion of the page begins now.

<table width="1000" border="0"><td width="200"><td width="800">

This creates a table within our content and sets the overall width with no border. It then specifies the width of the columns. The data in between identifies the menu items visible on the left of the page, which are considered the first column within the table.

<script type="text/javascript">

This identifies the following text as a JavaScript command.

function doPopAll(PopAll)...

This provides instruction to the browser which allows our tools to populate given data to the remaining fields. It is required for the next option.

<form onsubmit="doPopAll...

This section creates the "Populate All" button which populates the given data throughout the remaining tools.

Function doSearch01(Search01)

This tells the page we want it to "do" something, and the task is called Search01.

```
{window.open('http://google.com/search?q="' + Search01 + '"', 'Search01window');}
```

This instructs the page to build a URL, add a piece of data, and open the result in a tab.

```
</script>
```

This identifies the end of each script.

```
<form onsubmit="doSearch01(this.Search01.value); return false;">
```

This creates a form to generate the URL, looking for a specific value.

```
<input type="text" name="Search01" "id="Search01" size="30" placeholder="Email Address"/>
```

This creates a form input identified as Search01 with "Email Address" populated in the field.

```
<input type="submit" style="width:120px" value="Google" /><br /></form>
```

This creates the Submit button with specific text inside, inserts a new line, and closes the form.

```
</table></body></html>
```

This identifies the end of the "table", "body", and "HTML" sections, and closes the page.

This only represents the first search option within this tool, but it is quite powerful. This collects a target email address and queries Google to identify any websites containing this address within the contents. This technique will be explained in more detail later in the Email chapter.

This also demonstrates the need for a search tool versus simply visiting the search site. If you go to whoxy.com, you must navigate through the main page; change the drop-down menu to an email search; type in the target email address; solve the Captcha; and then wait for the results. Instead, we can navigate straight to our results with the following URL, replacing the test address with our target's email.

https://www.whoxy.com/search.php?email=test@test.com

You may be wondering where this URL came from. It is not advertised on the site, and is not an official option within the API (which is now a paid service, but this URL is free). That is our next tutorial. Navigate to whoxy.com within Firefox and allow the page to load. Conduct the following steps to identify the exact URL which submits a query to return data about your target.

- Right-click on the page and choose "Inspect Element".
- Click the "Network" tab in the new window at the bottom of the page.
- Change the top website search menu to "Email Address".
- Type an email address into this field and execute the search.
- Scroll through the new text in the Inspector window at the bottom of the page.
- Click on the result displaying "search.php" in the "File" column.
- Copy the URL in the window to the right under "Headers" as seen in Figure 16.03.

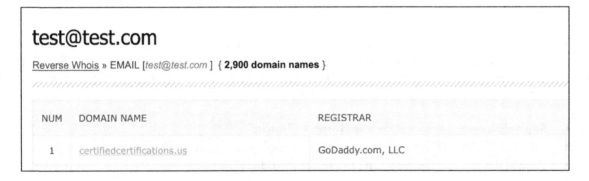

IntelTechniques Tools	Email Address	Populate All
Search Engines	Email Address	Google
	Email Address	Bing
Facebook	Email Address	Yandex
Twitter	Email Address	Trumail
	Email Address	Emailrep
Instagram	Email Address	Gravatar
LinkedIn	Email Address	HIBP
Communities	Email Address	Dehashed
	Email Address	Spycloud
Email Addresses	Email Address	Cit0day
Usernames	Email Address	Cybernews
	Email Address	PSBDMP
Names	Email Address	IntelX
Telephone Numbers	Email Address	LeakedSource
Maps	Email Address	HunterVerify
	Email Address	OCCRP
Documents	Email Address	SearchMyBio
Pastes	Email Address	SpyTox
	Email Address	ThatsThem
Images	Email Address	Protonmail
Videos	Email Address	DomainData
	Email Address	Whoisology
Domains	Email Address	AnalyzeID
IP Addresses	Email Address	Submit All
Business & Government	Email Address (Requires API Key)	PeopleDataLabs

Figure 16.01: The Email Addresses Tool.

test@test.com

Reverse Whois » EMAIL [*test@test.com*] **{ 2,900 domain names }**

NUM	DOMAIN NAME	REGISTRAR
1	certifiedcertifications.us	GoDaddy.com, LLC

Figure 16.02: A result from the Whoxy website.

▷	Headers	Cookies	Request	Response	Timings	Security		
∇ Filter Headers							Block	Resend

▶ GET https://www.whoxy.com/search.php?email=test@test.com

Figure 16.03: The static URL from a query as seen in Inspector.

With this method, we can identify the URL structures for our tool. Our tool presents a line of code which included the URL required for the search as follows.

```
{window.open('https://www.whoxy.com/search.php?email=' + Search22, 'Search22window');}
```

This line instructs the tool to open a new browser window; navigate to the Whoxy website followed by whatever text was entered into the search tool; and define that new window (or tab) with a unique name in order to prevent another search within our tool from overwriting the page. This results in our tool opening a new tab with our desired results (https://www.whoxy.com/search.php?email=test@test.com). Let's look at another search option within this same tool with a slightly different structure.

The Dehashed search option is unique in that it requires quotation marks surrounding the input. In other words, you must enter "test@email.com" and not simply test@email.com. This requires us to add an additional character after the target input has been provided. Below is the example for this query. Note that double quotes (") are inside single quotes ('), which appears quite messy in print. Always rely on the digital files to play with the actual content.

```
{window.open('https://dehashed.com/search?query="' + Search05 + '"', 'Search05window');}
```

This line instructs the tool to open a new browser window, navigate to the website https://dehashed.com/search?query=", followed by whatever text was entered into the search tool, plus another quotation mark (a single quote, double quote, and another single quote), and define that new window (or tab) with a unique name in order to prevent another search within our tool from overwriting the page. The lesson here is that you can add as many parameters as necessary by using the plus (+) character. You will see many examples of this within the files that you have downloaded. Remember, every search tool presented in this book is included in digital format. You only need to modify the options as things change over time.

Let's assume Dehashed made a change to their search, which appears in the tool as follows.

```
{window.open('https://dehashed.com/search?query="' + Search05 + '"', 'Search05window');}
```

This is because the URL structure of the search is as follows:

https://dehashed.com/search?query="test@email.com"

Assume that Dehashed changed the search structure on their site to the following:

https://dehashed.com/?query="test@email.com"&trial

Your new line within the tool would need to be manipulated as follows:

```
{window.open('https://dehashed.com/?query="' + Search05 + '"&trial', 'Search05window');}
```

Next, let's assume that you found a brand-new search service which was not included in the downloadable search tools. You will need to modify the tools to include this new option. Again, we will use the email tool as an example. Open the "Email.html" file within a text editor. Look through the text and notice that each search script possesses an identifier similar to "Search01", "Search02", "Search03", etc. These must each be unique in order to function. You will notice that the final option (after the Submit All feature) is "Search25". We now know that our next option should be "Search26". Assume that you found a website at emailleaks.com (which is no longer working) and you want to add it to the tools. A query of an email address presents a URL as follows.

https://emailleaks.com/ajax.php?query=test@email.com

You would next copy the "Search24" script and paste it at the end of the tool (before the Submit All feature). You can then edit the script, which should look like the following, using "Search26" and our new URL.

```
<script type="text/javascript">
function doSearch26(Search26)
{window.open('https://emailleaks.com/ajax.php?query=' + Search26, 'Search26window');}
</script>
<form onsubmit="doSearch26(this.Search26.value); return false;">
<input type="text" name="Search26" "id="Search26" size="30" placeholder="Email Address"/>
<input type="submit" style="width:120px" value="Email Leaks" /><br /></form>
```

All we changed within this copy and paste job was the target URL, the Search26 identifiers, and the descriptor. You can place this section anywhere within the tools, as it does not need to be at the end. Note it is titled Search26, so any new options added would need to start with Search27. These numbers do not need to be sequential throughout the tool, but they must be unique.

Submit All

Many of the online search tools offer a "Submit All" button at the bottom of the options. This executes each of the queries referenced above the button and can be a huge time saver. If you open one of the search tools with this option in a text editor, you will see the code for this at the bottom. It appears very similar to the other search options, but there are multiple "window.open" elements such as those listed below.

```
Window.open('https://haveibeenpwned.com/unifiedsearch/' + all, 'Search01window');
window.open('https://dehashed.com/search?query=' + all, 'Search05window');
```

In most of the tools, I have simply replicated the individual search options within one single "Submit All" feature. If you modify a search tool within the code next to the manual search, you should also update it under the final option to execute all queries. If you feel overwhelmed with all of this, do not panic. None of this is required at this point. **Your own custom offline search tools are already configured and functioning**. If a specific desired tool stops functioning, you can use this chapter to change your scripts.

You may have noticed that there are several files within the Tools folder. Launching any of these opens that specific tool, such as "Email.html", but a menu exists within each of the pages in order to navigate within the tool to the desired page. The file titled "index.html" is the "Main menu", and might be appropriate to set as your browser's home page. Clicking on the desired search option within the left side of the menu opens that specific tool. As an example, clicking on "X (Twitter)" presents numerous X (Twitter) search options. These will each be explained at the end of each corresponding chapter.

Simplified Modification

I am sure some readers are frustrated at the technology presented here. Some may look at this code and cite numerous ways it could be made better. I agree this is amateur hour, as I am not a strong HTML coder. Other readers may be confused at all of this. For those, there are two options which simplify things. First, ignore this entire chapter and simply use the free tools without any modification. Some options will break eventually as sites come and go, but that should not impact the other fields. Second, don't worry too much about adding new features. Instead, simply replace any searches that stop functioning. If Dehashed shuts down tomorrow, simply wait for a replacement. When that happens, modify only the URL and name, leaving the structure as-is.

You have a strong start with the current tools template. Very minimal modifications as things break will keep you in good shape. Any major updates which I perform to my own set of tools will be offered on my site for download. Check the "Updates" section at the following page.

https://inteltechniques.com/osintbook11

Populate All

You may have noticed that most of the tools have an option to populate all of the fields from a single entry. This is beneficial as it prevents us from copying and pasting target data within multiple fields. This code, which was presented earlier, tells your browser to populate anything you place into the first field within every field on that page which has an ID of "Search" plus any numbers. In other words, it would populate both examples on the previous page because they have id="Search25" and id="Search26". Test this within the Email search tool. Make sure each "id" field is unique, as no two can be the same on one page.

When I need to search a specific target, I do not copy the data into each search field and press the corresponding button for each service. I place the input directly into the "Populate All" option and then execute any individual searches desired. Alternatively, I place my target data into the "Submit All" option and let it go. If using Firefox, this will fail on the first attempt. This is because you have pop-ups blocked by default, and Firefox is trying to protect you from multiple new pages loading automatically. The following steps will prevent this.

- Open the Email.html search tool included in your downloaded offline search tools.
- Place any email address in the last option and press the Submit All button.
- A new tab will open, but close it.
- Back in the Email search tool, you should see an options banner at the top.
- Click the Preferences button and click the first option to "Allow pop-ups for file".

This will prevent your pop-up blocker from blocking that specific page. You would need to repeat the process for each of the other tools, such as X (Twitter), Facebook, etc., which can be quite a burden. If desired, you can disable the pop-up blocker completely, but that carries risks. You may visit a malicious website which begins loading new tabs. I do not see this as much as in years past, but the threat does still exist. If conducting your research within a VM, I do not see a huge risk in disabling this blocker. If you do, all of the tools will function without specific modifications to the blocker. Make this decision carefully.

- Click the Firefox menu in the upper right and choose Settings.
- Click on Privacy & Security and scroll to Permissions.
- If desired, uncheck the "Block pop-up windows" option.

While I would never do this on my primary browser used for personal activity on my main computer, I have disabled the pop-up blocker within my OSINT Original VM (and therefore all clones). It simply saves me headaches when trying to use automated tools. If only using the single queries within the tool, your pop-up blocker will not interfere. I highly recommend that you become familiar with these search tools before you rely on them. Experience how the URLs are formed, and understand how to modify them if needed. Each of these tools will be explained in the following chapters as we learn all of the functions.

License & Warranty

These tools are released to you for free. Full details of allowances and restrictions can be found in the "License.txt" file and "License" link within the tools download. The tools are provided "as is", without warranty of any kind. Please follow my blog for any updates. Ultimately, it is your responsibility to update your tools as desired as things change after publication. The torch has been passed.

Easy Access

Regardless of where you save your set of tools, I highly recommend that you create a bookmark within your browser for easy access. I prefer them to be within my bookmarks toolbar so that they are always one click away. Navigate to your search tools. If using the Linux, Mac, or Windows OSINT machines, they are in the Tools folder on your desktop. Double-click the file titled "Search.html" and it should open within your default browser, preferably Firefox. If the page opens in Chrome or another browser, open Firefox and use the file menu to select "Open File" and browse to the "Search.html" file. After the page loads, create a bookmark. In Linux and Windows, press "Ctrl" + "D" ("command" + "D" on Mac). When prompted, provide a name of "Tools" and save the page in the folder titled "Bookmarks Toolbar". You should now see a new bookmark in your browser's toolbar titled "Tools". If your Bookmarks Toolbar is not visible, click on "View", then "Toolbars", then "View Bookmarks Toolbar". You can now click this new button within your toolbar at any time and immediately load the Search Engines tool. Clicking through the other options in the left menu of that page should present all other search tool pages. I use this shortcut to launch my tools daily.

Online Version

As previously explained, I offer an updated live copy of all tools at **https://inteltechniques.com/tools/**. These tools are visually similar to my overall website theme, but the code powering them is identical to the strategy you have seen here and the offline files previously downloaded. As resources change, I will apply all modifications to my copy online, but I cannot modify your current offline set.

Some may still not be convinced they should maintain their own search tools and should just rely on my version on the website. The live tools could disappear at any time due to another takedown demand. Also, you cannot modify my live online version as you can your own copy. Finally, you must rely on my site being available during your investigations. The offline version is available on your desktop at any time.

Please use these responsibly. I am optimistic that we can keep this valuable resource for our daily investigations for years to come. Figure 16.05 displays an example of the updated online tools.

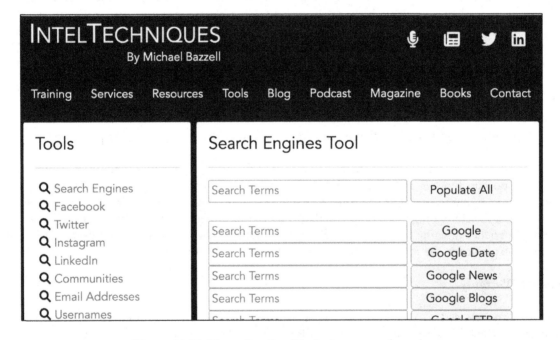

Figure 16.05: The online IntelTechniques search tools.

SECTION II
OSINT RESOURCES & TECHNIQUES

Some may consider this section to be the "guts" of the book. It contains the OSINT tips, tricks, and techniques which I have taught over the past twenty years. Each chapter was rewritten and confirmed accurate in December 2024. All outdated content was removed, many techniques were updated, and numerous new resources were added. The first four editions of this book only consisted of this section. Only recently have I adopted the preceding preparation section and the methodology topics toward the end. OSINT seems to have become a much more complex industry over the years. It is exciting to watch the community grow and I am honored to play an extremely small role.

This section is split into several chapters, and each explains a common type of target investigation. I have isolated specific topics such as email addresses, usernames, social networks, and telephone numbers. Each chapter provides every valuable resource and technique which I have found beneficial toward my own investigations. No book could ever include every possible resource, as many tools become redundant after a superior version has been identified. I do my best to limit the "noise" and simply present the most robust options for each scenario. This section should serve as a reference when you encounter a specific need within your own investigations.

Covert Accounts

Before proceeding with any of the investigation methods here, it is important to discuss covert accounts, also referred to by some as "Sock Puppets". Covert accounts are online profiles which are not associated with your true identity. Many social networks, such as Facebook and Instagram, now require you to be logged in to an account before any queries can be conducted. Using your true personal account could reveal your identity as an investigator to the target. Covert accounts on all of the social networks mentioned here are free and can be completed using fictitious information. However, some networks will make this task more difficult than others. Google, Facebook, X (Twitter), Instagram, and Yahoo are known to make you jump through hoops before you are granted access. We begin this chapter discussing ways around this.

Email: It is vital that you possess a "clean" email address for your covert accounts. Every social network requires an email address as a part of account registration, and you should never use an already established personal address. Later chapters explain methods for researching the owners behind email addresses, and those techniques can be applied to you and your own accounts. Therefore, consider starting fresh with a brand-new email account dedicated toward use for covert profiles.

The choice of email provider is key here. I do not recommend GMX, Proton Mail, Yahoo, Gmail, MSN, or any other extremely popular providers. These are heavily used by spammers and scammers, and are therefore more scrutinized than smaller providers. My preference is to create a free email account at **Fastmail** (https://ref.fm/u14547153). This established mail provider is unique in two ways. First, they are one of the only remaining providers which do not require a pre-existing email address in order to obtain a new address. This means that there will be no connection from your new covert account to any personal accounts. Second, they are fairly "off-radar" from big services such as Facebook, and are not scrutinized for malicious activity.

Fastmail will provide anyone unlimited free accounts on a 30-day trial. I suggest choosing an email address that ends in fastmail.us instead of fastmail.com, as that domain is less used than their official address. This is a choice during account creation. Once you have your new email address activated, you are ready to create covert profiles. Note that the free trial terminates your access to this email account in 30 days, so this may not be best for long-term investigations. Personally, I possess a paid account which allows me 600 permanent alias email addresses.

- **Facebook**: This is the most difficult in terms of new account creation. They will require you to provide a cellular telephone number where a verification text can be sent and confirmed. Providing VOIP numbers such as a Google Voice account will not work anymore. I have found it best to turn off any VPN, Tor Browser, or other IP address masking service and connect from a residential, business, or cellular internet connection. Clear out all of your internet cache and log out of any accounts. During account creation, provide the email address that you created previously. In most situations, you should bypass the requirement to provide a cellular number. If this method fails, there is something about your computer or connection that is making Facebook unhappy. Persistence will always equal success eventually. I find public library Wi-Fi our best internet option during account creation. Facebook is tracking your IP address and browser fingerprint, so if you fail to create a new account, you will need to start over from a fresh browser and network connection. **Instagram** is similar to (and owned by) Facebook. Expect the same scrutiny.

- **X (Twitter)**: Many of the X (Twitter) techniques presented later will also require an account. Even some third-party solutions will mandate that you be logged in to X (Twitter) when using them. I highly recommend possessing a covert account before proceeding. As long as you provide a legitimate email address from a residential or business internet connection, you should have no issues. You may get away with using a VPN to create an account, but not always.

- **Google/Gmail/Voice**: While Google has become more aggressive at refusing suspicious account registrations, they are still very achievable. As with the previous methods, Google will likely block any new accounts that are created over Tor or a VPN. Providing your Fastmail address as an alternative form of contact during the account creation process usually satisfies their need to validate your request. I have also found that they seem more accommodating during account creation if you are connected through a Chrome browser versus a privacy-customized Firefox browser (Google owns Chrome).

- **Network:** I always prefer to conduct online investigations behind a VPN, but this can be tricky. Creating accounts through a VPN often alerts the service of your suspicious behavior. Creating accounts from public Wi-Fi, such as a local library or coffee shop, are typically less scrutinized. A day after creation from open Wi-Fi, I attempt to access while behind a VPN. I then consistently select the same VPN company and general location upon every usage of the profile. This builds a pattern of my network and location, which helps maintain access to the account.

- **Phone Number:** The moment any service finds your new account to be suspicious, it will prompt you for a valid telephone number. Landlines and VOIP numbers are blocked, and they will demand a true cellular number. Today, I keep a supply of Mint Mobile eSIM activations, which can be purchased for $0.99 from Amazon. Each activation includes a telephone number with a one-week free trial. I activate the SIM card through an old Android phone, select a phone number, and use that number to open accounts across all of the major networks. As soon as the account is active, I change the telephone number to a VOIP option and secure the account with two-factor authentication (2FA).

- **2FA:** Once I have an account created, I immediately activate any two-factor authentication options. These are secondary security settings which require a text message or software token (Authy) in order to access the account. Typically, this behavior tells the service that you are a real person behind the account, and not an automated bot using the profile for malicious reasons.

- **Activity:** After the account is created and secured, it is important to remain active. If you create a new account and allow it to sit dormant for months, it is likely to be suspended the moment you log back in to the account. If you access the account weekly, it is less likely to be blocked.

You may assume that you can use your personal social network accounts to search for information. While this is possible, it is risky. Some services may never indicate to the target that your specific profile was used for searching. Others, such as Facebook, will eventually notify the target that you have an interest in him, usually in the form of friend recommendations. On any service, you are always one accidental click away from sending a friend request from your real account to the suspect. For these reasons, I never use a personal social network profile during any investigation. I maintain multiple covert accounts. The topic of undercover operations quickly exceeds the scope of this book. For our purposes, we simply need to be logged in to valid accounts in order to pacify the social networks. I will assume that you now have some accounts created. Let's dig into online search.

Profile Content

Possession of an empty profile on a social network may suffice for your investigations. However, lack of personal details might appear suspicious to both the provider and your target. Facebook is well known for suspending accounts which do not contain personal information, and your targets may conduct their own OSINT research into your publicly available details after you begin the hunt. For most scenarios, I believe you should populate a minimum amount of fake details into your covert profiles. You should never provide anything which may be associated with your true identity, such as interests, occupation, or location. Because of this, I rely heavily on randomly-generated and AI-produced content. The resources below have helped me within my own profile creation. Consider your own needs and employer policies before proceeding with your accounts.

Images: You may want a headshot within your profile which adds a layer of authenticity to your new covert account. This can also eliminate scrutiny from Facebook and X (Twitter) when their algorithms suspect your profile to be fraudulent. I recommend **This Person Does Not Exist** (thispersondoesnotexist.com). This site generates a very realistic image of a "person", which is entirely generated by computers. The image you see is not a real person and should not be visible anywhere else online. Refreshing the page generates a new image. If you find this helpful, I encourage you to generate numerous images for future use in the event the site disappears.

Name and Background: It may be easy to create your own alias name, but could you quickly generate a maiden name, birthday, birthplace, zodiac sign, username, password, religion, and political view? This is where services such as **ElfQrin** (elfqrin.com/fakeid.php) and **Fake Name Generator** (fakenamegenerator.com) can be beneficial. The example below was created instantly with these services.

- **Resume**: If you want to add another layer of realism to your new online identity, you might consider posting a resume online. If your target begins investigating your profile and finds the resume, you may appear to be a real person.
- **Physical Space**: You might consider **This Rental Does Not Exist** (thisrentaldoesnotexist.com). It uses the same artificial intelligence technology as This Person Does Not Exist to generate fake interior views of a home. These artificial images are intended to emulate a rental home or Air BNB profile, but they could be used if you ever need to post pictures of your "home".
- **Timeline and Friends:** Joining innocuous pop culture and hobby groups on Facebook is low-risk tactic for adding friends and content to your profile as Facebook automatically associates you with other members of those groups. This provides a near endless supply of potential friends and timeline content.

First name	Ella
Middle name	Theresa
Last name	Bowman
Mother's Maiden name	Sutton
Birthday	November, 07 1998 (Age: 23 years)
Birthplace	Walnut Creek, CA, USA
Zodiacal sign	Scorpio
User name	boe431
Password	f2b4qawha
Address	101 Maryland Ave Ne, Washington, DC 20002
Car	Wrangler

Hair color	Black (BLK)	Political side	Independent
Eyes color	Brown (BRO)	Favorite Color	Purple
Height	166 cm / 5 ft 5 in	Favorite Comfort Food	Chocolate
Weight	56 Kg / 123 pounds	Favorite Cereal	Raisin Bran
Shoe Size	7.5	Favorite Season	Spring
Blood Type	B+	Favorite Animal	Elephant
Religion	Jehovah's Witnesses	Lucky Number	2

CHAPTER SEVENTEEN
SEARCH ENGINES

The first stop for many researchers will be a popular search engine. The two big players in the United States are Google and Bing. This chapter will go into great detail about the advanced ways to use both and others. Most of these techniques can apply to any search engine, but many examples will be specific for these two. Much of this chapter is unchanged from the 10th edition.

Google (google.com)

There are entire books dedicated to Google searching and Google hacking. Most of these focus on penetration testing and securing computer networks. These are full of great information, but are often overkill for the investigator looking for quick personal information. A few simple rules can help locate more accurate data. No book in existence will replace practicing these techniques in a live web browser. In recent years, Google removed the number of search results from the default display. Selecting "Tools" on the filters bar will add that metric back to the interface. You cannot break anything. Play around and get familiar with the advanced options.

Quotation Marks

Placing a target name inside of quotation marks will make a huge difference in a quick first look for information. If I conducted a search for my name without quotes, the result is 147,000 pages that include the words "Michael" and "Bazzell". These pages do not necessarily have these words right next to each other. The word "Michael" could be next to another person's name, while "Bazzell" could be next to yet another person's name. These results can provide inaccurate information. They may include a reference to "Michael Santo" and "Barry Bazzell", but not my name. Since technically the words "Michael" and "Bazzell" appear on the page, you are stuck with the result in your list. In order to prevent this, you should always use quotes around the name of your target. Searching for the term "Michael Bazzell", including the quotes, reduces the search results to 31,800.

Each of these pages will contain the words "Michael" and "Bazzell" right next to each other. While Google and other search engines have technology in place to search related names, this is not always perfect, and does not apply to searches with quotes. For example, the search for "Michael Bazzell", without quotes, located pages that reference Mike Bazzell (instead of Michael). This same search with quotes did not locate these results. Placing quotes around any search terms tells Google to search exactly what you tell it to search. If your target's name is "Michael", you may want to consider an additional search for "Mike". If a quoted search returns nothing, or few results, you should remove the quotes and search again.

When your quoted search, such as "Michael Bazzell", returns too many results, you should add to your search. When I add the term "FBI" after my name, the results reduce from 31,800 to 12,000. These results all contain pages that have the words "Michael" and "Bazzell" next to each other, and include the term "FBI" somewhere on the page. While all of these results may not be about me, the majority will be and can be easily digested. Adding the occupation, residence city, general interest, or college of the target may help eliminate unrelated results. This search technique can be vital when searching email addresses or usernames. When searching the email address of "michael@inteltechniques.com", without quotes, I receive 14,200 results. When I search "michael@inteltechniques.com" with quotes, I receive only 7 results that actually contain that email address (which does not reach my inbox).

Search Operators

Most search engines allow the use of commands within the search field. These commands are not actually part of the search terms and are referred to as operators. There are two parts to most operator searches, and each are separated by a colon. To the left of the colon is the type of operator, such as "site" (website) or "ext" (file extension). To the right is the rule for the operator, such as the target domain or file type. The following will explain each operator and the most appropriate uses.

Site Operator

Google, and other search engines, allow the use of operators within the search string. An operator is text that is added to the search, which performs a function. My favorite operator is the "site:" function. This operator provides two benefits to the search results. First, it will only provide results of pages located on a specific domain. Second, it will provide all of the results containing the search terms on that domain. I will use my name again for a demonstration. I conducted a search of "Michael Bazzell" on Google. One of the results is a link to the website forbes.com. This search result is one of multiple pages on that domain that includes a reference to me. However, this search only displayed one of the many pages on that domain that possessed my name within them. If you want to view every page on a specific domain that includes your target of interest, the site operator is required. Next, I conducted the following exact search.

site:forbes.com "Michael Bazzell"

The result was all eight pages on forbes.com that include my name within the content. This technique can be applied to any domain. This includes social networks, blogs, and any other website that is indexed by search engines.

Another simple way to use this technique is to locate every page that is part of a specific domain. A search query of site:inteltechniques.com displays all 628 pages that are publicly available on my personal website. This can be a great way to review all the content of a target's personal website without attempting to navigate the actual site. It is very easy to miss content by clicking around within a website. With this technique, you should see all of the pages in a format that is easy to digest. Also, some of the pages on a website that the author may consider "private" may actually be public if he or she ever linked to them from a public page. Once Google has indexed the page, we can view the content using the "site" operator.

Real World Application: While conducting private background checks, I consistently use the site operator. A search such as "site:https://www.amazon.com/product-reviews" and the target name in quotes can reveal interesting information. A previous background check of an applicant that signed an affidavit declaring no previous drug or alcohol dependencies produced some damaging results. The search provided user submitted reviews that he had left on Amazon in reference to books that he had purchased that assisted him with his continual addiction to controlled substances. Again, this result may have appeared somewhere in the numerous general search results of the target; however, the site operator directed me exactly where I needed to look.

File Type Operator

Another operator that works with both Google and Bing is the file type filter. It allows you to filter any search results by a single file type extension. While Google allows this operator to be shortened to "ext", Bing does not. Therefore, I will use the original "filetype" operator in my search examples. Consider the following search attempting to locate PowerPoint presentation files associated with the company Cisco.

"Cisco" "PowerPoint"

The result is over 10,000,000 websites that include the words Cisco and PowerPoint in the content. However, these are not all actual PowerPoint documents. The following search refines our example for accuracy.

"Cisco" filetype:ppt

The result is 15,200 Microsoft PowerPoint presentations that contain Cisco within the content. This search only located the older PowerPoint format of PPT, but not newer files that may have the PPTX extension. Therefore, the following two searches would be more thorough.

"Cisco" filetype:ppt
"Cisco" filetype:pptx

The second search provided an additional 12,700 files. This brings our total to over 27,000 PowerPoint files, which is overwhelming. I will begin to further filter my results in order to focus on the most relevant content for my research. The following search will display only newer PowerPoint files that contain the exact phrase Cisco Confidential within the content of the slides.

"Cisco Confidential" filetype:pptx

The result is exactly 1,080 PowerPoint files of interest. There are many uses for this technique. A search of filetype:doc "resume" "target name" often provides resumes created by the target which can include cellular telephone numbers, personal addresses, work history, education information, references, and other personal information that would never be intentionally posted to the internet. The "filetype" operator can identify any file by the file type within any website. This can be combined with the "site" operator to find all files of any type on a single domain. By conducting the following searches, I was able to find several documents stored on the website irongeek.com.

site:irongeek.com filetype:pdf
site:irongeek.com filetype:ppt
site:irongeek.com filetype:pptx

If you do not receive any results for a filetype query, adding a keyword may increase the number results versus a query which only contains operators. Previously, Google and Bing indexed media files by type, such as MP3, MP4, AVI, and others. Due to abuse of pirated content, this no longer works well. I have found the following extensions to be indexed and provide valuable results.

7Z: Compressed File	JPEG: Image	PPTX: Microsoft PowerPoint
BMP: Bitmap Image	KML: Google Earth	RAR: Compressed File
DOC: Microsoft Word	KMZ: Google Earth	RTF: Rich Text Format
DOCX: Microsoft Word	ODP: OpenOffice Presentataion	TXT: Text File
DWF: Autodesk	ODS: OpenOffice Spreadsheet	XLS: Microsoft Excel
GIF: Animated Image	ODT: OpenOffice Text	XLSX: Microsoft Excel
HTM: Web Page	PDF: Adobe Acrobat	ZIP: Compressed File
HTML: Web Page	PNG: Image	
JPG: Image	PPT: Microsoft PowerPoint	

Hyphen (-)

The search operators mentioned previously are filters to include specific data. Instead, you may want to exclude some content from appearing within results. The hyphen (-) tells most search engines and social networks to exclude the text immediately following from any results. It is important to never include a space between the hyphen and filtered text. The following searches were conducted on my own name with the addition of excluded text. Following each search is the number of results returned by Google.

"Michael Bazzell" 31,800
"Michael Bazzell" -police 28,000
"Michael Bazzell" -police -FBI 22,100
"Michael Bazzell" -police -FBI -osint 6,010

"Michael Bazzell" -police -FBI -osint -books 4,320
"Michael Bazzell" -police -FBI -osint -books -open -source 604
"Michael Bazzell" -police -FBI -osint -books -open -source -"mr. robot" 92

The final search eliminated results which included any of the restricted words. The pages that were remaining referenced other people with my name. My goal in search filters is to dwindle the total results to a manageable amount. When you are overwhelmed with search results, slowly add exclusions to make an impact on the amount of data to analyze.

InURL Operator

We can also specify operators that will focus only on the data within the URL or address of the website. Previously, the operators discussed applied to the content within the web page. My favorite search using this technique is to find File Transfer Protocol (FTP) servers that allow anonymous connections. The following search would identify any FTP servers that possess PDF files that contain the term OSINT within the file.

inurl:ftp -inurl(http|https) filetype:pdf "osint"

The following will dissect how and why this search worked.

inurl:ftp - Instructs Google to only display addresses that contain "ftp" in the URL.

-inurl(http|https) - Instructs Google to ignore any addresses that contain either http or https in the URL. The separator is the pipe symbol (|) located above the backslash key. It tells Google "OR". This would make sure that we excluded any standard web pages.

filetype:pdf - Instructs Google to only display PDF documents.

"osint" - Instructs Google to mandate that the exact term osint is within the content of results.

Obviously, this operator could also be used to locate standard web pages, documents, and files. The following search displays only blog posts from inteltechniques.com that exist within a folder titled "blog" (WordPress).

inurl:blog site:inteltechniques.com

InTitle Operator

Similar to InURL, the "InTitle" operator will filter web pages by details other than the actual content of the page. This filter will only present web pages that have specific content within the title of the page. Practically every web page on the internet has an official title for the page. This is often included within the source code of the page and may not appear anywhere within the content. Most webmasters carefully create a title that will be best indexed by search engines. If you conduct a search for "osint video training" on Google, you will receive 2,760 results. However, the following search will filter those to 5. These only include web pages that had the search terms within the limited space of a page title.

intitle:"osint video training"

Note that the use of quotation marks prevents the query from searching "video training" within websites titled "osint". The quotes force the search of pages specifically titled "osint video training". You can add "all" to this search to force all listed words to appear in any order. The following would find any sites that have the words osint, video, and training within the title, regardless of the order.

allintitle:training osint video

An interesting way to use this search technique is while searching for online folders. We often focus on finding websites or files of interest, but we tend to ignore the presence of online folders full of content related to our search. As an example, I conducted the following search on Google.

intitle:index.of OSINT

The results contain online folders that usually do not have typical website files within the folders. The first three results of this search identified the following publicly available online data folders. Each possess dozens of documents and other files related to our search term of OSINT. One provides a folder structure that allows access to an entire web server of content. Notice that none of these results points to a specific page, but all open a folder view of the data present.

http://cyberwar.nl/d/
http://bitsavers.trailing-edge.com/pdf/
http://conference.hitb.org/hitbsecconf2013kul/materials/

OR Operator

You may have search terms that are not definitive. You may have a target that has a unique last name that is often misspelled. The "OR" (uppercase) operator returns pages that have just A, just B, or both A and B. Consider the following examples which include the number of results each.

"Michael Bazzell" OSINT 61,200
"Mike Bazzell" OSINT 1,390
"Michael Bazzell" OR "Mike Bazzell" OSINT 18,600
"Michael Bazell" OR "Mike Bazell" OSINT 1,160
"Michael Bazzel" OR "Mike Bazzel" OSINT 582

Asterisk Operator (*)

The asterisk (*) represents one or more words to Google and is considered a wild card. Google treats the * as a placeholder for a word or words within a search string. For example, "osint * training" tells Google to find pages containing a phrase that starts with "osint" followed by one or more words, followed by "training". Phrases that fit this search include: "osint video training" and "osint live classroom training".

Range Operator (..)

The "Range Operator" tells Google to search between two identifiers. These could be sequential numbers or years. As an example, OSINT Training 2015..2018 would result in pages that include the terms OSINT and training, and also include any number between 2015 and 2018. I have used this to filter results for online news articles that include a commenting system where readers can express their views. The following search identifies websites that contain information about Bonnie Woodward, a missing person, and between 1 and 999 comments within the page.

"bonnie woodward" "1..999 comments"

Related Operator

This option has been proven to be very useful over the past year. It collects a domain, and attempts to provide online content related to that address. As an example, I conducted a search on Google with the following syntax.

related:inteltechniques.com

The results included no references to that domain, but did associate it with my other websites, my X (Twitter) page, my Black Hat courses, and my book on Amazon. In my investigations, this has translated a person's personal website into several social networks and friends' websites.

Google Search Tools

There is a text bar at the top of every Google search result page. This allows for searching the current search terms within other Google services such as Images, Maps, Shopping, Videos, and others. The last option on this bar is the "Tools" link. Clicking this link will present a new row of options directly below. This provides new filters to help you focus only on the desired results. The filters will vary for each type of Google search. Figure 9.01 displays the standard search tools with the time menu expanded.

The "Any time" drop-down menu will allow you to choose the time range of visible search results. The default is set to "Any time" which will not filter any results. Selecting "Past hour" will only display results that have been indexed within the hour. The other options for day, week, month, and year work the same way. The last option is "Custom range". This will present a pop-up window that will allow you to specify the exact range of dates that you want searched. This can be helpful when you want to analyze online content posted within a known time.

Real World Application: Whenever I was assigned a missing person case, I immediately searched the internet. By the time the case is assigned, many media websites had reported on the incident and social networks were full of sympathetic comments toward the family. In order to avoid this traffic, I set the search tools to only show results up to the date of disappearance. I could then focus on the online content posted about the victim before the disappearance was public. This often led to more relevant suspect leads.

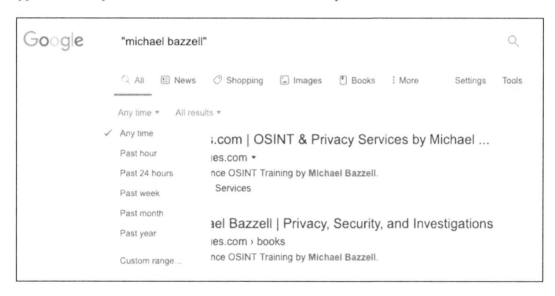

Figure 17.01: A Google Search Tools menu.

Dated Results

Google can be very sporadic when it comes to supplying date information within search results. Sometimes you will see the date that a search result was added to the Google index and sometimes you will not. This can be frustrating when you desire this information in order to identify relevant results. There is a fairly unknown technique that will force Google to always show you the date of each search result.

When you modify the "Any Time" option under the Search Tools menu, you will always see a date next to each result. If you are only searching for recent information, this solves the issue. However, if you are conducting a standard search without a specific date reference, the dates next to each result are missing. To remedy this, you can conduct a specific search that includes any results indexed between January 1, 1 BC and "today". The appropriate way to do this is to add "&tbs=cdr:1,cd_min:1/1/0" at the end of any standard Google search. Figure 17.02 displays the results of a search for the term "Michael Bazzell". The exact URL of the search was as follows.

https://www.google.com/search?q="michael+bazzell"

Notice that the result does not include a date next to the item. Figure 17.03 displays the results of this same search with the specific data added at the end. The exact URL of this search was the following address.

https://www.google.com/search?q="michael+bazzell"&tbs=cdr:1,cd_min:1/1/0

Notice that the result now has the date when the content was first indexed by Google. You can also now sort these results by date in order to locate the most recent information. The search tools menu also offers an "All results" menu that will allow you to choose to see "all results" or "Verbatim". The All Results will conduct a standard Google search. The Verbatim option searches exactly what you typed. One benefit of the Verbatim option is that Google will often present more results than the standard search. It digs a little deeper and gives additional results based on the exact terms you provided.

Figure 17.02: Google results without date injection.

Figure 17.03: Results with date injection.

Google Programmable Search Engines (programmablesearchengine.google.com)

Now that you are ready to unleash the power of Google, you may want to consider creating your own custom search engines, which Google has rebranded to Programmable Search Engines. Google allows you to specify the exact type of searches that you want to conduct, and then create an individual search engine just for your needs. Many specialty websites that claim to search only social network content are simply using a custom engine from Google. For our first example, we will create a basic custom search engine that only searches two specific websites.

After you log in to a Google account, navigate to the website listed above. If you have never created an engine, you will be prompted to create your first. Enter the first website that you want to search. In my example, I will search inteltechniques.com. As you enter any website to search, Google will automatically create another field to enter an additional website. The second website that I will search is inteltechniques.net. Provide a name for your custom engine and select "Create". You now have a custom search engine. You can either embed this search engine into a website or view the public URL to access it from within any web browser.

This basic functionality can be quite powerful. It is the method behind my custom Pastebin search engine discussed in a later chapter. In that example, I created a custom search engine that scoured dozens of specific websites in order to retrieve complete information about specific topics. This is only the first layer of a Google custom search engine. Google offers an additional element to its custom engines. This new layer, labeled Refinements, allows you to specify multiple actions within one custom search engine. The best way to explain this is to offer two unique examples.

For the first example, I wanted to create a custom search engine that allowed us to search several social networks. Additionally, we will isolate the results from each network across several tabs at the top of our search results. The first step will be to create a new custom search engine by navigating to "All search engines" and clicking "Add". Instead of specifying the two websites mentioned earlier, we will identify the websites to be searched as the following.

Facebook.com   X.com   Instagram.com
LinkedIn.com   YouTube.com   TikTok.com

While this is not a complete list of active social networks, it represents the most popular social networks at the time of this writing. At this point, our custom search engine would search only these websites and provide all results integrated into one search result page. We now want to add refinements that will allow us to isolate the results from each social network.

After you have added these websites, provided a name, and created your engine, select "Customize" in order to view the configuration of this custom search engine. On the left menu, click on "Search Features" and then in the main panel select "All Search Features settings". Selecting this should present a list of your engines. Select your test engine and click "Search features". This will present a new option at the top of the page labeled "Refinements". Click the "add" button to add a new refinement for each of the websites in this example. You should create these in the same order that you want them to appear within the search results. For this demonstration, I created the following refinements in order, accepting the default options.

Facebook   Twitter   Instagram
LinkedIn   YouTube   TikTok

When each refinement is created, you will have two options of how the search will be refined. The first option of "Search within sites with this refinement" will force Google to remain within the search request and not disclose other sites. The option of "Change priority of sites with this refinement" will place emphasis on matching rules, but will also reach outside of the rule if minimal results are present. I recommend using the first option. Scroll down to "Attach sites", select the corresponding filter, and then "Save" for each website.

You should now have a custom search engine that will not only search several specific social network websites, but it should also allow you to isolate the results for each network. Navigate back to "Setup" in the left menu and select the Public URL link to see the exact address of your new engine. Go to that address and you should see a very plain search engine. You can now search any term or terms that you want and receive results for only the social networks that you specified. Additionally, you can choose to view all of the results combined or only the results of a specific network. Figure 17.04 displays the results when I searched the term "osint". In this example, I have selected the Twitter refinement in order to only display results from twitter.com.

Figure 17.04: A Twitter refinement in a Google Programmable Search.

You can now bookmark this new search engine that you created and visit it whenever you have a target to search. You can take your custom search engines to another level by adding refinements that are not website specific. In the next example, we will make a search engine that will search the entire internet and allow us to filter by file type.

Create a new custom search engine and title it "Documents". Add only "google.com" as the website to be searched. We do not actually want to search google.com, but a website is required to get to the edit panel. Complete the captcha, click on "Create", and select "Customize". In the "Search Features" portion, enable the "Search the entire web" toggle. Delete google.com from the sites to be searched. You now basically have a custom search engine that will search everything. It will essentially do the same thing as Google's home page. You can now add refinements to filter your search results. Select "All Search Features settings" button at the top and add a new refinement. Title the new refinement "PDF"; change the default setting to " Change priority of sites with this refinement"; expand the "Advanced" menu, and enter the following in the "Rewrite query words" field.

ext:pdf

This will create a refinement that will allow you to isolate only PDF documents within any search that you conduct. Save this setting and create a new refinement. Title it DOC; change the default search setting; and place the following in the "Rewrite query words" field.

ext:doc OR ext:docx

This will create a new tab during your search results that will allow you to isolate Microsoft Word documents. By entering both the doc and docx formats, you will be sure to get older and newer documents. The word "OR" tells Google to search either format. Repeat this process for each of the following document types with the following language for each type.

XLS (Excel Spreadsheets) - ext:xls OR ext:xlsx OR ext:csv
PPT (PowerPoint Files) - ext:ppt OR ext:pptx
TXT (Text Docs) - ext:txt OR ext:rtf
WPD (Word Perfect Docs) - ext:wpd
ODT (OpenOffice Docs) - ext:odt OR ext:ods OR ext:odp
ZIP (Compressed Files) - ext:zip OR ext:rar OR ext:7z

Figure 17.05 displays the results of a search for the term osint within this new engine. The All tab is selected which reveals 717,000 results. Clicking the PowerPoint presentations option (PPT) reveals 45 files which contain the term. There are endless possibilities with this technique. You could make an engine that isolated images with extensions such as jpg, jpeg, png, bmp, gif, etc. You could also replicate all of this into a custom engine that only searched a specific website. If you were monitoring threats against your company, you could isolate only these files that appear on one or more of your company's domains.

Figure 17.05: A Documents File Type Google Custom Search.

Google Alerts (google.com/alerts)

When you have exhausted the search options on search engines looking for a target, you will want to know if new content is posted. Checking Google results every week on the same target to see if anything new is out there will get mundane. Utilizing Google Alerts will put Google to work on locating new information. While logged in to any Google service, such as Gmail, create a new Google Alert and specify the search term, delivery options, and email address to which to send the alert. In one of my alerts, Google will send an email daily as it finds new websites that mention "Open Source Intelligence Techniques" anywhere in the site. Another one of my alerts is for my personal website. I now receive an email when another site mentions or links to my website. Parents can use this to be notified if their child is mentioned in a website or blog. Investigators that are continuously seeking information about a target will find this beneficial.

Real World Application: A police detective was assigned a runaway case where a 15-year-old had decided to leave home and stay with friends at an unknown location. After several extensive internet searches, a Google Alert was set up using the runaway's name and city of residence. Within three days, one of the alerts was for a blog identifying the runaway and where she was currently staying. Within 30 minutes, the unhappy child was back home.

Bing (bing.com)

Google is not the only great search engine. While Google is the overwhelming choice of search engines used today, other sites should not be ignored, especially when having trouble locating any information on a subject. Bing is Microsoft's competition to Google and provides a great search experience. In 2009, Yahoo search (yahoo.com) began using the Bing search engine to produce search results. This makes a Yahoo search redundant if a Bing search has already been conducted. The same tactics described previously, and in the numerous Google books, can be applied to any search engine. The site operator and the use of quotes both work with Bing exactly as they do with Google. Bing also introduced time filtered searching that will allow you to only show results from the last 24 hours, week, month, year, or custom range. At the time of this writing Bing is including a set of "Generated using AI" results which are seldom pertinent in my experience. There are a couple of additional operators that are important that only apply to Bing. Bing offers an option that will list every website to which a target website links, and is the only search engine that offers this service.

Bing LinkFromDomain

I conducted a search on Bing of "LinkFromDomain:inteltechniques.com". Note that there are no spaces in the entire search string and you should omit the quotation marks. This operator creates a result that includes every website to which I have a link, located on any of the pages within my website. This can be useful to an investigator. When a target's website is discovered, this site can be large and contain hundreds of pages, blog entries, etc. While clicking through all of these is possible, sometimes links are hidden and cannot be seen by visually looking at the pages. This operator allows Bing to quickly pull links out of the actual code of the website.

Bing Contains

Earlier, I discussed searching for files with specific file extensions on Google. The "filetype" and "ext" operators that were explained both work on Bing the same way. However, Bing offers one more option to the mix. The "contains" operator allows you to expand the parameters of the file type search. As an example, a Bing search of "filetype:ppt site:cisco.com" returns 13,200 results. These include PowerPoint files stored on the domain of cisco.com. However, these results do not necessarily include links on the cisco.com website to PowerPoint files stored on other websites. A search on Bing for "contains:ppt site:cisco.com" returns 36,200 results. These include PowerPoint files that are linked from pages on the domain of cisco.com, even if they are stored on other domains. This could include a page on cisco.com that links to a PowerPoint file on hp.com. In most cases, this search eliminates the need to conduct a filetype search, but both should be attempted.

Google Images (images.google.com)

Google Images scours the web for graphical images based on a search term. Google obtains these images based on keywords for the image. These keywords are taken from the filename of the image, the link text pointing to the image, and text adjacent to the image. This is never a complete listing of all images associated with a subject, and will almost always find images completely unrelated to a target. In the case of common names, one should enclose the name in quotes and follow it with the city where the subject resides, place of employment, home town, or personal interests. This will help filter the results to those more likely to be related to the subject. When results are displayed, clicking the "Tools" button will present five new filter menus and an advanced search button. This menu will allow you to filter results to only include images of a specific size, color, time range, image type, or license type. The most beneficial feature of Google Images is the reverse image search option. This will be explained in great detail later in the book.

Bing Images (bing.com/images)

Similar to Google, Bing offers an excellent image search. Both sites autoload more images as you get toward the end of the current results. This eliminates the need to continue to load an additional page, and leads to faster browsing. Bing also offers the advanced options available on Google, and adds the ability to filter only files with a specified layout such as square or wide. Bing provides a "filter" option in the far right of results that provides extended functionality. The People tab offers restriction for images of "Just faces" and "Head & shoulders". It also provides suggested filters with every image search. Clicking image search links may provide additional photographs of the specific target based on the listed criteria. This intelligence can lead to additional searches of previously unknown affiliations.

International Search Engines

Search engines based in the U.S. are not the primary search sites for all countries. Visiting search sites outside of the U.S. can provide results that will not appear on Google or Bing. In Russia, Yandex is the chosen search engine. Yandex offers an English version at yandex.com. These results are often similar to Google's; however, they are usually prioritized differently. In the past, I have found unique intelligence from this site when Google let me down. In China, most people use Baidu. It does not offer an English version; however, the site is still usable. Striking the "enter" key on the keyboard after typing a search will conduct the search without the ability to understand the Chinese text. New results not visible on Google or Bing may be rare, but an occasional look on these sites is warranted.

Yandex (yandex.com)

In a previous edition of this book, I only made a brief reference to Yandex and quickly moved on. In the past few years, I have discovered many advanced features of Yandex which justify an expanded section. Visually, the Yandex home page and search results pages do not possess additional search operators. These options are only available by issuing a direct command within your search. While this can be more cumbersome than a Google search, the results can include much new data. Some of these searches can be overkill for daily use, but those who conduct brand reputation monitoring or extensive background checks may take advantage of this.

Exact terms: Similar to Google and Bing, quotation marks will search for exact terms. Searching "Michael Bazzell" inside of quotes would search those terms, and would avoid "Mike" or "Bazel".

Missing word: You can search an exact phrase without knowing every word of the phrase. A search for "Open Source * Techniques" inside of quotation marks will identify any results that include that phrase with any word where the asterisk (*) is located. This identified not only results with the title of this book, but also results for "Open Source Development Techniques" and "Open Source Responsive Techniques". This search can be very useful for identifying a person's middle name. "Michael * Bazzell" produced some interesting results.

Words within the same sentence: The ampersand (&) is used in this query to indicate that you want to search for multiple terms. "Hedgehog & Flamingo", without the quotation marks, would identify any websites that contained both of those words within one sentence. If you want the results to only include sentences that have the two words near each other, you can search "Hedgehog /2 Flamingo". This will identify websites that have a sentence that includes the words Hedgehog and Flamingo within two words of each other.

Words within the same website: Similar to the previous method, this search identifies the searched terms within an entire website. "Hedgehog && Flamingo", without quotation marks, would identify pages that have both those words within the same page, but not necessarily the same sentence. You can also control the search to only include results that have those two words within a set number of sentences from each other. A search of "Hedgehog && /3 Flamingo", without the quotation marks, would identify websites that have those two words within three sentences of each other.

Include a specific word: In Google and Bing, you would place quotation marks around a word to identify pages that contain that word in them. In Yandex, this is gained with a plus sign (+). Michael +Bazzell would mandate that the page has the word Bazzell, but not necessarily Michael.

Search any word: In Google and Bing, you can use "OR" within a search to obtain results on any of the terms searched. In Yandex, this is achieved with the pipe symbol (|). This is found above the backslash (\) on your keyboard. A search of "+Bazzell Michael|Mike|M", without quotation marks, would return results for Michael Bazzell, Mike Bazzell, and M Bazzell.

Exclude a word: Google and Bing allow you to use a hyphen (-) to exclude a word in a search. Yandex does not technically support this, but it seems to work fine. The official Yandex operator is the tilde (~). A typical search would look like "Michael Bazzell ~ Mike", without the quotation marks. This would identify websites that contained Michael Bazzell, but not Mike Bazzell. Using only one tilde will exclude only results where the unwanted term is in the same sentence as the keyword. I prefer to stick with the hyphen (-) until it no longer works.

Multiple identical words: This is a technique that I have needed several times in the past before I learned of Yandex's options. You may want to search for websites that contain a specific word more than once. An example might be if you are searching for someone that has two identical words in his or her full name. "Carina Abad Abad" would fit in this scenario. You could use quotation marks to identify the majority of the results, but you would filter out anything that was not exact such as Abad,Abad, Abad-Abad, or AbadAbad. This is where the exclamation point (!) comes in. A search of "!Carina !Abad !Abad", without quotation marks, would identify any results that included those three words regardless of spacing or punctuation.

Date specific searches: While Google provides a menu to filter your searches by date, Yandex's time period filter has no custom range option. You must specify the date range within the search using operators. The following queries should explain the options.

date:20111201..20111231 OSINT - Websites mentioning OSINT between December 1-31, 2011
date:2011* OSINT - Websites mentioning OSINT in the year 2011
date:201112* OSINT - Websites mentioning OSINT in December of 2011
date:>20111201 OSINT - Websites mentioning OSINT after December 1, 2011

Standard operators: Most of the operators explained earlier for Google and Bing should also work in Yandex. The commands for Site, Domain, Inurl, and Intitle should work the same way. Yandex maintains a list of operators at https://yandex.com/support/search/query-language/search-operators.html. All Yandex operators work together and multiple operators can be used to form very specific searches. Figure 17.06 displays the results for a search of any websites from 2013 with the phrase Michael Bazzell and the word OSINT while excluding the word Mike.

Figure 17.06: A custom Yandex search.

There are hundreds of additional international search engines. Of those, most are extremely specialized and do not offer great general search. The following have been most beneficial to my international investigations, in order of usefulness. I have included a direct search URL, which could be useful for your custom search tools.

Baidu http://www.baidu.com/s?wd=osint
Sogou https://www.sogou.com/web?query=osint
So https://www.so.com/s?q=osint
Mail.ru https://go.mail.ru/search?q=osint
Goo https://search.goo.ne.jp/web.jsp?MT=osint
Daum https://search.daum.net/search?w=tot&q=osint
Parseek http://parseek.com/Search/?q=osint
Naver https://search.naver.com/search.naver?query=osint
Coccoc https://coccoc.com/search?query=osint
Seznam https://search.seznam.cz/?q=osint
Rediff https://www.rediff.com/search/osint

I Search From (isearchfrom.com)

If you want to search Google within a version specified for another country, this site simplifies the process. Choose the country and language, and the tool will do the rest. While testing this service, I entered Japan as my country, English as my language, an iPad as my device, and OSINT as my search term. I was presented a google.co.jp search page in tablet view. Many results were similar to the U.S. version, but all were in a unique order. I find this useful when searching for international targets when I do not want bias toward a U.S. user. The "News" tab of foreign searches is often catered toward that geographical audience. This can display emphasis on news articles which would otherwise be buried in a typical Google result page.

Web Archives

Occasionally, you will try to access a site and the information you are looking for is no longer there. Maybe something was removed, amended, or maybe the whole page was permanently removed. Web archives, or "caches", can remedy this. I believe that these historical copies of websites are one of the most vital resources when conducting any type of online research. This section will explain the current options in order from most effective to least.

Google Cache (google.com)

Google recently removed the option to pull up cached pages directly from search results. The "Cached" option in the drop down menu is no longer present. Google has also clearly stated that they will no longer be supporting the "cache:" search operator. Currently we can regain some access to Google cache results by appending the target page to the specific Google URL of "https://webcache.googleusercontent.com/search?q=cache:". For example, https://webcache.googleusercontent.com/search?q=cache:phonelosers.org displays a cached copy of phonelosers.org. This version was taken four days prior to the current date, and displays information different from the current version. Google may eventually remove access to indexed pages altogether and I find myself more often relying on other search engines for access to cached versions of a target page.

Bing Cache (bing.com)

Unlike Google, Bing offers a cached view of many websites directly in their search results. Searching for a domain name, such as phonelosers.org, will present many results. The first result should link to the actual website. Directly next to the website name is a small green down arrow. Clicking it will present the option of "Cached". Clicking this link will display a previous version of the target website as collected by Bing. Figure 17.07 (first image) displays their menu option.

Yandex Cache (yandex.com)

The Russian search engine Yandex was already explained, but it is important to note now that it also possesses a cache option. If Yandex has a cached copy of a page, clicking on the three vertical dots next to a search result will show an option of "Saved copy". Figure 17.07 (second image) displays their cache menu option. Selecting the Saved copy option opens a new tab displaying the most recent Yandex archive of the page. The top banner displays the date and time of capture, the original website address, and a search option to highlight selected keywords within the result. Another benefit of the Yandex cache is that the results are sometimes older than those on Google or Bing. While this may sound counterintuitive, an older cache can be very helpful in an investigation.

The Wayback Machine (web.archive.org)

The Wayback Machine will provide a much more extensive list of options for viewing a website historically. Searching for phonelosers.org displayed a total of 1,280 captures of the site dating from 12/21/1997 through 8/14/2024 (Figure 17.08). Clicking the links presents quite a display of how the site has changed. Graphics are archived as well, proving that we should always think twice about which photos we post to the internet. Each view of the archived page will allow the user to click through the links as if it were a live page on the original web server. Clicking through the timeline at the top of each page will load the viewed page as it appeared on the date selected.

Wayback Search

Until 2016, you could not search keywords across Wayback Machine data. You had to know the exact URL of a target website, or at least the domain name. Today, we can search any terms desired and connect directly to archived data. At the time of this writing, a search bar was present at the top of every Wayback Machine page. If that should change, you can also conduct a search via a direct URL. The following address searched "phone losers" throughout the entire archive of information.

https://web.archive.org/web/*/phone losers

The results identify over twenty websites that include these terms. Within those sites are dozens of archived copies of each. This data represents decades of content at your fingertips. Much of it is offline and unavailable on the current public internet. Many domains have completely shut down. The results include several sites in addition to phonelosers.org, and you would not find these by searching the domain directly through the Wayback Machine. This is a reminder that we should check all available resources before completing our investigations.

Searching All Resources

Occasionally, there are websites that surface claiming to be able to extract and rebuild entire websites from online caches. In my experience, none of these have ever provided a complete historical view versus a manual approach. Engines such as Bing and Yandex generate a unique code when a cache is displayed. This action prevents most automated search tools from collecting archived information. I do not believe any option, other than navigating to each resource, will present you with the content that you need. I bookmark each of these services in an individual folder titled Archives and open each tab when I have a domain as a target. I have also created an online tool that will collect your target domain and forward you to the appropriate archive page. This will be explained later when discussing domain searches.

Finally, it is important to acknowledge that these resources can be beneficial when everything on a website appears to be present and unaltered. While caches work well on websites that have been removed and are completely empty, they also can tell a different story about websites that appear normal. Any time that I find a website, profile, or blog of interest, I immediately look at caches hoping to identify changes in content. These minor alterations can be very important. They highlight information that was meant to be deleted forever. These details can be the vital piece of your investigation puzzle. Most people have no idea that this technique exists.

Figure 17.07: Cache menu options on Bing and Yandex.

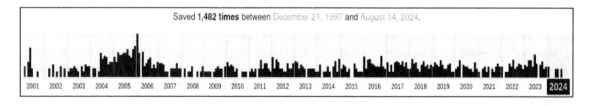

Figure 17.08: Wayback Machine results for an archived website.

Non-English Results

Not every piece of information that will be useful to you will be obtained by standard searches within English websites. Your target may either be from another country or have associates and affiliations in another country. While Google and Bing try to pick up on this, the technology is not perfect. Google has a search site and algorithm that change by location. For example, google.fr presents the French search page for Google. While this may produce the same overall results, they are usually in a different order than on google.com. Google no longer maintains a page with links to each international version of its search, but I have a preferred method.

2Lingual (2lingual.com)

This page will allow you to conduct one search across two country sites on Google. The Google search will display a plain search box and choices of two countries. The results will display in single columns next to each other. Additionally, the foreign results will be automatically translated to English. This feature can be disabled, if desired. The first few sponsored results (ads) will be similar, but the official results following should differ. This site can also be helpful when demonstrating to someone the importance of searching targets through multiple countries.

Google Translator (translate.google.com)

Many websites exist in non-English languages. As internet enthusiasts, we tend to focus on sites within our home area. There is a wealth of information out there on sites hosted in other countries which are presented in other languages. Google Translator will take text from any site or document and translate the text to a variety of languages. Usually, the service will automatically identify the language of the copied and pasted text. Selecting the desired output will provide the translation. Alternatively, you can translate an entire website in one click which will give a native view of the layout of the site. Instead of copying individual text to the search box, type or paste in the exact URL (address) of the website you want translated. Clicking the "Translate" button will load a new page of the site, which will be translated to English. This translation is rarely, if ever, perfect. However, it should give you an idea of the content presented on the page. This will also work on social network sites such as X (Twitter) and Instagram.

Bing Translator (bing.com/translator)

A few years after Google introduced free translation services, Bing created their own product. At first glance, it looks like a replica of Google's offering. However, Bing's translations are usually slightly different than Google's results. Similar to Google, you can also type or paste an entire foreign website to conduct a translation of everything on the target page.

DeepL (deepl.com/translator)

While smaller than Google or Bing, this may be the most accurate translator service I have found. The page appears and functions identical to the previous options, but the results may be substantially different.

Additional Online Translators

A few more online translation tools worth mentioning are **PROMT Online Translator** (https://www.online-translator.com/translation). **Libre Translate** (https://libretranslate.com/), **Lingva** (https://lingva.ml/), and **MyMemory** (https://mymemory.translated.net/). These services each provide independent translations. I recommend adding all of these as bookmarks and experimenting with each.

Google Input Tools (google.com/inputtools/try)

There is one last feature regarding foreign language searching that I have found useful. Google's Input Tools allow you to type in any language you choose. Upon navigating to the above website, choose the language of your target search. In Figure 17.09, I have chosen Russian as the language and typed "Online Investigation" on a standard English keyboard. The result is how that text might appear in traditional Cyrillic letters. I can now search for pages which include my keywords in Russian as well as in English. This technique is extremely important when you have located a username in a foreign language. As with all computer-generated translation services, the results are never absolutely accurate. I expect this technology to continue to improve.

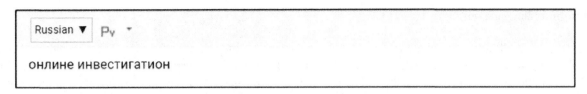

Figure 17.09: A Google Input Tools translation from English to Russian.

Google News Archive (news.google.com)

This can be an amazing resource of information about a target. In the past, if someone relocated to a new geographical area, he or she could leave the past behind and start over. Today, that is difficult. Google's News Archive is continually adding content from both online archives and digitized content from their News Archive Partner Program. Sources include newspapers from large cities, small towns, and anything in between. The link referenced above will allow for a detailed search of a target's name with filters including dates, language, and specific publication. In order to display this menu, click on the down arrow to the right of the search box. This can quickly identify some history of a target such as previous living locations, family members through obituaries, and associates through events, awards, or organizations.

Google Newspaper Archive (news.google.com/newspapers)

The previous option focused solely on digital content, such as your local newspaper website. Google's Newspaper archive possesses content from printed newspapers. All results on this site consist of high-resolution scanned newspaper pages. In my experience, this collection is not as extensive as the next option discussed. However, it is definitely worth a look, and will likely continue to grow.

Newspaper Archive (newspaperarchive.com)

This paid service provides the world's largest collection of newspaper archives. The high-resolution PDF scans of entire daily newspapers range in date from the 1800's until present. The first four editions of this book explained a method of using the Google Site operator and cached results to obtain practically any page of this newspaper collection without paying or subscribing. These vulnerabilities have all been patched and none of those techniques work today. Fortunately, Newspaper Archive still offers a 7-day free trial with unlimited access to every archive. While multiple trials can be obtained, each require a unique credit card number and email address. Many libraries have asked this service to scan their entire microfilm archives and make them freely available online. You will not find any mention of this free alternative on their home page, but a bit of searching will guide you to the right place. The following search on Google identifies hundreds of public libraries that pay for your access to their archives.

site:newspaperarchive.com "This archive is hosted by" "create free account"

The first part of the search tells Google to only look at the website newspaperarchive.com. The second part mandates that the exact phrase "This archive is hosted by" appears in the result. The final piece isolates only the newspaper collections that are available for free and without a credit card. This identifies the landing pages of the various libraries that have made their collections freely available. While you will still be required to register through the service, payment is not required for these collections. Consider the following usage that will likely present you with free views of Newspaper Archive whenever you need them.

On 12/13/2017, I navigated to newspaperarchive.com/advancedsearch/ and conducted an advanced search for anyone named Michael Williams from Cedar Rapids, Iowa. Newspaper Archive presented several results from the Cedar Rapids Gazette. Clicking on any of these results prompted me to create an account and forced me to enter a valid credit card number to proceed. I could not create an account from any of the pages without providing payment. Instead, I conducted the following Google search.

site:newspaperarchive.com "This archive is hosted by" "cedar rapids gazette"

The first result was a direct connection to crgazette.newspaperarchive.com. Clicking this link presented a page dedicated to searching over 40 newspapers within the Cedar Rapids and Des Moines areas. In the upper right corner was a link titled "Create Free Account". I clicked this link and provided generic details and a throwaway email address. The membership choices now include a completely free option, which will only allow access to the Iowa newspapers. After creating my free online account, I returned to the portal at crpubliclibrary.newspaperarchive.com and repeated the search of my target. Every link allowed me full unrestricted access to the high-resolution images.

While still logged in to this account, I navigated to delawarecolib.newspaperarchive.com, the direct page associated with the Delaware County Library (which I found through the original Google search in this section). I was not authorized to view this newspaper collection. However, after clicking "Create Free Account" on this page, I entered the same data as previously provided to the Iowa newspaper. After verifying my email address, I was allowed immediate access to this series of newspapers.

This technique will not obtain access to every collection on Newspaper Archive. However, it will provide a surprising amount of free access to huge collections internationally. During an hour of downtime, I created a free account on every library collection I could locate, using the same credentials on each. I can now log in to my single Newspaper Archive account and navigate the site from any page. When I reach a newspaper of interest after a search, I will be given full access if it is within a free collection. This is all thanks to the local libraries that have paid this site to give free access to the public. If the free trial of Newspaper Archive or the free library collections do not offer enough content, consider the following options.

Old Fulton (fultonhistory.com/Fulton.html):
57,000,000 scanned newspapers from the United States and Canada.

Library of Congress US News Directory (chroniclingamerica.loc.gov):
Scanned newspapers from the United States dated 1756-1963.

Library of Congress US News Directory (chroniclingamerica.loc.gov/search/titles):
Directory of newspapers from the United States dated 1690-Present.

Small Town Newspapers (stparchive.com):
Scanned and text versions of small town newspapers since 1890

Note that the search features on all of these options are mediochre at best. Always consider a Google search, such as site:stparchive.com "michael bazzell".

Google Advanced Search (google.com/advanced_search)

If the search operators discussed in this chapter seem too technical, Google offers an advanced search page that simplifies the process. Navigating to the above website will present the same options in a web page that are possible by typing out the operators. This will help you get familiar with the options, but it will be beneficial to understand the operators for later use. The Advanced Search page will allow you to specify a phrase for which you are searching, just like the quotes in a search will allow. The site and filetype operators used earlier can be achieved by entering the desired filters on this page. It should be noted that the file type option on this page is limited to popular file types, whereas the filetype operator can handle many other file extensions.

Bing Advanced Search (search.yahoo.com/web/advanced)

Bing does not technically provide an advanced search page similar to Google's. However, since Yahoo uses Bing's search, you can use Yahoo's advanced search page as a replacement. This page will allow you to easily create a search that filters by individual terms, exact phrases, omitted terms, specific domains, file formats, and languages.

Additional Google Engines

Google isolates some search results into specialized smaller search engines. Each of these focuses on a unique type of internet search. The following engines will likely give you results that you will not find during a standard Google or Bing search. While some results from these unique searches will appear within standard Google results, the majority will be hidden from the main page.

Google Patents (google.com/?tbm=pts)

Google probably has the best patent search option on the internet. It allows you to search the entire patent database within any field of a patent. This can be useful for searching names associated with patents or any details within the patent itself. If you need further help, Google offers an advanced patent search at google.com/advanced_patent_search.

Google Scholar (scholar.google.com)

Google Scholar is a freely accessible web search engine that indexes the full text of scholarly literature across an array of publishing formats. It includes most peer-reviewed online journals of Europe's and America's largest scholarly publishers, plus many books and other non-peer reviewed journals. My favorite feature of this utility is the case law and court records search. I have located many court records through this free website that would have cost money to obtain from private services.

Keyword Tool (keywordtool.io)

Keyword Tool displays autocomplete data from Google, Bing, YouTube, and the App Store. You have likely noticed that Google quickly offers suggestions as you type in your search. This is called autocomplete. If I were to type "macb" into Google, it would prompt me to choose from the most popular searches when people typed those letters. This information may lead you to new terms to search in reference to your investigation. The advantage of Keyword Tool over Google is that Google only provides the five most popular entries. Keyword Tool provides the ten most popular entries. Additionally, you can choose different countries to isolate popular terms. You can also see results from similar searches that Google does not display. Keyword Tool will redact some results and present pop-ups unless you sign up for a free trial. The pop-ups can be blocked using uBlock Origin as discussed earlier in this book.

Real World Application: I have successfully used this technique during the investigation of many businesses. I was once asked by a medium-sized business to investigate reports of a faulty product that they had recently recalled. They wanted to see customer complaints. After searching the typical review websites, I conducted a search with Keyword Tool. I discovered that the 9th most popular search involving this specific product name included a term that was a misspelling of the product name. It was different enough in spelling that my searches were missing this content. Knowing this information, I was able to locate more relevant data for the client.

This can also be very valuable for marketing and promotion. Assume I want to know what additional terms people search when they start with the word osint. Maybe I want to buy Google ads or tweak my website to be noticed more often. With this tool, I now know that the following are the most popular osint-related searches on Google.

osint meaning
osint websites
osint techniques
osint training

The YouTube tab tells me that people are searching for videos related to the following terms.

osint tools
osint investigations
osint phone number
osint analysis

Finally, I see that Bing users seem to be a bit more focused with the following queries.

osint resources
osint api
osint mind map
osint michael bazzell

Other Alternatives

Google and Bing are great, but they do not do it all. There will always be a need for specialized search engines. These engines usually excel in one particular search method which justifies the lack of search power in other areas. The sites listed in this next section represent the extreme minority when it comes to search traffic. It is often sites like these that implement the technologies that we later take for granted in more popular engines.

Searx (baresearch.org)

This meta-crawler was previously explained as a self-hosted option within our VM (preferred), but an online instance is also available. It presents results from Google, Bing, and others. It often gets dismissed as another comparison search site, but there are many other advantages to using this service. First, conducting a search will provide results from the main search engines, but will remove duplicate entries. This alone is a quick way to conduct your due-diligence by checking Google and Bing. Next, the top row of options will allow you to repeat this redundancy-reducing option by checking results on Images, News, and Videos sections. Next to each result on any search page is a "cached" link. Instead of opening the Google or Bing cache, clicking this will open the cached page of the target website through the Wayback Machine. Finally, a "proxied" option next to each result will connect you to the target website through a proxy service provided by Searx. This is basically a layer of privacy preventing the website owner from collecting data about you, such as your IP address. Technically, Searx opened the target site, and their data would be tracked instead of yours. There are ways for adversaries to bypass this "anonymity", but it is decent protection for most sites.

If you have executed the self-hosted option previously presented, then you may never need an online instance such as baresearch.org. Using your own self-hosted instance also prevents any third-party instances from snooping on your queries.

DuckDuckGo (duckduckgo.com)

This search engine with a clean interface offers two unique services. It has gained a lot of popularity because it does not track anything from users. Engines, such as Google, record and maintain all of your search history and sites visited. This can be a concern to privacy advocates and those with sensitive investigations. Additionally, it uses information from crowd-sourced websites such as Wikipedia and Wolfram Alpha to augment traditional results and improve relevance. You will receive fewer results here than at more popular search engines, but the accuracy of the results will improve.

Start Page (startpage.com)

Similar to DuckDuckGo, Start Page is a privacy-focused search engine that does not reveal your connection information to traditional search engines. The difference here is that Start Page only includes Google results versus DuckDuckGo's collaboration of multiple sources. The benefit to this is the ability to use Google's filters while still protecting your identity. This includes filtering by date, images, and videos. Another benefit is the ability to open any result through a "proxy" link. This option, labeled "Visit in Anonymous View " below each search result, opens the linked page through Start Page's servers and displays the content within their site. This protects your IP address from anyone monitoring connections at the target website. While this technique is not foolproof, it provides a valid layer of protection. My search strategy involves Start Page whenever I have a sensitive search that I do not want to associate with my computer or internet connection. This might include investigations that involve highly sensitive topics such as tech-savvy stalker suspects.

Qwant (qwant.com)

Qwant attempts to combine the results of several types of search engines into one page. It was launched in 2013 after two years of research. It has an easily digestible interface that displays results in columns titled All, News, Images, Videos, and Shopping. There is a Google "feel" to it and the layout can be changed to your own preferences. A default search of my own name provided the expected results similar to Google and Bing. Clicking on the tabs at the top introduced new results not found on the other engines. The results included recent posts from X (Twitter), Facebook, LinkedIn, and Myspace from and about people with my name.

Million Short (millionshort.com)

This website offers a unique function that is not found on any other search engine. You can choose to remove results that link to the most popular one million websites. This will eliminate popular results and focus on lesser-known websites. You can also select to remove the top 100,000, 10,000, 1,000, or 100 results. Million Short now requires that we register a free account, but they will accept addresses from forwarding/masking services.

Tor Search Engines

Tor is free software for enabling anonymous communication. The name is an acronym derived from the original software project name The Onion Router. Tor directs internet traffic through a free, worldwide, volunteer network consisting of more than six thousand relays to conceal a user's location and usage from anyone conducting network surveillance or traffic analysis. Using Tor makes it more difficult for internet activity to be traced back to the user. This also applies to a website that is hosted on the Tor network. Usually, these sites include illegal drug shops, child exploitation swaps, and weapon sales. Because these sites are not hosted on publicly viewable networks, they are hard to locate and connect. Tor-based search engines and a proxy aid this process.

Ahmia (ahmia.fi)

This is a very powerful Tor search engine. While no engine can index and locate every Tor website, this is the most thorough option that I have seen. It should be the first engine used when searching Tor related sites. The links in the results will not load if searching through a standard browser and connection. Using the Tor Browser discussed previously is the ideal way to use this service.

Tor Link (tor.link)

This engine appeared in 2022 and was quite promising. Although it will often provide fewer results than Ahmia, the results often include sites not present in the Ahmia results. This has complemented Ahmia well for many of my Tor-based investigations.

Onionland Search (onionlandsearchengine.net)

This service relies on Google's indexing of Tor sites which possess URL proxy links. However, I find some "hidden" sites with this utility which were not presented by the previous options.

Tor Search Sites

I believe some of the strongest Tor search engines exist only on the Tor network. You cannot access them from a standard internet connection, and the Tor Browser is required for native use (alternatively you can use the TOR functionality in Brave). My favorite is "Torch", which can be found at the following address if connected to Tor.

http://torchdeedp3i2jigzjdmfpn5ttjhthh5wbmda2rr3jvqjg5p77c54dqd.onion

Alternatives to Torch include **Haystack** and **Tor66**, which can each be accessed at the following addresses via the Tor network.

http://haystak5njsmn2hqkewecpaxetahtwhsbsa64jom2k22z5afxhnpxfid.onion.
http://tor66sewebgixwhcqfnp5inzp5x5uohhdy3kvtnyfxc2e5mxiuh34iid.onion

All of the options presented here, and several others, are available for automatic queries within your custom search tool, as presented in a moment. Please note that these sites appear, disappear, and reappear often.

Search Engine Collections

I believe I could fill several chapters with tutorials for the hundreds of search engines available today. Instead, I point you toward two of the best collections I have found.

Search Engine Colossus (searchenginecolossus.com)

This website is an index of practically every search engine in every country. The main page offers a list of countries alphabetically. Each of these links connects to a list of active search engines in that country. I stay away from this service when searching American-based subjects. However, if my target has strong ties to a specific country, I always research the engines that are used in that area through this website.

Fagan Finder (faganfinder.com)

This website offers an interactive search page which populates your query into hundreds of options. Enter your search term in the field and click any of the hundreds of buttons to begin a search. Many of the search services are targeted toward niche uses, but you may find something valuable there which you do not see on the custom offline search tool provided at the end of this chapter.

FTP Search

I believe that the searching of File Transfer Protocol (FTP) servers is one of the biggest areas of the internet that is missed by most online researchers. FTP servers are computers with a public IP address used to store files. While these can be secured with mandated access credentials, this is rarely the case. Most are public and can be accessed from within a web browser. The overall use of FTP to transfer files is minimal compared to a decade ago, but the servers still exist in abundance. I prefer the manual method of searching Google for FTP information. As mentioned earlier, Google and Bing index most publicly available data on FTP servers. A custom search string will be required in order to filter unwanted information. If I were looking for any files including the term "confidential" in the title, I would conduct the following search on Google and Bing.

inurl:ftp -inurl:(http | https) "confidential"

The result will include files from ftp servers (inurl:ftp); will exclude any web pages (-inurl:(http | https); and mandate that the term "confidential" is present (""). I have located many sensitive documents from target companies with this query. The above search yielded 107,000 FTP results. However, these specific hits are not the only valuable data to pursue. Consider the following example. I want to locate PDF documents stored on FTP servers that contain "cisco" within the title or content, and I conduct the following search on Google.

inurl:ftp -inurl:(http|https) "cisco" filetype:pdf

This results in 20,000 options within multiple FTP servers hosted on numerous domains. The first result is hosted on the Southwest Cyberport FTP server and connects to a PDF document at the following address. It appears to be a chapter of a textbook.

ftp://ftp.swcp.com/pub/cisco/03chap01.pdf

Manually changing the last "01" to "02" loads the second chapter of the book. However, it is easier to eliminate the document name altogether and browse the directory titled "cisco". The first of the following addresses displays the contents of that folder, while the second displays the content of the "pub" folder. Copy these directly into a web browser to see the results.

ftp://ftp.swcp.com/pub/cisco/
ftp://ftp.swcp.com/pub/

This type of manual navigation will often reveal numerous publicly available documents that traditional searches withhold. I have located extremely sensitive files hosted by companies, government agencies, and the military. Most File Transfer Protocol (FTP) servers have been indexed by Google, but there are other third-party options that are worth exploring. At the end of each description, I identify the number of results included for the search "Cisco" "PDF".

Napalm FTP (searchftps.net)

This FTP search engine often provides content that is very recent. After each result, it displays the date that the data was last confirmed at the disclosed location. This can help locate relevant information that is still present on a server. While it generated the most results of all four services, many of them were no longer available on the target FTP servers. Some could be reconstructed with cached copies, but not all.

"Cisco" "PDF": 3,384

Mamoht (mmnt.ru)

This Russian FTP server allows you to isolate search results by the country that is hosting the content. This is likely determined by IP address. While most of the filtered results will be accurate, I recommend searching through the global results before dismissing any foreign options. My favorite feature of this engine is the "Search in found" option. After conducting my search, I checked this option and my search field was cleared. I entered "router" and clicked search again. I was prompted with the 436 results within my original hits that also included the word router. While this could have been replicated manually, I appreciate the option.

"Cisco" "PDF": 789 results

For comparison, Google found 19,600 results for inurl:ftp -inurl:(http|https) "Cisco" "PDF".

FreewareWeb (freewareweb.com/ftpsearch.shtml)

This service is less robust than the previous options, but it should not be ignored. In 2022, I was searching for documents with a unique file extension. This was the only service which presented the documents I needed, which were contracts signed by my target.

NerdyData (nerdydata.com/reports/new)

Google, Bing, and other search engines search the content of websites. They focus on the data that is visually present within a web page. NerdyData searches the programming code of a website. This code is often not visible to the end user and exists within the HTML code, JavaScript, and CSS files with which most users are not familiar. This code can be extremely valuable to research in some scenarios. Viewing the source code of a website can be done by right-clicking on the background of a page and selecting "View Source". The following two examples should explain a small portion of the possibilities with this service.

In later chapters, you will learn about free services that try to identify additional websites that may be associated with your target website. The backbone of these services relies on the indexing of programming data of websites. Nerdy Data may be the purest way of searching for this data. If you were to look at the source code of one of my previous websites (no longer online), you would have seen at the bottom that I used a service called Google Analytics. This service identifies the number of visitors to a website and the general area where they are located. The following is the actual code that was present.

```
<script type="text/javascript">
try {var pageTracker = _gat._getTracker("UA-8231004-3");
pageTracker._trackPageview();
} catch(err) {}</script>
```

The important data here is the "UA-8231004-3". That was my unique number for Google Analytics. Any website with which I used the service would have needed to have that number within the source code of the page. If you searched that number on NerdyData a few years prior, you would have received interesting results. NerdyData previously identified three websites that were using that number, including computercrimeinfo.com and two additional sites that I maintained for a law firm. You can often find valuable information within the source code of your target's website.

Many web designers and programmers steal code from other websites. In the past, this would be very difficult to identify without already knowing the suspect website. With NerdyData, you can perform a search of the code of concern and identify websites that possess the data within their own source code. In 2013, I located a custom search website at the YGN Ethical Hacker Group that inspired me to create my own similar search service. I was curious if there were any other search websites that possessed this basic code that might give me more ideas. I looked at the source code of the website and located a small piece of code that appeared fairly unique to that service. I conducted a search on Nerdy Data for the following code.

```
<li>http://yehg.net/q?[keyword]&c=[category]  (q?yehg.net&c=Recon)</li>
```

This code was within the JavaScript programming of the search website. The search results identified 13 websites that also possessed the same code. Two of these results were hosted on the creator's website, and offered no additional information. Three of the results linked to pages that were no longer available. Three of the results linked to pages that were only discussing the code within the target website and how to improve the functionality. However, four of the results identified similar search services that were also using the programming code searched. This revealed new search services that were related to the website in which I was interested. NerdyData now restricts queries to 35 characters, but they will allow you to enter multiple strings by automatically connecting them with AND statements, so we just break longer code samples into smaller snippets.

This same technique could be used to identify websites that are stealing proprietary code; locate pages that were created to attempt to fool a victim into using a cloned site; or validate the popularity of a specific programming function being used on hacking websites globally.

IntelTechniques Search Engines Tool

At this point, you may be overwhelmed with the abundance of search options. I can relate to that, and I do not take advantage of every option during every investigation. During my initial search of a target, I like to rely on the basics. I first search Google, Bing, Yandex, and the smaller search engines. In order to assist with this initial search, I created a custom tool that will allow you to quickly get to the basics. Figure 17.10 displays the current state of this tool available in your downloads or at **https://inteltechniques.com/tools**. The search options will allow you to individually search directly through Google, Bing, Yahoo, Searx, Yandex, and many others. Across all options, each search that you conduct will open within a new tab within your browser. The search all takes place on your computer within your browser, directly to the sources.

The "Submit All" option will allow you to provide any search term that will be searched across all of the services listed. Each service will populate the results within a new tab in your internet browser. Regardless of the browser that you use, you must allow pop-ups in order for the tool to work. You can also use any of the search operators discussed previously within this tool, including quotation marks. I present a similar search tool at the end of most chapters which summarizes and simplifies the query processes for the techniques explained. I encourage you to become familiar with each of these. Once proficient, you can query target data across all options within a few minutes. This saves me several hours every week.

Search Terms	Populate All			
Search Terms	Google			
Search Terms	Google Date			
Search Terms	Google News			
Search Terms	Google FTP			
Search Terms	Google Index			
Search Terms	Google Scholar	Search Terms	Submit All
Search Terms	Google Patents	**Tor Required:**	
Search Terms	Bing	Search Terms	Torch
Search Terms	Bing News	Search Terms	Tor66
Search Terms	Yahoo	Search Terms	Haystack
Search Terms	Yandex	Search Terms	Ahmia
Search Terms	Baidu	Search Terms	SearchDemon
Search Terms	Searx	Search Terms	Excavator
Search Terms	Exalead	Search Terms	GDark
Search Terms	DuckDuckGo	Search Terms	Hidden Reviews
Search Terms	StartPage	Search Terms	OnionLand
Search Terms	Qwant	Search Terms	Phobos
Search Terms	Brave	Search Terms	Submarine
Search Terms	Wayback	Search Terms	DeepSearch
Search Terms	Ahmia	Search Terms	OnionCenter
Search Terms	Onionland	Search Terms	FreshOnion
Search Terms	Tor.link		

Figure 17.10: The IntelTechniques Search Engines Tool.

Artificial Intelligence (A.I.) Engines

Artificial Intelligence (AI) is all the rage today. People are flocking to ChatGPT and other providers to chat with machines and receive answers to practically any questions. **Contrary to many new online OSINT courses, I do NOT recommend the use of A.I. services within OSINT investigations**. This will upset some readers, but I offer the following reasons.

- Most online A.I. tools collect and use any data you enter to further train their systems. The specific details of your target might end up in someone else's chat box.
- The information is more often incorrect than accurate. In a moment, I provide an example which presented incorrect facts about me. We should not base our investigations on summarized content.

If you still want to proceed with A.I. as a part of your OSINT investigation process, offline Large Language Models (LLMs) can be a benefit to you. LLMs are the backbone behind AI services. They are machine learning models which can understand and generate human language text. They work by analyzing massive data sets of language. Fortunately, we can download these models and use them completely offline without sharing any data back to the companies which created them. There are many clients which allow access to this data, but most are complicated to install and configure. My preference is an open-source program called **Jan** (https://www.jan.ai). After installation, you will be prompted to browse the available models. For the following demonstration, I downloaded the 4 GB Mistral Instruct7B Q4 model. Once complete, I could select it under the Model tab.

I can now securely ask anything desired without jeopardizing my privacy. In one example, I asked about myself and where I live. The completely offline model summarized me and provided the city I live in as Omaha. However, I do not live in Omaha, I did not write one of the books listed, and my firm name was not correct. I hope you can see why I would never rely on this type of information. I believe these models can be used for research, learning, or entertainment, but never for investigations.

A far more appropriate use of these LLMs is for organizing data and creating sample code. They are great at creating sorted lists or building scripts to benefit our workflow. For example, a Windows user could use Jan with the Codestral 22B Q4 model to create a script which installs a full set of our preferred OSINT applications (Figure 17.11).

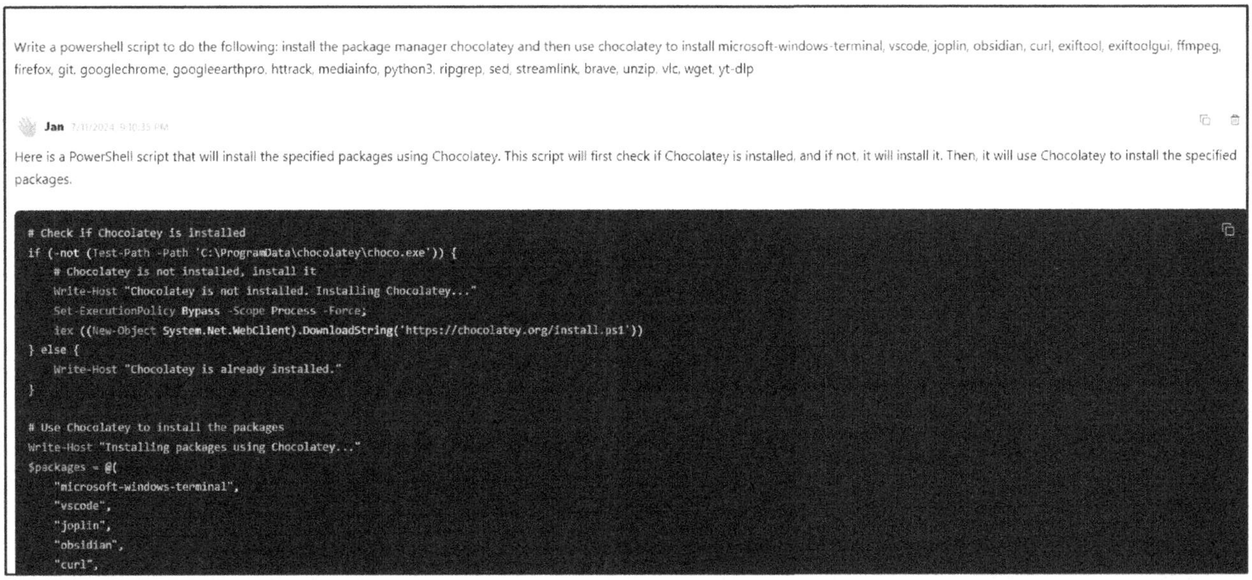

Figure 17.11: A Jan generated script.

CHAPTER EIGHTEEN
SOCIAL NETWORKS: FACEBOOK

I hesitate writing anything within this chapter. It seems that most valuable Facebook search techniques disappeared in 2019. There are still many methods we can apply, but the future outlook for targeted queries is dim. I worry this chapter will become outdated before anything else, but there are some stable searches which should have longevity. Before we dive in, let's take a look at the Facebook search issues timeline.

June 6th, 2019: This was the big date which began the decline of the Facebook graph. Previous profile queries all failed, and everything seemed doomed. Our ability to view "hidden" content via URL modifications was gone and we all scrambled for new techniques.

June 17th, 2019: Various researchers developed online search tools and browser extensions which brought back most of the Facebook Graph functionality. Hundreds of OSINT researchers flocked to these and we restored our missing techniques.

August 1st, 2019: On this date, all browser-based extensions which leveraged the Facebook Graph stopped working. Facebook implemented new encryption which terminated all functionality.

August 2nd, 2019: The Facebook username to user ID conversion tool on my website stopped working. It appeared that my web server was being blocked by Facebook. I switched the user ID conversion tool to a new web server, and all appeared to be working again.

August 3rd, 2019, 12:38 pm ET: Facebook began blocking my new web server.

September 8th, 2019: On this date, we saw methods such as using the Facebook Messenger application to search telephone numbers disappear, as well as most email search options. This appeared deliberate, and more evidence of Facebook's desire to lock down the platform.

2020: Facebook drastically changed their layout, removed the wildcard (*) search operator, blocked some of the "Base64" methods (explained in a moment), and continued to aggressively monitor the OSINT community's response to their actions.

2022: Many search methods have disappeared, reappeared, and disappeared again. You have been warned that some of the techniques here may no longer work by the time you read this. However, we still have many options!

Fortunately, many people still share intimate details of their lives within social networks such as Facebook. Information that was once held privately within a small group of friends or family is now broadcasted to the world via public profiles. This chapter should identify new techniques which can be applied to any Facebook target. It will explain numerous ways to obtain user information, which is public data, even if not visible within their official profile.

Official Facebook Options

Facebook's redesign in 2020 presented many new search options which can benefit online investigators. Once logged in, a simple search field will be present at the top of any Facebook page. This is a generic starting point. I encourage you to think of Facebook's current search landscape in two parts. The KEYWORD search is any generic term, name, location, or entity of interest. The FILTER search is the options which eliminates unwanted results. Let's start with a demonstration where we are looking for a profile of a person.

Typing in a target's real name should lead to results, many of which are unrelated to your investigation. Unlike other social networks, Facebook users typically use their real name when creating a profile. This profile is usually linked to an employer, graduating high school class, college alumni, or general interests. With billions of active users, it will be likely that you will locate several user profiles under the same name as your target. There are a few things that you can do to find the right person.

If your target's name is Tom Johnson, you have your work cut out for you. This does not mean that you will never find his Facebook page, but you will need to take additional steps to get to your target. When searching the name, several possibilities may appear in the results. This is obviously not the complete list of Tom Johnsons that are present on Facebook. At the bottom of this list is an option to "See All" the profiles with your target name. This is also not the complete list. Scrolling down should automatically populate more profiles. You could look through these and hope to identify your target based on the photo, location, or additional information displayed in this view. Instead, consider adding filters within the left menu.

Figure 18.01 displays my keyword search for "Tom Johnson" who lives in Chicago, Illinois, attended Vashon High School, and currently works at Foot Locker. This located only one result, as this was a very targeted query. The filters helped me get from thousands of targets to only one. However, this is not as easy as it sounds. There are multiple Vashon high schools and dozens of Foot Locker Facebook pages. In a moment, we will force Facebook to focus on specific entities.

Figure 18.01: A Facebook keyword search with filters applied.

Once a user's profile is located, the default view is the "Posts" tab. This will include basic information such as gender, location, family members, friends, relationship status, interests, education, and work background. This page will also commonly have a photo of the user and any recent posts on their page. Clicking through this data may uncover valuable evidence, but you may be missing other data. I will explain numerous methods throughout this chapter which should help identify all available content relevant to your investigation.

First, consider using the traditional filter options available on most Facebook pages. Figure 18.02 displays the main filter bar on the top of every Facebook profile page. This will seek Photos, Videos, Places, Groups, and other options associated with the profile. You may be able to click through the various sections in order to reveal all publicly available content. There is also an option to search within the current profile by clicking on the three horizontal dots above the target's timeline. A query such as "birthday" may reveal posts wishing a them a happy birthday and thus shed light on the target's date of birth. My preference is to query via direct URL so that I know I did not miss anything. Assume that your target is Mark Zuckerberg. His profile is available at the following URL.

https://www.facebook.com/zuck

This indicates his Facebook username is "zuck". We can apply this to the following URLs, each which connect directly to the associated public information page. These direct URLs will be beneficial to our Facebook tool presented soon. Since "zuck" does not share much, I replaced him with a random username of "mike" (not me).

Timeline: https://www.facebook.com/mike
About: https://www.facebook.com/mike/about
Employment: https://www.facebook.com/mike/about?section=work
Education: https://www.facebook.com/mike/about?section=education
Locations: https://www.facebook.com/mike/about?section=living
Contact Info: https://www.facebook.com/mike/about?section=contact-info
Basic Info: https://www.facebook.com/mike/about?section=basic-info
Relationships: https://www.facebook.com/mike/about?section=relationship
Family Members: https://www.facebook.com/mike/about?section=family
Bio: https://www.facebook.com/mike/about?section=bio
Life Events: https://www.facebook.com/mike/about?section=year-overviews
Friends: https://www.facebook.com/mike/friends
Following: https://www.facebook.com/mike/following
Profile Photos: https://www.facebook.com/mike/photos
Photo Albums: https://www.facebook.com/mike/photos_albums
Videos: https://www.facebook.com/mike/videos
Reels: https://www.facebook.com/mike/reels
Check-Ins: https://www.facebook.com/mike/places_visited
Visits: https://www.facebook.com/mike/map
Recent Check-Ins: https://www.facebook.com/mike/places_recent
Sports: https://www.facebook.com/mike/sports
Music: https://www.facebook.com/mike/music
Movies: https://www.facebook.com/mike/movies
TV Shows: https://www.facebook.com/mike/tv
Books: https://www.facebook.com/mike/books
Apps & Games: https://www.facebook.com/mike/games
Likes: https://www.facebook.com/mike/likes
Events: https://www.facebook.com/mike/events
Facts: https://www.facebook.com/mike/did_you_know
Reviews: https://www.facebook.com/mike/reviews
Reviews Given: https://www.facebook.com/mike/reviews_given
Reviews Written: https://www.facebook.com/mike/reviews_written
Places Reviews: https://www.facebook.com/mike/place_reviews_written

The Facebook search tool presented in a moment will allow you to execute all of these URL queries easily in order to minimize the effort to explore a profile. Let's conduct another example of searching through Facebook's official channels. Assume you want to see photos posted by Mark Zuckerberg while he was in San Francisco in 2015. First, we need to obtain access to Facebook's filters, which are not visible when looking at a target's profile. We can access the option to search within the current profile by clicking on the three horizontal dots above the target page's timeline. I enter "San" as my search term which will then cause the desired filters menu to appear on the left side of the page (Figure 18.03).

This method was sloppy since I am forcing Facebook to include the keyword of "San" within my search. It is also searching all posts on the profile, not specifically photos. At the time of this writing, there is no way to search Facebook's site by filters only. You must include a search term. In a moment, our tool will bypass this restriction with a new method. Photos can also be searched by generic location. Figure 18.04 demonstrates the "Photos" option after searching "Chicago". The filter on the left can filter results based on author, type, location, and date.

Let's conduct another keyword search within the official site. Assume you wanted to find any posts including the term "OSINT". After conducting the basic search, you should click "Posts". This expands the search and opens the Posts filter options. From there, you can filter by year or location. You could also click through the other categories such as Videos or Groups. All basic Facebook filters can be applied using direct URLs. Considering an interest in the term "OSINT", the following addresses replicate each of the filters of a standard Facebook search.

All: https://www.facebook.com/search/top/?q=osint
Posts: https://www.facebook.com/search/posts/?q=osint
People: https://www.facebook.com/search/people/?q=osint
Photos: https://www.facebook.com/search/photos/?q=osint
Videos: https://www.facebook.com/search/videos/?q=osint
Marketplace: https://www.facebook.com/marketplace/category/search/?query=osint
Pages: https://www.facebook.com/search/pages/?q=osint
Places: https://www.facebook.com/search/places/?q=osint
Groups: https://www.facebook.com/search/groups/?q=osint
Events: https://www.facebook.com/search/events/?q=osint
Links: https://www.facebook.com/search/links/?q=osint
Watch: https://www.facebook.com/watch/search/?q=osint

Figure 18.02: Facebook's main filter options.

Figure 18.03: Facebook filters in use.

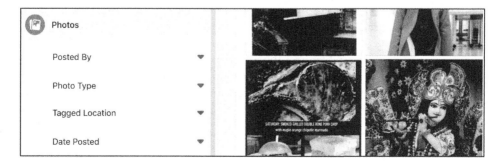

Figure 18.04: Photo results from Facebook filter options.

This presents the end of basic Facebook search techniques through the official site. Everything presented until now should apply for a while, and these URL structures should not change soon. Analyzing all of the evidence identified through these URLs should present substantial information. Many of these pages, such as a person's timeline, will load continuously. Pressing the space bar on your keyboard should load everything until the end. I have found taping down the space bar helpful for long pages. Some choose to use auto-scrolling browser extensions, but I prefer to avoid these as any detected scripts or automation increases the chances of Facebook suspending our user account. From here, we must dig deeper into profile data and apply some fairly technical methods in order to get to the next level.

Profile Details

At this point, you should be able to locate a target's profile by name with filters; analyze the publicly available content; and search by topic. That is just the tip of the iceberg. Facebook collects a lot of additional information from everyone's activity on the social network. Every time someone "Likes" something or is tagged in a photo, Facebook stores that information. Extracting these details can be difficult.

In order to conduct the following detailed searches, you must know the user number of your target. This number is a unique identifier that will allow us to search otherwise hidden information from Facebook. Prior to mid-2015, the easiest way to identify the user number of any Facebook user was through the Graph API. While you were on a user's main profile, you could replace "www" in the address with "graph" and receive the profile ID number of that user. This no longer works because Facebook removed the ability to search their graph API by username. However, we can still obtain this powerful number through a manual search option.

This technique involves viewing the source code of any user's Facebook profile. The process for this will vary by browser. In Firefox and Chrome, simply right-click on a Facebook profile page (not an image) and select "View Page Source". Be sure not to hover on any hyperlinks during the right-click. A new tab should open with the text-only view of the source code of that individual profile. Within the browser, conduct a search on this page for "userID". This will identify a portion of the code within this page that contains that specific term. As an example, the following is the source code visible in Zuck's profile.

"userID":"4"

Sometimes Firefox will search through the source code and highlight data, but the results don't match the terms searched. I do not know why this happens. Also note that your own Facebook ID number will likely return with this keyword search along with that of your target, so knowing the ID number for your own account will allow you to ignore those entries. When necessary, I copy all of the source code and paste it into a text editor, then search through it. In this example, the user ID of this profile is 4. We will use this number for numerous searches within the next instruction. Some users prefer to look at the URLs of a target's photos in order to identify the user ID, but I believe this is bad practice. If a user has no photos, this will not work. Also, Facebook's photo displays often hide this information from plain sight. I prefer to rely on the source code view or my Facebook tools for this identification. This number will allow us to obtain many more details about the account. Until July of 2019, there were dozens of online search tools which would identify the user ID number (4) when supplied a username (zuck). Almost all of these stopped functioning, including my own, when Facebook began aggressively blocking these search tools.

While you may find an online option which still functions, we should not rely on these. If you are exhausted from searching within each profile's source code in order to locate the user ID, I reluctantly offer the following site which currently attempts to automatically replicate this process.

https://findidfb.com/

Facebook Base64 Encoding

Prior to June of 2019, a simple URL could be used for all of our Facebook queries, but then Meta began requiring Base64 encoding for some queries. In essence, they added artificial complexity to some URL structures, likely in an effort to block content scraping and third-party services. Base64 structured queries are primarily required when using the target's Facebook ID number as part of our search. Let's break this down by looking at the following URL structure for queries.

https://www.facebook.com/search/posts/?q=posts&epa=FILTERS&filters=

https://facebook.com/	The Facebook domain
search/	Instructs Facebook to conduct a search
photos/	Specifies the type of information desired
?q=photos	Searches any photos (videos and posts works here too)
&epa=FILTERS&filters=	Finishes the URL with a filter demand

Next, we must formulate our target data and convert it to a specific type of encoding called Base64. This is likely used because it is extremely common and can be generated by any browser. Previously, I presented the following data.

{"rp_author":"{\"name\":\"author\",\"args\":\"[USERID]\"}"}

This tells Facebook that we are searching for information from a specific profile (author), and the [USERID] should contain your target's user ID number as determined earlier. If we were targeting "zuck", and knew his user number was "4", we would have the following data.

{"rp_author":"{\"name\":\"author\",\"args\":\"4\"}"}

Notice the position of "4" as the user number. Now, we must convert this data into Base64. I prefer the website https://codebeautify.org/base64-encode and we can check our work at the decoding version at https://codebeautify.org/base64-decode. When I copy and paste the previous data into this website, I receive the following.

eyJycF9hdXRob3IiOiJ7XCJuYW1lXCI6XCJhdXRob3JcIixcImFyZ3NcIjpcIjRcIn0ifQ==

The final two "==" are optional, and not necessary. When I paste this value into the decoder on this website, I receive the exact data originally entered. Let's take a look at the screen captures. Figure 18.05 (top) displays the desired text data, including my target's user ID number. Figure 18.05 (bottom) displays the result coded in Base64. Figure 18.06 (top) displays the opposite technique by converting the previous Base64 result back to the original desired data in Figure 18.06 (bottom). I realize this is confusing, but our search tools will simplify all of this in a moment.

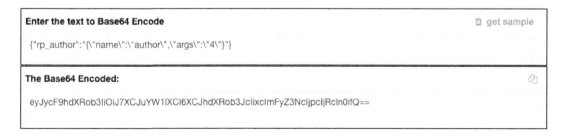

Figure 18.05: Encoding text to Base64 on https://codebeautify.org/base64-encode.

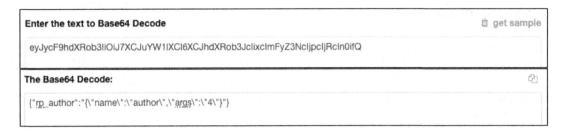

Enter the text to Base64 Decode   🗑 get sample

eyJycF9hdXRob3IiOiJ7XCJuYW1lXCI6XCJhdXRob3JcIixcImFyZ3NcIjpcIjRcIn0ifQ

The Base64 Decode: ⧉

{"rp_author":"{\"name\":\"author\",\"args\":\"4\"}"}

Figure 18.06: Decoding text to Base64 on https://codebeautify.org/base64-decode.

Let's take a look at the entire URL as follows. Below it is a breakdown.

https://www.facebook.com/search/posts/?q=posts&epa=FILTERS&filters=eyJycF9hdXRob3IiOiJ7XCJuY
W1lXCI6XCJhdXRob3JcIixcImFyZ3NcIjpcIjRcIn0ifQ

https://facebook.com/	The Facebook domain
search/	Instructs Facebook to conduct a search
posts/	Specifies the type of information desired
?q=posts	Searches any posts
&epa=FILTERS&filters=	Finishes the URL with a filter demand
eyJycF9hdXRob3IiOiJ7X...	{"rp_author":"{\"name\":\"author\",\"args\":\"4\"}"}

Figure 18.07 displays the results of this URL. Facebook has provided images posted by our target, some of which do not appear on his profile. Clicking "See All" opens even more images.

Figure 18.07: Post results from a Base64 search.

The results are public posts, but some may not be from his profile. In one investigation, I had a suspect with absolutely no posts within his timeline. However, this method identified hundreds of posts he made on other people's profiles. These included comments within posts and public messages to others. We can of course recreate these results by manually using the Facebook filters menu, but understanding the URL structuring allows us to add URL based queries to our OSINT tools. Remember, Facebook is constantly making changes and most recently queries for photos and videos have become unpredictable.

Let's make this simpler. In a moment, I will present the most common URL queries which I have found valuable to my investigations. Then, I will present the portion of my custom Facebook tools which automates this entire process. First, below is a summary of each search by section.

Posts by User/Year:	Posts by a specific user on any page (filtered by year)
Photos by User/Year:	Photos by a specific user on any page (filtered by year)
Videos by User/Year:	Videos by a specific user on any page (filtered by year)
Posts by Location/Year:	Posts submitted from a specific location (filtered by year)
Photos by Location/Year:	Photos submitted from a specific location (filtered by year)
Videos by Location/Year:	Videos submitted from a specific location (filtered by year)
Posts by Keyword/Year:	Posts matching a search term (filtered by year)
Photos by Keyword/Year:	Photos matching a search term (filtered by year)
Videos by Keyword/Year:	Videos matching a search term (filtered by year)
Events by Location:	Current and upcoming events by location (city or entity)
Profiles by Employer:	Profiles associated with employees of a specific business
Profiles by Location:	Profiles associated with residents of a specific city
Profiles by School:	Profiles associated with students of a specific school
Posts by Date:	Posts by keyword (filtered by date range)
Photos by Date:	Photos by keyword (filtered by date range)
Videos by Date:	Videos by keyword (filtered by date range)

If your target was the Facebook username "zuck" with user number "4", the first three URLs would be as follows. Notice that the Base64 encoding is identical on each and that I bolded the unique portions.

Posts by User:
https://www.facebook.com/search/**posts**/?q=**posts**&epa=FILTERS&filters=eyJycF9hdXRob3IiOiJ7XCJu YW1lXCI6XCJhdXRob3JcIixcImFyZ3NcIjpcIjRcIn0ifQ

Photos by User:
https://www.facebook.com/search/**photos**/?q=**photos**&epa=FILTERS&filters=eyJycF9hdXRob3IiOiJ7XC JuYW1lXCI6XCJhdXRob3JcIixcImFyZ3NcIjpcIjRcIn0ifQ

Videos by User:
https://www.facebook.com/search/**videos**/?q=**videos**&epa=FILTERS&filters=eyJycF9hdXRob3IiOiJ7XCJ uYW1lXCI6XCJhdXRob3JcIixcImFyZ3NcIjpcIjRcIn0ifQ

If your target was the city of Chicago, user number "108659242498155", the desired URLs would be as follows if no year was chosen. Selecting a specific year only changes the Base64 encoding.

Posts by Location:
https://www.facebook.com/search/**posts**/?q=**posts**&epa=FILTERS&filters=eyJycF9sb2NhdGlvbiI6IntcIm 5hbWVcIjpcImxvY2F0aW9uXCIsXCJhcmdzXCI6XCIxMDg2NTkyNDI0OTgxNTVcIn0ifQ

Photos by Location:
https://www.facebook.com/search/**photos**/?q=**photos**&epa=FILTERS&filters=eyJycF9hdXRob3IiOiJ7XC JuYW1lXCI6XCJsb2NhdGlvbiwiLFwiYXJnc1wiOlwiMTA4NjU5MjQyNDk4MTU1XCJ9In0

Videos by Location:
https://www.facebook.com/search/**videos**/?q=**videos**&epa=FILTERS&filters=eyJycF9hdXRob3IiOiJ7XCJ uYW1lXCI6XCJsb2NhdGlvbiwiLFwiYXJnc1wiOlwiMTA4NjU5MjQyNDk4MTU1XCJ9In0

We can now drill down within our queries. The following URLs would identify any time our target (zuck - user number 4) mentions "OSINT" within a post, photo, and video. Notice how the bolded areas have changed from the previous queries.

Posts by Keyword:

https://www.facebook.com/search/**posts**/?q=**OSINT**&epa=FILTERS&filters=eyJycF9hdXRob3IiOiJ7XC
JuYW1lXCI6XCJhdXRob3JcIixcImFyZ3NcIjpcIjRcIn0ifQ%3D%3D

Photos by Keyword:

https://www.facebook.com/search/**photos**/?q=**OSINT**&epa=FILTERS&filters=eyJycF9hdXRob3IiOiJ7X
CJuYW1lXCI6XCJhdXRob3JcIixcImFyZ3NcIjpcIjRcIn0ifQ%3D%3D

Videos by Keyword:

https://www.facebook.com/search/**videos**/?q=**OSINT**&epa=FILTERS&filters=eyJycF9hdXRob3IiOiJ7X
CJuYW1lXCI6XCJhdXRob3JcIixcImFyZ3NcIjpcIjRcIn0ifQ%3D%3D

We can now use additional filters to find events and profiles, as follows.

Events (Protest) by Location (City of Chicago-108659242498155):

https://www.facebook.com/search/**events**/?q=**protest**&epa=FILTERS&filters=eyJycF9ldmVudHNfbG9jY
XRpb24iOiJ7XCJuYW1lXCI6XCJmaWx0ZXJfZXZlbnRzX2xvY2F0aW9uXCIsXCJhcmdzXCI6XCIxMDg2
NTkyNDI0OTgxNTVcIn0ifQ%3D%3D

Profiles (Tom) by Employer (Harvard-105930651606):

https://www.facebook.com/search/**people**/?q=**tom**&epa=FILTERS&filters=eyJlbXBsb3llciI6Intcim5hbW
VcIjpcInVzZXJzX2VtcGxveWVyXCIsXCJhcmdzXCI6XCIxMDU5MzA2NTE2MDZcIn0ifQ

Profiles (Tom) by Location (City of Chicago-108659242498155):

https://www.facebook.com/search/**people**/?q=**tom**&epa=FILTERS&filters=eyJjaXR5Ijoie1wibmFtZVwiO
lwidXNlcnNfbG9jYXRpb25cIixcImFyZ3NcIjpcIjEwODY1OTI0MjQ5ODE1NVwifSJ9

Profiles (Tom) by School (Harvard-105930651606):

https://www.facebook.com/search/**people**/?q=**tom**&epa=FILTERS&filters=eyJzY2hvb2wiOiJ7XCJuYW1l
XCI6XCJ1c2Vyc19zY2hvb2xcIixcImFyZ3NcIjpcIjEwNTkzMDY1MTYwNlwifSJ9

In 2022, we saw a change to the way Facebook handles searching by date. I have found searching by a single date to be unreliable, but searching within a range of dates, even if the beginning and end are the same date, seem to function better. Because of the two dates, the URL created by the custom tools will be longer (twice the data). At the time of this writing, video queries were blocked, but searching for "top" entries was functioning and appeared to be displaying mostly videos. There is no limit to the date range, but these focus on one day.

Posts (OSINT) by Date (September 5, 2022-September 5, 2022):

https://www.facebook.com/search/**posts**/?q=**osint**&filters=eyJycF9jcmVhdGlvbl90aW1lIjoie1wibmFtZVw
iOlwiY3JlYXRpb25fdGltZVwiLFwiYXJnc1wiOlwie1xcXCJzdGFydF95ZWFyXCIpcIXwiMjAyMlxcXCIs
XFxcInN0YXJ0X21vbnRoXFxcIjpcIXwiMjAyMi05XFxcIixcXFwiZW5kX3llYXJcXFwiOlxcXCIyMDIyXFx
cIixcXFwiZW5kX21vbnRoXFxcIjpcIXwiMjAyMi05XFxcIixcXFwic3RhcnRfZGF5XFxcIjpcIXwiMjAyMi05
LTVcXFwiLFxcXCJlbmRfZGF5XFxcIjpcIXwiMjAyMi05LTVcXFwifVwifSIsInJwX2F1dGhvciI6IntcIm5hb
WVcIjpcIm1lcmdlZF9wdWJsaWNfcG9zdHNcIixcImFyZ3NcIjpcIlwifSJ9

Photos (OSINT) by Date (September 5, 2022-September 5, 2022):

https://www.facebook.com/search/**photos**/?q=**osint**&filters=eyJycF9jcmVhdGlvbl90aW1lIjoie1wibmFtZV
wiOlwiY3JlYXRpb25fdGltZVwiLFwiYXJnc1wiOlwie1xcXCJzdGFydF95ZWFyXFxcIjpcIXwiMjAyMlxcXC
IsXFxcInN0YXJ0X21vbnRoXFxcIjpcIXwiMjAyMi05XFxcIixcXFwiZW5kX3llYXJcXFwiOlxcXCIyMDIyX
FxcIixcXFwiZW5kX21vbnRoXFxcIjpcIXwiMjAyMi05XFxcIixcXFwic3RhcnRfZGF5XFxcIjpcIXwic3RhcnRfZGF5XFxcIjpcIXwiMjAyMi
05LTVcXFwiLFxcXCJlbmRfZGF5XFxcIjpcIXwiMjAyMi05LTVcXFwifVwifSIsInJwX2F1dGhvciI6IntcIm5
hbWVcIjpcIm1lcmdlZF9wdWJsaWNfcG9zdHNcIixcImFyZ3NcIjpcIlwifSJ9

Videos (OSINT) by Date (September 5, 2022-September 5, 2022):

https://www.facebook.com/search/**top**/?q=**osint**&filters=eyJycF9jcmVhdGlvbl90aW1lIjoie1wibmFtZVwi
OlwiY3JlYXRpb25fdGltZVwiLFwiYXJnc1wiOlwie1xcXCJzdGFydF95ZWFyXFxcIjpcXFwiMjAyMlxcXCIs
XFxcInN0YXJ0X21vbnRoXFxcIjpcXFwiMjAyMi05XFxcIixcXFwiZW5kX3llYXJcXFwiOlxcXCIyMDIyXFx
cIixcXFwiZW5kX21vbnRoXFxcIjpcXFwiMjAyMi05XFxcIixcXFwic3RhcnRfZGF5XFxcIjpcXFwiMjAyMi05
LTVcXFwiLFxcXCJlbmRfZGF5XFxcIjpcXFwiMjAyMi05LTVcXFwifVwifSIsInJwX2F1dGhvciI6IntcIm5h
WVcIjpcIm1lcmdlZF9wdWJsaWNfcG9zdHNcIixcImFyZ3NcIjpcIlwifSJ9

All of these queries will be easily created using our custom Facebook search tool in a moment, including filtration by dates for full profile analysis. As a reminder, I obtained the user ID number for the profile of "zuck" by searching the source code of the profile for "userID" or "pageID". However, location profiles do not possess this data. Fortunately, the user ID for cities is within the URL. When I searched for "City of Chicago" on Facebook, I clicked "Places" and selected the City of Chicago profile which possessed the following URL.

https://www.facebook.com/places/Things-to-do-in-Chicago-Illinois/108659242498155/

The last group of numbers (108659242498155) is the user ID number.

Business pages, such as those associated with Harvard, Pepsi, and others, do not present this data within the URL. Instead, we must search within the source code for "pageID", "page_ID", or "delegate_page_id" (including quotes). When searching this within the source code for the Harvard page, I observed the following.

"pageID":"105930651606"

Pepsi's page (pepsiUS) included the following.

"pageID":"56381779049"

Event profile numbers can be found by searching "eventID".

Group profile numbers can be found by searching "groupID".

While I always prefer manual extraction from the source code of my target Facebook profile, the Facebook ID tools previously presented should also identify profile numbers of business, event, and group pages.

It is extremely important to note that I did not discover this Base64 conversion technique. The online researcher NEMEC (https://x.com/djnemec) was the first to post about this method. Practically every online search tool generating these types of URLs, including mine, is due to the work of this person. I send many "thanks" on behalf of the entire OSINT community for this work.

2024 Photos Update

While updating this chapter, most Base64 queries involving photos failed. We considered removing those sections but decided against it. Since some random profiles still present photos with this technique, and there is a chance it could return for all profiles, the instructions are still present. Know that if you get no results on those queries, you are not alone.

IntelTechniques Facebook Tool

If you have not already skipped to the next chapter after all of this confusion, it is now time to simplify the process. Finally, let's use the custom Facebook search tool to replicate all of this work. This interactive document is included within the "Tools" you previously downloaded or at **https://inteltechniques.com/tools**. Figures 18.09 and 18.10 display the current version of the tool. The following pages explain each section with examples. The first input box in the "Facebook Profile Data" section allows you to enter a Facebook username, such as zuck, and the tool will populate that data within all of the search options in that section. This makes it easy to begin your queries. You can then use the submit buttons to search each entry, such as Timeline or Photos. Note there is no "Submit All" option here. This is due to Facebook's scrutiny into accounts which automate any queries. Submitting too many requests simultaneously will result in a suspended account.

The next section titled "Facebook Search Data" allows you to replicate the instruction on keyword searches throughout all twelve sections of Facebook, such as Posts, Photos, and Pages. This presents immediate results without relying on Facebook to present your desired data from a generic keyword search.

The "Base64 Conversion Queries" section presents the true power behind this tool. All of the technical search techniques presented within the previous pages are replicated here without the need to do any of the work. Instead of summarizing this section, let's run through a demonstration of each option.

Posts/Photos/Videos by User

I entered the user ID number of "4" (for the user zuck) in the first portion, as seen in Figure 18.11 (top). This allows me to query posts, photos, and videos posted by that user to any public pages. The drop-down menu allows me to filter by year, if desired, which is helpful if the target posted a lot of content. This option is available for all three queries. This often identifies content unavailable within the target's own profile.

Posts/Photos/Videos by Location

I entered the user number of "108659242498155" (Chicago) in the first portion, as seen in Figure 18.11 (bottom). This allows me to query posts, photos, and videos posted from that location to any public pages. The drop-down menu allows me to specify a year, if desired. This often identifies content unavailable through traditional search techniques.

FB Username	Populate All	FB Username	Reels
		FB Username	Check-ins
FB Username	Timeline	FB Username	Visits
FB Username	About	FB Username	Recent Check-ins
FB Username	Employment	FB Username	Sports
FB Username	Education	FB Username	Music
FB Username	Locations	FB Username	Movies
FB Username	Contact Info	FB Username	TV
FB Username	Basic Info	FB Username	Books
FB Username	Relationships	FB Username	Apps & Games
FB Username	Family	FB Username	Likes
FB Username	Biography	FB Username	Events
FB Username	Life Events	FB Username	Facts
FB Username	Friends	FB Username	Reviews
FB Username	Following	FB Username	Reviews Given
FB Username	Photos	FB Username	Reviews Written
FB Username	Photos Albums	FB Username	Notes
FB Username	Videos	FB User Number	Profile

Figure 18.09: The IntelTechniques Facebook Tool.

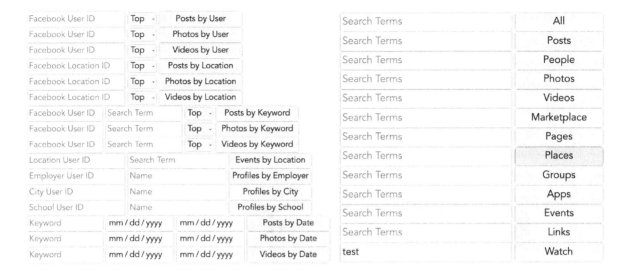

Figure 18.10: The IntelTechniques Facebook Tool.

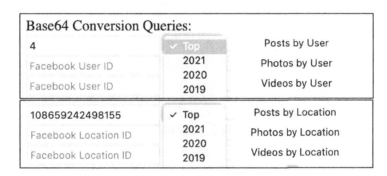

Figure 18.11: The IntelTechniques Facebook Tool options with date filtering.

Posts/Photos/Videos by Keyword

I entered the user number 4 (zuck) and a search term of "OSINT" in Figure 18.12. I can now select a year and filter only those posts, photos, or videos.

Figure 18.12: The IntelTechniques Facebook Tool year filters.

Events by Location

I entered the user number of "108659242498155" (Chicago) and added the keyword "protest". I was immediately presented dozens of active and future events matching my criteria.

People by Employer, City, and School

I entered the user number of "105930651606" (Harvard) in the first and third boxes, as seen in Figure 18.13. This allows me to query people's profiles by their employer or school affiliation. These search options require at least one additional piece of information. In this example, I searched the name "Tom". Notice the difference in the results within Figure 18.14. The left result identifies people named Tom who WORK at Harvard, while the right displays people named Tom who ATTENDED Harvard. This search option can quickly identify your target when you only know a small amount of information, or if they are using a false last name.

105930651606	Tom	Profiles by Employer
City User ID	Name	Profiles by City
105930651606	Tom	Profiles by School

Figure 18.13: The IntelTechniques Facebook Tool options for profile search.

Tom Tom Professor at Harvard University 116. Mittelschule Dresden	**Tom Priince (Nike)** 838 followers Pflegeassistent at pro civitate Harvard University
Tom Fraser Works at Harvard University Wentworth Institute of Technology	**Natalia Tom** Works at Dragon City Harvard University

Figure 18.14: Facebook results from an IntelTechniques Tool query.

I suspect that these queries will change over time. I do not present the source code of these specific queries within the book because they are quite complicated and lengthy. If this tool should be updated, I will make an announcement at **https://inteltechniques.com/osintbook11**.

Manual vs. Tool Queries

If you are paying close attention, you can see that there are many similarities between conducting a search directly within the official Facebook website and the options within my custom search tools. On the surface, these tools may seem redundant and unnecessary. However, I assure you that there are some key advantages to the Facebook tool. I present three quick examples where you can find content through the tool which is not available on the site.

Videos by Date: The official Facebook site allows filtration of videos by date, but you can only choose from "Today", "This Week", or "This Month". The tool allows detailed filters by year or exact date. The example below is from 2015.

Check out this 360 video timelapse of Facebook's campus. I'm really enjoying these 360 videos. They...
Check out this 360 video timelapse of Facebook's campus. I'm really enjoying these 360 videos. They feel like you're really...
Mark Zuckerberg ✓
Nov 17, 2015 · 2.5M Views

Posts by Location: I can query the official LAX page at facebook.com/LAInternationalAirport, but I cannot query for posts from other people at that location. However, the search tool allows me to focus on posts from any location which can be filtered by year. The following example was presented after entering location ID "74286767824" and choosing "2018".

> Dec 26, 2018 · 🌐 · So we are waiting to board and start our adventure to Rome! Sorry in advance for all the posts!

Posts by Date: I can search for any term on Facebook, but I can only filter by year. With the tools, I can focus on any individual date. In the following example, I searched for anyone mentioning my site on the day that it was briefly shut down due to legal demands, I quickly found evidence.

> Jun 6, 2019 · 🌐 · @IntelTechniques What a shame man, hate to hear that. Hope to have someway to access the same

I encourage you to experiment with both manual and automated search options. There is a small learning curve when querying Facebook, but the results are often fascinating.

Facebook Phone Number Search

In previous editions, I have included various techniques to identify a Facebook profile associated with a target telephone number. At one time, entering a cell number into a Facebook search showed you the name, email address, and photo of the user. That luxury is gone, but we do currently have one method which may be helpful. The following URL requests Facebook to locate an account for a password reset. Entering a telephone number will confirm if an account is associated to it, and will sometimes display the profile image for the user.

https://mbasic.facebook.com/login/identify/?ctx=recover

However, clicking "Try Another Way" within this technique should present even more details. While testing this method on an unknown target's number, I received the following.

Send code via email
n***@g******
n***@y******

This confirms that a Facebook account is associated with the number; there are two email addresses associated with the account; both email addresses begin with "n"; and the email service providers begin with "g" and "y". My guess is that this user has a similar email address with both Yahoo and Gmail.

It is important that this tactic is only used from a browser and connection where you are not already logged into a Facebook. This tactic can result in your session and associated IP address being flagged as potentially malicious. Multiple attempts on the same address or phone number may result in the target account holder being notified.

If use of breach data is within policy and scope of your investigation, there are some Facebook breach data sets floating around the internet and these can be of value in querying phone numbers to locate account holders. Locating, organizing, and querying breach data will be covered in a later section of this book.

Facebook ID Creation Date

Digital forensics enthusiast and private investigator Josh Huff at LearnAllTheThings.net has conducted a lot of research into the assignment of user ID numbers to Facebook profiles. We know that these numbers are assigned in chronological order, but the intelligence goes much further beyond that. His research could fill several pages and, in some situations, he can identify the month when a specific user account was created. For the sake of space and most useful details, he has provided the following to me for publication.

Facebook transitioned from 32-bit numbers, such as 554432, to 64-bit numbers that begin with 100000 between April and December of 2009. Therefore, if your target's number is less than 100000000000000, the account was likely created prior to April 2009. An account with a 15-digit ID number would have been created after December 2009. We can break down the numbers by year. The following are rough estimates that should only be used as a general guideline. Facebook appears to have begun issuing random numbers outside of these ranges in 2018.

2006: Numbers less than 600400000
2007: 600400000 - 1000000000
2008: 1000000000 - 1140000000
2009: 1140000000- 100000628000000
2010: 100000629000000 - 100001610000000
2011: 100001611000000 - 100003302000000
2012: 100003303000000 - 100004977000000
2013: 100004978000000 - 100007376000000
2014: 100007377000000 - 100008760000000
2015: 100008761000000 - 100010925000000
2016: 100010926000000 - 100014946000000
2017: 100014947000000 - 100023810000000
2018: 100023811000000 -

Facebook Friends Extraction

I was recently presented a Facebook scenario without any obvious solution. Assume that you find the Facebook profile of your target, and there is a large list of "Friends". You want to document this list, and a screenshot is not good enough. You want to capture the hyperlinks to each account and have a data set that can be manipulated or imported elsewhere. There are several outdated online tools that claim to "scrape" this data, but none of them work. In 2016, Facebook changed their Terms of Service (TOS) which now blocks any type of scraping of Friend data. Furthermore, the Facebook API no longer allows the display of this data either. There is a solution, and it will involve minimal geek work. First, identify the page of your target. For this example, I will use public profile at https://www.facebook.com/darya.pino/friends.

She has several friends, so I will hold down the space bar on my keyboard to load the entire page. I will now highlight her entire friends list and use "Ctrl" + "C" (Windows) or "command" + "C" (Mac) (or right-click > copy) to copy the data. I find it best to click directly above the left side of the first friend and hold until the lower right area of the last friend. The friends list should highlight. Now, open Microsoft Excel. Click on the "B" in column B to highlight the entire column. Paste the content with either "Ctrl" + "V" (Windows) or "command" + "V" (Mac) (or right-click > paste). This will appear disorganized, but the data is there. The images will be on top of the user data, which will not work for a final report. Use F5 to launch the "Go To" menu and select "Special". Select "Objects" and click OK. This will select all of those images. Hit the delete key to remove them. You will now see only the text data (with hyperlinks). Now click on the "A" in column A and paste the friend content again with either "Ctrl" + "V" (Windows) or "command" + "V" (Mac) (or right-click > paste). Right-click any cell in this column and choose "Clear Contents". This will remove any text, but keep the images.

Place your mouse in between columns A and B and resize column A to be a bit larger than one of the images. Do the same with Column B to fit in all of the text. Use the "Find and Replace" feature to find every instance of "Add Friend" and replace it with nothing. This will remove those unnecessary entries. In the "Home" menu, choose "Format" and then "Auto Fit Row Height". This will eliminate unnecessary spacing. Select Column B and Left Justify the text. If desired delete empty cells from the top of column B and select "Shift cells up" to further align the two columns. Your final result will be a clean spreadsheet with all of the images, names, and active links from your target's Facebook "friends" page. This is not the cleanest way of doing things, but it will work.

While working with my target's friends/followers lists on any platform, I take moment to do a quick search for any of my target's known first names, surnames, and usernames/aliases. This provides an opportunity to both identify contacts who are family members while also looking for other accounts belonging to my target. It is very common for individuals to follow a newly created account with existing accounts when they first create that profile as everyone wants the appearance of having friends and followers.

Email Search

As stated previously, we lost all standard email address search options within Facebook in 2019. However, there is one remaining technique which allows submission of some email addresses and provides identification of an associated profile if allowed in the user's settings. However, it is not simple or straightforward. It will take some work to set up, but will then be available as needed. This is often referred to as the "Page Role" trick. The premise is that you create a Facebook business page and then assign another profile to possess management rights. When you enter the email address of the target, Facebook confirms the name and profile to make sure you truly want to give away authorization to the person. We can then cancel the request without any notification to the target. The following steps replicate this technique.

- Open "Menu" and click "Page" in the upper-right corner, then create a new page.
- Assign a random name to your profile and select "Create page".
- Skip any additional requests for information.
- Once you see the new profile, click the "See dashboard" button in the upper-right.
- On the new menu, click "Page Access" in the left column.
- In the "People with Facebook access" section, click "Add new".
- Enter the target email address.

This should present any Facebook profiles associated with the address entered. Figure 18.15 displays a result. I entered an email address in this field and was presented the only Facebook profile which was associated with the account. I can now search this full name within Facebook, look for the image previously displayed, and scour the target profile for valuable information. Facebook continuously makes both minor and major changes to their search functions. Some of these instructions may not work one day and work fine the next. Your mileage will vary as Facebook scrutinizes your covert profiles, VPN protected networks, and overall "vibe" as a fake user. Hopefully, this chapter has given you new ideas on ways to completely analyze your next target on Facebook and ideas to circumvent the next roadblocks.

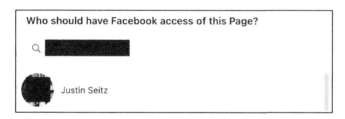

Figure 18.15: An email search through Facebook under the Page Access menu.

Facebook investigations are always a moving target. It is important to understand that if a technique fails to produce a positive result, this does not necessarily rule out that your target is on the Facebook platform. Always take multiple approaches, be creative, and expect to do some of your own problem solving. Throughout all of the services explained in this book, Facebook is the most likely to change often. Fortunately, any changes always bring new investigation opportunities. When we lost Graph search in 2019, we gained Base64 methods. When we lose the current strategies, something else will become available. As with all OSINT techniques, daily practice and understanding of the resources is more vital than the occasional nugget of data which is displayed on our screens.

CHAPTER NINETEEN
SOCIAL NETWORKS: X (TWITTER)

Until this point, every reference to "X" or "Twitter" has been labeled as "X (Twitter)". This is because Twitter was rebranded as X in 2024, but many people still refer to the service as Twitter and the posts as Tweets. For the rest of this book, I will only present references to the company as "Twitter", but URLs will be x.com. I think this will prevent some confusion and redundancies. The biggest change in this chapter is that you must log in to a Twitter account in order to benefit from optimal OSINT data. While you can see some content without an account, you will always be somewhat restricted. Posts will be hidden and often rearranged chronologically. Use the previous account creation lessons to ensure you have at least one Twitter account ready at all times.

Twitter is a social network and microblogging service that limits most posts to 280 characters. Paid subscribers are allowed more content. In 2024, Twitter reported that there were over 415 million Twitter users with over 335 active users monthly. Basically, users create a profile and post Tweets announcing their thoughts on a topic, current location, plans for the evening, or maybe a link to something that they feel is important. A user can "follow" other users and constantly see what others are posting. Likewise, a user's "followers" can see what that user is up to on a constant basis. The premise is simply sharing small details of your life for all of your friends to see, as well as the rest of the world. Most people utilize the service through a mobile app within a cellular phone. Obtaining information from Twitter can be conducted through numerous procedures, all of which are explained here. Similar to Facebook, we will start with official search options through Twitter's website. As a final reminder, you can view profiles and execute some queries without being logged in to a Twitter account, but most of these features and pages will only be accessible while logged in.

Twitter Search (x.com/explore)

This is the official site's search interface, but it is nothing different than the search field at the top of any Twitter profile or search result. I only present this because navigating to x.com often offers a signup page, but no option to search. We will use this standard search bar to conduct specific queries in a few moments.

Twitter Advanced Search (x.com/search-advanced)

This page will allow for the search of specific people, keywords, and locations. The problem here is that the search of a topic is often limited to the previous seven to ten days. Individual profiles should display Tweets as far back as you are willing to scroll. This can be a good place to search for recent data, but complete archives of a topic will not be displayed. The following explains each section.

All of these words: The order of wording is ignored here, and only the inclusion of each of the words entered is enforced.

This exact phrase: Every Twitter search takes advantage of quotes to identify exact word placement. Optionally, you can conduct the search here to get precise results without quotes.

Any of these words: You can provide multiple unique terms here, and Twitter will supply results that include any of them. This search alone is usually too generic.

None of these words: This box will filter out any posts that include the chosen word or words.

These Hashtags: This option will locate specific posts that mention a topic as defined by a Twitter hashtag. This is a single word preceded by a pound sign (#) that identifies a topic of interest. This allows users to follow certain topics without knowing usernames of the user submitting the messages.

Language: This filter removes results which are not written in the specified language.

From these accounts: This section allows you to search for Tweets from a specific user. This can also be accomplished by typing the username into the address bar after the Twitter domain, such as x.com/JohnDoe92. This will display the user's profile including recent Tweets.

To these accounts: This field allows you to enter a specific Twitter username. The results will only include Tweets that were sent to the attention of the user. This can help identify associates of the target and information intended for the target to read.

Mentioning these accounts: While these messages might not be in response to a specific user, the target was mentioned. This is usually in the form of using "@". Anyone mentioning me within a Tweet may start it with @inteltechniques.

Dates: The final option allows you to limit a search to a specific date range. We will do this manually in just a moment.

Overall, I do not ever use the Twitter Advanced Search page. You can replicate all of these queries with manual search operators within the search field available on every Twitter page. I will explain each as we go through the chapter. Knowing the Twitter search operators instead of relying on the advanced search page has many benefits. First, we can use these techniques to monitor live Twitter data, as explained later in this chapter. Next, manual searches allow us to better document our findings. This is vital if your discoveries will be used in court.

Later in the chapter, we will combine all of our new techniques within our own custom tool options, which will be much more powerful than these standard solutions. The results of any of these searches can provide surprisingly personal information about a target, or generic content that includes too much data to be useful. We must learn each technique within a specific order before we can combine them into powerful queries.

Twitter data can be used for many types of investigations. Law enforcement may use this data to verify or disprove an alibi of a suspect. When a suspect states in an interview that he was in Chicago the entire weekend, but his Twitter feed displays his Tweet about a restaurant in St. Louis, he has some explaining to do. Private investigators may use this content as documentation of an affair or negative character. Occasionally, a citizen will contact the authorities when evidence of illegal activity is found within a person's Tweets. The possibilities are endless. First, let's find your target's Twitter profile.

Twitter Person Search

Locating your target's Twitter profile may not be easy. Unlike Facebook, many Twitter users do not use their real name in their profiles. You need a place to search by real name. I recommend Twitter's official search page before relying on third parties. After searching any real name or username within the standard Twitter search field, click through the five menu options, which are each explained below.

Top: This displays popular tweets matching your query. If your target is popular, you may see something here. I typically avoid this tab as it allows Twitter to determine what evidence I should see instead of selecting content based on specific queries.

Latest: This presents a reverse-chronological list of data which matches your search. It always begins with the most recent post and goes backward. This works well when searching a topic, but not when locating a target's profile.

People: Scrolling through this list allows you to look through the photo icons and brief descriptions to identify your target. Clicking on the username will open the user's Twitter profile with more information. This is the best option for searching by real name or username.

Media: This searches for any photos or videos matching your query. This has been helpful when attempting to identify images or videos posted by unknown people who mentioned your target by name.

Lists: Some Twitter users create and share curated lists of accounts based on some connection, topical or otherwise. For example, you will find several public lists of OSINT professionals. Lists sometimes provide insight into a targets' interests, culture, and communities which they may be active in.

If searching by real name through the previous methods does not produce your target, your best option is to focus on the potential username. I will discuss username searches at length in a later chapter (Usernames). Overall, any associated usernames from other networks such as Instagram, Snapchat, and YouTube, should be tried on Twitter in the format of x.com/username.

Search by Email Address

Technically, Twitter does not allow the search of a username by providing an email address. If you attempt this type of search on Twitter, you will receive no results, even if a profile exists for a user with that email address. To bypass this limitation, you can sometimes use a feature offered within the mobile app version of Twitter. This technique will require a new Twitter account and the Twitter app present within a virtual Android device, as previously explained. There is always some risk that the emulation may be detected by Twitter services, but this tactic could also be replicated on a physical mobile device such as a burner phone.

Within Android, open the Contacts application and add the email address of your target within a new contact and save the entry. Open the Twitter app, navigate to the left menu and select "Settings and privacy", click on "Privacy and safety", then "Discoverability and contacts". You can then manage your data and allow Twitter to sync your Android contacts to their service.

Enabling this feature will not display your contacts within the application. Instead, look at your notification bar within Android. You should see a pending notification which states "Find your friends on Twitter". Clicking this should present the "Suggested Followers". Twitter will encourage you to add these profiles, but do not choose that option. If you do, your target will be sent a notification from your account. In 2022, I witnessed this strategy stop working within newer accounts, but appeared to still function within aged accounts. I suspect we will see this technique continue to fade away into 2025.

Search Operators

Similar to the way that search engines use operators as mentioned in previous chapters, Twitter has its own set of search operators that will greatly improve your ability to effectively search Twitter. Two of the most powerful options are the "to" and "from" operators. I use these daily in order to filter results. Consider the following examples using our target Twitter username of x.com/IntelTechniques. We can obviously navigate directly to the page, but it could be full of promoted Tweets, ReTweets, and whatever content the owner wants us to see. Instead, the following search within any Twitter window will limit our results only to the outgoing Tweets from the account. Clicking the "Latest" option in the Twitter menu will place these in reverse-chronological order.

from:IntelTechniques

This provides a better view into the thoughts of the author. Both the Twitter profile and this results page give us insight to the messages the user is sending out, but what about the incoming content? With most traditional Twitter investigations, we tend to focus on one side of the conversation. There is often a plethora of associated messages being sent to the attention of the target that go unchecked. In order to see all of the posts being publicly sent to the user, we would search the following.

to:IntelTechniques

We now see all of those incoming messages that the user cannot control. While one can prohibit them from being seen on the profile, users cannot block us from this search. When I have a missing person or homicide victim, I would much rather see the incoming messages versus the outgoing. We can also combine these options to create an extremely targeted query. At first glance, I did not see many incoming messages to IntelTechniques from protonprivacy. However, the following Twitter search tells a different story. It isolates only these posts.

to:IntelTechniques from:protonprivacy

We can also filter by replies with the following search. This would only display the tweets from our target which were replies to someone else.

from:IntelTechniques filter:replies

I do not find this very helpful. I prefer the opposite of this approach. The following search within Twitter would display only the tweets by my target which do NOT include replies.

from:IntelTechniques -filter:replies

Media, Highlights, Lists, Topics, Links, and Followers

You may want to filter all results from a target Twitter profile and only see those which have some type of media embedded. There is not a search operator to force this, but the following direct URL will display only these posts.

https://x.com/IntelTechniques/media/

Highlights are essentially a collection of "pinned" posts curated by the account holder.

https://x.com/inteltechniques/highlights/

Twitter Lists appeared recently, and there are two types which we might have interest. A traditional List is created by the target and may include people they know or like. The structure is as follows.

https://x.com/IntelTechniques/lists/

If your target is on someone else's List, which is something they cannot control, we can see that with the following.

https://x.com/IntelTechniques/lists/memberships

Once you identify a Twitter List of interest, you can dig deeper into the members. As an example, I am included on a List called Open Source Intelligence, which I identified from the previous URL. Clicking that List opened a new page with the following URL.

https://x.com/i/lists/1588523704245489664

1588523704245489664 is the List number. The following two URLs display the members of the List (the accounts included within the list) and the followers of the List (people who monitor the List for content).

https://x.com/i/lists/1588523704245489664/members
https://x.com/i/lists/1588523704245489664/followers

Twitter Topics is a feature which can quickly identify the interest of a Twitter user. When users add topics for their feeds, we cannot see their choices within their profiles. However, the following URL displays them all within one place.

https://x.com/IntelTechniques/topics

Next, we can focus only on tweets from a user which include a link to additional media. This could be an image, video, or website. The following presents only tweets with links from my own account.

from:IntelTechniques filter:links

We can also filter for popular posts. The following searches for any tweets from my own account which received at least 150 likes.

from:IntelTechniques min_faves:150

The following searches for any tweets from my own account which received at least 100 replies.

from:IntelTechniques min_replies:100

Finally, we can easily display a user's Followers (the people monitoring their profile) and Following (the people the target monitors) with the URLs below.

https://x.com/IntelTechniques/followers
https://x.com/IntelTechniques/following

Now, let's combine a few searches. The following query would identify any tweets sent to our target (IntelTechniques), from zerotrafficking, during the month of October of 2022, which included a link, and were replies from another post.

to:IntelTechniques from:zerotrafficking since:2022-10-01 until:2022-10-31 filter:links filter:replies

Replicating this search reveals only one result in the "Latest" tab, which may have been otherwise buried within the thousands of posts. Hopefully you can see the value of targeted queries. **Later in the chapter, I present the custom offline Twitter search tools which automate most of these queries.** However, it is vital to understand why these work in order to explain your methods when required.

Search by Location

If you are investigating an incident that occurred at a specific location and you have no known people involved, Twitter will allow you to search by GPS location alone. The Twitter Advanced Search allowed us to search by zip code, but that can be too broad. The following specific search on any Twitter page will display Tweets known to have been posted from within one kilometer of the GPS coordinates of 43.430242,-89.736459. Note that you may need to click the "Latest" tab after the query.

geocode:43.430242,-89.736459,1km

There are no spaces in this search. This will be a list without any map view. The "1km" indicates a search radius of one kilometer. This can be changed to 5, 10, or 25 reliably. Any other numbers tend to provide inaccurate results. You can also change "km" to "mi" to switch to miles instead of kilometers. If you want to view this search from the address bar of the browser, the following page would load the same results.

https://x.com/search?q=geocode:43.430242,-89.736459,1km&f=live

You can add search parameters to either of these searches if the results are overwhelming. The following search would only display Tweets posted within two miles of the listed GPS coordinates that also mention the term "fight".

geocode:43.430242,-89.736459,2mi"fight"

It would be inappropriate to finish this section without a discussion about the lack of geo-enabled Tweets. Several years prior, this search would have been highly productive, as an alarming number of Twitter users were unknowingly sharing their locations with every post. Today, it is the opposite. The default option for Twitter is NOT to share location. A user must enable this option in order to appear within these search results. In my experience, catching a criminal from a location-enabled Tweet is extremely rare. However, we should be aware of the possibility while understanding that lack of results does not rule out tweet activity for a queried location.

Mandatory and Optional Search Terms

You may have a scenario that requires a search of both mandatory and optional terms. Twitter does not provide a published solution for this. However, it does support this type of search. Assume you are investigating threats against your target named Michael Parker. You believe that people may be tweeting about him with reference to violence. Searching his name alone produces too many results. Placing the name within quotes forces Twitter to only give you results on those exact terms, which is your "mandatory" portion. Additional optional words could be added with the term "OR" between each. This term must be uppercase, and will only require one of the optional words be present within the search results. Consider the following query on Twitter.

"Michael Parker" kill OR stab OR fight OR beat OR punch OR death OR die

Posts Linking to Outside Content

Searching for keywords included in posted URLs is not only useful for general research but also can identify connections between the target account and sites outside of Twitter. Later in this book we will discuss tactics for researching breach data. Although Telegram has become the platform of choice for those posting links to breach data, I will occasionally find something worthwhile posted to Twitter. For example, the following Twitter query will filter for posts which include a link to mega.nz which is a popular file sharing platform.

url:mega.nz breach

Obviously this is a very broad search and similar to our search engine queries, we will likely add additional keywords and filters to dial it in to a more precise set of results. We may also wish to broaden the query even further to include sites other than mega.nz. The following query will look for posts with the provided keywords but will filter out any posts which do not contain links.

comb breach filter:links

COMB is a well-known breach data set that is fairly prolific, and this makes it a relatively good keyword to use when experimenting with queries. We will discuss COMB further when we reach the chapters covering breach data.

Date Range Search

If you are searching vague terms, you may want to filter by date. This option is now available on the advanced search page, but I believe it is important to understand how Twitter performs this task. Assume that you are investigating a bomb threat that occurred several weeks, months, or years ago. A search on Twitter of the terms "bomb threat" will likely apply only to recent posts. Instead, consider a date specific search. The following query on any Twitter page would provide any posts that mention "bomb threat" between January 1, 2015 and January 5, 2015.

since:2015-01-01 until:2015-01-05 "bomb threat"

My favorite use of this search technique is to combine it with the "to" operator or a name search (or both). This allows you to go further back in time than standard profile and Twitter feed searches typically allow. Consider an example where Twitter user humanhacker is your target. You can visit his live Twitter page and navigate back through several thousand Tweets. However, you will reach an end before obtaining all Tweets. This could be due to Twitter restrictions or browser and computer limitations. He currently has 15,000 Tweets. Even if you could make it through all of his Tweets, you are not seeing posts where he is mentioned or messages sent publicly to him. I recommend splitting this search by year and including mentions and messages directed toward him. The following search within Twitter displays all Tweets from the Twitter name humanhacker between January 1, 2012 and December 31, 2012.

from:humanhacker since:2012-01-01 until:2012-12-31

This may create a more digestible collection of Tweets that can be collected and archived appropriately. There may be no other way of identifying these messages since you cannot likely scroll back that far. In my investigations involving targets with several thousand posts, I conduct multiple searches within Twitter that span several years. The following would collect yearly sets of Tweets posted by humanhacker since 2006.

from:humanhacker since:2006-01-01 until:2006-12-31
from:humanhacker since:2007-01-01 until:2007-12-31
from:humanhacker since:2008-01-01 until:2008-12-31
from:humanhacker since:2009-01-01 until:2009-12-31
from:humanhacker since:2010-01-01 until:2010-12-31
from:humanhacker since:2011-01-01 until:2011-12-31
from:humanhacker since:2012-01-01 until:2012-12-31
from:humanhacker since:2013-01-01 until:2013-12-31
from:humanhacker since:2014-01-01 until:2014-12-31
from:humanhacker since:2015-01-01 until:2015-12-31
from:humanhacker since:2016-01-01 until:2016-12-31
from:humanhacker since:2017-01-01 until:2017-12-31
from:humanhacker since:2018-01-01 until:2018-12-31
from:humanhacker since:2019-01-01 until:2019-12-31
from:humanhacker since:2020-01-01 until:2020-12-31
from:humanhacker since:2021-01-01 until:2021-12-31
from:humanhacker sincc:2022-01-01 until:2022-12-31
from:humanhacker since:2023-01-01 until:2023-12-31
from:humanhacker since:2024-01-01 until:2024-12-31

This same technique can be modified to display only incoming Tweets to humanhacker for these years. Replace "from" with "to" to obtain these results. The 2018 posts would appear as follows.

to:humanhacker since:2018-01-01 until:2018-12-31

You can combine all of these options into a single result, but I only recommend this after you have attempted the more precise options mentioned previously. While the next search should theoretically display all of his outgoing Tweets, incoming Tweets, and mentions, it is not always complete. The following would include 2018.

"humanhacker" since:2018-01-01 until:2018-12-31

There are many uses for a date range search. Any supported Twitter search should work combined with dates. This might include a location search for a specific date related to an investigation. As a test of the possibilities, consider that you want to identify an email address for this target. His live Twitter page will not reveal this, as he no longer posts his email, likely to prevent spam. However, the following search is quite productive.

from:humanhacker email since:2006-01-01 until:2009-12-31

This isolates only his posts from the beginning of Twitter until the end of 2009. Only seven results are present, including the Tweet as seen in Figure 19.01 (top). These queries do not need to encompass an entire year. You could use this technique to focus on a specific month or day. Figure 19.01 (bottom) tells me what Chris was up to on October 2, 2017 with the following query.

from:humanhacker email since:2017-10-02 until:2017-10-03

Figure 19.01: An old Twitter post including an email address of the target.

Deleted, Suspended, and Missing Tweets

Twitter users may delete their own accounts if there is suspicion that an investigation is under way. If this happens, searching on Twitter will not display any of the posts. Furthermore, a person might only delete individual Twitter posts that are incriminating, but leave non-interesting posts on the profile to prevent raising suspicion associated with deleting an entire account. Some users may find their accounts suspended for violating Twitter's terms of service. In any of these scenarios, it is still possible to retrieve some missing posts using various techniques.

If I encounter a Twitter user that has recently deleted some or all of their messages, I conduct a cache search of their profile. There are various ways to do this, and I will demonstrate the most common. In this example, I conducted a search on Twitter for "deleted all my Tweets" on December 15, 2017. This provided many users who posted that they had just deleted all of their content. This helped me identify a good target for this type of demonstration. The first user I located was "WestCornfield". He had one Tweet and it referenced deleting all of his posts, and it is seen in Figure 19.02.

I attempted a search on Twitter of from:WestCornfield, which provided no results. I conducted a search of to:WestCornfield, which provided dozens of incoming messages from his friends. This was a good start. I then went to Google and conducted a search for "Twitter WestCornfield". The first search result was a link to the user's live Twitter page. Instead of clicking on the link, I chose the Google Cache view of his profile by clicking the small green "down arrow" next to the URL and selecting "Cached". Google has since removed the "cached" button from Google results, as previously discussed in the search engines section of this book, but other search engines still offer this embedded feature. We can also attempt the following URL to bring back limited Google Cache functionality, replacing "inteltechniques" with your own target.

https://webcache.googleusercontent.com/search?q=cache:https://twitter.com/inteltechniques

This view identified twenty deleted Tweets from this account. Two of these posts can be seen in Figure 19.03. Google identified this capture as taken on December 12, 2017. This may be enough for your investigation. Occasionally, I need to identify content that was deleted weeks or months before my investigation. The previous technique will likely not provide much assistance because the Google Cache is probably a recent copy of their live page. The cache may be missing Tweets you want to see. I next replicated this process on Bing and Yandex. Bing's cached view was taken on December 7, 2017 while Yandex's cached view was collected on November 3, 2017. Each of these possessed unique posts and images. Figure 19.04 displays a recovered post from Bing. Next, I returned to Google to obtain further data. I searched the following, which provided only results that possess a URL that begins with twitter.com, then my target's username, then "status". This will force Google to present direct links to actual posts.

site:twitter.com/westcornfield/status

During the original writing, the result was 56 posts. When I clicked on each of these, Twitter informed me that the post had been deleted. However, opening the cached version from the Google result displayed each of the posts. In Figure 19.05, you can see that Google is now identifying deleted posts as far back as October 2017. This process should also be repeated using the cached view options of Bing and Yandex. Next, we should check the Wayback Machine as mentioned in Chapter Nine. If you recall, you can search their archives by keywords or direct URL. The following address connects us directly to their archive of his account.

http://web.archive.org/web/*/twitter.com/WestCornfield

This identified a capture of his profile on December 6, 2017. Opening this archive displayed his Twitter profile dating back to November 8, 2017. Figure 19.06 displays this deleted Tweet.

While our target removed his content from his profile, he did not remove his history. In order to see the Twitter posts that he had previously liked before wiping out his page, we could previously navigate to a custom Twitter URL. They killed this feature, but we can still use the following.

http://web.archive.org/web/*/twitter.com/WestCornfield/likes

While every investigation is unique, I wanted to demonstrate the importance of checking every source. These searches took less than three minutes using my custom Twitter search tool discussed in the next section. While you will likely never rebuild an entire deleted account, the posts obtained with this technique are something you did not have before.

Figure 19.02: A live Twitter post announcing Tweet deletion.

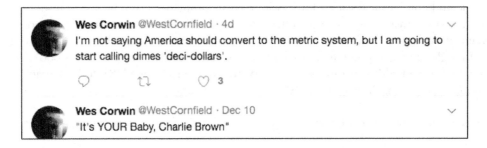

Figure 19.03: A Google cached Twitter posts recovered after deletion.

Figure 19.04: A Bing cached Twitter post recovered after deletion.

Figure 19.05: A Google cached Twitter message URL of a deleted post.

Figure 19.06: A recovered deleted Tweet from the Wayback Machine.

Twitter Post Details

Assume that you have identified an individual Tweet of interest. The URL of the message will appear similar to https://x.com/IntelTechniques/status/1821570065638256652. You have the tools to create a screen capture, but you may want a few more details. If there is an image embedded into the Tweet, you can click on it to see a larger version. However, this is sometimes not the original image size. In order to see the original full-size version, right-click the image and choose "View image". This will load a new URL such as the following.

https://pbs.twimg.com/media/GUeEPxjW4AA73pe?format=jpg&name=small

After removing "&name=small" from the URL, a larger image is available. You can save this image by right-clicking and choosing "Save image as". This example is as follows.

https://pbs.twimg.com/media/GUeEPxjW4AA73pe?format=jpg

Adding "=large" to the end of this URL or right-clicking and opening the image in a new tab will give us an even larger resolution version of the same image.

https://pbs.twimg.com/media/GUeEPxjW4AA73pe?format=jpg&name=large

Tweet Deck (tweetdeck.x.com)

Tweet Deck is owned by Twitter, and it can take advantage of the live Twitter "Firehose". This huge stream of data contains every public post available on Twitter. Many Twitter services do not have access to this stream, and the results are limited. In 2023, Twitter changed TweetDeck to require "X Premium" and attempting to go to https://tweetdeck.x.com will forward you to a page and ask you to sign up for premium. You could sign up for a premium account but that would require you to associate payment information with your burner account which could compromise your operational security. An alternative currently is to use an open-source browser extension called OldTweetDeck.

You can download OldTweetDeck from https://github.com/dimdenGD/OldTweetDeck where they also have concise steps for installation on Firefox and Chromium based browsers. The installation steps are straightforward. For example, you can install OldTweetDeck on any Firefox browser using these steps:

- Go to Release page and download OldTweetDeckFirefox.zip.
- Go to Firefox Configuration Editor (about:config).
- Change the preference xpinstall.signatures.required to false.
- Go to addons page (about:addons).
- Press "Install Add-on From File..." button.
- Select zip file you downloaded.
- Go to https://x.com/i/tweetdeck and use old TweetDeck.

Understand that this extension only restores most of TweetDeck's functionality and some features such as filtering by likes is going to fail due to Twitter making them private. This project's level of functionality will likely wane over time so your own results may vary.

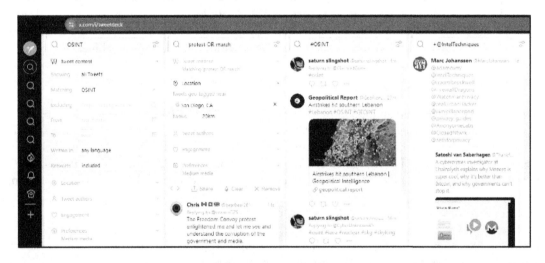

Figure 19.07: Tweetdeck via the OldTweetDeck browser extension.

Whether you choose to purchase a premium account or use the OldTweetDeck extension, once the page is loaded the functionality will be largely be the same. The plus symbol (+) in the upper left area will add a new column to your view. There are several options presented, but the most common will be "Search" and "User". The "Search" option will create a column that will allow you to search for any keywords on Twitter. The following is a list of search examples and how they may benefit the investigator.

"Victim Name": A homicide investigator can monitor people mentioning a homicide victim.
"School Name": A school can monitor anyone mentioning the school for suspicious activity.

"Subject Name": An investigator can monitor a missing person's name for relevant information.
"Event": Officials can monitor anyone discussing a special event such as a festival or concert.

The "User" option will allow you to enter a Twitter username and monitor all incoming and outgoing public messages associated with the user. If several subjects of an investigation are identified as Twitter users, each of the profiles can be loaded in a separate column and monitored. Occasionally, this will result in two of the profiles communicating with each other while being monitored.

You can also use the Geo search mentioned earlier within Tweet Deck. A column that searches "geocode:43.430242,-89.736459,1km" will display a live feed of Tweets posted within the specified range. A more precise search of "geocode:43.430242,-89.736459,1km fight" would add the keyword to filter the results. Figure 19.07 displays Tweet Deck with several searches.

The columns of Tweet Deck are consistently sized. If more columns are created than can fit in the display, the "Columns" option with left and right arrows will provide navigation. This allows for numerous search columns regardless of screen resolution. This is an advantage of Tweet Deck over the other services discussed. Tweet Deck is one of my Twitter staples. I use it at some point during every investigation. I recommend familiarizing yourself with all of the features before needing to rely on it during your searches.

Real World Application: In 2019, I was investigating a death threat toward a celebrity. I launched Tweet Deck and began monitoring. First, I created a search column with "to:myclient". This started a stream of numerous people mentioning my client, which was too much to monitor. Next, I created a column of "to:myclient kill OR die OR shoot OR death". This presented very few tweets being sent to the celebrity including specific hateful words. However, it did identify a suspect. A tweet was sent to the celebrity stating "I hope you die a fiery death tonight". I then created another column of "from:suspect to:myclient". This identified every tweet he was sending to the celebrity. Since I had to move on to other resources, I set one final Tweet Deck column of "from:suspect to:myclient kill OR die OR shoot OR death" and added an alert. This instructed Tweet Deck to play an audible sound if any new messages met the criteria. The same suspect was arrested a week later while attempting to burglarize her apartment.

Third-Party Resources

We have reached the end of the Twitter search options within the official website. Next, we will focus on third-party search tools. Most of these services require you to authenticate with a Twitter account before any queries can be submitted. This is largely due to Twitter's safeguards against fraud and abuse. I always recommend using a "junk" Twitter account when this is required. You will be asked to give the third-party service access to and control of the account in order to complete any tasks. This can be a security and privacy risk if using your true personal account. I will never give any service access to my personal Twitter account, but I often allow services to authenticate with one of my investigation accounts.

It is important to note that in 2023 Twitter closed their free API tier which resulted in almost all free third-party sites and services to close down. Third party services are now required to pay for API access so do not expect to get much back from free services, and most services which retained functionality are now premium only. The number of third-party resources has been reduced drastically, but I will share the handful of sties which may still be of use.

Twitter Location Information

While privacy-aware individuals have disabled the location feature of their accounts, many users enjoy broadcasting their location at all times. Identifying a user's location during a Twitter post is sometimes possible through various methods. Prior to 2014, identifying the GPS details of every post of many users was simple. Today, most of these identification techniques are no longer working. A manual Twitter search method for identifying posts by location was explained earlier. That technique is best for current or live information, and is limited to only recent posts. You may have a need for historical details from previous posts from a specific location. I have had better success with historical data than current content in regard to geolocation. I believe this is because most people unknowingly shared their location while Tweeting for many years. When Twitter changed the default location option to "Disabled", most users never intentionally re-enabled the feature. Fortunately, there are third-party websites that collected this historical data, and can assist with easy searching. The following options will work best when you are investigating events that occurred several years prior. While you may get lucky and receive some recent posts, the majority could be quite old.

Omnisci (www.heavy.ai/demos/tweetmap)

Omnisci is a massive database platform developed through collaboration between MIT and Harvard. Historically, each college had their own interface into this data, which supplied Twitter post locations from past Tweets. Each interface provided new ways of searching information. Both websites have been disabled, and the entire project has warped into Omnisci. This website can search by topic, username, or location. It can also combine all three options to conduct a detailed search. Results appear as blue dots on a dark map. Each dot represents a Tweet which possesses location data to the chosen area.

One Million Tweet Map (onemilliontweetmap.com)

This service only displays the most recent one million Tweets on an international map. They do not have access to every Tweet available, often referred to as the "firehose", but they offer new Tweets every second. I would never rely on this map for complete data about a location. However, monitoring a large event can provide live intelligence in an easily viewed format. I recommend using a mouse scroll wheel to zoom into your location of interest. Once you are at a level that you can see single Tweets, you can click any of them to see the content. The page will automatically refresh as new information is posted.

Tweet Mapper (keitharm.me/projects/tweet)

If your target possesses Tweets with location data, but the previous two options failed to locate anything, this map could reveal the data. The project appears to be abandoned, but I receive occasional results.

Fake Followers

There are a surprising number of Twitter accounts that are completely fake. These are bought and sold daily by shady people who want to make their profiles appear more popular than they really are. I have seen a lot of target profiles that have been padded with these fake followers. There are two websites that will assist in distinguishing the authentic profiles from the fraudulent. They both require you to be logged in to a Twitter account, and I will compare the results of each.

Twitter Audit (twitteraudit.com)

This option identified 9% of my followers as "fake" and provided very few details. It also allows for submission through a static URL, but you still need to request an audit once you get to the page. The following would display results for my own page. You will need to allow Twitter Audit to authenticate using a Twitter account, which is fairly common for third-party Twitter services. You also only get one free query per user account.

https://www.twitteraudit.com/inteltechniques

Miscellaneous Twitter Sites

Every week, a new site arrives that takes advantage of the public data that Twitter shares with the world. These sites offer unique ways of searching for information that Twitter does not allow on their main page. This partial list is a good start to finding information relevant to your target. I encourage readers to follow my blog, podcast, and Twitter account for any updates which surface after this book has been published.

TweetBinder (dash.tweetbinder.com/report/free)

TweetBinder is a site aimed at users in the marketing field, so it is largely activity analytics. However, I have found some useful information in the results occasionally. You can get a limited number of results with their free search or you can set up a free or premium account on their service to receive more robust results. If nothing else, this site can shed light on patterns of recent activity for the target account.

Memory.lol (github.com/travisbrown/memory.lol)

This project is a web service that provides historical information about social media accounts. Currently, it can be used to look up 542 million historical screen names for 443 million Twitter accounts. Most of this data has been scraped from either the Twitter Stream Grab or the Wayback Machine. As an example, the following URL produces the result seen immediately below it.

https://api.memory.lol/v1/tw/IntelTechniques

```
accounts
id       257644794
id_str   "257644794"
screen_names
IntelTechniques
0        "2015-04-06"
1        "2022-11-08"
```

I now know that the first time this profile, number 257644794, was seen within these resources was April 6th, 2015. I can also reverse this query when I know the user number. The following URL queries by number and identifies the username and same account details, as seen following the URL.

https://api.memory.lol/v1/tw/id/257644794

```
id       257644794
id_str   "257644794"
screen_names
IntelTechniques
0        "2015-04-06"
1        "2022-11-08"
```

This provides a quick way to identify usernames from profile IDs and vice versa.

Threadreader (threadreaderapp.com)

Threadreader is one of the few third-party sites which has retained functionality following Twitter's API changes. The purpose of the service is to make long Twitter threads easily readable and replicated onto a normal looking web page. Although technically a Twitter "bot", the Threadreader site can be used to view and even search Twitter content. The level of content will depend on the target account. One of my primary use cases for this site is simply a secondary means of viewing Twitter posts in scenarios where visiting the platform directly is not possible or desirable. Threadreader has a search bar on their main page and we can also use URL manipulation to run queries.

https://threadreaderapp.com/search?q=IntelTechniques

This would conduct a basic keyword search and does bring up dozens of results, but the results are not comprehensive. Likewise, some user accounts can be queried with the following format.

https://threadreaderapp.com/user/inteltechniques

Most accounts in our testing did not show results using this technique. An example of a working account is https://threadreaderapp.com/user/cyb_detective and this is likely due to that Twitter user utilizing the Threadreader service. As an added bonus, Threadreader does not require us to provide our own Twitter credentials or make an account in order to query for results on their service.

Pivoting to Alternate Microblogs

While Twitter placing their API behind a paywall has severely reduced the number of third-party tools and services for analyzing accounts, changes to the platform have also pushed many users to move to alternative microblogs. We can use this trend to our advantage. I have had significant success tracking Twitter users to alternate platforms while providing additional avenues of investigation. We simply take a target's username, vanity name, or any unique vernacular in their bio, and search it across the most popular Twitter competitors. Popularity of these microblog platforms will vary depending on the culture and demographics of your targets but many Twitter users have created alternate accounts on one or more of these platforms using account names identical to or variations on their Twitter username.

Instagram (instagram.com): Although technically not a micro-blog, many of my targets have migrated to posting Instagram content which they would have previously posted on Twitter. Likewise, groups which previously organized events on Twitter, now do so on Instagram, with the added intelligence benefit of an image or video being associated with every post.
Threads (threads.net): Threads is Meta's attempt to absorb users moving off of the Twitter platform. Any Instagram account can be used to instantly create an associated Threads account and we will discuss Threads further in the next chapter.
Bluesky (bsky.app): Bluesky is a federated platform which has absorbed many former Twitter users. It is particularly popular amongst those who work in technical fields and although previously only available by invitation, currently account creation on this platform is straightforward, making it relatively easy to investigate.
Mastodon (mastodon.social): Mastodon was one of the first federated platforms that was rumored to be the next Twitter killer. Although fairly popular it never reached the level of adoption of Twitter, but it is popular enough to be worth checking.

Often a simple google query is enough to locate any alternate accounts. For example, after seeing that a popular technology podcast has moved off of twitter, we could use the following query to locate the new accounts.

site:threads.net OR site:bsky.app OR site:mastodon.social OR site:instagram.com "techpod"

These reverse queries or "pivots" will be discussed in greater depth when we tackle username tactics in a forthcoming chapter.

IntelTechniques Twitter Tool

I found myself using many of these manual Twitter techniques daily. In order to prevent repetitive typing of the same addresses and searches, I created a custom tool with an all-in-one solution. Download the archive previously mentioned or visit **https://inteltechniques.com/tools/Twitter.html** to access this resource. This page includes embedded JavaScript that will structure and execute web addresses based on your provided information. The Twitter tool will replicate many of the Twitter searches that you have read about here. Clicking the button next to each option executes the query in a new tab in your browser. As a reminder, this page collects absolutely no information from your searches. They are all conducted within your own browser, and no data is captured by my server.

CHAPTER TWENTY
SOCIAL NETWORKS: INSTAGRAM

While Facebook and Twitter are likely going to offer the most bang for your buck in terms of web-based social network presence, Instagram has captured a large share of the market over the past two years. Instagram is a photo-sharing service that is now owned by Facebook. With well over 1 billion active monthly users, the amount of content available here is overwhelming. This application works alone or in correlation with Facebook and Twitter to distribute the photos. This service is very popular with most photo sharing Twitter users and should not be ignored. My preferred method of downloading a person's entire Instagram profile is through the Python tools Instalooter and Instaloader, as previously explained in the Linux, Mac and Windows chapters. These utilities will download all the images and videos from a profile, but there is much more data out there which may be valuable to your investigations. You will need to be logged in to an Instagram account for most techniques in this chapter. First, let's start with some basics.

If you visit Instagram.com, there is no search feature unless you log into an account. If you have already created a burner Facebook account, you can use that account to log into Instagram or you can create a new separate account. Once logged in you will find a search option in the left menu, however, this will only identify a handful of user accounts and recommended search terms. If you select one of the recommended search terms, you will then receive image results based on the query. Although each image corresponds to a post, this is not very efficient, as we would have to click on each image in order to see the corresponding account. Instagram's internal search also provides no additional filters, but in a moment we will use search engines to provide precise queries.

In previous editions of this book, I detailed several third-party Instagram search options that unlocked a lot of hidden content within user accounts. On June 1, 2016, Instagram tightened their API, and this killed most of the useful websites. My own Instagram tools page suffered drastically from the new restrictions in 2018 and 2020, and I had to start over with new options. Fortunately, you still have many search options for your next Instagram investigation. Let's start with keyword searching. I have found greater success with a custom Google search instead of an Instagram search field. The following query on Google will produce thousands of results that display Instagram posts that mention "OSINT" within the post title or comments.

site:instagram.com "OSINT"

This same term searched on an Instagram page only displayed users that have the term within the username. When searching "#OSINT" on Instagram, I was provided a list of hashtags that include the keyword. Each of these hashtags are associated with multiple Instagram posts. Consider the following example in order to identify the benefits of searching away from the Instagram website. While on an Instagram page, I searched for my target "Darren Kitchen" from Hak5. This presented several profiles associated with people having that name, but none of them were my target. Instead, I went to Google and conducted the following search.

site:instagram.com darren kitchen hak5

This produced one result, but it was not connected to my target. Since people seldom use last names on Instagram, I modified my search to the following.

site:instagram.com darren hak5

The first result was my target's profile (@hak5darren). Similar to Facebook and Twitter, a person's Instagram profile only tells a small portion of the story. Conducting the following search on Google revealed 215 results.

site:instagram.com "hak5darren"

These are the various pages and posts that contain the text of my target's username. Many of these are posts from the target, which we have already seen by looking at his profile. A few are from associates of the target and may otherwise be missed. I now only want posts that contain "@hak5darren" within the content. This is more likely to find other people mentioning my target.

site:instagram.com "@hak5darren"

Similar to the previous search, it forces Google to ignore the target's profile, and only focus on people that are posting "to" the target with @hak5darren instead of just his username alone. These searches can be modified to include or exclude keywords, usernames, real names, or any other terms with which you have interest. You could also repeat these on Bing and Yandex for better coverage. Figure 20.01 displays the difference in search results while Figure 20.02 identifies a post targeted toward a user. Hopefully, you now have a target profile of interest. Now we can dig into our target within Instagram and through third-party resources.

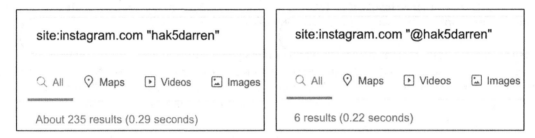

Figure 20.01: Google search queries for Instagram data.

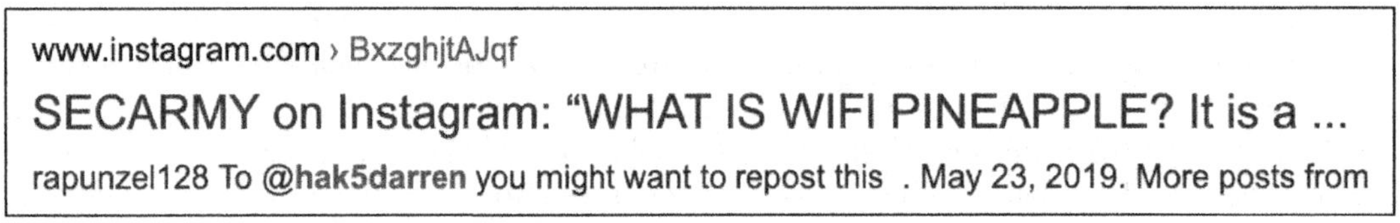

www.instagram.com › BxzghjtAJqf

SECARMY on Instagram: "WHAT IS WIFI PINEAPPLE? It is a ...

rapunzel128 To @hak5darren you might want to repost this . May 23, 2019. More posts from

Figure 20.02: Google search results of Instagram data.

Instagram Images

There is one obstacle with Instagram searches that needs to be addressed. When you identify a profile of interest, there will always be a profile image at the top of the page. This is usually a 150x150 pixel profile image and a full page of lower-resolution post images, all of which are small and heavily compressed. In 2015 and 2018, Instagram changed the way these thumbnails and original images are stored. The goal of this technique is to locate these low-resolution images and identify the full high-resolution images that were originally uploaded. For an example, I will pick on the user "hak5darren". His profile is at instagram.com/hak5darren. When I right-click on his profile picture, I am blocked from opening the image alone in a new tab. In fact, there is no right-click menu whatsoever. If I right-click on the images, I also receive no option to view the image alone, which previously would grant us a larger version. Instagram is actively blocking us, so we will need to dig into the raw files from the page using our browser's developer tools.

In the past we have searched for links to image files in the page code using "View page source", but our browser's built in developer tools provide a more direct method for locating and isolating these files. With the target Instagram profile loaded in my browser window, I right-click and choose "Inspect", or strike F12, to open the developer panel. Depending on your browser this panel will open to the side or below the target page. In the panel select the "Network" tab. Once on this tab, we can refresh the page using F5 to view a cascading list of files as the page reloads. To make things easier, we can use the image option in the filter bar in the developer panel to show only files with common image file extensions. Anytime we add or remove a filter we must refresh the page to generate a fresh list of files.

One of the benefits of this technique is that the files are listed in the order that they load, so image files at the top of the profile tend to be at the top of the file list. Therefore, one of the top images is likely to be our target's profile photo. If we select the desired file from the list, a window to the right of the file will provide additional information pertaining to that image. Within this window, the image itself will be displayed in the "Preview" tab for Chrome browsers or the "Response" tab for Firefox users.

Now that we can see the target image, we can right click on it and either save it or open it in a new tab. In my workflow, I prefer to open the file in a new tab which allows me to download it or perform a reverse image search. If you are working in Firefox and you are unable to interact with the image in the "Response" tab, move to the "Headers" tab where you can copy the direct link the image and then paste it into a new tab manually. Many people use the same profile picture across multiple platforms, so this reverse image search has a good chance of uncovering additional accounts belonging to our target. We will discuss reverse image searches further in a later chapter. We also now have the direct URL for the image which we can add to our case notes.

This is often our best option for viewing and archiving media files from pages which do not allow direct interaction with page content. Does this seem like too much trouble for every image of interest on Instagram? Yes, no argument here. If you prefer to allow a third-party service to replicate this for you, the following sites will download the best quality image available within a post. Regardless of your method, you should understand the functions allowing for the capture of these high-resolution images. I suspect that these methods will change slightly after this book is published. However, the replacement strategies explained in the examples should carry over into the unknown changes Instagram will apply next.

https://instadownloader.co/
https://igram.io/
https://igdownloader.com/
https://toolzu.com/downloader/instagram/photo/

Figure 20.03: Isolating files using the developer tools

Metadata Details

You should also consider digging into the source code of your evidence in order to identify further details that could be valuable. First, I like to identify the user number of an account. Similar to Facebook and Twitter, people can change their username on Instagram, but not their user number. Right-click on your target profile page and select the option to view the source code. This will open a new tab with a lot of pure text. Using either "Ctrl" + "F" (Windows) or "command" + "F" (macOS), conduct a search for exactly the following. The numbers directly after this data will be the user number of your target. In our previous example, his user number is 340416780.

"profile_id"

Sometimes Firefox will search through the source code and highlight data, but the results don't match the terms searched. I do not know why this happens, but selecting "Wrap long lines" within the Firefox source code page sometimes helps. When necessary, I copy all of the source code and paste it into a text editor, then search there. Your target may change their username, but they cannot change their user ID. If you know that your target's user ID is 340416780, but you can no longer access their profile based on the username, we can query the Instagram API to get the new details. However, you must first spoof your user-agent. In Chapter Two, I explained the Firefox extension called User-Agent Switcher and Manager. Open this menu within your Firefox browser; change the second drop-down menu to "Android"; change the first drop-down menu to "Instagram"; select the first option; click "Apply"; and navigate to the following page.

https://i.instagram.com/api/v1/users/340416780/info/

The text-only result should display pages of details, but I find the following of most interest.

```
"pk": 340416780,
"username": "hak5darren",
"full_name": "Darren",
"is_private": false,
"media_count": 949,
"geo_media_count": 0,
"follower_count": 5855,
"following_count": 257,
"external_url": "http://hak5.org",
"has_videos": true,
"has_highlight_reels": true,
"has_guides": false,
"can_be_reported_as_fraud": false,
"is_business": false,
"profile_pic_url": "https://scontent-sea1-1.cdninstagram.com/v/t51.2885-
19/13534173_1620017484977625_1916767107_a.jpg?stp=dst-
jpg_e0_s150x150&_nc_ht=scontent-sea1-
1.cdninstagram.com&_nc_cat=109&_nc_ohc=q_PLR6-
nj2IQ7kNvgHT9czS&_nc_gid=ed08cb087dc34ce3be64efaea67ff6ff&edm=AEF8tYYBAAAA&ccb
=7-5&oh=00_AYDoftauBBbsGYPujN8B__fEB9wrigM7Cw-FqlS_R-
5wHA&oe=66EA669A&_nc_sid=1e20d2"
```

If the target had changed his username, we would see it here. As an added benefit we are provided with a direct link to the target's profile image. While inconvenient, this is the most stable way to translate a user ID back into a username. Next, let's tackle exact timestamps. Instagram might tell you a photo was posted 67 weeks ago, and hovering over that notification should tell you the exact date, but it never tells you the time of the post. This detail can be crucial to a legal investigation. For this example, I located an image posted by our target at the following address.

https://www.instagram.com/p/CR854ZigEhR/

Right-click the profile and select the "Inspect" option within your browser. Click on the "Network" tab and reload the page. Click the small magnifying glass to conduct a search (not the filter URL option). Search for "taken" and notice the data which follows. My example displayed the following.

"items":[{"taken1627648763,"pk":"2629230846841735249","id":"262923

The number following "taken", which was 1627648763 is a Unix timestamp. Converting this from Unix to standard time on the website located at epochconverter.com reveals the image was uploaded on Friday, July 30, 2021 at 12:39:23 in universal time (GMT) format.

I realize these details are very minor. However, documenting this content can announce the difference between an average OSINT investigator and an expert. If you plan to serve any legal process later, knowing the user number and exact time of activity will be crucial.

Hashtags

A hashtag is a word or phrase preceded by a hash sign (#) used on social media websites and applications, especially Twitter and Instagram, in order to identify messages on a specific topic. If I wanted to view all posts tagged with "osint", the following direct URL would be appropriate.

https://www.instagram.com/explore/tags/osint/

I do not pay much attention to hashtags within my investigations. I prefer to focus more on search terms. Many people do not properly tag a post, and you can miss a lot by limiting your search to a hashtag. If I search for hashtags of #shooting, I may see valuable data. If a potential target only posts the term "shooting" without the "#", I would miss the post. This is why I rely much more heavily on searching within Google, as explained momentarily.

Followers & Following

Instagram now requires users to be logged in to an account in order to view the followers of a target or the profiles that a target follows (friends). Viewing these lists is not a challenge, but proper documentation can be tricky. The following explains how I choose to view and document every Instagram follower and friend of my target account, using hak5darren as an example.

After logging in to your account and navigating to the target profile, you will be able to simply click on "Followers" or "Following". In this demonstration, I chose the people he is "following", often referred to as friends. This opened a new window on my screen with the first twenty people displayed. Since hak5darren follows 215 people, I can scroll down the entire list to load all of the accounts. You will not be able to see all of the accounts at once because the window only displays ten within its boundaries. This causes screen capture tools to be useless in this scenario. If you are using either the Firefox browser we created within Linux or your own version of Firefox with the recommended Add-ons, you can easily copy this list.

After scrolling down to load all of the users, press either "Ctrl" + "A" (Windows & Linux) or "command" + "A" (Mac) on your keyboard. This will highlight or "select" the entire list. Next, right-click within this window and choose "Copy selected links". This copies all of the Instagram account hyperlinks within the target's following list into your computer clipboard. Open your desired documentation software, such as Word, Excel, or any text editor, and paste the contents into the application. I prefer Excel (or Calc within the free LibreOffice suite) for this task. Pasting the results confirmed 199 accounts, four of which are shown below. Repeat the process with "Followers".

196	https://www.instagram.com/dragorn/
197	https://www.instagram.com/smacktwin/
198	https://www.instagram.com/serafinamoto/
199	https://www.instagram.com/moon_spot/

In my experience, Instagram limits the number of accounts within this window to 1,000. This should be sufficient for most friends of the target, but may be limited when looking at the followers of famous people. While Instagram offers a text-only view of followers and following, it appears limited to 50 random profiles. I included these long links within the search tools, but I do not rely on them. I prefer this manual method. If your target's user ID was 340416780, the following URL presents the first 50 people he is following.

https://www.instagram.com/graphql/query/?query_hash=d04b0a864b4b54837c0d870b0e77e076&variables ={%22id%22:%22340416780%22,%22include_reel%22:true,%22fetch_mutual%22:false,%22first%22:50}

As you can see, this is quite messy and only presents partial information. While viewing who the target is following, I can also use the search bar in that window to do a quick query for accounts of known aliases. I often search for my target's surname to potentially locate family members. Remember, people will often follow their own account with their alternate accounts so searching for known aliases and usernames can be very beneficial. The "Following" window also has a tab for hashtags which will allow us to see a list of hashtags associated with our target. This can be good cultural intelligence on our target while also providing us with additional keywords which we may find useful when we move back to running queries in Google.

Likes & Comments

Similar to Twitter, users can "Like" or comment on each post. Unique from Twitter, this is only seen when you load the target post in your browser. In other words, if a user posts a comment to a photo published by our target, we do not see that comment within the account of the person who made it. We only see it within the specific post directly from the target. We also cannot search within Instagram by keyword in order to identify comments, but we can with Google as explained momentarily. First, let's focus on Likes.

Viewing an individual Instagram post reveals a heart icon below any comments. Clicking that icon "likes" the post from your account, so this should be avoided. Directly below the heart is a summary such as "557 Likes". Clicking on this opens a new window, which identifies each account that liked the post. Slowly scrolling through this list expands it until all accounts are present. Similar to the previous method of capturing friends and followers of a target, a manual approach is best here. Pressing "Ctrl" + "A" (Windows) or "command" + "A" (macOS) on the keyboard selects all of the content, and "Ctrl" + "C" (Windows) or "command" + "C" (macOS) copies it to your computer memory, which can be pasted into a spreadsheet or word processor. You can repeat this process for the comments within the post.

If you locate a comment which is valuable to your investigation, you may want to document the date and time of the post. This is not available within the standard view. As an example, look at the post at https://www.instagram.com/p/Bqi6r9uA0Y3. Inside the comments includes a response of "now I gotta go buy some beer" from a friend. At the time of this writing, Instagram displayed "303w" under the post, indicating it was posted 303 weeks previous to the current date. There is also a date for the post listed below the number of likes, but this may not be sufficiently accurate for our needs. While on the page, right-click and choose the "Inspect" option as we did previously. While on the "Inspector" tab, search for the terms (now I gotta go buy some beer) and expand the text immediately after the result, as displayed in Figure 20.04. You can now see that this comment was made on November 24, 2018, at 14:27:02 GMT. Alternatively, we could conduct the same keyword search in the "Network" tab of our developer tools in order to find the exact Unix time of the post.

```
▼<div class="_a9zs">
    <span class="_aacl _aaco _aacu _aacx _aad7 _aade">
    Damnit Darren, now I gotta go buy some beer...</span>
  </div>
▼<div class="_ab8w _ab94 _ab99 _ab9f _ab9m _ab9p _abaj _abb- _abcm"> flex
  ▼<div class="_aacl _aacn _aacu _aacy _aad6">
    ▼<a class="x1i10hfl xjbqb8w x6umtig x1b1mbwd xaqea5y xav7gou x9f619 x1y…d9i69 xkhd6sd
      x16tdsg8 x1hl2dhg xggy1nq x1a2a7pz _a9zg _a6hd" href="/p/Bqi6r9uA0Y3
      /c/17911737427262537/" role="link" tabindex="0"> event
       <time class="_a9ze _a9zf" datetime="2018-11-24T14:27:02.000Z" title="Nov 24,
       2018">207w</time>
```

Figure 20.04: "Like" data within an Instagram post.

Complete Post Analysis

Assume that you have located your suspect (https://www.instagram.com/hak5darren) and found an incriminating post on his account (https://www.instagram.com/p/BK1KWEthQkb). This is a high-priority investigation, and extensive manual documentation is justified. You have already attacked his account with

Instaloader, Instalooter, and Osintgram as explained in previous chapters. You possess all of the images from the account. The following outlines the next steps I would take toward this target.

- Use our browser's developer tools to inspect the loaded files for the target URL.
- If the media files have not been previously saved using scripts, save the image from the post manually as previously explained.
- Close the developer panel.
- Scroll through the comments, and expand any, if necessary, by clicking "+".
- Click the summary of likes below the heart icon.
- Scroll until all are loaded, select all with "Ctrl" + "A" or "command" + "A" on keyboard.
- Open a new spreadsheet through Microsoft Office or LibreOffice and paste the results.
- Rename this tab "BK1KWEthQkb" and open a new tab.
- Repeat the process with any other posts of interest.
- Return to the account (https://www.instagram.com/hak5darren) and click "Followers".
- Load the data, copy it, and paste it into the new sheet titled "Followers".
- Repeat the process for "Following".
- On the target profile, scroll down until all posts are loaded and select/highlight all.
- Right-click, choose "Copy selected links", and paste data into a new sheet titled "Posts".

You now have a spreadsheet with multiple pages inside it. The first provides the comments, details, and likes of a specific post. The second displays all of the target's followers. The third shows his friends, and the fourth provides the direct URL of every post for later analysis or extraction. Figure 20.05 displays a partial view of my example, highlighting the final sheet created. This was a lot of work, and I do not replicate these steps for every Instagram investigation. You must decide when the extra work is warranted. Unfortunately, there is no reliable automated solution which extracts all data.

Figure 20.05: A spreadsheet created from a target Instagram post.

Channels

While Instagram was originally introduced as a photo-sharing platform, it is quickly becoming dominated by user-submitted videos. Many profiles now include a video channel which was formerly called "IGTV". Meta has replaced the IGTV button on profile pages with "REELS", which are more similar to TikTok's format, but at this time channels can still be accessed directly via URL with the following structure.

https://www.instagram.com/ambermac/channel/

Opening a video page allows you to play the content and see any details such as likes and comments. Capturing the text data can be done using the techniques previously explained. However, saving the video introduces new challenges. While the video URL is embedded into the source code of the page, it requires heavy modification in order to replicate the content in a format which can be archived. Instead, we will rely on our browser to help us locate the stream. While viewing any Instagram video page, launch the "Inspector" tool within your Firefox or Chrome browser. You should be able to simply right-click on the page and select "Inspect Element". If this is not visible, you can launch Inspector from the Developer Tools within the browser menu (F12).

Within the developer tools, click the "Network" tab and play the video. If the video was already playing, reload the page. The inspector will display a lot of information which can seem overwhelming. Instead of manually filtering through these network connections, simply type "mp4" within the search field directly below the "Network" tab. This will result in multiple files being listed. Sort this list by file size and select the largest file. In the right side panel you will see a long URL in the "Headers" tab. Copy this link and paste it into a new browser tab. Now delete the last part of the URL which will be similar to "&bytestart=4635232&byteend=4933185" and hit enter. The new tab within your browser should present the video in full-size resolution. You can now right-click on the video and select the option to save it. Figure 20.07 displays results similar to what you should see in your developer tools.

This may all seem tedious and complicated. While there are browser extensions which simplify these processes, they are replicating the manual methods presented here. Knowing these manual functions allows you to explain the capture process when mandated. When I testified in criminal trials about my online evidence, I proudly explained the ways I captured evidence from the source rather than relying on third-party tools which do not disclose their exact methods.

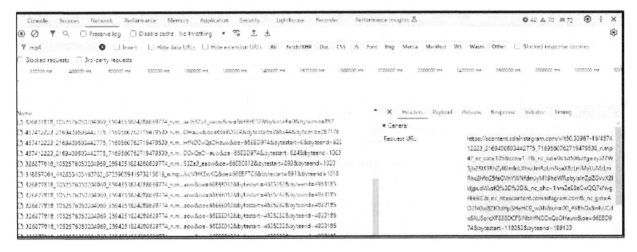

Figure 20.06: The "Inspector" utility within Firefox identifying an Instagram video MP4 file.

Tagged Users

Instagram allows users to be tagged within posts. On any target profile, you may see the "Tagged" link directly above the images. You can also navigate directly with the following structure.

https://www.instagram.com/hak5darren/tagged/

Google Instagram Search

We have exhausted all useful aspects of collecting data from within Instagram.com. The search functions are extremely limited there, so we must utilize a third-party search engine to find further data and connections. In my experience, Google is our best option, and you should be familiar with the queries conducted at the beginning of the chapter. Let's conduct a demonstration. Earlier, we searched site:instagram.com "hak5darren" and received hundreds of results. Browsing through these three pages reveals no evidence of a post including the word "Pager". However, I know he posted a photo with that term in the title. Searching the following reveals the target post.

site:instagram.com "hak5darren" "pager"

This confirms that Google indexed the post, but did not present it when I searched the suspect's Instagram username. This means that we should also query search terms when we conduct searches associated with a target. The search tools presented in a moment simplifies this, but let's conduct one more manual attempt. I see that "hak5darren" posts comments to "snubs" within his posts. I would like to search for any Instagram posts, within any accounts, which contain either a mention of or comment by both "hak5darren" and "snubs". The following is appropriate.

site:instagram.com "hak5darren" "snubs"

Twitter Instagram Search

Many people who post to Instagram broadcast the links on Twitter. Following this data can reveal our target's Twitter account and any unique comments from Twitter users. Because of these reasons, we should always check Twitter for Instagram posts. The user "hak5darren" on Instagram is also "hak5darren" on Twitter. The following Google search identifies posts on Twitter (site:x.com) which mention "hack5darren", and possess an Instagram image URL (instagram.com/p).

site:x.com "hak5darren" "instagram.com/p"

Third-Party Tools

Overall, the various Instagram search websites do nothing more than what we replicated in the previous instruction. However, these sites could identify that one piece of vital evidence which we missed. Therefore, it is always best to have as many resources as possible. I have found the following third-party resources beneficial to my investigations. Third-party Instagram tools appear and disappear rapidly. After publication, I will continue to update the Instagram search tool with new features, as explained soon.

Instagram Stories

Instagram Stories are vertical photos or videos, up to 15 seconds in length, which disappear 24 hours after posting. Instead of being displayed in the user's feed, they are displayed at the top of an active user's app when they are logged in. If there are active stories, we can click on the target's Instagram profile image to view them, but we must be logged into Instagram in order to do so. Since Stories disappear quickly, they are often used much more casually than the public Instagram feed. I have found the following utilities helpful for displaying and downloading this temporary content. I demonstrate each.

InstaFollowers (instafollowers.co/download-instagram-stories)

Of these, InstaFollowers has been the most beneficial. It was the only option which displayed "Stories Highlights" of previously expired content and easily allowed download of all stories directly through Instagram. Consider the following example. Using their search tool, I conducted a query for my target. Several "Stories" were presented with a "Download" button below each. That button forwarded me directly to the Instagram host of each video. Each link is quite long, but should load the video directly in your browser. Right-clicking should present the option to download the file.

StoriesDown (storiesdown.com/)

This service is very similar to the previous and should present most of the same data. These sites break or disappear often, so having multiple sites with redundant functionality is always a benefit.

Snapinsta (snapinsta.app)

A newer service which simplifies media download is Snapinsta. It allows download of images, videos, Reels, IGTV, and stories without the need to understand browser developer tools. However, it requires you to trust a third party with the identity of the target of your investigation. I prefer to go straight to the source.

Dumpor (dumpor.com)

From an evidence perspective, I believe it is best to obtain your Instagram data from the official website. However, account requirements might hinder your investigation. Some organizations prevent employees from using any covert account to access data about a target. If logging in to Instagram is prohibited, consider Dumpor. This service allows you to navigate through a person's Instagram posts without the need for an account. Dumpor also allows for easy downloading of media files by right-clicking on any image or video. You can search a username or tag from the main site, or submit a direct URL query as follows.

Username: https://dumpor.com/v/ambermac
Tag: https://dumpor.com/t/osint

Toolzu (toolzu.com)

In 2022, I found this site to be quite beneficial to Instagram investigations. It relies on the Instagram API, so you will not find any content which is not already public. However, the layout and analysis of profile data is unique. It also allows direct URL input, so it will play well with our tools. Consider the following.

https://toolzu.com/profile-analyzer/instagram/?username=@ambermac

Toolzu creates a summary of the account, but then extracts all profile data and analyzes if to provide details which are not available directly from Instagram. In this example, I now know that my target:

Posted over 2000 Instagram uploads
Has 35,600 followers
Posts 1.29 times weekly
Averages 5.54 posts per month
Is most likely to post on a Tuesday or Wednesday
Most commonly tags with Partner, TheFeed, CanadasSeniorCare, Seniors, and AmberMacMedia
Most commonly captions with newsletter, Canada, Tuesday, and technology
Interests include business (15,38%), travel (3,85%), marketing (3,85%), and art (3,85%)
Most commented post is https://www.instagram.com/p/CiSniiBgqKH/
Most liked post is https://www.instagram.com/p/CiSniiBgqKH/

Suspension Warning

I have some bad news. I have witnessed suspension of Instagram accounts when using third-party Instagram tools which require you to log in to an account. Always log in to a "junk" account and expect that you may be blocked. Logging back in to the account and completing a Captcha usually reverses the suspension.

Threads (threads.net)

In 2023, Twitter's popularity and number of active users began to decline. Meta responded to this change by opening up a competing microblogging service named Threads. Although hosted on its own domain, and having a format more similar to Twitter, Threads functions more as an extension to Instagram than it does its own platform. Threads in fact uses your existing Instagram login and anyone with an Instagram account can instantly use it to generate an associated Threads account. Threads uses Instagram credentials so every Threads user also has a corresponding Instagram account, but not every Instagram user has activated their corresponding Threads account. At some point in the future, Meta may choose to separate Threads from Instagram, but currently one is merely an extension of the other.

Locating targets on Threads is very straightforward. We can take our target's Instagram account name and easily check to see if they are also on threads using the following URL structure.

https://www.threads.net/@ambermac

We can also use our search operators to search for accounts or topics.

site:threads.net/@ "accountname"
site:threads.net/ "keyword"

Threads does have its own search functionality and unlike Instagram, you can perform some internal queries without being logged in, although you will receive additional filters if you are logged into a burner account. Likewise, when viewing without authenticating you will receive only a limited number of results for your queries. Unlike Instagram, the internal search feature on Threads does provide results for both accounts and posts. Threads search feature can be accessed at https://www.threads.net/search or we can use the following URL structure to manually formulate search queries.

https://www.threads.net/search?q=osint

The account identifiers will be identical to the target's Instagram account because on the back end it is all the same account. This means the account ID will be the same number as the Instagram account. Once an Instagram user joins Threads, they can change the bio and profile photo on the Threads account, so you may find some new data points if they have activated their Threads account. There will typically be overlap in followers, but there may be some unique followers on Threads.

Threads is still very new and has very limited functionality, so at this time the associated Instagram account tends to be a much richer source of intelligence. In my workflow, I analyze the target's Instagram first and then move on to their Threads account. Although Threads boasts a high number of users due to the integration with Instagram, many users are not actively posting to the platform.

The Threads mobile application does not boast any significant advantages over browser access. In our tests, the Threads application did not currently support contact exploitation, but this may change in future releases. Contact exploitation is where we use a clean virtual or physical phone, load our target's information in as a contact, and then prompt mobile applications on that device to locate "friends" by accessing our contacts list. The contacts list only has one entry, our target, so any account which shows up in the social media application would belong to our target. Hopefully this functionality will be added to the Threads application in the future.

I expect Threads to change rapidly as features are added as well as restrictions. Meta has a long history of increasing restrictions around access as their platforms gain in popularity. Currently Threads is in the honeymoon phase where it is easy to access and search, but this will likely change in the future.

Meta has already started to integrate Threads with some other microblogging ecosystems, such as Mastodon. Part of Threads' development roadmap is to add this interoperability and some functionality is in place for those who opt-in. Some of the other "fediverse" platforms are not very excited about Meta connecting to their communities, so it remains to be seen if this cross-platform communication will ever be fully supported.

IntelTechniques Instagram Tool

If this all seems like a lot of work for minimal information, consider using my custom Instagram Tool, which includes many of the search options previously discussed. It cannot replicate the source code techniques, but may save you time with username and keyword searching. The online version is available on my website at **https://inteltechniques.com/tools/Instagram.html**, and an offline copy is presented within your downloads portal.

CHAPTER TWENTY-ONE
SOCIAL NETWORKS: TIKTOK

The previous edition of this book included only a section about TikTok in the following chapter. The service was popular, but not a household name. In the past two years, TikTok has exploded with users. If you are investigating any person under 30 who is active within social media, they are very likely on TikTok.

TikTok (tiktok.com) is a Chinese-owned video-sharing social networking service which has become viral globally. It is used to create short videos which appear to viewers in an endless stream of content. Posts accept and display comments, both of which require login for access. There is a limited native search within the website, but we can formulate URLs to gain direct access to targeted details. The following URL structure displays the user profile for "snubsie".

https://www.tiktok.com/@snubsie

If you suspect your target possesses a username which includes "osint", but do not know the exact profile name, the following URL should assist. It displays every username which includes "osint" anywhere in the name.

https://www.tiktok.com/search/user?q=osint

Many users "tag" their posts with a keyword. The following displays posts which include the tag "osint".

https://www.tiktok.com/tag/osint

The search field within TikTok pages can be unreliable. Instead, we can formulate a URL with search terms. The following presents posts which include "osint" within the original post (requires account).

https://www.tiktok.com/search?q=osint

If you want to isolate this search to only display videos which include "osint", the following URL would apply (requires account).

https://www.tiktok.com/search/video?q=osint

Google indexes individual TikTok posts, so the following search query would present results which include the term "osint" within any post or author profile. This can be beneficial to discover deleted posts.

site:tiktok.com osint

Some TikTok users will broadcast live. Any current live streams can be found with the following URL.

https://www.tiktok.com/live

Once you find your target, navigating through the posts is similar to the techniques previously mentioned with Instagram. However, we do have a few unique offerings. Each profile possesses three identifiers within the source code view of the page. In the following example, I searched the following text within the source code view of the TikTok page of @willsmith, with the result in parentheses.

"id" (6727327145951183878)
"uniqueId" (willsmith)
"nickname" (Will Smith)

Note that nicknames are not unique. They are vanity names which can be reused. We can now search the user number within search engines in order to identify additional posts which may no longer be present within the TikTok website. Once you identify an individual post, it may appear as follows.

https://www.tiktok.com/@willsmith/video/7032216839878905134

This will usually include a video which can be played in full screen by clicking on it. Once in the player view, you can right-click the video and save it natively as an MP4 file. However, there could be issues with this easy technique. TikTok could remove the feature at any time and you are at their mercy for the file resolution. If they believe you are on a mobile device, you may receive a smaller file with lower resolution. I believe there is a better way to acquire TikTok files.

In the first section of this book, I explained my usage of a Terminal-based program called yt-dlp to acquire YouTube videos. This method also works great for TikTok. The following command within your OSINT VM (or any machine with yt-dlp installed) will download our target video.

```
yt-dlp https://www.tiktok.com/@willsmith/video/7032216839878905134
```

We can add `--write-info-json` at the end of the command to acquire the metadata associated with the file. This file included the following details within it.

```
"Accept-Language": "en-us,en;q=0.5",
"Sec-Fetch-Mode": "navigate", "Referer":
"https://www.tiktok.com/@willsmith/video/7032216839878905134"},
"channel": "Will Smith",
"channel_id": "MS4wLjABAAA222ObGXxt07F9BIh4QH3-g1P1DHyChT2LLi2cn-vAE2R53-H672ZO",
"uploader": "willsmith",
"uploader_id": "6727327145951183878",
"uploader_url": "https://www.tiktok.com/@willsmith",
"track": "original sound",
"artists": ["gakuyen"],
"duration": 9,
"title": "Sometimes we just be feelin' cute on this #kingrichard promo tour!",
"description": "Sometimes we just be feelin' cute on this #kingrichard promo tour!",
"timestamp": 1637315587,
"view_count": 4500000,
"like_count": 406400,
"repost_count": 542,
"comment_count": 1723,
"webpage_url_basename": "7032216839878905134", "
webpage_url_domain": "tiktok.com",
"extractor": "TikTok",
"extractor_key": "TikTok",
"upload_date": "20211119",
"ext": "mp4",
"vcodec": "h265",
"acodec": "aac",
"filesize": 1353054,
"width": 1080,
"height": 1920,"
```

This presents a ton of details, all generated directly by TikTok.

Most videos display an upload date within the content, but I always prefer to obtain a full date and time of upload. To do this, right-click a post and choose to view the page source. When this new tab of text opens, search (ctrl-f or cmd-f) for "~tplv". This should present a result similar to the following.

1637781925~tplv

The numbers directly before this search term represent a Unix timestamp, which was explained in previous chapters (Instagram). We can convert this number at unixtimestamp.com, which produces the following result.

Wed Nov 24 2021 19:25:25 GMT+0000

We now know the exact date and time of the post. Accessing some features and content on TikTok requires you to be logged in. I always recommend a "burner" account which is associated with a Gmail address or social network connection. When you attempt to create an account, you will see a list of accepted associations. In my experience, attempting to make a new account only associated with an email address will result in a demand to download their app to continue. I never recommend this. Instead, I open a new Firefox container assigned specifically to an investigative Google account. I then allow TikTok to build my account based on that data. From a privacy perspective, I hate these associations. If the Google account is free of any activity or personal information, I tolerate it. Associating an active Google account almost always bypasses the need to install the app, and allows full functionality within a browser

The commenting system on TikTok is very similar to Facebook and Instagram. Each comment post presents a username with hyperlink; the comment from that user; the date of the comment; the number of "likes"; and an option to expand further comments to that comment. Screen captures may work well for unpopular posts, but posts with many views may be a problem. **Export Comments** (exportcomments.com) will extract the first 100 comments from any post. A premium account is required to download larger content. There are several "scraper" applications and Chrome extensions which claim to aid in comment exportation, but I have found them all to be unreliable.

You can also see the comments within the browser element inspector under the section labeled https://www.tiktok.com/api/comment/list/. If you load our previous video, right-click outside the video area, choose Inspect, click the Network tab, and play the video, you should see comments populating within the page. Conduct a search within the lower Inspect area for "comment/list". This should limit you to a single file. Right-click that entry and select "Open in new tab". This should launch the JSON view of the comments. The following is a very partial entry from this text-only view, highlighting the most interesting data. This presents more granular detail from the comments, and is the same way that online extraction services pluck this data.

```
"comment_language": "en",
"create_time": 1637626005,
"desc": "TianeMarshaxのコメント,
"reply_score": 0.00056,
"text": "I thought Robert was on the loose. I nearly damn cried 😂",
"nickname": "TianeMarshax",
 "uid": "6866147955729728517",
```

Most users will display a small avatar icon next to their account details. If a larger image was uploaded, we can usually retrieve it through the source code. Let's test this for our current target (Will Smith). Navigate to https://www.tiktok.com/@willsmith, right-click the avatar and save the image. In my attempt, this downloaded a 55 kb jpeg image. Return to the avatar on the profile, but this time right-click and choose "Inspect". This should open a lower frame with this image selected. Right-click the highlighted image. Mine appeared as follows.

https://p19-pu-sign-useast8.tiktokcdn-us.com/tos-useast8-avt-0068-
tx2/62fcd65727a185278429a12d6bfecced~c5_720x720.jpeg?lk3s=a5d48078&nonce=4635&refresh_token=5
19f43cd9d35bc895cd7ee813fe3248f&x-expires=1726412400&x-
signature=E3aqvnZoVgUmkmD%2Fo825fBqfTcw%3D&shp=a5d48078&shcp=81f88b70

This opened the same 720p version of the profile image which we retrieved by simply downloading the icon. However, we want the largest image possible. Return to the profile, and right-click to select "View Page Source". Within this text, search for "jpeg". I observed only five files. One of which was the following.

"https:\u002F\u002Fp16-pu-sign-useast8.tiktokcdn-us.com\u002Ftos-useast8-avt-0068-
tx2\u002F62fcd65727a185278429a12d6bfecced~c5_1080x1080.jpeg?lk3s=a5d48078&nonce=83375&refresh
_token=f0f967025448777565f868d4cf4b1e7f&x-expires=1726412400&x-
signature=eh2w6gICA5RKyDTw46ZhT89%2BxOc%3D&shp=a5d48078&shcp=81f88b70"

Opening this link will fail. However, we can use the previous URL and this URL to combine the text needed to access the larger image. Notice in the 720p link, the image name started with "62fcd657". We see in this larger URL the same characters. If we copy every character beginning with "62fcd657" through the end of the URL and replace the text in the previous smaller image URL, we should receive the larger image. My URL was the following.

https://p16-pu-sign-useast8.tiktokcdn-us.com/tos-useast8-avt-0068-
tx2/62fcd65727a185278429a12d6bfecced~c5_1080x1080.jpeg?lk3s=a5d48078&nonce=83375&refresh_token
=f0f967025448777565f868d4cf4b1e7f&x-expires=1726412400&x-
signature=eh2w6gICA5RKyDTw46ZhT89%2BxOc%3D&shp=a5d48078&shcp=81f88b70

This presented a 1080p image, and is the largest available. Was this a lot of effort for little reward? Quite possibly. If you want an easier route, online extractors such as ttsave.app do the same thing for you. Personally, I prefer the manual way which I can articulate in my report. Figure 21.01 displays the process of using the browser's Inspect tool.

There are also numerous third-party TikTok services which provide analytics on target profiles. I prefer those which allow submission within the URL, such as the following, which display results for "vancityreynolds" (Ryan Reynolds, who was an owner of Mint Mobile, which may be of interest to listeners of my show).

https://tokcount.com/?user=vancityreynolds
https://tokcounter.com/?user=vancityreynolds
https://exolyt.com/user/vancityreynolds/full

These four sites confirm the following details about my target.

25.5M Followers	Latest Bio Details
15 Following	Profile Image
157M Likes	All Recent Posts
43.7k Average Post Comments	Daily Engagement Rate Changes
39.4M Average Plays	Follower Growth Chart
108k Average Shares	Daily Performance Score

Figure 21.01: Using our browser's developer tools to inspect comments

While most of these granular details will not be very helpful to an investigation, they should all be documented. I have included most of the TikTok search features within the Communities Search Tool presented in the next chapter. There were not enough options to justify its own page.

The popularity of the TikTok platform across many demographics has made it a fertile source of intelligence and I now regularly include it in my investigations. When assisting law enforcement colleagues with a recent case involving underground street racing, TikTok was pivotal in exposing involved individuals, video evidence of crimes, and intelligence on forthcoming events. Whereas the targets had privatized content on other platforms, they had used identical account names on the TikTok platform and were publicly posting valuable investigative leads. This tactic of searching known usernames across popular platforms is a key technique in our arsenal and TikTok's popularity makes it one of the best places to look for our target's alternate accounts and postings.

At the very least, understand how to properly create screen captures and full video exports as evidence. It is important to understand this platform and the many ways of exploring the content.

CHAPTER TWENTY-TWO
ONLINE COMMUNITIES

Online communities are very similar to social networks. The thin line which has separated the two is slowly disappearing. While social networks cater to a broad audience with many interests, these communities usually relate to a specific service or lifestyle. Some online communities do not get indexed by search engines; therefore, the presence of a target's participation will not always be found through Google or Bing. Any time that a target's interests or hobbies are located through the previous search techniques, you should also seek the online communities that cater to that topic. This can often identify information that is very personal and private to the target. Many people post to these communities without any regard to privacy. Some communities require registration to see the content, which is usually free. Occasionally, a cached version of the pages on the site is available without registering. This chapter will provide methods of infiltrating these communities to maximize the intelligence obtained.

While we see high usage on the most popular social network sites, such as TikTok and Instagram, we may not see much incriminating evidence. Instead of finding your suspect confessing to your investigation on Facebook or Twitter, you may be more likely to find his grandmother testifying to his innocence. Your suspect may feel exposed on the bigger sites, but a bit more private on smaller communities.

For OSINT purposes, I believe social networks are defined as generic areas which cater to a wide audience with various interests. We see much more general engagement between members within these platforms. People from all walks of life are on Facebook, regardless of their profession or age.

On the contrary, I believe online communities cater to a niche audience and are likely ignored by the masses which do not have a similar interest. I place LinkedIn, Snapchat, and dating services in this category. Most people on Tinder are single, and Snapchat primarily consists of a young audience. These are specialty sites with which my mother is unfamiliar (I hope).

It is impossible to mention even a fraction of potential communities which may contain online evidence about your target. Instead, I focus on those which have large numbers of members and are common to most internet users. My goal is to present various investigation tactics within each popular community which can be carried over to networks which are not discussed.

As an example, the Google "site" queries which will be used to identify LinkedIn content can also be used for hundreds of other networks. Please watch for techniques instead of specific resources or links. I promise that the following methods will need to be adjusted over time, but the overall strategies should prove to be useful when we see changes in the search infrastructure from the networks. Let's start with the most popular options and work our way down to the niche sites.

LinkedIn (linkedin.com)

When it comes to business-related social networking sites, LinkedIn is the most popular. It is owned by Microsoft and currently has more than 675 million subscribers internationally. The site requires searchers to create a free profile before accessing any data. As with any social network, I recommend creating a basic account with minimal details. The search field of any page offers a search using a real name, company, location, or title. These searches will often lead to multiple results which identify several subjects. The site was redesigned in 2020, which provides new options. The upper center portion of any search result page will offer some basic refinements to the search to filter by Jobs, Posts, Groups, People, Products, Companies, Schools, Courses, Events, and Services. These can also be queried by direct URL. The following includes a summary of each filter and the direct search URL which we will add to our custom search tools.

Jobs: (https://www.linkedin.com/jobs/index/?keywords=john%20wilson)

This presents current job openings and includes numerous additional filters. While beneficial for employment-seekers, I find this less useful than the other queries when my target is a person. However, it can be quite useful when investigating a company. Network penetration testers can use this to identify software applications used by the client, which could lead to identification of vulnerabilities.

Posts: (https://www.linkedin.com/search/results/content/?keywords=john wilson)
This option is similar to Facebook and presents posts including the provided search terms. This helps find content about (or by) our target. Further filters include search by date, author, and industry.

Groups: (https://www.linkedin.com/search/results/groups/?keywords=john wilson)
This option presents LinkedIn groups which contain your keyword within the title or description. It does not search for member names.

People: (https://www.linkedin.com/search/results/people/?keywords=john wilson)
This is the most common filter which presents profiles of people. Further filtering includes location and employer. This URL would find people named John Wilson.

Products: (https://www.linkedin.com/search/results/Products/?keywords=osint)
This search often nets limited results, but when researching a company, it may prove useful to also query their product and service offerings on LinkedIn.

Companies: (https://www.linkedin.com/search/results/companies/?keywords=john wilson)
This query strictly identifies companies which include the searched keywords. Further filters include location, industry, and company size.

Schools: (https://www.linkedin.com/search/results/schools/?keywords=john wilson)
This queries schools with the keywords in the title.

Courses: (https://www.linkedin.com/search/results/learning/?keywords=osint)
This search returns results for courses hosted on the LinkedIn Learning platform, which is built on what was originally Lynda.com until they were acquired by LinkedIn in 2015.

Events: (https://www.linkedin.com/search/results/events/?keywords=john wilson)
This queries events with the keywords in the title.

Services: (https://www.linkedin.com/search/results/services/?keywords=osint)
The results from a services query will list service pages which is primarily made up of contractors.

Knowing the real name of your target will be most beneficial. The results page should include the target's employer, location, industry, and possibly a photo. After identifying the appropriate target, clicking the name will open that user's profile if the user has not restricted access in the visibility settings of their account. If searching a common name, the filters will help limit options.

Profiles

The profiles on LinkedIn often contain an abundance of information. Since this network is used primarily for business networking, an accelerated level of trust is usually present. Many of the people on this network use it to make business connections. Some of the profiles will contain full contact information including cellular telephone numbers. This site should be one of the first stops when conducting a background check on a target for employment purposes. The target profile often contains previous employment information, alumni details, and work associates. Aside from searching names and businesses, you can search any keywords that may appear within someone's profile. Since many people include their phone numbers or email addresses in their profile, this can be an easy way to identify the user of that specific data. Visiting this profile identifies further information as well as confirmation of the target number. You can also search LinkedIn for a specific username, which may be directly associated with a profile. As an example, the following URL connects directly to a target.

https://www.linkedin.com/in/ambermac/

Posts

In years prior, LinkedIn was a place to create a profile and communicate directly with another person. Today, it is a true social network with Posts, Likes, and Comments. Conducting a keyword search through any LinkedIn page or my own custom tool will present anything applicable. From there, consider the following.

- Clicking the three dots within a post allows you to copy a static URL of the content, which is beneficial during documentation.
- Expanding all comments before generating a screen capture presents additional evidence within your documentation.
- Many posts are redacted to save space. Click "...see more" to enable this hidden content before generating a screen capture.
- Clicking the number next to the "clapping hands" icon presents a list of people interested in the post, which looks almost identical to the Instagram options.
- The Instagram media capture techniques previously presented work the same for LinkedIn. Use the Network tab in your browsers developer tools to filter for images or filter for "mp4" to isolate direct links to video files.

Timestamps

Much like other social networks, LinkedIn hides the dates and times behind generic announcements such as "posted 2 weeks ago". As online investigators, we need something more specific. Let's conduct a detailed example, which can be replicated across all of LinkedIn. Consider the post in Figure 22.01. The date of posting is "1w" in the upper-right corner, insinuating the post was published one week prior to today's date. In that image, I have already clicked the three dots in the upper-right which presented a new menu. I clicked "Copy link to comment", which was the following.

https://www.linkedin.com/feed/update/urn:li:activity:6996561887907692544?commentUrn=urn%3Ali%3Acomment%3A%28activity%3A6996561887907692544%2C6996572489061474307%29

Loading that URL in the browser presented the same comment, but it was technically a unique page from the original post which generated this response. Next, I right-clicked on the page and selected the option to "View Page Source", much like we did previously with Instagram. I searched through this code for the message, which is "Congratulations!" in this scenario. I then saw the following text, and I have bolded the important areas.

Congratulations!","$type":"com.linkedin.voyager.common.TextViewModel"}, "createdTime":**1668112871423**

The numbers represent Unix time, the same as with Instagram. We can visit the Epoch Converter site at epochconverter.com again to convert this number to GMT time, which happens to be Thursday, November 10, 2022 at 20:41:11. We now have a specific date and time of the post.

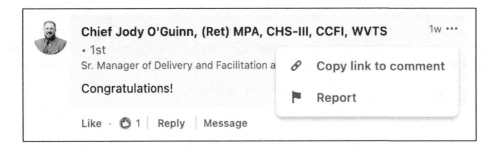

Figure 22.01: A generic timestamp on a LinkedIn post.

I believe this is the most reliable way to investigate this, but we have one additional option which does not require viewing any source code. Let's revisit the URL above, but break down the pieces. The first numbers (6996561887907692544) represented the original poster's activity number for the post. The second numbers (6996561887907692544) repeated this activity number again, but the third numbers (6996572489061474307) presented a unique activity number for the "Congratulations" response, which is our target. We can now create two unique addresses. The first URL below would present the original post. The second URL would present an error, but contains the timestamp of the "Congratulations!" response in the source code.

https://www.linkedin.com/feed/update/urn:li:activity:6996561887907692544
https://www.linkedin.com/feed/update/urn:li:activity:6996572489061474307

You could paste both of these URLs, or any other LinkedIn URL, into my LinkedIn timestamp tool, which is explained in a moment, to immediately see the timestamp of each post. My tool relies on JavaScript originally created at github.com/Ollie-Boyd. Figure 22.02 displays the result from this demonstration.

Figure 22.02: Timestamp results using https://inteltechniques.com/tools/Linkedin.html

Searching by Personal Details

You might get lucky and find your target with a simple name search. Unfortunately, this is rarely the case. With hundreds of millions of profiles, LinkedIn must make some assumptions when choosing the profiles to display after a search. This is especially true with common names. Let's conduct several queries as part of a demonstration of LinkedIn's URL structure. Searching "John Smith" produces practically useless results at the following URL.

https://www.linkedin.com/search/results/people/?**keywords**=john%20smith

Instead of the default "keywords" parameter, let's force a change with the following URL.

https://www.linkedin.com/search/results/people/?**firstName**=john

Changing to "firstName" displays content associated with people named John. This is still fairly unhelpful and includes a lot of content which is not applicable to our target. Now, let's specify the full name of our target in the following URL.

https://www.linkedin.com/search/results/people/?**firstName**=john&**lastName**=smith

The results now only include links to profiles of people with the real name of John Smith. This is much more useful and may be all you need to identify your target. With a name such as John Smith, we need to go a few steps further. The following URL adds his employer (Microsoft).

https://www.linkedin.com/search/results/people/?**firstName**=john&**lastName**=smith &**company**=microsoft

If you wanted to go further, we could specify his title (Manager) and school (Oklahoma) in the following URL. If you know these details about your target, you could start with this, but I find that providing too many details can work against you. Figure 22.03 displays the result of this URL, which identified the only person on LinkedIn which fit the criteria.

https://www.linkedin.com/search/results/people/?**firstName**=john&**lastName**=smith &**company**=microsoft&**title**=manager&**school**=Oklahoma

The previous URL query is the most precise option we have. This has been the most beneficial structure I have found to navigate directly to my target. However, it can fail. If your suspect did not provide the school attended or current employer to his profile, you will not receive any leniency from LinkedIn within this search. However, we can rely on Google to help us. Your target may have mentioned an employer somewhere else within the profile or listed a school within the "Interests" area. The following reveals many profiles associated with the target.

site:www.linkedin.com john smith Microsoft manager Oklahoma

Searching by Company

If you are searching for employees of a specific company, searching the company name often provides numerous profiles. We can easily structure the following URL which queries for a person (John Smith) associated with a specific company (Microsoft).

https://www.linkedin.com/company/microsoft/people/?keywords=john%20smith

Unfortunately, clicking on any of these profiles presents a very limited view with the name and details redacted. The name of the employee is usually not available, but the photo and job description are usually visible. You are now required to upgrade to a premium account, or be in the same circles as the target, in order to get further information. Instead, consider the following technique. Search for the business name of your target company, or the employer of your target individual. I typed "Uber" into the search bar and received the official business page on LinkedIn. Clicking the "See all 88,788 employees on LinkedIn" link presented me with numerous employee profiles such as the one visible in Figure 22.04. Notice the name is redacted and only "LinkedIn Member" is available. Clicking this first result prompts me with "Profiles out of your network have limited visibility. To see more profiles, build your network with valuable connections". We struck out, but there are ways that you can proceed in order to unmask these details. First, copy the entire job description under the "LinkedIn Member" title. In this example, it is "Account Executive at Uber". Use this in a custom Google search similar to the following.

site:linkedin.com "Account Executive at Uber"

The results listed will vary from personal profiles to useless directories. Since Uber is such a large company, I had to view many pages of results until I identified my target. When I opened the 24th search result, the LinkedIn page loaded, and her photo confirmed it was the correct target. The easier way would have been to search the images presented by Google. After the above search is conducted, click on the Images option within Google and view the results. Figure 22.05 (left) displays a section, which easily identifies the same image as the LinkedIn target. Clicking this will load the profile page with full name and details.

Another way to accomplish this is to navigate through the profiles in the "People also viewed" column. These pages include other profiles viewed that are associated with whichever person you are currently analyzing. These people may not be friends or co-workers with your target, but there is a connection through the visitors of their pages. As an example, I returned to the Google search at the top of this page. I clicked on the first search result, which was not my target. However, in the "People also viewed" area to the right, I saw my target, including her full name and a link to her complete profile. Figure 22.05 (right) displays this result. In 2024, LinkedIn replaced "People also viewed" with "More profiles for you" which functions similarly.

Finally, the last option is to conduct a reverse image search on the photo associated with the target's profile. Full details of this type of search will be presented later. For this demonstration, I will right-click on her photo and choose "Copy image location". On the Google Images page, I can click the camera icon and submit this URL. While the first result is not the target, clicking the page does present a link to the target's unmasked page. I will later explain many detailed ways to fully query reverse image search options within the upcoming Images chapter.

Figure 22.03: A LinkedIn result via direct URL.

Figure 22.04: Redacted employee results from a business search.

Figure 22.05: Google Images results (left) and un-redacted LinkedIn results (right).

Searching by City or Country

To complete a query and filter the results by country or city, I first conduct a keyword search as usual using the LinkedIn search field. I then scroll to the type of results I am interested in, such as "People" and click on See all people results". This will bring up additional filters including "Locations", which will allow you to add a specific city or country.

PDF Profile View

You may want a quick way to collect the publicly available details from the profiles that you find. One option is to have LinkedIn generate a PDF of the information. While on any profile, click the "More..." button and choose "Save to PDF". This will not extract any private details, but will make data collection fast.

Google Search

When all else fails, go to Google. It scrapes and indexes most of LinkedIn's profiles and pages. The following search would identify profiles of our target, followed by the direct URL.

site:www.linkedin.com john smith microsoft
https://www.google.com/search?q=site%3Awww.linkedin.com+john+smith+microsoft

Google Images

The results may be overwhelming. Often, I know the face of my target and I simply want to browse images from LinkedIn. The following URL queries Google for any images (&tbm=isch) associated with my target's name (john+smith) on LinkedIn (site:linkedin.com). In a moment, we will replicate all of this with my tools.

https://www.google.com/search?q=site:linkedin.com+john+smith&tbm=isch

Google Videos

Many LinkedIn posts contain embedded videos. While a keyword search directly on LinkedIn may not find them, a query on Google should. The following URL replicates our image search, but focuses only on videos (&tbm=vid)

https://www.google.com/search?q=site:linkedin.com+john+smith&tbm=vid

Bing Search

While Google is typically our most powerful search engine, I prefer Bing for LinkedIn queries. Microsoft owns both Bing and LinkedIn, and indexes LinkedIn data well. The following search on Bing replicates our Google attempt, followed by the direct URL.

site:linkedin.com john smith microsoft
https://www.bing.com/search?q=site%3Alinkedin.com+john+smith+microsoft

Yandex Search

Finally, we should always consider Yandex as a LinkedIn search engine. The following search on Yandex replicates our Google attempt, followed by the direct URL.

site:linkedin.com john smith microsoft
https://www.yandex.com/search/?text=site%3Alinkedin.com+john+smith+microsoft

IntelTechniques LinkedIn Tool

These search techniques may seem complicated, but we can simplify them with our custom search tool. The "LinkedIn" section of the offline tool, which you previously downloaded, possesses several advanced search features. Most techniques mentioned in this section are available as automated queries within this tool. The online version is available at **https://inteltechniques.com/tools/Linkedin.html**.

Snapchat (snapchat.com)

Overall, Snapchat is a difficult OSINT resource. It is available officially as a mobile application, and there is minimal native web search. The majority of the content is set to auto-destruct after a specific amount of time, and is privately delivered from one user to another. In 2018, we started to see much more public content, and in 2020, we saw better search options. In 2024, we witnessed many of our favorite search techniques disappear. Today, Snapchat is locked down more than ever before. While there are some extended search options within the app itself, I will only focus on traditional web resources here. Let's start with official options within the Snapchat website. However, you will always receive better results within the Snapchat mobile application.

Keyword Search: (https://www.snapchat.com/explore/osint) This queries the search term throughout Snapchat. I find it to fails often, but should be attempted.

User Search: (https://www.snapchat.com/add/inteltechniques) This option may forward to the "Story" page, which can also serve as the landing page for that profile. The privacy settings on the target account may limit our results.

Google/Bing/Yandex

You should expect by now that we can use traditional search engines to query specific sites and services. A query of site:snapchat.com "inteltechniques" would search for any mention of "inteltechniques" within Snapchat across the three major search engines. I include Snapchat query options within the Username Tool, which is explained later.

Google Networks

Every Google account has been issued a specific numeric ID which associates the account with any Google service used. This includes Gmail addresses, YouTube accounts, photo albums, and other areas. My goal is always to identify the Google ID and then research any areas which may be associated with my target. First, we must find the ID itself. There are several ways, let's start with the manual option.

- Log in to any covert Google account and navigate to mail.google.com/chat.
- Right-click on the page and select "Inspect".
- Click "Find a Chat" and enter your target's email address.
- Strike enter but do not send any communication.
- In the "SearchHTML" field, enter the email address of your target.

Striking enter or return on your keyboard should cycle through the results. One of the results should contain data such as "data-member-id="user/human/100202552162672367520". The numbers after "human/" is the Google User ID of your target. I typically document this within my report for future reference. The following URL should display any public map contributions made by this target. However, this technique seems to be less reliable every year.

https://www.google.com/maps/contrib/100202552162672367520

Let's conduct a real example using my friend Justin Seitz as the target. We know his personal email address is justin.seitz@gmail.com (he is the creator of Hunchly and provided permission to do this). This means that he has a valid Google account, so he should also have a Google ID. I used the premium Epieos tool (epieos.com) to search his email. The result appears in Figure 22.06 (left). This identifies his Google ID as "100202552162672367520". Clicking "Reviews" presents the content in Figure 22.06 (right).

Figure 22.06: Google ID number (left) associated with a map review (right).

We now know his interests and potential area of residence. We can also use this technique to confirm association from our target to malicious negative reviews. My success rate of viewing public photo albums with this method is low, but the availability of mapping data has been high. This will immediately display reviews of businesses and photos of locations which have been shared by your target with the Google Maps service.

Tumblr (tumblr.com)

Tumblr was purchased by Yahoo in 2013, Verizon became the owner when it acquired Yahoo in 2017, but then sold Tumblr to WordPress owner Automatic in 2019. While I believe neither Yahoo or Verizon took advantage of the reach of this network, I suspect we will see Tumblr continue to thrive over the years under control of Automatic. Tumblr is half social network and half blog service. At the time of this writing, there were hundreds of millions of blogs and hundreds of billions of posts. These posts can include text, photos, videos, and links to other networks. The search method and layout are no longer user-friendly. The search feature will only identify blogs that were specifically tagged by the creator with the provided search terms. I suggest using a custom Google search. As an example, I conducted a search of "osint" within the official Tumblr search and received three results. I then conducted the following search in Google and received the appropriate 611 results.

site:tumblr.com "osint"

Once you find a blog associated with your target, consider the Photo Gallery Tool explained in Chapter Four. It will retrieve all of the images and videos. Opening each post within a browser allows you to see and capture all "likes" and "reblogs". Similar to other networks such as Instagram, people can "tag" items with specific terms. The following URL presents any posts tagged "osint". At the time of this writing, the tag URL presented many more items than a keyword search on Tumblr.

https://www.tumblr.com/tagged/osint

Usernames cannot be queried, but a direct URL may locate the content. If your target uses "inteltechniques" on other sites, you may find applicable content at the following URL.

https://inteltechniques.tumblr.com

Most profiles contain a search field dedicated to the author's posts. It can also be queried with a direct URL. If you wanted to search for any posts by "inteltechniques" which contain the term "osint", the following URL would apply.

https://inteltechniques.tumblr.com/search/osint

Many Tumblr blogs display a large layout which hides many of the posts. Therefore, I always prefer to browse a user's posts with the "Archive" display.

https://inteltechniques.tumblr.com/archive

I have incorporated some of these queries into the Username Tool, which is explained in a later chapter. While accessing the Tumblr site you may receive popups requiring you to login to an account. You can remove these popups by blocking them with uBlock Origin using blocking rules or the zapper tool (the lightning icon in uBlock Origin).

Telegram (telegram.org)

Much of the content on Telegram is encrypted private communications between individuals. However, "Channels" were added in 2015 and have become quite popular. These are publicly visible and often include content replicated from other social networks and websites. There is no official search option on telegram.org, but options exist based on the public data. I have found site searches on Google to be the most helpful. The following examples may help explain. I searched "osint" within different official Telegram domains and received very unique results from each.

site:telegram.me "osint" (2620 results)
site:t.me "osint" (22 results)
site:telegra.ph "osint" (255 results)

Although the results tend to be limited, I sometimes have luck structuring a query to search specifically for groups.

site:t.me/joinchat "osint"

We can also use URL manipulation to manually query usernames, although the level of detail included in the results will vary based on the target account's profile settings.

https://t.me/inteltechniques

Limited results will likely open within browser windows if you do not have Telegram installed, and may launch the Telegram desktop application if it is available. **Note that I will dive much deeper into Telegram usage within the data breaches chapter.**

Telegram Analytics (tgstat.ru - telemetr.io)

I believe these are the most robust Telegram Channel search options currently available. A keyword search presents channels which are associated with the terms and immediately displays analytics including subscribers, growth, and post reach. Clicking on the channel name presents further details about post behaviors and history. Some search features on these sites require that we create a free account using a burner email address such as SimpleLogin (app.simplelogin.io).

Access to Private Profiles

There have been several "hacks" in the past that would allow a type of "back door entry" into a profile that is marked as private. By the time these methods become known, the vulnerability is usually corrected by the social network host. Websites or applications that publicly claim to be able to access this secured data are most often scams or attempts to steal your own passwords. In my experience, it is best to avoid these traps and focus on finding all available public information. At the time of this writing, an application had recently surfaced that claimed to be able to obtain all information from within private Facebook accounts. The program did not work, but installed a malicious virus instead. If it seems too good to be true, it probably is.

Contact Exploitation

Previously, I explained how to add cell phone numbers and email addresses as contacts to an Android virtual machine in order to supply them to various apps. When programs received the numbers directly from the contacts list, it believed the contacts were "friends"; therefore, they often identify the names and accounts associated with each number or email. I refer to this technique as contact exploitation, and the Android technique is not the only option for this type of activity. This technique works throughout several social networking environments. I keep covert Gmail accounts solely for adding my target's contact information and asking networks to find friends based on this data. I am often presented with profiles in my target's true name as well as alias accounts.

We now know that locating someone's social network profile can reveal quite a lot about them. Just knowing a target name can make use of the people search engines that will identify places to seek more information. Unfortunately, sometimes the investigator does not know the target's name. A common scenario is an investigation into some type of event. This could be a specific violent crime, a bomb threat on a campus, or inappropriate chatter about a particular business. All of these scenarios require search engines that monitor social network traffic. There is an abundance of these types of services. Some will work better on reactive investigations after an incident while others show their strength during proactive investigations while monitoring conversations. Many of the sites mentioned here will find the same results as each other.

Overall, some of the strongest methods of searching social network traffic have already been discussed in the Facebook and Twitter chapters. Searching for traffic at the source, such as on x.com, will usually provide more accurate and updated content than on an aggregated website of multiple sources. Furthermore, searching specific services through Google or Bing may sometimes quickly locate results that would be difficult to obtain anywhere else. The use of the site operator previously explained will take you far. Aside from direct searches on social networks and targeted search engine queries, there are other options. The accuracy of the services mentioned in the rest of this chapter varies monthly. Hopefully, you will find some of these websites to have value in your investigations. I believe that the options in this chapter should be used to supplement, not replace, the results obtained from previous methods.

Social Searcher (social-searcher.com)

I had previously discouraged users from attempting searches on the first version of Social Searcher. Since then, I have begun to rely on their free service to digest data located on the main social networks. You can provide any keywords, usernames, or terms and receive the most recent results from Facebook, Twitter, Instagram, and the overall web. It allows email alerts to be created for notification of new content matching your query. One of the unique features of this website is the free ability to export search results into CSV format. This output contains the username, date & time, and entire message among other information. Having this in a spreadsheet format can be incredibly beneficial. This document also included dozens of Reddit and other network posts. The document could be imported into any other collection system.

International Social Networks

While this book is heavily focused on social networks popular in the United States, they tend to be fairly global with an international presence. This is especially true for Facebook and Twitter. However, there are many social networks which are not popular within the United States that are the primary networks to local residents abroad. This section attempts to identify and explain the most popular foreign networks that may be used by your international targets.

Russia: VK (vk.com)

VK is basically a Russian version of Facebook. You can create a new free account or log in using your existing Facebook credentials. Most search options function without logging in to an account. The page at vk.com/people offers advanced search options which allow filtering by location, school, age, gender, and interests. Most profiles publicly display a user's birthday, location, and full photo collection.

Russia: Odnoklassniki (ok.ru)

Odnoklassniki works similar to most other social media platforms. It is intended to be a way to communicate with friends, as well as an opportunity to network with other people with similar interests. The service is concentrated on classmates and old friends, and translates to "Classmates" in Russian. The official search page is located at ok.ru/search, but you will need to create an account to take full advantage of the options. I have found a targeted site search on Google to be most effective. Searching for Michael Smith could be conducted with "site:ok.ru michael smith". The links connect directly to profiles, which can be browsed as normal. These will appear very similar to Facebook profiles. The upper-right portion of a profile will announce the date of the user's last login. Most of the profile details are public, and do not require any type of URL trickery in order to expose the details.

China: Qzone (qq.com)

Qzone is typically used as a blogging and diary platform. Most of the loyalty to the platform is due to the popularity of the instant messaging tool "QQ". This is a one-to-one messaging platform, so opportunities for public search are not present. The search options on qq.com pages provide results similar to Chinese search engines such as Baidu. The searches are not restricted to the social network profiles. I have found searching on Google or Baidu to work best for English queries. The format of "site:user.qzone.qq.com michael smith" should begin your query, although results will be sparse. We can use the password recovery page located at https://accounts.qq.com/psw/find to query email addresses, although anytime we use this method assume that the platform will notify the account holder that a password recovery was attempted.

Newer Social Networks

These social networks represent only a portion of the available options. Overall, resort to custom Google searches when new services appear. As I write this, I am monitoring newer sites such as **Parler** (parler.com), **Gab** (gab.com), **Gettr** (gettr.com), and **Mastodon** (mastodon.social), all of which claim to be the next generation of social networks. The search techniques previously presented throughout this book also apply to these new platforms. Let's briefly dissect each.

Parler was previously shutdown, but has been recently been reopened after being acquired by a new company in 2023. Conducting queries on Parler is very straightforward and we can start by using our Google site: operator.

site:parler.com "keyword"

Once you identify a target profile, such as "inteltechniques", or a topic, such as "bomb", the following should disclose details.

https://app.parler.com/inteltechniques
https://app.parler.com/search?type=user&s=inteltechniques
https://app.parler.com/search?type=hashtag&s=bomb

Clicking through options such as "Media", "Following", and comment notifications should present data similar to Twitter and Instagram. There is no real magic here, what you see is what you get.

Gab has been widely described as a haven for extremists including neo-Nazis and white supremacists, and has attracted users who have been banned from other social networks. We have the following direct query URLs assuming your target is "inteltechniques" and your keyword of interest is "osint". Note that an account is required to view most data.

https://gab.com/inteltechniques
https://gab.com/search/top?q=osint
https://gab.com/search/people?q=osint
https://gab.com/search/groups?q=osint
https://gab.com/search/statuses?q=osint
https://gab.com/search/links?q=osint
https://gab.com/search/feeds?q=osint
https://gab.com/search/businesses?q=osint
https://gab.com/search/marketplace?q=osint
https://gab.com/search/hashtags?q=osint

We can also use our site: operator on Google although results tend to be limited. If we start with site:gab.com osint, one of the top results is https://gab.com/Numbers_Stations. We can click on the three vertical docs next to that Google result to open the "About the source" panel. If we click on "More about this page" we will see an option at the bottom which reads "See previous versions on Internet Archive's Wayback Machine". Selecting that will take us to previously saved versions of the target Gab profile on Archive.org. This has proven useful for locating old posts and deleted content.

Gettr is a Twitter clone targeted toward far-right political beliefs. The structure of all accounts and feeds follows the Twitter examples previously presented. The following would apply if I were a member.

https://www.gettr.com/user/inteltechniques
https://www.gettr.com/user/inteltechniques/followers
https://www.gettr.com/user/inteltechniques/following
https://gettr.com/user/inteltechniques/recommend
https://www.gettr.com/search?q=to:inteltechniques
https://www.gettr.com/search?q=from:inteltechniques
https://www.gettr.com/user/inteltechniques/comments
https://gettr.com/user/thedahmercase/live
https://gettr.com/user/thedahmercase/gtok
https://www.gettr.com/user/inteltechniques/medias
https://www.gettr.com/user/inteltechniques/likes

Search is straightforward and we have options for using both Google and Gettr's own search feature.

site:gettr.com "osint"
https://gettr.com/search?q=osint

Mastodon received a lot of attention in late 2022. As Elon Musk began taking over Twitter, many people exited and sought alternative options. Mastodon is a very popular Twitter clone, so many people ended up there. While search engines will push you toward joinmastodon.org, that domain will not offer many search possibilities. You might find mastodon.social, but it is only one of many communities which allow connection through the Mastodon network. This is because Mastodon is a *decentralized* social network which can be self-hosted and is available on numerous servers. Services such as Twitter are *centralized*. You must connect through x.com and Twitter has the power to prevent your access. You can join and participate in Mastodon from a number of servers, each independent of any Mastodon domains. This can cause a lot of confusion. Let's start with mastodon.social, but we will rely on official APIs for our OSINT research. Assuming your target was "alexwinter" and he was present on the "mastodon.social" instance, the following would apply.

https://mastodon.social/@alexwinter
https://mastodon.social/@alexwinter/with_replies
https://mastodon.social/@alexwinter/following
https://mastodon.social/@alexwinter/followers
https://mastodon.social/@alexwinter/media

These URLs would display his profile and all messages; messages with replies; the people following him; the people he follows; and posts which contain media. This should seem very familiar after the Twitter chapter. While his username on "mastodon.social" is simply "alexwinter", his full Mastodon username, including the community where he joined, is "@alexwinter@mastodon.social". This means that someone could join Mastodon through another server with his exact username. The following are examples of multiple accounts with a username of "JohnDoe".

https://social.tchncs.de/@JohnDoe
https://social.linux.pizza/@JohnDoe
https://mastodon.top/@JohnDoe

This is why you should never rely on one site, such as mastodon.social. While it may connect you to everything on the Mastodon network, your results could be filtered without you knowing. Next, let's compare a typical graphical view of a profile with the API option. I will return to https://mastodon.social/@alexwinter. I can see the date he joined, an image, and general biographical details. Let's compare that to the following URL.

https://mastodon.social/api/v2/search?q=alexwinter&limit=40&type=accounts

This URL reveals the following text-only result.

id	"109292970397906870"
username	"alexwinter"
acct	"alexwinter@mastodon.social"
display_name	"Alex Winter"
locked	false
created_at	"2022-04-25T00:00:00.000Z"
note	"Boring, suburban dad, mostly making things at Trouper Productions."
url	"https://mastodon.social/@alexwinter"
followers_count	6229
following_count	468
statuses_count	138
last_status_at	"2022-11-12"
verified_at	null

I believe this provides more explicit details, and can be easily copied into a report. The "limit=40" is the maximum number of results which can be returned. Next, let's repeat this with a different server, specifying something different than the server which the user joined.

https://infosec.exchange/api/v2/search?q=alexwinter&limit=40&type=accounts

The results are identical since each server is relying on the overall Mastodon API for this data. We can also use the API to query hashtags. Mastodon has greatly improved cross instance search results so that we now receive almost identical results when we compare the following API queries.

https://mastodon.social/api/v2/search?q=osint&limit=40&type=hashtags
https://infosec.exchange/api/v2/search?q=osint&limit=40&type=hashtags
Similarly, the following two URLs display very similar results.

https://mastodon.social/tags/osint4good
https://infosec.exchange/tags/osint4good

These new search options are included within the Communities Tool, which is discussed later in the chapter. There is no way to predict which social networks will be the next big thing. However, possessing a sharp set of Google and OSINT skills will take you far. If desired, you could add these options to the custom search tools explained in Section One. Until I see wide-spread usage of these platforms, I will wait.

Reddit (reddit.com)

This social news aggregation, web content rating, and discussion website went from a place for those "in-the-know" to a resource often cited on mainstream media. More users than ever post, reply to, and read the user-submitted content in the form of either a link or text, each submitted to a specific category known as a Subreddit. Other users then vote the submission up or down, which is used to rank the post and determine its position on the website's pages. The submissions are then discussed on the "comments" page of every entry. The Subreddits cover practically any topic you can imagine. If your target has the slightest interest in the internet, he or she has probably been to Reddit. As of 2024, there were over 850 million registered users.

Reddit Search

The official search option on Reddit has been plagued with problems since inception. The search field in the upper right of every page will allow you to query any terms you desire, but the results have not always been optimal. In 2016, I saw the search function improve drastically, and even with some added new features. When typing terms into the search field on any Reddit page, the results will be from all pages, including thousands of Subreddits. While you should understand this option, and even execute target searches from the home page on occasion, we should consider some advanced search options. We can replicate that standard keyword search within a URL. This is beneficial for bookmarking searches of interest that need checked often. The format for a search about OSINT is as follows.

https://www.reddit.com/search?q=OSINT

The results from such a generic search can be quite overwhelming. With the following URL, we can force Reddit to only deliver results if our search term is within the title of a post, and not simply present within comments.

https://www.reddit.com/search?q=title:OSINT

If you know the name of the Subreddit, you can navigate directly with the following structure.

https://www.reddit.com/r/OSINT/

If you locate a username of interest while searching Reddit, you can load all of that user's posts and comments by clicking on the name. Alternatively, the following URL can be used.

https://www.reddit.com/user/inteltechniques

If you want to see a summary of all original posts, the following URL can be used.

https://www.reddit.com/user/inteltechniques/submitted/

If you want to see a summary of all original comments, the following URL can be used.

https://www.reddit.com/user/inteltechniques/comments/

If you have a target website, and you want to know if the URL has ever been posted as a submission link, the following URL will display all results.

https://www.reddit.com/search?q=site:inteltechniques.com

If Reddit is not providing the results you think you should be receiving, you should return to our previous instruction on Google searching. The following query would identify any posts, categories, or users that included the word "surveillance".

site:reddit.com "surveillance"

If you wanted to force Google to restrict its searching to a specific Subreddit, such as OSINT, you would add "/r/osint" after the first portion. If you wanted to restrict the searching to a specific user, you would add "/user/inteltechniques" to the end. The following are two examples.

site:reddit.com/r/osint "surveillance"
site:reddit.com/user/inteltechniques "surveillance"

Each of these queries could be replicated within both Bing and Yandex. While Google is good at indexing new content within Reddit, I have witnessed better performance from Yandex when the content was associated with pornography and other adult content.

"Old" View

Since 2018, Reddit has been changing the layout and function of their website. This also includes many additional trackers which collect information about your usage. I prefer the "old" view of Reddit, which can be achieved by replacing "www" with "old" within any Reddit link. This is personal preference, and I believe the old view provides a more compressed experience which displays more content within each page.

Deleted Content

If you have identified any Reddit content of interest, you should consider checking any online third-party archives. These historic representations of an account will often disclose previously deleted or modified content. It is extremely common for Reddit users to edit or delete a comment entirely, especially if it was controversial. I have investigated numerous Reddit accounts where the evidence I expected to find was not present. First, I always search the standard archive options which were previously explained. The following direct URLs would attempt to display historic versions of a Reddit user's profile. The first only works occasionally. You could replace the Reddit user URL within each of these with a Subreddit address or Reddit post URL.

webcache.googleusercontent.com/search?q=cache:https://www.reddit.com/user/mikeb
web.archive.org/web/*/https://www.reddit.com/user/mikeb

You may get lucky with these queries, but the results are often limited. These will display the historic view of a Reddit account at a specific moment in time. While this may provide evidence for your investigation, you should also identify any further deleted content. In order to dig much deeper, we must understand Pushshift (pushshift.io) and PullPush (pullpush.io).

Pushshift was an active archive which contained most of the content which was publicly posted to Reddit from 2005 through 2023. This provided an amazing collection of data, including most deleted posts. Any time your target wiped out various Reddit posts before you could collect the evidence, Pushshift revealed the deleted content. This site allowed you to take advantage of their robust application programming interface (API). In 2023, Reddit drastically changed their own API which eliminated Pushshift's ability to access any new content.

The sites are still up, but the functionality has been shuttered. A new project called PullPush acquired the data and returned the search functionality.

First, let's assume that you are only interested in a specific user that has deleted all content. Figure 22.07 displays a partial post which I created on Friday, July 19, 2019. On September 1, 2019, I deleted all of my posts from Reddit, including that initial content. Figure 22.08 displays the confirmation my account was empty. As I wrote this in 2024, the following URL queried the data set for posts that have been archived by PullPush for user inteltechniques.

https://api.pullpush.io/reddit/search/comment/?author=inteltechniques

This URL presented a lot of information about my deleted posts, but I was most interested in the data visible in Figure 22.09. It displayed the entire deleted comment and the subreddit location. Furthermore, it provided a Unix time of 1563580052, which converts to Friday, July 19, 2019 5:47:32 PM GMT.

IntelTechniques commented on Hi guys any reading material to get into osint so I can teach my self.

IntelTechniques 6 points · 1 month ago
I estimate 10% of the book is outdated/inaccurate. Mostly the Facebook section

Reply Share ···

Figure 22.07: A Reddit post prior to deletion.

hmm... u/IntelTechniques hasn't posted anything

Figure 22.08: A Reddit post after deletion.

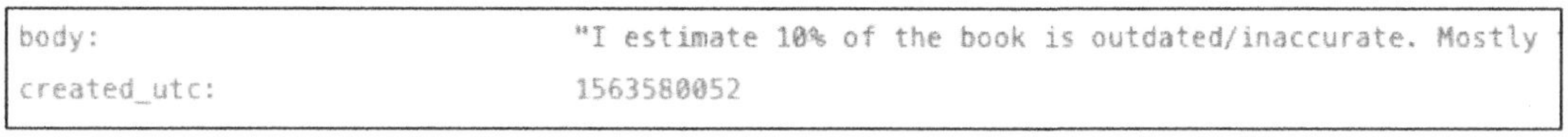

```
body:                    "I estimate 10% of the book is outdated/inaccurate. Mostly
created_utc:             1563580052
```

Figure 22.09: A PullPush result of a deleted post.

This URL will display up to 99 of the most recent posts, regardless of whether they are still on Reddit or have been removed. This is a great start, but our target may have thousands of posts. The following URL adds two options at the end to force sorting in ascending format and force display of 100 comments within a single page.

https://api.pullpush.io/reddit/search/comment/?author=inteltechniques&sort=asc&size=100

Likewise, we can force a descending view with the following URL.

https://api.pullpush.io/reddit/search/comment/?author=inteltechniques&sort=desc&size=100

If you are seeking a specific post with unique wording, you can accomplish this with the following URLs. The first example would identify public and deleted posts mentioning my username in ascending order while the second is in descending order.

https://api.pullpush.io/reddit/search/comment/?q=inteltechniques&sort=asc&size=100
https://api.pullpush.io/reddit/search/comment/?q=inteltechniques&sort=desc&size=100

Each of these searches may present too much content and may not be easy to digest. We can filter unwanted content in order to produce less results. The following would repeat our previous queries, but only display content from the Subreddit Privacy.

https://api.pullpush.io/reddit/search/comment/?q=inteltechniques&subreddit=privacy&sort=asc&size=100
https://api.pullpush.io/reddit/search/comment/?q=inteltechniques&subreddit=privacy&sort=desc&size=100

In order to demonstrate the value of this, consider the following random example. On November 8, 2020, a Twitter user posted the Tweet seen in Figure 22.10. Reddit user Defaultyboi6829 posted on Twitter "Good thing I deleted my Reddit account". Today, in 2024, we can confirm this account was deleted by viewing https://old.reddit.com/user/Defaultyboi6829. I navigated to the following URLs, which each displayed 100 deleted posts in ascending and descending order from this user. His latest post was a disagreement about Minecraft with another user as seen in Figure 22.11. Evidence of this interaction is not present anywhere on the live view of Reddit.

https://api.pullpush.io/reddit/search/comment/?author=Defaultyboi6829&sort=asc&size=100
https://api.pullpush.io/reddit/search/comment/?author=Defaultyboi6829&sort=desc&size=100

Good thing I deleted my Reddit account

11:34 AM · Nov 8, 2020 · Twitter for iPhone

Figure 22.10: A Twitter post announcing deletion of a Reddit account.

```
author:                            "Defaultyboi6829"
author_created_utc:                1551167898
author_flair_background_color:     null
author_flair_css_class:            null
author_flair_richtext:             []
author_flair_template_id:          null
author_flair_text:                 null
author_flair_text_color:           null
author_flair_type:                 "text"
author_fullname:                   "t2_3aw21crz"
author_patreon_flair:              false
body:                              "The first comment I was like ok and the second comment I was like WHAT ITS AN ENDERMAN"
```

Figure 22.11: A deleted Reddit post.

Note that all of these searches only identify results which are comments and not user submissions. A submission is a new topic, and a comment is a post within a specific submission. In order to replicate all of these queries for user submissions, simply replace "comment" in each example to "submission". The following URLs only displays my deleted submissions.

https://api.pullpush.io/reddit/search/submission/?author=inteltechniques&sort=asc&size=100
https://api.pullpush.io/reddit/search/submission/?author=inteltechniques&sort=desc&size=100

In a moment, I will demonstrate my offline search tools which you can use to simplify this entire process. The ability to extract deleted content from a community as large as Reddit is a substantial OSINT technique. I encourage you to monitor Reddit for new features and changes in order to update your own tools as needed.

I am sure many readers are wondering what will happen if PullPush goes away in the same way PullPush disappeared. If desired, you could download this entire archive of Reddit consisting of every live and deleted post from June of 2005 through December of 2023 from the following locations.

https://academictorrents.com/details/9c263fc85366c1ef8f5bb9da0203f4c8c8db75f4

I will warn you that this consists of 2.52 Terabytes of data (compressed), and accessing the content quickly exceeds the scope of this section. However, you may want to dive in after reading the upcoming section about data breaches and accessing large amounts of data.

Images

Reddit is well-known for hosting entertaining images and memes. The majority of linked images on Reddit are now self-hosted, but I still see a lot of images hosted on a photo-sharing site called **Imgur** (imgur.com). This can be very beneficial when you are investigating an image post that has been removed from Reddit. If a user posted a photo to Imgur, then linked it to a Reddit post, and then deleted the post, the image is still online. You will no longer have a link to the image, and randomly searching Imgur will be unproductive. Instead, we can browse all of the Reddit images on Imgur with a direct URL. The following address will display the current images, in reverse chronological order, associated with the Subreddit titled NetSec. Scrolling will continuously load older images.

https://imgur.com/r/netsec

If you find an image of interest, you should consider searching the name of the image within PullPush. Let's run through an example. Assume that you suspected your target was posting images of his antique vehicle on the Subreddit /r/projectcar, but he deleted the posts before you could find them. You should first navigate to the following page of related images on Imgur.

https://imgur.com/r/projectcar

Assume you then located a potential suspected vehicle image at the following address.

https://imgur.com/J0C7Mi9

You should right-click on the image and select "View Image" to open view the full-size version in a new tab.

https://i.imgur.com/J0C7Mi9.jpg

The filename of the image is J0C7Mi9. The following two URLs search this image within both submissions and comments within all of Reddit, including deleted posts.

https://api.pullpush.io/reddit/search/submission/?q=J0C7Mi9
https://api.pullpush.io/reddit/search/comment/?q=J0C7Mi9

The second URL provides the following data within the result. Note that I had to refresh the query a few times to obtain the data. This is a scenario where possessing all of the content from the previous download links could work in your favor. You could query through all data without relying on PullPush's search term queries.

Author: mrmoto1998
body: [Obligatory pic of the moldsmobile](https://imgur.com/J0C7Mi9.jpg)
created_utc: 1568129504
link: /r/projectcar/comments/d296fl/tore_up_some_carpet_in_the_moldsmobile/eztg3jk/

You now know the author, date, and original link of the post on Reddit. The previous example may be an extreme case scenario, but the possibilities are endless. The important message is to search any keyword data through PullPush when your investigation is associated with Reddit. Next, you should consider a reverse image search. This will be explained in detail later, but you should know now that you have a Reddit-specific reverse image search option called Karma Decay. Assume that you located an image on Imgur at the following URL.

https://imgur.com/r/funny/0DnE1aB

You can navigate to karmadecay.com, supply this address, and immediately see if that image has been posted to any other locations within Reddit. If you wanted to bookmark a direct URL for future checking, you could use the following to obtain the same result.

http://karmadecay.com/imgur.com/r/funny/0DnE1aB

Investigation Subreddits

There are many Subreddits that can provide a unique benefit to an investigator, three of which are outlined here. There are several versions of each of these, but those that I present here have the most history of being helpful. You will find additional options with a bit of searching.

Reddit Bureau of Investigation (reddit.com/r/rbi)

This active community helps other Reddit users solve crimes and other problems. Internet gurus will help find deadbeat parents; computer specialists will aid in tracking stolen devices; and private investigators will assist with investigation techniques. I have used this option several times during my career. The most successful cases involved hit and run traffic crashes. In 2013, I assisted a northern Illinois police department with the investigation of a fatal car crash. The offender fled the area and an elderly woman died. Three small pieces of the offending vehicle were left at the scene. After posting this information to local media outlets, I submitted it to RBI. Within minutes, several vehicle body shop employees were tracking down the parts and eventually tied them to a specific year and model of a 10-year-old vehicle. This information led to the arrest of the subject. Another victim of an unrelated hit and run traffic crash posted a blurry photo of the suspect vehicle and asked for assistance. Within hours, a Reddit user identified the license plate through digital correction techniques.

Pic Requests (reddit.com/r/picrequests)

A constant frustration in my work is blurry, out of focus, or grainy digital images. Commonly, I will receive surveillance photos that are too dark or light to identify anything of value in the image. Occasionally, I will find images on social networks that could be beneficial if they were just a touch clearer. Pic Requests saves the day. This Subreddit consists of digital photo experts that can perform Photoshop magic on practically any image. Many Reddit users will request old photos colorized, torn photos digitally repaired, or unwanted subjects removed from an image. I have uploaded several surveillance images to this group with a request for assistance. The users have been incredibly helpful by identifying digits in blurred license plates and turning dark surveillance footage into useful evidence.

What Is This Thing? (reddit.com/r/whatisthisthing)

I am consistently amazed at the results from this Subreddit. What Is This Thing is a place where you can post a digital photo of practically anything, and someone will know exactly what it is while providing detailed and cited additional information. Many users post images of old antiques and intricate items hoping to identify something valuable in their collection. I use it to identify tattoo meanings, graffiti, suspicious items mailed to politicians, vehicle parts, and just about anything else that is presented to me during my investigations.

Real World Application: In 2012, I was asked to assist with a death investigation of a "Jane Doe". I submitted a sanitized version of a tattoo on her back that appeared to be Chinese symbols. Within five minutes, a Reddit user identified the symbols, their meaning, and references to the region of China that would probably be related to my investigation. A reverse image search of his examples led to information about a human trafficking ring with which the victim was associated. This all occurred over a period of one hour.

If you plan to use these techniques on Reddit, please consider a few things. You should create a free account now and hold on to it. Creating a new account and asking for help minutes later can be viewed as rude. I like to use accounts that appear to have been established a long time ago. If you are visible as an active member of Reddit with a history of comments, this might encourage other active members to assist you. You should never be demanding in your requests. Remember, these people are volunteering to help you. Many of them possess a skill set that cannot be found elsewhere. I also never upload any content that is not already publicly available. If digital images were released to the press, I have no problem releasing them to Reddit. If my target image is already on a public social network, I see no reason it cannot be linked through Reddit.

While Reddit seems to get most of the attention in this type of community, there are alternative options that are rapidly growing. These include 4chan, Hacker News, and others. I will briefly discuss the most common search options, which can be replicated with my Custom Communities Tool that is explained later.

4chan (4chan.org)

4chan is a mess. It is an image-board website and users generally post anonymously, with the most recent posts appearing above the rest. 4chan is split into various boards with their own specific content and guidelines, modeled from Japanese image-boards. The site has been linked to internet subcultures and activism groups, most notably Anonymous. The site's "Random" board, also known as "/b/", was the first board to be created, and is the one that receives the most traffic. This site is full of bullying, pornography, threats, and general illicit behavior. It has also been the focus of numerous investigations. There is no search feature. In this scenario, we will use 4chansearch.com. The following examples are direct URLs that take advantage of this third-party search option, each using "OSINT" as a search term.

Active Search: http://4chansearch.com/?q=OSINT&s=4
Archives Search: http://4chansearch.com/?q=OSINT&s=7
Archives Alternative: https://archive.4plebs.org/_/search/text/OSINT/order/asc/
Google Search: https://www.google.com/search?q=site:4chan.org%20OSINT

Hacker News (news.ycombinator.com)

While this site is targeted toward a tech-savvy community, general discussion topics are followed by millions of users daily. Fortunately, we have a lot of control with searching specific posts, keywords, users, and favorites. The following searches locate data based on a keyword (OSINT) and user (inteltechniques).

Text Search: https://hn.algolia.com/?query=OSINT&type=all
Username Search: https://news.ycombinator.com/user?id=inteltechniques
User Posts: https://news.ycombinator.com/submitted?id=inteltechniques
User Comments: https://news.ycombinator.com/threads?id=inteltechniques
User Favorites: https://news.ycombinator.com/favorites?id=inteltechniques
Google Search: https://www.google.com/search?q=site:news.ycombinator.com+OSINT

Nextdoor (nextdoor.com)

This popular online community allows for people within a specific neighborhood or geographical area to communicate privately within a controlled space. People within a neighborhood in Texas cannot see posts from a neighborhood in Illinois. In order to join a specific neighborhood, one must either receive an invite from another neighbor or request a physical invite be sent via postal mail to an address within range. This presents problems for OSINT. If you are investigating posts within your county, there are a few things you can do to extend your range.

While logged in to a Nextdoor account, navigate to "Settings" then "Neighborhoods". By default, you can only see activity within your specific neighborhood. However, clicking the "Explore Neighborhoods" button should present surrounding areas which you can join. In my experience, you can usually see the majority of your county by joining all available groups. Law Enforcement and other public sector teams have an additional option of creating an overt "public agencies" account (https://nextdoor.com/agency/apply) for use in monitoring their jurisdiction.

Meetup (meetup.com)

Meetup consists of users and groups, with all communication related to events where people actually meet in real life. Each user creates a profile that includes the person's interests, photos, and username. A group is created by one or more users and is focused on a general interest in a specific location. An example would be the "Houston Dog Park Lovers", which is a Houston-based group of dog owners that meet at dog parks. Each group will post events that the members can attend. The majority of the events posted on Meetup are visible to the public and can be attended by anyone. Some groups choose to mark the details of the event as private and you must be a member to see the location. Membership is free and personal information is not required.

You can search Meetup by interest or location on practically any page. Once you locate a group page, you can browse the members of the group. This group page will also identify any future and past events sponsored by the group. These past events will identify the users that attended the event as well as feedback about the event. This site no longer offers the option to search by username. In order to do this, you will need to use a search engine as described in a moment. A user profile will often include links to social networks and messages from associates on the website. Additionally, these profiles will identify any future Meetup events that the user plans on attending. Because of this, the site has been used in the past by civil process servers, detectives, and the news media to locate people that had been avoiding them. The following Google search structures have been most helpful in my experience, although access to certain results may require the use of a burner Meetup account.

Name Search (Michael Smith): site:meetup.com "michael smith"
Event Search (Protest): site:meetup.com inurl:events Protest
Event Search (Chicago): https://www.meetup.com/find/?location=us--il--Chicago&source=EVENTS
Event Search (Chicago & Protest): https://www.meetup.com/find/?keywords=protest&location=us--il--chicago&source=EVENTS
Post Search (Protest): site:meetup.com inurl:discussions Protest
Google Keyword Search (OSINT): site:meetup.com OSINT

Dating Websites

When investigating cheating spouses, background information, personal character, or applicant details, dating sites can lead to interesting evidence. The presence of a dating profile does not mean anything by itself. Millions of people successfully use these services to find mates. When a target's profile is located, it will usually lead to personal information that cannot be found anywhere else. While many people may restrict personal details on social networks such as Facebook, they tend to let down their guard on these intimate dating websites. In my experience, the following will apply to practically every dating website.

- You must have an account to browse profiles, which is usually free.
- You must have a premium (paid) account to contact anyone.
- If a target uses one dating service, he or she likely uses others.

Instead of explaining each of the dating services, I will focus on methodology of searching all of them. While each website is unique and possesses a specific way of searching, they are all very similar. Overall, there are three standard search techniques that I have found useful, and they are each identified below.

Username: Every dating website requires a username to be associated with the profile, and this data is searchable. Surprisingly, most users choose a username that has been used somewhere else. I have seen many dating profiles that hide a person's real name and location, but possess the same username as a Twitter account. The Twitter account then identifies name, location, and friends. Additional username tools are presented later.

Text Search: This is a technique that is often overlooked. Most dating network profiles include an area where the users can describe themselves in their own words. This freeform area often includes misspellings and obvious grammatical errors. These can be searched to identify additional dating networks since many users simply copy and paste their biography from one site to another. In 2013, I was teaching an OSINT course in Canada. During a break, one of the attendees asked for assistance with a sexual assault case that involved the dating website Plenty Of Fish. The unknown suspect would meet women through the online service and assault them. All of the information on his profile was fake, and the photos were of poor quality and unhelpful. Together, we copied and pasted each sentence that he had written in his bio for the profile. Eventually, we found one that was very unique and grammatically worded poorly. A quoted Google search of this sentence provided only one result. It was the real profile of the suspect on Match.com, under his real name, that contained the same sentence describing himself. The high-quality photos on this legitimate page were used to verify that he was the suspect.

Photo Search: In later chapters, I explain how to conduct reverse-image searching across multiple websites. This technique can compare an image you find on a dating network with images across all social networks, identifying any matches. This will often convert an "anonymous" dating profile into a fully-identifiable social network page. This applies to any dating networks, and photos will be your best way of identifying your target.

The list of popular dating websites grows monthly. The following are the current most popular services.

Match (match.com)
Plenty of Fish (pof.com)
eHarmony (eharmony.com)
OK Cupid (okcupid.com)
Hinge (hinge.co)
Bumble (bumble.com)
Christian Mingle (christianmingle.com)
Ashley Madison (ashleymadison.com)
Adult Friend Finder (adultfriendfinder.com)
Farmers Only (farmersonly.com)
Elite Singles (elitesingles.com)
Zoosk (www.zoosk.com)
Friendfinder-X (friendfinder-x.com)
Badoo (badoo.com)

Tinder (tinder.com)

A section about online dating would not be complete without a reference to Tinder. The simplest explanation of Tinder is that it connects you with people in your immediate geographical area who are also using the service. Some call it a dating app, some refer to it as a "hook-up" app. Either way, it is probably the most popular dating service available today.

While this service was once natively available only through a mobile app, they have recently begun allowing account access via their website. However, I find this to be full of frustration. In order to access Tinder via their web interface, you must provide either Facebook account information or a mobile telephone number. I never advise connecting any third-party service to any covert Facebook account, so that option is out. Instead, you can provide a Google Voice number, which is a bit more acceptable. Supply a covert Google Voice telephone number and prepare for the issues.

First, Tinder will send you a text message with a code to verify your number. Supplying this code to Tinder passes the first hurdle. If you are using a VPN, you will immediately be sent to a series of tests to verify you are human. If you have been annoyed by Google Captcha pop-ups in the past, Tinder's options take frustration to a new level. In most scenarios, you will be asked to complete a series of 20 small tasks. In my experience, completing them perfectly results in a failure report 99% of the time. Tinder simply does not like a combination of a VOIP number and a VPN. Providing a real cellular number seems to pacify Tinder somewhat. Providing a true number and internet connection without a VPN seems to make it happy. However, you sacrifice privacy and security in order to do so. If you accept these risks, you can proceed with the web-based access to Tinder. After I explain the process, I will present my chosen solution.

In order to access Tinder from your web browser, several things must be perfectly aligned in order to prevent account blocking. Tinder gets bombarded with fraudulent accounts, and their radar for investigative use is very sensitive. The following instructions assume that you do not have an existing Tinder account.

- Connect to a public Wi-Fi location, without a VPN, near your target.
- Click the Login button at tinder.com and choose "Log In With Phone Number".
- Supply a Google Voice number.
- Confirm the text message received on Google Voice number.
- Complete registration with alias name and photo.

These instructions may seem simple, and too good to be true. They are. Tinder has begun blocking any type of GPS spoofing, even if done manually through the browser inspector. They focus much more on the networks through which you are connected. The previous edition explained ways to spoof GPS within your browser and pretend to be at another location. In my experience, these tricks simply do not work anymore. If you are able to connect through the web version of Tinder, it is unlikely to be of any use. Furthermore, your "matches" will likely be far away from your actual location. Personally, I no longer try to make this work.

Instead, I keep an old Android phone ready for any Tinder investigations. I have the Tinder app installed along with the "Fake GPS Location" app. I keep the Tinder app logged in using a covert Google Voice number. Before I open Tinder, I set my desired location through the Fake GPS Location application. Upon loading Tinder, I can control the search settings through the app. I usually choose to limit the search to a few miles away from my target's location. In my experience, this will not work on an iPhone due to GPS spoofing restrictions. Since Tinder actively blocks emulators, connecting through VirtualBox or Genymotion does not work. This will simply require a dedicated Android device.

Real World Application: I have two recent experiences with covert Tinder accounts to share. The first is a human trafficking investigation with which I was asked to assist. The investigation unit received information that a well-known pimp had recruited several children to enter his world of prostitution. He was not promoting them on websites, as he believed it was too risky. Instead, he posted profiles to Tinder while located at a run-down motel. From several states away, I spoofed my GPS on my Android device to the motel of interest. I set my search settings for females within five miles aged 18-19. I immediately observed two images of what appeared to be young girls in a shady motel room. I "swiped right" to indicate interest, and was immediately contacted by the pimp pretending to be one of the girls. We agreed on a price and he disclosed the room number. The local agency working the case began immediate surveillance while a search warrant was obtained. While waiting, they arrested two men before the "date" could begin, and also arrested the pimp after a search warrant was obtained for the room.

The other example I have presents a much different view of Tinder usage. An attorney reached out requesting assistance with a cheating spouse investigation. He was looking for evidence which confirmed the husband was involved with other women. He provided several images of the man and common locations which he was known to frequent. After many failures, I had Tinder launched with the GPS spoofed to the suspect's office. I claimed to be a woman looking for a man his age, and I was eventually presented an image of my target. I swiped right, as did he, and we began a conversation. The evidence piled up immediately.

What photo should you use? First, uploading one photo and vague information to your account looks suspicious. Providing images of other people without their consent is wrong. Using stock photography from the internet will quickly get you banned from Tinder. I rely heavily on Fiverr (fiverr.com). I search for people willing to send unique photos of themselves for a few dollars. I once paid a 21-year-old woman $30 for five "selfies" while dressed in different outfits. I received a signed consent form allowing me to upload them to Tinder with the intent of luring cheating spouses. At first, she assumed I was a pervert with a unique fetish. After my explanation, she loved the idea and was eager to assist. Another option is to use copy and crop images generated by services such as https://thispersondoesnotexist.com/. This tactic has been successful in the past but has limitations such as the inability to generate more than one photo of the same likeness.

Tinder Profiles

Tinder users can optionally create a username within the network. Instead of being limited to the identity of "John, 30, NYC", a user can claim a specific username such as John911. This generates a web profile which can be seen publicly (often unknowingly to the user). The following format would display a user with that username. Both should connect to active profiles with multiple photos of each target.

https://www.gotinder.com/@John911
https://www.gotinder.com/@TomB

If you open the source code view of these profiles, we can dig deeper. Searching "birth_date" for user TomB reveals "1996-09-26" while ""_id" displays "53d8b9d0b3158f947bccd832". We now know the date of birth and Tinder user ID of our target. If he should change his name or username, we still have a unique identifier which could be checked within a new profile. For those in law enforcement, this account ID number will also be critical should we intend to serve Tinder with any legal requests, such as subpoenas or warrants. When submitting legal requests, we should always include the account name and account number of the target profile.

Discord (discord.com)

Discord is a free voice, video, and text chat application and digital distribution platform which was originally designed for the video gaming community. Today, it is heavily used within various hacking, doxing, and other communities associated with cybercrime. Some call it a modern-day IRC replacement. Discord allows users to create virtual servers which further divide into text and voice channels. Discord stores unlimited logs of all channels within every server. Anybody who joins a Discord server has full access to all server history. Access to a Discord server is granted through invites in the form of a URL. Discord is classified as a "deep web" resource, as Discord servers are unable to be indexed by conventional search engines such as Google. I present two initial thoughts on Discord investigative techniques.

- You must receive some type of invite in order to join a server. Once you have an invite, joining is easy and covert details are accepted. You can often find generic invite links within related forums or simply by asking a member of the server. Administrators will know that you joined, but will only see the details you provided during registration. Invite links expire often so do not be surprised if some invitation links located in Google are no longer valid.
- Once you are in the server, you should have access to complete chat history since inception. In 2018, I was asked to assist the podcast Reply All with an investigation into the OG Users Discord. Members of this group stole social network accounts from random people and sold them to each other and the public. The primary avenue for communication was through a designated Discord server. The episode is titled *130-The Snapchat Thief* if you want to hear more.

Let's conduct a demonstration of finding, joining, and archiving a Discord server. First, I navigated to **Disboard** (disboard.org). This free service indexes numerous Discord servers which have open invitations. I conducted a search for the term "osint" and received one result of "Team Omega Cybersecurity and Analysis". The static Disboard link was the following.

https://disboard.org/server/join/605819996546924544

This immediately forwarded to the Discord link at the following address. This is the official invitation link which could be shared by members of the channel. I found it through Disboard because someone from the group likely posted the details with the intent of increasing usage. If you do not find any servers of interest on Disboard, try **Discord Me** (discord.me).

https://discord.com/invite/DbtGker

I was greeted with a login window asking for the name I wished to use in the channel. I provided OSINTAuthor and completed a Captcha. I was immediately given an error which demanded a cellular telephone number in order to join this server. This is common when using a VPN, hardened browser, and guest login. Therefore, I never recommend this route. Instead, register for a Discord account at https://discord.com/register, but take a few precautions. In my experience, creating the account from within Chrome appears less "suspicious" than Firefox. Connecting from a network without a VPN seems to allow registration while an IP address from a VPN results in another telephone demand. Therefore, I create a handful of accounts any time I am at a hotel or library. I create them from within my Windows VM using Chrome on the public Wi-Fi without a VPN. These accounts can be stored until needed.

I prefer to conduct all Discord investigations within their official Windows application while inside a virtual machine. Conduct the following steps to replicate my Discord machine.

- Create a Windows 10 virtual machine as previously discussed (Section One).
- Title your new VM "Discord" and conduct the following inside the Windows VM.
- Download and install the Discord app from https://discord.com/download.
- Download the first file titled "DiscordChatExporter.zip" from the website located at https://github.com/Tyrrrz/DiscordChatExporter/releases.
- Extract the contents of the zip file to your Windows VM Desktop.
- Launch DiscordChatExporter.exe from within the new folder.
- Launch the Discord app, provide your account credentials, and connect to the target Discord server (example: https://discord.com/invite/2SUWKFnHSm).
- Now we must locate our Discord token by logging into Discord on your browser of choice.
- Press "Ctrl" + "Shift" + "I" on the keyboard to launch the developer tools.
- Move to the Network tab of the developer tools and reload the page by hitting F5.
- Locate and select an entry that starts with "messages".
- In the right panel, open the "Headers" tab and scroll down to "Request Headers".
- Your token will be listed after "Authorization:".
- Select and copy the entire token key (without the quotes).
- Paste the token into the DiscordChatExporter program and click the arrow.
- Select the desired target server on the left and the target channel on the right.
- Choose the "CSV" export format and leave the dates empty.
- Choose the save location and click "Export".

The result is a text-only CSV file with the entire contents of the exported server and channel. You should repeat this process for each channel of your target server. In 2019, I located a Discord server used to share file-sharing links to recent data breaches. I exported all of the content, which included thousands of links to mega.nz, Google

Drive, Dropbox, and other hosts. The day after I created the export, the Discord server was removed due to policy violations. However, I already had the full export and could investigate the links at my own pace. If desired, you could export an HTML report which would be much more graphically pleasing. I prefer the CSV option because I can import and manipulate the text easier than an HTML web page. If you prefer to run the export in an environment similar to the Discord application, there is a third party viewer available at https://github.com/slatinsky/DiscordChatExporter-frontend.

Discord user IDs are easily located by first selecting the target user within the application or web client. This will bring up a window with basic user details. Click on the three dots on the top right of this panel and then select "Copy User ID". We can now add this to our report or legal requests. We can reverse search user IDs using the third party tools at https://discordlookup.com and https://discord.id/.

Discord is not the only platform for this type of communication, but I find it to be the most popular with amateur cyber criminals. **Slack** (slack.com) appears very similar, but it is targeted more toward professionals. **Element** (element.io) and **Tox** (tox.chat) each possess encrypted communications and better overall security, but adoption is lower than Discord. I believe you should be familiar with all of these environments, and be ready for an investigation within any of them. I keep an investigation VM with all four applications installed and configured. This can be a huge time-saver when the need arises.

Board Reader (boardreader.com)

Online forums provide a unique place for discussion about any topic. If you can think of the subject, an entire site full of people is probably hosting a discussion about the topic. These are usually referred to as user forums. Sometimes, these sites are excluded from being indexed by search engines. This can make locating them difficult. A new wave of forum search sites fills this void. Board Reader queries many forum communities, message boards, discussion threads, and other general interest groups which post messages back and forth. It also offers an advanced search which allows you to choose keywords, language, date range, and specific domain. If you have trouble filtering results on other forum search sites, this can be useful.

Craigslist Forums (forums.craigslist.org)

This forum is categorized by topic instead of location, but location filtering is supported. These forums are not indexed by most search engines, so a manual search is the only way to see the content. In order to search these areas, you may be required to create a free user account. As usual, you can use fictitious information in your profile. After logging in, you can search by keyword on this main page, but not by screen name. This option will identify posts matching the search terms within any of the topics.

The "Handle" option would search by username, but the search field for this query was removed in 2020. Fortunately, we can replicate it with a URL. The following URL displays all posts within the past 31 days by Craigslist user "honeygarlic".

https://forums.craigslist.org/?act=su&handle=honeygarlic

This page also provides two valuable pieces of information. The first line identifies the date the account was created and number of days since inception. Our example appears as follows.

since: 2004-06-16 06:40 (5992 days)

Next, we are notified if the user has deleted any posts in the past 31 days, as follows.

0% of this handle's posts in the last 31 days have been deleted

As a general rule, most people will use the same username across several sites. Craigslist is no exception. If you have identified a username of a target, a search on the Craigslist forums is worth a look. Although you will not get a result every time you search, the commentary is usually colorful when you do. When you locate a username of a target on the Craigslist forums, searching that username on other sites could provide an abundance of information.

Online Prostitution

Craigslist was once used by many prostitutes nationwide as an avenue to meeting "Johns". Likewise, many people used the site to locate a prostitute. In 2009, Craigslist was forced to remove the "Erotic Services" section that hosted these posts announcing this activity. In 2018, Backpage was forced offline and seized by various government agencies. Today, it is difficult to find a post offering prostitution on Craigslist and impossible on Backpage. This does not mean that the prostitutes and their clients simply stopped the potentially illegal behavior. Instead, they found new resources. There are many sites online that aid in prostitution and human trafficking. A few of the big players are listed here. I encourage you to investigate which services are applicable to your cities of interest.

https://5escorts.com

https://www.bedpage.com

https://cityoflove.com

https://www.eros.com

https://www.escort-ads.com

https://escortbabylon.net/

https://escortindex.com

https://www.humaniplex.com

https://ibackpage.com

https://onebackpage.com

https://preferred411.com

https://privatedelights.ch

https://sipsap.com

https://skipthegames.com

https://www.slixa.com

https://www.tsescorts.com

https://theotherboard.com

https://www.tnaboard.com

Escort Review Websites

These types of services may be difficult for some readers to understand. I was also surprised when I first found them. This is where prostitution clients communicate with each other and leave reviews of their experiences with the prostitutes. These "Johns" document the slightest details of the experience including price, cleanliness, and accuracy of the photograph in the ad. Furthermore, this is the first location that will announce an undercover operation by the police. This is important for law enforcement, as this could create an officer safety issue. It is also how the police can determine when a new name or photo should be used in future covert ads. Another purpose for this data is to create documentation of the reviews of an arrested prostitute. This can prove to be valuable in court for the prosecution of offenses. There are several of these services, and every metropolitan area will have a preferred website by the customers. A Google search of "Escort reviews Anaheim" will get you to the popular options. Of course, replace Anaheim with your city of interest.

The Erotic Review (theeroticreview.com)

If you do not know of any individual services that prostitution clients are using in your area, The Erotic Review is a safe bet. Practically every metropolitan area has a presence here. Much of this site will not be available unless you join as a premium member. However, there should be plenty of visible free content for basic investigations. Most of the posts are unsuitable for this book. At the time of this writing, this site was blocking U.S. IP addresses. Switching my VPN to Canada or any other country bypassed the restriction.

Real World Application: While participating in an FBI Operation, I focused on locating juvenile prostitutes and women forced into the sex industry by pimps. One easy way to determine if a sex worker was traveling extensively was to search her number through various escort websites. If it returned numerous cities with postings, that was a strong indication that she was a full-time sex worker and was likely not traveling alone. Every contact that we made with traveling prostitutes resulted in the identification of their pimps.

Online Newspaper Comments

Practically every newspaper now has some sort of online presence. Most digital editions allow readers to leave comments about individual articles. These comments can usually be seen at the bottom of each web page. While the value that these comments add to the newsworthiness of each piece of news is debatable, the content can be important to an investigation. In years past, most newspapers hosted their own digital comment delivery system within their website. This often resulted in a large headache while trying to maintain order, prevent feuds between readers, and delete direct threats. Today, most news websites use third-party services to host these comments. The most popular are Facebook and Disqus. When Facebook is utilized, most people use their real names and behave better than when using only a username on Disqus. Any complaints about the comment activity can be referred to Facebook since they technically store the content. Searching Facebook comments can be conducted through the technique previously explained.

In order to search for content within the Disqus comment system, you can conduct a custom Google search. First, it is important to understand how the Disqus system is recognized by Google. There is an option to log in to a Disqus account and you can "upvote" or "downvote" each comment to show your approval. The words visible on this page that were provided by Disqus are important for the search. The word "comments" will be visible on every Disqus provided environment and there will also be a link to disqus.com. Therefore, the following search on Google should provide any websites that have the Disqus comment delivery system and also have a reference to OSINT.

"osint" "disqus" "comments"

This may produce some non-Disqus results that happen to possess all three words, but those should be rare. This will also identify many pages that do not contain any comments whatsoever. In order to only receive results that actually have comments, alter your search to the following.

"osint" "disqus" "1..999 comments"

This instructs Google to only display results that contain the keywords "OSINT" and "Disqus" and also contain the exact phrase of any number between 1 and 999 followed immediately by the term "comments". This would provide results that contain any number of comments with the exception of "0" or over "1000". The "1..999" portion is the Google range operator that will display any number within the specified range.

Craigslist Auctions (craigslist.org)

Craigslist is one big online classified ad for every area of the world. The site can ease the pain of finding an apartment; provide numerous options for buying a vehicle locally; or assist in locating just about any item or service that you can imagine that is within driving distance of your home. It is also a landing spot for stolen goods, illegal services, and illicit affairs. While Craigslist offers a search option, the results are limited to active posts only. You can also only search within one category at a time. You can browse through the posts individually, but this will be overwhelming.

Government and private investigators have found much success in locating stolen goods within this site. To start, you must find the Craigslist site for your area. Often, simply visiting craigslist.org will direct you to the landing page for your geographical area. If this does not happen, navigate through your country, then your state, then your metropolitan area to see listings around you. If the theft occurred recently, a live search in the "for sale" section may produce results. I do not recommend searching from the main page, as there are no advanced options. Instead, click on any section title. For example, clicking on the "for sale" section will take us to that area. The top of the page will have a search field that will search all of the categories in this section. Additionally, we can filter by price range, posts that contain images, or terms that only appear in the title of the post.

Craigslist also has features that allow you to view results by list view, gallery view, or map view. These locations will only refer to the city of the item, and not exact GPS location. The gallery view can be used as a "photo lineup" to identify a stolen item. The map view can be beneficial when only looking for items within surrounding areas. Four new options on the upper left of every result page allow you to sort the items by newest listings (default), relevance, lowest price, and highest price. Most pages with items for sale will also allow you to filter the results so that only items being sold by individuals are listed. This would eliminate businesses and dealers. The default is to show both, and I recommend it unless you are overwhelmed by the number of results.

If a thief sells the item on Craigslist, he or she will usually delete the post after the transaction is complete. If the post is deleted, it will not be listed in the results of a search on Craigslist. This is where Google and Bing come into play. Both Google and Bing collect information from Craigslist posts to include in their search results. This collection can never be complete, but a large archive of posts is available. Searching Google or Bing with "site:craigslist.org" (without quotes) will search through archived posts on Craigslist that are both active and removed. Similar to the previous example, you can search "site:craigslist.org laptop Edwardsville" (without the quotes). This search produced 572 results that match these criteria on Google. These include the current posts that were available with the live search on craigslist.org as well as posts that have been recently deleted from Craigslist. If you wanted to focus only on a specific regional area of Craigslist, changing the search to "site:stlouis.craigslist.org laptop Edwardsville" would filter results. This example would only show listings from the St. Louis section of Craigslist. You can use any region in your custom searches.

The results that are still current will link to the actual post and display all content of the post. If a search result links to a post that has been deleted from Craigslist, a standard "page not found" error will be returned. You can still get additional information from this deleted post by looking through the text supplied on this search page. The brief description will often disclose an email address or telephone number. Some listings may have a cached view, but lately this has been rare. In a scenario where thousands of search results are presented by Google or Bing, you can add search terms to filter to a more manageable number of posts. Adding the make or model number of the product may quickly identify the stolen property.

You can also search by terms other than the product of interest. Many people that use Craigslist do not want to communicate through email sent from the website. Most users will include a telephone number in the post as a preferred method of communication. The overwhelming majority of these telephone numbers belong to the cellular telephone of the user submitting the post. This can be a huge piece of intelligence for an investigator attempting to identify a person associated with a telephone number. It is common that a criminal will purchase a cellular telephone with cash and add minutes to it as needed. This makes it difficult for someone to identify the criminal from the phone number. Ironically, the same criminal will post the telephone number as well as a name on a public internet site for the world to see. Sometimes, a person will post both a cellular and a landline telephone number on the same post. This allows an investigator to associate these two numbers, and a quick internet search should identify the owner of the landline telephone number.

Another way to search Craigslist posts is to identify screen names. Craigslist discourages inserting a screen name or email address within a post; however, most people have figured out how to bypass this limitation. Instead of someone typing their email address within their posts, they will insert spaces between the first portion of the email address (username) and the second portion of the email address (domain name). For example, instead of the user typing their email address as JohnDoe911@gmail.com, he or she may identify the account as "JohnDoe911 at gmail com". This would be enough to prevent Craigslist's servers from identifying the text as an email address and prohibiting the post. Fortunately for the investigator, this information is indexed by Craigslist and other search engines to be retrieved.

You can search any keyword on either the official Craigslist site or on Google and Bing using the "site" operator. In my experience, Bing offers more results of archived Craigslist posts than Google. If you do not have success with Bing, Google should be searched as well. Many private investigators used to find the "personals" section of interest. The "Casual encounters" area was well known for extramarital affairs, but was shut down due to rampant exploitation. If you want to only search all live Craigslist posts, regardless of which geographical area it exists, you can use sites such as searchcraigslist.org, adhuntr.com, and searchalljunk.com.

Craigslist has a few advanced search operators that may be of interest. It supports a phrase search with quotation marks such as "low miles". It accepts the hyphen (-) operator to exclude terms such as honda black -red. This search finds postings that have 'honda' and 'black' but not 'red'. A pipe symbol (|) provides "OR" searches such as honda | toyota. This search finds postings that have 'honda' or 'toyota' (or both). You can group terms together in parentheses when queries are complicated. A search of red (toyota | honda) -2000 -2001 finds listings that have 'red' and either 'honda' or 'toyota' (or both) but do not have 2000 or 2001. Wildcards are as follows.

Hond* civ* (match "honda civic", "honda civil", etc.)
wood floo* (matches "wood floors", "wood flooring", etc.)
iphone* (matches "iphone", "iphones", "iphone5", etc.)

Craigslist's email alert feature has made third-party tools for this purpose unnecessary. After logging in to your account, you can customize alerts to send an email to you when specific search terms are located.

Real World Application: Many thieves will turn to the internet to unload stolen items. While eBay requires banking information or a credit card to use their services, most thieves prefer Craigslist's offer of anonymity. My local police department successfully located a valuable stolen instrument this way and set up a sting to arrest the thief. Often, the thief will be willing to bring the item to you in order to get some quick cash. Another tip that has helped me during investigations is to look for similar backgrounds. When I had a group of gang members stealing iPhones from vehicles and pockets, they would sell them right away on Craigslist. Since there were hundreds of legitimate iPhones listed, identifying the stolen units can be difficult. By looking for similarities in the backgrounds, I could filter the list into interesting candidates. Finding unique backgrounds, such as tables or flooring, within several posts can be suspicious. Additionally, I have found posts that include "hurry", "must sell today", and "I will come to you" to be indicators of illegal activity.

eBay Auctions (ebay.com)

eBay is an online auction site. Since the site requires a user's financial information or valid credit card to post items for sale, many thieves have moved to Craigslist to unload stolen goods. eBay offers an advanced search that will allow filters that limit to auctions from a specific location, or specified distance from the location. On any search page, there is an "Advanced" button that will display new options. Of these options, there is a category titled "Item Location". The second option in this category is titled "Items within". Here, you can select a zip code and filter results to a minimum of 10 miles from the zip code selected. This will now allow you to search for any item and the results will all be from sellers near a specific zip code. This location option will remain active as you search for different keywords. These searches will only search current auctions that have not expired. In order to search past auctions, select the "Completed listings" option under the category of "Search including". If you want to conduct your searches directly from a URL, or if you want to bookmark queries that will be repeated often, use the following structure. Replace TERMS with your search keywords and USER with your target's username. Visibility of some results may require that you be logged into an eBay account.

Keyword: ebay.com/dsc/i.html?&LH_TitleDesc=1&_nkw=TERMS
Sold: ebay.com/sch/i.html?_from=R40&_nkw=TERMS&LH_Sold=1&LH_Complete=1
Complete: https://www.ebay.com/sch/i.html?_from=R40&_nkw=TERMS&LH_Complete=1
Username: https://www.ebay.com/usr/USER
User Feedback: https://feedback.ebay.com/ws/eBayISAPI.dll?ViewFeedback2&userid=USER
User Items: https://www.ebay.com/sch/USER/m.html
User: http://www.ebay.com/sch/ebayadvsearch/?_ec=104&_sofindtype=25&_userid=USER

Flippity (flippity.com)

An alternative to the location feature on the official eBay site is Flippity. This site performs the same function as mentioned previously, but with less work on the user's part. The results of your search will appear on a map with the ability to minimize and expand the radius as desired. This is a quick way to monitor any type of items being sold in a specific community.

GoofBid (goofbid.com)

Not everyone uses spellcheck. Some people, especially criminals, will rush to list an item to sell without ensuring that the spelling and grammar are correct. You could conduct numerous searches using various misspelled words, or you can use GoofBid. This site will take your correctly spelled keyword search and attempt the same search with the most commonly misspelled variations of the search terms. Another alternative to this service is **Fat Fingers** (fatfingers.com).

Search Tempest (searchtempest.com)

If you find yourself searching multiple geographical areas of Craigslist and eBay, you may desire an automated solution. Search Tempest will allow you to specify the location and perimeter for your search. It will fetch items from Craigslist, eBay, and Amazon. You can specify keywords in order to narrow your search to a specific area. Advanced features allow search of items listed within the previous 24 hours, reduction of duplicates, and filtering by categories. While I encourage the use of these types of services, I always warn people about becoming too reliant on them. These tools could disappear. It is good to understand the manual way of obtaining data.

OfferUp (offerup.com)

This service is steadily stealing the audience currently dominated by Craigslist. OfferUp claims to be the simplest way to buy and sell products locally. A search on their main page allows you to specify a keyword and location. The results identify the usual information including item description and approximate location. OfferUp follows the eBay model of including the seller's username and rating. The unique option with OfferUp is the ability to locate the approximate GPS coordinates associated with a post instead of a vague location. This information is not obvious, but can be quickly obtained. While on any post, right-click and choose to view the page source. Inside this new tab of text should be two properties titled place:location:latitude and place:location:longitude. You can search for these in your browser by pressing "Ctrl" + "F" (Windows) or "command" + "F" (Mac). Next to these fields should display GPS coordinates. In my experience, these precise identifiers will either identify the exact location of the target, or a location in the neighborhood of the suspect. I would never rely on this all the time, but I have had great success getting close to my targets through this technique.

Amazon (amazon.com)

Amazon is the largest online retailer. Users flock to the site to make purchases of anything imaginable. After the receipt of the items ordered, Amazon often generates an email requesting the user to rate the items. This review can only be created if the user is logged in to an account. This review is now associated with the user in the user profile. An overwhelming number of users create these product reviews and provide their real information on the profile for their Amazon account. While Amazon does not have an area to search for this information by username, you can do it with a search engine. A search on Google of site:amazon.com followed by any target name may link to an Amazon profile and several item reviews. The first link displays the user profile including photo, location, and the user's review of products purchased.

This technique of using Google or Bing to search for profiles on websites that do not allow such a search can be applied practically everywhere. Many sites discourage the searching of profiles, but a search on Google such as "site:targetwebsite.com John Doe" would provide links to content matching the criteria. The difficulty arises in locating all of the sites where a person may have a profile. By now, you can search the major communities, but it is difficult to keep up with all of the lesser-known networks.

FakeSpot (fakespot.com)

There is an abundance of fake reviews on Amazon, which can make it difficult to determine which reviews accurately describe a product and which are provided by employees associated with the seller. FakeSpot attempts to identify products that are likely misrepresented by the review community. During a search for a remote-controlled drone, I found that the Amazon "Best Seller" possesses over 53% fake reviews, and top reviewers "tri nguyen" and "EUN SUN LEE" appear to be automated reviewers based on other products. This service also supports analysis of reviewers on Yelp and Trip Advisor. FakeSpot now requires you to install a browser extension. If this service is valuable to your investigations, I find this service effective. If you rarely need this type of data, I would avoid any unnecessary extensions.

Pinterest (pinterest.com)

Pinterest is an online "pinboard" where users can share photos, links, and content located anywhere on the internet. It is a way to rebroadcast items of interest to a user. People that follow that user on Pinterest can keep updated on things that the user is searching and reading. The search feature on the main website is useful for keyword searches only. It will search for any term and identify posts that include those words within the description. A search of my last name displayed several photos of people. Clicking each of these links will present the full-page view of the photo and any associated comments. This page will also identify the full name of the person that uploaded the content and the original online source. Clicking on the full name of the user will open the user profile which should include all "pinned" content. Unfortunately, you cannot search a person's full name or username on Pinterest and receive a link to their profile page. To do this, you must use Google. The following direct search URLs will identify the usernames (bill) and keywords (CRAFTS) present on Pinterest.

Username: https://www.pinterest.com/bill/
User Pins: https://www.pinterest.com/bill/pins
Created Boards: https://www.pinterest.com/bill/_created/
Saved Boards: https://www.pinterest.com/bill/_saved/
Pins Search: https://www.pinterest.com/search/pins/?q=CRAFTS
Boards Search: https://www.pinterest.com/search/boards/?q=CRAFTS
Google Search: https://www.google.com/search?q=site:pinterest.com+CRAFTS

BugMeNot (bugmenot.com)

This utility may violate your departmental policies about online research. BugMeNot allows users to share their logins for various websites with the world. Technically, users of this service are giving the public consent to use their credentials in order to access data behind a login. However, this could violate the terms of service for a specific website. I once needed to access a private web forum which was hidden behind a login portal. This forum was not accepting new members. Searching the URL on BugMeNot revealed a username and password shared by a member of the forum for public use. This allowed me to access the site and find my desired data.

IntelTechniques Communities Tool

Similar to the previous search tools, this option attempts to simplify the various search techniques presented within this chapter. The entire tool is quite large, and could not fit into a graphical representation on a single page here. This tool should replicate all of the specific URLs cited within this topic. While the chances of your target appearing here are lower than large social networks, this resource should not be ignored. In my experience, the details obtained about a target from online communities are usually much more intimate and personal than the public blasts on the larger sites. The online version is updated often and can always be accessed on my site at **https://inteltechniques.com/tools/Communities.html.**

CHAPTER TWENTY-THREE
EMAIL ADDRESSES

Searching by a person's real name can be frustrating. If your target has a common name, it is easy to get lost in the results. Even a fairly unique name like mine produces almost 20 people's addresses, profiles, and telephone numbers. If your target is named John Smith, you have a problem. This is why I always prefer to search by email address when available. If you have your target's email address, you will achieve much better results at a faster pace. There may be thousands of John Wilsons, but there would be only one john.wilson.77089@yahoo.com. Searching this address within quotation marks on the major search engines is my first preference. This should identify web pages which include the exact details within either the content or the source code. This is the "easy stuff" which may present false positives, but should provide immediate evidence to the exposure of the target account. I then typically search the username portion of the email address by itself in case it is in use within other providers, such as Gmail, Hotmail, Twitter, LinkedIn, etc. Let's conduct an example assuming that "john.wilson.77089@yahoo.com" is your target. You could place this email within quotes and execute through each service manually, or use the following direct search URLs to expedite the process.

Google Email: https://google.com/search?q="john.wilson.77089@yahoo.com"
Google Username: https://google.com/search?q="john.wilson.77089"
Bing Email: https://bing.com/search?q="john.wilson.77089@yahoo.com"
Bing Username: https://bing.com/search?q="john.wilson.77089"
Yandex Email: https://yandex.com/search/?text="john.wilson.77089@yahoo.com"
Yandex Username: https://yandex.com/search/?text="john.wilson.77089"

The custom search tools presented at the end of this chapter and the next will automate this entire process. Next, you should verify the target email address.

Emailrep.io (emailrep.io)

This is an email verification service with many additional features. Below is an actual search result, and I provide an explanation after each detail [within brackets]. As you will see, this is an impressive free search, and at the top of my list for every investigation.

"email": "redacted@gmail.com",   [Email address provided]
"reputation": "high",   [Likelihood to be a real email address]
"suspicious": false,   [Indications of spam or malicious use]
"references": 20,   [Number of online references]
"blacklisted": false,   [Blocked by spam lists]
"malicious_activity": false,   [Known phishing activity]
"malicious_activity_recent": false,   [Known recent phishing activity]
"credentials_leaked": true,   [Password present within data leaks]
"credentials_leaked_recent": false,   [Password present within recent leaks]
"data_breach": true,   [Address present within known breaches]
"first_seen": "07/01/2008",   [Date first seen online]
"last_seen": "02/25/2019",   [Date last seen online]
"domain_exists": true,   [Whether domain is valid]
"domain_reputation": "n/a",   [Reputation of domain]
"new_domain": false,   [Domain recently registered]
"days_since_domain_creation": 8795,   [Days since the domain was registered]
"spam": false,   [Marked as spam]
"free_provider": true,   [Free provider such as Gmail]
"disposable": false,   [Disposable provider such as Mailinator]

"deliverable": true,	[Inbox able to receive mail]
"accept_all": false,	[Address is a catch-all]
"valid_mx": true,	[Domain possesses an email server]
"spf_strict": true,	[Domain email security enabled]
"dmarc_enforced": false,	[Dmarc email security enabled]
"profiles": "youtube","google","github","twitter"	[Profiles associated with email]

This provides detail we cannot find anywhere else. In this example, I now know that my target email address has been in use for at least twelve years and appears within at least one data breach. This encourages me to explore the breach search methods explained in a moment. The following "explainer" which was included at the end of my result provides even more value.

"Not suspicious. This email address has been seen in 3 reputable sources on the internet, including Twitter. It has been seen in data breaches or credential leaks dating back to 07/18/2017, but not since 02/25/2019. SPF and DMARC are strictly enforced, so this email address is not spoofable. We've observed no malicious or suspicious activity from this address. "

If the result had reported no identifiable history, that can be an indication that we are dealing with a burner email address. I often see this type of result when investigating addresses used to deliver threats or extortion emails. I now know to expect limited success with further queries on the address and I am able to report back to my client that we are likely dealing with an email account setup specifically for the purpose of the crime committed. Email address history and reputation can also be brought to light using breach data, which we will discuss in detail later in this book.

An additional email verification option is **Email Hippo** (tools.verifyemailaddress.io). This service provides minimal data, but may identify something missing from the previous superior option. When I searched each of my Gmail accounts, I received "OK" as a response. When I changed one character, I immediately received "BAD" as a result. As you validate your target addresses through Email Hippo, the responses appear at the bottom as a collection. Choosing the Export option allows you to download all results. This service limits free daily usage by IP address and browser cookies.

Email Assumptions

You may know about one address, but not others. It can be productive to make assumptions of possible email addresses and use the verifiers to see if they exist. For example, if your target's name is Jay Stewart and he has an email address of jay112003@yahoo.com, you should conduct additional searches for the addresses of jay112003@gmail.com, jay112003@hotmail.com, jay112003@live.com, and others. If you already know your target's username, such as a Twitter handle, you should create a list of potential email addresses. If I had no email address or username for my target (Jay Stewart), but I knew that he worked at the Illinois Medical District Commission (medicaldistrict.org), I may start searching for the following email addresses.

jstewart@medicaldistrict.org
jay.stewart@medicaldistrict.org
j.stewart@medicaldistrict.org
stewartj@medicaldistrict.org

These are merely assumptions of potential addresses. Most, if not all, of them do not exist and will provide nothing for me. However, if I do identify an existing address, I now have a new piece of the puzzle to search. These addresses can be verified against the previous three tools.

Email Format (email-format.com)

If the previous email assumption techniques were unproductive or overkill for your needs, you may want to consider Email Format. This website searches a provided domain name and attempts to identify the email structure of employee addresses. When searching medicaldistrict.org, it provided several confirmed email accounts under that domain and made the assumption that employee emails are formatted as first initial then last name. Our target would have an email address of jstewart@medicaldistrict.org according to the rules. I use this service to help create potential email lists from names collected from Facebook, Twitter, and other social networks. I can then verify my list with the services previously mentioned.

Gravatar (gravatar.com)

This service is responsible for many of the small image icons that you see next to a contact in your email client. You may notice that some incoming emails display a square image of the sender. This is configured by the sender, and this image is associated with any email address connected. You do not need to wait for an incoming message in order to see this image. While the Gravatar home page does not offer an email address search option, we can conduct a query directly from the following URL, replacing the email address with your target information. This image can then be searched with a reverse image query as explained later.

https://en.gravatar.com/site/check/test@test.com

Compromised Accounts

Email addresses are compromised regularly. Hacker groups often publicly post databases of email addresses and corresponding passwords on websites such as Pastebin. Manually searching for evidence of compromised accounts can get complicated, but we will tackle this later in the book. Several online services now aid this type of investigation. These services provide one minimal piece of information about any email address entered. They disclose whether that address appears within any publicly known hacked email databases. While most will never disclose the owner, any email content, or passwords, they will confirm that the target's email account was compromised at some point. They will also identify the service which was targeted during the breach.

This helps us in two ways. First, it confirms an email address as valid. If your suspect account is todd007@gmail.com, and that address was compromised in a breach in 2015, you know the address is valid, it was active, and is at least a few years of age. Second, you know the services which need to be investigated. If todd007@gmail.com was included in the Dropbox and LinkedIn breaches, you should attempt to locate those profiles. Compromised account data is absolutely the most beneficial technique I have used within my investigations in the past five years. We will dive much deeper into data sets later, but let's focus on online services first. These are also good websites to check your own address in order to identify vulnerabilities.

Have I Been Pwned (haveibeenpwned.com)

This is a staple in the data breach community. This site allows entry of either a username or email address, but I find only the email option to be reliable. The result is a list and description of any public breaches which contain the provided email address. The descriptions are very helpful, as they explain the type of service associated and any details about the number of users compromised. In a test, I searched an old email of mine that was used to create several covert accounts many years prior. The result was notification that the email address had been compromised on six websites, including Bitly, Dropbox, LinkedIn, Myspace, River City Media, and Tumblr. The data present here is voluntarily contributed to the owner of the site. Cyber thieves steal various credential databases and allow Have I Been Pwned (HIBP) to confirm the legitimacy. HIBP then makes the content searchable and credits the thief by name. The thief can then charge more money for the stolen goods as HIBP has vetted the content. It's a weird game. Searching content within the HIBP website is straightforward.

Some "white hat" hackers eagerly share the data leaks and breaches which they discover in order to receive acknowledgement from the site. Once HIBP has verified the legitimacy and source of the data, it becomes much more valuable in the black markets. Many researchers have accused this website of encouraging data theft, as it can be sold for a higher amount once the owner has vetted the content. Many criminals who deal with stolen credentials dislike this site and its owner. They do not share their goods and try to keep them off of the radar of the security community. Therefore, we must always utilize every resource possible.

Dehashed (dehashed.com)

While Have I Been Pwned is often considered the gold standard in regard to breached account details, we cannot ignore Dehashed. It takes a more aggressive approach and seeks breached databases for their own collection. Using the same email address provided during the previous test, I received two additional breach notifications. These included lesser-known breaches which had not yet publicly surfaced on HIBP. When combining results from both of these services, you would now know that this target email address was likely a real account (you received results); it had been used online since 2012 (the date of the oldest breach according to HIBP); it is connected to an employment-minded individual (LinkedIn); and it exists in spam databases as a U.S. consumer (River City Media).

I believe that Have I Been Pwned and Dehashed complement each other, and one should never be searched without the other. This search alone often tells me more about a target email address, even if it never identifies the owner. Dehashed allows unlimited search once you create a free account, but will not disclose passwords without a premium account. They advertise the ability to see all associated passwords for a small fee. I have tried this service in the past, and it worked well. However, I believe that paying a company to disclose stolen passwords might exceed the scope of OSINT. It may also violate your own employer's policies. Please use caution. Unfortunately, Dehashed now requires you to be logged into a free account in order to conduct any queries, even at a free access level.

Spycloud (spycloud.com)

This service is a bit different. They are extremely aggressive in regard to obtaining fresh database breaches. They possess many data sets which are not present in HIBP. However, they do not display details about accounts which you do not own. We should not manually query addresses through the main Spycloud landing page as this will result in the target address receiving an email from Spycloud. Our only option is general details through their free API. The following URL submits a query for test@email.com.

https://portal.spycloud.com/endpoint/enriched-stats/test@email.com

The results are in JSON format, which may appear like pure text within your browser. The following result was presented to me when I searched an email address within my own domain. They basically tell you that the email address queried is present within multiple database breaches, but the identity of each is not available. I use this service to simply verify an email address.

```
    "discovered": 7,
    "records": 8,
    "discovered_unit": "Months"
  "company": {
    "discovered": 1,
    "records": 11,
    "discovered_unit": "Month",
```

Hudson Rock (hudsonrock.com)

When searching an email address, Hudson Rock identifies whether it has been seen within stealer log data. Stealer logs are explained much later in the book, but presence within them indicates that the email owner's computer has been compromised by a virus. We can query their API with the following URL.

https://cavalier.hudsonrock.com/api/json/v2/preview/search-by-login/osint-tools?email=test@email.com

Cybernews (cybernews.com/personal-data-leak-check)

This service only provides a "true" or "false" identifying the presence of the email within a breach. The following URL submits a text-only query. This could verify an email address exists.

https://check.cybernews.com/chk/?lang=en_US&e=test@test.com

Passwords

The previous options only display the services which are associated with a target email account due to that data being stolen and publicly released. Passwords are not visible unless you pay a premium to Dehashed or Spycloud. Other sites present more robust options for displaying redacted and unredacted passwords for billions of accounts without any fees. I believe this is OSINT data, but your employer's policies may disagree. Let's approach cautiously with some demonstrations.

Leak Peek (leakpeek.com)

The benefit of this service is that it displays a partial view of passwords associated with email addresses within a breach. It possesses a decent data set of 8 billion credentials. This consists of a "Combo List", which will be acquired later. The following examples identify the masking protocol used to block portions of each password.

test@email.com:55Ji*******
test@email.com:Big6****

Note that Leak Peek allows query by email address, username, password, keyword, and domain. We will use this resource again within upcoming chapters.

Breach Directory (breachdirectory.org)

The results here seem very similar to Leak Peek, but redundancy is always valuable. However, full passwords are available if you are willing to do some work. Consider the following results for test@email.com.

Ex7l****   dc3245ecdcf2e40b140e121a014cc37f70239f41
Exig***   7e39ea215613a23a6b33f1dabc340ccf65dfa243

The left column displays the typical redacted passwords and the right column displays SHA-1 hash values of the full passwords. I will explain much more detail about hash values later in the book. For now, this is a representation of the entire password, but we must decrypt the has to reveal the true password. There are several online options, and I will explain my recommended approach with the data breaches chapter. For demonstration, I will use **MD5 Decrypt** (md5decrypt.net/en/Sha1). I entered dc3245ecdcf2e40b140e121a014cc37f70239f41 into this website and received the following response.

dc3245ecdcf2e40b140e121a014cc37f70239f41 : **Ex7layer**

I now know the full password without creating any account or downloading any breach data. These services are only an introduction into breach data. We have a lot more to discuss later in the book.

PSBDMP (psbdmp.ws)

Up to this point, all of these services display content received directly from known data breaches. PSBDMP takes a different approach. It monitors Pastebin for any posts including email addresses and/or passwords. There is no reliable search option, but their free API presents detailed results with the following URL structure.

https://psbdmp.ws/api/search/test@test.com

The following is an actual result.

"id": "69yKWrZE",
"length": 25004,
"time": "2019-07-05 14:30",
"text": "$contact->setEmail('test@test.com');

The "id" is the Pastebin identifier. We can access the original file with the following URL.

https://pastebin.com/69yKWrZE

By visiting the Pastebin URL, we can see the full data, including the following excerpt.

$contact->setFirstName('John');
$contact->setLastName('Doe');
$contact->setEmail('test@test.com');
$contact->setEmail('example@mail.com');
$contact->setPhoneCountryCode('123');
$contact->setPhone('12345678');

If this had not been intentional test data, the results could have been very valuable for an investigation. We can also use this service to search for exposed password details. If I wanted to know if "password1234" had ever appeared within current or deleted Pastebin files, I would navigate to the following.

https://psbdmp.ws/api/search/password1234

The following is an actual result, displaying the Pastebin file, date, and credentials.

"id": "fEV4hrbe",
"length": 189357,
"time": "2016-12-12 19:34",
"text": "rd123 sketches5973:password1234 sketches5973:passw"
We can also sort through their archives with the following Google query.

site:psbdmp.ws "test@gmail.com"

The first result is https://psbdmp.ws/WjwCkNL4. Clicking that link presents a dead page. However, modifying the URL as follows presents the original content.

https://pastebin.com/WjwCkNL4

I once had an investigation where Google had indexed a PSBDMP Pastebin hit, but searching the Pastebin site through Google did not reveal the data. I also once investigated a Pastebin link to a client doxing at https://pastebin.com/qbkWTxCW. Pastebin had already removed the data and it was no longer accessible. A URL of https://psbdmp.ws/api/search/qbkWTxCW contained the full text file archived from Pastebin by

PSBDMP. I believe the free version of PSBDMP provides great value for online investigators. Their paid API can be more beneficial if you have a need for that service. I have only used it a few times, and still have a few free trial credits remaining. More details can be found at https://psbdmp.ws.

IntelligenceX (intelx.io)

You can search IntelligenceX for free and receive partial results, or create a free trial to see everything. In my experience, you are only limited to the number of burner "trial" email addresses with which you have access. While I have used this site for the free tier and an occasional free trial, I do not recommend any of the paid services. We will replicate the same results for free throughout the book and within our own tools. In fact, many of the tools on their site were copied verbatim without attribution from the tools which are included free here.

LeakIX (leakix.net)

This service indexes various areas of the internet looking for data leaks which may contain sensitive information. We can query through the site or directly via the following URL structure, which identifies an email address associated with a website owner's WordPress account.

https://leakix.net/search?scope=leak&q=%22test@test.com%22

The following is a partial result.

Japan GMO Internet,Inc 2022-06-21 01:45 2022-11-06 01:55 https://www.houyoukai.sai-net.work
ASN: 7506, Open ports: 443, Certificate domains: www.houyoukai.sai-net.work, houyoukai.sai-net.work
Found Wordpress users (CVE-2017-5487):
User #1 testtest-com Name: test@test.com

Email Reputation

When I am investigating an email address, I want to know its reputation or spam score. If the address has been blacklisted or reported as spam, I won't waste too much time attempting to identify the true owner. The following is a reliable service which we can query with the following URL.

https://cleantalk.org/email-checker/michael@inteltechniques.com

An example record may appear as follows.

Record	Sites	Blacklisted	Real	Disposable	Updated
spam@gmail.com	14	True	Fake	True	Nov 14, 2022 22:52:42

Hunter (hunter.io/email-verifier)

This service advertises the ability to display email addresses associated with a specific domain. However, the "Verifier" tool can also be valuable. This URL allows query of an individual email address. It immediately provides details similar to the first two services mentioned in this chapter, such as the validity of the address. From there, it sometimes displays internet links which contained the email address within the content at some point. This appears to be sourced from their own database, as many links are no longer present on the internet, and not indexed by Google. I once searched my target email address here and confirmed that it was present within a forum associated with terrorism. The forum had recently been removed, but this evidence was permanent. Hunter.io accepts URL queries with the following structure.

https://hunter.io/verify/test@gmail.com

OCCRP (data.occrp.org)

Self-identified as "The global archive of research material for investigative reporting", this service possesses an amazing amount of data. We will dig into this resource within a later chapter, but we should acknowledge the email options here. A query of any email address immediately displays documents associated with the account. Additionally, any keyword search which provides results can be filtered by email address. Let's conduct an example. When I search for "inteltechniques", I receive two results, both of which appear to be PDF files from a journalism conference in 2017. I could download and read the documents, or click the filters to the left. When I click on the "Email" option, I am notified that the following email addresses are included within these documents. This is great way to find additional email addresses which may be associated with your target.

jaimi.dowdell@gmail.com
james.grimaldi@wsj.com
mark.maremont@wsj.com

A manual query of the address test@test.com on their website resulted in 42 results and a URL structure of https://data.occrp.org/search?limit=30&q=test%40test.com. We can edit this URL and resubmit it in the following format to receive additional results.

https://data.occrp.org/search?test@test.com

Spytox (spytox.com)

This is a "White Pages" style of query and you will potentially see a name, city, and telephone number associated with the account. The paid options are never worth the money.

XLEK (xlek.com)

I often find email addresses of my targets within this service (which is now called USA-Official), but it does not allow you to query by email address. We will need to rely on Google to assist. Assume your target is "mike@gmail.com". I receive better results if I split up the search terms in my query. The following Google queries produce over 200 results.

site:xlek.com "mike" "gmail.com"
site:usa-official.com "mike" "gmail.com"

These results include the actual target email address queried and anything else which also matches, such as "johnson.mike@gmail.com" and "smith.mike@gmail.com". This overall strategy should apply toward any people search websites which display email addresses but do not provide a specific email search field.

That's Them (thatsthem.com)

The majority of email addresses and usernames I have searched through this service returned no results. However, on occasion I received detailed results such as full name, address, phone number, and vehicle information. Although this is rare, I believe That's Them should be on your list of email and username search resources.

Search People Free (searchpeoplefree.com/cyberbackgroundchecks.com)

This data set is suspected to be generated from various marketing database leaks. Because of this, we usually receive much more complete results. Most results include full name, age, current home address, previous addresses, telephone numbers, family members, and business associations.

Proton Mail (protonmail.com)

Proton Mail provides arguably the most popular secure and encrypted email service. Because of this, many criminals flock to it. In 2020, at least half of my criminal email investigations were associated with a Proton Mail account. When this happens, I want to know the date of account creation. The following steps should be conducted while logged in to a free Proton Mail account.

- Create a new "Contact", add the target email address, then save it.
- Access the contact and click the "Email Settings" icon.
- Click the "Show advanced PGP settings" link.

The result should display the creation date of the "Public key". This is usually the creation date of the email account, but not always. If your target generated new security keys for an account, you will see that date instead. Fortunately, this is very rare. Figure 23.01 displays the result when searching the email address of a colleague. I now know he has had this account since at least March 10, 2016. If the result displayed a recent date, I would suspect it was a new "burner" account created for a malicious purpose.

FINGERPR...	CREATED	EXPIRES	TYPE	STATUS
900a5c16b...	Mar 10, 2016	-	RSA (2048)	PRIMARY

Figure 23.01: A Proton Mail public key announcing account creation date.

This technique requires you to possess a free or paid Proton Mail account. It provides the easiest way to generate, view, and document the details. However, we can replicate this entire process without a requirement to log in to an account, but the results are not as reliable. Assume your target email is notmyemail@protonmail.com. First, we must query it to determine if it is present within the Proton Mail system with the following URL.

https://api.protonmail.ch/pks/lookup?op=get&search=notmyemail@protonmail.com

If your browser prompts you to download a file titled "pubkey.asc", this indicates that the address exists. If you receive a message of "No Key Found", then it does not. If the address exists, navigate to the following URL.

https://api.protonmail.ch/pks/lookup?op=index&search=notmyemail@protonmail.com

That URL currently provides the following response.

```
info:1:1
pub:74ecf3959bac5eba2bd636e204fac101b757d18f:1:2048:1623879788::
uid:notmyemail@protonmail.com <notmyemail@protonmail.com>:1623879788::
```

The last set of digits (1623879788) represents an Epoch Unix timestamp, which was explained in Chapter Twelve during the source code review of Instagram profiles. We can convert that number into a date and time at https://www.unixtimestamp.com/index.php. This tells me that the account was created on or before Wednesday, June 16, 2021 at 21:43:08 GMT. Be warned that I have experienced false positives with both of these URLs if you are connected to a VPN server which is abusing this process or you conduct multiple queries within a few seconds. Technically, they should obtain the same data from the same source, but I have had many failures. This is why I prefer the manual method explained at the beginning of this section.

If your target has an email address associated with their own domain and hosted through Proton Mail, you may want to know if the address was created within Proton Mail or if it is simply a catch-all address which forwards to a single inbox. This can help you determine if your target email address might be used across multiple sites (created address) or if it was supplied for a single purpose knowing that any email sent to it would be forwarded (catch-all). The following URL queries an email address hosted at Proton Mail and discloses whether the address forwards to another address.

https://mail-api.proton.me/pks/lookup?op=index&search=**test@michaelbazzell.com**

In this scenario, Proton reports the following, which tells you the email address receiving the inbound emails.

uid:**office@michaelbazzell.com** <office@michaelbazzell.com>:1609097370::

Domain Connections

Every domain name registration includes an email address associated with the site. While many people will use a privacy service to hide personal details, this is not always the case. Fortunately, many free services have been collecting domain registration details and offer queries of current and archived domain registration data. They will identify domain names that were registered with the target email address entered. This is beneficial when you have a tech-savvy target that may have registered websites of which you are not aware. This also works on domains that no longer exist. As a test, I provided an email address of brad@notla.com. The following results identify the details found by each service. The use of affiliate IDs obtained by services such as Analyze ID will be explained during the domain instruction presented later.

Whoxy (whoxy.com/reverse-whois)
Full Name & Mailing Address
Telephone Number
Nine Owned Domain Names
Registrar and Host Details

Whoisology (whoisology.com)
Full Name & Mailing Address
Telephone Number
Twenty Owned Domain Names
Registrar and Host Details

AnalyzeID (analyzeid.com)
Amazon Affiliate ID
AdSense Affiliate ID
Five Owned Domain Names

Imitation

The assumptions of email addresses can be valuable in discovering potential valid accounts, as mentioned earlier. Imitation of any target email addresses can reveal more details, and confirm association with online activities. Consider the following example. Your target email address is bill@microsoft.com, and you want to know if he is a Mac or Windows user. You could first navigate to account.apple.com and attempt to make an Apple account with that address. If allowed to proceed past the first screen, then that user does not already have an account associated with the target address. If you are informed that the email address is already in use, then you know that your target is an Apple user, and that specific address controls the account. You could navigate to signup.live.com and attempt to create an account with the address. If denied, you know that your target is already a Windows user and that address controls the account.

This method can be replicated across practically all websites and services. I have used this technique to confirm that target email addresses are associated with services from Yahoo, Gmail, Facebook, Twitter, and many others. I have also identified real-world services in use by my target by attempting to create accounts with local cable, power, and water companies, supplying the target email account and being notified that the address was "already in use". Knowing the local cable provider of a suspect can seriously limit the geographical area where he or she could be residing. Be sure not to fully execute any account creations with your target email address. This method should only be used on an initial account creation screen, and never submitted.

Email Provider

If your target's email address ends in gmail.com or yahoo.com, the identity of the email provider is quite obvious. However, business addresses and those with custom domain names do not notify you of the service that hosts the email. A domain's email provider is the company listed in the domain's MX record. The email provider may be the same as the domain's hosting company, but could also be a separate company. You may need to know the email provider in order to issue a court order for content or subscriber data. You may simply want to document this information within your investigation for potential future use. Regardless of your needs, the following will obtain the email provider from almost any address.

Navigate to **MX Toolbox** (mxtoolbox.com) and enter the domain of the email address, such as phonelosers.org. The result should include a hostname and IP address. These identify the email provider for the target domain. In this example, the host is mx1.mailchannels.net. This tells me that Mail Channels is likely the email host. This technique helps me identify the email providers or hosts behind business email accounts. If I am trying to connect an individual to a shell company, this may associate the same small provider with each target. I believe every thorough OSINT report should include a brief mention about the domain email provider. This should be checked as the investigation continues. Changing providers could be a sign of paranoia or intent to conceal evidence. Law enforcement can use this information in order to secure a proper search warrant.

OSINT Rocks (osint.rocks)

This newer service attempts to recreate several Linux utilities we discussed in previous chapters but through a web browser. It currently allows email address and username queries through Ghunt, Sherlock, Holehe, and others. However, this requires you to submit your target data to a third party instead of relying on your own locally-installed tools. You can also use **Gmail OSINT** (gmail-osint.activetk.jp) to replicate the features of Ghunt, but the previous warning still applies. If these services are no longer online, you can also use the email search feature at **Castrick** (castrickclues.com).

IntelTechniques Email Addresses Tool

Similar to the previous IntelTechniques search tools, I have created a custom email address search tool as previously explained in Section I. This is my most used tool, and the option which requires the most updates. As you find new or updated resources, you will likely want to keep this tool functioning 100 percent.

CHAPTER TWENTY-FOUR
USERNAMES

Once you have identified a username for an online service, this information may lead to much more data. Active internet users often use the same username across many sites. For example, the user "amanda62002" on Myspace may be the same "amanda62002" on Twitter and an unknown number of other sites. When you identify an email address, you may now have the username of the target. If a subject uses mpulido007@gmail.com as an email address, there is a good chance that he or she may use mpulido007 as a screen name on a number of sites. If the target has been an internet user for several years, this Gmail account was probably not the first email address used by the target. Searches for potential addresses of mpulido007@yahoo.com, mpulido007@hotmail.com, and mpulido007@aol.com may discover new information. Manual searching of this new username information is a good start. Keeping up with the hundreds of social websites available is impossible.

Prior to 2024, this book contained a handful of username query websites. In the past two years, we have been bombarded with new username search resources. I will no longer explain any of the sites, as usage is simple. Instead, I will focus on services which allow username query directly from a URL. This will be beneficial for our custom search tools. Visiting the following services will allow you to search usernames across several websites, and will report links to profiles that you may have missed. Replace "inteltechniques" with your target to avoid dealing with an unnecessary home page. If a service says that a username is "taken" "exists" or "unavailable", then you know that someone possesses that username on a specific service and you should conduct manual research.

https://www.idcrawl.com/u/inteltechniques
https://instantusername.com/?q=inteltechniques
https://www.namechecker.org/#inteltechniques
https://namechk.com/namechk-plugin-search-results/?n=inteltechniques
https://namevine.com/#/inteltechniques
https://profilediscover.com/inteltechniques/
https://www.social-searcher.com/search-users/?q6=inteltechniques
https://usernamechecker.checkistan.com/#inteltechniques
https://usersearch.org/results_normal.php?URL_username=inteltechniques
https://usersearch.org/results_advanced.php?URL_username=inteltechniques
https://usersearch.org/results_advanced1.php?URL_username=inteltechniques
https://usersearch.org/results_advanced2.php?URL_username=inteltechniques
https://usersearch.org/results_advanced4.php?URL_username=inteltechniques
https://usersearch.org/results_advanced5.php?URL_username=inteltechniques
https://usersearch.org/results_advanced6.php?URL_username=inteltechniques
https://usersearch.org/results_advanced7.php?URL_username=inteltechniques
https://usersearch.org/results_dating.php?URL_username=inteltechniques
https://usersearch.org/results_forums.php?URL_username=inteltechniques
https://usersearch.org/results_crypto.php?URL_username=inteltechniques

Manual Query

You may desire a quick peek into the profile associated with a username across the most common networks. I added the following options to the Username Tool, assuming "inteltechniques" is the target username.

https://x.com/inteltechniques
https://facebook.com/inteltechniques
https://instagram.com/inteltechniques
https://www.tiktok.com/@inteltechniques

https://tinder.com/@inteltechniques
https://inteltechniques.tumblr.com
https://www.snapchat.com/s/inteltechniques
https://medium.com/@inteltechniques
https://youtube.com/inteltechniques
https://www.reddit.com/user/inteltechniques

Search Engines

As previously explained, we can query search engines directly via URL as follows.

https://www.google.com/search?q=%22inteltechniques%22
https://www.bing.com/search?q=%22inteltechniques%22
https://yandex.com/search/?text=%22inteltechniques%22

Compromised Accounts

In the previous chapter, I explained how I use Have I Been Pwned (haveibeenpwned.com) and Dehashed (dehashed.com) in order to identify online accounts associated with a target email address. While HIBP does not always work with usernames, Dehashed performs well. Similar to the previous instruction, enter your target's username with the intent to discover any data breaches which include these details. The custom search tool contains multiple breach queries, as I find that information to be the most valuable at the beginning of an investigation. If my target username is "inteltechniques", I find the following direct query URL to be most beneficial for username search, although they now require the use of a burner account to show results on Dehashed. This should look familiar to the options presented in the previous chapter.

https://dehashed.com/search?query="inteltechniques"

While we cannot submit queries via direct URL through all data breach sites, the following allows manual entry of usernames. All of these were explained in the previous chapter.

https://haveibeenpwned.com
https://leakpeek.com/
https://breachdirectory.org
https://psbdmp.ws

Gravatar (gravatar.com)

This service was explained in the previous chapter in regard to email addresses, but can also apply to usernames. The following URL would search my own information and display any email account images associated with my username.

https://en.gravatar.com/inteltechniques

Link Tree (linktr.ee)

This popular link aggregation service allows members to announce all of their networks on one page. We can also take advantage of this via direct URL, such as the following.

https://linktr.ee/ambermac

Email Assumptions

We can also make assumptions in order to identify target accounts. Assume that your suspect is IntelTechniques on Twitter. A search of the email addresses of IntelTechniques@gmail.com, IntelTechniques@hotmail.com, and IntelTechniques@yahoo.com at HIBP or Dehashed might reveal an active account that appears within a compromised database. Unfortunately, this manual search is time consuming and takes a lot of redundant effort. Therefore, consider using this option within the custom search tools.

These tools contain two search fields near the bottom of the page. Each queries a provided username through HIBP and Dehashed. The code appends the most popular email domains after the supplied username, and conducts a search within a new tab for each. If you provide IntelTechniques as the target username, the following email addresses are queried within independent browser tabs.

IntelTechniques@gmail.com
IntelTechniques@yahoo.com
IntelTechniques@hotmail.com
IntelTechniques@protonmail.com
IntelTechniques@live.com
IntelTechniques@icloud.com
IntelTechniques@yandex.com
IntelTechniques@gmx.com
IntelTechniques@mail.com
IntelTechniques@mac.com
IntelTechniques@me.com

Any positive results indicate that an address exists matching the search criteria, and that address was present within a breach. If you look at the code behind the tools, it appears as follows.

setTimeout(function(){window.open('https://dehashed.com/search?query=%22' + all3 + '@gmail.com%22', '1leak3window');},1000);

The Timeout function places a short pause in between searches. This ensures that we do not upset the server by conducting too many automated queries at once. If desired, you could replace "gmail.com", or any other options, with an email provider more appropriate for your investigations. If you are outside the U.S., you may want to replace several of these. You could also add more at the end. If I were to add "qq.com" after the last option, it would appear as follows. The 35000 is the next Timeout option to ensure that we have 3000 milliseconds in between each search execution.

setTimeout(function(){window.open('https://dehashed.com/search?query=%22' + all3 + '@qq.com%22', '13leak3window');},35000);

Similar to how compromised database searches are the most powerful email search option that I use, querying usernames in this manner can be equally important. This search tool eliminates any laborious process and removes any excuses not to conduct this type of search every time.

The previous option made assumptions about usernames within email addresses which may appear on breach search sites. We can replicate that method within a standard search engine. The following URL populates a search on Google of the target username with the addition of the most popular email address domains, including quotation marks and the OR operator, as previously discussed. If your target username is IntelTechniques, you could manually conduct the following Google search.

"IntelTechniques@gmail.com"OR"IntelTechniques@yahoo.com"OR"IntelTechniques@hotmail.com"OR"IntelTechniques@protonmail.com"OR"IntelTechniques@live.com"OR"IntelTechniques@icloud.com"OR"IntelTechniques@yandex.com"OR"IntelTechniques@gmx.com"OR"IntelTechniques@mail.com"OR"IntelTechniques@mac.com"OR"IntelTechniques@me.com"

If desired, you could copy this query and paste it into Bing and Yandex, but I have found the results to be very unreliable. Your custom search tool makes this much easier. Enter your username in the "Email Search" option at the end in order to replicate this search. It will usually generate the most results the fastest.

Skype Username (web.skype.com)

Identifying a Skype username can be an important lead. It could direct you toward additional searches of the newly found data. Unfortunately, usernames are not obviously available when researching a real name on Skype. However, a quick method will reveal any Skype username when searching by name or email address. While logged in to a Skype account within the website or application, navigate to the search area. This section allows you to enter a real name or email address, and then conducts a search of the Skype user directory. Any results will appear immediately below. Clicking on these results displays the user's basic profile details including a photo. If the user chose not to include a photo, a silhouette graphic appears. Right-click on either image format and choose to "Open image in a new tab" (Chrome) or "View image" (Firefox). The new tab will contain the image that was already available. However, the address in the URL will reveal the Skype username of the target.

University Homepages

These automated searches for usernames can be very productive. However, they will not locate accounts within all online communities. One large untapped resource is the massive presence of university personal web pages and usernames. Most universities issue each student a university email address. These usually follow a standard naming convention such as the following.

lastname.firstname@university.edu

If you can identify the convention that the school uses and know the full name of the target, you can often determine the email address of the student. This address can be searched in order to identify any social networks that may have been missed. Furthermore, the first part of that address is usually the username that would have been issued to the student for a homepage. The target may have never used this email address online and a search result may appear empty. That does not mean there is not data available. The chance that the target created some type of homepage while attending the university is high. Finding the content is easy.

Hopefully, the searches explained earlier have helped in identifying a university that the target attended. A search for the university's website will reveal the domain name that the university uses. For example, Southern Illinois University at Edwardsville's website is siue.edu. We can now take that information and conduct a specific search for any personal pages on their domain. The search should be similar to **site:siue.edu laura**.

I picked the name of Laura at random just to identify any student or employee personal website on the SIUE domain. One of the results was a link to a personal website belonging to "Laura Swanson". The link was similar to **www.siue.edu/~lswanso/**.

This indicates that the naming convention for personal websites is a tilde (~) followed by the first initial and then the first six letters of the last name. If the target of interest was "Scott Golike", the personal website would probably be at **www.siue.edu/~sgolike/**.

We can also assume the possibility of his school issued email account to be sgolike@siue.edu. A few searches using previously discussed techniques should confirm if this address belongs to the target. A search using the email to Facebook profile technique may identify an abandoned profile. We can now navigate to this personal school page and see if there is any content. If there is, we can collect the data and conduct an analysis for intelligence and further research leads. If there is no page at this address, it does not mean that there has never been data there. This only indicates that there is no current content on this website. When students graduate, universities will usually remove all of the personal content from the servers. As discussed previously, this is never an excuse to stop looking. You can now take the URL of a target and conduct a search on The Wayback Machine (wayback.archive.org).

As an example, I can navigate to the first personal link for "Laura Swanson". Figure 24.01 (first) displays a portion of the live page at www.siue.edu/~lswanso/. If this page did not exist and the site contained no content, you could check on The Wayback Machine. Figure 24.01 (second) shows the search results for this personal page and identifies numerous archives dating back to 1997 for this site. Checking all of these options presents the many different versions of the site including one from 2005, as seen in Figure 24.01 (third), and the first capture from 1997, as seen in Figure 24.01 (fourth). This presents new data that would not have been uncovered with conventional searches. When a personal website is located, earlier versions should be archived.

Real World Application: While assisting another agency, information had developed in regard to a suspect in a priority investigation. After all online search attempts revealed nothing of value in locating the subject, a deleted student personal page was located using this method. It contained a list of friends, roommates, family members, and interests that were not previously known. This information helped locate the individual within hours.

It should be noted that some institutions will not follow a standard naming convention for all students and faculty. Additionally, there will be occasions when two or more students will have a name similar enough to create the same username. Usually, there is a plan in place to thwart these duplications. Sometimes it is as simple as adding the number "2" after the username. Universities are not the only places that create personal web pages based on a member name. Several internet service providers allow each subscriber a personal space online as part of the provider's main website. Comcast provides 25 MB of storage in a folder with the title of the subscriber's username. For example, if the email address of the customer was crazycheetah70@comcast.net, the username for the service would be crazycheetah70. The URL to view the personal web page would be as follows.

home.comcast.net/crazycheetah70

The following is a sample list of personal web page addresses from additional internet providers, using "crazycheetah70" as a username example. You should also search for internet providers in the target's area and attempt to find deleted pages on The Wayback Machine, Google Cache, Bing Cache, Yandex Cache, and the other services discussed in Chapter Nine.

360.yahoo.com/crazycheetah70
crazycheetah70.webs.com
crazycheetah70.weebly.com
webpages.charter.net/crazycheetah70
sites.google.com/crazycheetah70
about.me/crazycheetah70
angelfire.com/crazycheetah70
geocities.com/crazycheetah70
reocities.com/crazycheetah70
crazycheetah70.tripod.com
home.earthlink.net/~crazycheetah70
home.comcast.net/~crazycheetah70

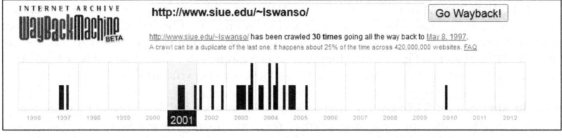

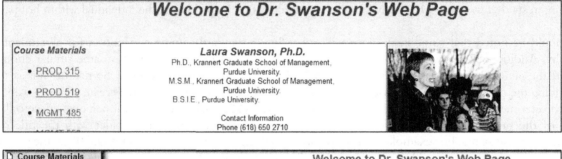

Figure 24.01: Historic versions of university pages.

Ghunt Gmail Verification (gmail-osint.activetk.jp)

You can confirm a username is associated with a Google (Gmail) account with this resource. It can also identify the profile image, last edit date, Gaia ID, the type of account, any gaming connections, and any mapping or reviews information. This service relies on Ghunt, which we previously installed within our VM. We can query with the following URL by replacing inteltechniques with your target data.

https://gmail-osint.activetk.jp/inteltechniques

IntelTechniques Usernames Tool

Similar to the custom email search tool, this page assists with an automated search of some of the techniques mentioned previously. This page allows you to execute manual queries or use the option to attempt all search possibilities. As a reminder, you must allow pop-ups for these pages if you want to use the "Submit All". An online version exists at **https://inteltechniques.com/tools/Username.html**.

CHAPTER TWENTY-FIVE
PEOPLE SEARCH ENGINES

Just as Google and Bing specialize in searching content on the internet, people search engines specialize in finding content about a particular person. Many of these sites utilize search engines such as Google and Bing to help compile the data, and then present a summary style interface that is easy to consume. The sites listed here each have their own strengths and weaknesses. Standard searches are free on all of them; however, each site generates revenue in some form. Usually, this is by displaying advertisements that often appear to be a report function within the site. I do not recommend purchasing any of the premium paid services until all free options have been exhausted.

These details are often focused on targets in the United States, but many services are starting to reach past North America. Searching a target's real name often leads to the discovery of home addresses, telephone numbers, email accounts, and usernames. The following resources are presented in order of most beneficial within my investigations to least. Please note that many of these sites are now blocking access from IP addresses associated with VPNs. This is due to malicious "scraping" behavior by competing sites. If you receive an "access denied" error, it is likely your VPN is being blocked by the service.

True People Search (truepeoplesearch.com)

This service has provided the most comprehensive and consistent free report based on real name. The results usually include current address, previous addresses, telephone numbers (including cellular), email addresses, relatives, and associates. There are no blatant ads, but the "Background Reports" links forward you to a paid service which will likely return the same details. This is my first stop when trying to locate an individual in the U.S. The direct search URL is as follows.

https://www.truepeoplesearch.com/results?name=michael%20bazzell

Fast People Search (fastpeoplesearch.com)

This service appears to rely on the exact same database as True People Search. However, it possesses one huge advantage. True People Search gained a lot of media attention as a "stalking" assistant, which resulted in numerous articles instructing individuals to remove their profiles with an opt-out link. Many people have removed their information, but practically none of them replicated the procedure on Fast People Search. If your target removed his or her profile from the previous option, it might still be present here. The direct search URL is as follows.

https://www.fastpeoplesearch.com/name/michael-bazzell

Nuwber (nuwber.com)

A newcomer in 2017 was Nuwber. I first learned about this service from various members of the privacy forum at my website. They were discussing the importance of removing their own personal details from this site through various opt-out procedures available at the time. I found my own information to be quite accurate. Therefore, this makes for a great OSINT resource. The default landing page allows search of a first and last name. The results are presented by location, and each profile often includes full name, age range, home address, telephone number, and neighbors. The direct search URL is as follows.

https://nuwber.com/search?name=michael-bazzell

Open Data USA (usa-official.com)

This was another service that surprised many privacy-conscious people. A typical entry contains a target's full name, current home address, current home telephone number, email addresses, previous home addresses, additional telephone numbers, possible relatives, and age. I recently located a target's email address from this service, which was not present on any other site. Using the techniques mentioned in previous chapters, I was able to create a full dossier. The default page does not present a direct URL, but the inspector presents following.

https://usa-official.com/Michael-Bazzell

Family Tree Now (familytreenow.com)

In 2016, this website emerged and launched an uproar online. This site is targeted toward those who want to conduct family history research, and its specialty is connecting a person to his or her relatives. The results do not display home addresses, but simply the age of the target and a large list of family members. After gaining a lot of online popularity, many people started complaining about the availability of this sensitive information. While this type of service is nothing new, people were outraged at this violation of their privacy. Since Family Tree Now sources all of their data from public databases, they defended their product, which is still available today. This attention may have been the inspiration for this company to take things to another level with True People Search. The direct search URL is as follows.

https://www.familytreenow.com/search/genealogy/results?first=Michael&last=Bazzell

Cyber Background Check (cyberbackgroundchecks.com)

I suspect this site is associated to the first two entries in this chapter. However, I have located unique data. Therefore, it should be included in our tools. The direct search URL follows.

https://www.cyberbackgroundchecks.com/people/michael-bazzell

Intelius (intelius.com)

Intelius is a premium service that provides reports about people for a fee. Most of the information is from public sources, but some of it appears to come from private databases. Searching for any information on the main website will always link you to a menu of pricing options. The information will never be displayed for free. However, the page that lists the report options does possess some interesting information. This free preview identifies an exact age, possible aliases, cities lived in, previous employers, universities attended, and relatives. If the subject is married, this will usually identify the spouse. In most situations, it will identify the maiden name of the person's wife. Anything that you do not see on this main screen, you must pay a fee. I never recommend purchasing any of this data. Users are usually disappointed with the results. The direct search URL is as follows.

https://www.intelius.com/people-search/Michael-Bazzell

Radaris (radaris.com)

This service has many similarities to Intelius. However, the data set is unique. The business model is to entice you into purchasing an entire profile. I only use the service for the limited free content available in the preview. After searching a name, select the most appropriate target and choose "Full Profile" in the lower right of the result. This will open the full view of any free information. This will often include the target's middle name, age, current address, previous address, landline telephone number, and links to social networks. The Background Check options forward you to a premium website which I do not recommend. The direct URL follows.

https://radaris.com/p/Michael/Bazzell/

Spytox (spytox.com)

This service provides limited data during a free search, but the records are often updated from premium resources. In my experience, the free option only provides city, state, and phone. The direct URL follows.

https://www.spytox.com/michael-bazzell

Search People Free (searchpeoplefree.com)

This database looks awfully familiar to True People Search and Fast People Search, but I occasionally locate an individual present here and nowhere else. One benefit here is that the email addresses identified within the results are hyperlinks. They connect to additional names on occasion. The direct search URL is as follows.

https://www.searchpeoplefree.com/find/michael-bazzell

That's Them (thatsthem.com)

In late 2014, a new website quietly entered the crowded scene of people search services. On the surface, it was just another service that aggregated publicly available information. Consequently, a closer examination revealed That's Them to contain information that is not available anywhere else for free. This service has many options, and most will be discussed in this book. For the purposes of this chapter, I will focus on the "Name and Address" search option in the top menu of the website. Entering a full name with city and state is preferred, but not required. Results often display the person's age range, cell phone number, landline number, full address, religion, financial details, home IP address and any associated email addresses. I searched my own name to test the accuracy of the results. My profile correctly identified similar information as well as the exact VIN number of a previous vehicle. This type of data is impressive without any fees. I have found their details of religion and financial information to be unreliable. Note that the options to purchase additional information are advertisements from third-party companies, and should be avoided. The direct search URL is as follows.

https://thatsthem.com/name/Michael-Bazzell

Spokeo (spokeo.com)

Spokeo is probably the most well-known of all the people search engines. There are two very distinct versions of this service, free and premium. The premium service will provide a large amount of accurate data, but at a cost. The free version provides an interface that is easy to navigate. The results from a target name search will be presented after choosing a state and city. Only the states and cities where the target name has a presence will be shown. Choosing this target will display a profile with various information. Within this data will be several attempts to encourage you to purchase a premium account. Basically, anything that you do not see within this profile will cost you money. Any links from the profile will present a membership plan with pricing. The profile will often display full name, gender, age, and previous cities and states of residency. However, it no longer presents the actual current address. Spokeo is one of many sites which present an animate gif file while you wait on the results. This is unnecessary and is in place to make you believe data is being queried in real time. The following static search URL bypasses this annoyance.

https://www.spokeo.com/Michael-Bazzell?loaded=1

Advanced Background Checks (advancedbackgroundchecks.com)

This is another service which includes advertisements for premium options. It appears to present data very similar to Intelius. Surprisingly, the majority of their data archive is free without any payment. The main search results appear redacted and entire addresses and telephone numbers are masked. With many other services, clicking these details prompt the user for payment. Instead, this service opens a new page revealing the entire record. This often includes home address, home landline telephone number, age, and relatives. Clicking the "See full info" button reveals previous addresses, additional telephone numbers, and aliases. Overall, this service is extremely useful for U.S. targets. The direct search URL is as follows.

https://www.advancedbackgroundchecks.com/names/michael-bazzell

Yasni (yasni.com)

On the surface, Yasni appears to be another standard people search engine. Much of the content received will be duplicate data, but there are a few areas where Yasni works differently. The home page will give three search options. For most OSINT purposes, the last option is the desired search. It will accept a real name or username and forward you to a results page. Real name search will present a large number of links associated with your target's name. As with other engines, many of these results will be about a person other than your target. The first box on the results page will include a "lives/works in" option that will display the cities of the users identified with the search. Clicking on a location that looks appropriate for your target will load a new results page that will provide all search results about your specific target. Yasni will identify news articles, websites, and social networks related to your target. By default, the search is conducted internationally. Yasni is a German site and searching outside of the United States is one of the strengths of the service. The search bar includes an option to filter the results by specific countries, but the United States is not listed as an option. If you have a target that lives in another country, Yasni is a great tool. The direct search URL is as follows.

https://www.yasni.com/jason+edison/check+people

Zaba Search (zabasearch.com)

This site appears to have several search options at first glance. Unfortunately, all but one will forward to an Intelius site, which will require a fee. There is one very specific free option on this page. Providing any real name and state of residence will provide a results page with full name, date of birth, address, and phone number. In my experience, this often includes unlisted telephone numbers and addresses. Clicking on practically anything else on this results page will take you to a sponsored link. When I use this resource, I only rely on the information obtained on the first result page. The direct search URL is as follows.

https://www.zabasearch.com/people/michael+bazzell/

People Search Now (peoplesearchnow.com)

This database appears to have the same parent company as True People Search, and possesses the same data. However, this search should be included in the event that a target has removed details from other related websites. Due to increased awareness of exposed personal information, I am seeing many people request removal of personal online data. The direct URL is as follows.

https://www.peoplesearchnow.com/person/michael-bazzell

WebMii (webmii.com)

This service emphasizes information associated with social networks. I have never located any home addresses or telephone numbers, but I have found online images that were not available on any other search engine. This is not the most productive option, but one to consider when desperate for details. The direct search URL is as follows.

http://webmii.com/people?n="Michael%20Bazzell"

Social Searcher (social-searcher.com)

I explained this service within the username chapter, but it also applies here. It focuses on social media presence, including mentions within posts. The direct search URL is as follows.

https://www.social-searcher.com/search-users/?q6=Michael+Bazzell

Truth Finder (truthfinder.com)

There is nothing very special about this service, as it will likely have data similar to the other sites already mentioned. However, there is one major annoyance. When you search this site, you are bombarded by fake progress meters that insinuate that a huge report is being prepared about your target. On average, a real name search takes over 14 minutes due to these constant "please be patient while we find more details" notifications. The solution to this is to submit a direct URL as follows.

https://www.truthfinder.com/results/?firstName=Michael&lastName=Bazzell&state=ALL

People By Name (peoplebyname.com)

The title of this site is misleading. It only allows the query of a telephone number, which is not beneficial when searching by name. However, the following URL structure displays all profiles associated with the name.

http://www.peoplebyname.com/people/Bazzell/Michael

White Pages (whitepages.com)

This is the official White Pages website that will conduct a reverse name or address search. The results often include known residents and neighbors. This data is pulled from public information and is rarely complete. The direct search URL is as follows.

https://www.whitepages.com/name/Michael-Bazzell

Clustr Maps (clustrmaps.com)

There is nothing too exciting here, as it is more of the same. Since this service offers a direct URL query, we should add it to our arsenal. The URL structure follows.

https://clustrmaps.com/persons/Michael-Bazzell

Public Records (publicrecords.directory)

This service displays a few unique details about an individual. It taps into various voter registration databases, campaign contribution disclosures, and vehicle registration data. None of these categories appear consistently within search results, but a search here is always justified. There is no direct URL submission option, so a manual search is your only option.

Rocket Reach (rocketreach.co)

This impressive site does not identify home addresses. Instead, it focuses on business details likely scraped from LinkedIn and online resumes. Conducting a search on the website only presents a login form and an account is mandatory. However, Google can help us. I conducted the following search.

site:rocketreach.co "michael bazzell"

This resulted in three Rocket Reach profiles, all of which could be viewed without an active account. The first was someone else with my name. It disclosed the following details.

Location: Baltimore, Maryland, United States
Work: Senior Artist @ Firaxis Games, Senior Artist @ MicroProse Software, Artist @ Innerprise Software
Education: Maryland Institute College of Art, Bachelor Of Fine Arts (Communication, Illustration), 1985 - 1989
Michael Bazzell's Email: @firaxis.com @kryptotoyz.com @erols.com
Michael Bazzell's Phone Numbers: 410667XXXX 410726XXXX

The site then teases the ability to uncover the redacted results for free. However, this requires a free account.

Official USA (officialusa.com)

While many targets will not be present within this data set, those who are will be quite exposed. A typical result includes full name, home address, email address, phone number, and home sale records. This service works best when queries are submitted manually. Submit your target's name in the "Search for all governments" field on the main page and doing so will open a results page which will allow you to filter and refine your query.

Addresses (addresses.com)

This service appears to be using other public datasets, but the redactions of details seem to be less than the other premium sites. It is common to see full telephone numbers, addresses, and family connections. The URL structure follows.

https://www.addresses.com/people/michael-bazzell

ID Crawl (idcrawl.com)

This service attempts to build a full online profile from a name. Results are hit or miss, but the following direct URL access makes for an easy query.

https://www.idcrawl.com/michael-bazzell

Classmates (classmates.com)

Classmates is a very underrated resource for the internet searcher. Unfortunately, you must create a free account to take advantage of the worthy information inside the site. This free account can contain fictitious information and it is necessary to complete a profile on the site to access the premium features. After you are logged in, you can search by first and last name. If you know the school that was attended, the results will be much more accurate. This should provide the school attended as well as the years the target attended the school. My new interest in this site is due to the availability of scanned yearbooks. The collection is far from complete, but there are a surprising number of complete yearbooks available to browse. Analyzing this content can be very time consuming, as the yearbook must be manually browsed one page at a time. The information obtained should be unique from any internet search previously conducted.

Rebate Tracking

I find this technique more "interesting" than valuable to an investigation, but you might locate a nugget of information which assists you. As an example, let's look at the store Menards. Menards is an American home improvement company which pushes rebates in order to make products appear low-priced. When you buy a product, you can retrieve a rebate slip and mail it off. In a few weeks, numerous checks in small amounts begin arriving at your home. This game provides small discounts, but at what risk? This is where the online rebate center comes in. Let's start with a visit to https://rebateinternational.com/RebateInternational/tracking.do. This page allows you to enter a first initial, last name, numeric portion of an address, and postal code of your target. This result appears similar to Figure 25.01.

Redeemed Date	Rebate #	Description	Purchase Date	Rebate Amount	Rebate Status	Check #
	668	DEFENSE ZONE SANITIZER	03/17/2021	$3.55	Mailed on 04/21/2021	XXXXXX5347
	658	SAVE 11%	03/17/2021	$1.09	Mailed on 04/21/2021	XXXXXX5347
	657	SAVE 11%	03/10/2021	$4.31	Mailed on 04/21/2021	XXXXXX5347
03/10/2021	633	DEFENSE ZONE HAND SANITIZ	12/28/2020	$2.99	Mailed on 03/05/2021	XXXXXX0196
12/28/2020	554	SAVE 11%	05/26/2020	$3.93	Mailed	XXXXXX5704

Figure 25.01: A Menards rebate tracking screen.

We now see the purchased items, purchase dates, rebate amounts, and payment details. This gives us a glimpse into the shopping habits of the target and could lead to patterns of behavior which might expose someone's routines. It could also provide pretext value. I could initiate an email phishing attack focused on a specific purchased item announcing a problem with the rebate. That would be so targeted that the recipient would probably click whatever link I sent. This rebate service even stores all purchases within a static URL which is prone to abuse. If my name were Michael Smith and I lived at 1212 Main Street in Houston, Texas, my URL would be the following.

https://rebateinternational.com/RebateInternational/trackResults/M/Smith/1212/77089

Note that this URL does not require any credentialing and is open to brute-force scraping. Next, let's take a look at Lowe's home improvement. They offer a rebate confirmation website at https://lowes-rebates.com/en-us/RebateStatus which allows entry of a cellular number or home address, as seen in Figure 25.02.

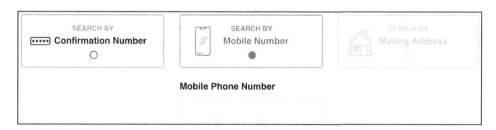

Figure 25.02: A Lowe's rebate tracking entry.

This allows us to potentially translate an unknown cell number into a name and address or vice-versa, as well as obtain shopping history of the target. These two examples are only a small selection of the possibilities. You will find online portals for Micro Center, Budweiser, Miller, Kohls, Auto Stores, and other retail establishments. I have found the following three Google searches to assist with finding companies which offer similar options.

https://www.google.com/search?q=intitle:"rebate center"
https://www.google.com/search?q="track+my+rebate"
https://www.google.com/search?q="track+your+rebate"

Utility Inquiries

If you know your target's telephone number and postal code, you may be able to uncover an entire home address. Consider the following example with the home telephone and internet service provider CenturyLink. The following address connects to their internet troubleshooting page.

https://www.centurylink.com/home/help/internet/test-your-internet-at-the-network-interface.html

Clicking "Open Troubleshooter" in the lower right area opens a query page asking for the telephone number and postal code. Submitting this data then presents a confirmation screen which includes the customer's name, full address, and telephone number. I have found many local utilities which offer similar search portals.

IntelTechniques Names Tool

The abundance of free person search tools can get overwhelming. They each have strengths and weaknesses, and none of them are consistent on accurate results. In years past, I would manually visit each site and enter my target information. This would usually result in small, yet valuable, pieces of information from each service. Today, I use a custom search tool that I created to search all possible sites simultaneously. This free tool is in your offline downloads and online at **https://inteltechniques.com/tools/Name.html**. You can either enter the first and last name of your target within the search fields of each service, or enter this information only once at the final set of search fields. This latter option will launch several new tabs and conduct your search across each service. During my live training courses, I am often questioned about the absence of the ability to enter a middle initial or name. While I could make this an option, I find that a lot of people search websites do not always possess a middle name. Entering this data could harm an investigation by omitting valuable results.

Resumes

Resume searching was mentioned earlier. Those methods will identify many documents, especially if the word "resume" is inside the file or file name. These results are only a portion of available content that could be extremely valuable to your investigation. I believe that resumes are an ideal target since they usually contain sensitive information that is not posted anywhere else. Many people will include a cellular number and personal email address on a resume, but would never consider placing these details on a social network. If the resume is publicly available, regardless of whether the target realizes this, we can gather good intelligence. The following techniques aim to assist in locating this valuable data. Detailed searches within Google or Bing will identify many resumes hosted publicly on websites and cloud-based document storage services. If my target's name is Michael Bazzell, I have found the following exact searches valuable on Google, Bing, and Yandex.

"Michael Bazzell" "Resume"
"Michael Bazzell" "Curriculum Vitae"
"Michael Bazzell" "CV"
"Michael Bazzell" "Resume" filetype:doc
"Michael Bazzell" "Curriculum Vitae" filetype:doc
"Michael Bazzell" "CV" filetype:doc
"Michael Bazzell" "Resume" filetype:pdf
"Michael Bazzell" "Curriculum Vitae" filetype:pdf
"Michael Bazzell" "CV" filetype:pdf
"Michael Bazzell" "Resume" site:docs.google.com
"Michael Bazzell" "Curriculum Vitae" site:docs.google.com
"Michael Bazzell" "CV" site:docs.google.com

While these queries will likely locate any resumes with text, they will fail on many resume images. Numerous resume hosting websites have realized that various data scraping engines scour their resume collection and "steal" their content. This has encouraged some services to store images of resumes that do not contain text that can be easily searched. While this is a decent layer of protection, it is not enough to keep out of Google results. Since Google scans images for Optical Character Recognition (OCR), it knows what words are within an image. After conducting the previous queries within traditional search engines, attempt them through Google Images (images.google.com). A search of "Mary Johnson" "Resume" on Google Images revealed hundreds of images of resumes. A manual inspection of each identified many pieces of sensitive information.

Indeed (resumes.indeed.com)

Indeed has a powerful collection of resume data. Because the term "resume" is not present in any of the content pages, you will likely not obtain this data during your standard searches. Entering your target name on Indeed under the "Find Candidates" option may present new results. Contact information is usually redacted. However, detailed work experience, education, and location are commonly present.

Ripoff Report (ripoffreport.com)

If your target conducts any type of business with the public, he or she will likely upset someone at some point. If your target regularly provides bad service or intentionally commits fraud within the business, there are likely many upset victims. Ripoff Report is a user-submitted collection of complaints about businesses and individuals. I have had investigations into shady people and businesses where these reviews were beneficial.

Gift Registries

Decades ago, people were surprised at the gifts presented to them after a wedding or birth. Today, we create online registries identifying the exact products desired, and within moments someone can purchase and ship the "thoughtful" gift with very little effort. As an investigator, I have always enjoyed the plethora of personal details within these registries, which tend to stay online long after the related event. Before identifying the best resources, let's take a look at the types of details we can acquire from some random targets.

- **Partner Name**: When I am investigating someone, that person usually knows they are under a microscope. He or she tends to stop posting to social media and starts scrubbing any online details. However, their partner tends to ignore the threat of investigation and continues to upload sensitive information applicable to the target. Therefore, online wedding and baby registries help me identify the most lucrative target aside from the original suspect. In an example from the wedding registry website theknot.com, I received over 200 results for Michael Wilson, which also includes the name of the future spouse.
- **Maiden Name**: In the example above, the results only identified future weddings. However, modifying the year in the search menu allows us to view past weddings. This will divulge a woman's maiden name. This can be beneficial in order to better locate a Facebook page or other family members that may be off my radar. I can also use this to then search old yearbooks, criminal details, and previous addresses.
- **Date / State**: Many counties will only share marriage certificates if the requestor knows the exact names of each party and the exact date of the event. We have everything we need in order to file a request. Marriage certificates often include full details of all parents, witnesses, and the officiant. Furthermore, I now have their anniversary date which can be helpful during a phishing attack or social engineering attempt. You might be surprised at the number of people that use their anniversary as a security question to an online account.
- **Ceremony Details**: The Knot and other wedding registry sites offer the couple a free website to announce details about the upcoming (or past) event. This usually includes an embellished story about how they met, fell in love, and he proposed. While this could be good knowledge for social engineering, I am usually more interested in the wedding party. This will usually include the closest friends of my target, which will be next on my investigation list.

- **Items**: While it may be fun to look at the items desired by a couple, there is much we can learn about their lives based on these details. In an example from Figure 25.03, I now know that a random Michael Wilson, who is getting married in San Antonio, will be going to his honeymoon in Maui (#2), snorkeling (#3), at the airport carrying a Lowepro backpack (#4), checking red/black suitcases (#5), capturing everything on a Canon HD camcorder (#6), dining at the Lahaina Grill (#7), and staying at a fancy nearby hotel (#8). Other recent examples associated with actual targets identify the types of phones used, vehicles driven, and subjects of interest. While The Knot requires both a first name and last name to conduct a search, providing two asterisks (**) as the first name will present every entry online including the provided last name.
- **Children**: The items within a baby registry will usually provide little to no value. Knowing the brand of diapers preferred or favorite crib style has never helped me in the past. However, knowing a due date and location of the target can be beneficial for future searching. Unfortunately, The Bump only allows searching of upcoming births, and not any past profiles. Fortunately, Google has our backs. A Google search of site:registry.thebump.com "Michael Wilson" revealed multiple baby registries associated with Michael Wilson.

The most fruitful registries in regard to identifying personal preferences of a target are the various gift registries. Of all these, Amazon is the most popular. The following are the most common wedding, baby, and gift registries, with direct links to the most appropriate search pages. I highly encourage you to conduct a detailed Google "Site" search after attempting the proper method.

The Knot: https://www.theknot.com/registry/couplesearch
The Bump: https://registry.thebump.com/babyregistrysearch
Amazon Baby: https://www.amazon.com/baby-reg/homepage/
Amazon Wedding: https://www.amazon.com/wedding/
Walmart Wedding: https://www.walmart.com/lists/find-wedding-registry
Walmart Baby: https://www.walmart.com/registry/baby/search
Target Wedding: https://www.target.com/gift-registry/
Target Baby: https://www.target.com/gift-registry/baby-registry
Ikea Wedding: https://info.ikea-usa.com/giftregistry
Bed Bath & Beyond Wedding: https://bedbathandbeyond.myregistry.com/
Macy's Wedding: https://www.macys.com/registry/wedding/registrysearch
Registry Finder: https://registryfinder.com
My Registry: https://www.myregistry.com

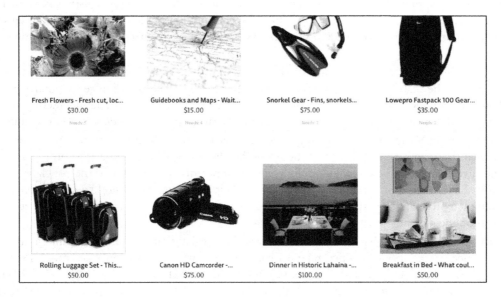

Figure 25.03: A search result from a gift registry website.

Find a Grave (findagrave.com)

While I assume that your goal is to find living targets, you should also have a resource for locating proof of deceased individuals. I have used this website numerous times to locate the graves of recently deceased people. While not necessarily "proof" of death, it provides a great lead toward locating a death certificate and living family members. In 2021, I began finding better results at **People Legacy** (peoplelegacy.com).

Addresses

The target of your investigation may be an address of your suspect. You may want to know who else lives at a residence. The name search websites which were previously discussed allow search of a residential address.

Voter Registration (www.blackbookonline.info/USA-Voter-Records.aspx - voterrecords.com)

Many people will have their address and telephone number unlisted in public telephone books. This prevents their information from appearing on some websites. If any of these people are registered voters, their address may still be public. In order to locate this data, you will need to connect to the county clerk of the county of residence. The link here will display a list of all fifty states. Clicking the state of the target will present all of the counties with known online databases of voter registration content. These will often display the full name of the voter and full address. This can be sorted by name or address depending on what information you have about the target. Later chapters present additional voter registration search options.

Unclaimed Property

Every state in the U.S. possesses an unclaimed property website. Common forms of unclaimed property include savings or checking accounts, stocks, uncashed dividends, online payments, refunds, and leftover utility balances. Most of these pages only require a last name to conduct a search. The results almost always include full name, home address, property type, and amount owed. This can provide a great search resource, and a possible pretext for a phone call. A complete collection of these sites with easy access to each state is at **Unclaimed** (unclaimed.org).

Google (google.com)

If all else fails, or you believe you are missing something, check Google. Searching the address should identify any leftover information about your target address. When searching, place the street address in quotes excluding the city. An example search may appear similar to "1234 Main" "Bethalto" IL. This chapter is heavily focused on U.S. targets. If you have a subject of interest outside of America, I have found the following to be beneficial.

Australia: www.peoplesearch.com.au
Canada: www.canadapages.com
Canada: www.infobel.com/en/Canada
France: www.infobel.com/en/France
Germany: www.infobel.com/en/Germany

Spain: www.infobel.com/en/Spain
UK: www.192.com
UK: www.peopletraceuk.com
UK: www.gov.uk/government

Premium Search Option: Skopenow (Skopenow.com/IntelTechniques)

The previous resources are free to use. However, your result accuracy will vary. Many free sites will present outdated information which was scoured from unreliable resources. If you are looking for a paid provider which can display current home addresses, telephone numbers, email addresses, associates, and much more information, I highly recommend Skopenow. You will need to create an account and be vetted, but the results are way better than any free resources. Pricing for this service varies, but connecting via the previous URL informs Skopenow that you learned about them through this book, and they will know that you crave OSINT information from them.

CHAPTER TWENTY-SIX
TELEPHONE NUMBERS

There are hundreds of websites that claim the ability to search for information on telephone numbers and addresses. These vary from amazingly accurate results to sites that only include advertisements. If I have a target telephone number, there are three phases of my search. First, I want to identify the type of number and provider. The type could be landline, cellular or internet, and the provider could be the company supplying the service. Next, I want to identify any subscriber information such as the name and address associated with the account. Finally, I want to locate any online web content with a connection to the target number. This can all lead to more intelligence and additional searches. The majority of cellular numbers can now be identified if they are registered in someone's name. If you have an address, you will want to identify any associated people or telephone numbers. This chapter will highlight the sites which can assist with these tasks.

Carrier Identification

Ten years ago, I often queried telephone number porting websites to identify the provider of my target's telephone number. This would identify the cellular company that supplied service to my suspect. I would use that information within my court order to demand subscriber data about the target. Knowing the provider was essential as to not waste time requesting records from companies that had no data to provide. The websites used back then have either disappeared, or now charge a substantial fee for access. Five years ago, I noticed that an overwhelming amount of my target telephone numbers were connected to Voice Over Internet Protocol (VOIP) services such as Google Voice and Twilio. This would often be indicated by a result of "Broadband" or "Internet" instead of something obvious such as "Verizon". Until recently, the absence of a specific provider was a hurdle during investigations. Today, we have more sophisticated services that can identify exact provider details on practically any number.

Free Carrier Lookup (freecarrierlookup.com)

I begin with this option because it has been the most stable and does not limit searching as others do. This site requests any domestic or international telephone number and produces a report which includes the country, type of service, and provider associated with the number. While many online services can identify the provider of a cellular or landline number, this option provides the best details about VOIP numbers. I submitted several telephone numbers associated with various providers that I could personally confirm. The following identifies the results of these searches. The first column represents the provider as I knew it, the second column is the type, and the third is the provider displayed by Free Carrier Lookup. This is far from complete, but I wanted to demonstrate the ability to convert internet-based numbers into identifiable companies.

Verizon	Mobile	Verizon Wireless
AT&T	Mobile	AT&T Wireless
Google Voice	VOIP	Google/Level 3
Sudo	VOIP	Twilio/Level 3 (SMS-Sybase) (MMS-SVR)
Blur	Landline	Twilio/Level 3 Communications
TextNow	VOIP	Enflick/Bandwidth.com (SVR)
On/Off	VOIP	Peerless Network

If this service cannot provide the data you need, or if you want another source to provide more confidence in the result, you should also consider the sites **Carrier Lookup** (carrierlookup.com) and **Phone Carrier Check** (phonecarriercheck.com). If both of these services disappear by the time you need them, a Google search of "carrier lookup" should provide new alternatives.

NANPA (nationalnanpa.com)

This site is dedicated to the North American Number Plan for switched telephone networks for the US, Canada, and the Caribbean. An advantage of this service is that the data is being provided by the number authority themselves and not an untrusted third party. NANPA allows us to identify the original carrier by searching the number block (the first six digits of the 10 digit phone number) from their Central Office Code Utilized Report which is available at https://nationalnanpa.com/reports/reports_cocodes.html. Although this will only identify the provider of the number block, those in law enforcement can call 877-416-6551 to find out if the number has been recently ported to an alternate carrier. While other carrier identification services can be useful, this service tends to be the most accurate.

Scout (scout.tel/phone-number-lookup)

This newer service provides a few pieces of information about a telephone number which I have not seen available anywhere else. The following is a partial result of a target telephone number query.

administrative_area_level_3	Alton Township
administrative_area_level_2	Madison County
administrative_area_level_1	Illinois
operating_company_name	AT&T
line_type	mobile
ported	false
risk_rating	unlikely
risk_level	28

We now know that this number was not ported from another carrier; it is a mobile number; and it possesses a low risk rating. These ratings increase for VOIP, forwarding, and masked numbers, and might indicate that the number you are searching is not assigned to any specific individual. A free API key from RapidAPI is required.

Caller ID Databases

Once you have identified the provider, you should focus on the subscriber data associated with the number. We will tackle this in several different ways, as many things changed in 2019. First, we should focus on the most reliable options, which often require registration for a free trial. This chapter becomes quite technical quickly, but the tools at the end will simplify everything.

In 2013, I began experimenting with reverse caller ID data. These are the same databases that identify a telephone number on your landline caller ID display. Often, this will include the name associated with the number. Until recently, this was something that only appeared on landline numbers, but that has changed. Now many cellular telephone numbers have name information associated with them. This name information is usually extracted from the cellular telephone service provider. I was immediately shocked at the accuracy of these results while searching cellular telephone numbers that were otherwise untraceable. On many of my investigations, this technique has eliminated the need to obtain court subpoenas to discover subscriber information.

The reason we can access this data is because it is necessary for telephone systems that do not already possess caller ID options. New systems that operate over the internet, referred to as VOIP systems (Voice Over Internet Protocol), do not receive caller ID data natively. This is something that we have taken for granted while it was provided by our telephone companies. Today, many businesses must purchase access to this data from resellers. This presents us with an opportunity.

I scoured the internet for every business that provides bulk caller ID data to private companies. Some offer a free website for testing; some require you to submit queries through their servers; and others make you register for a free trial. I have tested all of them and identified those that are easy to access and give the best results.

First, I will focus only on easy and reliable ways to search an individual number through specific web addresses. I explained more robust options via APIs, including an automated script, within Section One.

Twilio (twilio.com/lookup)

This company was briefly discussed in Section One. A feature of their internet-based phone service is the ability to identify incoming calls through caller ID. Fortunately for us, they provide a page on their site that allows queries against their database, but it requires you to register for a free trial account. Locate the "Sign up" button and create a free account. Click the confirmation link in the email and you should be all set. If you are required to verify a telephone number, Google Voice numbers are accepted. You should be presented with a $15 credit within Twilio. This should provide numerous searches.

Once you are logged in to an account, click "Explore Products" in the left menu. Scroll down to the "Lookup" feature on the right. This is the screen which allows querying of numbers, and you may want to bookmark this page. I usually only select the "Include caller name" unless I want confirmation of the carrier. These searches are $0.01 each, which means you should be able to conduct 1500 queries on this single trial. While a bit of an annoyance to set up the first time, the work is justified. Make sure you have a valid email and Google Voice account ready before registering. If Twilio demands to know why you created an account, I would not mention OSINT or this book. They often cater to people who own a "small businesses which wants to transition from landlines to VOIP telephone service". That was a hint. If pushed further, tell them you are a developer who has been asked to review their API, and explain you will only need internal testing without an outside number.

On the Lookup search page, insert the target number and allow the page to generate a result, which will appear directly below. The result will include the type of provider and any name associated with the billing. If I only had one website to search, this would be it. Below is an actual redacted result.

```
PHONE NUMBER      +16180000000
NATIONAL FORMAT   (618) 000-0000
COUNTRY CODE      US
CALLER NAME       M Bazel
CALLER TYPE       null
CARRIER NAME      Google (Grand Central) - Level3 - SVR
CARRIER TYPE      voip
```

There are many other caller ID services, but they all require usage of API keys via Terminal commands. I explained more on this in Section One.

Apeiron (apeiron.io/info)

This service possesses data similar to Twilio, but is completely free and available through a traditional website. The results are not as comprehensive as the previous option, but could be valuable if cannot use Twilio.

Truecaller (truecaller.com)

This service stands alone as the most creative telephone number lookup service. True Caller is an app for smart devices that displays caller ID information of incoming calls. If you receive a call on your phone, and the number is not in your contacts, True Caller searches its database and provides any results on your screen. You can then choose to accept or deny the call. This is fairly standard and is not the interesting aspect of this service. The fascinating part to me is the source of their caller database. It is mostly crowd-sourced.

When you install the app, you give it permission to collect all of your contacts and upload them to the original database. Basically, millions of users have uploaded their contact lists for the world to see. The next amazing thing to me is the ability to search within this data on the True Caller website. You must connect to the service via a covert Microsoft or Google account, but that is not difficult. The first time you sign in make certain that "Enhanced Search" is not checked and "I reside in California" is selected. Doing so will reduce the amount of data collected from you by Truecaller during your session. When I first found this service, I was skeptical. I entered the cellular number of my government issued cellular telephone expecting to see no results. The response was "Mike Bazell". My jaw dropped. My super-secret number was visible to the world. This means that someone in my circle, likely another government employee, installed True Caller on his or her phone and had my information in their contacts. Until someone else populates data for this number, it will always be present in the database. Until someone else populates data for this number, it will always be present in the database.

Real World Application: During my final year of government investigations, I queried a target number associated with a homicide through this service. The result was "Drug Dealer Matt". One of the target's customers must have installed True Caller. One of three potential suspects was named Matt, who earned our spotlight, and later an arrest.

Spy Dialer (spydialer.com)

This service offers a typical telephone number search tool, which also appears to extract data from crowd-sourced databases. I suspect that much of this data was acquired many years ago, but this can still be beneficial. Sometimes, I want historical data about a number, even if it is no longer issued to the target.

Caller ID Test (calleridtest.com)

This site was designed to input a telephone number and test the Caller ID display feature. It is nothing more than a standard lookup service, but I have found the data to be unique from other sources on some occasions. Unfortunately, I have also found the availability of this service to be unreliable. While the site is usually present, the results don't always populate. However, this resource should be checked when others have failed.

Telephone Search Websites

In previous editions of this book, I summarized a handful of people search websites which allowed the query of a telephone number. These sites all possess unique data sets and each should be searched. Most of the results originate from sources such as property tax data, marketing leaks, phonebooks, and various data breaches. Instead of explaining each site, which becomes quite redundant, I will display the static URL of a search submission. Many of these links avoid unnecessary loading screens and advertisements. This will help us with the automated tool at the end. Overall, we cannot control the results, and telephone search is mostly "what you see is what you get". Replace the demo number (618-462-0000) with your target number.

411 https://www.411.com/phone/1-618-462-0000
800 Notes https://800notes.com/Phone.aspx/1-618-462-0000
Advanced Background Checks https://www.advancedbackgroundchecks.com/618-462-0000
America Phonebook http://www.americaphonebook.com/reverse.php?number=6184620000
Caller Smart https://www.callersmart.com/phone-number/618-462-0000
Cyber Background Checks: https://www.cyberbackgroundchecks.com/phone/618-462-0000
Dehashed https://dehashed.com/search?query=6184620000
Fast People Search https://www.fastpeoplesearch.com/618-462-0000
Info Tracer https://infotracer.com/phone-lookup/results/?phone=6184620000
Numpi https://numpi.com/phone-info/6184620000
Nuwber https://nuwber.com/search/phone?phone=6184620000
OK Caller https://www.okcaller.com/6184620000
People Search Now https://www.peoplesearchnow.com/phone/618-462-0000
Phone Owner https://phoneowner.com/phone/6184620000
Search People Free https://www.searchpeoplefree.com/phone-lookup/618-462-0000
Spytox https://www.spytox.com/reverse-phone-lookup/618-462-0000

Sync.me https://sync.me/search/?number=16184620000
That's Them https://thatsthem.com/phone/618-462-0000
True People Search https://www.truepeoplesearch.com/results?phoneno=(618)462-0000
US Phonebook https://www.usphonebook.com/618-462-0000
White Pages https://www.whitepages.com/phone/1-618-462-0000
WhoseNo https://www.whoseno.com/US/6184620000
Yellow Pages https://people.yellowpages.com/whitepages/phone-lookup?phone=6184620000
Zabasearch https://www.zabasearch.com/phone/6184620000
Google https://www.google.com/search?q=618-462-0000
Bing https://www.bing.com/search?q=618-462-0000
Yandex https://yandex.com/search/?text=618-462-0000

Search Engines

Google and Bing were once a great place to find basic information about a target phone number. These sites can still provide valuable information, but the amount of spam that will display in the results is overwhelming. Many of the links presented will link to sites that will charge a fee for any information associated. This information is usually the same content that could have been located with an appropriate free search. I do not recommend giving in to these traps. While we can't ignore a traditional search of telephone numbers, we can customize the queries in order to achieve the best results. Before explaining advanced telephone owner identification, we should take a look at appropriate search engine structure.

Most people use traditional search engines as a first step toward identifying the owner of a telephone number. The number is usually provided in a standard format such as 202-555-1212. This can confuse some search engines because a hyphen (-) is often recognized as an operator to exclude data. Some engines might view that query as a search for 202 but not 555 or 1212. Additionally, this search might identify a website that possesses 202-555-1212 within the content but not one that contains (202) 555.1212. If this is your target number, all of the following should be searched in order to exhaust all possibilities. The quotation marks are important to prevent the hyphen from being seen as an operator.

"2025551212"	"202 555 1212"	"(202) 555.1212"	"(202)555.1212"
"202-555-1212"	"(202) 5551212"	"(202)5551212"	
"202.555.1212"	"(202) 555-1212"	"(202)555-1212"	

This may seem ridiculous, but I am not done. Many websites forbid users to post a telephone number, such as many auction sites, but people try to trick this restriction. They will type out a portion of their number to disclose contact information. While not a complete list of options, the following should also be searched.

"two zero two five five five one two one two"	"202 five five five one two one two"
"two zero two five five five 1212"	"202 555 one two one two"
"two zero two 555 one two one two"	"202 five five five 1212"
"two zero two 555 1212"	

This list would not capture a post that included (202) 555 twelve twelve, but you get the point. After submitting these through Google, you should attempt each through Bing. In my effort to always provide search tools which automate and simplify these techniques, I have added this feature to your telephone tools presented at the end of the chapter. The right-middle portion of this page, displayed later in Figure 26.03, allows you to enter a numerical and written target telephone number. Clicking the submit button launches a series of JavaScript commands that launch eight new tabs within your browser. The first four are custom Google searches with the target data and the last four repeat the process on Bing. The following four searches are conducted on both services, using the example data entered previously.

"2025551212"OR"202-555-1212"OR"202.555.1212"OR"202 555 1212"

"(202) 5551212"OR"(202) 555-1212"OR"(202) 555.1212"OR"(202)5551212"OR"(202)555-1212"OR"(202)555.1212"

"two zero two five five five one two one two"OR"two zero two five five five 1212"OR"two zero two 555 one two one two"OR"two zero two 555 1212"

"202 five five five one two one two"OR"202 555 one two one two"OR"202 five five five 1212"

Notice that these queries use quotation marks to obtain exact results and the OR operator to search multiple options independently from each other. You will likely receive many false positives with this method, but you are less likely to miss any relevant results.

Sly Dial (slydial.com)

This service contacts the cellular provider of the target telephone number and sends you straight to the outgoing voicemail message. This can allow you to hear their voice and name without ringing the phone and hoping they do not pick up. Sly Dial does not work through a website and you do not need to create an account to use the service. Instead, you must call a general Sly Dial telephone number and follow the automated prompts. You must listen to a brief advertisement before your call is placed. Finally, the service will play the target's outgoing voicemail message through this audible telephone call. Since a website is not involved, there is no option to download an audio file of the call.

Sly Dial does not usually ring the suspect's telephone. It will likely not show "missed call" or any other indicator that a call occurred. In my testing, less that 5 percent of the attempts actually cause the target telephone to ring only one time. Calling the missed call back reveals nothing about the identity of the number. Ultimately, there is a very small chance that the target will know that someone attempted a call. In the rare occurrence that the telephone rings, the target will never know the identity of the person making the calls. To use the Sly Dial service, call 267-759-3425 (267-SLYDIAL) from any telephone service including landlines, cellular lines, or VOIP. Follow the directions during the call. If this number does not work, visit slydial.com for updates. I want to stress the following one additional time. Use these services at your own risk. If accidentally notifying your target that you are conducting these types of activities could compromise your investigation, avoid this technique.

Old Phone Book (oldphonebook.com)

I first noticed this niche service in late 2018. It provides historical White Pages landline listings from 1994-2014. The sources are official databases collected from many years of telephone CD-ROMs. These were purchased by various companies throughout several decades as a more convenient option than traditional phone books. The data is quite impressive, and the following direct URLs allow us to add these to our tools. Results include historic addresses attached to each year. Figure 26.01 displays an actual redacted result from the official website. This provides an old address, and assumes that the target moved to a new address between 1998 and 2001. This search is vital for background checks.

http://www.oldphonebook.com/searchphone2.php?syear=1994&sphone=6184620000
http://www.oldphonebook.com/searchphone2.php?syear=1995&sphone=6184620000
http://www.oldphonebook.com/searchphone2.php?syear=1996&sphone=6184620000
http://www.oldphonebook.com/searchphone2.php?syear=1997&sphone=6184620000
http://www.oldphonebook.com/searchphone2.php?syear=1998&sphone=6184620000
http://www.oldphonebook.com/searchphone2.php?syear=2001&sphone=6184620000
http://www.oldphonebook.com/searchphone2.php?syear=2002&sphone=6184620000
http://www.oldphonebook.com/searchphone2.php?syear=2003&sphone=6184620000
http://www.oldphonebook.com/searchphone2.php?syear=2007&sphone=6184620000

http://www.oldphonebook.com/searchphone2.php?syear=2008&sphone=6184620000
http://www.oldphonebook.com/searchphone2.php?syear=2013&sphone=6184620000
http://www.oldphonebook.com/searchphone2.php?syear=2014&sphone=6184620000

Figure 26.01: A partial redacted result from Old Phone Book.

Craigslist (craigslist.org)

Craigslist has already been discussed in earlier chapters, but the phone search options should be further detailed. Many people use Craigslist to sell items or services. The posts that announce the item or service available will often include a telephone number. These numbers will belong to a landline or cellular provider. This can be a great way to identify unknown telephone numbers. Some posts on Craigslist will not allow a telephone number to be displayed on a post. It is a violation of the rules on certain types of posts. Some people choose not to list a number because of automated "scrapers" that will grab the number and add it to databases to receive spam via text messages. Either way, the solution that most users apply to bypass this hindrance is to spell out the phone number. Instead of typing "314-555-1212", the user may enter "three one four five five five one two one two". Some will get creative and post "314 five five five 1212". This is enough to confuse both Craigslist's servers as well as the spammers. This can make searching difficult for an analyst. The hard way to do this is to conduct several searches similar to the following.

site:craigslist.org "314-555-1212"
site:craigslist.org "314" "555" "1212"
site:craigslist.org "three one four" "five five five" "one two one two"
site:craigslist.org "314" "five five five" "1212

This list can get quite long if you try to search every possible search format. One search that will cover most of these searches in a single search attempt would look like the following.

site:craigslist.org "314"|"three one four" "555"|"five five five" "1212"|"one two one two"

The "|" symbol in this search is the same as telling Google "OR". In essence, we are telling Google to search "314" or "three one four", then "555" or "five five five", and then "1212" or "one two one two". With this search, you would receive a result if any combination of the following was used.

314-555-1212
3145551212
314 555 one two one two
three one four 555-1212

This search will not catch every possible way to post a phone number. For example, if the user had typed "314 555 twelve twelve", the above technique would not work. The researcher must consider the alternative ways that a target will post a number on a website. It may help to imagine how you would post the target number creatively on a site, and then search for that method. Additionally, searching for only a portion of the number may provide results. You may want to try searching only the last four digits of the number. This may produce many unwanted results, but your target may be within the haystack. An automated option is included in the search tools.

Grocery Reward Cards / Loyalty Cards

Most grocery chains have adopted a reward/loyalty card system that mandates the participant to enroll in their program. The consumer completes an application and receives a plastic card to use during checkout for discounts. Many of these stores only offer a sale price if you are a member in the program. Most consumers provide a cellular telephone number to the program and use that number during checkout. This eliminates the need of possessing a physical card in order to receive the discount. Instead, they type their cell number into the card swiping machine to associate the purchase with their membership. These programs contain a huge database of telephone numbers and the registered users. There is no online database to access this data. However, you can obtain this data if you are creative.

Assume your target telephone number is 847-867-5309. If you have tried every technique mentioned at this point to identify the owner and failed, you may consider a query with a local grocery chain. The easiest method is to enter the store, purchase a pack of gum, and enter the target telephone number as the reward/loyalty program number. You will likely receive a receipt with the target's name on the bottom. Figure 26.02 (left) displays a portion of the actual receipt that I received when using this number. If you prefer to avoid entering a store, drive to the company's gas station outside of the store. Figure 26.02 (right) displays the notification I received when entering this same number at the pump. Note that this number is fictional. However, it has been registered at practically every grocery store in the United States. Try to use it the next time you make a purchase.

Figure 26.02: A receipt (left) and gas pump (right) identifying the owner of a cell number.

The Other Board (theotherboard.com)

NSFW! If you have any suspicion that the target of your investigation is involved in prostitution, drugs, or any related activity, The Other Board should be checked against the telephone number of your subject. This website aggregates all of the prostitution classifieds and review sites into one search. It extracts the telephone numbers from all online classified pages and allows you to search by the target telephone number. One of my training examples identified 37 online photos, 20 escort ads, several reviews by "Johns", ages used by the target, the last known location, and locations visited based on postings in online classifieds. Any time I have a target telephone number that is likely involved in criminal activity, I conduct a brief search on this site, via URL, as follows.

https://theotherboard.com/escort-reviews?phone=6185551212

Another option for this type of query is **The Erotic Review** (theeroticreview.com), with the following structure. Notice that the area code is separate from the number.

https://www.theeroticreview.com/reviews/newreviewsList.asp?Phone=5551212&AreaCode=618

Contact Exploitation

I mentioned this technique previously during the Android emulation chapter. If I receive no valuable information about a target telephone number with the previous options, I proceed to my Android emulator. I add the number as a friend named "John" in the contacts of the device. I then open any applicable application, such as Twitter, Instagram, and dating apps, and ask them to "find my friends". More often than not, an app links me to a social network profile which is associated with the only number in my contact list.

Real World Application: I was asked to assist an attorney in a child custody and divorce case. He provided the cellular telephone numbers of the suspected cheating husband and an unknown number of a potential mistress identified from telephone records. I added both numbers to the contacts list in my Android emulator and checked every app daily. This method identified a dating profile which included the husband's photo, but with a different name. On the same day which he was served divorce papers, I observed both numbers show up in the encrypted communications app Signal. While it did not identify the person on the other end of the communication, the coincidence of the two numbers joining Signal on the same day is revealing. While writing this chapter, I successfully identified the owner of a "burner" number because he connected it to his WhatsApp account. I added the number to my Contacts within my Android emulator; Opened WhatsApp; and asked it to find any "friends". It immediately displayed an image of a face associated with the number. A reverse image search (explained later) identified a social network in my target's true name. I have also used this technique to identify Skype profiles associated with a cellular number.

Calls.ai (sync.ai/calls-ai)

This Android application is impressive. It queries a large database of crowd-sourced contact details from unknown sources. Most telephone number search results reveal only a first name, but I find them to be highly accurate. Conduct the following to use this app.

- Launch your Android virtual machine through Android Studio.
- Launch the Google Play Store or Aurora Store and search "Calls.ai".
- Install Calls.ai from Sync.ai.
- Launch the Calls.ai app and allow default permissions.
- When prompted, associate with the Google account within the VM.
- Click the search option in the lower left and input any number.

As a test, I searched three cellular numbers which were assigned to me when I worked for the government. All three returned with positive results displaying "Mike", Michael" and "Bazzel". None of these phones were publicly attached to my name until someone shared their contact details with the world. While it is a nuisance to open an Android VM each time I need to conduct a search, the results from Calls.ai, Truecaller, and others justifies the time.

WhatsApp Mobile Tools (whatsapp.checkleaked.cc)

WhatsApp requires a telephone number to use the service, which can be a cell or VoIP number. This service attempts to query a number to provide details about the user. I tested this with a VoIP account and added a name and description to my WhatsApp profile. I received the following response, which I found impressive.

"isUser": true,
"isGroup": false,
"localized_display_name": "OSINT Training"
"isBlocked": false,
"about": "My Test Description",
"Public Name": "MB",

We can also submit via URL with the following structure: https://whatsapp.checkleaked.cc/12025551212

IntelTechniques Telephone Tool

Of all the automated search tools, this one may save the most time. You can submit an area code, prefix, and number and execute all queries. The number and word area on the search tool replicates the techniques mentioned previously which attempt to search both the numbers and words of a target telephone number within Google, Bing, and Craigslist.

CHAPTER TWENTY-SEVEN
ONLINE MAPS

The presence of online satellite images is not news anymore. Most of you have already "Googled" your own address and viewed your home from the sky. This view can get surprisingly detailed when using the zoom feature. Alleys, sheds, and extended driveways that are hidden from the street are now visible thanks to this free service. Many tactical units will examine this data before executing a search warrant at a residence. Aerial maps are helpful for viewing the location of exiting doors, escape routes, stairs, and various obstructions. The rapidly growing availability of the Street View option now gives us more data. This chapter explains detailed use of Google, Bing, and other mapping services. At the end, I present my custom maps tool which provides an automated solution to collecting every possible view associated with your target of interest.

Google Maps (maps.google.com)

Google constantly makes changes to their online Maps service, attempting to streamline the entire Maps experience to make everything easier to use. Over the past two years, we have witnessed features come and go, only to randomly re-appear. The following basics of Google Maps are now default for all users.

Search Bar: The Google Maps search bar can now accept practically any type of input. A full address, partial address, or GPS coordinates will immediately present you with a mapped view. Company names and types of businesses, such as "café" will highlight locations that may be of interest. This search field is the first stop. Attempt any search relevant to your investigation and you may be surprised at how accurate Google is. You can collapse this entire menu by clicking the left arrow next to the search field. This will return you to a full screen view of the map.

Satellite View: The lower left area of any map will offer a satellite view. The satellite view is a direct view from the sky looking almost straight down. A satellite view of your target location is always vital to every investigation.

Globe View: The Globe view (click "More" under layers and select the option) is similar, but usually offers a unique view from a different date. It also presents a rotation option. While in the Globe view, click on the "3D" icon and then the small "rotation" icon to the right of the map. This will shift the view 45 degrees and a second click will shift an additional 45 degrees. This presents new angles of your target.

Street View: If the Street View option is available, Google has been in the area and captured a photo of the location from the street. Dragging and dropping the small orange person in the lower right menu will open a street view from ground level at the area specified. You can navigate through this view by clicking forward, clicking and dragging, or scrolling and zooming. This view can be zoomed in by double-clicking and panned left and right by dragging the mouse while holding a left click. Double-clicking an area of the street will refresh the window to the view from that location. Clicking the map in the lower left will return you to the standard map view.

Historic Street View: In late 2014, Google began offering the ability to view all stored street view images for any single location. This option is available within the standard street view layout within the search area of the upper left corner. Click on "See more dates" in order to launch a new menu in the lower area. This new view will allow you to select from several street view captures which each present different views. The month and year of image capture will also appear for documentation. Figure 27.01 displays this method which presents additional views from an area. Additional options include views from several years prior. This can often reveal additional vehicles or missing structures associated with an investigation.

Figure 27.01: Historic Street View options from Google Maps.

Distance Measurement: Google Maps reintroduced the distance measurement tool after completely disabling the classic maps interface in 2015. While in map or satellite view, right-click on your starting point and choose "Measure distance". Click anywhere on the map to create a path you want to measure. Further clicks add additional measuring points. You can also drag a point to move it, or click a point to remove it. The total distance in both miles or kilometers will appear under the search box. When finished, right-click on the map and select clear measurement.

GPS Coordinates: Clicking on any point will load a small window in the bottom center that identifies the exact GPS coordinates of the chosen location. If this is not visible, right-click any point and select "What's here". Searching via GPS will be more precise than other queries.

URL Queries: For the purposes of the search tool, which is explained at the end of the chapter, we always want to identify the GPS coordinates of our target. In my examples throughout the chapter, 41.947242 is the latitude coordinate and -87.65673 is the longitude. The static search URLs I explain throughout this chapter will assist us in quickly querying multiple services once we identify a target location. The static URL displaying various Google Maps views of our target location is as follows.

Google Standard Map View:
https://www.google.com/maps/@?api=1&map_action=map&center=41.947242,-87.65673&zoom=18

Google Map View with Terrain:
https://www.google.com/maps/@?api=1&map_action=map&center=41.947242,-87.65673&zoom=18&basemap=terrain

Google Satellite View:
https://www.google.com/maps/@?api=1&map_action=map&center=41.947242,-87.65673&zoom=18&basemap=satellite

Google Street View

Google Street Views possess multiple options, including a 360-degree horizontal scope and vertical pitch. I have created the following URLs which we will use in our custom tools. These offer a view of north, east, south, and west with no pitch. After each URL loads, you can use the cursor to drag the view to fit your needs.

Google Street View (Down):
https://www.google.com/maps/@?api=1&map_action=pano&viewpoint=41.947242,-87.65673&heading=0&pitch=-90&fov=100

Google Street View (North):
https://www.google.com/maps/@?api=1&map_action=pano&viewpoint=41.947242,-87.65673&heading=0&pitch=0&fov=90

Google Street View (East):

https://www.google.com/maps/@?api=1&map_action=pano&viewpoint=41.947242,-87.65673&heading=90&pitch=0&fov=90

Google Street View (South):

https://www.google.com/maps/@?api=1&map_action=pano&viewpoint=41.947242,-87.65673&heading=180&pitch=0&fov=90

Google Street View (West):

https://www.google.com/maps/@?api=1&map_action=pano&viewpoint=41.947242,-87.65673&heading=270&pitch=0&fov=90

Bing Maps (bing.com/maps)

Similar to Google Maps, Bing offers a map view, satellite view, angled view, and street view. In my experience, the imagery provided by Bing will always be unique to the images available in Google Maps. A side-by-side comparison can be seen in a few pages with the custom maps tool. Bing does not always present the various 3D view options, which they call "Bird's Eye View". Fortunately, we can replicate all views with the following custom URLs.

Bing Standard Map View:

https://www.bing.com/maps?cp=41.947242~-87.65673&lvl=20

Bing Satellite View:

https://www.bing.com/maps?cp=41.947242~-87.65673&lvl=20&sty=a

Bing Satellite View (North):

https://www.bing.com/maps?cp=41.947242~-87.65673&lvl=20&sty=o&w=100%&dir=0

Bing Satellite View (East):

https://www.bing.com/maps?cp=41.947242~-87.65673&lvl=20&sty=o&w=100%&dir=90

Bing Satellite View (South):

https://www.bing.com/maps?cp=41.947242~-87.65673&lvl=20&sty=o&w=100%&dir=180

Bing Satellite View (West):

https://www.bing.com/maps?cp=41.947242~-87.65673&lvl=20&sty=o&w=100%&dir=270

Bing Street View (North):

https://www.bing.com/maps?cp=41.947242~-87.65673&lvl=20&dir=0&pi=0&style=x

Bing Street View (East):

https://www.bing.com/maps?cp=41.947242~-87.65673&lvl=20&dir=90&pi=0&style=x

Bing Street View (South):

https://www.bing.com/maps?cp=41.947242~-87.65673&lvl=20&dir=180&pi=0&style=x

Bing Street View (West):

https://www.bing.com/maps?cp=41.947242~-87.65673&lvl=20&dir=270&pi=0&style=x

Zoom Earth (zoom.earth)

This multiple satellite imagery website presents views from NASA, Bing, and ArcGIS. Occasionally, the ArcGIS data is more recent than Google or Bing. The smooth interface will easily provide a comparison of the available images for any location. One advantage of Zoom Earth is the ability to view satellite images in true full-screen mode. This allows creation of full-screen captures without branding, menus, or borders. This could be more appropriate for live demonstration instead of a standard Google or Bing window. The static URL with satellite view is as follows. The "20z" is the maximum zoom level.

https://zoom.earth/#view=41.947242,-87.65673,20z

Here (wego.here.com)

This service has experienced a lot of transformation over the past ten years. Originally a Nokia company with a unique set of satellite imagery, it now mostly contains identical images to Bing Maps. However, I find unique images on occasion, and we should always consider every resource. The static URL with satellite view is as follows.

https://wego.here.com/?map=41.947242,-87.65673,20,satellite

Yandex (yandex.com/maps)

Satellite views from Yandex are often poor quality and low resolution when focused on the U.S. However, international locations tend to possess clearer results. The static URL with satellite view is as follows.

https://yandex.com/maps/?l=sat&ll=-87.65673%2C41.947242&z=20

Apple Maps (beta.maps.apple.com)

In 2024, Apple released their mapping service via web browser instead of forcing people to use their apps. The following direct URLs access standard, satellite, and hybrid maps. The zoom feature (z=1) has been unreliable in this beta version, but I anticipate it to improve.

https://beta.maps.apple.com/?t=m&z=1&ll=41.9479061%2C-87.6558203
https://beta.maps.apple.com/?t=k&z=1&ll=41.9479061%2C-87.6558203
https://beta.maps.apple.com/?t=h&z=1&ll=41.9479061%2C-87.6558203
https://beta.maps.apple.com/?t=r&z=1&ll=41.9479061%2C-87.6558203

Dual Maps (data.mashedworld.com/dualmaps/map.htm)

This website provides a satellite view of a location on both Google Maps and Bing Maps simultaneously. The Google view on the left will also contain a search field in the upper right corner. Searching an address in this field will center both maps on the same address. This will provide a comparison of the satellite images stored on each service. This can quickly identify the service that has the better imagery. While this can provide a quick side-by-side comparison, upcoming automated solutions are preferred.

Historic Imagery

Researching different satellite views of a single location can have many benefits. These views are all of the current content stored within each service. However, these mapping services continuously update their offerings and usually present the most recent option. You may want to view the previous content that was available before an image was updated.

Historic Aerials (historicaerials.com)

If you need satellite imagery from several years prior, you can visit Historic Aerials. The quality will often be poor, especially as you view imagery from previous decades. After you enter an address, you will be presented all available options on the left side of the page. Figure 27.02 displays several results of the same location over a twenty-year period. These views will be unique from all of the previously mentioned services.

World Imagery Wayback (livingatlas.arcgis.com/wayback)

I began using this site in 2018 as an alternative to Historic Aerials. The quality is superior, the number of satellite views is higher, and the functionality is smoother. Figure 27.03 displays four images acquired from the service of a specific location. Each provides a unique view from 2014, 2015, 2016, and 2017.

https://livingatlas.arcgis.com/wayback/#active=20337&mapCenter=-87.65673%2C41.94782%2C18

Old Maps Online (oldmapsonline.org)

If you simply need road maps from the past 100 years, this service has you covered. There are no images or satellite views, but street details from previous decades could be useful. You might learn that a target location possessed a different street name in the past or identify the approximate year when a specific road was built.

Real World Application: Combining several satellite views can provide much information about a target's residence. Before the execution of a search warrant, it is beneficial for police to collect as much map information as possible. This will give updated views of a drawn map, satellite imagery directly above the house, four angled views from the sky, and a complete view of the house and neighboring houses from the street, including vehicles. This can be used to identify potential threats such as physical barriers, escape routes, and video surveillance systems in place.

In 2020, I assisted a former colleague with a missing person investigation. Google and Bing maps were queried, but nothing helpful was found. However, a search on Mapillary (explained next) revealed a vehicle parked outside the victim's residence which was otherwise unknown to investigators. This clue opened a new path of investigation which ultimately led my colleague to the victim. We must always thoroughly check every resource.

Figure 27.02: Multiple views of a location through Historic Aerials.

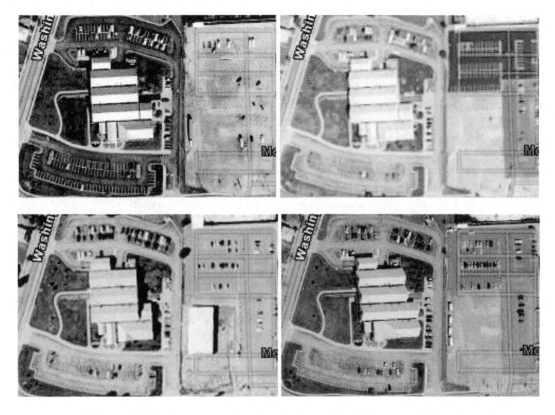

Figure 27.03: Historic satellite images from World Imagery Wayback.

Crowd-Sourced Street Views

Street View maps from services such as Google and Bing are nothing new. Most of you can view the top and front of your home from multiple online websites. With street view options, these services are fairly responsible and block most faces and license plates. This makes it difficult for investigators trying to identify a suspect vehicle parked at a home or present at a crime scene prior to the incident. We have two services that offer unique street-level views that may remove these limitations.

Mapillary (mapillary.com/app)

This service appears similar to other mapping websites when first loaded. You see a typical map view identifying streets, landmarks, and buildings. Enabling the satellite view layer displays images from the Open Street Map project. The real power is within the crowd-sourced street view images. While in any map view, colored lines indicate that an individual has provided street-level images to Mapillary, usually from a GPS-enabled smart phone. This is actually quite common, as many people record video of their driving trips which could be used in case of an accident. These services make it easy and automated to upload these images. The sites then embed these images within their own mapping layers for the public to see. Clicking these colored lines reveals the street view images in the lower portion of the screen. Expanding these images allows you to navigate through that individual's images similar to the Google Street View experience. Figure 27.04 displays a street view layered over a satellite view. The username of the Mapillary member and date of image capture appears in the lower left.

In some of these images, the services appear to be redacting license plates with a typical "Blur Box" as seen in Figure 27.05 (left). A few feet later, the box disappears and a partially legible license plate is revealed, as seen in Figure 27.05 (right). It seems like these services are attempting to determine when a license plate is legible, and then blurring it. When the plate is farther away and more difficult to read, it is ignored. This can work in our favor. In Figure 27.06 we can use selective cropping and photo manipulation to obtain the registration. The left image appears unaltered as it is difficult to read. The right image was cropped; inverted with Photoshop;

brightness turned down to 0%; and contrast heightened to 100%. The result is a legible license plate. I believe most registration plates can be made visible within these services. The following URL conducts a query for our target location.

https://www.mapillary.com/app/?lat=41.947242&lng=-87.65673&z=18

Karta (kartaview.org)

After exhausting your options on Mapillary, continue to Karta, previously called Open Street Cam. The site functions in the same way, but possesses unique images. These sites allow you to identify the uploader's username, mapping history, number of posted images, and profile image. You can also select to watch all of the captured images from a specific user as he or she travels daily. I can't begin to imagine the amount information available about a user's travel habits if he or she were to become a target of an investigation. While there is not coverage of every area like we see with Google Maps, the databases are growing rapidly, and should be included when using other mapping tools. We will use the following URL structure for our automated tools.

https://kartaview.org/map/@41.947242,-87.65673,18z

Land Viewer (eos.com/landviewer)

This resource will not present detailed views of your target's home. The images here are often generated from weather satellites, and restrict zoom levels to a city view. Most locations offer four active satellites that constantly retrieve images and five inoperative satellites that store historic imagery dating back to 1982. I have only used this resource to document potential weather at a crime scene (clouds, rain, or clear). The static URL follows.

https://eos.com/landviewer/?lat=41.947242&lng=-87.65673&z=11

Landsat Look (landsatlook.usgs.gov/explore)

This is very similar to Land Viewer, but with additional historic images. Each map view possesses several unique satellite view options ranging from 1972 to present.

Figure 27.04: A crowd-sourced street view from Mapillary.

Figure 27.05: A vehicle with a blurred registration plate (left) and clear (right).

Figure 27.06: An illegible registration plate (left) and manipulated view (right).

Acre Value (acrevalue.com)

This site relies on Mapbox for aerial imagery, but offers a unique service unavailable in other mapping applications. It attempts to identify property boundaries for an address. Figure 27.07 displays an example. Acre Value requires a paid account in order to see property owner details. However, we can extract this information from the site with a few steps. First, right-click the page and launch the Inspector, as previously discussed, and click the "Network" tab. Next, click on the property of interest, as visible in Figure 27.07. You should see a "xhr" entry within the Inspector, which should appear similar to the following.

https://www.acrevalue.com/map/api/plot/?id=1673576598

You can open this link in a new tab or click the "Response" tab on the right to view the data. This will potentially display the property owner.

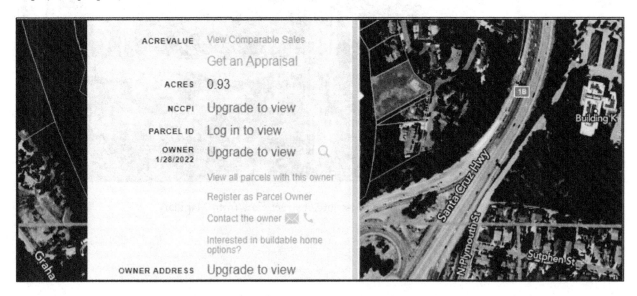

Figure 27.07: An Acre Value map listing.

"owner": "ELDRIDGE, CHARLES D & SANDRA J",
    "county_fips": "06087",
    "id": "1673576598",
    "plot_type": "parcel",
    "prediction": null,
    "soil_label": "NCCPI",
    "soil_value": 15.220648845321122,
    "apn": "06028118000",
    "acreage": 0.9311936516181484,
    "slope": 25.73647948663312,
    "fema": 0,
    "easements": 0,

Apple Maps Alternative (satellites.pro)

While not an official Apple product, Satellite Pro provides Apple Maps aerial views during search queries. A direct URL of our target location follows.

https://satellites.pro/USA_map#41.94721,-87.656502,18

Real Estate (zillow.com, trulia.com, realtor.com, etc.)

These websites display information about homes which are currently available for sale or have previously sold. I usually search this option in hopes of locating interior images of a suspect home. This can often identify personal belongings, interests, and family information. It can be a long-shot, but has been vital to several of my investigations. Figure 27.08 displays the interior of a home near our target location from Zillow. The following direct-access URLs are available for quick viewing and will be used for our search tool.

https://www.zillow.com/homes/for_sale/?searchQueryState={"isMapVisible"%3Atrue%2C"mapBounds"%3A{"west"%3A-87.6558203%2C"east"%3A-87.6558203%2C"south"%3A41.9479061%2C"north"%3A41.94790612}%2C"filterState"%3A{"sort"%3A{"value"%3A"globalrelevanceex"}%2C"ah"%3A{"value"%3Atrue}}%2C"isListVisible"%3Atrue%2C"mapZoom"%3A11}

https://www.trulia.com/for_sale/41.947242,41.947242,-87.65673,-87.65673_xy/

https://www.realtor.com/realestateandhomes-search/Miami_FL?view=map&pos=41.948901,-87.659305,41.945557,-87.654155,18

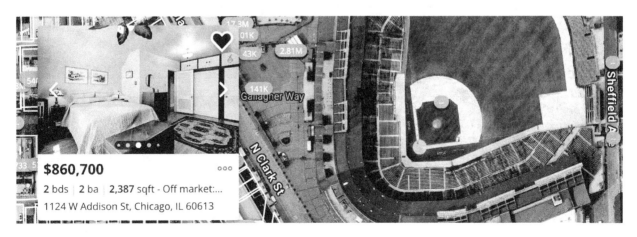

Figure 27.08: A Zillow satellite view with a nearby home selected to view interior images.

IntelTechniques Maps Tool (https://inteltechniques.com/tools/Location.html)

The first portion of this tool allows entry of a physical address in traditional format which can execute several searches previously mentioned. The first field presents a mapping API page which includes the GPS coordinates of your target. These will be used in the second portion of the page. This area allows entry of GPS coordinates for several mapping options. The "Populate All" simplifies entry into the query options. Each search will open results in a new tab. It currently fetches images from all options mentioned in this chapter which allow a static URL with GPS for submission. Figures 27.09 through 27.36 on the following pages display the results from these providers when searching Wrigley Field in Chicago, using the search tool to generate each result. Remember to allow pop-ups within your browser if you want all of the data to populate within new tabs automatically.

Figures 27.09 through 27.14: Google Satellite, Google Globe, Bing Satellite, Here Satellite, Google Globe North, and Google Globe East.

Figures 27.15 through 27.21: Google Globe South, Google Globe West, Google Street views of North, East, South, and West, and Bing Bird's Eye view of North.

Figures 27.22 through 27.28: Bing Bird's Eye views of East, South, and West, and Bing Street views of North, East, South, and West.

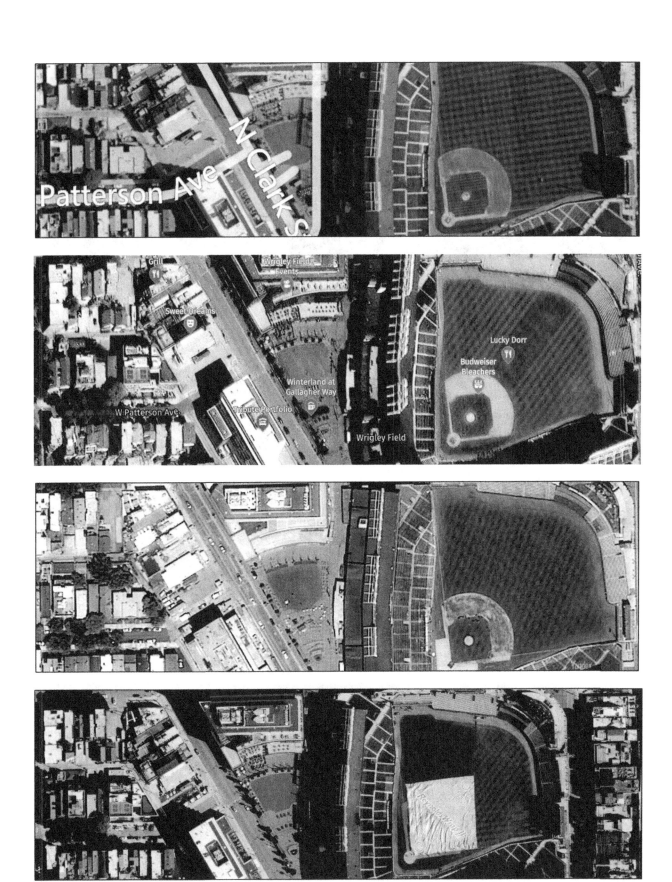

Figures 27.29 through 27.32: Zoom Earth, Here, Yandex Satellite, and Apple.

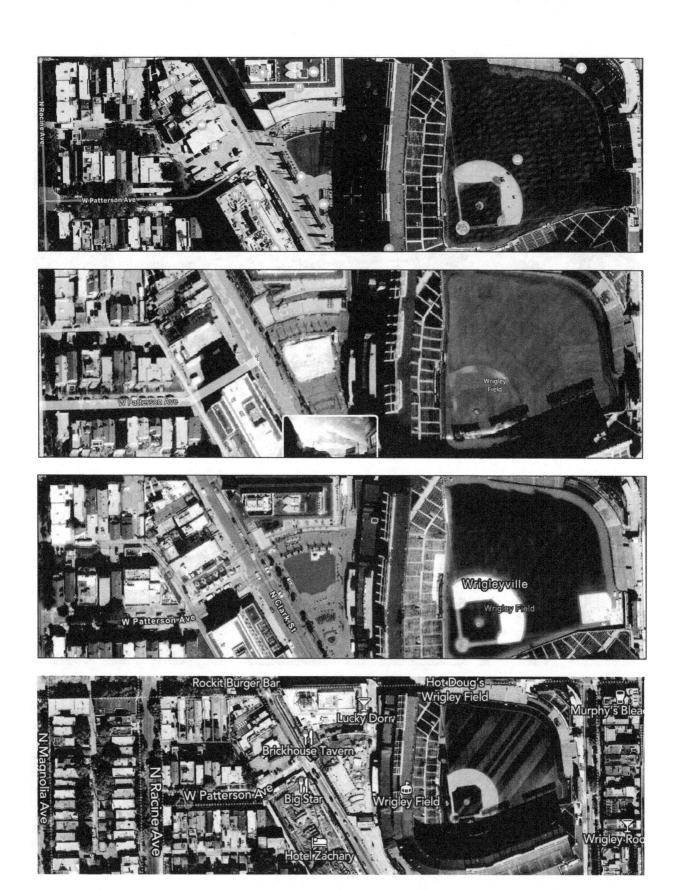

Figures 27.33 through 27.36: Satellite Pro (Apple), Mapillary, World Imagery, and Acre Value.

Map Shadows

If you look closely at the previous images, you can see many shadows. We can use these to make a guess at the date and time of capture. In fact, analyzing shadows within any images, even those which do not originate with satellite imagery, can help identify the date and time of capture. There is no exact science to this (yet), but we have online tools available to assist our efforts. Consider the image in Figure 27.33. The shadow of Wrigley Field is due west of the building and does not appear to project north or south of the building. We can use **Shade Map** (shademap.app) to identify the most likely date and time of this satellite capture. After loading the site, search for Wrigley Field and allow the location to load. Next, we can begin manipulating the map.

Click the date in the lower-left and drag the month bar until the shadows seem to match the horizontal position within our target image in Figure 27.33. In my attempts, the month of March displayed shadows which did not extend north or south of the building at an angle. This month displayed shadows which extended directly east and west. Next, choose the time of day which matches the position of the shadows. My attempts identified 6:28 am Mountain (7:28 am Central) as the ideal match. Therefore, my best guess is that the satellite image captured in this example was approximately 7:30 am local time in late March. Figure 27.37 displays my result. I would never document an assumption of an exact date and time, but a range could be appropriate. Documenting that the shadows indicate capture between February and April from 7:00 to 8:00 am could suffice.

While this book may be printed with black ink, hopefully you can match the overall shadows. Replicate this on your own computer to see the true value. This technique could also be used when you identify a photograph posted to social media. If you know the approximate location and time of year, it should be fairly easy to establish the approximate time of capture.

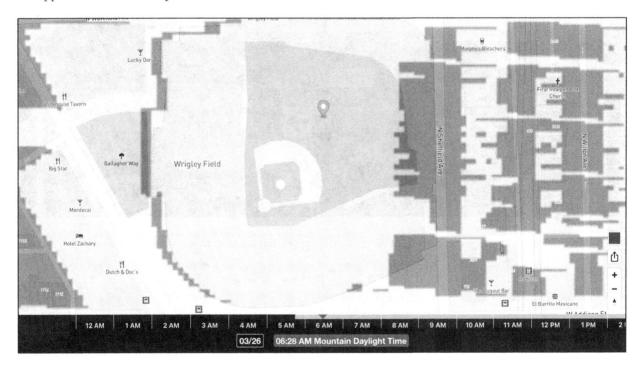

Figure 27.37: A Shade Map result.

Scribble Maps (scribblemaps.com)

The default view of mapping services such as Google and Bing may be enough for your situation. Occasionally, you may want to modify or customize a map for your needs. Law enforcement may want to create a map to be used in a court case; a private investigator may want to customize a map to present to a client; or a security director may want to use this service to document the inappropriate Tweets that were found during the previous instructions. Scribble Maps offers one of the easiest ways to create your own map and add any type of visual aids to the final product.

The default view of your new map at Scribble Maps will display the entire world and a menu of basic options. I close this menu by clicking the small "x" in the upper right corner. You can then manually zoom into an area of interest or type in an address in the location bar at the top of the map. This will present you with a manageable area of the map. The lower right corner will allow you to switch from a traditional map view to a satellite or hybrid view.

The menu at the top of the map will allow you to add shapes, lines, text, and images to your map. Practicing on this map can never be replaced with any instruction printed here. Mastering the basics of this application will make occasional use of it easy. Figure 27.38 displays a quick sample map that shows a title, a line, a marker, and graphics. The menu can be seen in the upper left portion. When finished, the "Menu" button will present many options to print, save, or export your map. I also highly recommend **Free Map Tools** (freemaptools.com). This service provides multiple advanced options such as mapping a radius around a point of interest.

Figure 27.38: A basic custom map created with Scribble Maps.

CHAPTER TWENTY-EIGHT
DOCUMENTS

The open source intelligence discussed up to this point has focused on websites which include valuable information about a target. A category of intelligence that is often missed during OSINT research is documents. This type of data usually falls into one of three classes. The first is documents that include information about the target within the contents of the file. These can include online PDF files that the target may not know exist. The second class is documents that were actually created by the target. These files can make their way into public view unintentionally. Finally, the third class includes the metadata stored within a document that can include vital information about the true source of the document. The following techniques explain manual searching and retrieving of these documents and automated software solutions for analysis of found content.

Google Searching (google.com)

A very basic way of locating documents that are publicly available on a specific website, or related to a specific topic, is to use Google. The "filetype:" (or easier "ext:") search operators previously explained can be used for this task. An example of search queries for all Microsoft Word documents stored on the domain of inteltechniques.com would be the following.

site:inteltechniques.com ext:doc
site:inteltechniques.com ext:docx

If you wanted to locate all documents that reference a specific topic, you can use the filetype operator without a specific website listed. An example of a search query for all Excel spreadsheets that contain the acronym OSINT would be the following.

ext:xls "OSINT"
ext:xlsx "OSINT"

If you wanted to search for a specific person's name within any spreadsheets, such as John Doe, you would type the following single query.

ext:xls OR ext:xlsx "John Doe"

The following table includes the most common document file types and the associated file extensions. As previously explained, both Google and Bing are capable of searching any file type regardless of the file association. Remember that Bing demands "filetype" while Google seems to prefer "ext". Please note that this is a partial list, and I identify new possibilities constantly.

Microsoft Word	DOC, DOCX
Microsoft Excel	XLS, XLSX, CSV
Microsoft PowerPoint	PPT, PPTX
Adobe Acrobat	PDF
Text File	TXT, RTF
Open Office	ODT, ODS, ODG, ODP

If you wanted to search all of these file types at once, the following string in Google or Bing would find most documents on the topic of OSINT. You could change that term to anything else of interest.

"OSINT" filetype:pdf OR filetype:doc OR filetype:xls OR filetype:xlsx OR filetype:docx OR filetype:ppt OR filetype:pptx OR filetype:txt

This query basically tells the search engine to look for any reference to the term OSINT inside of a PDF, Microsoft Word, and other documents, and display all of the results. The Google Custom Search Engine (CSE) described in Chapter Seventeen is a great resource for this exact type of search. However, I highly recommend having an understanding of the manual search process. It will give you much more control than any automated solution. Additionally, Google CSEs limit the number of results. Therefore, I no longer recommend exclusively relying on it for a Document search. It simply cannot compete with a properly structured Google or Bing query. The custom search tools presented at the end of the chapter will further simplify all of this.

Google Docs (docs.google.com)

The idea of storing user created documents on the internet is gaining a lot of popularity. Keeping these files "in the cloud" eliminates the need for personal storage on a device such as a CD or flash drive. In addition, storing files on the internet allows the author to access and edit them from any computer with an internet connection. A common use of these document-hosting sites is to store them only during the editing phase. Once the document is finished and no longer needed, the user may forget to remove it from public view. Google is one of the most popular document storage websites. It allows users to embed the stored documents into their own websites if desired. Searching the site is relatively easy.

Many Google Mail (Gmail) users take advantage of Google's free service for document storage called Google Docs or Google Drive. When a document is created, it is private by default and not visible to the public. However, when people want to share documents with friends or coworkers, the sharing properties must be changed. While it is possible to privately share files with individual Google users, many people find it easier to make the documents public. Most of these users probably assume that the files will not be seen by anyone other than the intended recipients. After all, who would go out searching for other people's documents? We will.

The Google Docs and Google Drive websites do not offer the option to search these public files, but you can do this using Google search. Now that Google allows search engines to index most of the public files, you should be able to find them with some specific search methods. The following search examples will explain a few of the options that would be conducted on google.com. The exact search is listed with the expected result. These should be used as a starting point for the many possibilities of document searching.

site:docs.google.com "resume" - 29,800 online resumes
site:docs.google.com "resume" "Williams" - 985 resumes with the name Williams
site:docs.google.com "Corey Trager" - 1 document (resume) belonging to the target
site:docs.google.com 865-274-2074 - 1 document containing the target number

Google categorizes the documents that are created by the user. The examples below identify searches that would display documents by type.

site:docs.google.com/presentation/d - 325,000 PowerPoint presentations
site:docs.google.com/drawings/d - 18,600 Google flowchart drawings
site:docs.google.com/file/d - 945,000 images, videos, PDF files, and documents
site:docs.google.com/folder/d - 4,000 collections of files inside folders
site:docs.google.com/open - 1,000,000 external documents, folders, and files

In 2013, Google began placing some user generated documents on the "drive.google.com" domain. Therefore, any search that you conduct with the method described previously should be repeated with "drive" in place of "docs". The previous search for the telephone number would be the following.

site:drive.google.com 865-274-2074

Microsoft Docs (docs.microsoft.com)

Similar to Google Drive, Microsoft Docs offers that ability to store and share documents. The service is not as popular as Google Drive. However, there are thousands of publicly visible documents waiting to be found. The shared files are stored on the docs.microsoft.com domain. A query for resumes would be as follows. This search could be conducted on Google or Bing. The result on Google was 63,400 resume files with personal information.

site:docs.microsoft.com "resume"

Amazon Web Services (amazonaws.com)

Amazon Web Services (AWS) is a large collection of servers that supply storage and internet application hosting in "the cloud". Instead of purchasing expensive hardware, many companies and individuals rent these servers. There are numerous documents available for download from these servers when searched appropriately. I cannot overstate the value of searching Amazon's servers. This is where most of the voter data that was heavily discussed during the 2016 election originated. I have personally located extremely sensitive documents from this source on numerous occasions. The following structure will identify files indexed on google.com.

site:amazonaws.com

The following search examples will explain a couple of the options. The exact search is listed with the expected result. These should be used as a starting point for the many possibilities of document searching.

site:amazonaws.com ext:xls "password" - 114 Excel spreadsheets containing "password"
site:amazonaws.com ext:pdf "osint" - 260 PDF files containing "osint"

Another option is the Amazon CloudFront servers. CloudFront is a content delivery network (CDN) offered by Amazon Web Services. Content delivery networks provide a globally-distributed network of proxy servers which cache content, such as web videos or other bulky media. These are provided more locally to consumers, thus improving access speed for downloading the content. We can apply the same previous search techniques on this domain. The following search yielded 129 results on various CloudFront servers containing "OSINT".

site:cloudfront.net OSINT

Refseek (refseek.com)

Refseek is a search engine singularly focused on document search and claims to search over five billion sites, books, journals, and newspapers. We can structure queries with https://www.refseek.com/documents?q=osint.

Searcholic (searcholic.com)

Searcholic primarily returns results for PDFs and video content such as YouTube channels with the added benefit of displaying thumbnails for most results.

Core (core.ac.uk)

Core is a UK based search engine specializing in searching for research papers and other academic documents. We can structure queries with https://core.ac.uk/search/?q=osint.

Base (base-search.net)

Base boasts the ability to conduct queries across 400 million documents and twelve thousand content providers. We can structure queries with https://www.base-search.net/Search/Results?lookfor=osint.

Gray Hat Warfare (buckets.grayhatwarfare.com)

AWS hosts more than simple documents. Many companies host large databases and data sets within "buckets" on AWS servers. Custom Google searches may locate some of this content, but never a full index of all data. This is where Gray Hat Warfare excels. It has created a searchable database of over one billion files, all publicly stored with AWS servers. Free users are limited to the first 350 million of these files, which is substantial. A search of "OSINT" revealed only 11 results while "password" displayed over 41,000. The results are often large files which must be opened carefully. A search of "password xls" provided three documents with active credentials. A direct search URL is as follows.

https://buckets.grayhatwarfare.com/files?page=1&keywords=password

Google Cloud Storage (cloud.google.com)

This is Google's response to Amazon's AWS. It is a premium file storage web service for storing and accessing data on the Google Cloud Platform infrastructure. It is heavily used by all types of businesses and tech-savvy individuals. The number of publicly available sensitive documents is growing at an alarming rate. Below are a few examples.

site:storage.googleapis.com ext:xlsx OR ext:xls - 2,310 Spreadsheets
site:storage.googleapis.com "confidential" - 9,502 Documents
site:storage.googleapis.com "confidential" ext:pptx - 11 PowerPoint files marked as confidential

Presentation Repositories

With unprecedented online storage space at all of our fingertips, many people choose to store PowerPoint and other types of presentations in the cloud. Several free services have appeared to fill this demand. Of those, the following have the majority of publicly available documents.

Slide Share (slideshare.net)	Slidebean (slidebean.com)	Power Show (powershow.com)
ISSUU (issuu.com)	Prezi (prezi.com)	

Slide Share and ISSUU allow native searching within their websites. However, Prezi does not have this option. For all, I recommend a custom Google search with the site operator. If I want to locate presentations including the term OSINT from Prezi, I would use a query of site:prezi.com "osint".

Scribd (scribd.com)

Scribd was a leading cloud storage document service for several years. Since 2014, it has shifted its focus toward e-book sales. However, the plethora of stored documents is still accessible. This can be valuable for historical content posted, and likely forgotten, by the target. A search field is at the top of every page on the site within their collapsible menu. Searching for your target name should produce any public books stored through this service that includes the target name on any page of the publication. Clicking "Documents" in the menu will present more relevant information.

Most of these documents are intentionally stored on the site and any evidence of criminal activity will not be included. Instead, the primary use of the site for OSINT investigations is the large number of documents related to businesses. Entering any large corporation name should display several pages of viewable documents related to the company. Often, these include documents that the company's security personnel would not authorize to be online. Searching for "FOUO", an acronym for "for official use only", produced hundreds of results. While none of these appeared to be officially classified, they were not intended to be posted to a public website. If you are presented with an unmanageable number of results, the filter options appear directly above the first document result. These will allow you to search by language, size, file type, and date uploaded.

Identifying the user that uploaded a document is as easy as locating the document. In the left of any page containing a document, there is an area that will identify the subject that uploaded the file. This also acts as a link to this user's profile on the website. The profile will display any information that the user supplied as well as a feed of recent activity of that user on the site. This can help identify other documents uploaded by a specific user.

PDF Drive (pdfdrive.com)

This service scans the internet for new PDF files and archives them. This can be helpful when the original source removes the content. The static URL of https://www.pdfdrive.com/search?q=osint queries the entire domain.

WikiLeaks (search.wikileaks.org)

Some websites are created for the sole purpose of leaking sensitive and classified documents to the public. Wikileaks is such a site. When an Army soldier named Bradley Manning was arrested in 2010 for uploading classified government information to the site, Wikileaks became a household name. People then began to flock to the site to catch a glimpse of these controversial documents and videos. The official Wikileaks site finally provides a working search option. It will allow you to enter any search terms and will provide results of any leaked documents that contain these terms. Both the government and the private sector should be familiar with this site and the information that is identified with their respective agency.

Cryptome (cryptome.org)

Another site that strives to release sensitive and classified information to the public is Cryptome. Most of the information is related to freedom of speech, cryptography, spying, and surveillance. Much of the content could be considered conspiracy theories, but several official documents get released daily. Cryptome does not provide a search for their site and there are no third-party providers that cater to this service. Therefore, we must rely on Google or Bing to find the documents. A query of site:cryptome.org "osint" should function well.

Paste Sites

Paste Sites are not technically storage services for documents. They are websites that allow users to upload text for public viewing. These were originally designed for software programmers that needed a place to store large amounts of text. A link would be created to the text and the user could share the link with other programmers to review the code. This is still a common practice, but other users have found ways to abuse this technology. Many hacking groups will use this area of the internet to store compromised account information, user passwords, credit card numbers, and other sensitive content. There are dozens of sites that cater to this need, and very few of them have a search feature.

Pastebin (pastebin.com)

Pastebin is the most popular paste site in the United States. Criminal hacker groups often use this site to release illegally obtained data to the public. A previous release included the home addresses and personal information of many police officers near Ferguson, Missouri during protests and riots. More recently, stolen bank records and credentials from Venezuela were posted with encouragement to infiltrate the company. This is one of the sites that will allow for a search from within the site. This function performs a search through Google in the same way we could with the "site" operator. Typing in a target name, email address, or business name may reveal private information not intended for the public. For law enforcement, typing in the last four digits of a stolen credit card number may identify a link to the thief. If successful, the target is most likely outside of the country. Regardless, this is a valuable piece to the case and an impressive explanation to the victim. Unfortunately, most of the users leave a default username of "Guest". Pastebin no longer allows a direct URL search, but relies on Google for indexing. A query of site:pastebin.com "osint" should work well.

New paste sites come and go monthly. There is no way to present a current and complete list. However, I will focus on the most stable and prominent options which allow search. In a moment, I present a custom search tool which queries all of these at once. The following sites can be individually queried with the site operator, such as site:doxbin.org "osint". Please note that these sites come and go often.

0bin.net	gist.github.com	paste.centos.org	paste.ubuntu.com	privatebin.net
cl1p.net	hastebin.com	paste.debian.net	paste2.org	slexy.org
codepad.org	heypasteit.com	paste.ee	pastebin.com	snipplr.com
controlc.com	ideone.com	paste.frubar.net	pastebin.fr	textsnip.com
doxbin.org	ivpaste.com	paste.lisp.org	pastebin.gr	tidypub.org
dpaste.com	jsbin.com	paste.opensuse.or	pastefs.com	wordle.net
dpaste.de	justpaste.it	g	pastehtml.com	zerobin.net
dpaste.org	justpaste.me	paste.org	pastelink.net	
friendpaste.com	p.ip.fi	paste.org.ru	pastie.org	

Document Metadata

When an original document is found online, it is obviously important to analyze the visible content of the file. This includes the file name, written text, and an original location of the document. Digging deeper will expose more information. There is data embedded inside the document that cannot be seen by simply looking at the content of the file. This data is called metadata and can be very valuable to any type of investigation. It can often include the computer name on which the document was created, the username of the computer or the network, the software version used, and information about the network to which the computer is connected. The best way to view all of this information is to use software-based metadata viewers, but you can also view this "hidden" information online through a web browser.

Several online sites will allow you to upload documents for analysis. To do this, click the "browse" button on the pages detailed below. This will enable a file explorer that will allow you to select the document that you want analyzed. The result often identifies a created and modified date, the original title, three applications used to create the document, and a username. A further search of this username through the previously discussed techniques could produce a wealth of information about the author of the document. The following websites allow you to upload a locally stored document or submit a URL of a file for analysis. Please use caution with this technique. If the document is already posted online, there is very little risk of allowing a URL analysis. However, a locally stored file that has never been on the internet may require a second thought. If the content is sensitive, you may not want to upload to any service. If the file contains classified information, you could be jeopardizing your clearance. In these situations, use the methods discussed in a moment. If this is not a concern the following websites work well.

Extract Metadata (extractmetadata.com)
Online Exif Viewer (onlineexifviewer.com)
Exifdata (exifdata.com)
ExifInfo (exifinfo.org)
Get Metadata (get-metadata.com)

Document Metadata Applications

If I need to analyze the metadata stored within documents, I prefer to do so locally on my machine. I do not want to share any potential investigation details with an online resource. This is especially true if the documents are not already online. You may possess a folder of files which were retrieved from a suspect computer or emailed directly to you. In these scenarios, we should be cautious as to not distribute any evidence electronically to any websites. I present two solutions, with a third unstable option.

ExifTool (exiftool.org)

You already possess a document metadata viewer within your custom Linux virtual machine. It is called ExifTool and we installed it during the previous chapters. This is a terminal-based solution, but the function is quite simple. Assume that you have used the previous techniques to download several Word documents in .docx file format onto your Desktop in a folder titled Evidence. The following steps within Terminal would navigate to the proper folder, generate a spreadsheet with the metadata included within the documents, and title it Report.csv on your Desktop in the Evidence folder.

```
cd ~/Desktop/Evidence
exiftool * -csv > ~/Desktop/Evidence/Report.csv
```

Let's conduct an example and take a look at the results. I performed the following Google search:

ext:docx "osint"

This provided 371 results, all of which were Microsoft Word documents. I downloaded the first four into the Evidence folder on my Desktop. After executing the commands above, I launched the spreadsheet. Figure 28.01 displays a small portion of the interesting results. This tells me the names of the individuals who created and last modified the documents; the companies involved; the software which was used; and even the amount of time they spent editing the content. This is extremely valuable information which should be collected during every investigation in which documents are obtained.

Application	AppVersion	Company	CreateDate	Creator	LastMo	By		TotalEditTime
Microsoft Office Word	12		2011:03:18 20:29:00Z	marko.pri	marko.	ac		1.2 hours
Microsoft Macintosh Word	15		2016:04:25 14:56:00Z	Kirk Haye	Kirk Ha			26 minutes
Microsoft Office Word	12		2017:08:03 09:53:00Z	Hakon201	Hakon2			4 minutes
Microsoft Office Word	14	United States Army	2016:06:13 08:31:00Z	john.t.rich	IMO-P(	lin, Jonas A		3 hours

Figure 28.01: Document metadata results from ExifTool.

FOCA (github.com/ElevenPaths/FOCA)

You may desire a Windows-based solution which possesses a user-friendly interface. FOCA was once the premier document metadata collection and extraction tool. It was created to search, download, and analyze documents and their metadata in one execution. Unfortunately, Google and other search engines began blocking the search and download behavior of the software. Fortunately, the analysis portion still works perfectly. The following steps will download and install FOCA to your Windows VM or any other Windows device.

- Install the "Basic" version of SQL server express which is available directly from Microsoft (https://www.microsoft.com/en-us/sql-server/sql-server-downloads).
- Navigate to https://github.com/ElevenPaths/FOCA/releases.
- Click the hyperlink for the most recent "zip" file.
- Double-click the .zip file and extract the contents.
- Launch FOCA.exe.
- If prompted, select "Download and install this feature" to install the .net framework.

FOCA should launch and present a window with many options. Today, the vast majority of the features no longer work, but the document analysis is helpful. Assume you possess the same four documents mentioned previously on the Desktop of your Windows VM.

- Open FOCA and click the Metadata folder in the left menu.
- Drag and drop the documents into the FOCA window.
- Right-click any of the documents and choose "Extract all metadata".

- Right-click any of the documents and choose "Analyze metadata".

You can now click through the menus on the left to view any metadata details such as email addresses, names, and computers associated with these files. The benefit of this method is the user interface, but you sacrifice a reporting option. The previous ExifTool method is not as pretty, but the spreadsheet result is helpful. Ultimately, I believe you should be familiar with both options and rely on the method most appropriate for you.

Real World Application: Dennis Lynn Rader, also known as the BTK killer, sent a floppy disk to the Wichita Police Department containing a Microsoft Word document in reference to his killings. The police examined the metadata of this document and determined that it was made by a subject named "Dennis". Links to a Lutheran church were also located within this data. Conducting OSINT searches on these two pieces of information helped to identify the suspect and make an arrest.

Manual Metadata Extraction

There are some documents which store much more metadata within the content than what is presented within the official metadata associated with the file. I see this most commonly with PowerPoint files. Let's conduct a demonstration. I searched ext:pptx "osint" within Google. The first result was a PowerPoint presentation, which I downloaded. The previous methods announced all of the standard metadata we would expect to see. I then changed the name of the PowerPoint presentation file from "OpenSourceIntelligence-OSINT.pptx" to "OpenSourceIntelligence-OSINT.zip". This tells my computer that this file is now an archive.

I then decompressed the zip file which presented dozens of new files. These are the content behind the scenes of the PowerPoint itself. They include all of the images inside the presentation, which can then easily be analyzed for their own metadata, and text extraction of all words in the slides. The "app.xml" file confirms that the author was using PowerPoint from Microsoft Office 2016 (AppVersion>16.0000) and several files include unique identifiers for this user. Comparing these to other downloaded documents could prove that the authors of each were the same.

In a bit of irony, this PowerPoint file randomly selected from the Google results included the OSINT flowcharts which I present at the end of my books, but the owner claimed them as his own work with "Copyright of the Cybersecmentorship.org". Apparently, this technique can also help expose copyright infringement and blatant plagiarism.

Free OCR (free-ocr.com)

You may occasionally locate a PDF file that has not been indexed for the text content. These types of PDF files will not allow you to copy and paste any of the text. This could be due to poor scanning techniques or to purposely prohibit outside use of the content. You may desire to capture this text for a summary report. These files can be uploaded to Free OCR and converted to text documents. OCR is an acronym for optical character recognition. Basically, a computer "reads" the document and determines what the text is inside the content. The result is a new document with copy and paste capability.

Text Archives (archive.org)

The Internet Archive possesses massive collections of text files, books, and other documents. These files can be accessed with the "=TXT" parameter after a search. A direct URL for documents mentioning "inteltechniques" within the title or content would be the following.

https://archive.org/search.php?query=inteltechniques&sin=TXT

Google Books (books.google.com)

Google has scanned most books printed within the past decade and the index is searchable. Many of these scans also include a digital preview of the content. A direct URL query appears as follows.

https://www.google.com/search?tbm=bks&q=inteltechniques

Pirated Books (annas-archive.org)

I am hesitant to present this resource, but I have found it extremely valuable in my investigations. Many people use a service called Library Genesis to download illegal pirated e-books. Library Genesis does not offer any type of indexing of content, but Annas Archive acquires all of their content and provides a search interface. This allows us to search within the content of millions of pirated books without actually downloading any content and allows us to find references to specific targets within publications. While it may be tempting to download the PDF of the book, please don't. This likely violates your laws, policies, or ethics. The following URL would query "osint" within the entire collection.

https://annas-archive.org/search?q=osint

Additional resources such as **File Pursuit** (filepursuit.com) attempt to replicate this service.

Book Sales (amazon-asin.com)

I have never had an investigation rely on book sale information, but I find it interesting. Amazon offers a lookup tool which displays details about the number of copies being sold of any book on their site. First, you must identify the ASIN assigned to the book. This is typically visible within the details section of the book's listing page or the page URL. The previous edition of this book is B0BRDR9P4Q. The following URL accesses all available details, but supposedly will switch to a paid model soon.

https://amazon-asin.com/asincheck?q=B0BRDR9P4Q

By visiting this page, you can access the fee I pay to Amazon for each sale ($7.90); the fee I pay to Amazon for fulfillment ($5.84); the fee I pay to Amazon for royalties (40%); the "Listing Quality" (Poor); Potential sales (Low); Estimated Daily Sales (11-13 books); Estimated Daily Income ($447.00 - $528.00); Main Search Keywords (open source intelligence techniques); and Amazon Buyer Keywords (100 techniques americas test kitchen). As you can see with that last entry, these results are not all accurate. Well, maybe the Potential Sales entry (Low). I never believe everything I see here, but it can be an indicator of sales versus a competing book.

Rental Vehicle Records

The details of rental vehicles are not technically documents, but the data seemed to fit this category the best. The following options have been controversially received during training and may not be appropriate for everyone. I present these methods to you as theories, and you should evaluate if the techniques are suitable for your research. Several vehicle rental companies offer an option to access your receipts online. This is probably designed for customers that leave a vehicle at the business after hours and later need a receipt. While the processes to retrieve these documents are designed to only obtain your own records, it is easy to view others.

Enterprise (enterprise.com)

At the bottom of every Enterprise web page is an option to "Get a receipt". Clicking this will present a form that must be completed before display of any details. Enterprise will need the driver's license number and last name. Providing this information will display the user's entire rental history for the past six months to three years. Testing with my own data provided two years' worth of results. Each document will link to the entire receipt from that rental. These receipts include the start date and time, end date and time, vehicle make and model, pick up location, total mileage, lease name, and form of payment. This information could be very beneficial to any drug case or private investigation.

Hertz (hertz.com/rentacar/receipts/request-receipts.do)

Similar to Enterprise, Hertz has a link at the bottom of this page titled "Get a receipt". You can search by driver's license number or reservation with last name. The receipt will be similar to the Enterprise demonstration.

Alamo (alamo.com)

Alamo titles their receipt retrieval link "Past Trips/Receipts" and it is located in the bottom portion of every page. The process is identical to the previous two examples. The only difference is that you must choose a date range. I usually select a start date of one year prior to the current date and the end date of the current date.

Thrifty (thrifty.com/Reservations/OnlineReceipts.aspx)

This service requires a last name and either a driver's license number or credit card number.

Dollar (dollar.com/Reservations/Receipt.aspx)

Similar to Thrifty, this service requires a last name and either a driver's license number or credit card number.

Government Document Archives

In additional to using search engines and third party document search sites, I will often seek out repositories of government documents related to my target. This often involves searching for online repositories associated with their specific city, county, and state. This will vary from target to target, but we can also use national resources such as the National Archives which are available at https://www.archives.gov/. The following is a sample URL query which results in dozens of PDFs, spread sheets, and other documents related to my keyword.

https://search.archives.gov/search?query=osint&submit=&utf8=&affiliate=national-archives

There are additional archive tools available at https://www.archives.gov/research/start/online-tools. An alternative service for locating government documents is https://www.govinfo.gov/.

Gender Analyzer (uclassify.com/browse/uclassify/genderanalyzer_v5)

This tool attempts to identify the gender of the person who wrote the text. This can be very hit or miss, but I have found it to be reliable in most of my testing. When supplied five blog posts I wrote within the past two months, it believed that 72% of my words were written by a male person.

IntelTechniques Documents and Pastes Tools

If these resources seem overwhelming, consider my custom document search tools available online at **https://inteltechniques.com/tools/Documents.html** or the file titled "Documents.html" in your download from previous chapters. The first section queries documents by file types. It allows entry of any terms or operators in order to locate PDF, DOC, DOCX, XLS, XLSX, CSV, PPT, PPTX, KEYNOTE, TXT, RTF, XML, ODT, ODS, ODP, ODG, ZIP, RAR, 7Z, JPG, JPEG, PNG, MPG, MP4, MP3, and WAV documents. The second section allows entry of any terms or operators in order to locate files stored within Google Docs, Google Drive, Microsoft Docs, Amazon AWS, CloudFront, SlideShare, Prezi, ISSUU, Scribd, PDF Drive, and others. The "Pastes" search tool at **https://inteltechniques.com/tools/Pastes.html** presents a Google custom search engine (CSE) which queries all paste sites mentioned previously.

CHAPTER TWENTY-NINE
IMAGES

Thanks to cameras on every data cellular phone, digital photograph uploads are extremely common among social network users. These images can create a whole new element to the art of open source intelligence analysis. This chapter will identify various photo sharing websites as well as specific search techniques. Later, photo metadata will be explained that can uncover a new level of information including the location where the picture was taken; the make, model, and serial number of the camera; original uncropped views of the photos; and even a collection of other photos online taken with the same camera. After reading this information, you should question if your online photos should stay online.

Google Images (images.google.com)

During my live training sessions, I always encourage attendees to avoid individual searches on various photo sharing websites such as Flickr or Tumblr. This is because most of these searchable sites have already been indexed by Google and other search engines. Conducting a search for "Oakland Protest" on Flickr will only identify images on that specific service that match. However, conducting the same search on Google Images will identify photos that match the terms on Flickr and hundreds of additional services. Similar to Google's standard search results, you can use the Search Tools to filter by date. Additionally, you can further isolate target images by size, color, and type, such as photographs versus line drawings. I no longer conduct manual searches across the numerous photo sharing sites. Instead, I start with Google Images.

Bing Images (bing.com/images)

Similar to Google, Bing also offers an image search. While it is not as beneficial as the Google option, it should never be overlooked. On several occasions, I have located valuable pictorial evidence on Bing that was missing from Google results. The function is identical, and you can filter search results by date, size, color, type, and license type. When searching for relevant data about a target, I try to avoid any filters unless absolutely necessary. In general, we always want more data, not less. The search techniques explained in Chapter Seventeen all apply to queries on Google Images and Bing Images.

Reverse Image Search

Advancements in computer processing power and image analysis software have made reverse image searching possible on several sites. While a standard search online involves entering text into a search engine for related results, a reverse image search provides an image to a search engine for analysis. The results will vary depending on the site used. Some will identify identical images that appear on other websites. This can be used to identify other websites on which the target used the same image. If you have a photo of a target on a social network, a reverse analysis of that photo may provide other websites on which the target used the same image. These may be results that were not identified through a standard search engine. Occasionally, a target may create a website as an alias, but use an actual photo of himself. Unless you knew the alias name, you would never find the site. Searching for the site by the image may be the only way to locate the profile of the alias. Some reverse image sites go further and try to identify other photos of the target that are similar enough to be matched. Some will even try to determine the sex and age of the subject in the photo based on the analysis of the image. This type of analysis was once limited to expensive private solutions. Now, these services are free to the public.

Google Reverse Image Search (images.google.com)

One of the more powerful reverse image search services is through Google. Rolled out in 2011, this service, now called Google Lens, is often overlooked. On any Google Images page, there is a search field. Inside of this field on the far right is a camera icon that appears slightly transparent. Figure 21.03 (first) displays this search field. Clicking on this icon will open a new search window that will allow for either a web address of an online image, or an upload of an image file on your computer. In order to take advantage of the online search, you must have the exact link to the actual photo online. Locating an image within a website is not enough. You will want to see the image in a web browser by itself, and then copy the address of the image. If I want to view the image from the actual location, I must right-click on the image and select "view image" with my Firefox browser. Chrome users will see "open image in new tab" and Edge users will see "properties" which will identify the URL of the image. This link is what you want in order to conduct a reverse image analysis.

In late 2022, I witnessed many changes to Google's reverse image search process. Today, if you paste a URL into Google's reverse image search, the default result will be "Visual matches" within "Google Lens", which can be seen in Figure 29.01. These are typically images similar to the target, but not a replica of the target. Clicking the "Find image source" button takes you to a new tab with results matching your target image. Adding text context to the search field in this new tab can improve accuracy. As an example, a reverse-search of a photo from LinkedIn might produce many inaccurate results, but including the name or employer of your target will often display only applicable evidence.

Another way to use this service is to search for target text details within the Google Images search page at images.google.com. The images in the results will present additional options when clicked. A larger version of the image will load inside a black box. The options surrounding the image will allow you to visit the page where the image is stored; view the image in full size; crop a portion of the image; or cycle through similar images.

I miss the way Google handled these queries before Google Lens, but we are stuck with whatever they provide us. Let's focus on each feature and identify exact URL submission options. I will start with the following image of a friend of mine (sorry Marcos), which can be seen in Figure 29.01 (left). The original URL follows.

https://s.hdnux.com/photos/01/30/23/25/23147846/3/1200x0.jpg

I can submit this URL directly to Google Lens with the following URL.

https://lens.google.com/uploadbyurl?url=https://s.hdnux.com/photos/01/30/23/25/23147846/3/1200x0.jpg

If I have a name or keyword, and only want to search images through Google, the following URL applies

https://www.google.com/search?tbm=isch&q=Marcos+Pulido

Once within the Google Lens page, you can navigate to the image source or manipulate the current target photo. In this example (Figure 29.01), I cropped the image using the embedded frame, and focused on the unknown person in the lower-left of the image. The result can be seen in Figure 29.02. On occasion, this has been helpful in identifying other people or objects within an image. It also provides an option to extract text from a photo, but I have not needed that yet.

Bing Reverse Image Match (bing.com/images)

In 2014, Bing launched its own reverse image search option titled "Visual Search". This feature can be launched from within any page on Bing Images by clicking the camera icon to the right of the search field. Figure 29.03 (second) displays this option. This service does not seem to be as robust as Google's. In my experience, I often receive either much fewer results, although they do match. On a few occasions, I have received matched images that Google did not locate.

TinEye (tineye.com)

TinEye is another site that will perform a reverse image analysis. These results tend to focus on exact duplicate images. The results here are usually fewer than those found with Google. Since each service often finds images the others do not, all should be searched when using this technique. Figure 29.03 (third) displays the search menu. The icon on the left prompts the user to provide a location on the hard drive for image upload while the search field will accept a URL.

Yandex Images (yandex.ru/images)

Russian search site Yandex has an image search option that can conduct a reverse image search. Similar to the other methods, enter the full address of the online image of interest and search for duplicate images on additional websites. In 2015, Yandex began allowing users to upload an image from their computers. In 2020, I began noticing accurate results from Yandex which were not visible in results from Google, Bing, or TinEye. Today, Yandex may be your best reverse image search option. Figure 29.03 (fourth) displays the reverse image search icon in the far-right portion.

Baidu Images (image.baidu.com)

Similar to Yandex, the Chinese search engine Baidu offers a reverse image search. Baidu currently offers no English version of their website and only presents Chinese text. Navigating to the above website offers a search box that contains a small camera icon to the right. Clicking this presents options for uploading an image (button to left) or providing the URL of an online image within the search field itself. The results will identify similar images on websites indexed by Baidu. Figure 29.03 (fifth) displays the search page only available in Chinese. In my experience, this reverse search option fails more than it functions, and it has been removed from the custom search tools explained in a moment.

Figure 29.01: A Google Lens search via URL.

Figure 29.02: A Google Lens focused search result.

Regardless of the services that you are executing, I urge you to use caution with sensitive images. Similar to my view of analyzing online documents for metadata, I believe that submitting online photos within these engines is harmless. If the photo is already publicly online, there is very little risk exposing it a second time. My concern involves child pornography and classified photos. As a former child pornography investigator and forensic examiner, there were several times that I wanted to look for additional copies of evidence online. However, I could not. Even though no one would know, and the photos would never appear any place they should not, conducting reverse image searches of contraband is illegal. It is technically distributing child pornography (to Google). While working with a large FBI terrorism investigation, I had possession of ten photos on which I wanted to conduct a reverse image search. The photos were part of a classified case, so I could not. Overall, never submit these types of photos from your hard drive. It will always come back to haunt you.

Whenever I have any public images that call for reverse image searching, I always check all five of these services. While I rarely ever get a unique result on Baidu, it only takes a few seconds to check every time. This diligence has paid off in the past. These manual searches do not need to be as time consuming as one may think. We can automate much of this process to save time and encourage thorough investigations. First, we should take a look at direct URL submission. For the following examples, assume that your target image is the cover of my privacy book from the web page at inteltechniques.com/book7.html. The actual target image is stored online at the URL of https://inteltechniques.com/img/EP4-3D.png. The following direct addresses would conduct a reverse image search at each service listed.

Google: https://www.google.com/searchbyimage?image_url=https://inteltechniques.com/img/EP4-3D.png&client=app

Google Lens: https://lens.google.com/uploadbyurl?url=https://inteltechniques.com/img/EP4-3D.png

Bing: https://www.bing.com/images/search?view=detailv2&iss=sbi&q=imgurl:https://inteltechniques.com/img/EP4-3D.png

TinEye: http://www.tineye.com/search/?url=https://inteltechniques.com/img/EP4-3D.png

Yandex: https://yandex.com/images/search?rpt=imageview&url=https://inteltechniques.com/img/EP4-3D.png

Baidu: https://graph.baidu.com/upload?image=https%3A%2F%2Finteltechniques.com%2Fimg%2FEP4-3D.png

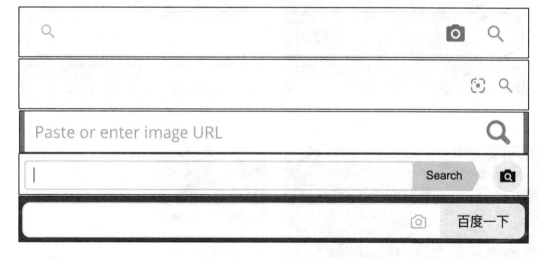

Figure 29.03: Reverse image search options from Google, Bing, TinEye, Yandex, and Baidu.

Cropped Reverse Image Searching

Beginning in 2018, I noticed that both Google Images and Bing Images were returning fewer results than in previous years. It seemed as though each were trying to limit the number of matching photos, possibly with the intent to present only relevant images based on previous search history or whatever they "think" we want from them. In 2019, I had an investigation focused around an online image. When I conducted a reverse image search, I received one result, which was a copy I already knew existed. When I cropped the image to only display my target, I received more search results. I find this technique applicable to Google and Bing, but I believe it works best with Yandex. The following is a demonstration of this method, using a public image posted to Twitter.

Figure 29.04 (left) is the original image obtained from Twitter. A reverse image search through Google, Bing, and Yandex revealed numerous results, but none of them contained my target displayed on the far left. I cropped the image, as seen in Figure 29.04 (right), to display only the target and resubmitted to Yandex. This immediately identified numerous images of the target. Figure 29.05 displays one of these images. Both Google and Bing displayed no results from this cropped image. I cannot stress enough the importance of reverse-searching images through Yandex. I find their service superior to all others.

Figure: 29.04: An original image (left) and cropped version (right).

Figure 29.05: A reverse image search result from Yandex.

FaceCheck (facecheck.id)

While the major search engines will find most generic images, there are two services which stand out for faces and vehicles. I will explain each. FaceCheck surfaced in 2022, and is currently a free alternative to the paid service Pimeyes. It applies artificial intelligence to compare an online or uploaded image to a database of billions of photos which were previously shared online. This is not exact pixel comparison and the matching images do not need to be from the same place or time. This is a series of servers which analyze your target image and attempt to identify any stored images of the same person. The results are creepy to say the least. The online interface encourages you to upload an image, which I am cautious to do. This will likely add it to their collection. Instead, I only submit images which are already online and have likely already been indexed by this service. Let's revisit the following image from the Google Lens demonstration.

https://s.hdnux.com/photos/01/30/23/25/23147846/3/1200x0.jpg

The following URL submits this image, which is a feature otherwise hidden from their service.

https://facecheck.id/#url=https://s.hdnux.com/photos/01/30/23/25/23147846/3/1200x0.jpg

This populated the image and began the analysis, as seen in Figure 29.06. Notice that it automatically determined the face within the image and cropped out any unhelpful details. The final result was twelve images of my target, all of which were captured on various dates with different clothing and background, as partially seen in Figure 29.07. I can click each to access the original location and details. This has uncovered the true identities of countless people associated with my investigations. I suspect this will become a paid service someday, so take advantage of the free version while it lasts.

Figure 29.06: A target image and analysis by FaceCheck.

Figure 29.07: FaceCheck results identifying additional images of a target.

CarNet (carnet.ai)

This is another service which appeared in 2022, and has been extremely beneficial to my investigations. It allows you to upload an image, or provide a URL, of a suspect vehicle, and it will use machine learning to identify the year, make, and model when possible. Let's conduct a demonstration. As I wrote this, someone posted on Reddit asking for assistance identifying the vehicle within the following link, as seen in Figure 29.08 (left).

https://i.redd.it/xf4m1q7t6d0a1.jpg

I uploaded the blurry image into CarNet, which immediately identified it as a 2013-2017 4th generation Holden/Commodore, grey in color. That didn't sound familiar to me, so I assumed it was wrong. Someone much more knowledgeable about vehicles was credited on Reddit as posting the correct answer, a rare "Chevrolet SS built off the Australian Holden Commodore", as seen in Figure 29.08 (right). I have found this service extremely valuable when trying to identify vehicles captured on video doorbells and dash cameras.

Figure 29.08: An image of an unknown vehicle.

Reddit Repost Sleuth (repostsleuth.com)

This service is a reverse image search engine that only provides positive results that appear on the website Reddit. It was originally launched as a way for users to identify when someone reposted a photo that had previously been posted on the website. The user could then "down-vote" the submission and have it removed from the front page. We can use this in investigations to locate every copy of an individual photo on Reddit. You can either provide a link to an image or upload an image from your computer. The following static URL submits our target image for reverse analysis on Reddit.

https://www.repostsleuth.com/search?url= https://inteltechniques.com/img/EP4-3D.png

Root About (rootabout.com)

This is another specialized reverse image search utility which only queries against images stored on the Internet Archive and within Open Library (also an Internet Archive product). Any results will likely contain public images such as published photos and book covers. I have yet to receive any benefit to my investigations with this service, but it should still be available in your arsenal of tools. Root About does not support search via a direct URL.

Wolfram Image Identification Project (imageidentify.com)

While this is not a traditional reverse image search, it does provide value. The goal of this service is to identify the content of an image. If you upload a photo of a car, it will likely tell you the make, year, and model. An upload of an image containing an unknown Chinese word may display a translation and history details. The site prompts you to upload a digital file, but you can also drag and drop an image from a web page in another tab.

Real World Application: These reverse image search sites can have many uses to the investigator. In 2011, I searched a photo of damage to a popular historic cemetery that was vandalized. The results included a similar photo of the suspect showing off the damage on a blog. An arrest and community service soon followed. Later, while working with a private investigator, I was asked to locate any hotels that were using the client's hotel images on websites. A reverse image search identified dozens of companies using licensed photos without authorization. This likely led to civil litigation. More recently, a federal agent asked me to assist with a human trafficking case. He had a woman in custody who spoke little English. She was arrested during a prostitution sting and was suspected of being a victim of trafficking. A reverse image search from one online prostitution ad located all of her other ads which identified the regional areas that she had recently been working, a cellular telephone number connected to her pimp, and approximate dates of all activity.

Pictriev (pictriev.com)

Pictriev is a service that will analyze a photo including a human face and try to locate additional images of the person. The results are best when the image is of a public figure with a large internet presence, but it will work on lesser-known subjects as well. An additional feature is a prediction of the sex of the target as well as age.

Twitter Images

For the first several years of Twitter's existence, it did not host any photos on its servers. If a user wanted to attach a photo to his or her post, a third-party photo host was required. These have always been free and plentiful. Often, a shortened link was added to the message, which forwarded to the location of the photo. Twitter now hosts photos used in Twitter posts, but third-party hosts are still widely used. The majority of the images will be hosted on Instagram, which was previously explained. If you have already identified your target's Twitter page, you will probably have the links you need to see the photos uploaded with his or her posts. Many Twitter messages have embedded images directly within the post. Twitter now allows you to search keywords for photo results. After you conduct any search within the native Twitter search field, your results will include a filter menu on the top. The "Photos" results will only include images which have a reference to the searched keyword within the message or hashtag. You can also filter this search for people, videos, or news. The URL query for all Twitter images associated with "osint" would be https://x.com/search?q=osint&f=media.

Facebook Images

Facebook also allows a query for images. The traditional method is to search a keyword and navigate to the Photos filter. However, we can replicate this via URL at https://www.facebook.com/search/photos/?q=osint.

Tumblr Images

Tumblr blogs have a heavy emphasis on images, and search engines do not always index associated keywords well. Therefore, we should consider a query specifically on the site. The URL query for images associated with "osint" would be https://www.tumblr.com/search/osint. All of these options are included within the custom search tools which are presented at the end of this chapter.

Photo-Sharing Sites

In order to find a photo related to a target, the image must be stored on a website. The most common type of storage for online digital photos is on a photo-sharing site. These sites allow a user to upload photographs to an account or profile. These images can then be searched by anyone with an internet connection. Almost all of these hosts are free for the user and the files will remain on the site until a user removes them. There are dozens of these services, many allowing several gigabytes worth of storage. While I mentioned earlier that a Google Images or Bing Images search was most appropriate for all photo sharing hosts, Flickr deserves a mention.

Flickr (flickr.com)

Flickr, purchased by Yahoo and now owned by SmugMug, was one of the most popular photo-sharing sites on the internet. Many have abandoned it for Twitter and Instagram, but the mass number of images cannot be ignored. The majority of these images are uploaded by amateur photographers and contain little intelligence to an investigator. Yet there are still many images in this "haystack" that will prove to be beneficial to the online researcher. The main website allows for a general search by topic, location, username, real name, or keyword. This search term should be as specific as possible to avoid numerous results. An online username will often take you to that user's Flickr photo album. After you have found either an individual photo, user's photo album, or group of photos by interest, you can begin to analyze the profile data of your target. This may include a username, camera information, and interests. Clicking through the various photos may produce user comments, responses by other users, and location data about the photo. Dissecting and documenting this data can assist with future searches. The actual image of these photos may give all of the intelligence desired, but the data does not stop there. A search for photographs related to the Occupy Wall Street protesters returned over 157,000 results.

Flickr Map (flickr.com/map)

Flickr attempts to geo locate all of the photos that it can. It attempts to identify the location where the photo was taken. It will usually obtain this information from the Exif data, which will be discussed in a moment. It can also tag these photos based on user provided information. Flickr provides a mapping feature that will attempt to populate a map based on your search parameters. I believe this service is only helpful when you are investigating a past incident at a large event or researching the physical layout of a popular attraction.

Flickr API

There are three specific uses of the Flickr Application Programming Interface (API) that I have found helpful during many online investigations. The first queries an email address and identifies any Flickr accounts associated with it. The second queries a username, and identifies the Flickr user number of the connected account. The final option queries a Flickr user number and identifies the attached username. Unfortunately, all of these features require a Flickr API key. I have included a throwaway key within the search tools explained at the end of the chapter. However, it may not function for long after the book is published. If the key should be terminated by Flickr, simply request your own free key at https://www.flickr.com/services/api/. Once issued, replace my test key (27c196593dad58382fc4912b00cf1194) within the code of the tools to your own. A demonstration may help to explain the features. First, I submitted the following URL to Flickr in order to query my target email address of test@test.com.

https://api.flickr.com/services/rest/?method=flickr.people.findByEmail&api_key=27c196593dad58382fc4912b00cf1194&find_email=test@test.com

I immediately received the following result.

User id="8104823@N02" username>intellectarsenal

I now know that my target possesses a Flickr account associated with the email address, the username for the account, and the unique user number which will never change. Next, assume that we only knew the username. The following URL could be submitted.

https://api.flickr.com/services/rest/?method=flickr.people.findByUsername&api_key=27c196593dad58382fc4912b00cf1194&username=intellectarsenal

The response includes the following.

User id="8104823@N02"

Once you have identified the user number, we can submit the following URL.

https://api.flickr.com/services/rest/?method=flickr.people.getInfo&api_key=27c196593dad58382fc4912b00cf1194&user_id=8104823@N02

This returns the most details, including the following result from our target.

username>intellectarsenal
photosurl>https://www.flickr.com/photos/8104823@N02/
profileurl>https://www.flickr.com/people/8104823@N02/

Navigating to the profile displays details such as the join date, followers, and photo albums. This may seem like a lot of work for a minimal number of details, but this is quite beneficial. There is no native email address search on Flickr, but we can replicate the function within the API. You may not find young targets sharing images here, but the massive collection of photos spanning the past decade may present new evidence which was long forgotten by the target.

Exif Data

Every digital photograph captured with a digital camera possesses metadata known as Exif data. I have already explained several applications which extract this data from documents and images, but we need to have a better understanding of the technology. This is a layer of code that provides information about the photo and camera. All digital cameras write this data to each image, but the amount and type of data can vary. This data, which is embedded into each photo "behind the scenes", is not visible by viewing the captured image. You need an Exif reader, which can be found on websites and within applications. Keep in mind that some websites remove or "scrub" this data before storing it on their servers. Facebook, for example, removes the data while Flickr does not. Locating a digital photo online will not always present this data. If you locate an image that appears full size and uncompressed, you will likely still have the data intact. If the image has been compressed to a smaller file size, this data is often lost. Any images removed directly from a digital camera card will always have the data. This is one of the reasons you will always want to identify the largest version of an image when searching online. The quickest way to see the information is through an online viewer.

Exifinfo (exifinfo.org)

Although offline Exif data analyzers are generally preferred, there are occasions where it is beneficial to have an online option. For years this was Jeffrey's Exif Viewer, but that project has been recently discontinued. There are many alternatives, but Exifinfo is easy to use and presents the data in a concise format. The site accepts both image URLs and uploads, but as a reminder we should not upload sensitive photos to third party sites on the internet if they do not already exist in publicly available resources. A good rule of thumb is that if you originally located the image on the open web, then it likely okay to upload it to one of these services. We have an offline Exif viewer in our virtual machine which is a more appropriate option for sensitive images.

Another consideration when pulling Exif data from files is that it is always possible that someone has tampered with the original metadata. This is not a common occurrence but we should keep in mind that at some point in our career we will no doubt run into an image where the Exif data has been purposefully changed from its original state. Exifinfo boasts the following data results, although bear in mind that the data has to be present in the file in the first place so photos from sites which scrub metadata, such as Facebook, will result in very limited file information.

Capture and last edited date and time stamps (with varying precision)
GPS location coordinates (degrees of latitude & longitude)
A small thumbnail of the original image
The author's name and copyright details
Compass heading
Device information including manufacturer, and model
Capture information including lens type, focal range, aperture, shutter speed, flash settings
The original filename

An example of an Exifinfo result can be seen in Figure 29.09. For images with GPS data there is an option on the Exifinfo interface to open the location in OpenStreetMap or you can paste the location coordinates into your mapping service of choice. Exifinfo promises to delete uploaded files immediately after processing, and the resulting analytical data is only stored for three days. This makes it one of the most transparent and privacy respecting online options. The backend of this service utilizes the open source project https://exiftool.org/ which we can run locally if we want an additional offline option.

Figure 29.09: An Exifinfo result identifying location with map view.

Cropped Images

Another piece of information that we can look for inside the Exif data is the presence of a thumbnail image within the photograph. Digital cameras generate a small version of the photo captured and store it within the Exif data. This icon size image adds very little size to the overall file. When a user crops the image, this original smaller version may or may not get overwritten. Programs such as Photoshop or Microsoft Photo Editor will overwrite the data and keep both images identical. Other programs, as well as some online cropping tools, do not overwrite this data. The result is the presence of the original and uncropped image within the Exif data of the cropped photo. An example of this is seen in Figure 29.10. A cropped photo found online is examined through an Exif analyzer. The cropped full-size large photo is seen on the left. The embedded smaller original photo was not overwritten when cropped. We can now see what the image looked like before it was cropped. This technique has been used by police to identify child pornography manufacturers. These pedophiles will crop themselves out of illegal images to avoid identification. When photos of the children are found by police, an original uncropped image may be enough to identify and prosecute a molester. This is not limited to law enforcement. Some tech-savvy fans of television personality Catherine Schwartz examined a cropped photo on her blog in 2003. Inside the Exif data was the uncropped version which exposed her breasts and quickly made the rounds through the internet. We must remember this unfortunate lesson when we consider posting our own content to the internet.

Real World Application: In a civil litigation, a subject claimed an injury that prohibited him from work, walking, and a normal life. The suit claimed damages from pain and suffering and sought a monetary judgment for future lack of ability to work. A brief scan of the subject's online photo album revealed fishing trips, softball games, and family adventure vacations. With Exif information data intact, exact dates, times, locations, and cameras were identified and preserved. The subject withdrew his lawsuit.

Figure 29.10: An Exif summary result displaying an original uncropped photo.

Stolencamerafinder (stolencamerafinder.com)

This site was designed to help camera theft victims with locating their camera if it is being used by the thief online. For that use, you would find a photo taken with the stolen camera, and drop it into Stolen Camera Finder. This analysis identifies a serial number if available based on the metadata of the image or you can enter the serial number into the site manually. The service will search for that serial number within their database of online photos and previous reports of stolen cameras. They also offer a map feature which displays the locations of stolen devices in their database, although this function is less useful for my investigations as I am typically starting with a specific photo or serial number. The website urges users to sign up for a premium service that will make contact if any more images appear in the database, but I have never needed this.

Online Barcode Reader (online-barcode-reader.inliteresearch.com)

Barcodes have been around for decades. They are the vertical lined images printed on various products that allow registers to identify the product and price. Today's barcodes are much more advanced and can contain a large amount of text data within a small image. Some newer barcodes exist in order to allow individuals to scan them with a cell phone. The images can provide a link to a website, instructions for downloading a program, or a secret text message. I generally advise against scanning any unknown barcodes with a mobile device since malicious links could be opened unknowingly. However, an online barcode reader can be used to identify what information is hiding behind these interesting images.

Figure 29.11 displays the barcode search options from Online Barcode Reader. These include 1D, PDF417, Postal, DataMatrix, QR, and ID barcodes. After selecting the type of barcode image, you can select any PDF, TIFF, JPEG, BMP, GIF, or PNG file on your computer up to 12 MB in size. This could be a photo that possesses a barcode in the content or a digital code downloaded from a website. Screen captures of codes also work well. While sitting on a plane with Wi-Fi, I captured a photo of an abandoned boarding pass in the magazine holder in front of me. The barcode reader identified text information stored inside the code that was not present in text on the document.

Figure 29.11: Barcode input samples from Online Barcode Reader.

Additional barcode identification options are as follows.

Online Barcode (onlinebarcodereader.com)
Zxing (zxing.org)
Cognex (manateeworks.com/free-barcode-scanner)
Online Decoder (online-barcode-reader.com)

Image Manipulation

It is common to find images on the internet that have been manipulated using software such as Photoshop. Often it is difficult, if not impossible, to tell if these photos have been manipulated by visually analyzing them. A handful of websites use a technique to determine which portions of the photo have changed.

Foto Forensics (fotoforensics.com)

This site allows you to upload a digital image. After successful upload, it will display the image in normal view. Below this image will be a darkened duplicate image. Any highlighted areas of the image indicate a possible manipulation. While this site should never be used to definitively state that an image is untouched or manipulated, investigators may want to conduct an analysis for intelligence purposes only. Figure 29.12 displays original and manipulated images while Figure 29.13 displays the analysis of the images from Foto Forensics. This site will provide an analysis of an image from the internet or a file uploaded from a computer. It is important to note that any images uploaded become part of the website's collection and a direct URL is issued. While it would be difficult for someone to locate the URL of the images, it could pose a security risk for sensitive files.

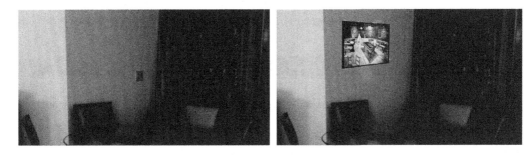

Figure 29.12: An original photograph (left) compared to a manipulated photograph (right).

Figure 29.13: The original photograph (left) and manipulated image (right) on Foto Forensics.

Forensically (29a.ch/photo-forensics)

Forensically is a robust image analyzer that offers a huge collection of photo forensic tools that can be applied to any uploaded image. This type of analysis can be vital when image manipulation is suspected. Previous tools have offered one or two of the services that Forensically offers, but this new option is an all-in-one solution for image analysis. Loading the page will present a demo image, which is used for this explanation. Clicking the "Open File" link on the upper left will allow upload of an image into your browser for analysis. Images are NOT uploaded to the server of this tool; they are only brought into your browser locally. Figure 29.14 (left) is the standard view of a digital photo. The various options within Forensically are each explained and example images are included.

The Magnifier allows you to see small hidden details in an image. It does this by magnifying the size of the pixels and the contrast within the window. There are three different enhancements available at the moment: Histogram Equalization, Auto Contrast, and Auto Contrast by Channel. Auto Contrast mostly keeps the colors intact; the others can cause color shifts. Histogram Equalization is the most robust option. You can also set this to none.

The Clone Detector highlights copied regions within an image. These can be a good indicator that a picture has been manipulated. Minimal Similarity determines how similar the cloned pixels need to be to the original. Minimal Detail controls how much detail an area needs; therefore, blocks with less detail than this are not considered when searching for clones. Minimal Cluster Size determines how many clones of a similar region need to be found in order for them to show up as results. Block Size determines how big the blocks used for the clone detection are. You generally don't want to touch this. Maximal Image Size is the maximal width or height of the image used to perform the clone search. Bigger images take longer to analyze. Show Quantized Image shows the image after it has been compressed. This can be useful to tweak Minimal Similarity and Minimal Detail. Blocks that have been rejected because they do not have enough detail show up as black. Figure 29.14 (right) demonstrates this output.

Figure 29.14: A normal image view (left) and Clone Detector (right) in Forensically.

Error Level Analysis compares the original image to a recompressed version. This can make manipulated regions stand out in various ways. For example, they can be darker or brighter than similar regions which have not been manipulated. JPEG Quality should match the original quality of the image that has been photoshopped. Error Scale makes the differences between the original and the recompressed image bigger. Magnifier Enhancement offers different enhancements: Histogram Equalization, Auto Contrast, and Auto Contrast by Channel. Auto Contrast mostly keeps the colors intact; the others can cause color shifts. Histogram Equalization is the most robust option. You can also set this to none. Opacity displays the opacity of the Differences layer. If you lower it, you will see more of the original image. Figure 29.15 (left) displays manipulation.

Noise Analysis is basically a reverse de-noising algorithm. Rather than removing the noise it removes the rest of the image. It is using a super simple separable median filter to isolate the noise. It can be useful for identifying manipulations to the image like airbrushing, deformations, warping, and perspective corrected cloning. It works best on high quality images. Smaller images tend to contain too little information for this to work. Noise Amplitude makes the noise brighter. Equalize Histogram applies histogram equalization to the noise. This can reveal things but it can also hide them. You should try both histogram equalization and scale to analyze the noise. Magnifier Enhancement offers three different enhancements: Histogram Equalization, Auto Contrast, and Auto Contrast by Channel. Auto Contrast mostly keeps the colors intact; the others can cause color shifts. Histogram Equalization is the most robust option. You can also set this to none. Opacity is the opacity of the noise layer. If you lower it, you will see more of the original image. The result can be seen in Figure 29.15 (right).

Figure 29.15: Error Level Analysis (left) and Noise Analysis (right) in Forensically.

Level Sweep allows you to quickly sweep through the histogram of an image. It magnifies the contrast of certain brightness levels. To use this tool simply move your mouse over the image and scroll with your mouse wheel. Look for interesting discontinuities in the image. Sweep is the position in the histogram to be inspected. You can quickly change this parameter by using the mouse wheel while hovering over the image, this allows you to sweep through the histogram. Width is the amount of values (or width of the slice of the histogram) to be inspected. The default should be fine. Opacity is the opacity of the sweep layer. If you lower it, you will see more of the original image.

Luminance Gradient analyzes the changes in brightness along the x and y axis of the image. Its obvious use is to look at how different parts of the image are illuminated in order to find anomalies. Parts of the image which are at a similar angle (to the light source) and under similar illumination should have a similar color. Another use is to check edges. Similar edges should have similar gradients. If the gradients at one edge are significantly sharper than the rest it's a sign that the image could have been copied and pasted. It does also reveal noise and compression artifacts quite well. Figure 29.16 (left) displays this view.

PCA performs principal component analysis on the image. This provides a different angle to view the image data which makes discovering certain manipulations and details easier. This tool is currently single threaded and quite slow when running on big images. Choose one of the following Modes: Projection of the value in the image onto the principal component; Difference between the input and the closest point on the selected principal component; Distance between the input and the closest point on the selected principal component; or the closest point on the selected principal Component. There are three different enhancements available: Histogram Equalization, Auto Contrast, and Auto Contrast by Channel. Auto Contrast mostly keeps the colors intact; the others can cause color shifts. Histogram Equalization is the most robust option. You can also set this to none. Opacity is the opacity of the sweep layer. If you lower it, you will see more of the original image. Figure 29.16 (right) displays this view.

Figure 29.16: The Luminance analysis (left) and PCA analysis (right) within Forensically.

MetaData displays any Exif metadata in the image. Geo Tags shows the GPS location where the image was taken, if it is stored in the image. Figure 29.17 displays the result.

Thumbnail Analysis shows any hidden preview image inside the original image. The preview can reveal details of the original image or the camera used. Figure 29.18 displays the online image (left) while the original thumbnail displays a different view (right).

The next time you identify a digital image as part of your online investigation, these tools will peek behind the scenes and may display evidence of tampering.

Make	SONY		GPSVersionID	2,2,0,0
Model	ILCE-6000		GPSLatitudeRef	N
Orientation	1		GPSLatitude	47.35
XResolution	300		GPSLongitudeRef	E
YResolution	300		GPSLongitude	8.498
ResolutionUnit	2			
Software	darktable 1.6.6			
ModifyDate	2015:08:14 13:32:39			
YCbCrPositioning	2			
Rating	1			
RatingPercent	20			
DateTimeOriginal	Thu Jul 31 2014 09:05:43 GMT-0700 (PDT)			

- View on OpenStreepMap
- View on Google Maps
- Other Images around here on Flickr

Figure 29.17: Metadata from Forensically.

Figure 29.18: An online image (left) and original thumbnail image (right) on Forensically.

Image Enlarging & Upscaling

There may be times when you have an image of poor quality which you may wish to enhance. Typically, this is not advised since you may be manipulating evidence, but there are scenarios where this may be justified. A blurry image of a license plate could warrant the manipulation of an image for clarity. Let's look at two options.

IMG Enlarger (imglarger.com)

This option requires a free account, and only magnifies the overall image. It simply doubles everything in size. I have not found this extremely valuable.

IMG Upscaler (imgupscaler.com)

This option does not require an account and uses various software programming to truly enhance an image. In 2021, I uploaded a blurry vehicle with a license plate which barely identified half of the digits. This tool clarified two additional digits which led to the discovery of the full registration.

Aperisolve (aperisolve.com)

This new service replicates some of the methods previously explained, but adds a few unique options. I uploaded the image from the FaceCheck example and allowed the service to conduct a full analysis. It displayed the typical file attributes and metadata, but then displayed the image with various superimposed values and attempted to identify any steganography patterns. This allowed me to hunt for any hidden artifacts which may not have been present within the previous utilities. Overall, I reserve this tool for situations when I suspect modification to a file which may include hidden data.

GeoSpy (geospy.ai)

This one gets creepy. It analyzes an image and tries to identify the location based on the image itself, and not any metadata. I was skeptical, so I uploaded an image of a random stone bridge posted by someone I know on Twitter. The result accurately declared "This image depicts a stone bridge over a creek in the Watchung Reservation in Millburn, New Jersey."

Detecting AI Generated Images

The widespread increase in services offering "AI" generated images is drastically increasing the number of inauthentic photos and images on the internet. Anytime I run across a questionable image, I complete a reverse image search to potentially locate other instances or versions of the target file. Another step is to use one of the metadata or error level analysis tools previously mentioned to reveal indications that the photo is not authentic. In addition to these steps, there are multiple third party sites which boast the ability to detect artificially generated content. **Sightengine** (sightengine.com) and **Is It AI** (isitai.com/ai-image-detector/) performed well in our tests, although both platforms require that we create a free account. Figure 29.19 displays an example.

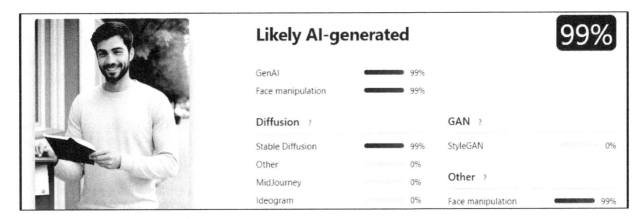

Figure 29.19: AI image detection using Sight Engine.

Manual Visual Analysis

This is the process of analyzing the visual data in the images posted by our target. I typically carry out this step last and only on major investigations as it is time consuming. Visual analysis is simply closely inspecting the images visually for leads displayed in the depictions themselves. I typically start with any photos shared by my target in which they may have unintentionally disclosed location or identity information. Selfies and social media photos tend to be a gold mine. These are often taken at one's home, workplace, or vehicle, potentially narrowing down my target's residence, employer, and other details which might assist in identifying or locating them. Aside from potential investigative leads, these images can be a gold mine should the case result in enforcement action. On a child exploitation case, a series of photos the suspect posted to social media disclosed the presence, make, and model of several computers which we were able to later seize only because the photos tipped us off that they existed. When finally serving a search warrant, we were also able to provide a briefing on counter surveillance and security measures in the suspect's residence prior to sending in tactical teams, which reduced the risks involved and prevented the target from having the opportunity to destroy evidence.

IntelTechniques Images Tool

I have created an offline and online (**https://inteltechniques.com/tools/Images.html**) tool which automates most techniques presented within this chapter. The first search options replicate the reverse-search techniques explained for Google, Bing, and others. The "Submit All" option on this page executes keyword searches across all popular networks into separate tabs on your browser.

CHAPTER THIRTY
VIDEOS

Online videos may now be more common than online photographs. The cameras in smart data phones can act as video cameras. In some situations, uploading a video to the internet is easier than a photograph. Most social networks now act as independent video hosts for their platforms. Video sharing sites such as YouTube have made video publication effortless. For investigations, a video can contain a huge amount of intelligence. When any abnormal event happens, people flock to their phones and start recording. These videos may capture criminal acts, embarrassing behavior, or evidence to be used in a civil lawsuit. Obtaining these videos is even easier than creating them.

YouTube (youtube.com)

The most popular video-sharing site is YouTube. The official YouTube site declares that 500 hours of video are uploaded every minute, resulting in nearly 80 years of content uploaded every day. It further states that over a billion videos are viewed each day. These impressive statistics confirm the need to include videos as part of a complete OSINT analysis. YouTube is easy to search from the main search field on every page. This field can accept any search term and will identify video content or username. Users that upload videos to YouTube have their own "channel". Their videos are uploaded to this channel, and locating a user's channel will identify the videos uploaded by that user.

Many people use YouTube as a social network, leaving comments about videos and participating in discussions about various topics. If you locate a video of interest, it is important to also retrieve this text information. Each comment below a video will include the username that created the comment, which will link to that user's profile.

A search for "school bus fight" returned over 500,000 video links on YouTube. Adding a search term such as the city or school name may help, but it may also prohibit several wanted videos from appearing. The "Filter" option can be expanded to help limit the search scope. This button is above the first video result. This provides additional filter options including the ability to sort by the upload date (date range), type (video vs. channel), duration (short or long), and features (video quality). In the "school bus fight" example, the "uploaded this week" option was chosen. This resulted in only 700 videos which could easily be examined for any intelligence. The lower left portion of any video page includes a link to the profile of the user who submitted this video. This profile page includes all of the videos uploaded by that user and additional profile information. Several YouTube "hacks" have surfaced over the years. Many of these stopped working as YouTube made changes to the environment. Of those still functioning, I find the following techniques helpful to my investigations.

Bypass Age and Login Restriction

Several YouTube videos have been tagged as violent, sexual, or otherwise inappropriate for young viewers. Others demand that you log in to a Google account in order to view the content for unclear reasons. Either way, this is an unnecessary roadblock to your investigation. As an OSINT investigator, I prefer to not be logged in to any personal or covert account while I am researching. Any time you are searching through a Google product while logged in to an account, Google is documenting your every move. This can be unsettling. One easy technique should remove this restriction. Navigate to the following website and notice the inability to view the video. If you are not logged in to a Google account with a verified age, you should see a warning about mature content. This video cannot be played.

https://www.youtube.com/watch?v=SZqNKAd_gTw

We can now append the beginning of this URL with "nsfw", as follows.

https://www.nsfwyoutube.com/watch?v=SZqNKAd_gTw

You should be able to play the video through this page. Please be warned that the content in this example contains very disturbing video, hence the blockage by YouTube. The download techniques explained in Chapter Ten should also bypass this restriction.

Bypass Commercials with Full Screen

It seems lately that every long YouTube video I play possesses a 30 second commercial at the beginning. This is very frustrating when analyzing a large number of videos. The same URL trick will bypass this annoyance. Navigate to the following address and notice the commercial at the beginning.

http://www.youtube.com/watch?v=IEIWdEDFlQY

Alter this address slightly in order to force the video to play in full screen in your browser. This will also bypass any commercials. The URL should appear like the following.

https://www.youtube.com/embed/IEIWdEDFlQY

Display Thumbnails of Videos

When a user uploads a video, YouTube captures and displays a frame for that media. This is the still frame you see when searching videos and before a video is played. These possess a static URL, which will be helpful when we discuss reverse video searching. As an example, navigate to the following address to load a demo video.

https://www.youtube.com/watch?v=1nm1jEJmOTQ

Using that same video ID, navigate to the following address to view the main still frame. This is the image visible when a video is loaded within YouTube before playing.

https://i.ytimg.com/vi/1nm1jEJmOTQ/hqdefault.jpg

The address that displayed the main image is not your only option. An additional high-resolution image can usually be extracted from this specific video with the following address.

https://i.ytimg.com/vi/1nm1jEJmOTQ/maxresdefault.jpg

Furthermore, we can extract four unique frames with the following URLs.

https://img.youtube.com/vi/1nm1jEJmOTQ/0.jpg
https://img.youtube.com/vi/1nm1jEJmOTQ/1.jpg
https://img.youtube.com/vi/1nm1jEJmOTQ/2.jpg
https://img.youtube.com/vi/1nm1jEJmOTQ/3.jpg

In a moment, our tools will query all of these images for download and reverse image searching.

Identify and Bypass Country Restriction

Many videos on YouTube are allowed to be viewed in some countries and blocked in others. If you encounter a video that will not play for you because of a country restriction, you have options. We will use the following video as a demonstration.

http://youtube.com/watch?v=cgEnBkmcpuQ

Visiting this URL from a U.S. IP address should present " Video unavailable - The uploader has not made this video available in your country". Before proceeding, consider identifying from which geographical areas a video is restricted. After you have identified a video with possible country restrictions, paste the video ID into the following URL. Our video ID is cgEnBkmcpuQ.

http://polsy.org.uk/stuff/ytrestrict.cgi?ytid=cgEnBkmcpuQ

The result is a page with a world map. Countries in grey are allowed to view the target video while countries in red are not. Another service which replicates this is WatanNetwork. The following URL displays their map.

https://watannetwork.com/tools/blocked/#url=cgEnBkmcpuQ

While I cannot natively play this video due to my location, I can easily view the default and high resolution still frames with the technique described in the previous section. The following exact URLs display content otherwise not viewable.

https://i.ytimg.com/vi/cgEnBkmcpuQ/hqdefault.jpg
https://i.ytimg.com/vi/cgEnBkmcpuQ/maxresdefault.jpg

If a video is blocked from playing in your location, you can usually use a VPN which should allow viewing. Identify which countries are not blocked using the previous methods and select a server in one of those areas. The internet is full of "YouTube Proxy" websites which promise to play any blocked video, but I have found them to be unreliable.

YouTube Metadata

Most of the details of a YouTube video can be seen on the native page where the video is stored. Occasionally, some of this data may not be visible due to privacy settings or profile personalization. In order to confirm that you are retrieving all possible information, you should research the data visible from YouTube's servers. The most comprehensive way to do this is through Google's YouTube API. Any Google account can request a free API key from Google at developers.google.com. You will need to create a new project and enable a YouTube API key. For your convenience and the search tools, I have already created the following key.

AIzaSyDNALbuV1FZSRy6JpafwUaV_taSVV12wZw

I suspect this key will be abused and disabled at some point, but I will keep the key used in the tools updated. Creating your own key prevents outages. We can now use this for the following query based on our target video.

https://www.googleapis.com/youtube/v3/videos?id=cgEnBkmcpuQ&part=snippet,statistics,recordingDetail s&key=AIzaSyDNALbuV1FZSRy6JpafwUaV_taSVV12wZw

This presents a text-only view of all metadata associated with the target video (cgEnBkmcpuQ). While any YouTube video page displays estimated dates, like, dislikes, and comment counts, the metadata is more precise. The following is partial data extracted from our demonstration. I believe every YouTube investigation should document all metadata.

"publishedAt": "2012-07-24T18:33:57Z",
"channelId": "UCP6YCSvxq2HEX33Sd-iC4zw",
"viewCount": "656405279",
"likeCount": "1421566",
"dislikeCount": "717133",
"favoriteCount": "0", "commentCount": "1173"

YouTube Profiles

If you ever locate a video of interest, you should investigate the profile which hosts the content. As stated earlier, every YouTube video is associated with a profile. Clicking the uploader's name directly below a video should display this content. However, the profile page displays only a portion of available results. Let's conduct a demonstration. Assume you have identified a suspect video which is associated with the profile at https://www.youtube.com/user/SnubsieBoo. Viewing this page tells you that she has approximately 35,000 subscribers and videos. However, we can dig deeper into her account with the following URL.

https://www.youtube.com/feeds/videos.xml?user=SnubsieBoo

This text-only page presented a lot of data, but I am most interested in the following.

```
<name>Shannon Morse</name>
<yt:channelId>UCNofX8wmSJh7NTklvMqueOA</yt:channelId>
<link="https://www.youtube.com/channel/UCNofX8wmSJh7NTklvMqueOA"/>
<published>2006-08-16T23:23:03+00:00</published>
```

These details tell us her Channel ID assigned to her username and the exact date and time she created her YouTube account. All of this should be documented within our investigation. After this content, you can see the metadata of each video, which includes the following.

```
<published>2020-11-21T15:00:05+00:00</published>
<updated>2020-11-21T15:00:05+00:00</updated>
<media:starRating count="48" average="4.75" min="1" max="5"/>
<media:statistics views="374"/>
```

This tells us the exact creation and modification times of each video along with viewer details. Again, this text can be helpful in our report. If you created your own API key as explained in the previous page, you can query more details. The following uses my own key and her Channel ID.

https://youtube.googleapis.com/youtube/v3/channels?part=snippet&id=UCNofX8wmSJh7NTklvMqueOA&key=AIzaSyDNALbuV1FZSRy6JpafwUaV_taSVV12wZw

The results tell us she is in the United States ("country": "US") and has a custom YouTube URL at https://www.youtube.com/ShannonMorse ("customUrl": "shannonmorse"). Finally, we can retrieve a full-size image of her profile photo within this code. The following URL appears after "High". This links to a high-resolution (800x800) image of her profile picture, which is otherwise only available as a 160x160 icon. All of the search options on this page are available in the Videos Tool presented later.

yt3.ggpht.com/ytc/AAUvwnix3Pc9x9SX4z85pV6MtKGGTndGxIGqV8_dWJ9bsPw=s800-c

Reverse Image Search

You learned about reverse image searching in the previous chapter. Since YouTube allows us to extract frames from any video without playing the video itself, we can easily automate reverse image searching of those images. We already know that the maximum resolution image for our target video is available at https://i.ytimg.com/vi/cgEnBkmcpuQ/maxresdefault.jpg. Therefore, the following URL would conduct a reverse image search via Google, which should identify additional copies of this video. The Videos Tool will replicate this across Bing, Yandex, and TinEye using the methods explained in previous chapters.

https://www.google.com/searchbyimage?image_url=https://i.ytimg.com/vi/cgEnBkmcpuQ/maxresdefault.jpg&client=app

This URL presents 305 results, including links to the target video available within dozens of additional video platforms. While this works well on YouTube videos, complete reverse video searching across multiple networks will be explained later in this chapter. The search tools presented at the end automates all of these techniques.

Immediate Download Options

My preferred method for extracting YouTube and other online videos was explained in previous chapters while discussing YouTube-DL and yt-dlp within a Linux, Mac, or Windows OSINT machine. **This will always be the most stable and reliable option, and you should be proficient with the video download strategies explained within Chapter Ten.** However, if you have no software or browser plugins available to you, there is another easy option. While you are watching any YouTube video, you can add "deturl.com/" to the address in order to download the video to your computer. To test this, navigate to the following.

https://www.youtube.com/watch?v=t2mU6USTBRE

Now, add "deturl.com/" to the beginning, as indicated in the following address.

https://deturl.com/www.youtube.com/watch?v=t2mU6USTBRE

You will be presented a new page with many options including the ability to download the video; download only the audio; convert the video to a different format; and bypass the age restriction as discussed earlier. Additional options include yout.com and y2mate.com.

YouTube Comments

As a reminder, the Video Download Tool previously presented for Linux, Mac, and Windows possesses YouTube-Tool, which extracts comments from video pages. I believe this type of documentation should be a part of every investigation associated with a YouTube video. However, you can also search through all video comments with an online tool. **YouTube Comment Finder** (ytcomment.kmcat.uk) allows a query of any term against all comments posted to a video. This is beneficial when a target video possesses thousands of comments which cannot be loaded into a single page.

The previous video currently has over 42,000 comments. After populating the YouTube URL into YouTube Comment Finder, we can search within those comments. Assume I wanted to know if anyone mentioned MTV within these 42,000 comments. A query for that term immediately displayed the seven results which include MTV. Furthermore, all results display the name of the poster; the full comment; the number of likes and replies; a link to the native comment on the YouTube page; and the exact date and time of post, as seen below.

Brian Teel
This video could never be made today. MTV would be boycotted just for playing it.
Show Comment | Likes: 0 | Replies: 0 | 2/20/2022, 17:07:38

This is a great benefit to our investigations. I wanted to reverse-engineer the method for this query in case the YouTube Comment Finder site ever shut down. It seems they are querying the Google API for the data. The following is the structure, assuming you are searching through the comments of YouTube ID "t2mU6USTBRE".

https://www.googleapis.com/youtube/v3/commentThreads?part=id,snippet&videoId=**t2mU6USTBRE**&pageToken=&order=Relevance&maxResults=100&searchTerms=&textFormat=plainText&key=AIzaSyDNALbuV1FZSRy6JpafwUaV_taSVV12wZw

The results are not as pretty as displayed through the previous website, but the text-only view from an official Google source could be desired. The following displays the API view of the same comment.

"kind": "youtube#commentThread",
"etag": "qdR5vhARYWedx117YcpTnx9vECY",
"id": "Ugyk7ac2hEf7tOAAnA54AaABAg",
"snippet": {
  "videoId": "t2mU6USTBRE",
  "topLevelComment": {
    "kind": "youtube#comment",
    "etag": "Tp1XaLoiR_MaAFs-XL_6I8Y5Ur4",
    "id": "Ugyk7ac2hEf7tOAAnA54AaABAg",
    "snippet": {
      "videoId": "t2mU6USTBRE",
      "textDisplay": "This video could never be made today. MTV would be boycotted just for playing it.",
      "textOriginal": "This video could never be made today. MTV would be boycotted just for playing it.",
      "authorDisplayName": "Brian Teel",
      "authorProfileImageUrl":
"https://yt3.ggpht.com/ytc/AMLnZu8KhBLuYE6dKaC2N43QqL2eeLiPb3a36xPkuyk=s48-c-k-c0x00ffffff-no-rj",
      "authorChannelUrl": "http://www.youtube.com/channel/UCMF3qEhJlHmXYarRyGe5MTQ",
      "authorChannelId": {
        "value": "UCMF3qEhJlHmXYarRyGe5MTQ" },
      "canRate": true,
      "viewerRating": "none",
      "likeCount": 0,
      "publishedAt": "2022-02-21T00:07:38Z",
      "updatedAt": "2022-02-21T00:07:38Z"}},
  "canReply": true,
  "totalReplyCount": 0,
  "isPublic": true

YouTube Channel Crawler (channelcrawler.com)

As previously explained, anyone can search YouTube and filter by Channels. This allows you to only see results which possess one or more videos within a designated Channel. Unfortunately, the results place emphasis on the most popular channels. Within an investigation, it is much more likely that your target will not have thousands of views or followers. Instead, a channel with no subscribers is more common. Finding these poorly-visited channels is quite difficult with official search options.

Instead, we can find these lesser-known collections with YouTube Channel Crawler. Let's conduct an example demonstration. I queried the term "Guns" within YouTube, clicked the filters option, and chose to only display Channels. I received numerous results, and every Channel featured over 100,000 subscribers. I would never find my target there. Now, let's use our crawler. I chose the term of "Guns", no limit to the results, a maximum of 40 subscribers and 40 total views, and did not specify a date range. Figure 30.01 displays partial results. As you can see, these Channels receive very little attention, but were at the top of my results due to the filters I applied.

Figure 30.01: Channel results on YouTube Channel Crawler.

YouTube Unlisted Videos

YouTube videos can be classified as "Public", "Private", or "Unlisted". Public videos appear within YouTube search results; private videos require an invitation from the host; and unlisted videos sit in between. Unlisted videos will not appear within search results, but they can be seen by anyone possessing the direct URL. There are two methods to discover unlisted videos. First, we can conduct a search on Google such as the following.

site:youtube.com "This video is unlisted" intitle:osint

This can be unreliable, as it presents videos which contain "This video is unlisted" within the description provided by the uploader. I find **Unlisted Videos** (unlistedvideos.com) to be more reliable. Conduct a keyword search on this site to identify videos which are unlisted and not present within search results.

YouTube is not the only video sharing service on the internet. Wikipedia identifies dozens of these sites, but searching each of them can become tedious. These sites are no longer restricted to pages of video files with standard extensions such as mp4, mpg, and flv. Today, services such as Instagram allow embedded videos which do not conform to yesterday's video standards. Many new services present the viewer with animated gif files that only appear as true videos. Fortunately, search engines like Google, Bing, and Yandex offer a search across all of the types.

Google Videos (google.com/videohp)

A search on YouTube for "school bus fight" returned over 500,000 results. However, Google Videos returned 3 million results. These include the results identified in the previous YouTube search plus any videos from other sites that meet the search criteria. This will often lead to duplicate videos that have been posted by news websites and social networks. Google can filter these results by duration time, date and time captured, and video source. The top menu of any Google video results page will display these options. A Google search for the term "female street fight", including filters for videos with a short duration that were posted this week from any source, returned over 900 results. These results could either be further filtered with search terms or quickly viewed by still frame to determine relativity to the investigation.

Bing Videos (bing.com/videos)

One feature that makes Bing a favorite site for searching videos is the instant video playback option. When viewing a video search results page, simply hovering the cursor over the video still shot will start the video playback from the beginning of the video. This eliminates the need to navigate to each video page for playback to determine the value of the video. Bing also offers filtering by length and source. The "select view" toolbar at the top of each search result page will allow you to sort the results by either the best match or the most recent. Whether using Google or Bing to locate videos, I recommend turning off the safe search feature. This feature is designed to prohibit some videos with adult content from displaying. With investigations, it is often these types of videos that are wanted.

Yandex Videos (yandex.com/video)

In 2020, Yandex's video search option became a contender for OSINT usage. While Google and Bing are constantly removing videos, which violate their policies associated with violent and inappropriate content, Yandex seems to allow anything. Similar to my recommendations for general search and images, Yandex Videos should always be queried when researching any video file. Direct query URLs for all three services follows.

https://www.google.com/search?tbm=vid&q=osint
https://www.bing.com/videos/search?q=osint
https://yandex.com/video/search?text=osint

Social Network Videos

Google, Bing, and Yandex index social networks for video pages, but these search engines can never replicate internal queries through popular networks such as Twitter, Facebook, Reddit, and others. We should always consider a keyword search directly within these services. The following assumes "osint" is your search term and provides a direct URL for each network query.

Twitter: https://x.com/search?q=osint&f=media
Facebook: https://www.facebook.com/search/videos/?q=osint
Reddit: https://www.reddit.com/search?q=site:v.redd.it%20AND%20osint&type=media
TikTok: https://www.tiktok.com/tag/osint

When you locate videos embedded within social networks, use the previous methods to download any evidence. I always start with the Video Download Tool. If it is a live stream, I use the Video Stream Tool. If neither are available or functioning, browser extensions may work. If you get desperate, try various free third-party tools such as **Twitter Video Downloader** (twittervideodownloader.com), **FDown** (fdown.net), and **Instagram Downloader** (igdown.net).

Deleted Videos

It has become very common for people to remove their YouTube videos. This often happens when unwanted attention is generated and the user regrets the post. The following technique will not always work, but I have had many successes within my own investigations. Consider the following video which has been removed from YouTube.

https://www.youtube.com/watch?v=9ZmsnTDLykk

The Internet Archive has been mirroring YouTube videos for years and often possesses their own independent copies. We can look for this with the following URL.

https://web.archive.org/web/https://www.youtube.com/watch?v=9ZmsnTDLykk

This identifies 276 captures of this video page. However, these are HTML archives, and the video will not play within any of them. These pages are beneficial for locating comments associated with your target video, but not for the video content itself. We can use the following URL to play the full resolution version of the archived video.

https://web.archive.org/web/2oe_/http://wayback-fakeurl.archive.org/yt/9ZmsnTDLykk

We can now right-click on the video to save our own offline copy. You would only need to replace your target YouTube video ID with the one listed here (9ZmsnTDLykk). Our search tools will replicate this for you at the end of the chapter.

Reverse Video Searching

There was a brief mention earlier of conducting a reverse image search on the still captures of a YouTube video. This would use the same techniques as mentioned in Chapter Twenty-Nine for images. While there is no official reverse video search option, applying the techniques to still captures of videos can provide amazing results. This method is not limited to YouTube. We can conduct reverse image searches on videos from many sites. As the popularity of online videos is catching up to images, we must always consider reverse video searches. They will identify additional websites hosting the target videos of interest. Before explaining the techniques, consider the reasons that you may want to conduct this type of activity.

- School resource officers and personnel are constantly notified of inappropriate video material being posted online. Identifying these videos, consisting of fights, malicious plans, and bullying, may be enough to take care of the situation. However, identifying the numerous copies on other websites will help understand the magnitude of the situation.

- Global security divisions monitoring threats from protest groups will likely encounter videos related to these activities. However, identifying the numerous copies on various websites will often disclose commentary, online discussions, and additional threats not seen in the primary source video.

- Human trafficking investigators can now reverse search videos posted to escort providers similar to the now seized site Backpage. The presence of identical videos posted to numerous geographical areas will highlight the travel and intentions of the pimps that are broadcasting the details.

There are limitless reasons why reverse video searching should be a part of your everyday research. The following methods will get you started with the most popular video websites. These techniques can be replicated as you find new services of interest.

YouTube: As explained earlier, YouTube offers four still frames for every video uploaded plus a high-resolution image. Obtain the URLs outlined during that instruction, and provide each to Google, Bing, Yandex, TinEye, and Baidu as a reverse image search as previously explained. The Videos Tool presented later will automate this process.

Vimeo: Vimeo does not natively offer URLs with a video ID that display screen captures of multiple frames. However, they do provide a single high definition still capture for every video. This is stored in the Application Programming Interface (API) side of Vimeo, but it is easy to obtain. As an example, consider your target is at https://vimeo.com/99199734. The unique ID of 99199734 is assigned to that video. You can use that number to access the video's API view at https://vimeo.com/api/oembed.json?url=https://vimeo.com/99199734. This address will display a text only page with the following content.

Type: "video",
version: "1.0",
provider_name: "Vimeo",
provider_url: "https://vimeo.com/",
title: "Billy Talent 'Try Honesty'",
author_name: "S M T",
author_url: "https://vimeo.com/user10256640",
is_plus: "0",
html: "<iframe src="https://player.vimeo.com/video/99199734" width="480" height="272" frameborder="0" title="Billy Talent 'Try Honesty'" webkitallowfullscreen mozallowfullscreen allowfullscreen></iframe>",
width: 480,
height: 272,
duration: 247,
description: "Music Video Directed by Sean Michael Turrell.",
thumbnail_url: "https://i.vimeocdn.com/video/513053154_295x166.jpg",
thumbnail_width: 295,
thumbnail_height: 167,
upload_date: "2014-06-25 21:29:06",
video_id: 99199734,

The portion relevant to this topic is the thumbnail URL. Following that description is an exact address of the "medium" image used at the beginning of each Vimeo video. Removing the "_295x166.jpg" from the end of the URL presents a full size option, such as the following.

https://i.vimeocdn.com/video/513053154

We will use this static URL within our tools. Also note that this view identifies the exact date and time of upload. The video page view only identified the date as "1 Year Ago". A reverse image search of the thumbnail URL, using our video search tools in a moment, will produce additional websites which host the same (or similar) video.

Others: Repeating this process for every video sharing website can get redundant quickly. Instead, consider the following. Practically every online video possesses a still image that is displayed to represent the video before being played in search results. This image is likely a direct link that can be seen in the source code. Searching "jpg" and "png" may quickly identify the proper URL. Providing this image to various reverse image search websites will likely display additional copies of the target video within unknown websites.

Internet Archive (archive.org)

The premise of this site is to permanently store open source movies, which can include commercial and amateur releases. The search option at the beginning of every page allows for a specific section of the site to be searched. Selecting "community video" will provide the best results for amateur video. A large number of anti-government and anti-American videos are present and ready for immediate download. Unlike YouTube, this site does not make it easy to identify the user that uploaded the videos. Furthermore, it does not link to other videos uploaded by the same user. To do this, you will need to look for some very specific text data. As an example, consider that Internet Archive user Enver_Awlaki is your target. His video profile is located at http://www.archive.org/details/Enver_Awlaki. One of his video pages is stored at the address of https://archive.org/details/Awlaki_to_americans.

Below the video frame in the center of the page are several options on the lower right. These allow you to specify video files with different file types. Below these options is a link titled "Show All". Clicking the link provides a view of the files associated with the video as seen in Figure 30.02. The eighth link on this list forwards to the metadata associated with the video. This data includes the title, description, creator, email address used to upload, and the date of upload, as seen in the text below the example.

```
Enver_Awlaki.thumbs/          26-Feb-2011 09:08      -
Enver_Awlaki_archive.torrent  26-Jun-2016 22:58      33.4K
Enver_Awlaki_avi.avi          26-Feb-2011 00:05      417.1M
Enver_Awlaki_avi.gif          26-Feb-2011 09:13      308.9K
Enver_Awlaki_avi.ogv          26-Feb-2011 10:46      186.6M
Enver_Awlaki_avi_512kb.mp4    26-Feb-2011 09:52      202.4M
Enver_Awlaki_files.xml        26-Jun-2016 22:58      36.6K
Enver_Awlaki_meta.xml         26-Jun-2016 22:58      686.0B
Enver_Awlaki_wmv.gif          26-Feb-2011 09:04      312.1K
```

Figure 30.02: An Internet Archive video options page.

<mediatype>movies</mediatype><collection>opensource_movies</collection>
<title>Awlaki_to_americans</title><description>UmmaNews</description>
<uploader>ibnumar@islamumma.com</uploader>
<addeddate>2012-03-31 22:47:36</addeddate>
<publicdate>2012-04-01 00:09:10</publicdate>

This view quickly identifies the email address of ibnumar@islamumma.com as the verified uploader of the video content. It also displays the exact date and time of upload and publication. In this example, notice that the author waited over an hour to publish the content. Since 2016, I have seen the Internet Archive become a very popular place to store video, especially from international subjects that may be blocked from traditional American services such as YouTube.

TV News Archive (archive.org/details/tv)

At the time of this writing, the TV News Archive, another part of archive.org, had collected 2,094,000 television news broadcast videos from 2009 to present. Furthermore, it extracts the closed captioning text from each video and provides a search option for this data. This allows you to search for any words verbally stated during these broadcasts in order to quickly locate videos of interest. A search of the term "Bazzell" resulted in 35 videos that mentioned someone with my last name within the broadcast. Selecting any result will play the video and all text from the closed captioning. The menu on the left will allow filtering by show title, station, date, language, and topic. I have found this resource valuable when vetting a potential new hire for a company.

Video Closed Captions (downsub.com)

YouTube and other providers attempt to provide captioning subtitles for as many videos as possible. This automated process transcribes any spoken dialogue within the audio of the video file and documents the words to text. To see this text while watching a video, click on the closed captioning icon (cc) in the lower right area of the video box. When the icon changes to a red color, the subtitles will display. These subtitles are contained within a small text file associated with the video. It also includes timestamps that identify the frame in which each piece of text is spoken. YouTube does not provide a way to obtain this text file, but Downsub does. Copy an entire URL of any YouTube video with closed captioning. Paste this link into this website and execute the process. This will display download links for the captioning inside the video. Links for each language will download text files with an .srt file extension. These automated captions are not usually completely accurate. Slang and mumbled speech may not transcribe properly. Any time you collect and submit a YouTube video as part of a report, I recommend obtaining this caption file as well. Even though the actual text may not be accurate, it can help during official proceedings with identifying a specific portion of a video.

Live Video Streams

If you are investigating any live event that is currently occurring, live streaming video sites can be a treasure of useful intelligence. These services offer the ability for a person to turn a cell phone camera into an immediate video streaming device capable of broadcasting to millions. The common set-up is for a user to download a host service's application to a smartphone. Launching the application will turn on the video camera of the phone and the video stream is transmitted to the host via the cellular data connection or Wi-Fi. The host then immediately broadcasts this live stream on their website for many simultaneous viewers to see. An average delay time of five seconds is common.

There are now several companies that provide this free service. The following are listed in my order of preference for investigative needs. Each site has a search option to enter the keywords that describe the live event you want to watch. You may also see Twitter links to these services while monitoring targets.

YouTube (youtube.com/live)
TikTok (tiktok.com/live)
Twitch (twitch.com)
Bitchute (bitchute.com)
LiveU (liveu.tv/resources/tv)
YouNow (younow.com)
UScreen (uscreen.tv)

Consider the Video Stream Tool presented in Section One when you want to view and capture any live video streams. It provides the most robust and stable option, especially if you keep your tools updated with the automated scripts.

Real World Application: During several large events, I have used live streams to capture the majority of my intelligence. In one investigation, I was assigned the task of monitoring social networks during a large protest that had quickly become violent to both officers and civilians. While Twitter and Facebook occasionally offered interesting information, live streams provided immediate vital details that made a huge impact on the overall response of law enforcement, fire, and EMS. The live video streams helped me identify new trouble starting up, victims of violence that needed medical attention, and fires set by arsonists that required an immediate response.

Listen Notes (listennotes.com)

This is not a video utility, but I believe it fits best within this chapter as a media service. Listen Notes queries a keyword through millions of audio podcasts and presents any results. As an example, I conducted a search of the term "privacy" and received 10,000 matches of that word within the indexed podcasts. We can take this a step further with an email address search. I searched "privacypodcast@protonmail.com" and received one result based on show notes of an old episode. As the number of podcasts continue to grow, and audio to text technology improves, this technique will become more useful in our investigations.

Video Analysis

If you have discovered a target video on a YouTube or Vimeo page, you may want to analyze individual frames without using the utilities presented within Chapter Ten. You can use **Anilyzer** (anilyzer.com) for this task. Enter the video URL; select the appropriate provider; and click "Watch Video". you can now click through each still frame or modify the playback speed to fit your needs. I use this tool when I need a quick way to scrutinize a handful of frames, especially with surveillance videos.

YouTube Handles

In 2022, YouTube began rolling out user-defined handles as a way to connect to your favorite media. This was already somewhat available within the URL. As an example, the following two links connect to the same content. The first is a user's page and the second is their handle.

https://www.youtube.com/ambermac
https://www.youtube.com/@ambermac

I currently do not see much investigative value, aside from an additional URL to query when researching usernames. I believe most people who possess a custom YouTube handle already possess a profile with the same name.

IntelTechniques Videos Tool

If you feel overwhelmed at this point, I understand. Navigate to the "Videos" page in your Tools download, or online at **https://inteltechniques.com/tools/Videos.html**, to access an all-in-one option similar to the previous tools. This should replicate and simplify the processes which were explained throughout this chapter. I hope you find it helpful. Please note that some fields only require a YouTube video ID, while others require search terms or usernames.

CHAPTER THIRTY-ONE
BROADCAST STREAMS

Within the previous chapter, I explained the analysis and collection of online videos. While I did briefly mention live video streams on services such as YouTube, there is a whole other online world of live broadcast streams. These are typically not pre-recorded, and often are not archived after the broadcast. Before we dive into the techniques, let's discuss the reason these streams could be important to our investigations. I will break this chapter up into four topics, each of which are explained below.

Live Television News: Most international television news services broadcast their shows live on the internet. This can be very valuable when you are investigating a live incident far from your current location. If you are in California, it may be difficult to watch the local news in Chicago to monitor current events there. Through online video streams, we can watch live local, state, national, and international news broadcasts from anywhere in the world. We will also use our own custom tools to easily access the streams important to you.

Live Commercial Radio: Similar to TV broadcasts, most commercial radio stations broadcast over the internet. This access can be equally valuable when trying to listen to a live news broadcast from another state or country.

Live Web-Controlled Radios: Online radio broadcast streams are great, but they never replicate the true listening experience one would receive if listening locally through a receiver. There is often a delay; targeted commercials might play during the middle of a broadcast; and you might receive a different stream of audio based on your location (for marketing purposes). Sometimes, you might want to listen to a pure audio broadcast exactly as it would be heard in another state or country through a radio receiver. We will access physical radios, which are connected to external antennas, from all over the world via the internet. We will even control them, change the stations, and hear the same audio that we would receive if we were present at that location. This also applies to shortwave frequencies and pirate radio stations. As one of many examples, we can tune into a radio present in Ireland, which has an antenna targeting AM reception, and listen to stations live in that region, including all BBC content, and shortwave pirates broadcasting from the ocean. I believe this is one of the most fascinating pieces of technology we have today.

Live Web-Controlled Scanners: Similar to the previous topic, we will eavesdrop on local scanner radios which will allow us to hear emergency radio traffic in real time all over the world. If you are investigating a live event, there is no better source of news than the police, fire, and EMS working at the scene. If we miss anything, we can tap into online archives of the transmissions.

Nerd alert! I confess that I tend to geek-out on audio and video broadcasts, especially those in other countries. This might stem from my early days of local, shortwave, and scanner radio monitoring. 13-year-old me could have never understood how I could connect to practically any live video or audio stream anywhere in the world in real time. While you may not have the same fascination as I do for various broadcasts, please approach with an open mind. These broadcasts can be extremely valuable to your own investigations.

Live Television News Streams

Only a few years ago, the local news which was served to your television was determined by your location. An antenna might receive the analog or digital feed from a local news station's building, or cable television might bring in that same video stream. If you lived in Chicago, you received Chicago news. More recently, satellite television began offering local news stations, often as an affiliate for ABC, CBS, or NBC, along with national programming. Some satellite services even offered the ability to purchase channels from other major metropolitan areas. Today, most local, national, and international news services offer their content via the internet through their websites. This is nothing new, and I assume most readers already know they can retrieve this content. However, I believe there is a better way.

When you visit a website to stream local news, you also receive all associated web trackers, advertising scripts, and forced commercials before and during the broadcast. Some stations will not let you maximize the video window because they don't want your eyes interrupted from their flashy ads and popup annoyances. My preference is to identify the video stream and view it through my own web-based tools which bypass most annoyances. The following tutorial will walk you through a few common scenarios which will help identify the streams for your own needs. At the end, I present my custom online and offline tools which already have most of this content embedded into them. You can decide if my tools suffice for your work or if you should create your own. A lot of the content within this section may seem technically complicated. Please know that all of the coding is optional, and you can rely on my tools if desired. However, an understanding of the technology and creation of your own tool now can lead to fewer headaches later. Let's begin.

CBS offers a choice of 24-hour national and local news coverage. A national feed can be found at cbsnews.com. Clicking the play icon streams their live national feed in your web browser on top of the other elements within their web page. However, I prefer to access the video feed itself. In Chapter Nine, I explained the use of the Firefox add-on called Stream Detector. We can also use this to identify these live news streams. Before clicking the play option, make sure that Stream Detector is installed and active within Firefox. After beginning the live video stream, you should notice new results within the Stream Detector tool. Figure 31.01 displays my results.

Type	Filename	Size	Source	Timestamp	✖
HLS	1753312.m3u8	-	IntelTechniques Video Feed Tool	10/12/2022 1:49:24 PM	✖
HLS	master.m3u8	-	IntelTechniques Video Feed Tool	10/12/2022 1:49:24 PM	✖
HLS	master.m3u8	-	IntelTechniques Video Feed Tool	10/12/2022 1:49:23 PM	✖

Figure 31.01: A Stream Detector result.

I prefer to read these results from the bottom to the top, and I typically look for the first entry of any "m3u8" file in the list. In this scenario, the first entry loaded within the page was "master.m3u8". Left-clicking this file copies it into your computer's clipboard. At the time of this writing, the first "master.m3u8" file possessed the following complete URL.

https://dai.google.com/linear/hls/event/Sid4xiTQTkCT1SLu6rjUSQ/master.m3u8

This file serves as a "playlist" or set of instructions to play a live video stream. Placing this URL directly in your browser will likely download the file, but not play the video stream. Instead, we should create our own HTML file like we did with the rest of our tools within Section One. I titled my file cbs.html and placed it within the "video" folder in my online and offline tools package. The entire content appears in the following section.

```
<head><link href="https://vjs.zencdn.net/7.20.3/video-js.css" rel="stylesheet"
/></head>
<body>
<video
id="CBS"
autoplay="true"
class="video-js"
controls
preload="auto"
width="640"
height="480"
data-setup="{}">
<source
src="https://dai.google.com/linear/hls/event/Sid4xiTQTkCT1SLu6rjUSQ/master.m3u
8" type="application/x-mpegURL" /></video>
<script src="https://vjs.zencdn.net/7.20.3/video.min.js"></script></body>
```

Now, let's pick apart the important pieces. The line starting with <head> begins our file and incudes a link to an online repository of our video player (Video JS). This is the code which will play the video stream in a nice format. Within the <body> section, we can set our desired settings for the video output. This includes a unique identifier (CBS); the setting to automatically begin the stream (autoplay); and the desired width and height (640x480). You could modify any of these for your own needs. The <source section includes our URL which we retrieved from Stream Detector, and the final script source is required by our video player. Figure 31.02 displays the result when I open this file within a web browser. You can see the live file (or view the source code) at **https://inteltechniques.com/tools/video/CBS.html**. If you ever have issues, or simply want to update your version of Video JS, visit **https://videojs.com/getting-started/**. Notice the bottom controls of the player. This is Video JS in action. We can pause the stream; change the volume; load closed captioning; or display the stream full-screen with these controls.

Figure 31.02: A live video stream.

I suspect you are wondering why we took all of that effort to display a live video stream when we could have just visited the source website and play it from there. Aside from the tracking and website annoyances previously mentioned, this method allows us to build our own tool which can display any customized list of video streams. I currently maintain an online page at **https://inteltechniques.com/tools/Video.html** which possesses live feeds from most major U.S. cities as well as numerous international feeds. If you downloaded the custom offline tools as explained in Chapter Sixteen, you also possess an offline version of this page which you could easily modify to suit your own investigative needs. The following source code is an abbreviated version within both the online and offline tools.

```
<script type="text/javascript">
function dosearch(menu)
{window.open(menu, 'inner');}
</script>
<form onsubmit="dosearch(this.menu.value); return false;">
<select name="menu" id="menu">
<option value="" selected>Select</option>
<option disabled="">US:</option>
<option value="video/ABC.html">ABC National</option>
<option value="video/CBS.html">CBS National</option>
<option value="video/FOX.html">FOX National</option>
<option value="video/NBC.html">NBC National</option>
</select>
<input type="submit" style="width:80px" value="Launch" /></form>
<iframe name="inner" class="inner" width="640px" height="480px"
overflow="hidden" frameborder=0 scrolling="no"></iframe>
```

In this example, you can see a reference to the CBS.html file which we previously created. It is one option within the drop-down menu. You could add any files you created which contain a live stream. The "iframe" line tells the browser to load the chosen file within a frame on the page to keep the menu present. Figure 31.03 displays the online tool with the CBS option selected. I purposely left the menu visible to see a portion of the options included within my demo tools.

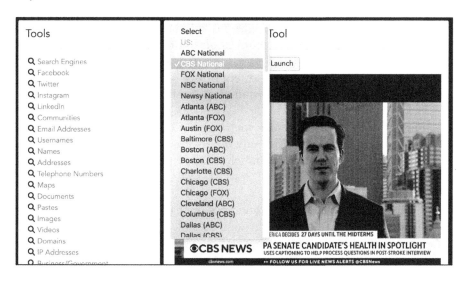

Figure 31.03: A custom streaming tool page.

Now that you have one CBS station completed, you could replicate the process for the CBS local coverage streams for Atlanta, Baltimore, San Francisco, Boston, Chicago, Dallas, Denver, Detroit, and many others. You can find each page under the "Local" section at cbsnews.com, or simply copy them from the pages I already created within the online and offline search tools. This allows you to instantly connect to a live news stream in every major U.S. city at any time. I have this running daily. As I write this in Los Angeles, I received word of a series of shootings in Chicago which I wanted to hear more about. I could wait for minimal coverage on CNN, or I could watch the live Chicago feeds from Fox and CBS to receive better details. There are countless ways in which this tool could be valuable to investigators.

Many live news streams broadcast on YouTube. Consider Al Jazeera as an example. If you navigate to **https://www.youtube.com/watch?v=bNyUyrR0PHo**, you will be presented their current live stream page. I can do without all of the Google tracking, user comments, and constant chat flowing down the screen. Instead, I want to embed this stream into my tools. I created a file called AlJazeera.html which contained the following entire content.

```
<body>
<iframe width="640" height="480" src="https://www.youtube-
nocookie.com/embed/bNyUyrR0PHo?controls=0&autoplay=1" frameborder="0"
allow="accelerometer; autoplay; clipboard-write; encrypted-media"
allowfullscreen>
</iframe>
</body>
```

This code sets the size of the video; identifies the stream source; informs the browser to automatically play the content; and allows the video to be maximized to full screen playback. Notice the portion I bolded (**bNyUyrR0PHo**). This matches the YouTube live stream ID from the previous YouTube URL. You can now replace this single identifier within this code to make a file for any other live YouTube stream. Let's do one more example. The European live streaming news source from Germany called DW News possesses a YouTube live stream at https://www.youtube.com/watch?v=tZT2MCYu6Zw. The following code would embed this stream into a new file.

```
<body>
<iframe width="640" height="480" src="https://www.youtube-nocookie.com/embed/
tZT2MCYu6Zw?controls=0&autoplay=1" frameborder="0" allow="accelerometer;
autoplay; clipboard-write; encrypted-media" allowfullscreen>
</iframe>
</body>
```

Live examples of both of these pages can be analyzed at the links below. They are also both included in the Live Video Streams Tool at **https://inteltechniques.com/tools/Video.html**.

https://inteltechniques.com/tools/video/AlJazeera.html
https://inteltechniques.com/tools/video/GermanyDW.html

CBS and YouTube might provide all the coverage you need, but those are just the tip of the iceberg. You can locate practically any online live news stream; identify the stream file with Stream Detector; and create a new page for your own set of tools. From there, you can rely on the following channel aggregators to find new live streams of interest.

TubiTV (tubitv.com/live): This service streams hundreds of channels to your browser for free. You can also use their stream URLs to populate your own tool. As one example, I use their live ABC national stream located at https://live-news-manifest.tubi.video/live-news-manifest/csm/extlive/tubiprd01,ABC-News.m3u8 within my tool set. I also collected numerous local news channel URLs from their "Local" page.

Pluto (pluto.tv/en/live-tv): This service also presents hundreds of free live streaming channels including several national and international news feeds. They tend to block their links when posted within another website. However, they should work fine within your own offline tools ran from a folder on your computer. Figure 31.04 (left) displays the result when I tried to play a Pluto stream from my website's online tools. Their security settings prevent this. However, Figure 31.04 (right) shows the result when I launch the same file from my offline tools on my Desktop via my browser. Always try all options when you encounter issues.

USTV247 (tv247.us): This site might be illegally streaming premium services such as HBO, but they also offer streams which can be found for free. For example, their PBS stream is currently being broadcasted from the URL of https://tv247.us/watch/pbs-us-live-stream/. Place this into a new html file relying on the Video JS code, and you have PBS in your tool set. My example is located within my online search tools at https://inteltechniques.com/tools/video/PBS.html, however, this page goes down often as USTV247 blocks my copying of their stream (the irony). If they block cross-site scripting for a channel you would like, placing it within your offline tools should bypass the restriction.

LocalNow (localnow.com/channels): If you are still craving local news options, LocalNow should have you covered. Use Stream Detector to identify feeds of interest and place them within an HTML file using Video JS as previously explained.

Roku (therokuchannel.roku.com): This option has limited live content, but it may be useful to you.

The rest is up to you. The tutorials here, along with the files I have already created for you in the offline search tools, should be all you need to create your own customized tool.

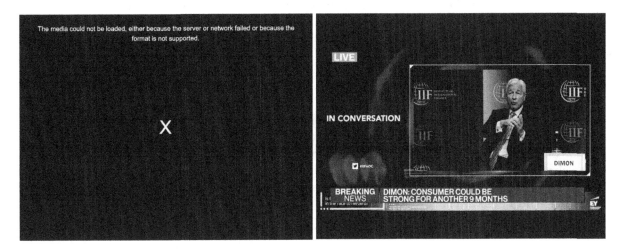

Figure 31.04: A blocked stream (left) which was bypassed in offline tools (right).

Live Commercial Radio

Live radio streams are old news. Most commercial AM and FM stations have a website which will stream their live broadcasts online. Some even offer second and third alternate streams with different content. If you have a favorite station, you may already stream a high-quality version of their content while you work. However, there is much more to discuss.

Similar to my reasons to stream news video within my own tool, I prefer to stream audio feeds outside of the provider's website. Some radio streaming websites insert additional advertisements before the radio stream, which are delivered through the website. Some make you sit through a video ad before the stream begins. If we can identify the desired streams, we can add them to our own tool which can bypass several annoyances. It also offers us a clean way to select the audio feed without interruptions.

Let's begin with something basic and easy. If you navigate to the BBC World News site at bbc.com/news/world, you will not find a link to their 24/7 audio stream. However, if you go directly to their "Sounds" site located at https://www.bbc.co.uk/sounds/play/live:bbc_world_service, their embedded web player will begin playing their World Service radio stream. Unfortunately, this is an MPD file which will not play by itself within our tools. A search for "BBC radio streaming URLS" presented me with numerous results which displayed pure streaming URLs for our needs. I now know that http://stream.live.vc.bbcmedia.co.uk/bbc_world_service is what I want. I can place this directly into my browser and stream live audio from the BBC. I could bookmark this URL for future use. If only every service was this easy.

Many live radio streams will be in "m3u8" format. Much like the video streams which use this format, we will need to play these streams through a third-party player. I currently rely on HLS Player (hlsplayer.org). Let's conduct another example. Al Jazeera Radio has a direct stream located at the following URL.

https://live-hls-audio-web-aje.getaj.net/VOICE-AJE/index.m3u8

However, inserting this into your browser simply downloads the m3u8 file. If we add our HLS Player link before the stream, it will play fine through our browser. The following link loads the Al Jazeera Radio URL into an embedded player for direct access to the audio stream.

https://www.hlsplayer.org/play?url=https://live-hls-audio-web-aje.getaj.net/VOICE-AJE/index.m3u8

Before we create our custom audio streaming tool to handle all of this, we should first consider sources for the streaming URLs we will need. Searching for your favorite stations might yield all of the results you need. I prefer to begin my search at **Radio Browser** (www.radio-browser.info). This crowd-sourced service attempts to possess direct audio streams for every radio station in the world. Searching your target streams' call letters, name, station, number, or location should get you results. My search of BBC immediately identified the URL we used in the previous example without much effort. This database powers many online streaming applications, including **Radio Garden** (radio.garden) and Radio Browser's own map of streams (radio-browser.info/map). We will use their API in our search tools next.

Hopefully, you now have an idea of the types of radio streams which you might like available to you when needed. Let's work through the first portion of the Live Audio Streams tool included with your offline search tools and online at **https://inteltechniques.com/tools/Radio.html**. The first four forms allow you to query a commercial radio station by search term, call letters, broadcast state, or broadcast country. These all query the Radio Browser database via their API and provide results as JSON text in a new tab. Search for the "url" of each result. Many results can be played directly within the browser. Those with "m3u8" at the end will need the HLS Player added to the URL as previously explained.

The next section includes a pre-configured "Radio News Stream" option. Selecting one of the streams and clicking "Play" will load the audio controls within the page and allow immediate streaming of the chosen content. Let's take a look at the source code for this section below.

```
<script type="text/javascript">
function dosearch2(menu2)
{window.open(menu2, 'inner');}
</script>
<form onsubmit="dosearch2(this.menu2.value); return false;">
<select name="menu2" style="width:200px">
<option>Radio News Stream</option>
<option value="https://www.hlsplayer.org/play?url=https://live-hls-audio-web-aje.getaj.net/VOICE-AJE/index.m3u8">Al Jazeera News</option>
<option value="http://stream.live.vc.bbcmedia.co.uk/bbc_world_service">BBC News</option>
<option value="https://www.hlsplayer.org/play?url=https://cbcradiolive.akamaized.net/hls/live/2041053/ES_R1SRE/master.m3u8">CBC News</option>
<option value="https://www.hlsplayer.org/play?url=https://live.amperwave.net/manifest/audacy-cbsnewsaac-hlsc.m3u8">CBS News</option>
<option value="http://radio.ukr.radio:8000/ur1-lv-mp3">Ukraine News</option>
</select>
<input type="submit" style="width:50px" value="Play" /></form>
```

The selection in bold is the area which determines which audio feeds will play when selected. Notice that selections such as the BBC do not need the HLS Player while Al Jazeera does. I included only a few entries here as a demonstration. You should consider modifying your own offline search tools to include the streams most valuable to you. I keep my local news stations ready to go. The quality is superior to the AM or FM broadcasts and I can easily stream from my mobile device if desired. The sky is the limit for your own tools.

Live Web-Controlled Radios

This may be my favorite portion of this chapter. If you have listened to my podcast or read my magazine, you know that I am fascinated by analog radio reception. Whether that means pulling in distant AM stations with my handheld radio or tuning into pirate shortwave broadcasts using an external outdoor antenna, there has always been something magical about eavesdropping on audio which was not meant to be heard in my location. While I still break out the portable radio on occasion, I rely most on internet-connected, remote-controlled radios located all over the world. Let's start with some manual access and control options before we automate our tasks within our custom tools.

I have mentioned **WebSDR** (websdr.org) within previous editions of this book. It allows you to connect to select analog radios via the internet and control the frequencies to which they are tuned. One can then listen to a radio broadcast exactly as it is heard from a specific location. I still visit WebSDR occasionally, but I now much prefer **KiwiSDR** (kiwisdr.com) for this purpose. We will start at their listing of publicly-accessible radios on their site at **kiwisdr.com/public**. At the time of this writing, there were 651 radio receivers online from all over the world.

The KiwiSDR is a software-defined radio (SDR) board that attaches to a BeagleBone miniature computer. It then connects to an internet connection for broadcast to the world. Most owners attach a high-quality indoor or outdoor antenna appropriate for their location. Most devices allow up to four simultaneous connections from the internet, and each visitor can control the tuning of the radio without impact to other listeners. These kind anonymous internet hosts provide a great service to us listeners.

While I am writing this, I am in Los Angeles. I can listen to practically any southern California radio station through any cheap receiver. However, assume I am interested in a broadcast from China or London. While commercial radio stations in those countries likely have an official audio stream, anything outside of the common AM and FM bands is not otherwise online. I can connect to these international radios; tune to any frequency between 1 KHz and 30,000 KHz; and hear exactly what I would receive if I were physically present at the radio's location. I find this astonishing. OK, let's get to the demonstration.

I randomly selected a radio in the UK. The following URL connected me to receiver located in West Wales which possessed a Wellbrook ALA1530LN active loop antenna. You do not need to connect to this specific receiver, any other option available should appear exactly the same as my example.

http://sdrwales.hopto.org:8073/

Figure 31.05 displays the default view of most KiwiSDR interfaces. The first thing I like to do is to eliminate the purple popup "Welcome" menu, as it blocks my view and provides no value to me. Clicking the arrow in the upper right corner of that menu collapses it to the left side. This shows more of the waterfall display, which identifies frequencies which have active audio broadcasts. Seeing this overall 1 KHz to 30,000 KHz coverage immediately tells me how well this radio receives broadcasts within various bands.

Next, I tune to the desired frequency. Since the BBC broadcasts their live news service on the longwave spectrum at 198 KHz, I entered that within the frequency field (visible in the figure) and struck enter. This presented a crystal-clear live broadcast of the BBC longwave broadcast. However, many of these receivers default to a "LSB" or "Lower Side Band" mode. I prefer traditional "AM" mode, so I clicked the "AM" button for better sound. Next, I do not like the large banner at the top of the page, which is not visible within the figure. Clicking the grey "up" arrow should dismiss this. If the volume is low, sliding the volume bar up should correct the issue.

None of these actions are difficult, but they can become tedious when tuning to multiple frequencies during a session. Instead, I rely on keyboard shortcut keys for this. I typically type "xayyyVVVVVzzzzz" any time I connect to a stream. The following explains these keys.

x:	Closes all popup windows
a:	Selects the "AM" mode
yyy:	Removes all three banners from the top
VVVVV:	Amplifies the volume five times
zzzzz:	Zooms into the chosen frequency

The result of these actions can be seen in Figure 31.06. This presents a much cleaner view. You can see that I am tuned to a strong stream, but holding down alt and clicking the right arrow six times would take me to another longwave UK broadcast at 252 KHz. Clicking around would allow me to listen to longwave, AM, and shortwave broadcasts. The visible waterfall helps me locate strong streams without manually connecting to each frequency. Shift-z (uppercase "Z") zooms back out at any time.

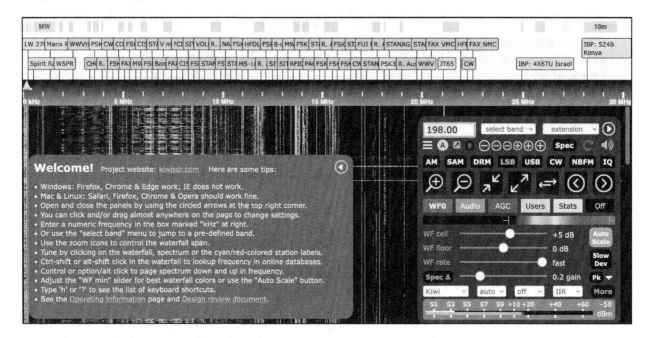

Figure 31.05: A default interface to KiwiSDR.

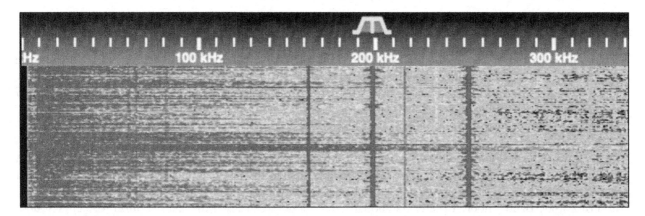

Figure 31.06: A cleaner interface to KiwiSDR.

To make things even easier, we can modify our URL to make all of these actions on our behalf. Using our original West Wales URL, the following URL connects to our desired radio; tunes to the BBC longwave frequency; closes all menus; eliminates all three banners; enhances the volume; and zooms into the band.

http://sdrwales.hopto.org:8073/?f=198am&keys=xyyyVVVVVzzzzz

You could bookmark this URL and immediately access this station with a minimal view at any time. You could replicate this and create URLs for numerous stations from unique locations. There are many options here. Before you commit, consider my online and offline search tools which you previously downloaded. I will use my Live Audio Streams tool at **https://inteltechniques.com/tools/Radio.html** as an example, but you could modify your own offline version if desired, as explained within Chapter Sixteen. While writing this chapter, I expanded the Remote Radio Access menu and selected a UK radio in Amersham. I then entered my desired frequency (198 KHz), and clicked "Play". The tool automatically conducted all of my desired tasks, and displayed the waterfall. You no longer need to remember the keyboard shortcuts or URL modifications. The tool should take care of everything. You could enter a different frequency or use your mouse to select strong signals. Of course, you can always replicate this from the main KiwiSDR site. I have simply chosen many international radios which work well for my needs.

I also find the site at **http://rx.linkfanel.net/** to be extremely helpful. It is linked within my tools and titled "Launch Live Shortwave Receiver Map". Figure 31.07 displays a partial view. This is a map version of all online KiwiSDR receivers. You can zoom into any location and select the receiver desired. This map also identifies areas which are currently in darkness, which typically aids in shortwave radio reception. As I write this, it is noon in California. That is a very bad time to listen to shortwave broadcasts due to sunlight propagation. However, it is nighttime in Australia, so I might want to connect to radios there if I want to find clear shortwave stations broadcasting to the entire world.

Figure 31.07: An international map of online KiwiSDR receivers.

I realize this can seem overwhelming at first. There are unlimited listening options which quickly change. Please allow me to explain how I take advantage of these receivers for fun and as part of my investigations. The fun part is obvious. I enjoy tracking down international shortwave broadcasts. I have heard many pirate stations on shortwave being broadcast from ships within international waters. These are often full of music, but I have also intercepted shows about hacking and disappearing from society. They also allow me to tune into a live KFI AM 640 stream when I am traveling internationally and need some familiar voices. There is something soothing about a real feed and not a digitally-compressed stream with commercials catered to my location. I want the real thing.

However, this is a book about online investigations, so I should stick to that. I find these radios to be vital to that need. I can tune into local radio stations which are broadcasting updates about current events. If I want to get a local take on the current situation in Ukraine, local stations in that area might give me more insight. A surprising number of these are in English. If I want to listen to a shortwave broadcast from China about international affairs, it is a click away. Some of these receivers are also capable of receiving Citizens' Band (CB) frequencies. I can listen to individuals using their CB radios in practically any U.S. city from my home.

My main investigative use is HAM radio. These receivers allow access to all low and high amateur radio frequency bands. This allows me to listen to HAM operators from practically anywhere in the world. While a lot of this chatter is from hobbyists testing their equipment, I can also receive real-time updates about major events. If there is a wildfire or missing person rescue in an area, be assured that HAM operators are discussing updates unavailable to any news outlet. Is there police activity and road closures due to a barricaded subject? There is likely an amateur radio operator discussing the events in real-time. There is no limit to the power of this technique. I encourage you to familiarize yourself now, and everything will be easy when needed.

Live Web-Controlled Scanners

The receivers in the previous section cover everything from the bottom of the radio spectrum until 30 MHz (30,000 KHz). This will include most traditional radio broadcasts within longwave, AM, and shortwave. They will not receive anything within upper frequencies commonly used for emergency services, aviation, marine, or VHF amateur radio. For those, you would need a "scanner" type of radio, which typically begins at 25 MHz and can reach over 1 GHz. While we do not have scanner receivers which allow us to control the tuning, we do have numerous scanners which are pre-tuned and connected to the internet for our listening.

Broadcastify (broadcastify.com) is our best resource. This site has been a steady part of my arsenal for over a decade. It allows you to listen to live and archived streams of radio traffic from emergency transmissions. Broadcastify is the largest platform of live streaming audio from public safety, aircraft, rail, and marine related communications in the United States. From the "Listen" > "Browse Feeds" menu, you can drill down through states and counties to select your area of interest. From there, you rely on the willingness of internet strangers to share their audio feeds to the world. I can be in Los Angeles and listen to a stranger's police scanner monitoring frequencies in Chicago. I confess that on occasion, I listen to the police department which hired me in the 90's to hear what my former colleagues are doing. If you are investigating any event in real-time, this can be a wonderful free service.

I recently heard about an active shooter within a neighborhood where a few friends live. Instead of waiting for tomorrow's copy of the local newspaper to know what happened, I tuned into the live police frequencies for that district. I heard all updates in real-time, and could let my friends know. I was recently stuck in traffic due to a road closure and a lot of police activity. Connecting through my mobile device let me know that a bad accident had shut down the highway and that a specific alternate route was being planned. This allowed me to jump ahead of the crowd and be on my way. However, the real power is in the archives.

Every scanner broadcast is recorded at all times. A paid membership provides access to these archives. This has been a huge benefit to my investigations. I can go back in time to hear the original dispatch and all follow-up radio transmissions. Even better, I can do this without a subpoena or FOIA request. I have been a scanner enthusiast for much of my life, but this takes everything to a new level. In the early 90's, I would have never suspected that I could hear all frequencies at any time and "rewind" communications from anywhere.

A premium membership is $30 annually. This provides commercial-free listening; non-stop streaming; access to archives; custom listening templates; and programming functions through scanner software. The free tier allows limited streaming with commercials and manual query of frequencies. I know many people who get by with the free version. The first time you need access to the archives, the cost of membership will likely be justified. This service allows journalists to play dispatch recordings without waiting on a public release from a government agency. The scanner section of my Live Audio Streams tool allows you to select a state or country and immediately be taken to the Broadcastify page, which allows you to listen to any online streams or archives.

Scanner to Text (copcrawler.com)

This service takes advantage of the previous police scanner utilities and applies artificial intelligence (AI) speech-to-text products to create text files of all transmissions. Due to poor audio quality, the results can vary, but the following random example matched the audio well.

0.00: This is badge six on scene 310946 with EMS.
8.00: 40 call-in at Boulders of Lake Ridge
16.00: 3324
21.00: Check area in reference to a possible disturbance

This allows you to query text and quickly identify which audio recordings match your term of interest, and allows you to play the associated audio within the page.

Community Watch Dogs

In recent years there has been a noticeable increase in social justice causes and other community watchdog groups creating and sharing portals for viewing public video feeds. Locating these feed collections can be a time saver, especially when working on an event or critical incident in a remote city or region. An example which offers a dashboard for pulling up department of transportation camera feeds for a handful of major US cities is https://www.pig.observer/nyc/. This particular dashboard allows us to add and remove camera feeds via an interactive map of the city. Always keep in mind that these sites often collect IP data from site users and many of these groups are not friendly to law enforcement and government. I always use VPN and a secure browser when utilizing these services. Figure 31.08 displays an example.

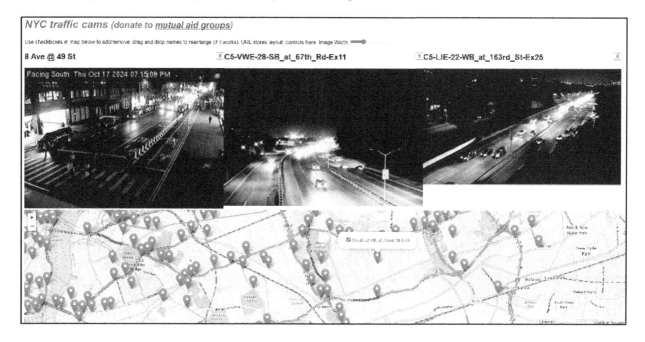

Figure 31.08: Camera feeds on observer.com.

Live Web Cam Search (www.earthcam.com/search/advanced_search.php)

Online cameras are everywhere. Most are private and cannot be accessed by the public. However, an alarming number of feeds are available to anyone with an internet connection. This site allows advanced query in order to locate your desired camera. You can search by location, camera name, or category. This can be very beneficial for those working within intelligence centers whenever a disaster or other large-scale event has occurred. You can quickly get a live view of the commotion.

CHAPTER THIRTY-TWO
DOMAIN NAMES

A specific web page may quickly become the focus of your investigation. Websites, also known as domains, are the main sites at specific addresses. For example, the website that hosts my blog, www.inteltechniques.com/blog, is on the domain of inteltechniques.com. The "www" or anything after the ".com" is not part of the domain. These addresses should always be searched for additional information. If your target has a blog at a custom domain, such as privacy-training.com, the content of the site should obviously be examined. However, digging deeper into the domain registration and associated connections can reveal even more information. Every time I encounter a domain involved in my investigation, I conduct full research on every aspect of the domain, including historical registration, visual depiction, and hidden content. I rely heavily on the automated tools presented at the end of the chapter to make the work easy.

Current Domain Registration & Hosting

Every website requires information about the registrant, administrative contact, and technical contact associated with the domain. These can be three unique individuals or the same person for all. The contact information includes a full name, business name, physical address, telephone number, and email address. These details are provided by the registrar of the domain name to the service where the name was purchased. This service then provides these details to Internet Corporation for Assigned Names and Numbers (ICANN). From there, the information is publicly available and obtained by hundreds of online resources. While ICANN declares that the provided information is accurate, this is rarely enforced. While most businesses supply appropriate contacts, many criminals do not. While we must consider searching this publicly available information, often referred to as Whois details, we will also need to dig deeper into domain analysis in order to obtain relevant results. First, we will focus on the easy queries.

Whois queries (pronounced "who is") are very simple searches, but are not all equal. While this data is public, it could change often. Some Whois search sites display the bare bones details while others provide enhanced information. There are dozens of options from which to choose, and I will explain those that I have found useful. After the demonstrations, I present my own custom online tool that automates many processes.

The biggest hurdle with Whois data is privacy controls. Many domain owners have started using private registration services in order to protect their privacy. These services provide their own data within the Whois search results, and only these companies know the true registrant. While a court order can usually penetrate this anonymity, I will discuss public resources to help in these situations later. Some web hosts now provide free masking services for domain owners, which is making this problem worse. Historical record queries will be vital if you see this happening. Until then, let's focus on current registration data. For the first example, I will use a target domain of cnn.com. Assume that this website is the focus of your investigation and you want to retrieve as much information as possible about the site, the owner, and the provider of the content. For the standard Whois search, as well as many other options, I prefer ViewDNS.info.

ViewDNS Whois (viewdns.info/whois)

This service provides numerous online searches related to domain and IP address lookups. Their main page (viewdns.info) provides an all-in-one toolbox, but the above website connects you directly to their Whois search. Entering cnn.com here presents the following information.

Domain Name: cnn.com
Updated Date: 2020-10-20T13:09:44Z
Creation Date: 1993-09-22T00:00:00.000-04:00
Admin Organization: Turner Broadcasting System, Inc.

Admin Street: One CNN Center
Admin City: Atlanta
Admin State/Province: GA
Admin Postal Code: 30303
Admin Country: US
Admin Phone: +1.4048275000
Admin Fax: +1.4048271995

The administrative and technical contacts were identical to the registrant shown above. This data identifies the company which owns the site and associated contact details. We also know it was created in 1993 and the record was updated in 2020. This is a great start, if the provided details are accurate. I have found that ViewDNS will occasionally block my connection if I am connected to a VPN. An alternative Whois research tool is who.is.

ViewDNS Reverse IP (viewdns.info/reverseip)

Next, you should translate the domain name into the IP address of the website. ViewDNS will do this, and display additional domains hosted on the same server. This service identified the IP address of cnn.com to be 151.101.1.67 and stated the web server hosted dozens of additional domains related to this company. These included weather.cnn.com and cnnbusiness.com. If the results had included domains from websites all over the world without a common theme, it would have indicated that this was a shared server, which is very common.

ViewDNS Reverse Whois (viewdns.info/reversewhois)

This utility attempts to search the domain in order to locate other domains owned by the same registrant. In our example, it located 28 additional domains associated with our target. If the domain possessed private registration, this technique would fail.

ViewDNS Port Scanner (viewdns.info/portscan)

This online port scanner looks for common ports that may be open. An open port indicates that a service is running on the web server that may allow public connection. A search of cnn.com revealed that ports 21, 80, and 443 are open to outside connections. Port 80 is for web pages and port 443 is for secure web pages. These are open on practically every website. However, port 21 is interesting. ViewDNS identifies this as a port used for FTP servers, as was discussed previously. This indicates that the website hosts an FTP server and connecting to ftp.cnn.com could reveal interesting information.

ViewDNS IP History (viewdns.info/iphistory)

This tool translates a domain name to IP address and identifies previous IP addresses used by that domain. A search of cnn.com reveals the following details. The first column is the IP address previously associated with the domain, the second column identifies the current user and company associated with that IP address, and the last column displays the date these details were collected by ViewDNS.

IP Address	Location	IP Address Owner	Last seen
151.101.65.67	United States	RIPE NCC	2020-11-23
151.101.193.67	United States	RIPE NCC	2020-11-23
151.101.1.67	United States	RIPE NCC	2020-11-23
157.166.255.19	United States	Turner Broadcasting System, Inc.	2011-04-04
157.166.255.18	United States	Turner Broadcasting System, Inc.	2011-04-04
157.166.226.25	Atlanta	Turner Broadcasting System, Inc.	2011-04-04

ViewDNS DNS Report (viewdns.info/dnsreport)

This option presents a complete report on the DNS settings for the target domain. This tool is designed to assist webmasters and system administrators diagnose DNS related issues, but we can use it to peek into their settings, including DNS and mail server details.

The utilities hosted at ViewDNS are always my first stop for a couple of reasons. First, the site has been very reliable over the past ten years. More vital, it allows query via static URL. This is beneficial for submission directly from our tools. The following displays the URL structure for the previous techniques, with cnn.com as the target.

https://viewdns.info/whois/?domain=cnn.com
https://viewdns.info/reverseip/?host=cnn.com&t=1
https://viewdns.info/reversewhois/?q=cnn.com
https://viewdns.info/portscan/?host=cnn.com
https://viewdns.info/iphistory/?domain=cnn.com
https://viewdns.info/dnsreport/?domain=cnn.com

Historical Domain Registration

As stated previously, many domains now possess private registration. This means that you cannot see the owner of a domain publicly. Many hosts are now offering private registration as a free service, further complicating things for investigators. If you query a domain and see a name entry such as "WhoisGuard Protected", you know that the domain is protected. There are two ways to defeat this. The first requires a court order, which is outside the scope of this book. The second way to reveal the owner is through historical domain records. If the domain has been around a while, there is a very good chance that the domain was not always private. There are several free and paid domain history services, and I present my favorites in order of usefulness.

Whoxy (whoxy.com)

This is one of the very few premium services which offer a decent free tier. Searching my own domain, which currently possesses private registration, reveals valuable results. The general registration data was "protected" and confirms what I found on ViewDNS. Scrolling down the page reveals powerful historical records. These identify my real name, multiple email addresses used during various registrations, and a date next to each entry to tie it all together. Figure 32.01 displays one of the results. This confirms that during July of 2015, my site was briefly registered without privacy protection. The "9 Domains" link reveals even more information. Figure 32.02 displays this result which identifies numerous domains which I had previously created from 2007 through 2018. This resource has single-handedly exposed more private domain registrations than any other free service during my investigations throughout 2022. Furthermore, it allows submission via URL which will benefit our search tools, as follows.

https://www.whoxy.com/inteltechniques.com

The search option in the upper right allows us to query email addresses, names, and keywords. This can be extremely valuable when you do not know which domain names your target has owned. Searching "OSINT" reveals a surprising amount of people and companies purchasing domains associated with this topic. Whoxy offers many paid services if the free tier is not sufficient. Of the paid services, this one is the most affordable, allowing you to purchase small amounts of information without committing to any specific level of subscription.

Owner: Michael Bazzell (9 domains)

Geolocation: Alton, Illinois, United States (129 million domains from **United States** for **$3,500**)

Email: info@yourcomputernerds.com (7 domains) UPDATED

Nameservers: ns01.domaincontrol.com, ns02.domaincontrol.com

Status: clientDeleteProhibited, clientRenewProhibited, clientTransferProhibited, clientUpdateProhibited

Figure 32.01: A Whoxy historical domain registration result.

DOMAIN NAME	REGISTRAR	CREATED	UPDATED	EXPIRY
inteltechniques.com	NameCheap, Inc.	21 Jul 2013	14 Apr 2018	21 Jul 2019
inteltechniques.online	GoDaddy.com, LLC	31 Mar 2018	31 Mar 2018	31 Mar 2019
privacy-training.com	GoDaddy.com, LLC	11 Jun 2016	31 May 2017	11 Jun 2018
yourcomputernerds.com	GoDaddy.com, LLC	18 Dec 2007	20 Oct 2015	18 Dec 2016
missouriinternationalexports.com	GoDaddy.com, LLC	1 Apr 2008	25 Mar 2016	1 Apr 2017
illinoisinternationalexports.com	GoDaddy.com, LLC	1 Apr 2008	25 Mar 2016	1 Apr 2017
humphreyinternationalexports.com	GoDaddy.com, LLC	1 Apr 2008	25 Mar 2016	1 Apr 2017

Figure 32.02: Additional domains owned by a target from Whoxy.

Whoisology (whoisology.com)

This service appeared in 2014 and becomes more powerful every month. Like Whoxy, it provides historical domain records as a reverse-domain search utility. The home page of Whoisology presents a single search field requesting a domain or email address. Entering either of these will display associated websites and the publicly available Whois data. This is where the publicly available free features end. Any further details require registration. I encourage all readers to create a free account. Once logged in as a free user, you receive much more detail within your searches. The first basic feature that you see is the display of standard Whois data which will identify the registered administrative contact, registrant contact, technical contact, and billing contact. These will often be the same individual for most personal websites. The advanced feature within this content is the ability to immediately search for additional domains associated within any field of this data. As an example, a search for the domain of phonelosers.org reveals the following data.

Name	Brad Carter (88)
Email	brad@notla.com (7)
Street	PO Box 465 (1,091)
City	Albany (42,428)
Region	Oregon (492,506)
Zip / Post	97321 (3,080)
Phone	8144225309 (4)

The name, address, and other data can be found on any Whois search website. However, the numbers in parentheses identify the number of additional domains that match those criteria. In this example, there are a total of 88 domains registered to Brad Carter, and seven domains registered to the email address of brad@notla.com. Clicking on any of these pieces of data will launch a new page with all of the matching domain information. As an example, clicking on brad@notla.com will display the 7 domain names associated with his email address. Clicking 8144225309 will display the 4 domain names associated with his telephone number. One of these is a new domain that is not directly associated with him. However, since it was registered with the same phone number, there is now a connection.

This type of cross-reference search has not been found through many other services. Another powerful feature of Whoisology is the historical archives. This service constantly scans for updates to domain registrations. When new content is located, it documents the change and allows you to search the previous data. As an example, a search of computercrimeinfo.com reveals the current administrative contact telephone number to be 6184628253. However, a look at the historical records reveals that on October 16, 2012, the domain contact number was 6184633505. This can be a great way to identify associated telephone numbers that have since been removed from the records. Whoisology will also provide details from the search of an email address. In my experience, Whoisology will provide a more detailed and accurate response than most other resources. However, this comes at a cost. Whoisology continues to minimize the free options in order to maximize sales. Your usage may vary by the time you try the free services. A search of the email address brad@notla.com revealed the following domains associated with that account.

notla.com
phonelosers.com
bigbeefbueno.com
callsofmassconfusion.com
snowplowshow.com
phonelosers.org

If you ever encounter an investigation surrounding a domain or any business that possesses a website, I highly encourage you to conduct research through Whoxy and Whoisology. They also offer access through their API at a cost. The individual queries through their website are free. Whoisology restricts free accounts to only one historical record and three searches every 24 hours. Because of this, Whoxy receives my overall recommendation. I believe Whoisology offers the most data for those looking to purchase a subscription in order to query numerous domains, but it can be quite expensive. **WhoisXMLAPI** (whoisxmlapi.com) offers limited free trial access to their historical domain data, but it requires access through their API, as previously explained within Chapter Twelve.

Archive.org Domain Registration Data (web.archive.org)

You now know there are many ways to identify the owner of a domain through historical Whois captures. You might get lucky through a free preview of previous registration data or be required to purchase access in order to see all records dating back decades. We have one last free option which has been successful for me throughout several investigations. We can query the Wayback Machine for the exact historical URL of a domain registration. If you navigate directly to https://who.is/whois/phonelosers.org, you can see that the domain possesses WhoisGuard protection and the owner's identity is masked. This is displayed in Figure 32.03 (left). However, it is possible that the Wayback Machine captured this exact page. The following URL displays any results.

https://web.archive.org/web/http://who.is/whois/phonelosers.org

This URL defaults to a capture from 2017 which displays the owner's name, address, telephone number, and email. This can be seen in Figure 32.03 (middle). Clicking the earliest archive presents a capture of this data from 2010, as seen in Figure 32.03 (right). We now have accurate historical domain registration data without a premium membership, and two additional telephone numbers to investigate. This is not the only domain registration service indexed by archive.org. The following direct links query domain registration history from Who.is, Domain Tools, Whoxy, and Whoisology. Replace cnn.com with your target domain. The domain tools presented at the end of this chapter replicate each of these options.

https://web.archive.org/web/http://www.who.is/whois/cnn.com/
https://web.archive.org/web/https://whois.domaintools.com/cnn.com
https://web.archive.org/web/https://www.whoxy.com/cnn.com
https://web.archive.org/web/https://whoisology.com/cnn.com

```
┌──────────────────────────────┐ ┌──────────────────────────────┐ ┌──────────────────────────────────┐
│ WhoisGuard Protected         │ │ Brad Carter                  │ │ Name: Brad Carter                │
│                              │ │ Phone losers of America      │ │ Organization: Phone losers of    │
│ P.O. Box 0823-03411          │ │ PO Box 465                   │ │ America                          │
│ Panama                       │ │ Albany                       │ │ Address 1: PO Box 465            │
│ Panama                       │ │ Oregon                       │ │ City: Albany                     │
│                              │ │ 97321                        │ │ State: Oregon                    │
│ PA                           │ │ US                           │ │ Zip: 97321                       │
│ +507.8365503                 │ │                              │ │ Country: US                      │
│ +51.17057182                 │ │ +1.8144225309                │ │ Phone: +1.5057964020             │
│ a75ea473ac4449e786c8aa9a6cf57316 │ brad@notla.com            │ │                                  │
└──────────────────────────────┘ └──────────────────────────────┘ └──────────────────────────────────┘
```

Figure 32.03: Results from who.is (left) and the Wayback Machine (middle and right).

Historical Content Archives

I previously mentioned The Internet Archive and explained how it collects copies of websites over time. This is very useful when we need to see the ways in which a website has changed. This is especially true if our target domain is no longer online. The direct URL for a domain query at their service is as follows.

http://web.archive.org/web/*/cnn.com

This view presents a graphical way to browse through various archives at a specified domain. However, we can also conduct a URL-based query which presents all full URLs which have been archived by the service. This text-only view can be accessed with the following URL structure.

https://web.archive.org/cdx/search/cdx?url=cnn.com/*&output=text&fl=original&collapse=urlkey

The result from this URL is tens of thousands of URLs, many of which no longer exist on the domain, but can be accessed via The Internet Archive. This text view is easy to copy and paste into a report.

If you queried my website, IntelTechniques.com, you should be notified that my domain is not indexed by their service. This is because I placed code within my site requesting the pages to be ignored by The Internet Archive's indexing engine. However, this request is ignored by other providers. Archive.org is not the only service which provides archived domains.

Archive Today (archive.is / archive.ph / archive.md)

This service also collects copies of websites and ignores all requests for deletion. My own site can be found at the following URL, which displays 183 captures dating back to 2013.

https://archive.is/*.inteltechniques.com

Mementoweb (mementoweb.org)

This service offers a "Time Travel" option which presents archives of a domain from several third-party providers. The following URL queries my own domain, which found 5 new archives.

http://timetravel.mementoweb.org/list/19991212110000/http://inteltechniques.com

Library of Congress (www.loc.gov/web-archives)

This option allows you to search by domain to discover all publicly available content in the Library of Congress Web Archives. A direct URL is as follows.

https://webarchive.loc.gov/all/*/http://inteltechniques.com

Portuguese Web Archive (arquivo.pt)

I was surprised to see my site indexed here with 12 historic archives dating back to 2017. The query URL structure is similar to https://arquivo.pt/url/search?hitsPerPage=100&q=inteltechniques.com.

Historical Screen Captures

You should document the current visual representation of your target website. This may be a simple screen capture, but you may have advanced needs. When I am investigating a domain, I have three goals for visual documentation. I want documentation of the current site, any historical versions archived online, and then future monitoring for any changes. Previous chapters presented numerous methods for capturing live web pages and techniques for locating archives. Let's briefly revisit these methods and then apply new resources.

Search Engine Cache

Searching your target domain within Bing and Yandex should present numerous results. The first is almost always the home page, and clicking the green down arrow presents a cached version of the page with some providers. This should be conducted first in order to identify any cached copies, as previously explained.

Website Informer (website.informer.com)

I am mostly interested in the screen capture available to the right of a search result. Figure 32.04 (upper left) displays their capture of my site in May of 2019.

URLScan (urlscan.io)

Similar to the previous option, this service provides very little valuable details. However, the screen captures are often unique. Figure 32.04 (upper middle) displays a result from August of 2018.

Easy Counter (easycounter.com)

The screen capture presented here was very similar to Website Informer, but it was cropped slightly different. This appears to be from May of 2019 and is seen in Figure 32.04 (upper right).

Domain Tools (whois.domaintools.com)

These screen captures are in high resolution and current. Figure 32.04 (lower left) displays the result from my domain captured in August of 2022.

Domains App (dmns.app)

This service offers the highest resolution image, which is very high quality. However, you must know the exact URL to receive a result. The following URL structure reveals a full-page screen capture of my site from April 2022. Figure 32.04 (lower middle) displays the result.

https://files.dmns.app/screenshots/inteltechniques.com.jpg

Hype Stat (hypestat.com)

Finally, the lowest-quality option we will receive is from Hype Stat. This is typically an older image. Figure 32.04 (lower right) displays their selection for my site from 2020.

The following direct URLs will be used for our search tool, displaying my own site as an example.

https://website.informer.com/inteltechniques.com#tab_stats
https://urlscan.io/domain/inteltechniques.com
https://www.easycounter.com/report/inteltechniques.com
https://whois.domaintools.com/inteltechniques.com
https://files.dmns.app/screenshots/inteltechniques.com.jpg
https://hypestat.com/info/inteltechniques.com

Figure 32.04: Historical screenshot captures from six resources.

Follow That Page (followthatpage.com)

Once you locate a website of interest, it can be time consuming to continually visit the site looking for any changes. With large sites, it is easy to miss the changes due to an enormous amount of content to analyze. This is when sites like Follow That Page come in handy. Enter the address of the target page of interest, as well as an email address where you can be reached. This service will monitor the page and send you an email if anything changes. Anything highlighted is either new or modified content. Anything that has been stricken through indicates deleted text. Parents are encouraged to set-up and use these services to monitor their child's websites. It does not work well on some social networks such as Facebook, but can handle a public Twitter page fine.

Visual Ping (visualping.io)

If you found the service provided by Follow That Page helpful, but you are seeking more robust options, you should consider Visual Ping. This modern Swiss website allows you to select a target domain for monitoring. Visual Ping will generate a current snapshot of the site and you can choose the level of monitoring. I recommend hourly monitoring and notification of any "tiny change". It will now check the domain hourly and email you if anything changes. If you are watching a website that contains advertisements or any dynamic data that changes often, you can select to avoid that portion of the page. Figure 32.05 displays the monitoring option for phonelosers.org. In this example, I positioned the selection box around the blog content of the main page. I also chose the hourly inspection and the "Tiny Change" option. If anything changes within this selected area, I will receive an email announcing the difference.

Figure 32.05: A portion of a web page monitored by Visual Ping for changes.

Email Address Identification

Lately, I am eager to identify any email addresses associated with a specific domain. This can lead to the discovery of employees and can be used for further breach data queries. We now have three reliable resources which should be queried any time we are investigating a domain name.

Hunter (hunter.io)

Previously, I explained how Hunter could be used to verify email addresses. This tool can also accept a domain name as a search term, and provides any email addresses that have been scraped from public web pages. The free version of this tool will redact a few letters from each address, but the structure should be identifiable. The Hunter website should take you where you need to be, but I find myself getting caught in Captcha loops and trial restriction notices. I now submit queries from the following URL structure.

https://hunter.io/try/search/cnn.com

The result is a list of email addresses with minor redactions. It also includes the online source of the information which was scraped by Hunter. The following is an example.

http://edition.cnn.com/specials/cnn-investigates-team Jun 15, 2022
j**.martin@cnn.com
http://cnnpressroom.blogs.cnn.com/2011/05/17/cnn-launches-international-news-app May 1, 2022
c**re.duffy@cnn.com

Website Informer (website.informer.com)

Once I have exhausted Hunter, I switch to Website Informer. The results are typically fewer, but they are not redacted. The URL submission I use follows.

https://website.informer.com/cnn.com/emails

SkyMem (skymem.info)

Finally, this service also displays full email addresses which are not redacted. The following URL allows our search tool to automate the process.

https://www.skymem.info/srch?q=cnn.com

As with most OSINT tools, these three services will likely never provide the same results. This is why it is so important to exhaust all options in order to acquire the most data possible.

Blacklight (themarkup.org/blacklight)

You may want to know about any malicious activity embedded into a target website. Blacklight displays this data. When querying cnn.com, I am notified of the following invasive activity.

34 Advertisement Trackers
52 Third-Party Cookies
Notifications to Facebook
Interactions with Adobe, Google, and others

Domain Analytics

Domain analytics are commonly installed on websites in order to track usage information. This data often identifies the city and state from where a visitor is; details about the web browser the person is using; and keywords that were searched to find the site. Only the owner of the website can view this analytic data. Analytics search services determine the specific number assigned to the analytics of a website. If the owner of this website uses analytics to monitor other websites, the analytic number will probably be the same. These services will now conduct a reverse search of this analytic number to find other websites with the same number. In other words, it will search a website and find other websites that the same owner may maintain. Additionally, it will try to identify user specific advertisements stored on one site that are visible on others. It will reverse search this to identify even more websites that are associated with each other. None of this relies on Whois data. A couple of examples should simplify the process.

Spy On Web (api.spyonweb.com)

Spy On Web is one of many sites that will search a domain name and identify the web server IP address and location. It also conducts a Whois query which will give you registration information of a website. More importantly, it identifies and cross-references website analytic data that it locates on a target domain. A search for the website phonelosers.org reveals a "Google AdSense" ID of ca-pub-3941709854725695. It further identifies five domains that are using the same Google AdSense account for online advertising. This identifies an association between the target website and these new websites. We now know that whoever maintains phonelosers.org places ads on the page. We also know that those same ads and affiliate number is present on five domains. This means that our target likely maintains all of the following domains. Recently Spy On Web has moved to requiring registration and query submission via their API, but they offer a limited free tier.

www.notla.com   www.phonelosers.org
www.oldpeoplearefunny.com   www.signhacker.com
www.phonelosers.com

Hacker Target (hackertarget.com/reverse-analytics-search)

This service stands out due to their immediate availability of historic analytics IDs across multiple subdomains. Consider a search of cnn.com. Hacker Target displayed dozens of associated Google IDs, such as the following.

cnnworldlive.cnn.com,UA-289507
center.cnn.com,UA-96063853
games.cnn.com,UA-74063330

We could search these IDs through this or other sites to track additional associated domains.

DNSLytics (dnslytics.com/reverse-analytics)

The final analytics option I offer is DNSLytics. Enter the analytics ID found with any of the previous techniques and you may find associations not present within other options. The two direct URL options follow.

https://dnslytics.com/reverse-analytics/inteltechniques.com
https://dnslytics.com/reverse-adsense/inteltechniques.com

SSL Certificates

Most target websites will possess an SSL certificate which allows for a secure connection through HTTPS. The history of these certificates can be quite lucrative. Consider my own domain through a free service called **CRT.sh** (crt.sh) through a direct URL of https://crt.sh/?q=inteltechniques.com. Most of the data identifies various certificate updates which do not provide any valuable information. However, through the history you can see that I once purchased a group SSL certificate from GoDaddy. Clicking on any of these entries displays the other domains I secured with this option, including dates of activity, as follows. This identifies other domains to investigate.

inteltechniques.com   yourcomputernerds.com
privacy-training.com   computercrimeinfo.com

OSINT.sh (osint.sh)

This multiple-use service offers a lot to digest. I find the following direct URLs most beneficial.

https://osint.sh/subdomain: Display all subdomains of a target domain
https://osint.sh/stack: Display all technologies in use by a target domain
https://osint.sh/ssl: Display all SSL certificates associated with a target domain
https://osint.sh/whoishistory: Display historic registrations associated with a target domain
https://osint.sh/analytics: Display all domains associated with a Google Analytics ID
https://osint.sh/adsense: Display all domains associated with a Google AdSense ID
https://osint.sh/domain: Display all domains associated with keywords
https://osint.sh/reversewhois: Display all domains publicly associated with an email address
https://osint.sh/ocr: Extract text found within a document stored at a target domain URL

Website Source Code

Every website possesses valuable information "under the hood" within its source code. We should always search within this code and understand the various technologies used to create the site. For this, I rely on the following services.

NerdyData (search.nerdydata.com)

NerdyData is a search engine that indexes the source code of websites. I use this to locate websites which steal the source code of my search tools and present them as their own. In one example, I searched "function doSearch01(Search01)", which is the JavaScript I use within the search tools. NerdyData immediately identified a competitor's website which was selling access to my scripts.

If you have located a Google Analytics ID, AdSense ID, or Amazon ID of a website using the previous methods, you should consider searching this number through NerdyData. A search of our target's Google AdSense number revealed five domains that possess the same data. The search of the Amazon number revealed three domains. If this service presents more results than you can manage, consider using their free file download option to generate a csv spreadsheet.

Real World Application: While investigating an "anonymous" website that displayed photo evidence of a reported felony, I discovered that the registration information was intentionally inaccurate. A search of the website on these services identified a Google Analytics ID and an additional website that possessed the same number. That additional website was the personal blog of the suspect. An arrest was made the same day.

Built With (builtwith.com)

A quick analysis of a target website may identify the technologies used to build and maintain it. Many pages that are built in an environment such as WordPress or Tumblr often contain obvious evidence of these technologies. If you notice the YouTube logo within an embedded video, you will know that the creator of the site likely has an account within the video service. However, the presence of various services is not always obvious. Built With takes the guesswork out of this important discovery. Entering the domain of phonelosers.org into the Built With search immediately identifies the web server operating system (Linux), email provider (DreamHost), web framework (PHP, WordPress), WordPress plugins, website analytics, video services, mailing list provider, blog environment, and website code functions. While much of this is geek speak that may not add value to your investigation, some of it will assist in additional search options through other networks. Another option for this type of search is **Stats Crop** (statscrop.com).

Subdomains

A subdomain is a domain that is a part of another domain. For example, if a domain offered an online store as part of their website example.com/shop.html, they might use a subdomain of shop.example.com. A subdomain finder is a tool which performs an advanced scan over the specified domain and tries to find as many subdomains as possible. This often discloses interesting evidence otherwise not visible within the main page. I rely on several tools.

PentestTools (https://pentest-tools.com/information-gathering/find-subdomains-of-domain)

This unique tool performs several tasks that will attempt to locate hidden pages on a domain. First it performs a DNS zone transfer which will often fail. It will then use a list of numerous common subdomain names and attempt to identify any that are present. If any are located, it will note the IP address assigned to that subdomain and will scan all 254 IP addresses in that range. In other words, it will attempt to identify new areas of a website that may not be visible from within the home page. The following example may help to clarify.

The website at phonelosers.org is a blog that appears to have no further content to be analyzed. Searching for it on Pentest-Tools provides additional intelligence. It identifies the following subdomains present the server.

webmail.phonelosers.org   ftp.phonelosers.org   mail.phonelosers.org
ssh.phonelosers.org   www.phonelosers.org

We now know that this domain possesses a webmail server, SSH connection, FTP server, and mail server. This method has helped me locate "hidden" pages which contain several forum messages from users of the site.

Columbus Project (columbus.elmasy.com)

This new service emerged in late 2022, and is the fastest of all present options. The web-based search should suit most users, but they also offer an API via Terminal with the following command, replacing "cnn.com" with your target domain.

curl -H "Accept: text/plain" "https://columbus.elmasy.com/lookup/cnn.com"

I find myself using the API via terminal when I have numerous domains to query and I want to easily document the results. I can add " > cnn.com.txt" at the end of the command to output a text file with all found subdomains.

If these options do not provide the results you need, consider **SubDomain Finder** (subdomainfinder.c99.nl) and **DNS Dumpster** (dnsdumpster.com). These services rely on Host Records from the domain registrar to display potential subdomains. DNS Dumpster also generates a domain map which may be downloaded as an image or Excel spreadsheet. While searching a target domain related to a stalking investigation, it displayed a blog hidden from the main domain. This presented more information than I could easily digest.

Robots.txt

Practically every professional website has a robots.txt file at the "root" of the website. This file is not visible from any of the web pages at the site. It is present in order to provide instructions to search engines that crawl the website looking for keywords. These instructions identify files and folders within the website that should not be indexed by the search engine. Most engines comply with this request, and do not index the areas listed. Locating this file is relatively easy. The easiest way to view the file is to open it through a web browser. Type the website of interest, and include "robots.txt" after a forward slash (/). The file for CNN can be found at the following address, with partial contents underneath.

http://www.cnn.com/robots.txt

Disallow: /cnnbeta
Disallow: /development
Disallow: /partners

The file identifies online folders which include a new beta website, temporary development page, and list of their partners. Much of this content would not be found in a search engine because of the "Disallow" setting. These Disallow instructions are telling the search engines to avoid scanning the folders "cnnbeta", "development", and "partners". It is likely that there is sensitive information in these directories that should not be available on Google or Bing. You can now type these directories after the domain name of your target to identify additional information. Based on the robots.txt file in this demonstration, typing the following addresses directly into a browser may generate interesting results.

https://www.cnn.com/cnnbeta
https://www.cnn.com/development
https://www.cnn.com/partners

Most robots.txt files will not identify a secret area of a website that will display passwords, raunchy photos, or incriminating evidence. Instead, they usually provide insight into which areas of the site are considered sensitive by the owner. If you have a target website and have exhausted every other search method, you should also visit this file. It may direct you toward a new set of queries to find data otherwise ignored by search engines.

If this technique produces no results, you can conduct a Google or Bing query to identify any files. A search of "site:cnn.com robots ext:txt" on either search engine identifies robots.txt files from the entire website. We can also query the Wayback Machine to display changes of this file over time at the following URL structure.

https://web.archive.org/web/*/cnn.com/robots.txt

Search Engine Marketing Tools

The ultimate goal of most commercial websites is to generate income. These sites exist to bring in new customers, sell products, and provide the public face to a company. This has created a huge community of services that aim to help companies reach customers. Search Engine Optimization (SEO) applies various techniques affecting the visibility of a website or a web page in a search engine's results. In general, the higher ranked on the search results page and more frequently a site appears in the search results list, the more visitors it will receive. Search Engine Marketing (SEM) websites provide details valuable to those responsible for optimizing their own websites. SEM services usually provide the overall ranking of a website; its keywords that are often searched; backlinks; and referrals from other websites. SEO specialists use this data to determine potential advertisement relationships and to study their competition. Online investigators can use this to collect important details that are never visible on the target websites. Three individual services will provide easily digestible data on any domain. I will use my own domain for each example in order to compare the data. Only the free versions will be discussed.

Similar Web (similarweb.com)

Similar Web is usually the most comprehensive of the free options. However, some of these details usually contradict other services. Much of this data is "guessed" based on many factors. A search of inteltechniques.com produced the following partial information about the domain.

- The majority of the traffic is from the USA, followed by UK, DE, FR.
- There is no paid search or advertisements on search engines.
- There are 56 websites that possess links to the target, and 15 are visible.
- "Buscador" led more people to the site than any other search term followed by OSINT.
- Over 50,000 people visit the site monthly.
- There are five main online competitors to the target, and the largest is onstrat.com.
- 71% of the visitors navigated directly to the domain without a search engine.
- 12% of the traffic was referrals from other websites and search engines.
- The referrals included my other website (computercrimeinfo.com).
- 3% of the traffic to this site originated from social networks Facebook and Twitter.
- Similar websites include onstrat.com and automatingosint.com.

Spyfu (spyfu.com)

This service replaced Alexa and Moon Search for me after those services were shut down. It provides site rankings, competitors, common keywords, Google advertisement data, and backlinks. The data will probably be redundant at this point, but the service should be queried. An additional website which provides a similar service to Spyfu is **Majestic** (majestic.com).

Shared Count (sharedcount.com)

This website provides one simple yet unique service. It searches your target domain and identifies its popularity on social networks such as Facebook and Twitter. A search of labnol.org produced the following results. This information would lead me to focus on Pinterest and Facebook first. It tells me that several people are talking about the website on these services.

Facebook Likes: 348   Facebook Total: 1034
Facebook Shares: 538   Twitter Tweets: 0
Facebook Comments: 148   Pinterest Pinned: 1

Reddit Domains (reddit.com)

Reddit was discussed previously as a very popular online community. The primary purpose of the service is to share links to online websites, photos, videos, and comments of interest. If your target website has ever been posted on Reddit, you can retrieve a listing of the incidents. This is done through a specific address typed directly into your browser. If your target website was phonelosers.org, you would navigate to the exact URL of reddit.com/domain/phonelosers.org. This example produced 16 Reddit posts mentioning this domain. These could be analyzed to document the discussions and usernames related to these posts.

Small SEO Tools: Backlinks (smallseotools.com/backlink-checker)

After you have determined the popularity of a website on social networks, you may want to identify any websites that have a link to your target domain. This will often identify associates and people with similar interests of the subject of your investigation. There are several online services that offer a check of any "backlinks" to a specific website. Lately, I have had the best success with the backlink checker at Small SEO Tools. A search of my own website, inteltechniques.com, produces 264 websites that have a link to mine. These results include pages within my own websites that have a link to inteltechniques.com, so this number can be somewhat misleading. Several of the results disclosed websites owned by friends and colleagues that would be of interest if I were your target.

Host.io Backlinks (host.io)

In 2021, I discovered this service which seems to offer many additional backlinks which were not present within the previous option. The following direct URL displays 45 domains which are linking to my website.

https://host.io/backlinks/inteltechniques.com

Host.io Redirects (host.io)

This option displays any URLs which are forwarding their traffic to your target site. The following direct URL displays my own results. You can quickly identify three domains which I own that are forwarding visitors to my main site. Searching for historic records of these domains should reveal outdated websites and details.

https://host.io/redirects/inteltechniques.com

A summary of all details about a domain stored with Host.io can be found via the following direct URL.

https://host.io/inteltechniques.com

Small SEO Tools: Plagiarism Checker (smallseotools.com/plagiarism-checker)

If you have identified a web page of interest, you should make sure the content is original. On more than one occasion, I have been contacted by an investigator that had been notified of a violent threat on a person's blog. I was asked to track down the subject before something bad happened. A quick search of the content identified it as lyrics to a song. One of many options for this type of query is the plagiarism checker at Small SEO Tools. You can use this tool by copying any questionable text from a website and paste it into this free tool. It will analyze the text and display other websites that possess the same words. This service uses Google to identify anything of interest. The benefit of using this tool instead of Google directly is that it will structure several queries based on the supplied content and return variations of the found text. Clicking the results will open the Google search page that found the text. Another option for this type of search is **Copy Scape** (copyscape.com).

Octopus (octopus.do)

There are times when a visual representation of a site can be helpful in quickly identifying pages or sections worthy of deeper investigation. Octopus generates a very simple and easy to navigate diagram of the site pages with the benefit of labels and small text based descriptions. There are additional settings which allow you to customize how the data is displayed on the page. These diagrams can also be nice additions to our reports.

XML Sitemaps (xml-sitemaps.com)

This service "crawls" a domain and creates an XML text file of all public pages. Scanning my own site and blog displayed direct URLs of 493 unique pages. Exporting the XML file provided documentation of the process.

This is a great companion to visual site mappers, as the text can be easily imported into reporting systems. This often presents previously unknown content.

Threat Data

This represents a new category for this chapter and I am quite embarrassed it took me so long to realize the value of the content. I use the term "Threat Data" to encompass the top four websites which monitor for malicious content. For a network security analyst, this data might identify potentially malicious sites which should be blacklisted within internal networks. For us OSINT researchers, the data represented here can provide a unique glimpse into our target domain. Instead of explaining every facet of these services, I will only focus on the new evidence received after a query of various domains. All of these services are available in your search tools.

VirusTotal (virustotal.com)

This option displays the most useful information in regard to OSINT, and this is likely the most popular threat data service of the four. Much of the details presented here are redundant to the previous options, so let's focus only on the unique data. The "Details" menu provides the most public data. The Whois and DNS records should be similar to other sites. The "Categories" area provides the general topics of the target site. For mine, it displays "Information Technology". This can be useful to know a small detail about sites which have disappeared. The "HTTPS Certificate" section can become interesting very quickly. The "Subject Alternative Name" portion of this section identifies additional domains and subdomains associated with the SSL certificate of your target site. When I search cnn.com, I receive dozens of additional URLs which could prove to be valuable. Below is a partial view.

dev.client.appletv.cnn.com,dev.cnnmoney.ch,dev.content.cnnmoney.ch,dev.hypatia.api.cnn.io

I now know that cnn.io is directly associated with the target, which should then be investigated. The "Relations" tab identifies many new subdomains such as customad.cnn.com, go.cnn.com, and store.cnn.com. The "Files" section displays unique content from practically any other resource. It identifies files downloaded **from** the target site for analysis and files which have a reference **to** the target site.

Let's analyze my own site as an example. Figure 32.06 displays two files which are present on my site. Both of these files have been analyzed by VirusTotal from either user submission or automated scanning. The first column displays the date of the scan and the second column identifies whether any virus databases detected the files as malicious (none out of 60 tested positive for a virus). The final two columns identify the file type and name. If I were to remove these files today, this evidence would stick around.

Figure 32.07 displays the result in the "Files Referring" section. These are files and programs, which are not present on my site, that refer to my domain. All of these display positive results for being malicious. These are basically files stored on other websites which mention my domain. If you were investigating me, you should try to find these files for further analysis. The fourth file is a virus disguised as a digital copy of this book, attempting to fool would-be downloaders. If your target is mentioned within off-site files, you can learn a lot from analysis. Always use a virtual machine without network access if you plan to download or open anything found here.

| 2018-11-14 | 0 / 59 | ZIP | ffmpeg.zip |
| 2018-11-25 | 0 / 60 | PDF | workbook.pdf |

Figure 32.06: A VirusTotal result identifying files from a domain.

Scanned	Detections	Type	Name
2019-08-29	1 / 48	Win32 EXE	OSCAR.exe
2019-08-04	1 / 60	ZIP	Doxing eBooks.zip
2019-05-14	3 / 73	Win32 EXE	HawkEye.exe
2019-05-09	1 / 60	Office Open XML Document	Open Source Intelligence Techniques
2019-02-11	1 / 60	ZIP	Hacklog2.zip
2019-01-15	2 / 58	PDF	Hacklog. Web Hacking - vol. 2.pdf
2019-01-06	1 / 60	ZIP	Doxing eBooks.zip

Figure 32.07: A VirusTotal result identifying files referring to a domain.

Finally, the "Community" tab can be a treasure of details if anything exists about your target domain. This is where members of the VirusTotal community can leave comments or experiences in reference to the target site. While there are no comments currently on my profile, I have seen helpful details on target "hacking" related sites. These included owner details and new domains created for illegal phishing purposes. Most sites will not have any comments, but this option should be checked while browsing through the other sections.

Threat Intelligence (threatintelligenceplatform.com)

This service replicates many of the features already presented. However, I usually look to three specific sections in the domain report. The "Connected Domains" area identifies any external domains which are linked from your source. This can often display hidden links to third-party services otherwise unknown from previous queries. On my domain, you see a link to the icon service I use because I gave attribution within the footer of my page. In previous investigations, I have found additional domains owned by the suspect. From there, I focus on the "Potentially dangerous content" and "Malware detection" sections. Both of these offer a historical view into any malicious content hosted on the target domain. This can include suspicious files or phishing campaigns. While recently investigating a domain which currently possessed no content, this service confirmed the presence of a phishing page designed to steal credentials.

Threat Crowd (ci-www.threatcrowd.org)

This service provides a unique view of the domains associated with your target. It can display server IPs, primary domains, and additional domains which were once associated with the target.

Censys (censys.io)

Censys provides a detailed summary of the basics, which is quite redundant at this point. However, there are three key pieces of information I access here on most domains. I previously mentioned the importance of checking the Subject Alternative Names of a domain's SSL certificate. Most services conduct scans of the entire internet in order to retrieve this data. The moment a certificate is issued, it is provided in real-time to Censys. Censys thus does not need to rely on internet scans to discover certificates, and more importantly Subject Alternative Names. Therefore, I always click the "Details" button on the summary page and look for any interesting data by searching "alt_name" within the results. Next, I have relied on the HTTP Body text information stored within the "Details" page of the HTTP and HTTPS sections. This is basically the HTML code which makes the web page display properly within a browser. It is the same data you would see by viewing the source code of a target page. If the target website should disappear, this entire section of code could be copied; pasted into a text file; saved with an html extension; and opened within a browser to reveal the overall look and structure. I prefer to capture this data in the event of a modified or removed target web page. Finally, I believe Censys has the overall best data about the security certificates associated with a domain. It provides hyperlinks to every certificate within the chain and extreme details about each. Much of this data is not valuable to an OSINT report, but I prefer to collect a screen capture for potential later analysis or comparison to live data. Overall, threat data is often considered minor bits of information designated only for the digital security community. OSINT practitioners should also be aware of the content available within these sites. While the majority of details are not immediately useful, small nuggets of valuable information which cannot be found anywhere else awaits you.

WordPress Data

Many websites displayed at domains are WordPress blogs. These can be customized in any way to have the appearance of a traditional website. You may want to identify any vulnerabilities which exist within the WordPress installation which may disclose interesting details about the site. The following providers display the basics without the need to install any software. Please note the terms of service when you use these options. A search of my own domain revealed the version of WordPress; blog IP address; hosting provider; title of the blog; any blacklist entries; installed plugins; custom themes; login usernames; linked websites; and overall security of the site.

https://sitecheck.sucuri.net/
https://hackertarget.com/wordpress-security-scan/

Domain Reputation

In the chapter about email addresses, I explained the importance of investigating an address's reputation for sending spam or delivering malicious content. We can do the same for domains with the following URLs.

https://www.spam.org/search?type=domain&convert_block=1&group_ips=1&data=inteltechniques.com
https://www.mywot.com/en/scorecard/inteltechniques.com

Threat Analysis (dracoeye.com)

This service conducts a passive security audit for any domain. This can display spam reports, malware flags, virus possibilities, server details, blacklists, and many other details. Queries can be submitted via URL as follows.

https://dracoeye.com/search/inteltechniques.com

Data Breaches and Leaks

Similar to email addresses and usernames, domains can possess valuable breach data. You should already be familiar with breach data providers, so I will focus only on methodology here.

Dehashed (dehashed.com)

This service and search options function identical to the email queries. Provide the domain, and the results display the breaches which possess at least one email address matching the provided data. The URL query structure is https://dehashed.com/search?query="inteltechniques.com". Dehashed now requires that we create a free account prior to receiving results on queries through their site, but they do accept addresses from most masking services during registration.

IntelX (intelx.io)

This service presents partial Pastebin files which include your target domain. A direct query URL is https://intelx.io/?s=inteltechniques.com. A free trial is required to see all results.

Leakpeek (leakpeek.com)

This service requires a free account to search domains, and a direct URL is not available.

Shortened URLs

Social networking sites, such as Twitter, have made the popularity of shortened URL services soar. When people post a link to something they want their friends to see, they do not want the link to take up unnecessary space. These services create a new URL, and simply point anyone to the original source when clicked. As an example, I converted a URL to a blog post from "https://inteltechniques.com/blog/2019/08/03/book-release-extreme-privacy/" to "https://bit.ly/32Up8h7".

You have likely seen these during your own investigations, and many people pay them little attention. There is actually a lot of information behind the scenes of these links that can reveal valuable information associated with your investigation. For a demonstration, I created the following shortened links, all of which forward to my home page. After, I will explain how to access the hidden data behind each service.

bitly.com/29A4U1U
http://tiny.cc/v973ez
goo.gl/Ew9rlh
https://www.naturl.link/6VPA30

Bitly allows access to metadata by including a "+" after the URL. In our scenario, the direct URL would be bitly.com/29A4U1U+. In this example, the results only identified that 21 people have clicked on my link. However, creating a free account reveals much more detail. After logging in, I can see any websites that referred the user to the link and extremely generic location data, such as the country of the user. This is a good start.

Tiny.cc adds a "~" to the end of a link to display metadata. In our example, the direct URL would be tiny.cc/v973ez~. The results on this page identify the number of times the URL was clicked, the number of unique visits, the operating systems of those that clicked the link, and the browsers used. This service also displays generic location data, such as the country of the user. Tiny.cc blocklists certain domains (including mine now), so your results may vary depending on your target.

Google gives us the same detail as above. However, Google has announced that they will be ending their shortener services in August of 2025, so this is another Google feature which soon be deprecated. Naturl Link is a good option if you are looking for a simple shortener which requires no account creation or other hoops to jump through. It is a lesser known shortener service, but could not be easier to use. If you are investigating a shortened URL link that was not mentioned, consider using the catch-all online service located at **CheckShortURL** (checkshorturl.com).

UNFURL (dfir.blog/unfurl/)

This service appeared in late 2022, and I find it very valuable. You can enter any full internet address to gather behind-the-scenes details by expanding the data associated within the URL. This could be to identify details behind a Twitter post, Instagram photo, or shortened URL. As one of many examples, I often find Twitter links posted in various places. Clicking these will forward me to the intended URL target, but I want more details. I also find this very beneficial for the investigation of magnet Torrent links. Any time I find a Torrent link, I copy and paste the entire URL into this tool. It typically displays the web seed, address tracker, source, file details, and domains. I encourage you to submit any URLs or domains of interest to this tool. You will soon discover the possibilities as related to your types of investigations.

Cloudflare

While identifying web hosts and IP addresses behind your target domain, you are likely to encounter sites hiding behind Cloudflare. This company provides security for websites which often prevents online attacks and outages. They also help keep web host and owner details hidden when investigating criminal websites. There is no magic solution to uncover the owner of a website behind Cloudflare's protection, but we do have a few investigative options, as follows.

Historical: Use the previous methods to search historical domain registration records. While Whois sites may show Cloudflare today, historical registration records may show the actual web host used prior to Cloudflare. The result may or may not be the current host.

Censys (censys.io): Most websites possess Secure Socket Layer (SSL) certificates. Searching a domain name through the Censys "Certificates" search may identify historical SSL ownership records. The direct URL of "https://censys.io/certificates?q=inteltechniques.com" displays my own domain. The results identify my SSL host authority as Sectigo in 2020, Comodo (Namecheap) in 2018, and GoDaddy in 2016. You now know my domain host history. This area of Censys can be beneficial to any domain regardless of Cloudflare protection, which is a feature often overlooked. We can also query a specific SSL certificate to potentially see other associated domains. The previous search identified "7583b0cb25632de96575dd0f00ff99fed81b9069" as the SSL certificate which I possessed in 2016. Searching this within Censys under the "Certificate" menu provides the domains of computercrimeinfo.com, inteltechniques.com, privacy-training.com. We now have other domains to investigate. Some of them may reveal the current domain registration provider and web host.

Third-Party Tracking: Some websites will hide their domain registration and host behind various protection services, but continue to use analytics, tracking, and Google services. Consider the previous methods of searching Analytics, and any other unique identifiers across other sites owned by the same target.

Advanced DNS

I mentioned **Domains App** (dmns.app) previously as a way to query stored historical screen captures. We can also use this resource to see much more DNS details than the services explained at the beginning of this chapter. This can often include an email address within the DMARC data which is not visible elsewhere. Consider an example for michaelbazzell.com. We can query with the following direct URL.

https://dmns.app/domains/michaelbazzell.com/dns-records

The results identify the usual DNS suspects, including my web host and server IP address. However, there is new data in the last sections.

"protonmail-verification=f84a8f78b21c92a4493fe5d9d5cb1150385846e9"
"v=spf1 include:_spf.protonmail.ch mx ~all"
"v=DMARC1; p=none; rua=mailto:donotspamme@michaelbazzell.com"

We now know that all email for that domain is handled within a Proton Mail account. We also see a new email address in the final DMARC section. For many domains which apply this extra level of email security and verification, you will find a legitimate email address which may have escaped your other analysis. As I write this, I learned of a personal email address included within results for a domain which is part of a current investigation. I have included this option within the search tool explained next.

IntelTechniques Domain Tool

Similar to the previous custom search tools mentioned here, I have created a page for easier domain searching. While it does not possess every service discussed in this chapter, it can automate queries across the most beneficial options. Each box allows entry of a target domain name. The "Submit All" option will open several tabs within your browser that present each query listed on the page. The final section provides easy access to shortened URL metadata. The online version at **https://inteltechniques.com/tools/Domain.html** is updated often.

CHAPTER THIRTY-THREE
IP ADDRESSES

IP addresses are often obtained from an internet investigation, email message, or connection over the internet. When legal process is served to online content providers, a list of IP addresses used to log in to the account is usually presented as part of the return of information. Serving legal orders to identify and obtain IP addresses is outside the scope of this book. However, several techniques for collecting a target's IP address using OSINT are explained in this chapter. The previous instruction assumed that you were researching a domain name. These names, associated with websites, simply forward you to a numerical address that actually hosts the content. This is referred to as an Internet Protocol (IP) address.

The way that you encounter IP addresses as a target of your research will vary widely. Law enforcement may receive an IP address of an offender after submitting a subpoena to an internet provider. Any online researcher may locate an IP address while researching a domain with the previous methods. While only one website can be on a domain, multiple domains can be hosted on one IP address. The following resources represent only a fraction of available utilities. Note that many of the domain name resources mentioned in the previous chapters also allow for query by an IP address. Let's begin with the basic resources at ViewDNS.

ViewDNS Reverse IP (viewdns.info/reverseip)

This page was previously used to translate a domain name into an IP address. It will also display additional domains hosted on an individual IP address. This service identified 134 domains hosted on 104.28.10.123. These included domains from websites all over the world without a common theme. This indicates that he uses a shared server, which is very common. If I would have seen only a few domains on the server, that may indicate that he is also associated with those specific domains.

ViewDNS IP Location (viewdns.info/iplocation)

This utility cross-references an IP address with publicly available location data connected to the server hosting any domains associated with the IP address. A search of 54.208.51.71 revealed the following information.

City: Ashburn
Zip Code: 20147
Region Name: Virginia
Country Code: US
Country Name: United States

ViewDNS Port Scan (viewdns.info/portscan)

This online port scanner looks for common ports that may be open. An open port indicates that a service is running on the web server that may allow public connection. A search of 54.208.51.71 revealed that ports 21, 53, 80, and 443 are open to outside connections. Port 21 is for FTP connections, 53 is for DNS settings, 80 is for web pages, and port 443 is for secure web pages.

ViewDNS IP Whois (viewdns.info/whois)

This service was used earlier to display registration information about an individual domain. Entering an IP address will attempt to identify details about any domain registrations associated with the address. A search of 54.208.51.71 revealed it to belong to Amazon and provided the public registration details.

ViewDNS IP Traceroute (viewdns.info/traceroute)

This tool identifies the path that ViewDNS took from their servers to the target IP address. This can identify IP addresses of servers that were contacted while you tried to establish communication with the address. These will occasionally identify associated networks, routers, and servers. Additional IP addresses can be searched for further details. The numbers after the IP addresses indicate the number of milliseconds that each "hop" took.

ViewDNS Reverse DNS (viewdns.info/reversedns)

This simply finds the reverse DNS entry for a given IP, which is usually the host name.

Similar to the Domain chapter, ViewDNS allows queries of IP addresses via URL, as follows.

https://viewdns.info/reverseip/?host=70.39.110.82&t=1
https://viewdns.info/iplocation/?ip=70.39.110.82
https://viewdns.info/portscan/?host=70.39.110.82
https://viewdns.info/whois/?domain=70.39.110.82
https://viewdns.info/traceroute/?domain=70.39.110.82
https://viewdns.info/reversedns/?ip=70.39.110.82

Bing IP (bing.com)

Once you have identified an IP address of your target, you can search for websites hosted on that IP address. A specific search on Bing will present any other websites on that server. If your target is stored with a large host, such as GoDaddy, there will not be much intelligence provided. It will only list websites that share a server, but are not necessarily associated with each other. If the user is hosting the website on an individual web server, this search will display all other websites that the user hosts. This search only works on Bing and must have "ip:" before the IP address. An example of a proper search on Bing would look like ip:54.208.51.71. The results of this search identify every website hosted by a specific local website design company. The direct URL follows.

https://www.bing.com/search?q=ip%3A54.208.51.71

IPLocation (iplocation.net)

IPLocation offers unlimited free IP address searches, and queries five unique services within the same search results. The results are the most comprehensive I have seen for a free website. While GPS coordinates of an IP address are available, this most often returns to the provider of the internet service. This usually does not identify the exact location where the IP address is being used. The country, region, and city information should be accurate. If an organization name is presented in the results, this indicates that the address returns to the identified company. The exception here is when an internet service provider is identified. This only indicates that the IP address belongs to the specified provider. Most results translate an IP address into information including business name, general location, and internet service provider. This can be used to determine if the IP address that a target is using belongs to a business providing free wireless internet. If you see "Starbucks", "Barnes & Noble", or other popular internet cafés listed in the results, this can be important intelligence about the target. This can also confirm if an IP address is associated with a VPN service. The direct URL query follows.

https://www.iplocation.net/ip-lookup?query=70.39.110.83&submit=IP+Lookup

That's Them (thatsthem.com/reverse-ip-lookup)

The previous resources rely on conventional IP address data, which is sourced from various registration documentation and scanning of servers. Very little information is sensitive or personal in nature. That's Them enters into an environment that is a lot more invasive. This service, mentioned previously during person, email, and telephone search, collects marketing data from many sources to populate its database. This often includes IP address information. These details could have been obtained during an online purchase or website registration. Regardless of the source, the results can be quite beneficial. At the time of this writing, I searched an IP address associated with a business email that I received. The result identified a person's name, home address, company, email address, and age range. All appeared accurate. This tool will work best when searching static business IP addresses, and not traditional home IP addresses that can change often. While I get no results much more often than positive results, this resource should be in everyone's arsenal. The direct URL follows.

https://thatsthem.com/ip/70.39.110.82

I Know What You Download (iknowwhatyoudownload.com)

While discussing invasive websites, this resource might be the most personal of all. This service monitors online torrents (ways to download large files which often violate copyright laws) and discloses the files associated with any collected IP addresses. I searched the previous IP address collected from an associate, and received an immediate hit. Figure 33.01 displays the result. It identifies that the target IP address was downloading two specific movies on December 28, 2017 at 9:53 pm. Clicking on the movie title presents every IP address captured that also downloaded the same file. Again, this will work best with IP addresses that rarely change, such as a business, organization, or public Wi-Fi network. I have used this to determine the files being downloaded from the network with which I was currently connected. On one occasion, this revealed an employee that was downloading enormous amounts of pornography on his employer's network. He should have used a VPN, which would have masked his online activity from me. In order to see the power of this type of service, try searching a known VPN address such as an address provided by Private Internet Access (PIA) 173.244.56.138. While I know that no one reading this book has ever downloaded pirated content, this should serve as a reminder why VPNs are essential. The direct URL query follows.

https://iknowwhatyoudownload.com/en/peer/?ip=70.39.110.82

| Dec 28, 2017 9:53:21 PM | Dec 28, 2017 9:53:21 PM | Movies | Looper |
| Dec 28, 2017 9:53:19 PM | Dec 28, 2017 9:53:19 PM | Movies | The Beguiled |

Figure 33.01: A search result from I Know What You Download.

Exonerator (metrics.torproject.org/exonerator.html)

The Onion Router (Tor) was explained in Chapter Nine. It is a network that provides anonymity by issuing IP addresses to users that connect to servers in other countries. If you possess an IP address of your target, but cannot locate any valuable information using the previous techniques, it is possible that the address was part of the Tor network and there is no relevant data to be located. Exonerator is a tool that will verify the usage of an IP address on the Tor network. Provide the IP address and a date of usage, and the service will display whether it was used as a Tor connection. While a date is required, you could provide the current date if your target time frame is unknown. Most IP addresses are typically always or never a part of the Tor network.

Wigle (wigle.net)

Wigle is a crowd-sourced database of wireless access points. Users in all areas of the country conduct scans of wireless devices in their area; identify details of each device; and submit this data to Wigle in order to map the found devices on the site. This allows anyone to browse an area for wireless access points or search an address to locate specific devices. Additionally, you can search for either a specific router name or MAC address and locate any matching devices. The results include links that will display the results on an interactive map. Most of the world has been covered. In order to take advantage of the search features, you will need to register for a free account. Generic or misleading information can be used that does not identify you.

There are many investigative uses for this service. You can identify the wireless access points in the immediate area of a target's home. As an example, a search of the address of a gas station revealed a map of it with the associated routers. In this view, I can identify the router names including potential sensitive information. It displays wireless router SSID's of AltonBPStore, tankers_network, Big Toe, and others. Clicking View and then Search in the upper left of the page presents a detailed query engine. A search of tankers_network, as identified previously in the map view, displays details of the wireless access point. It has a MAC address of 00:1F:C6:FC:1B:3F, WPA encryption, was first seen in 2011, and operates on channel 11.

An investigator could also search by the target's name. This may identify routers that have the target's name within the SSID. A search of "Bazzell" identifies seven access points that probably belong to relatives with my last name. These results identify the router name, MAC address, dates, encryption method, channel, and location of the device. This can easily lead an investigator to the home of a target.

Many internet users will use the same name for their wireless router as they use for their online screen name. Assume that your target's username was "Hacker21224". A search on Wigle for "Hacker21224" as a router name might produce applicable results. These could identify the router's MAC address, encryption type, and GPS coordinates. A search on Google Maps of the supplied GPS coordinates will immediately identify the home address, a satellite view of the neighborhood, and a street view of the house of the target. All of this intelligence can be obtained from a simple username. These results would not appear on any standard search engines.

If you find Wigle valuable to your investigations, I recommend you create a free account. While logged in, you can use their advanced search (wigle.net/search) or submit direct queries via URL as follows.

https://wigle.net/search?ssid=bazzell
https://wigle.net/search#fullSearch?postalCode=62002

Shodan (shodan.io)

Shodan is a search engine that lets you find specific computers (routers, servers, etc.) using a variety of filters. General search engines, such as Google and Bing, are great for finding websites; however, they do not search for computers or devices. Shodan indexes "banners", which are metadata that a device sends back to a client. This can be information about the server software, what options the service supports, or a welcome message. Devices that are commonly identified through Shodan include servers, routers, online storage devices, surveillance cameras, webcams, and VOIP systems. Network security professionals use this site to identify vulnerabilities on their systems. Criminals use it to illegally access networks and alter devices. We will use it to locate specific systems near a target location. In order to take advantage of Shodan's full search capabilities, you must create a free account. Only a name and email address is required. The following example will identify how to locate live public surveillance cameras based on location. The target for this search is Mount Pleasant, Utah. The following search on Shodan produced 9,684 results.

country:US city:"Mount Pleasant"

There are two flaws with this search. First, you may receive results from other cities named Mount Pleasant. Second, you will likely receive too many results to analyze effectively. A search of "geo:39.55,-111.45" will focus only on the specific GPS location of interest (Lat=39.55, Long= -111.45). There were 238 results for this search. This is much more manageable and all of the results will be devices in the target area. Adding more specific search criteria will filter the results further. A search of "geo:39.55,-111.45 netcam" identified only one device. The result displays this device as a "Netcam". It also identifies the internet service provider as "Central Utah Telephone" indicating the user has a DSL connection.

To connect to the device, you would click on the IP address identified as 63.78.117.229. Clicking through each of these options may be time consuming. You can add a search term to filter your results. Replicating this search for a GPS location in a large city will produce many results. Clicking the IP address will take you to the page that will connect to each device. You must be careful here. Some devices will require a username and password for access. You could try "admin" / "admin" or "guest" / "guest", but you may be breaking the law. This could be considered computer intrusion. However, many of the webcam and netcam results will not prompt you for a password and connect you to the device automatically. There is likely no law violation when connecting to a device that does not prompt you for credentials. Your local laws may prohibit this activity.

Shodan Maps (maps.shodan.io) allows you to conduct any of these searches based on location alone while **Shodan Images** (images.shodan.io) displays collected webcam captures from open devices. Figure 33.02 displays a home using an automated lighting and climate control system in Missouri located with Shodan Maps. These two options are premium services and require a modest fee. All Shodan features allow input of the following types of information for filtering.

City: Name of the city (ex. City:"San Diego")
Country: 2-letter country code (ex. Country:US)
GPS: Latitude and longitude (ex. Geo:50.23,20.06)
OS: Operating system (ex. Os:Linux)
IP Address: Range (ex. Net:18.7.7.0/24)
Keyword: (ex. Webcam)

Figure 33.02: A Shodan Maps search result.

Shodan Beta (beta.shodan.io) offers complete details of a specified IP address. This can be queried with the following three URLs.

https://beta.shodan.io/host/147.135.65.22
https://beta.shodan.io/host/147.135.65.22/raw
https://beta.shodan.io/host/147.135.65.22/history

The first presents the standard view while the second offers text-only details which may be more valuable to a report. The final option looks at all available details about the domain throughout several scans over time. Each entry displays a date in the format of 2020-04-26T07:49:17 (April 26, 2020 at 7:49 am).

Zoom Eye (zoomeye.hk)

This Shodan competitor provides a similar service, often with unique results. A direct URL query follows.

https://www.zoomeye.hk/searchResult?q=70.39.110.82

Threat Crowd (ci-www.threatcrowd.org)

As mentioned in the previous chapter, Threat Crowd is a system for finding and researching artifacts relating to cyber threats. Searching an IP address can reveal an association to malicious software being spread over the internet. A positive result will display the type of malware, associated domain names, dates of discovery, and any comments by other researchers. Most readers that actually need this type of service likely already know more about it than me. However, it should be a consideration when investigating suspicious IP addresses. A URL query follows.

https://www.ci-www.threatcrowd.org/ip.php?ip=70.39.110.82

Censys (censys.io)

Similarly, Censys is a search engine that enables researchers to ask questions about the hosts and networks that comprise the internet. Censys collects data on hosts and websites through daily scans of the internet, in turn maintaining a database of how hosts and websites are configured. Researchers can interact with this data through a search interface. As an example, a search of 173.189.238.211 reveals it to be associated with a Schneider Electric BMX P34 2020 device through a Windstream provided internet connection, located near Kansas City, Kansas. A URL query follows.

https://censys.io/ipv4/70.39.110.82

Ipv6 Addresses

The IP addresses previously mentioned were all version four (Ipv4), such as 192.168.1.1. Due to limited availability, many providers are switching to Ipv6, which allows many more addresses. A typical example may appear as 2001:0db8:85a3:0000:0000:8a2e:0370:7334. While many of the utilities mentioned here are adapting to this input, we should query these types of addresses through designated Ipv6 engines. Some sites may require either full or compressed IPv6 addresses, and you can convert one format to the other online at https://iplocation.io/ipv6-expand/. I have tested dozens, and I find the following two to work best, both of which are included in the search tool.

https://search.dnslytics.com/ip/2001:db8::8a2e:370:7334
https://myip.ms/view/comp_ip6/176883/2001:db8:85a3::8a2e:370:7334

Email Headers

I no longer teach email header analysis in my live courses. The vast majority of users rely on web-based email such as Gmail or Yahoo. These services do not disclose the IP address of an individual user within the email headers. The only email headers that I have encountered over the past three years that contained valuable IP addresses were business users that sent emails within a desktop client such as Outlook. If you would like to analyze an email header in order to identify the IP address and sender information, you have two options. You can look through a few sites and teach yourself how to read this confusing data, or you can use an automated service.

IP2Location (ip2location.com/free/email-tracer) provides a large text box into which an entire email header can be copied for analysis. The response includes the IP address and location of the sender; interactive map identifying the originating location; internet service provider; and links to additional information from an IP search. Anyone wanting more information from an email threat should start here. An alternative site that conducts similar actions is **MX Toolbox** (mxtoolbox.com/EmailHeaders.aspx).

Obtaining a Target's IP Address

You may want to know the IP address of the person you are researching as provided by their internet service provider. This address could be used to verify an approximate location of the person; to provide law enforcement details that would be needed for a court order; or to determine if multiple email addresses belong to the same subject. All of those scenarios will be explained here.

IP Logger (iplogger.org)

For many years, this was my favorite option for identifying the IP address of a target. There are many options now, and most of them will be explained here. This specific technique involves some trickery and the need to contact the target from a covert account. For this demonstration, assume your target has a Facebook page that he checks regularly. You can send him a private message that includes "bait" in the form of an online link. A detailed set of instructions should explain the processes. The main website presents several options, but only the "URL & Image Shortener" service will be explained.

Link: You can generate a URL which will redirect to any website that you provide. IP Logger will save the IP address of each user who clicked the link. In the box provided, enter any address that you want the target to see when clicking on a link. This could be something generic such as cnn.com. After submitting, you will receive a series of links. This page also serves as the log of visitors, and I recommend documenting it. In an example, I received the following link at the beginning of this list.

http://www.iplogger.org/3ySz.jpg

Although the link appears to be a jpg image, clicking this link or typing it into a browser forwards the target to cnn.com. This action collects his or her IP address, operating system, and browser details. These details, along with the date and time of capture, can be viewed at the link generated previously. A URL shortening service such as Bitly (bit.ly) would make the link look less suspicious.

Real World Application: I was once communicating with an unknown subject on a web forum about hacking and stolen credit card numbers. I wanted to find out his IP address in order to discover his true identity with a court order. I told the hacker I had an image of a freshly stolen debit card that I was willing to share. He requested proof, so I created an IP Logger link based on a generic online image, and embedded that link into the web forum where we were communicating. Within a few moments, I visited the log for this image and discovered his IP address in Newark, New Jersey.

Canary Tokens (canarytokens.org)

A newer option for IP identification is Canary Tokens. It offers redundant functionality as the previously mentioned product, but may be more useful to you. Ultimately, you should familiarize yourself with all options and choose which works best for you. Lately, I have found Canary Tokens to be the superior option of all. It allows creation of a PDF or DOCX file that contains a tracker, and is the most user-friendly of the services. After choosing a tracking option, it walks you through the process. I maintain Canary Token files at the following addresses. They are used as traps for people that conduct Google searches attempting to find my home address. Opening any of these alerts me to your IP address and general location. At the time of this writing, the most recent opening of one of these documents occurred only two days prior. The culprit lives in Matawan, New Jersey, possesses MCI as an internet provider, and had downloaded an Xbox 360 game through a torrent.

https://inteltechniques.com/canary/canary.pdf
https://inteltechniques.com/canary/canary.docx

Remember that VPNs and Tor may create inaccurate results. Use caution when sending trackers, and make sure you are not violating any laws or internal policies. I find these services slowly becoming less useful.

LinkBait (github.com/AmIJesse/LinkBait)

There is a glaring problem with all of these public IP logging services. They are well-known and may be blocked by email providers. Gmail typically blocks any domains associated with either IP Logger or Canary Tokens. A tech-savvy target may recognize these tactics which could jeopardize your investigation. This is why I rely on my own self-hosted option made by my colleague Jesse. The link above includes all files required to host your own IP Logger on your website. You simply need to copy the PHP file into a web-accessible directory on your Apache web server, including shared web hosts. I renamed the file to "index.php" and placed it on my website at https://inteltechniques.com/site/index.php. If you visited that page by clicking a link I had sent to you, a text file would have been generated in that folder. The title would have included the date and your IP address. The following represents a partial view of the content submitted by your computer. This page is not currently live because I do not want to log visitors to my site.

```
70.39.126.131
Mozilla/5.0 (Macintosh; Intel Mac OS X 10.14; rv:81.0) Gecko/20100101
Firefox/81.0
touch: false / mic: Found / gpu: AMD Radeon Pro 560X OpenGL Engine
Screen Height: 1080
Language: en-US
Fonts: 109 fonts: American Typewriter...
Detected OS   = Mac OS X  [generic] [fuzzy]
MTU           = 1392
Network link  = OpenVPN UDP bs128 SHA1 lzo
MTU not 1500, VPN probable.
"country":"United States"
"regionName":"California","city":"Los Angeles","isp":"Sharktech"
"timezone":"Denver"
browserVersion: 5.0 (Macintosh) / Screen Width: 1920
System Time: 2020-10-14 16:2:6
router: https://192.168.1.1
browser: Mozilla / platform: MacIntel
Discord: Not Running
Logins: Google Services
```

I would then know that you clicked the link from a Mac computer through Firefox. I would have details about your hardware and know all of the fonts installed to the operating system. I would know that you are connected to PIA VPN from a west coast server, but your system time is set to Mountain. I would also know you are logged in to a Google product. If you would like to see what details your computer would submit to this script, I have a test page available at the following URL.

https://inteltechniques.com/logger/

This page does not collect your details or store them on my server and nothing is logged. It simply generates the same queries through JavaScript through your own browser and displays them within your screen. Theoretically, any website could replicate these tactics and collect data about your visit. This is why investigators should always use caution and practice good operational security. I dive deep into this topic in my book *Extreme Privacy*.

IntelTechniques IP Addresses Tool

Similar to the domain tool mentioned previously, this page automates some of the most common IP address searches. The first box accepts any IP address. Clicking the Populate All button will insert this address into all the search options where manual queries can be conducted. The final option will open several tabs within your browser. The online version at **https://inteltechniques.com/tools/IP.html** is updated often.

CHAPTER THIRTY-FOUR
GOVERNMENT & BUSINESS RECORDS

Open source government and business information has never been easier to obtain. A combination of a more transparent government, cheaper digital storage costs, and marketing data leaks has placed more information online than ever before. There is no standard method of searching this data. One county may handle the queries much differently than another county, and business records vary by state. The following resources and techniques should get you started in the United States.

County General Records (www.blackbookonline.info/USA-Counties.aspx)

Counties all over America have digitized the majority of their public records and allow unlimited access over the internet. Searching for your county's website will likely present many information options. This can become overwhelming and it can be easy to get lost within the pages of the site. My initial preference when just beginning an investigation is to use Black Book Online's free county public records page. It allows you to drill down from state to county. The resulting page isolates all available records for viewing. As an example, I chose Illinois and then Madison County as my target. I was presented with the following databases, each linking directly to the source.

Coroner Reports	Recorded Documents	Unclaimed Property
Delinquent Tax Sale	Registered Lobbyists	Crime Map
Government Expenditures	Press Releases	Building Contractors
Property Tax Search	Voter Registration Verification	Building Permits
Public Employee Salaries	Voter Registration Addresses	Foreclosed Properties

County Court Records (www.blackbookonline.info/USA-County-Court-Records.aspx)

A Google search of your county of interest should identify whether an online court records database is available. As an example, St. Clair County in Illinois possesses a website that has their entire civil and criminal court records online (co.st-clair.il.us/departments/circuit-clerk/courts). Searching only a last name will present profiles with full name, date of birth, physical identifiers, case history, fines, pending appearances, and more. Navigating the website will expose charged crimes even if they were dismissed. This can be extremely useful in civil litigation. There are several websites that help connect you to publicly available county government records, such as Black Book Online. It allows you to drill down to your local records. The main page will prompt for the state desired. The result will be a list of links that access each county's court information. Some rural areas are not online, but an occasional search should be done to see if they have been added. Repeating my previous search of Madison County, Illinois revealed the following court related databases.

Circuit Court Complete Docket	Traffic Citations
Circuit Court Attorney Docket	Crash Reports
Family and Civil Pro Se Dockets	Police Blotter
Felony State's Attorney Jury Trials	Daily Crime Log
Traffic, Misdemeanor, DUI Docket	Jail Inmate Search

If the Black Book Online options do not provide optimal results, please consider **Public Records Online** (publicrecords.onlinesearches.com) or a new robust online service which appeared in 2021 called **Netronline** (publicrecords.netronline.com). This option seems to receive more updates of both content and design than Black Book Online. Ultimately, all of these simply connect you to the source of the records. Use the option which works best in your area.

PACER (pacer.gov)

PACER is an acronym for Public Access to Court Electronic Records. It is an electronic public access service of United States federal court documents. It allows users to obtain case and docket information from the United States district courts, United States courts of appeals, and United States bankruptcy courts. It holds more than 800 million documents. PACER charges $0.10 per page. The cost to access a single document is capped at $3.00, the equivalent of 30 pages. The cap does not apply to name searches, reports that are not case-specific, and transcripts of federal court proceedings. Account creation is free and if your usage does not exceed $15 in a quarter, the fees are waived. I have possessed an account for several years and have never been billed for my minimal usage. PACER has been criticized for being hard to use and for demanding fees for records which are in the public domain. In reaction, non-profit projects have begun to make such documents available online for free.

RECAP (courtlistener.com/recap)

RECAP (PACER backwards) allows users to automatically search for free copies during a search in PACER, and to help build up a free alternative database at the Internet Archive. It is an extension for the Firefox and Chrome browsers. Each PACER document is first checked if it has already been uploaded by another user to the Internet Archive. If no free version exists and the user purchases the document from PACER, it will automatically upload a copy to the Internet Archive's PACER database. While the browser extension assists greatly with searching, a search page exists on RECAP at the address above.

UniCourt (unicourt.com)

This court document search site appeared in 2018 and currently possesses an impressive database. The search options are straightforward, and results appear quickly, but you are limited to three searches without a paid membership. In my experience, clearing your browser's cache and selecting a new VPN IP address seems to reset this restriction. This is a premium site with full court documents hidden from guests, but we can obtain a fair amount of free information. Let's conduct an actual example.

Searching "Facebook" within the official site provides numerous results. However, after clicking through three case summaries, you will likely receive a notification to purchase a monthly premium membership. This may be acceptable if you plan to use the service heavily, but there are many additional free resources available. Consider conducting your queries through Google instead. Since the case summaries are publicly available, Google appears to have indexed most, if not all, of the pages. The following Google search produced over 10,000 results.

site:unicourt.com "facebook"

The first result connected to the following static URL.

https://unicourt.com/case/ca-la23-adam-blumenkranz-vs-facebook-123515

This page returned the following case details without a subscription or registration.

Case Summary	Case Type	State
Case Number	Jurisdiction	Defendant Names
Filing Date	Judge Name	Plaintiff Names
Update Date	Courthouse	Respondent Names
Case Status	County	Docket Entries

The documents area is restricted, but the docket entries are public. In this case, the details provide dates and actions taken within the litigation. Below is a partial example. UniCourt is now a staple within my investigations, but I rely on Google to find a direct link to the data.

03/14/2018   Case Management Statement; Filed by FACEBOOK, INC. (Defendant)
03/14/2018   Reply Filed by FACEBOOK, INC.; MARK ZUCKERBERG (Defendant)
02/21/2018   NOTICE OF CONTINUANCE; Filed by Attorney for Defendant
02/21/2018   Continuance of Hearing and Order; Filed by FACEBOOK, INC.

Judy Records (judyrecords.com)

This service is so good that they were sued for providing too much access. Although the site was shut down for a period of time, it has since reopened with most of its functionality intact. The search feature accepts traditional search operators. By placing my name in quotes, I immediately identified an Illinois Supreme Court case in which I was mentioned. The site is completely free with no business model.

Trellis (trellis.law)

While not as abundant as Judy Records, Trellis does offer value for those seeking court records. If you want to query via URL, you must add each state indexed by the service, as demonstrated below. A free account is required to see full court docket information.

https://trellis.law/cases/bazzell?state=az&state=ca&state=ct&state=de&state=fl&state=ga&state=il&state=ma&state=nv&state=nj&state=ny&state=oh&state=pa&state=ri&state=tx&state=wa

FOIA Search (foia.gov/search.html)

The Freedom Of Information Act (FOIA) allows us to demand government records from various entities. Filing a specific request exceeds the scope of this book, but you should know that a lot of public information is already available online. This site appears to rely on Bing to index government websites, so I assumed that this resource was unnecessary. However, my attempts to replicate some of the results within Google were unsuccessful. As an example, I searched for "Darrell Bazzell" on the FOIA site and received a specific result from a 2001 committee session. I replicated this search within Google and could not retrieve the same entry. Therefore, this service should be available within your arsenal of tools. A static submission URL is as follows.

https://search.foia.gov/search?affiliate=foia.gov&query=osint

MuckRock (muckrock.com)

This service buries government entities with FOIA requests and then publishes all responses. A direct URL search query structure follows.

https://www.muckrock.com/foi/list/?q=inteltechniques

Open Corporates (opencorporates.com)

Practically every state offers a searchable database of all businesses created or registered within the state. This will usually identify the owner(s), board members, and other associated subjects. **Dun & Bradstreet** (dnb.com) offers a business search within the home page, but many registered companies do not participate with them. In my experience, the best overall business lookup entity is Open Corporates. This free service indexes all 50 states in the U.S. plus dozens of additional countries. The records usually identify corporate officers' names, addresses, and other contact details. The basic search option allows queries by business name, entity registration number, or officer name. Clicking the advanced option allows query by physical address, but requires you to create a free account. This website is superior to targeted Google queries, because it indexes and scrapes data directly from government websites. This can assist with identifying historical results that no longer appear within the original source. I visit this resource every time I encounter a business name during my research, or identify a target that would likely be associated with an organization. Open Corporates allows search submission via URL as follows.

https://opencorporates.com/companies?q=inteltechniques
https://opencorporates.com/officers?q=bazzell

AIHIT (aihitdata.com)

This service is unique in that it uses artificial intelligence (AI) in order to populate and update business records. I do not know how much of this is legitimate process and not marketing hype, but I consistently find unique data here. The default search options query business names and registration numbers, and usually provide the same results as the previous options. However, the "More Fields" area allows entry of an email address, telephone number, or name of an individual. I have used this option to search personal email addresses and retrieve associated businesses. Fortunately, AIHIT allows search submission via URL as follows.

https://www.aihitdata.com/search/companies?k=email@gmail.com
https://www.aihitdata.com/search/companies?t=Michael Bazzell
https://www.aihitdata.com/search/companies?c=inteltechniques

OCCRP Aleph (aleph.occrp.org)

This self-described "global archive of research material for investigative reporting" includes numerous business records, transcripts, and other data sets. All can be filtered to display email addresses, phone numbers, names, and specific file types. Queries are free, but results might be limited if you are not signed in with a free account. The query URL structure follows.

https://aleph.occrp.org/search?q=michael%20bazzell
https://aleph.occrp.org/search?q=inteltechniques

Public Accountability (www.publicaccountability.org)

This service allows query of any name or term and provides government licenses, campaign contributions, federal grants, federal loan details, government employee data, and much more.

Open Payrolls (openpayrolls.com)

Open Payrolls might be the largest searchable nationwide government salary database consisting of nearly 85 million salary records from over 14,800 employers. It allows you to locate employee salaries for federal agencies, states, counties, cities, universities, colleges, and K-12 schools. A direct query URL follows.

https://openpayrolls.com/search/michael-bazzell

EINTaxID (eintaxid.com)

There is no official way to query a tax ID (EIN) for a company, but this service attempts to uncover those assigned to large companies. Sites such as **Little Sis** (littlesis.org) connects the dots between the world's most powerful people and organizations. Searching a name or company can reveal details associated with donations, political support, board members, and other relationships. The query URL follows.

https://littlesis.org/search?q=michael bazzell

SSN Verify (www.ssn-verify.com)

A simple way to verify if a social security number is valid is at SSN Verify. This does not provide the personal information attached to the number, only verification that the number is valid. A typical response will include the state that issued the number, the year issued, verification that the number was assigned, and a rough estimated age range of the person assigned the number.

Social Security Death Index (genealogybank.com/explore/ssdi/all)

This public index of death records is stored on a genealogy site. The only required information is the first and last name. The results will identify birth year, death year, state of last residence, and state of SSN issue.

Legacy (legacy.com/search)

There are many websites that search for death-related information such as social security indexes and ancestry records. A leader in this area is Legacy. This site indexes online obituaries and memorials from approximately 80 percent of all online newspapers. The results can identify family members and locations.

Asset Locator (www.blackbookonline.info/assetsearch.aspx)

Black Book Online's Asset Locator is the most comprehensive list of sources for the search of real estate, judgments, bankruptcies, tax liens, and unclaimed funds. This page will allow you to select the type of asset you are researching and the state of the target. This will then create a new page with all the options for that state. It will provide direct links to the sites for a search of the target. This often includes online databases of public employee salaries, vehicle registrations, property tax records, and dozens of other categories.

Voter Registration Records

The elections of 2016 and 2020 caused a lot of controversy in regard to the use and collection of voter registration data. While these personal details are public record, many people did not believe it was appropriate for politicians to use this personal data as a part of their campaign strategies. Regardless of your opinion on these matters, much of the voter registration details are available online. The most beneficial sites I have found are **Voter Records** (voterrecords.com) and **VoterRef** (voteref.com). You can search both by name or browse by state. Any results will identify full name, home address, mailing address, gender, party affiliation, age, and relatives. Currently, databases are available for Alaska, Arkansas, Colorado, Connecticut, Delaware, Florida, Michigan, Nevada, North Carolina, Ohio, Oklahoma, Rhode Island, Utah, Washington, and others. NCSL maintains a list of US states and availability of public data at https://www.ncsl.org/elections-and-campaigns/access-to-and-use-of-voter-registration-lists.

Vehicles

Many people assume that information related to vehicle registration and licensing is only available to law enforcement through internal networks. While a full driver's license search and complete license plate query is not publicly available, a surprising portion of related data is online for anyone to view. The following methods will display all publicly available details.

Department of Transportation (vpic.nhtsa.dot.gov)

The DOT has a website which provides free access to vehicle identification number (VIN) data. All information on this website is public information, and the data comes from vehicle manufacturers. You can search by VIN within their database to find detailed vehicle information. I submitted a unique VIN and received the following response.

Year: 2010
Make: VOLKSWAGEN
Model: JETTA
VIN: 3VWRL7AJ6AM13xxxx

Trim Level: TDI
Style: SEDAN 4-DR
Manufactured: Mexico
Weight: 4,500 lbs

The following options also allow you to enter any VIN and retrieve the year, make, and model of the vehicle associated. The first option will often display estimated mileage based on service records.

Vin Decoderz (vindecoderz.com)
Check That VIN (checkthatvin.com)
Search Quarry (searchquarry.com)

FaxVin (faxvin.com)
Vehicle History (vehiclehistory.com)
VinCheck (vincheck.info)

NICB VIN Check (nicb.org/vincheck)

While the previous searches will identify details about vehicles, they will not display any information about theft or salvage records. The National Insurance Crime Bureau (NICB) allows a search of any VIN and will display two unique pieces of information. The VINCheck Theft Record will identify vehicles that have been reported stolen, while the VINCheck Total Loss Records identifies VINs that belong to salvaged vehicles.

Cycle VIN (cyclevin.com)

VINs from motorcycles may not be searchable on standard VIN engines due to the number of characters in them. Cycle VIN will display a year and make, as well as any indication that the VIN exists in its proprietary database. If it does, $25 will obtain title and mileage information. I only use this as a free resource for verifying motorcycle VINs to the correct year and make.

Vehicle Registration

Several free services identify the year, make, and model of a vehicle after supplying the VIN. However, it is more likely that we know the license plate registration details rather than a VIN. Fortunately, we have many options for researching these plates. The following services provide a search option based on the vehicle registration plate and state. Results are hit-or-miss, and rarely include a name, but many will identify the VIN for further research.

Auto Check (autocheck.com)
Records Finder (recordsfinder.com/plate)
CarFax (carfax.com/vehicle-history-reports)
Search Quarry (searchquarry.com/vehicle_records)
Free Background Search (freebackgroundcheck.org)
Carvana (carvana.com/sellyourcar/getoffer/vehicle)
VinCheck (vincheck.info/free-license-plate-lookup/)
Vehicle History (vehiclehistory.com/license-plate-search)
Find By Plate (findbyplate.com)

While the previous license plate search websites offer a straight-forward query option, they are limited to the data available within publicly-traded vehicle databases. California plates often reveal accurate data, but states such as South Dakota and Montana are not as generous with the sharing of their own registrations. Because of this, we may want to query services which pay a fee in order to access premium data sets. My favorite of these is **Kelley Blue Book** (kbb.com/instant-cash-offer). The premise of this site is to identify the value of your own vehicle and potentially receive an offer to purchase it from KBB. That may have a benefit to you, but I prefer to harness the OSINT capabilities of this service.

As a test, I submitted a vehicle's registration number which was displayed on a television show playing in the background while I wrote this section. The result correctly identified the vehicle as a 2010 Dodge Avenger. This example was a California plate, so I felt like I was cheating a bit. Instead, I conducted a search of the license plate "MRBIG" within South Dakota and Wyoming, which are both known to protect vehicle registration data from public view. The results appear below.

2008 MAZDA MX-5 Miata

2019 Ram 2500 Crew Cab

While only a small piece of information, this works in conjunction with other search techniques. After exhausting all of these searches, you should be able to obtain the VIN, make, model, year, engine, and style of the vehicle. These options will not typically provide the name of the owner.

O'Reilly Auto Parts (oreillyauto.com)

If the previous search options fail to identify the VIN, year, make, and model of a vehicle based on the license plate, try O'Reilly. As a service to potential customers, it allows you to enter your license plate in order to identify applicable parts for your vehicle. Select the "Garage" in the upper-right and enter the license plate and state. I provided the state of California and the plate of "HACKER". I received the following response.

2007 GMC Sierra 1500 SLE, V8,6.0, 5967,364,Electronic, SFI,GAS, FI,MFI

When I searched the same plate on VinCheck, I received a VIN of 3GTEK13Y87G527460. I now have a decent beginning to my investigation of a license plate.

Progressive (progressive.com)

While not an official vehicle search, the insurance provider Progressive offers an interesting piece of information. I first learned about this technique from S.L., a member of my online OSINT forum. When you view the home page at progressive.com, you are prompted to request a free insurance quote. If you provide the zip code and address of any target, you receive a summary of the year, make, and model of all vehicles registered at that address. You can supply any random data besides the physical address and receive the results. This was likely designed to make the quote process more efficient and accurate, but investigators should appreciate the utility.

Marine Traffic and Boat Information

There is an abundance of details available about global marine traffic within ownership records and real-time monitoring. Marine Traffic (marinetraffic.com) provides an interactive map that displays the current location of all registered ships and boats. Clicking on any vessel provides the name, speed, collection time, and destination. Boat Info World (boatinfoworld.com) allows the search of a boat name and provides the following details.

Boat Name	Lloyd's Registry Number	Vessel Build Year
Boat Owner	Call Sign	Ship Builder
Record Date	Coast Guard Vessel ID	Hull Shape
Registered Address	Service Type	Propulsion Type
Hull ID	Boat's Length	
Hailing Port	Boat's Gross Tons	

Aircraft Information

Monitoring aircraft during flight and searching historical ownership records is relatively easy. Commercial planes constantly announce their location with automated reporting systems and tail numbers act similarly to a vehicle's registration plate. Today, this information is publicly available on multiple websites. Plane Finder (planefinder.net) displays an interactive global map identifying all known aircraft currently in flight. Hovering over a selection displays the carrier, flight number, originating departure, destination, speed, and altitude. Historical ownership records are available on multiple websites and none are completely accurate. I recommend Black Book Online's aviation page (www.blackbookonline.info/Aviation-Public-Records.aspx). At the time of this writing, it provided direct links to the following databases.

Aircraft N-Number Search	Certified Pilots
Aircraft Ownership Search	Cockpit Voice Recorder Database
Airline Certificates	Flight Tracker
Airport Profiles	Military Aviation Crash Reports

Campaign Contributions

Any contributions to political campaigns are public record. Searching this is now easy thanks to three separate websites. These sites will search using information as minimal as a last name. Including the full name and year will provide many details about the target. This includes occupation, the recipient of the contribution, the amount, the type of contribution, and a link to the official filing that contains the information. After an initial search is conducted, you will receive additional search tabs that will allow you to filter by zip code, occupation, and year. Melissa Data allows you to search a zip code and identify all political donations for a specified year. The results from these sites may be redundant, but often contain unique data. Once I know the state where my target lives, I will search for that state's own campaign contribution portal. For example, if my target were in Massachusetts, queries through https://m.ocpf.us/reports/searchitems may uncover results for my case.

Open Secrets (opensecrets.org)
Melissa Data (lookups.melissa.com/home/)

Selective Service Verification (sss.gov/verify)

This website requires a last name, social security number, and date of birth of the target. The result will identify the person's full name, selective service number, and date of registration.

High Programmer (highprogrammer.com/cgi-bin/uniqueid)

Most states use some type of algorithm to create a driver's license number for a person. Often, this number is generated from the person's name, sex, and date of birth. After you have determined your target's middle initial and date of birth from the previous websites mentioned, you can use this data to identify the target's driver's license number. High Programmer will automate this process for the following states.

Florida	Michigan	New York
Illinois	Minnesota	Washington
Maryland	New Hampshire	Wisconsin

BinDB (www.bindb.com/bin-database.html)

While not technically government data, I felt that this option fits best in this chapter. This website will allow you to enter the first six digits of any credit card number and identify the brand, issuing bank, card type, card level, country, bank website, and customer care line.

Real World Application: While working in the homicide division, I often identified credit or debit card numbers of my victims. If the actual card was located, I did not need this service. However, if only the number was located, this service helped to identify the financial institution and a contact number. In one specific investigation, I had learned that the victim had eaten at a local restaurant the evening prior to her suspicious death. Visiting the restaurant allowed me to acquire the debit card that she used for payment. Searching this number through BinDB identified the issuing bank. Calling presented an automated self-service feature for members of that bank. Entering the newly found debit card number and the zip code of the victim allowed me to access the previous 30 days of charges to her account. This identified an unknown ATM withdrawal on the day of her killing. Retrieving video from that ATM machine displayed a passenger in her vehicle. This initiated a new investigation which eventually led to the killer.

Criminal Information

If a target has a criminal past, there is probably evidence of this on the internet. County court searches will identify most of this information, but this requires a separate search on each county's website. There are a handful of services that attempt to locate nationwide information by name. **Family Watch Dog** (familywatchdog.us) is one of the leading sites in identifying public criminal information about sex offenders. The main page includes a "Find Offender" tab. You can search here by address or name. The name search only requires a last name to display results. This will identify registered sex offenders that match the criteria specified. This will include a photograph of the target and details of the offense.

Both federal and state prisons offer prisoner details online. The amount of detail will vary by state, but most will include photographs of the target and details of the crime. In most states, this information is maintained in public view after the target is released, if the subject is still on probation or parole. Federal prisoners can be located at www.bop.gov/inmateloc. A first and last name is required for a search. Each state maintains its own database of prisoner information. Conducting a search on Google of "Inmate locator" plus the state of interest should present official search options for that state.

VINELink (vinelink.com) is an online portal to VINE, a victim notification network. VINE has been providing victims and concerned citizens with information for decades, allowing individuals to access reliable information about custody status changes and criminal case information. After choosing the state of interest, you can select from the following options.

Find an Offender: Get info and register to be notified of custody status changes.
Find an Offender Court Case: Get info and register to be notified of offender court dates.
Find Sex Offender Registry Status: Get info about sex offender registry status changes.
Find a Protective Order: Get info and register to be notified of protective order status changes.

Warning: Every city, county, state, and country reports criminal matters uniquely. While you may find something of interest through traditional OSINT resources, absence of online criminal information does not indicate that a crime was not committed. More often than not, I cannot locate online information about a known crime or criminal. These resources should be considered secondary to a detailed inquiry through the courts or law enforcement.

Regional Government Databases

As previously mentioned, when investigating targets who are working or living in the US, I routinely check city, county, and state databases for pertinent records. Business and licensing information is often maintained by the office of the Secretary of State. Property tax records are typically maintained at the county level, by the assessor's office or similar. Counties also often operate jails and public assistance services, although the availability of public searchable databases will vary depending jurisdiction. Cities will have their own records pertaining to licensing, permitting, and municipal courts. Once I narrow down a location for my target, a simple search engine query for publicly available databases for that region often opens up public data sources which I may not have discovered otherwise.

IntelTechniques Business & Government Tool (https://inteltechniques.com/tools/Business.html)

While minimal, this tool should assist with replicating some of the searches mentioned within this chapter.

CHAPTER THIRTY-FIVE
VIRTUAL CURRENCIES

In simplest terms, virtual currencies can be spent for goods and services without connection to a person or bank account. It has no physical presence, and is mostly used online as digital payment. Bitcoin is virtual currency. A bitcoin address, which is an identifier you use to send bitcoins to another person, appears similar to a long string of random characters. In our demo, we will use 12t9YDPgwueZ9NyMgw519p7AA8isjr6SMw, which is the real address that was used to collect ransom from victims after malicious software had taken over their computers. Think of a Bitcoin address as an email address. That address stores their "virtual" money.

Blockchain (blockchain.info)

This website allows search of a Bitcoin address and displays the number of transactions, total amount of Bitcoin received ($), final balance, and a complete transaction history. We can track every incoming and outgoing payment. This will almost never be associated with any real names, but it provides a great level of detail about the account. We learn that this account has received 19.69355613 Bitcoin worth $1,333,710 USD at the time of this writing.

Bitcoin Who's Who (bitcoinwhoswho.com)

Our next stop is a service that provides a bit more analysis about the suspect account. We immediately learn that it is a suspect ransomware account, and that the address has appeared on various news outlet websites. Furthermore, we see transaction IP addresses, which are likely behind VPNs. Overall, I use Blockchain for transaction details and Bitcoin Who's Who to get a better idea of why I might care about the account.

BlockChair (blockchair.com)

This service is very similar to Blockchain, but I find it has better representation across multiple virtual currencies. Additionally, we can query each currency via URL, which will assist in our tools. Let's start with a search of a Bitcoin address at the following URL.

https://blockchair.com/bitcoin/address/1EzwoHtiXB4iFwedPr49iywjZn2nnekhoj

The results are typical, and include balance and transaction data. The power of BlockChair is the ability to search Bitcoin, Ethereum, Ripple, Bitcoin Cash, Litecoin, Bitcoin SV, Dash, Dogecoin and Groestlcoin. We will use the following URLs for each, replacing "xxx" with the target address.

https://blockchair.com/bitcoin/address/xxx
https://blockchair.com/ripple/account/xxx
https://blockchair.com/bitcoin-cash/address/xxx
https://blockchair.com/litecoin/address/xxx
https://blockchair.com/bitcoin-sv/address/xxx
https://blockchair.com/dash/address/xxx
https://blockchair.com/dogecoin/address/xxx
https://blockchair.com/groestlcoin/address/xxx

Chain Abuse (chainabuse.com)

This service focuses on one feature. It notifies you if others have reported a target virtual currency address as associated with malicious activity. This often provides valuable information about an investigation. Consider an actual report located at the following URL.

https://www.chainabuse.com/address/1KUKcwCv64cXQZa4csaA1cF3PPTio6Yt2t

The results include a summary of the activity and the email addresses sending malicious email.

| Sep 21, 2019 | sextortion | peter6389dd@excite.co.uk | "Hacked computer email" |
| Sep 21, 2019 | ransomware | addntfogjnfi@activeware.com | Claims to hack computer |

CloverPool (cloverpool.com)

CloverPool, formerly BTC.com provides a summary and full list of transactions for any BTC, ETH, BCH, LTC, or ETC address. We can conduct queries directly using the following URL structure.

https://explorer.cloverpool.com/btc/address/xxx

Wallet Explorer (walletexplorer.com)

The previous utilities examined an individual virtual currency account, such as a Bitcoin address. Many people possess numerous addresses and store them all within a virtual wallet. This is where Wallet Explorer can be extremely beneficial. While researching one of our target Bitcoin addresses within this free service, the results identified a wallet of "00037fd441" which contained the target address. Clicking on the link to this wallet revealed multiple new transactions from additional Bitcoin addresses previously unknown. This step is vital in order to track all transactions associated with your suspect. The following URLs search an address and a wallet.

https://www.walletexplorer.com/address/1EzwoHtiXB4iFwedPr49iywjZn2nnekhoj
https://www.walletexplorer.com/wallet/00037fd441938ba4

Bitbo (bitbo.io)

The calculator at https://tools.bitbo.io/satoshi-usd/ allows us to convert Satoshi's to USD or Bitcoins.

Breadcrumbs (https://breadcrumbs.app)

Whereas many of the platforms previously discussed are intended for consumers and business, Breadcrumbs is built for use on investigations. Although it is a premium service, they offer twenty searches a month once you register for a free account. Account creation is easy and they accept masked emails, such as SimpleLogin. One nice feature of Breadcrumbs is the inclusion of a customizable graph showing transactions and associated addresses. This can be very useful in illustrating the movement of funds and can be a nice addition to our case reports. Breadcrumbs also provides a monitoring feature which tracks activity on a virtual currency address over time and will generate a downloadable .csv spreadsheet.

Virtual Currency APIs

In order to create the custom search tool presented at the end of this chapter, I needed a very simple way to query virtual currency addresses for various tasks. Many of the websites which allow searching of Bitcoin addresses do not permit submission via URL. Instead, I will take advantage of various Application Programming Interfaces (APIs) which allow us to query directly and receive a text-only result. The following URLs are used within the tool, with an explanation of each. Each display of "xxx" is where the virtual currency address or amount would be inserted.

Validation: The following URL provides an indication whether a provided address is valid or invalid. This is a great first search to make sure you have a proper address. The response will be the Unix date the address was first seen within the network. An error notifies you of a bad address.

https://blockexplorer.com/api/addr/xxx

Value: The following URL presents the current value of one Bitcoin.

https://blockchain.info/q/24hrprice

Received: This URL displays the total amount of Bitcoin received by a specific address. It is important to note that this amount will be in "Satoshi". A Satoshi is equal to 0.00000001 Bitcoin. Put another way, one bitcoin contains 100 million Satoshis. This unit of measurement is popular because a single Bitcoin is currently worth approximately $70,000. The Satoshi is a more precise number We can use the previously mentioned calculator at bitbo.io to convert BTC to Satoshi units.

https://blockchain.info/q/getreceivedbyaddress/xxx

Sent: This URL displays the total amount of Bitcoin sent by a specific address. It is important to note that this amount is also presented in "Satoshi" (0.00000001 Bitcoin).

https://blockchain.info/q/getsentbyaddress/xxx

Balance: This utility displays the current balance of an address in "Satoshi".

https://blockchain.info/q/addressbalance/xxx

BTC > USD Value: The following URL will always display the current value of any amount of Bitcoin in USD. This price fluctuates hourly. Replace "xxx" with your value of Bitcoin.

https://api.coinconvert.net/convert/btc/usd?amount=xxx

USD > BTC Value: The following URL will always display the current Bitcoin value of any amount of USD. This price fluctuates hourly. Replace "xxx" with your value of USD.

https://blockchain.info/tobtc?currency=USD&value=xxx

Summary: This URL displays a brief summary of a Bitcoin address including total received, total sent, balance, total transactions, first transaction, and most recent transaction. Replace "xxx" with your target address.

https://chain.api.btc.com/v3/address/xxx

First seen: This Blockchain query displays the date which a virtual currency address transaction was first seen within the public blockchain. Note that this result will appear in Unix time format, but our tools will allow you to convert this to traditional time format. Replace "xxx" with your virtual currency address.

https://blockchain.info/q/addressfirstseen/xxx

Investigation Summary

Now that you understand the details available about a virtual currency address, let's run through a typical investigation. Assume you are investigating a Bitcoin address of 1EzwoHtiXB4iFwedPr49iywjZn2nnekhoj. It was used as part of an extortion email, and you have been tasked to find any information about the address. First you input the address into the search tool. The following information would be presented after each of the options.

BTC Validation: Valid (The address is a proper format)
1 BTC Price: $19,978.23 (The current value of one Bitcoin)
Satoshi Received: 716409285544 (The total amount of received currency)
Satoshi Sent: 716371585974 (The total amount of sent currency)
Satoshi Balance: 37699570 (The total amount of the current balance)
Satoshi > USD: (Used to convert Satoshi to USD as follows)
        Received: $136,925,336.62
        Sent: $136,914,950.52
        Balance: $7,205.23
Summary:
        "address": "1EzwoHtiXB4iFwedPr49iywjZn2nnekhoj",
        "received": 716409285544,
        "sent": 716371585974,
        "balance": 37699570,
        "tx_count": 3534,
        "unconfirmed_tx_count": 0, "unconfirmed_received": 0, "unconfirmed_sent": 0,
        "unspent_tx_count": 3,
        "first_tx": "6cc1542feb7abcff6364e0d31fc75097e0ecf7dae897ad6de6a2c1c5a1261316",
        "last_tx": "e11525fe2e057fb19ec741ddcb972ec994f70348646368d960446a92c4d76dad"

Creation Date: 1331482301 (Unix time when the address was first seen)
Date Conversion: Mar-11-2012 10:11:41 (Time in UTC)
Blockchain: A detailed list of all transactions.
Chainabuse: One report of malicious activity and a new email address to research.
BitcoinWhosWho: Links to online references to the address on Reddit.
WalletExplorer Address: Transaction details and wallet ID of 00037fd441.
WalletExplorer Wallet: Several pages of additional Bitcoin addresses within the suspect's wallet.

You could now repeat the process with the new Bitcoin addresses with hopes of identifying more email addresses. The email address search tool may identify further information about your target. While this is all very time consuming, the tools should simplify the queries.

Scam Search (scamsearch.io)

This free service was previously explained as a resource for searching email addresses, usernames, and telephone numbers to identify association with online scams. It can also be used to query virtual currency addresses. Searching "1FVuyuSN41aa3JN9sn8qkuD2PmaMEMHHnc" reveals email addresses, IP addresses, and locations associated with an online extortion suspect.

IntelTechniques Virtual Currency Tool

This online (https://inteltechniques.com/tools/Currencies.html) or offline tool simplifies the various techniques explained in this chapter. Each option, including API requests, open in a new browser tab.

SECTION III
LEAKS, BREACHES, LOGS, & RANSOMWARE

The tenth edition of this book had a single section devoted to data leaks, breaches, and logs. It was possibly the most controversial section, and contained the content which was most discussed and debated. This new edition, which contains nine chapters dedicated to these topics, attempts to expand on the original teachings.

Obligatory Warning: The techniques that you will read about in this section are for educational use only. Many, if not all, of the methods described here could violate organizational policy if executed. While I will only discuss publicly available data, possession could violate your security clearance or be determined illegal by state or federal law. Distribution (not necessarily possession) of the types of content that will be discussed here may be illegal in most cases. However, I will explain ways in which you can apply these practices in a legal way, and keep yourself employed. Overall, please do not take any action from this instruction unless you have verified with your organization's legal counsel or supervisory personnel that you have the authority to do so. Please do not let this warning persuade you to abandon the guide. I promise there is something here for everyone.

In previous books, I discussed the services Have I Been Pwned (HIBP) and others as online resources for compromised email search. These services possess huge databases of publicly available content which were originally stolen from the host companies and distributed over the internet. When you search an email address on these services and are informed that it was compromised within the LinkedIn data breach, this means that a partial copy of this stolen data resides within these breach lookup services. HIBP and others are often applauded as a great resource to monitor your own accounts for any reported compromises. Well, what if we created our own unredacted collection of this data? Is there additional value? I believe so.

This is where things get tricky. While you can find copies of thousands of stolen databases all over the internet, what are the legalities of downloading and possessing the data? First, let me say that I am not an attorney and I offer no legal advice. I have spoken with many attorneys and prosecutors about this, and the feedback was similar from each. If the data is publicly available, possession alone would likely be legal. This is similar to viewing an email stolen from Hillary Clinton posted on WikiLeaks or an internal document stolen from Google posted on a blog. If you do not violate the laws and policies applicable in your city, county, state, or country when you encounter this publicly available, yet stolen, data, then you could likely get away with viewing stolen credentials existing in the various database leaks online.

What matters most is that you never take any illegal action with the data which you possess. In a moment, I will explain how to access valid email addresses and passwords of billions of accounts. Using this data as an investigation technique is one extreme, but attempting to use this data to access someone's account is another. There is no situation where casually gaining access to a target's account is acceptable, unless you have a valid search warrant or court order to do so. Since some of you are in law enforcement, this chapter may identify new strategies for you when you have the legal authority to access an account. We will start with some very basic legal "leaked" data in just a moment.

Some will argue that this type of book is reckless and teaches criminals how to do bad things. I disagree. The criminals are way ahead of us. They have been using and sharing these techniques for many years. We can either ignore this type of data and hope for the best, or we can face it head on and be better investigators. I choose the latter. I once again encourage you to generate your own opinions as you read along. You may disagree with me at times, which is ideal. That means you are really thinking about how all of this applies to you. Please continue to read with an open mind and willingness to try new things.

CHAPTER THIRTY-SIX
INVESTIGATIVE BENEFITS

Before proceeding, we should discuss some definitions for the types of data which will be discussed and beneficial uses for each. We can then tackle the hardware and software requirements. First, let's define the scope. There are many lengthy definitions and explanations of this type of data, but let's keep things simple. For the purposes of this guide, the following apply.

Leaks: This type of data is accidentally released, or "leaked", through public online resources. It could be public voter data which was legally acquired and then shared online; a marketing database of public information which was archived through a third-party site; a misconfigured database which is publicly leaking all details if you know where to look; or a plethora of other possibilities. The common theme is that no one intentionally compromised a secure server and stole anything. Of the types of data, this is the most likely to be legally accessed.

Breaches: This type of data takes us into the criminal world. Breaches occur when a criminal compromises a source of data illegally and copies the content. Examples include the Twitter and LinkedIn breaches where people's email addresses and passwords were stolen and published online. There are now tens of thousands of data breaches floating around, which have introduced billions of plain-text passwords for the majority of people online. While accessing or downloading this publicly-available data might not get you into legal trouble, further publishing it might. Also, your organization's policies might prevent you from this access. Possession and research of this data is extremely common, even by us law-abiding internet citizens. More warnings are to come.

Logs: This data, sometimes referred to as "Stealer Logs" or "Password Logs" is illegally obtained from infected machines. This occurs when a criminal tricks a victim into installing a virus which extracts data and sends it to an accessible third-party server. This often includes stored passwords, session cookies, documents, photos, and other sensitive information. This may sound like a rarity, but hundreds of thousands of victim's logs are uploaded every day. This type of data can expose the passwords of people who are not within any known data breaches, and the content is much more likely to be accurate.

Ransomware: This type of data is also illegally acquired. Criminals install a virus within a company's network; infect many machines; make a copy of all data; encrypt all files on the network; and hold the decrypted copies hostage. They then offer to decrypt all data for a ransom, and threaten to publish the stolen content if payment is not received. Every day, new private company data is published online for anyone to see. This often includes passwords, sensitive documents, and copies of passports.

Offense: There are many reasons for interest in leaks, breaches, logs, and ransomware. I always split them into the sides of "offense" and "defense". Let's discuss a few of both, beginning with offense.

Identify Home Addresses: Some people do a very good job of keeping their names and home addresses off of the internet. You may strike out with people search websites. However, they often slip-up when ordering products to their home or registering to vote. Breach and leak data will often disclose true home addresses when no other online resource was successful.

Identify Alias Account Holders: In a later chapter, I will explain how I uncover the true owners of many "burner" email addresses due to common recycling of passwords. When my suspect uses a junk email account, and it appears within a data breach, I may see his password is "badguy432!@". When I discover an additional email address which had a password of "badguy432%$", I call that a lead. A surprising number of suspects will use the same password across their real account and those used for criminal purposes. Once their information appears within multiple data breaches, we can put together the pieces. I will provide many examples later.

Associate Social Network Accounts to People: Every day, my company uses breach data to connect a social network account to a real person. When a service has a data breach, the otherwise hidden email addresses and cellular telephone numbers are often disclosed along with the username for the product. This can immediately uncover the account holder's true identity. When used in conjunction with the previous two examples, we often solve entire cases from breach data alone.

Identify Telephone Number Owners: Very few of us own a landline these days which is listed in a phone book. Many of us use VOIP numbers and prepaid cellular plans in order to protect ourselves. Criminals also do this. When I want to identify the owner of a telephone number harassing a client, I assume the standard OSINT techniques will fail. However, I typically identify some valuable information about these number from within breach data.

Machine Identifiers: When my target shows up within stealer logs, I am often presented a unique hardware identifier and screen capture of their desktop. This is priceless information which would never show up within a website. Over the past year, stealer logs have been the most beneficial type of data to acquire for us.

Identify Additional Email Addresses: Once you know a target's unique username, searching that detail within breach data often reveals additional email addresses very similar to the username. This can allow us to pivot to new target data which could quickly open up an investigation.

Business Details: If you are investigating a company which has suffered a data breach, possessing the stolen data can reveal much more than any website or business listing page. Knowing the number of customers, types of encryptions, and other details can provide more value than public data.

Defense: The following are only a few defense considerations.

Identify Stolen Assets: If you are employed by a company which has suffered a data breach, you may want to track down the stolen data. This helps understand the magnitude of the breach better than any claims or demands from the criminal. I believe every victim of a data breach should investigate the incident and obtain the data being shared publicly. This is one of our most requested services by clients.

Aid Disclosure Notifications: When a company is hit with a cyber-attack, there are many laws and regulations which require notification to those impacted by the stolen data. Knowing the exact data being shared within criminal groups can help identify the proper disclosure requirements for impacted victims.

Defend Future Attacks: I rely on our daily update of leaks, breaches, logs, and ransomware in order to protect my clients. Every week, we are able to notify a potential victim of newly exposed information which could be devastating to them if abused. In many cases, we can intercept this data before the criminals begin to use it. We can then help the client block access before bad things happen.

These are only a few benefits to this type of data. I query our leaks, breaches, logs, and ransomware data every day. My staff uses it to quickly identify new leads and to protect our clients. I cannot overstate the value of this data, and the value of possessing your own offline copy.

Many online services which provide breach data queries are very limited. Most start as a free service but then move to a paid model. Your organization may have policies preventing the purchase of stolen data. Most of these services require an online account in order to conduct any queries. Your organization might prohibit this type of access, and you risk the service collecting and analyzing your target queries. Finally, many of these services eventually shut down. What would happen if your favorite breach data search engine disappeared tomorrow? By the end of this guide, I hope that you have no concern for this.

We have a lot to discuss, and I am excited to work through the process together.

CHAPTER THIRTY-SEVEN
HARDWARE CONFIGURATION

Let's have a conversation about hardware. If you begin acquiring this type of data, it can become overwhelming very quickly. Every day, our systems ingest anywhere from 50 GB to 5 TB of data. Storing and processing this amount of data can be both time consuming and resource intensive. Even if you stick to public leaks, the data can quickly fill your drives. Because of this, there are many hardware considerations. Don't worry, I offer affordable solutions.

First, your selection of computer is vital. The following may sound contradictory to previous teachings, but I no longer recommend a virtual machine for large data collections. Downloading huge files within a VM will be slightly slower than on a host machine. Decompressing large files within a VM will be much slower, and VM disk space will be quickly depleted. You could connect an external drive to the VM for storage, but the data transfer speed will be a huge bottleneck to the overall efficiency of data queries. Unless you are simply dabbling in this area, I would stay away from VMs while trying to conduct any extensive breach work.

Much like my opinions about investigative actions within *OSINT Techniques, 10th Edition*, I also never recommend using your primary personal host computer for this type of work. I would never download breach data onto the same machine which I use for personal communications, banking, or other private tasks. This is because the type of data we will be discussing is full of bad players, malicious files, viruses, and other shady concerns. I would never jeopardize the host operating systems of my personal machines to the risks associated with stolen data. What do I do? I possess a machine solely for breaches, leaks, logs, and ransomware. It possesses minimal applications and blazing fast hardware. When I am not actively downloading data, it is offline. However, that may be extreme for you.

In the previous book, I stressed the importance of a dedicated OSINT computer which possessed virtual machine software for investigations. In some scenarios, I have no objection to also using this OSINT machine's host operating system for breach data collection, but there are caveats which I will explain in a moment.

In a perfect world, you have a macOS or Linux machine dedicated to breach data collection and analysis, a macOS or Linux machine dedicated to OSINT research, and another macOS or Linux machine for personal use. However, I realize that is asking a lot and I understand that we do not live in a perfect world. If your dedicated OSINT machine has Linux or macOS as the host operating system, I believe it is acceptable to use it for the techniques explained throughout this guide. I also respect that many readers will prefer Microsoft Windows due to familiarity and availability. Let's dive deeper into all of these considerations.

Apple macOS: In previous chapters, I praised macOS as a great operating system for OSINT machines. I stand by this. The blazing fast virtual machines and Android emulation cannot be beat by Linux or Windows. The hardened operating system is considered by many, including me, to be more secure than Linux or Windows (but not as private as Linux). This OS also works well for data collection, with modification.

The disk speed should be your highest priority. Once you possess hundreds of gigabytes of data, queries will take some time. As you work with larger datasets to make them more efficient to query, the disk speed will determine if a command executes within seconds, minutes, hours, or days. I never recommend a "spinning disk" hard drive, such as a standard 2.5" or 3.5" SATA drive. At a bare minimum, I recommend a newer Solid-State Drive (SSD) for the operating system. This will be used to download data and to work with active files.

I believe any MacBook Pro with a newer M series processor (M1, M2, M3) is optimal for the tasks presented here. The internal storage drives for these systems are all comparable to newer NVMe drive speeds (7,000 MB/s), and more than sufficient for our needs. Internal drives for macOS systems prior to the M series processors are fast, but typically cap at 2,500 MB/s. Much older machines which possess spinning disks or early

SSDs will not be suitable. I present more on disk speed in a moment. I recommend at least 16 GB of RAM, with 32 GB preferred. Overall, I believe a newer M Series MacBook Pro is the optimal machine for breach data collection. It will be fast and fluid, and many people are already familiar with navigating the system. However, any Linux computer comes in at a very close second place, as explained next.

Linux: If you have a Linux-capable machine available to dedicate to data collection, you will also be safe from most threats. The processor speed is not the biggest concern, but it should be considered. If you can, upgrade to a computer which is capable of housing an NVMe drive directly onto the motherboard. This small device which resembles a stick of RAM can have read and write speeds of up to 7,000 MB/s. Let's compare them.

Average USB 3.0 Flash Drive:	125 MB/s
Traditional Spinning Disk Hard Drive:	135 MB/s
Solid State Drive (SSD):	600 MB/s
PCIe Gen 3.0 NVMe Drive:	3500 MB/s
PCIe Gen 4.0 NVMe Drive:	7000 MB/s

In other words, a modern NVMe drive will provide 60 to 70 times faster data access. When you start dealing with large data sets, you will want to squeeze every drop of data bandwidth possible. Computer RAM is also important, and quite inexpensive. The more RAM you have, the more data which can be manipulated at a faster rate. At a minimum, I believe you should possess 16 GB of RAM, but I prefer 32 GB.

I do not have any brand loyalty for Linux machines for this purpose. I care more about the hardware specifications. Any processor on a motherboard which supports PCIe Gen 4.0 NVMe Drives will probably be sufficient for the tasks. Machines without this will also perform well, you will only see a speed decrease when processing large amounts of data. For many years, I conducted this type of work without a 7,000 MB/s drive. When I began, I was using slow spinning drives. If you can, start with existing repurposed hardware and identify your own needs.

For most Linux breach data machines, I recommend the latest Long-Term Support (LTS) version of Pop!_OS or Ubuntu (I prefer Pop!_OS). They will have most of the utilities we need by default, and adding the others will be easy. They can also be installed on practically any hardware with default configuration. If you prefer another flavor of Linux, it should also work the same.

Microsoft Windows: I would never consider a Windows host computer for data collection. However, I will provide tutorials to make them work. The problems are two-fold. First, data manipulation and queries are typically slower within Windows than Linux or macOS, and configuring your system to replicate the commands within other operating systems will take some effort. However, we can get past that. My big complaint is risk. Most of the shady data which we will acquire has been stolen from Windows machines.

Often, we encounter virus files which were involved in the theft. We do not want to infect our own Windows machines while attempting to build our data collections. We encounter stealer log criminals who infect their own Windows systems and upload stored credentials every day. I do not want you to join their ranks. If you are very careful, you can make Windows work for you throughout this guide, but you have been warned. I highly recommend dedicating a Linux or macOS system for this purpose.

I know that the data I download is toxic, but I don't care. If I encounter a virus included within some stealer log data, I know it is likely targeted toward the Windows operating system and would have no impact on my macOS or Linux machines. If I encountered a rare macOS or Linux threat, I know that there is no personal information on this machine which could expose me. If the machine becomes infected, it is no big deal to wipe it out and reinstall the OS.

External Drives

I suspect many readers are not ready to commit to new hardware with multiple large internal NVMe drives for these tasks. Therefore, I want to offer some considerations which cost less. If you are just beginning your journey into data collection, consider a proper external drive for storage of your content. You can use your fast internal drive for downloading and processing of your data, and then move your final product to an external drive. This USB drive will be slower than anything internal, but we will only use it when we need to query the data. Once we build our databases which index all data, the query speed will be very similar to that of an internal drive. I would never consider a mechanical or flash drive for this process. Instead, I would rely on fast portable SSD. For most readers, I recommend a 4 TB external USB-C SSD.

I have had great success with the SanDisk Extreme Portable SSD (amzn.to/3yPcMJ2) and the SanDisk Extreme PRO Portable SSD (amzn.to/3MKbvZl). The "Pro" version boasts twice the speed of the regular version (2,000 MB/s vs. 1,000 MB/s), but this can be misleading. Many computers do not support "USB 3.2 Gen 2x2", and your computer may only take advantage of half the advertised speed anyway. Do your research first. Even the standard version should provide 1,000 MB/s of read access, which is eight-times faster than most mechanical drives. You may encounter many reports of SanDisk SSD failures. This was a valid concern for a large batch of devices, but was then corrected with a firmware update. Some reports claim there is still a problem with these drives. Always check for firmware updates when you buy any device. I have never had any issues with mine, but I have also had success with the SAMSUNG T7 Shield 4TB SSD ($240 - amzn.to/3SBo7qM). Again, do your research.

Also consider disk space. While the $90 1 TB drive might be enticing, how quickly will you fill it up? I believe the SanDisk 2 TB Extreme Portable SSD (amzn.to/3yPcMJ2) is a great starter drive. It can be purchased for $125 and should be compatible with any modern computer. The 4 TB model (amzn.to/3sADepQ) typically costs $250, but gives you double the storage space. I will be using the SanDisk 4 TB Extreme Portable SSD (amzn.to/3sADepQ) for all of my demonstrations, but any SSD should work. Always check the USB connections. If your computer only possesses a USB-A port, then you want to make sure you buy a drive which includes this connection. I always prefer a USB-C port on the computer and direct USB-C to USB-C cable to make that connection to the external drive. Do your homework before you commit.

Once you have an SSD full of exciting data, you will want to make a backup. Any drive could fail, and we do not want to start over. I possess a 4 TB traditional spinning disk as my backup drive. These can be found online and in retail stores for less than $100. I will be using a Toshiba Canvio Basics 4 TB Portable External Hard Drive (amzn.to/3sBAJUk) for my demonstrations. Since it is only used for backup data, and I will never query directly from it, speed is no concern. Once you have your external drives available, they should be reformatted and encrypted. In later chapters, I explain how to use an external USB SSD for fast breach queries and a cheaper drive for backups. It is vital to encrypt the data within these drives. What if they are lost, stolen, or seized? We should protect this type of sensitive data. I always recommend encrypting drives before they store any data.

External Apple macOS Drives

Encrypting external drives within macOS is not always easy. Sometimes, macOS hides the settings we need to protect an external device. As an example, I inserted a USB SSD which was formatted as "FAT32", which is common for universal drive access. I wanted to erase the drive and encrypt it. However, the Disk Utility application (Applications > Utilities) only displayed the following options. Right-clicking the drive in Finder also did not present an option to encrypt the drive.

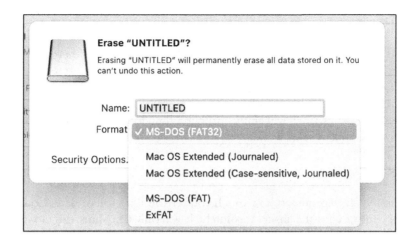

The first step to take within the Disk Utility application is to select "Show All Devices" under the "View" menu. Next, select the device (not the formatted volume) within the left menu and click the "Erase" button. This may still only present volume formats which cannot be encrypted. Be sure to change the "Scheme" to "GUID Partition Map". You should now see an option of "APFS (Encrypted)" under "Format". This option will encrypt the entire external drive with macOS encryption. I believe this is the best option for users who will only need to access this drive from a macOS system. If you want to follow along with my tutorials and use my script, make sure to name the drive "DATA" and any backup drive "BACKUP".

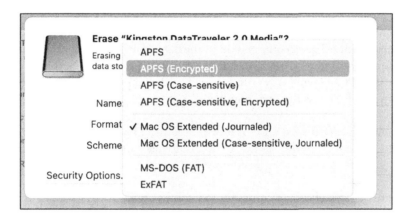

External Linux Drives

Linux systems are more user-friendly for encrypting external drives. The following applies to Pop!_OS and Ubuntu, but the steps should be similar for most Linux systems.

- In Ubuntu, launch "Files" and right-click your external drive.
- Select "Format" and provide a name of "DATA" for your SSD.
- Choose "Internal disk for use with Linux systems only (Ext4)".
- Select the "Password protect volume" option.
- Click "Next" and supply a secure password when prompted.
- Confirm the password when prompted.
- Click "next" until you reach the "Format" option and click it.
- Repeat the process for your backup drive, but name it "BACKUP".

When you encrypt the drives, the process may take some time to complete. You will need to unlock it with the password every time it is inserted into your machine.

External Windows Drives

This is where things get tricky. If you have a professional version of Windows, then you should be able to right-click the drives within Explorer and "Turn On BitLocker". This is always the preferred option. If BitLocker is not available on your system, you could encrypt the entire disks with VeraCrypt, but this can present more problems. I have seen many drives with full-disk encryption via VeraCrypt within Windows refuse to unlock, and then have severe speed issues whenever things properly functioned. This is yet another reason I prefer to stay away from Windows for this type of work.

Hardware Summary

Is this all overkill? Possibly. It depends on how much you rely on this type of data. Could you get by with just using more traditional hardware for this task? Absolutely. It will only take more time to download, decompress, process, clean, store, and query the data every day.

If you begin to rely on this data often, you might find yourself looking at faster machines with embedded ultra-fast storage in order to make the process more tolerable. A MacBook Pro with 4 TB of internal 7,000 MB/s storage is a luxury, but you will pay for it. A Linux machine with a 4 TB internal NVMe drive will be more affordable, and just as fast. However, I want to be realistic. The current most affordable MacBook Pro with 4 TB of internal storage is $3700. A 4 TB External SSD is less than $250. The latter is more approachable.

There is no harm using older equipment in order to understand the strategies presented within this section. The limit to your resources will become apparent as soon as you start dealing with large data sets.
As an example, I downloaded 250 GB of compressed stealer logs to an older Intel-based MacBook Pro laptop with a 2,100 MB/s internal SSD. The decompression of the data took over an hour. Parsing the passwords from the text files took another four hours. I replicated the exact same process on both a new MacBook Pro and a new Linux machine with a PCIe Gen 4.0 NVMe Drive. The decompression on each took a few minutes, and the extraction of passwords took less than ten minutes.

I deal with enough data to justify the expense of a dedicated machine for this purpose. When we start talking about stealer logs, the vast number of files alone can be a bottleneck on most machines. It is common to extract over two million very small files within a single compressed archive.

I will now assume that you have chosen a computer, operating system, external drive for storage, and external drive for backups. We can now begin configuring our software.

CHAPTER THIRTY-EIGHT
SOFTWARE CONFIGURATION

Once you have your desired computer, you should configure the software required for the lessons within this guide. If you are using a Linux machine for these tasks, you already have most of the utilities needed for our commands. Programs such as cut, sed, and awk are included within most Linux systems. However, others are not. This chapter will separate all required configurations by operating system. I will tackle all necessary modifications to macOS, Linux, and Windows in their own sections. Once you have completed this chapter, all remaining tutorials should work the same on each operating system. However, your desktop may appear different than mine.

Apple macOS

The first application I install on any new macOS operating system is a package manager called Homebrew, often shortened to Brew. This application is very beneficial when there is a need to install utilities which would usually already be present on a Linux computer. It also simplifies installation of applications which would otherwise require manual download or access to Apple's App Store. Brew is my favorite software for macOS computers. The easiest way to install Brew is to visit the website brew.sh then copy and paste the following command into the Terminal application (Applications > Utilities > Terminal). After completion, you are ready to use Brew to install and update applications.

```
/bin/bash -c "$(curl -fsSL https://raw.githubusercontent.
com/Homebrew/install/HEAD/install.sh)"
```

You will likely receive a notice from macOS that you need to install "Developer Tools". Click "Install" and "Agree", then allow the process to complete. After Brew installation is complete, you will likely be presented with one or two commands which need to be manually executed within Terminal. My installation presented the following notice.

```
==> Next steps:
- Run these two commands in your terminal to add Homebrew to your PATH:
    (echo; echo 'eval "$(/opt/homebrew/bin/brew shellenv)"') >> /Users/ventura/.zprofile
    eval "$(/opt/homebrew/bin/brew shellenv)"
```

This is unique to my installation, as my chosen username was "ventura" at the time. Copy any commands presented here and paste them within the same Terminal window, executing each by striking return. Let's test everything with a few commands.

- `brew doctor` - This command confirms that Brew is configured properly and that all paths are set. You should receive a notice that "Your system is ready to brew".
- `brew update` - This command checks for any pending updates to Brew itself. You should receive a response of "Already up to date".
- `brew upgrade` - This command updates any installed programs. You should receive no response since we have not installed anything.
- `brew analytics off` - This command disables Brew's embedded analytics which monitor the number of times an application is installed using Brew. These metrics are only used to understand how users interact with the product, but I prefer to limit my exposure.

If everything is working, you are now ready to use Brew as a software installation repository. Treat this as a replacement for the App Store, but it does not require an Apple ID. If you are using a macOS host which already possesses Brew, your results will appear slightly different than mine. However, there is no conflict with these tutorials and those within the book. Let's use Brew to install our first application.

```
brew install wget
```

This command ensures the Wget is installed, which we will use to download data from the internet within terminal. Next, we should install Ripgrep. This is a faster version of Grep, which queries any file or folder for specific text. We will use this to conduct general queries within specified large data sets when we need quicker results than a standard text search.

```
brew install ripgrep
```

While Ripgrep is much faster than a standard Grep query, it has limitations. We will install Qgrep to take our queries to the next level. Qgrep allows us to create compressed databases of our data and receive search results in a fraction of the time Ripgrep takes to go through all of the data. First, navigate to the following URL within your browser.

https://github.com/zeux/qgrep/releases/tag/v1.3

Download the most recent "macos" zip file to your default "Downloads" folder. Then, execute the following within Terminal.

```
mkdir ~/Documents/Qgrep
cd Downloads
unzip qgrep* -d ~/Documents/Qgrep
chmod +x ~/Documents/Qgrep/qgrep
```

The first command creates a new directory titled "Qgrep" within the Documents folder of the current user. The second command navigates to the Downloads folder. The third command unzips the file which you downloaded, and places the data into the new folder you created in your Documents. The final command makes the Qgrep file (program) executable.

Apple systems already possess sed, awk, cut, and many other commands which we will use throughout this guide. However, we should not use these default applications. The macOS versions of these programs are slower, less robust, and possess fewer features than the traditional Linux versions. Therefore, we need to download better options and make them the default for our usage. Let's start with "Sed". This program will be essential for replacing, removing, and modifying text within large data files. The following command installs the application.

```
brew install gnu-sed
```

You can now use Sed, but you must use the command "gsed" if you want to use the "GNU" version which is identical to the default Linux options. Executing "sed" within Terminal will still rely on the macOS version, which is undesired. The following command will tell us how to change this.

```
brew info gnu-sed
```

You should receive something similar to the following.

```
GNU "sed" has been installed as "gsed".
If you need to use it as "sed", you can add a "gnubin" directory to your
PATH from your bashrc like:
```

```
PATH="/opt/homebrew/opt/gnu-sed/libexec/gnubin:$PATH"
```

Copy and paste the "PATH" line into Terminal and press Return. You should now have "sed" as the new version, but let's test with the following command.

```
sed --version
```

The result should include something similar to "sed (GNU sed) 4.9". If you see an error, you are still using the macOS version. However, we have a new problem. If you were to completely close Terminal and open a new instance, Apple's version of Sed will become the default again. This is quite an annoyance, but easily repaired. Instead of simply executing the previous "PATH" command, we must create a hidden file in your home directory called .zshrc (assuming you are using the latest version of macOS). We can do this with the following command.

```
touch ~/.zshrc
```

Next, we must open this file inside of a text editor to modify it with the following command.

```
open -a TextEdit ~/.zshrc
```

Finally, paste the previous PATH command into this file and save it, but do not close it. We should now be able to close and open Terminal and see that the new version of Sed is the default. Let's replicate this process and install a better version of Awk, which is a scripting language used for manipulating data. We will use it to sort our large stealer logs later. First, take a look at the default version with the following command.

```
awk --version
```

The result should appear similar to the following.

```
awk version 20230909
```

This confirms we are using the default macOS version of Awk. The following command installs the GNU version of Awk.

```
brew install gawk
```

We can now execute this new version of Awk with "gawk" inside of Terminal. However, "awk" will still rely on the macOS version. The following command will tell us how to change this.

```
brew info gawk
```

You should receive something similar to the following.

```
GNU "awk" has been installed as "gawk".
If you need to use it as "awk", you can add a "gnubin" directory to your
PATH from your ~/.bashrc and/or ~/.zshrc like:

PATH="/opt/homebrew/opt/gawk/libexec/gnubin:$PATH"
```

Paste this PATH command on a new line into the .zshrc file which we previously created and save the file. Close and reopen Terminal and you should now have "awk" as the new version, but let's test with the following command.

```
awk --version
```

The result should include something similar to "GNU Awk 5.3.0". If you see anything similar to "awk version 20230909", you are still using the macOS version. Let's do this again with the Cut command, which will be vital for extracting columns of data later.

The following command installs the GNU version of Cut, along with many other valuable programs.

```
brew install coreutils
```

We can now execute this new version of Cut with "gcut" inside of Terminal. However, "cut" will still rely on the macOS version. The additional programs within this repository will also require you to append "g" before each execution. The following command will tell us how to change all of these utilities to the default GNU version.

```
brew info coreutils
```

You should receive something similar to the following.

```
Commands also provided by macOS and the commands dir, dircolors, vdir
have been installed with the prefix "g".
If you need to use these commands with their normal names, you can add a
"gnubin" directory to your PATH with:

PATH="/opt/homebrew/opt/coreutils/libexec/gnubin:$PATH"
```

Paste this PATH command on a new line into the .zshrc file which we previously created and save the file. Close and reopen Terminal and you should now have "coreutils" as the new version, but let's test with the following command.

```
cut --version
```

The result should include something similar to "cut (GNU coreutils) 9.4". If you see an error, you are still using the macOS version. This should also make the GNU version of Sort and other utilities the default. Perform one last test with the following command.

```
sort --version
```

The result should include something similar to "sort (GNU coreutils) 9.4".

At this point, my .zshrc file appeared as follows. If you are using a macOS host which was used to create an OSINT build following the previous book, you may see extra lines in the file, which are fine.

```
PATH="/opt/homebrew/opt/gnu-sed/libexec/gnubin:$PATH"
PATH="/opt/homebrew/opt/gawk/libexec/gnubin:$PATH"
PATH="/opt/homebrew/opt/coreutils/libexec/gnubin:$PATH"
```

When we start applying our techniques to automated scripts, we will need a program called Zenity to present a selection menu. It can be installed in macOS with the following command (Zenity is already present within Pop!_OS and Ubuntu).

```
brew install zenity
```

FreeFileSync

Later in this guide, I will explain the importance of data backups. For now, install our synchronization program, FreeFileSync, with the following steps.

- Navigate to https://freefilesync.org/download.php.
- Download the macOS version.
- Double-click the downloaded file to extract the installer.
- Double click the "FreeFileSync" package.
- Complete the installation with the default options.

Telegram

This is the only program which I have reservations about. While it will be vital for our acquisition of data, it also presents mild risk. Telegram is the wild west. Anything goes. There is no content moderation or policing of any kind. You can find anything there, even things which should not be found. I do not believe the Telegram application itself is harmful, but there is no lack of viruses available to download within it. This is why I prefer to conduct data collection on an isolated machine away from my personal documents and financial logins. Telegram can be installed with the following Homebrew command.

```
brew install --cask telegram
```

Transmission

Many large data sets will only be available as a torrent file through the BitTorrent file distribution system. Transmission is our best software for this purpose. It can be installed within macOS with the following command.

```
brew install --cask transmission
```

jq

The application jq is a lightweight and flexible command-line JSON processor. We will later use it to parse long JSON entries into a single line of data. It can be installed within macOS with the following command.

```
brew install jq
```

Tor Browser

Your stock web browser can only access public websites. This web browser can do the same, but can also access sites on the Tor network. When we get into ransomware conversations and data collection, this will be required. It can be installed with the following command.

```
brew install --cask tor-browser
```

Python

Your macOS system should now have Python ready within Homebrew, but we can make sure with the following commands

```
brew install python
brew unlink python && brew link python
python3 -m pip install pip
```

BBEdit

I highly recommend the free version of BBEdit (barebones.com/products/bbedit) for all macOS users. It opens incredibly large files and allows you to easily view and modify the content. I know of no other text viewer which will open a 5 GB file in seconds and allow immediate find and replace functionality.

Linux

Linux users are all set on most of the software requirements, but there are a few programs which we will need to install. We should first make sure our system is updated and then confirm that we have two essential programs installed with the following commands within Terminal. I highly recommend that you add a shortcut to Terminal within your Linux Dock. For Pop!_OS and Ubuntu, you can do this by clicking the nine dots in the Dock; navigating to Terminal; right-clicking the Terminal icon; and selecting "Add to Favorites".

```
sudo apt update
sudo apt upgrade -y
sudo apt install -y wget
sudo apt install -y curl
sudo apt install -y python3-pip
```

The first two commands update our Linux software. The third command ensures the Wget is installed, which we will use to download data from the internet within terminal. The final command installs Curl, which will also help us retrieve data within Terminal.

Next, we should install Ripgrep. This is a faster version of Grep, which queries any file or folder for specific text. We will use this to conduct general queries within specified large data sets when we need quicker results than a standard text search.

```
sudo apt install -y ripgrep
```

While Ripgrep is much faster than a standard Grep query, it has limitations. We will install Qgrep to take our queries to the next level. Qgrep allows us to create compressed databases of our data and receive search results in a fraction of the time Ripgrep takes to go through all of the data. First, navigate to the following URL within your browser.

https://github.com/zeux/qgrep/releases/tag/v1.3

Download the most recent "ubuntu" zip file to your default "Downloads" folder. Then, execute the following within Terminal.

```
mkdir ~/Documents/Qgrep
cd Downloads
unzip qgrep* -d ~/Documents/Qgrep
chmod +x ~/Documents/Qgrep/qgrep
```

The first command creates a new directory titled "Qgrep" within the Documents folder of the current user. The second command navigates to the Downloads folder. The third command unzips the file which you downloaded, and places the data into the new folder you created in your Documents. The final command makes the Qgrep file (program) executable.

FreeFileSync

Later in this guide, I will explain the importance of data backups. For now, install our synchronization program, FreeFileSync, with the following steps.

- Navigate to https://freefilesync.org/download.php.
- Download the Linux version.
- Right-click the downloaded file within Files and select "Extract Here".
- Double-click the new FreeFileSync folder.
- Right-click the FreeFileSync file and choose "Run".
- Complete the installation with the default options.

Note that FreeFileSync does not play well with ARM-based processors, but a typical Linux Intel or AMD laptop should not have any issues. Some software app stores have FreeFileSync ready to install, which is much easier.

Telegram

This is the only program which I have reservations about. While it will be vital for our acquisition of data, it also presents mild risk. Telegram is the wild west. Anything goes. There is no content moderation or policing of any kind. You can find anything there, even things which should not be found. I do not believe the Telegram application itself is harmful, but there is no lack of viruses available to download within it. This is why I prefer to conduct data collection on an isolated machine away from my personal documents and financial logins. If you are using Ubuntu, you can install Telegram with the following command.

```
sudo snap install telegram-desktop
```

If you are using a Linux system without Snap, then the following applies.

- Navigate to https://desktop.telegram.org.
- Expand the "Show All Platforms" option.
- Click "Get Telegram for Linux" to download the file.
- Right-click the downloaded file within Files and select "Extract Here".
- Double-click the "tsetup" and "Telegram" subfolder.
- Right-click the Telegram file and choose "Run".

Transmission

Many large data sets will only be available as a torrent file through the BitTorrent file distribution system. Transmission is our best software for this purpose. It can be installed within Pop!_OS and Ubuntu with the following command.

```
sudo apt install transmission
```

jq

The application jq is a lightweight and flexible command-line JSON processor. We will later use it to parse long JSON entries into a single line of data. It can be installed within Linux with the following command.

```
sudo apt install -y jq
```

Tor Browser

Your stock web browser can only access public websites. This web browser can do the same, but can also access sites on the Tor network. When we get into ransomware conversations and data collection, this will be required. The Linux installation of Tor Browser changes often. Always follow the latest instructions on their official website at https://tb-manual.torproject.org/installation/.

Microsoft Windows

I want to stress again that conducting breach data work within Windows is risky. It is also more complicated. While the following steps will configure your system to replicate most of the techniques within the remaining chapters, expect occasional hurdles. The experience with Windows will never be as fluid as Linux or macOS. During the Mac setup, we used Homebrew as a package manager. For Windows, we will use Chocolatey. It can be installed with the following steps.

- Click the Windows menu button (lower-left) and type "powershell".
- Right-click on Windows PowerShell and select "Run as Administrator".
- Enter the following command and press Enter (Confirm if required).

```
Set-ExecutionPolicy AllSigned
```

- Execute the following single command within PowerShell.

```
Set-ExecutionPolicy Bypass -Scope Process -Force;
[System.Net.ServicePointManager]::SecurityProtocol =
[System.Net.ServicePointManager]::SecurityProtocol -bor 3072; iex
((New-Object
System.Net.WebClient).DownloadString('https://community.chocolatey.org/
install.ps1'))
```

If everything is working, you are now ready to use Chocolatey as a software installation repository. You do not need to open PowerShell any more. We will use Command Prompt to install our desired applications.

- Click the Windows menu button (lower-left) and type "cmd".
- Right-click on Command Prompt and select "Run as Administrator".
- Enter the following commands and press Enter after each.

```
choco install -y wget
```

This command ensures the Wget is installed, which we will use to download data from the internet within terminal. Next, we should install Ripgrep. This is a faster version of Grep, which queries any file or folder for specific text. We will use this to conduct general queries within specified large data sets when we need quicker results than a standard text search.

```
choco install -y ripgrep
```

While Ripgrep is much faster than a standard Grep query, it has limitations. We will install Qgrep to take our queries to the next level. Qgrep allows us to create compressed databases of our data and receive search results in a fraction of the time Ripgrep takes to go through all of the data. First, navigate to the following URL within your browser.

https://github.com/zeux/qgrep/releases/tag/v1.3

Download the most recent "windows-x64" zip file to your default "Downloads" folder. Then, execute the following within Command Prompt.

```
mkdir C:\users\%username%\Documents\Qgrep
cd C:\users\%username%\Downloads
choco install -y unzip
unzip qgrep* -d C:\users\%username%\Documents\Qgrep
```

The first command creates a new directory titled "Qgrep" within the Documents folder of the current user. The second command navigates to the Downloads folder. The third command installs the unzip program. The fourth command unzips the file which you downloaded, and places the data into the new folder you created in your Documents.

Windows systems do not possess sed, awk, cut, and many other commands which we will use throughout this guide. The following commands install the applications which will replicate the actions within the previous Linux and macOS tutorials.

```
choco install -y sed
choco install -y awk
choco install -y curl
choco install unxutils
```

FreeFileSync

Later in this guide, I will explain the importance of data backups. For now, install our synchronization program, FreeFileSync, with the following command. You may be required to manually confirm the installation and then exit any popup window.

```
choco install -y freefilesync
```

Telegram

This is the only program which I have reservations about. While it will be vital for our acquisition of data, it also presents mild risk. Telegram is the wild west. Anything goes. There is no content moderation or policing of any kind. You can find anything there, even things which should not be found. I do not believe the Telegram application itself is harmful, but there is no lack of viruses available to download within it. This is why I prefer to conduct data collection on an isolated machine away from my personal documents and financial logins. Telegram can be installed with the following Chocolatey command.

```
choco install -y telegram
```

Transmission

Many large data sets will only be available as a torrent file through the BitTorrent file distribution system. Transmission is our best software for this purpose. It can be installed within Windows with the following command.

```
choco install transmission
```

jq

The application jq is a lightweight and flexible command-line JSON processor. We will later use it to parse long JSON entries into a single line of data. It can be installed within Windows with the following command.

```
chocolatey install jq
```

Tor Browser

Your stock web browser can only access public websites. This web browser can do the same, but can also access sites on the Tor network. When we get into ransomware conversations and data collection, this will be required. The Windows installation executable can be found at https://tb-manual.torproject.org/installation/.

Virtual Private Network (VPN)

This is a vital layer of protection when working with leaks, breaches, and logs. We should start with an extended understanding of the Virtual Private Network, which I will only present as VPN for the rest of this guide. Let's work through the "what" before we tackle the "why" and "how".

First, let's take a visual look at a traditional home network configuration without any protection. Your home internet connection begins at the modem, which could be a fiber, cable, satellite, or DSL connection. It is the first device within the home which accepts data from your provider and makes it available to your devices. From there, most people possess a Wi-Fi router which wirelessly broadcasts the availability of internet access to any other device in the home. Any device connected to your internet service is using the same public Internet Protocol (IP) address. When your laptop, tablet, or any other internet-capable device connects to any website or service, it shares the same public IP address assigned to your home internet connection. In many cases you are the only person in the world using this IP address at any given time.

I estimate that 99% of households possess a similar scenario to this example. Some may argue that there is no threat in sharing your true IP address with every site you visit and service you use. I disagree. While a true IP address does not disclose the home address of the user directly, it does present numerous threats, as outlined next.

- **Internet Activity:** Assume that I am suing you through civil court, and I have convinced a judge to grant me a court order to collect your internet activity. Since I know where you live, I can assume the provider of your internet service. A court order could be issued to your ISP for your internet activity. If your ISP logs your traffic, which most do, the response would tell me every domain which you visited and the dates and times of occurrence. I could use this to prove you were visiting specific websites or transmitting large amounts of data to designated services. I have witnessed child custody disputes enter online history as evidence, which was then presented without any context to discredit a parent's abilities to care for a child.

- **Search Queries:** When you connect to Google and conduct a search for "inteltechniques", the response URL presented to you, including the search results from the query, is https://www.google.com/search?q=inteltechniques. Does your Internet Service Provider (ISP) know you conducted a search on Google? Yes. Do they know you searched for "inteltechniques"? No. This is because Google encrypts the actual search URL. The provider of your internet connectivity can only see the domain name being accessed. It cannot see any details about specific pages or any credentials entered. This is why https versions of websites are so important. Your browser can see this entire URL, but it does not directly share any details with your provider. However, if a site does not include proper SSL protocols, then any search query on that site could be captured by your ISP.

- **Location:** Next, assume I want to know where you live. I know your email provider is Gmail, and a subpoena to them would reveal your IP address at a specific date and time. If this IP address belongs to your internet service provider, a second subpoena will disclose the address of service (your home). This could be applied to any website you have ever visited.

- **Fingerprinting**: Every website you visit collects and stores your IP address. If you are the only person in the world with that address, they know when you return to the site and any activity conducted. They know every click you make, and attribute that to you. This is one way so many websites seem to know what you are searching, buying, and discussing before you provide the full details within your devices.

- **Download History:** Shady law firms monitor questionable files such as pirated movies, music, and other media. Once an IP address is seen downloading content without authorization, they issue subpoenas to identify the home with the offending connection. They then issue threats of lawsuits unless an extortion is paid. Does your nephew use your home Wi-Fi without supervision at any time? You could be liable for any of his activity.

- **Breach Data**: Every day, services are breached and the databases they possess are published online. Almost all of these include data containing the home IP address of the user. If you have followed my other guides to possess a private home which is not publicly associated with your name, this could unravel all of your hard work. I can search your name within breach data and see your true home IP address. I can then use the previous methods to discover your home address. If you have multiple accounts in alias names, I can tie them all together thanks to your unique public IP address.

If you believe any of this could be a threat to you, then you need a properly configured VPN. VPNs provide a good mix of both security and privacy by routing your internet traffic through a secure tunnel. The secure tunnel goes to the VPN's server and encrypts all the data between your device and that server. This ensures that anyone monitoring your traffic before it reaches the distant server will not find usable, unencrypted data. Privacy is also afforded through the use of a distant server. Because your traffic appears to be originating from the VPN's server, websites will have a more difficult time tracking you, aggregating data on you, and pinpointing your location. Let's now revisit the previous threats with the assumption a VPN was used.

- **Internet Activity:** Your ISP cannot see your internet activity when a VPN is used. They only see that a connection was made to the VPN, and then all traffic is encrypted. They have no log of your online activity. Reputable VPN companies have a "No Logging" policy which prevents them from storing the IP address assigned to you at any given time. They would be unable to identify your traffic from everyone else.

- **Search Queries:** After connecting to your VPN, you conduct the same search as before. Does your ISP know you conducted a search on Google? No. Does your VPN provider know you conducted a search on Google? Yes. Does your VPN provider know you searched for "inteltechniques"? No. If you encounter a website without proper SSL, your queries will be visible to the VPN provider, but not attributed directly to you.

- **Location**: VPNs offer numerous server locations which you can select and change at any time. You can make your website traffic appear to be occurring from London, New York, Los Angeles, Australia, or any location in between. No online service will ever know your true location.

- **Fingerprinting**: The IP address provided by the VPN will be shared with hundreds or thousands of other users at any given time. However, websites will then rely on other ways to try to track you. We will tackle this later.

- **Download History:** When a law firm subpoenas your VPN IP address to begin their extortion campaign, they will discover the owner of the address is a VPN company which cannot provide the information they need. They will move on to the next victim.

- **Breach Data**: When you appear in the next data breach, the IP address associated with your account will be a VPN provider, and that address will be useless to anyone wanting to use this information in a malicious manner.

VPNs are not a perfect anonymity solution. It is important to note that VPNs offer you privacy, not anonymity. The best VPNs for privacy purposes are paid subscriptions with reputable providers. There are several excellent paid VPN providers out there and I strongly recommend them over free providers. Free providers often monetize through very questionable means, such as data aggregation. Paid VPN providers monetize directly by selling you a service, and reputable providers do not collect or monetize your data. Paid providers also offer a number of options which will increase your overall privacy and security.

I think I have worked through the "what" and "why", it is now time to tackle the "how". This is where you must select a VPN provider. If you already possess a VPN service which you like, then you should proceed with that option. Please do not change providers solely because of my preference. However, please be informed of my considerations when choosing a VPN provider and ensure that your selection passes all of the tests.

Recommending a VPN provider today is similar to claiming a preference for the best version of Linux. No matter what I say, I will offend someone. Please note that any reputable VPN provider is better than none at all. However, I do believe there are some much better than others. Okay, enough beating around the bush. I currently use and recommend Proton VPN as my exclusive VPN provider, and almost all of my clients possess a Proton VPN account. Please allow me to explain my opinions, and my reasons for not recommending your favorite service. Overall, I mostly care about the following categories when choosing a VPN provider.

- **No Logging:** As stated previously, most reputable VPNs offer a "No Logging" policy which prevents them from saving logs about customer usage. However, some VPN companies claim this logging policy without following it. To be fair, the idea of absolute zero logs is a myth. There must be some sort of logging of connections for the service to function. I care mostly about whether the service stores these logs and has access to them when demanded. Services such as PureVPN have been caught giving away logs of user activity when demanded by court order, and breaches have disclosed that other services such as Fast VPN store user data indefinitely. There is no way to truly know the logging of your VPN data, so we should all monitor any news about this data being released. Proton VPN (and many others) have never had a known exposure of user logs. Proton VPN's logging policy can be found online at https://protonvpn.com/support/no-logs-vpn.
- **Audits:** This is where we can have some comfort. Since we are not able to monitor VPN servers directly, we must rely on third-party audits of services. Any reputable VPN provider will not only hire companies to audit their service, but will also publicly share those audits with the world. In April of 2022, Proton VPN announced that they hired Securitum to conduct a full audit of their logging practices. Proton shares the audits for all of their products (Mail, VPN, Calendar, and Drive) on their official website located at https://proton.me/blog/security-audit-all-proton-apps. I never trust any company to abide by their rules. I place more trust in the third parties allowed to access the code.
- **Open Source:** When VPN companies provide their application's source code publicly, it allows anyone to examine the code for any malicious intent. I do not have the abilities to do this myself, but I appreciate that many other people much smarter than I am are scrutinizing the code of these services. However, we never truly know if the open-source code is the same as what is being used in the live environment. This is why those audits by third parties are so important. Publicly disclosing the code of a VPN application is a nice layer, but I do not care about that as much as the other categories presented here.
- **Jurisdiction:** This will vary for every reader. You might want to consider the legal jurisdiction of your provider. Many privacy purists are very picky about the location of a VPN company's headquarters. Do you live in the United States and worry that your government will execute federal court orders to obtain your activities? Then you may not want to choose a U.S. service (or any service within cooperating jurisdictions). Proton VPN is hosted in Switzerland, and they only respond to Swiss court orders. They cannot disclose any user activity, but they could disclose payment details or account identifiers if forced. However, I believe that we place too much emphasis on jurisdiction. If you are using a U.S. server, there could always be infiltration regardless of the jurisdiction. Any country could decide to cooperate with your country at any time. I would rather rely on a Swiss company than a Russian or Chinese provider which may not be following any rules. As a U.S. citizen, I do prefer my provider to be outside of U.S. court order authorization, especially for civil cases. However, I am not naive. If my government placed all of their power into investigating me, I am sure that Swiss (or any other) courts would not protect me. My chief threat is not the government. It is data breaches, ISPs, and online services. If you are truly worried your government is monitoring you at all times, a VPN will not save you.

- **Ownership:** Who owns your chosen VPN service? Is it a small independent company with a handful of employees or a large conglomerate which owns 20 VPN brands? The first option may seem better since only a small group of people can access your data, but some may find the second option better to disappear within the thousands of other users. I prefer something in between. I prefer the VPN company to be independently-owned and not a brand under a larger VPN umbrella company. However, I also want a large user base to exist so that my traffic can disappear within all of the other activity. Proton VPN works for me.

- **Advertising:** If you search for "VPN reviews" online, you will immediately find numerous "unbiased" review sites. However, if you look closely, you will see something peculiar. The same handful of VPN providers seem to make the list every time. Also, these providers are never the services commonly used within the privacy communities. This is because these are mostly paid placements. In some cases, large VPN companies own the entire website and simply recommend their own products. I ignore all VPN review sites. I also ignore any providers which participate in this activity. This is another reason I prefer Proton VPN. They do not create fake review sites to push their product.

- **Connection Options:** Most VPN providers offer several servers within numerous countries. This is not unique to Proton VPN, but I am happy with their selection.

- **Firewall Capabilities:** Most reputable VPN providers allow their product to be used within a home firewall. If you are unsure, look for tutorials from your chosen provider by searching the VPN name along with "pfSense" or "OpenVPN". Within my testing, Proton VPN works very well with firewall software.

I should now explain my reasons for choosing Proton VPN over other respected providers. The first to discuss is Mullvad. Proton VPN and Mullvad are commonly the most recommended VPN providers within various privacy communities. I believe the privacy policies of Mullvad are great, and I have no concern over their presence in Sweden. My issue is with the reliability of the service. I tested Mullvad in late 2021 and late 2022. In 2021, I experienced slow speeds and dropped connections while using their official application. In 2022, this seemed to have been fixed, but I could not maintain a reliable connection within my firewall via OpenVPN. Many others have complained of the same failures online. A VPN is no good if it fails. If you use Mullvad and have no issues, I see no reason for you to change. Since I have experienced bad results with their service and support, I choose Proton VPN. I also do not like that anyone can brute force Mullvad user numbers to access an account without password.

I should address an important disclosure. Most VPN companies offer an affiliate program which rewards people for introducing their product to new users. I have had an affiliate partnership with both Proton VPN and PIA for several years. If you use my referral at **https://go.getproton.me/aff_c?offer_id=26&aff_id=1519**, Proton knows that you were referred by me, and I receive a small one-time financial reward. I receive absolutely no details about you or your order.

Some will say that this affiliate payment is the only reason I recommend their product. My response to that is three-fold. First, I would not risk my reputation recommending a product which I do not use and trust. Second, PIA was paying me more for a referral than Proton VPN, and I have stopped recommending PIA for many users. Finally, another VPN company offered me the highest reward ($60) for every referral, but I would never use their product. Therefore, I declined the offer.

I would recommend Proton VPN without the affiliate partnership, but I want to be transparent about our relationship. I also allow these affiliate payments to directly support our efforts to keep this guide updated. If you sign up for Proton VPN and want to support my show, please use the previous referral link. If you cringe at the idea of using any referral link, then you can find the absolute same pricing by simply purchasing from protonvpn.com, and I receive nothing. I was not paid anything by Proton VPN for inclusion in this guide. I maintain a page which always displays my VPN preferences at **https://inteltechniques.com/vpn.html**. It also contains any affiliate links.

When purchasing a VPN service, you will need to make payment online. This is tricky because we want a VPN to hide our traffic, but then we have to tell the company something about us when we make the payment. This leaves a digital trail which could be tracked back to us. Therefore, you need to consider your own threat model when paying for a VPN service.

I prefer to pay via Bitcoin from my offline software wallet stored on my computer. There is no Bitcoin exchange involved and I can provide any name desired for the VPN. Proton maintains a website for instructions to pay for service via Bitcoin on their site at https://protonvpn.com/support/vpn-bitcoin-payments.

If you have the ability to pay via Bitcoin from a local wallet, I believe you should. However, that does not make you magically invisible. You will still be connecting from your home internet connection, so the VPN provider will always see that unique identifier. You will also be paying bills in your name, sending email from your account, and conducting other sensitive activity while connected to this VPN. My point is that VPNs do not make us bullet-proof. This is why we choose providers with proper privacy policies, but we never expect to be completely untraceable.

Because of this, I do not have a strong objection to purchasing your VPN service with a standard credit card. Since Proton VPN has a respected no IP logging policy, they can never translate a public-facing VPN IP address back to your home address. They can also never translate your true home IP address to a VPN address once used. In other words, Proton VPN could never provide the internet activity associated with a name, or the user of specific access to a website.

Some will scoff at these remarks. Some will say that you should only pay for a VPN with cash in the mail (some services do offer this). However, I believe it is overkill. The digital trail will still be present. If you are a fugitive looking for a way to check your email without getting caught, a VPN is not for you. If you are looking to prevent abusive technologies from monitoring your online activity, a VPN can be quite helpful.

Once you have purchased a VPN service, you need a way to connect to it for daily use. For most readers, and almost every client I have consulted, I recommend possessing the standard application provided by the VPN company on any device where it might be needed. These branded apps should suffice for most needs. Proton VPN can be downloaded from https://protonvpn.com/ for both mobile and desktop devices. Once installed, simply provide your account credentials and you can launch your VPN connection.

While I am at home, I rely on a network-wide firewall with VPN, as explained within my digital guide *Extreme Privacy: VPNs & Firewalls*. When I am on this home network, I do not need any VPN application running on my devices. I only need to launch them when I am away from home and need VPN protection (or prefer a different IP address than that which is in use at my home).

I strongly advise that you always protect your internet usage through a VPN while conducting any of the tasks described throughout this guide.

It is now time to practice our Terminal commands and work with some data. Please do not skip the following chapter! The included tutorials explain usage of several important commands which will be abbreviated in later chapters about leaks, breaches, logs, and ransomware. At the minimum, please familiarize yourself with the overall techniques.

CHAPTER THIRTY-NINE
TERMINAL COMMANDS

In the previous print edition of this book, I offered several Terminal commands which helped clean specific data sets. Those commands are still here within this new digital edition, but I want to offer more explanation and tutorials. Mastering Terminal commands will make your journey into data collection much easier. Therefore, this chapter has two goals. First, I want to dive into each command which we will use throughout this section to offer better understanding of the actions instead of the results. Second, I want to offer numerous practice examples which allow you to test what you have learned before moving on.

Everything in this chapter should be conducted within Terminal. For Linux and macOS users, that means opening the Terminal application and inputting text directly into the window. For Windows users, that means opening Command Prompt and replicating each command. Note that Windows file paths require a backslash (\) instead of the traditional forward slash (/). As long as you are working within the target directory, this should not be much of an issue. Please note my previous warnings about data work within Windows.

Let's start with something basic. The cd command allows us to change the working directory within Terminal while the ls command displays the contents of the current directory. We have already relied on this heavily in the first section of this book, but let's revisit to make sure we are all capable of the task. Open Terminal within macOS or Linux and execute the following commands, striking Enter/Return after each.

```
ls
cd /
ls
```

The first command should have displayed the files within your home directory, which may have identified folders such as Desktop, Documents, Downloads, and other default directories. The second command changed the directory to the root of your operating system, and the third command should have revealed a different set of folders. Next, let's replicate this within Command Prompt in Windows.

```
dir
cd \
dir
```

The first command should have displayed the files within your home directory, which may have identified folders such as Desktop, Documents, Downloads, and other default directories. The second command changed the directory to the root of your operating system, and the third command should have revealed a different set of folders. Notice the backslash for Windows instead of the forward slash.

Since we will mostly be working within the home directory, Linux and macOS users can use the tilde (~) in the upper left area of your keyboard to navigate to the default home directory, regardless of the computer username. An example follows.

```
cd ~/
```

If you wanted to navigate directly to the Downloads folder within your home folder, you would conduct the following.

```
cd ~/Downloads
```

Navigating to your Documents or Desktop would be as follows.

```
cd ~/Documents
cd ~/Desktop
```

Windows users have another hurdle here. It does not accept a tilde, and insists on "%username" to change into the default user's home directory. The same commands as before would appear as follows.

```
cd C:\users\%username%\
cd C:\users\%username%\Downloads\
cd C:\users\%username%\Documents\
cd C:\users\%username%\Desktop\
```

We can now use the mkdir (make directory) command to create a new folder titled "Datatest" within our Documents folder with the following macOS/Linux command.

```
mkdir ~/Documents/Datatest
```

We can switch to this folder with the following.

```
cd ~/Documents/Datatest
```

We can use the rm (remove) command to delete this folder. Execute the following.

```
rm ~/Documents/Datatest
```

You should have received an error about Datatest being a directory. This is because rm by itself can only delete a file. The following command will delete the folder and all contents. Be careful with this.

```
rm -r ~/Documents/Datatest
```

If you wanted to move a folder instead of delete it, the following will make a directory called Datatest within your Documents folder and move it to your Downloads folder.

```
mkdir ~/Documents/Datatest
mv ~/Documents/Datatest ~/Downloads/Datatest
```

Windows users have more hurdles. The same commands as before would appear as follows. Note that the final two lines are one single command.

```
mkdir C:\users\%username%\Documents\Datatest
cd C:\users\%username%\Documents\Datatest
rm -r C:\users\%username%\Documents\Datatest
mkdir C:\users\%username%\Documents\Datatest
mv C:\users\%username%\Documents\Datatest
C:\users\%username%\Downloads\Datatest
```

I will assume that you can now navigate through directories within Windows systems. While all of the following commands will function within any operating system, any path changes will only be presented for macOS and Linux machines. Use these lessons to replicate on Windows when needed.

The Cat command (short for concatenate) reads data from a file and provides its data as output. It can be used to view the contents of an existing file or combine several files into one. We will mostly focus on the latter, but let's try both. Within Terminal (or Command Prompt), navigate to your Downloads folder to conduct the following.

```
cd ~/Downloads
curl -O https://inteltechniques.com/data/osintdata/cat-1.txt
curl -O https://inteltechniques.com/data/osintdata/cat-2.txt
cat cat-1.txt
```

The first command switched our working directory to the Downloads folder. The next two commands downloaded two files which I have on my website. The final command displays the content of the first file, which should appear as follows.

```
1
1
1
```

Your first simple assignment (Assignment #1) is to display the content within the second file downloaded. All commands for these practice exercises are within the final page of this chapter. Your results should appear as follows.

```
2
2
2
```

We now want to combine these two files into one file called cat-final.txt with the following command.

```
cat cat-1.txt cat-2.txt > cat-final.txt
```
Your result should appear as follows.

```
1
1
1
2
2
2
```

You could add as many files as desired before the ">" which would be combined into the designated file. We will use ">" often, which is basically telling Terminal to output the data into a specific file. Let's remove the three files with the following commands.

```
rm cat-1.txt cat-2.txt cat-final.txt
```

It is now time to test your abilities. I have four files at the following locations:

https://inteltechniques.com/data/osintdata/cat-1.txt
https://inteltechniques.com/data/osintdata/cat-2.txt
https://inteltechniques.com/data/osintdata/cat-3.txt
https://inteltechniques.com/data/osintdata/cat-4.txt

Attempt to download these four files within your Downloads directory, combine them all into a new file called cat-test.txt, delete the four files downloaded, and display the content within the newly-created file. Again, the commands for this are at the end of the chapter, this is specifically Assignment #2.

Did you see 1's, 2's, 3's, and 4's within the file? If so, you passed. The Cat command may seem simple and unnecessary, but I promise it will pay off. When we start downloading hundreds of small log files which need combined into one, this utility will be vital.

The next command will probably be the most used in your arsenal. Sed, short for stream editor, is used to perform basic text transformations on an input file. It allows us to replace specific text throughout an entire file with different text or nothing at all. It is similar to "find and replace" within a text editor, but it is much faster without file size restrictions. When we need to modify a 100 GB file, we will use Sed since that file could not be opened through a traditional text editor. Some examples should help explain.

Assume you have a large file titled customers.csv with thousands of lines similar to the following.

username:test1,email:test@gmail.com,password:pass123,ip_address:10.2.2.3,phone:5551212,id:32
username:test2,email:test2@gmail.com,password:pass456,ip_address:10.2.2.4,phone:5551213,id:33
This might actually be acceptable for most data collection enthusiasts, but I am bothered by the wasted data. The presence of "username", "email", "password", etc. on every line is unnecessary. If this file only contained 200 entries, it would be no big deal. If the file contained 500,000,000 lines and had a size of 200 GB, we would really be wasting drive space. Our queries would also take much longer due to the searching of unneeded data. Let's fix this with the following command.

```
sed "s/username//gI" customers.csv > customers-cleaned.csv
```

We should now dissect this command.

sed	The command executable.
"s/	The command to substitute.
username/	The text we want to find.
/	The text we want to replace (nothing in this example).
g	The command to replace every occurrence in the document.
I"	The command to ignore case (UPPERCASE = lowercase).
customers.csv	The input file.
>	The command to output to another file.
customers-cleaned.csv	The output file name.

The result of this command would be the following.

:test1,email:test@gmail.com,password:pass123,ip_address:10.2.2.3,phone:5551212,id:32
:test2,email:test2@gmail.com,password:pass456,ip_address:10.2.2.4,phone:5551213,id:32

This removed "username" but left the colon (:) in the line. We could have modified our query better with the following.

```
sed "s/username\://gI" customers.csv > customers-cleaned.csv
```

The results would now appear as follows:

test1,email:test@gmail.com,password:pass123,ip_address:10.2.2.3,phone:5551212,id:32
test2,email:test2@gmail.com,password:pass456,ip_address:10.2.2.4,phone:5551213,id:33

Notice the presence of the backslash (\) before the colon. This is because a colon is not a standard letter or number. We must always "escape" any special characters with a backslash. I rarely conduct a Sed operation with both an input and output file. I prefer to edit the files "in-place" with the "-i" switch. Note that the "I" option at the end only works for the GNU version of Sed, which we previously installed. The following command would replicate our modification to the customers.csv file without the need to create a new file, and would ignore all case (UPPERCASE or lowercase).

```
sed -i "s/username\://gI" customers.csv
```

Linux and macOS users should have no problem with this command. Windows users have yet another hurdle. The "-i" is not allowed within Windows, as that version of Sed does not include the in-place option. Windows users will need to modify their commands to match the previous example which creates a new file with the omitted details. Did I mention that I prefer macOS and Linux machines? The following command would remove the information and create a new file within Windows.

```
sed "s/username\://gI" customers.csv > customers-cleaned.csv
```

It is now time to practice. Your assignment (#3) is to download the file from the following URL and remove "username:", "email:", "password:", "ip_address:", "phone:", and "id:" from it using Sed. Don't forget to escape the underscore (_). This will require eight commands (found on the last page of this chapter) including the instructions to switch to your Downloads directory and download the file. For extra credit, Cat the file to view the contents.

https://inteltechniques.com/data/osintdata/sed-customers.csv

Your result should appear as follows.

test1,test@gmail.com,pass123,10.2.2.3,5551212,32
test2,test2@gmail.com,pass456,10.2.2.4,5551213,33

If you had a 200 GB original file, your new file would be almost half of the size. This is a substantial savings of disk space, and will be vital once you start collecting large data sets. We are barely scratching the surface with the power of Sed. Consider the following examples, assuming you want to modify a file titled 1.txt. If this all seems overwhelming, please do not worry. We will conduct many more examples using real data throughout the rest of this section.

Replace "OLD" with "NEW":	sed -i "s/OLD/NEW/gI" 1.txt
Replace all commas with hyphens:	sed -i "s/\,/\-/gI" 1.txt
Remove all data until the first comma:	sed -i "s/^\([^,]*,\)//gI" 1.txt
Remove all data until the first colon:	sed -i "s/^[^:]*://gI" 1.txt
Remove all single quotes:	sed -i " s/\'//gI" 1.txt
Remove all double quotes:	sed -i "s/\"//gI" 1.txt
Remove all data between "A" & "B:	sed -i "s/\(A\).*\(B\)/\1\2/" 1.txt
Remove all data between "{" and "}":	sed -i "s/{[^}]*}//gI" 1.txt
Remove all digits between commas:	sed -i "s/\,[0-9]*\,//gI" 1.txt
Remove any line beginning with "A":	sed -i "/^A/d" 1.txt
Remove empty lines:	sed -i "'/^$/d" 1.txt
Remove first 10 lines:	sed -i "1,10d" 1.txt
Remove first ten characters:	sed -i "s/^.\{10\}//" 1.txt
Remove everything after the last "_":	sed -i "s/_[^_]*$//" 1.txt
Remove hyphens from phone numbers:	sed -i "s/\([0-9]\{3,\}\)-/\1/g" 1.txt

I realize we are getting very technical early in this guide. If you feel overwhelmed, don't worry. I promise this will make more sense when we deal with real data.
Before we move on, we should discuss the likelihood of errors on macOS and Linux machines due to unreadable characters. If your downloaded data includes non-ASCII characters, such as ¡, µ, ¶, and many others, the Sed command may not function. This is especially true for the Cut and Sort commands. Therefore, we should start

preceding every command with "LC_ALL=C" within macOS and Linux. This command sets the system's language to ASCII. This should avoid character errors and, in some cases, make our queries faster. Let's apply it to our next tutorial about the Cut command.

Cut is extremely powerful. It allows us to easily remove entire columns of a comma separated value (CSV) file without the need to identify specific text with Sed. Assume you have downloaded a file titled cut-1.txt with text similar to the following.

```
internal_id,customer_id,email,password,value
1,kjh234g5,test1@gmail.com,pass123,ydt-655-hhjk4-yui7-6ddgghejkr776djhdi8f
2,asd9f87,test2@gmail.com,pass456,ydt-655-hhjk4-yui8-6ddgghejkr776djhdi8f
3,;l2k3j45,test3@gmail.com,pass789,ydt-655-hhjk4-yui9-6ddgghejkr776djhdi8f
```

You might have no need to store the "internal_id", "customer_id", and "value". We often see large data sets with too much content which will never be beneficial to us. This is where Cut comes in. It allows us to select specific columns to extract while ignoring the others. My command to extract only the desired columns would be the following.

```
LC_ALL=C cut -d, -f3,4 cut-1.txt > cut-2.txt
```

We should understand each part of the command, as follows.

LC_ALL=C	Sets character type to avoid errors (macOS and Linux).
cut	The "cut" command.
-d,	Identifies the delimiter, which is a comma here (,).
-f3,4	Identifies the desired columns to keep, by number.
cut-1.txt	Identifies the input file.
>	Directs the result to output somewhere.
cut-2.txt	Determines the new file name.

The results of this command are as follows.

```
email,password
test1@gmail.com,pass123
test2@gmail.com,pass456
test3@gmail.com,pass789
```

Assignment #4 will test your understanding of the Cut command. Your assignment is to extract only the "email", "password", and "phone" columns using the Cut command from the file located at the following URL. Your result file should be titled cut-cleaned.txt.

https://inteltechniques.com/data/osintdata/cut-1.txt

The original data appears as follows.

```
internal_id,email,customer_id,password,phone,value
1,test1@gmail.com,kjh234g5,pass123,202-555-1212,ydt
2,test2@gmail.com,asd9f87,pass456,202-555-1213,ydt
3,test3@gmail.com,l2k3j45,pass789,202-555-1214,ydt
```

Your final result should appear as follows.

```
email,password,phone
```

```
test1@gmail.com,pass123,202-555-1212
test2@gmail.com,pass456,202-555-1213
test3@gmail.com,pass789,202-555-1214
```

Later in this section, we will use the Cut command to extract desired columns from numerous files in one command. Next is an equally vital command called Sort. This allows us to not only sort the contents of a file alphabetically, but it also removes duplicate lines when we provide specific parameters. This is important because a lot of the data we will acquire is full of redundant entries eating up your valuable disk space. Assume you have a file called sort.txt which contains the following content.

```
test1@gmail.com:pass123
test2@gmail.com:pass456
test1@gmail.com:pass123
test2@gmail.com:pass456
test1@gmail.com:pass123
```

The following command would remove the duplicates; sort the remaining content alphabetically; and create a new file called sorted.txt.

```
sort -u sort.txt > sorted.txt
```

This new file would have only the following content.

```
test1@gmail.com:pass123
test2@gmail.com:pass456
```

Windows users should have noticed an error with this command. That is because Windows wants "/unique" instead of "-u" to complete the command. Windows hurdles seem to be the common theme here, and Windows users would execute the following command.

```
sort /unique sort.txt > sorted.txt
```

This was a very basic example, but you will encounter extremely large data which will need more tweaking. The following is my preferred command when I need to sort large data. This command will only work on macOS and Linux systems.

```
LC_ALL=C sort -u -b -i -f -S 80% --parallel=8 sort.txt > sorted.txt
```

The following is a breakdown.

LC_ALL=C	Sets the character type to avoid errors.
sort	The "sort" command.
-u	Instructs to only save unique entries (no duplicates).
-b	Ignores leading blanks.
-i	Ignores non-printable characters.
-f	Ignores case when UPPERCASE and lowercase are the same.
-S 80%	Sets buffer size to use 80% of the system's RAM.
--parallel=8	Uses 8 processor threads to run processes concurrently.
sort.txt	Identifies the input file.
>	Directs the result to output somewhere.
sorted.txt	Determines the new file name.

I chose 8 threads because my machine can support it. You may need to lower or raise this number based on your own hardware. I believe 80% of RAM buffer will work fine on most machines. It is now time for you to test your skills. Assignment #5 challenges you to sort a file titled sort-1.txt located at the following URL.

https://inteltechniques.com/data/osintdata/sort-1.txt

Download this file to your Downloads folder; sort for unique entries and save the file as sort-2.txt; remove the original file; and display the content of the new file within Terminal. The results should appear as follows.

test1@gmail.com:pass123
test2@gmail.com:pass456
test3@aol.com:pass789
test3@gmail.com:pass789

Sometimes, you will encounter data which is simply too large to process. I once retrieved a 260 GB text file full of names, DOBs, and SSNs which possessed several duplicates. Sorting a 260 GB file on a machine with 8 GB of RAM will likely crash the computer and required a reboot. I never like to sort files which are more than twice as large as my amount of RAM. Since I possess 32 GB of RAM in my machine, I try to keep my sorting limited to files which are under 64 GB each. However, I was able to successfully sort a 100 GB Stealer Logs file with 32 GB of RAM, as explained in a later chapter, but the process was quite taxing on my drive. Sometimes, I need to split a large file into several pieces, and then sort those pieces back into one file which excludes all duplicates. To do this, we must first understand the Split command.

Split allows us to turn one large file into several smaller files. There are many options with this command, but we will focus only on those most relevant to our use. Assume I have a 260 GB file titled SSN.txt in my Downloads directory which contains thousands of duplicate entries. I will first split this one file into multiple files, each containing 25 GB of data (25,000,000,000 bytes), with the following commands.

```
cd ~/Downloads
split -C 25000000000 --additional-suffix=.txt SSN.txt
```

The result should be multiple files titled xaa.txt, xab.txt, xac.txt, etc., which each have a 25 GB file size. We can now sort each of these independently with the following macOS/Linux command.

```
for f in x*.txt; do LC_ALL=C sort -u -b -i -f -S 80% --parallel=8  $f >
sorted_$f; done
```

This command finds all files which begin with "x" and end with ".txt" inside the working directory; executes our sort command on each file; saves each result with "sorted" added to the beginning of the file; and quits when finished. The result is several files titled sorted_xaa.txt, sorted_xab.txt, sorted_xac.txt, etc. Each file has been sorted to only contain unique entries, with all duplicates removed. We can now use our sort command with the merge flag (-m) to quickly merge all sorted files into one large file which only contains unique entries (macOS/Linux).

```
LC_ALL=C sort -S 80% --parallel=8 -m -u sorted* > SSN-Sorted.txt
```

LC_ALL=C	Sets the character type to avoid errors.
sort	The "sort" command.
-S 80%	Sets buffer size to use 80% of the system's RAM.
--parallel=8	Uses 8 processor threads to run processes concurrently.
-m	Merges pre-sorted files into one
-u	Instructs to only save unique entries (no duplicates).
sorted*	Identifies all input files which start with "sorted".
>	Directs the result to output somewhere.

SSN-Sorted.txt   Determines the new file name.

Notice I omitted the flags for ignoring some characters since we have already sorted those out in the previous command. With my data example, the file of SSN entries went from 260 GB to 210 GB by removing duplicates. We will revisit all of this when we start sorting large files of stealer log data. I understand the frustration of Windows users. While we can make most of these commands work, there will always be hurdles. The remaining chapters of this book will allow Windows machines to acquire all of the data presented. However, minimizing and cleaning that data will be troublesome. I encourage Windows users to focus more on data acquisition than processing the content. Queries will work fine in future chapters, but the time required to search the data will be more. All of this will always be easier for macOS and Linux users.

It is now time to test your skills. Assignment #6 brings together a lot of what you have learned in this chapter, and we will be using real breach data. This will require a lot of work, but it will be great exercise for future demonstrations. I have a 19 MB file at the following URL which contains true Whois data. We will get much more of this data later, but this is a good way to test our skills. Inside this file is many names and addresses of domain owners who did not protect the information. However, it also contains many duplicates and columns of data which are unneeded.

https://inteltechniques.com/data/osintdata/Whois.txt

Your challenge is to conduct the following.

- Download the file into your Downloads directory.
- Remove all double quotes (") from the file.
- Extract the "domain_name", "registrant_name", and "registrant_address" columns into a file titled "who.txt".
- Split the who.txt file into 1 MB chunks.
- Delete the Whois.txt and who.txt files.
- Sort each split file for unique entries, each saved as a file beginning with "sorted".
- Merge the "sorted" files into one file called Whois-Sorted.txt.
- Remove the sorted* and xa* files.

Your Whois-Sorted.txt file should be 1.1 MB and include entries similar to the following.

00000777.com,Peng Goh,G.P.O. Box 732
0012222.com,Peng Goh,G.P.O. Box 732
0013333.com,Peng Goh,G.P.O. Box 732

This file is not very useful, but it served as a good demonstration. We will identify much better data sets later. The splitting of such a small file and then merging the contents was unnecessary, but I wanted you to practice these steps for preparedness when large data is acquired.

We will use the Awk command several times throughout this section. There are unlimited uses for this utility, but let's take a look at one way it may be beneficial. Assume you have a large file with entries similar to the following.

test1@gmail.com:pass123
test2@gmail.com:pass456
null
test3@gmail.com:pass789
null
test4@gmail.com:pass321

Many times, we will encounter data which has empty, or "null" lines which eat up space for no reason. Using Awk, we can remove any lines which do not contain a specific character. The following would remove any lines which do not contain a valid email address, with "@" inside the line, within a file titled awk-1.txt, which is saved to awk-2.txt.

```
awk '/@/' awk-1.txt > awk-2.txt
```

The result follows.

```
test1@gmail.com
test2@gmail.com
test3@gmail.com
test4@gmail.com
```

Another utility I often use is Word Count (wc). The following commands display the number of lines within our files.

```
wc -l awk-1.txt
wc -l awk-2.txt
```

The results from these two files were "6" and "4" respectively. I often use this to determine how many entries are within a data breach. As I am writing this, I found a data leak from a person search website. The file was over 100 GB, and the wc command revealed it possessed 21,304,654 entries.

You should now practice querying data. We previously installed Ripgrep, which allows us to quickly search within any data type for results matching our query. A typical query, which would search through all data within a file titled passwords.txt for the word "michael", would appear as follows. Excluding the file name would search all files within the working directory.

rg -a -F -i -N michael passwords.txt

The following is the breakdown.

rg	The command to launch Ripgrep.
-a	The switch to search all data as text.
-F	The switch to treat the pattern as a literal string.
-i	The switch to ignore case.
-N	The switch to exclude the line number.
michael	The search term.
passwords.txt	The file to search.

In this demonstration, I added a switch (-) for each option, which is overkill. We can add all of the options within one command and only one switch. In other words, our original Ripgrep query of rg -a -F -i -N michael passwords.txt can be replicated much more simply as rg -aFiN michael passwords.txt. Ripgrep is a very powerful query tool with many options. Let's work through the most common query parameters which we will use over the next several chapters.

rg -aFiN T@Gmail.com	Search EXACTLY t@gmail.com or T@GMAIL.com
rg -aiN Test@Gmail.com	Search ALL test and gmail and com
rg -aFN T@Gmail.com	Search ONLY T@Gmail.com and not t@gmail.com
rg -aFi Test@Gmail.com	Search EXACTLY test@gmail.com and show line #
rg --help	Show Ripgrep help menu

Each of these commands will search within all of the files contained in the current folder. If you are in Terminal within your Downloads folder and conduct these queries, they will search every file present within that folder, which may be undesired. As you begin to collect multiple large files, you will want to specify the file desired. The following would only search through a specific voter file.

```
rg -aFiN Test@Gmail.com Voter-FL-2018.txt
```

If you want to search two specific pieces of data within a single file, the following would apply. It would display only lines within our file which contain BOTH "Michael" and Bazzell".

```
rg -aFiN "Michael" | rg -aFiN "Bazzell" Voter-FL-2018.txt
```

If you want to search two potential pieces of data within a single file, the following would apply. It would display only lines within our file which contain EITHER "Bazel" or Bazzell".

```
rg -aFiN "Bazel|Bazzell" Voter-FL-2018.txt
```

Overall, we will almost always use the combination of rg -aFiN "target". You can play with this now against any test files you have downloaded. I think we are finally ready to start acquiring some real data.

I think I have exhausted the patience of many readers who want to dive into data acquisition. There are many more commands which will need explained and tested, but we can tackle those within the remaining chapters. The following page provides the solutions to the assignments presented within this chapter. The following chapter finally begins our journey into data collection.

Assignment #1
```
cat cat-2.txt
```

Assignment #2
```
cd ~/Downloads
curl -O https://inteltechniques.com/data/osintdata/cat-1.txt
curl -O https://inteltechniques.com/data/osintdata/cat-2.txt
curl -O https://inteltechniques.com/data/osintdata/cat-3.txt
curl -O https://inteltechniques.com/data/osintdata/cat-4.txt
cat cat-1.txt cat-2.txt cat-3.txt cat-4.txt > cat-test.txt
rm cat-1.txt cat-2.txt cat-3.txt cat-4.txt
cat cat-test.txt
```

Assignment #3
```
cd ~/Downloads
curl -O https://inteltechniques.com/data/osintdata/sed-customers.csv
sed -i "s/username\://gI" sed-customers.csv
sed -i "s/email\://gI" sed-customers.csv
sed -i "s/password\://gI" sed-customers.csv
sed -i "s/ip\_address\://gI" sed-customers.csv
sed -i "s/phone\://gI" sed-customers.csv
sed -i "s/id\://gI" sed-customers.csv
cat sed-customers.csv
```

Assignment #4
```
cd ~/Downloads
curl -O https://inteltechniques.com/data/osintdata/cut-1.txt
LC_ALL=C cut -d, -f2,4,5 cut-1.txt > cut-cleaned.txt
```

```
cat cut-cleaned.txt
```

Assignment #5
```
cd ~/Downloads
curl -O https://inteltechniques.com/data/osintdata/sort-1.txt
LC_ALL=C sort -u -b -i -f -S 80% --parallel=8 sort-1.txt > sort-2.txt
rm sort-1.txt
cat sort-2.txt
```

Assignment #6
```
cd ~/Downloads
curl -O https://inteltechniques.com/data/osintdata/Whois.txt
sed -i "s/\"//g" Whois.txt
cut -d, -f2,11,13 Whois.txt > who.txt
split -C 1000000 --additional-suffix=.txt who.txt
rm Whois.txt who.txt
for f in x*.txt; do LC_ALL=C sort -u -b -i -f -S 80% --parallel=8  $f >
sorted_$f; done
LC_ALL=C sort -S 80% --parallel=8 -m -u sorted* > Whois-Sorted.txt
rm sorted* xa*
```

CHAPTER FOURTY
DATA LEAKS

The chapter on data breaches and leaks within the previous edition of this book began with a demonstration involving voter data. I included links to websites which hosted the entire voter databases of nine states. The person who hosted those sites had filed FOIA requests for the public voter data, and published the results when received. In early 2022, all nine sites began forwarding to a genealogy site which did not possess any voter data. However, data never dies.

In early 2023, a new site called **BreachForums** (breachforums.is) surfaced to replace the previously-seized **BreachForums** (breached.to) site which was created to replace the previously-seized **RaidForums** (raidforums.com) site. The latest site is basically a clone and serves as a marketplace for breaches and leaks. **I do not recommend visiting this site until you have a full understanding of the consequences.** I also do not ever recommend purchasing credits which allow download of stolen data. There is no need, as we will access the data in other ways without paying criminals through a shady website.

In June of 2022, BreachForums released an official database of complete voter registration details from twenty-eight states. This included the original leaked data I discussed in the previous edition, plus numerous additional states acquired from other leaks. All of this data is technically public, but it was never meant to be published in this way. The original source of this voter data was official government agencies, and the data was obtained legally. The **publication** in this format is likely against some, if not all, state laws.

If you believe **possession** of this type of invasive data is illegal, consider Ohio's stance. If you navigate to https://www6.ohiosos.gov/ords/f?p=VOTERFTP:HOME:::::: and click on the "Statewide Voter File" tab, you can download the entire database of registered voters directly from the official Ohio government domain. This is truly public data and avoids the use of third-party providers.

The data set for Washington state is also available from the government if you promise not to further distribute or sell the content. You can download the entire database directly at https://www.sos.wa.gov/elections/vrdb/extract-requests.aspx.

Other states' voter databases are also out there, and we will find them together. The data sets include millions of people's names, dates of birth, and home addresses (some otherwise unpublished), along with numerous email addresses and cellular telephone numbers. I hope by now you could see how this might be beneficial to online investigations. Let's begin with some official data from Ohio.

I navigated to https://www6.ohiosos.gov/ords/f?p=VOTERFTP:HOME:::::: and clicked the "Statewide Voter Files" tab. I then downloaded all four options which consisted of approximately 425 MB of compressed data. After decompressing the files, I was presented 4.6 GB of text files, each beginning with "SWVF". Now, let's apply the lessons learned within the previous chapter to slim down this data. First, I combined all four files into one file titled Ohio.txt with the following Terminal command while in the Downloads directory.

```
cat SWVF* > Ohio.txt
```

I then removed the unnecessary individual files with the following.

```
rm SWVF*
```

I now want to view the contents of the new text file, but it is quite large. While my computer could open this entire file within a text editor, it is never a good idea. When we start downloading 50 GB files, we will crash our computers if we try to open them. Instead, we will use Ripgrep. The following command displays only the first two lines within Terminal.

```
rg -m2 "" Ohio.txt
```

The result is overwhelming, as each line of this text file is enormous. However, this is a digital guide, so I will include the entire output on the following page. The first 80% of the file is line one while the last 20% is line two. The first line identifies the column headers (descriptions), while the remaining lines are the actual content. This first line can be quite helpful. It allows us to understand what the data is and why we may want it. The second line was modified for publication here.

We can see the valuable data within the second line. Most of the beneficial content is at the beginning. For this demonstration, I only want the names, addresses, and dates of birth of the voters, so I will eliminate all undesired data with the following Cut command.

```
cut -d, -f4,5,6,8,12,13,14,15,16,17 Ohio.txt > Ohio-clean.txt
```

This extracts only columns 4, 5, 6, 8, 12, 13, 14, 15, 16, and 17, saving that data to a new file called Ohio-clean.txt. The output is similar to the following.

"SMITH","DAVID","E","1975-05-20","33 MAIN","","WINCHESTER","OH","45697",""

Compare that to the ortiginal entry as follows.

"OH0016289533","01","3086","SMITH","DAVID","E","","1975-05-20","1991-10-08","ACTIVE","R","33 MAIN","","WINCHESTER","OH","45697","","","","","","","","","","","","","","","","","02","04","SOUTHER N OHIO ESC","","","ADAMS COUNTY/OH VALLEY LSD (ADAMS)","","LIBERTY TOWNSHIP","01AAI","05","90","14","LIBERTY TOWNSHIP","","","R","X","","","R","X","","","X","R","X","","","","X","","R","X","","","X","","","R","","X"," ","","","","","X","R","","","X","R","","X","R","X","","","","X","R","X","","","X","R","","","X","","","X","R", "","X","","","X","R","X","","","","X","R","R","X","","","X","","","X"

I do not like all of those unnecessary quotes, so I will remove them with the following command.

```
sed -i "s/\"//gI" Ohio-clean.txt
```

The result is as follows.

SMITH,DAVID,E,1975-05-20,33 MAIN,,WINCHESTER,OH,45697,

Not only is that cleaner, but the 4.6 GB file is now only 549 MB. I believe this file is finished, and it can be added to our external SSD. The easiest way to do this is via the default file explorer application for your operating system. I prefer to create a new folder at the root of my external SSD titled "Voter" for this type of data. If you named this external drive "DATA", as previously explained, we can search the file with the following commands within macOS.

```
cd /Volumes/DATA/Voter
rg -aFiN Bazzell Ohio-clean.txt
```

As a reminder, the first command navigated to our external drive. The easiest way to do this is to type "cd", followed by a space, and then drag the desired folder from the Finder into the Terminal box. This also works in Pop!_OS and Ubuntu, however, the Linux command to change into the external drive is different.

```
cd /media/$USER/DATA/Voter
rg -aFiN Bazzell Ohio-clean.txt
```

This "rg" command queries our file for the presence of "Bazzell". The following is the redacted result.

```
BAZZELL,     ████ON,1935-0█████  SALE█████G PL,,ENGLEWOOD,OH,45322,
BAZZELL,     █████N,1964-06█████HELTO█TERING,OH,45429,
BAZZELL,     █████ER,JAMES,█████9,936████DR,,KETTERING,OH,45429,
```

Many states either offer their voter registration as a download option within their website or via a request directly to their offices. If I can extract raw data from the official source, that is always preferred, but I never make any requests to the government. The data is almost always floating around other places. Currently, you can download 110 GB of voter registration data from the BreachForums site previously mentioned. I cannot provide a direct link to the content, but I can help you find it. The following Google query should provide an abundance of links to investigate.

site:breachforums.is voter

One of the first results during my test was titled "USA Voter Databases Collection" which contained full voter registration files for 28 states. However, one must possess eight "credits" in order to download the data. I never recommend purchasing credits, as this gives money to criminals and is often unnecessary. Most of these breach forums allow users to earn credits for free by posting and commenting within various areas of the site. One should be able to generate eight credits by leaving eight comments within an area about recent events. This is quite annoying, but it should get the job done. I typically try to find alternative sources, such as Telegram.

We previously installed Telegram onto our devices. However, you must possess a Telegram account in order to access any data. This requires registration through the Telegram mobile app. This can be completed from a mobile device or an Android emulator, as explained in *OSINT Techniques, 10th Edition*. If Telegram requires a phone number for your account, they should accept Google Voice and other VoIP numbers. Creating the account can be a pain, but the effort is justified.

Once you have Telegram Desktop open and logged in to an active account, we can begin searching. First, query "Open Data" within the search field and look for a room similar to the following.

Once you see the room, click the "Join Channel" option to save it to your favorites. Next, search for "voter" within the search field and scroll down to the "Messages" section of the results. This immediately displayed the following.

Clicking these links opened that portion of the channel. This presented three interesting compressed voter registration databases. Mine appeared as follows.

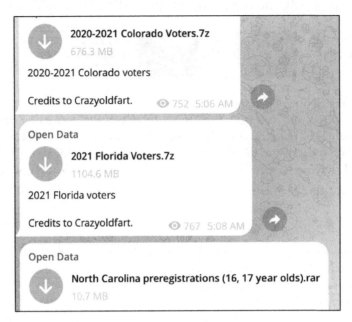

Clicking the down arrows began the download process. The first file contained Colorado voter data. After decompressing the 676 MB 7z file, I possessed 3.1 GB of data. If desired, you could replicate the previous demo to combine and clean all of the data. Repeating the process and searching for "Data Stream" then "Voter" presented the following. Within a few minutes, I had downloaded six state's voter rolls.

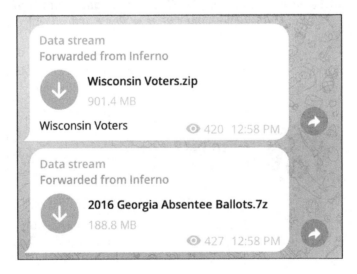

You will likely find that many of the voter data sets on Telegram are outdated. Some are from 2015 or earlier. Since voter registration data is always changing, you may want to research newer sources. In 2020, RaidForums offered a huge download consisting of current voter registration from 19 states. That website is now gone, but the data lives on. Shortly after the domain was seized, someone created a torrent file which allows download of every official data set from the defunct website.

I am not allowed to provide a direct link to this data, but I can tell you how I found it. Searching "Raidforums databases" produced over 100,000 results, most of which provided no valuable content. However, the following search within Google produced ten interesting results.

raidforums "magnet:?" database 2020

The "magnet:?" term forces Google to only display results which include that specific text with those characters. This will identify sites which contain an actual torrent link within them, instead of sites which simply discuss the data. The first two links both offered a torrent magnet link, similar to the following fictitious example.

magnet:?xt=urn:btih:651570d629b83e95353c47f9e1

I copied and pasted this data into my browser, which then prompted me to choose an application to open the data stream. I chose Transmission (some systems will choose this by default). This launched Transmission and prompted me to choose the download location. If you have modified your default Transmission settings, your experience might be different. I chose my Downloads folder and clicked "Open". The torrent file was added and launched. I double-clicked the torrent and clicked the "Files" tab. It took a few minutes for the metadata to be retrieved, but I eventually saw a list of data within this torrent.

I immediately deselected all of the files. In some systems (macOS), you may see a button labeled "None" which will do this for you. Within others (Linux), you will need to deselect the highest "Database Leaks" checkbox. This prevents immediate downloading of all 486 GB of this data. After I deselected all boxes, I scrolled down to the "Voter Databases" folder and selected it. My system began downloading the data from all states, including millions of people's names, home addresses, and dates of birth.

I hope you can now see the value of voter data, but we are just getting started. It is important to note that each state stores their data in a unique format. The Ohio example was just to begin the conversation about merging and cleaning of data. There is much more to discuss. Many of the voter files are already stored within comma-separated value files (CSV). Ripgrep will easily search through those for you and you may not need to take any further action. Some are text files with a slightly different format. Please remember that this tutorial is not intended to provide a single solution to all data you might encounter. We are only dipping our toes into the world of leaked data.

I have collected CSV files of leaked data which possessed over 200 columns of data. Many times, the majority of this content is not valuable and taking up precious space. The smaller your files are, the faster you can search them with Ripgrep. I could replicate this for the other state sets if desired. I could also clean up all of the other states and make one huge file called Voter.txt if I really want to minimize things. As you see, there are always many ways to do this.

Consumer Data

You may have noticed the wealth of information within the previously explained torrent file. Most of the databases within this download contain user credentials and fit better in the next chapter. However, let's focus on some more data within this torrent before we move on. I began the download for the USA Consumer data. We never truly know the source of any data leak, but these were supposedly extracted from an unknown consumer reporting agency through a poorly configured server.

The USA Consumer file contains almost 12 million entries, each of which displays the email address, full name, home address, and telephone number of all victims. The website which they used to enter information was also collected. A typical entry appears as follows.

wjan@yahoo.com,Jane,Burns,26 Main St,CA,Fullerton,94011,,,(650) 722-2000,http://www.coolsavings.com,Coupon Offers

Next, I opened Telegram and searched for a popular channel called "LEAKS AGGREGATOR" and joined. I then searched for "consumer" and perused the options. I found a series of files titled "2021_1_USA_Consumer", each of which appeared to be for a specific state. The Texas collection was so big it needed split into two compressed files, totaling 2.5 GB. The decompressed files were almost 20 GB, and were split into 21 CSV files. Each contained 414 columns of text, including full names, home addresses, email addresses, telephone numbers, and interests.

I went ahead and downloaded all nine files, which contained consumer data for eight states. This presented 5.56 GB of compressed data which decompressed to 59 GB of CSV files. I then conducted the following to clean the data, based on the previous tutorials. First, I needed to Cat all the files into one large file. Since the files are spread over multiple subdirectories, I needed to modify my commands. Below is a partial screen capture of the files located within the Telegram Desktop folder located in my Home Downloads folder.

I executed the following command, which combined all of those files, regardless of being in subfolders, into one 59 GB file called 1.txt.

```
cd ~/Downloads/Telegram\ Desktop
cat * */* > 1.txt
```

The "* */*" command basically tells Terminal to look into the current folder and one level deep into any subfolders. I then cleaned the data with the following commands.

```
cut -d, -f3,4,5,8,10,17,18,43,410,411,412 1.txt > 2.txt
sed -i "s/\"//gI" 2.txt
mv 2.txt ~/Downloads/Consumer-Cleaned.txt
rm -r *
```

Based on the previous tutorials, can you identify each command's usage? The first command cut the columns in which I was most interested from the original file into a file called 2.txt. The second command removed all of the quotes. The third command moved my cleaned file into my Downloads directory with a more descriptive name. The final command deleted all of the files which I no longer need in the original folder, making it ready for the next attack. The final file was 1.6 GB, containing 31,631,871 entries, which each appeared as follows.

personfirstname,personmiddleinitial,personlastname,housenumber,streetname,state,ZipCode,FullPhoneNumber,email,datasource,ip
SMITH,J,MIKE,64,Main,VT,05488,8028682000,me@hotmail.com,diaperbeagle.com,24.127.95.2

This type of consumer data is all over the internet. Most of it contains enormous amounts of unhelpful data, but you may want to archive the original versions of everything you find. In this case, we went from 59 GB to just over 1 GB, and maintained the most commonly searched data. Let's go ahead and query for anyone with my last name with the following commands.

```
cd ~/Downloads
rg -aFiN bazzell Consumer-Cleaned.txt
```

The result should include the following redacted sample.

```
CHARLES,C,BAZZELL         thryn,TX,75067,66      3,cbazz      l.com,hbwm.com,209.217.94.       48.222.31
ROSLYN,Y,BAZZELLE         O Box,TX,77253,71      0,rbazz      otmail.com,www.xmllead.com       48.222.31
```

Marketing Lists

Let's move on to something in a grey area. There are many companies that collect millions of email addresses and create spam lists. These then get sold to companies selling fake pharmaceuticals or designer handbags, and those unwanted messages end up in your inbox. We are all on a spam list somewhere. These are very expensive to buy, especially the good ones. One such database is the Kyle Data, or "Special K", spam list. This database contains 178,288,657 email addresses. There are no passwords, but it does contain other sensitive data. In November of 2015, a web page at updates4news.com temporarily possessed active links to this entire data set. This page is long gone by now. Fortunately for us, the Wayback Machine archived all of it. The following direct link displays hundreds of CSV spreadsheets, each containing millions of email addresses.

https://web.archive.org/web/20151110195654/http://www.updates4news.com:80/kyledata/

If desired, you could use the Firefox extension called DownThemAll to automatically download all of this data overnight into a folder on your desktop titled "SpecialK". You could also grab it from the previously explained torrent file. You could then execute a command through Terminal within that folder of `cat * > SpecialK.txt`. The result would be a single file, 19.73 gigabytes in size. That is very big, but also very powerful. Let's take a look at the content. Assume I was looking for a target who possessed an email address of robynsnest2006@yahoo.com. Assuming that I had made a single file titled SpecialK.txt within my Downloads folder on my machine, my commands in Terminal would be as follows. The result of the search is directly after the search command.

```
cd ~/Downloads
rg -aFiN robynsnest2006@yahoo.com SpecialK.txt
```

MANHATTAN BEACH, robynsnest2006@yahoo.com,yahoo.com, Robyn Bazzell, 2015-04-07, 72.129.87.179, paydayloaneveryday.com, CA, 90266

This tells me that my target lives in Manhattan Beach, CA 90266. Her name is Robyn Bazzell, and on 04/07/2015 her marketing data was collected from the website paydayloaneveryday.com. At the time, her computer IP address was 72.129.87.179. We basically just converted an email address into a full dossier on our target. This type of data is simply not available on public websites. If you doubt the validity of this data, please consider searching your own content. This is only one of dozens of interesting databases stored within the Wayback Machine. It is up to you to exercise your skills from this guide to locate them all.

Social Security Death Index (SSDI)

Hopefully, you agree that possessing your own collection of this type of data could be useful. Let's add another collection of publicly available data. An individual previously purchased the entire Social Security Death Index, which is public data, and uploaded it for public consumption. This entire database can be downloaded from the public Archive.org at **https://archive.org/download/SocialSecurityDeathIndex/2013-05-31/**. After downloading the multiple files, you can combine them as stated previously into a single file and name it SSDI.txt.

Assuming you placed the text file in the Downloads folder, the following commands would navigate to the folder and search for anyone in the file with my last name.

```
cd ~/Downloads
rg -aFiN bazzell SSDI.txt
```

The results will include multiple entries with the following format.

433220353 BAZZELL   DOROTHY   S   0118201303191921

The first set of numbers is the Social Security Number of the deceased individual, followed by the last name, first name, and middle initial. The last set of numbers represents the date of death (01/18/2013) and the date of birth (03/19/1921). I am bthered by these unnecessary tabbed spaces. The following command will replace each tab with a comma, which compresses the data and makes it easier to read. This is much cleaner and will make future search results easier to digest. Note that the spaces in the command are created by pressing the control, v, and tab keys at the same time. This represents a "tab" to the command.

```
sed -i "s/     /\,/gI" SSDI.txt
```

The result would appear as follows.

433220353,BAZZELL,DOROTHY,S,0118201303191921

Let's recap where we are at right now. You might have single, very large, text files that each include all of the registered voter data for various states. These often include dates of birth, names, telephone numbers, addresses, and email accounts. You also have the entire SSDI. You can now search through all of that data with a simple search. If you wanted to identify any entries within all of the files inside a specific folder, with a last name of Bazzell, the following would be the most appropriate search. You could also now search by social security number, date of birth, or date of death.

```
rg -aFiN Bazzell
```

SnapChat Numbers

Let's conduct another Archive.org demonstration. This one is quite dated but allows us to add some historical phone data to our collection. In January 2014, Snapchat had 4.6 million usernames and phone numbers exposed. The breach enabled individual usernames, which are often used across other services, to be resolved to phone numbers. This file is titled SnapChat.7z and can be found online at archive.org/download/SnapChat.7z. This link contains the entire breach inside one text file. Conducting the following search would query a specific Snapchat username for any leaked data. Directly after this command is the result.

```
rg -aFiN mikenap115 SnapChat.txt
```

('21220392XX', mikenap115, ", ")

This identifies the cellular telephone number of our target to include 212-203-92xx. While the last two numbers are redacted, you could try all 100 combinations within the previously discussed telephone search options. It is a great start. You could have also conducted this query on websites which possess this data. However, those sites require an absolute username. It cannot search partial names. If we only knew that our target had a SnapChat name that included the term "topher4", this database would provide the following users of interest.

('30351923XX', 'topher451', ", "),
('41572499XX', 'topher413', ", "),

('71974140XX', 'topher456', '', ''),
('75426428XX', 'topher481', '', ''),

We can also now search by telephone numbers. If you know your target has a cellular number of 303-519-2388, you could conduct the following search, with the partial result appearing after.

```
rg -aFiN 30351923XX SnapChat.txt
```

('30351923XX', 'topher451', '', ''),
('30351923XX', 'ben_davis', '', ''),
('30351923XX', 'rosemcdonald', '', ''),
('30351923XX', 'cuzzycook', '', ''),
('30351923XX', 'angelgallozzi', '', ''),
('30351923XX', 'kmo85', '', ''),
('30351923XX', 'rinisob', '', ''),

Your target may not appear in the results, but minimal investigation could result in a powerful new lead. You should note that the full numbers were never publicly leaked, and the group that conducted this attack redacted the results to exclude the last digits.

Public Data Sets (Usenet)

Many large data sets which are beneficial to investigations are not technically "leaks". This chapter has focused mostly on data which was never meant to become publicly available. However, there are numerous archives full of public information which should be considered for your data collection. Most archives cannot be searched through traditional resources such as Google. Instead, we must acquire the data, condense it, and conduct our own queries. As a demonstration, I will explain how I utilize Usenet archives as a vital part of my investigations.

Usenet was my first introduction into newsgroups in the early nineties. My internet service provider allowed full access to thousands of topics through Outlook Express. I could subscribe to those of interest and communicate via email with people from all over the world. This sounds ridiculously common today, but it was fascinating at the time. I located a newsgroup about my favorite band, and I was quickly trading bootleg cassettes and exchanging gossip about the music industry. I was freely sending messages without any consideration of any abilities to permanently archive everything.

Today, the Internet Archive presents huge repositories of data containing over thirty years' worth of Usenet messages. It is presented in over 26,000 archives, each containing between 1 to 20,000 files. It is massive, and would take years to download manually. Fortunately, we can use a download script created by the Internet Archive to automatically obtain all desired data.

The following tutorial will install the necessary software into our macOS or Linux machine; download the entire Usenet archive; extract email addresses and names of each member; acquire newsgroup data to associate with each person; and condense the data into a usable format. This will take some time and may be overwhelming for some readers at this stage. The final product is worth the effort, and I offer a download link at the end if you want to avoid the hassle. If you are up for the challenge, please follow along to learn how to deal with large Archive.org data sets. Let's begin.

First, we need to install the Internet Archive script within our macOS or Linux machines. Unfortunately, this tool is unreliable within Windows. Enter the following Terminal commands for Linux systems.

```
sudo apt update
sudo pip install -U internetarchive
```

Conduct the following within macOS.

```
brew install internetarchive
```

We now have the application installed and ready to use from any folder. Next, we need to identify the Internet Archive collections which we want to acquire. For this demonstration, I will focus on the following two data sets.

https://archive.org/details/giganews
https://archive.org/details/usenethistorical

These are two independent Usenet archives. Each contains unique records and some redundant data. Let's take a look at the second collection. The first folder is titled Usenet-Alt and contains over 15,000 files extracted from decades of conversations within the "Alt" communities. Opening the file titled alt.2600.fake-id.mbox reveals names, email addresses, dates, and entire messages dating back to 1997. The following is an excerpt.

From: "David N." <david.nine@juno.com>
Subject: Need Fake Texas DL
Date: 1998/07/11
Newsgroups: alt.2600.fake-id
I need a quality bogus TX DL for my 17 year old sister. Can you help me out?

Possessing a database of every email address and name from thirty years of Usenet posts can be very beneficial. Downloading every message can be overkill. This entire data set is over a terabyte in size. Instead of trying to download everything, I only want specific portions of the data. The Giganews collection includes two files for each archive. The first is the "mbox" file which includes the full messages along with user information. These are very large and could take months to download. The second is a "csv" file which only includes the date, message ID, name, email address, newsgroup, and subject of each post. This is a much more manageable amount of data which includes the main information desired (name and email address). We will only download the minimal information needed for our purposes.

First, we must create a text file which includes every archive within each collection. The following commands navigate to your Desktop and create text files for the Giganews and Usenet Historical archive.org data sets.

```
cd ~/Desktop
ia search 'collection:giganews' -i > giganews1.txt
ia search 'collection:usenethistorical -i > usenethistorical1.txt
```

Let's dissect the Internet Archive commands. "ia" is the application, "search" identifies the type of query, "collection:giganews" identifies the target data on archive.org, "-i" instructs the application to create an item list, and " > giganews1.txt" provides the desired output. These text files on your Desktop contain the names of all the archives within the collections. The following is an excerpt.

usenet-alt.2600
usenet-alt.2600a
usenet-alt.2600crackz

We can now instruct Internet Archive to begin downloading the necessary files. The following command downloads only the "csv" files from the Giganews collection. It can take several hours if you have a slow internet connection. If you do not have sufficient space within your VM, consider saving these to an external drive as previously instructed.

```
ia download --itemlist giganews1.txt --glob="*.csv.gz"
```

You should now have thousands of folders, each containing multiple compressed CSV files. This is not very useful or clean, so let's extract and combine all the valuable data. The following command will decompress all the files and leave only the actual CSV documents. It should be executed from whichever directory contains all of the downloaded folders. In my demonstration, it is in the Desktop.

```
gunzip -r .
```

"gunzip" is the command to extract the data from the compressed files (use "unzip" if your macOS machine does not recognize this command), "-r" conducts the command recursively through any sub-folders, and " ." continues the action through every file. Below is a modified excerpt from one of the files. It identifies the date of the post (12/04/2003), name of the author (John Smith), email address associated with the account (John-smith@smh.com), specific newsgroup used (microsoft.windowsxp), and the subject of the post (Help me!).

#date   from   newsgroups   Subject   20031204   John Smith <John-smith@smh.com> microsoft.windowsxp   Help Me!

We still have thousands of files, which is not ideal. The following command will combine every CSV file into a single text file titled Giganews2.txt. Furthermore, it will only extract the columns of data most valuable to us, as explained afterward.

```
find . -type f -name \*.csv -print0 | xargs -0 cut -f1,3,4,5 > Giganews2.txt
```

Let's break down each portion of this command, as it can be quite useful toward other data sets.

find	This is the command to "find" data to manipulate.
.	This instructs the command to find all files.
-type f	This searches for a regular file type.
-name *.csv	This filters to only find a specific file extension (csv).
-print0	This directs output to a file instead of the screen.
|	This is a "pipe" character which separates commands for instruction.
xargs -0	This builds our next command from the previous data as input.
cut -f1,3,4,5	This extracts only the data from columns 1, 3, 4, and 5 from each CSV.
>	This instructs the command to send the data to another file.
Giganews2.txt	This identifies the output file name.

The final result should be a very large file which contains all of the valuable content from within every downloaded file. In a moment, we will use this data to research our targets. The Usenet Historical collection is stored in a different format, so these instructions will need to be modified. The following steps will extract the beneficial data from that collection, and should appear similar to the previous actions. First, we must download the entire archive with the following command.

```
ia download --itemlist usenethistorical1.txt --glob="*.zip"
```

Next, we must extract the "mbox" files from their compressed containers with the following.

```
find . -name "*.zip" -exec unzip {} \;
```

Finally, we must extract the "From:" line from each file with the following command.

```
rg -aFiN "From: " > UsenetHistorical2.txt
```

This leaves us with a single large file titled UsenetHistorical2.txt. Below are a few lines.

```
alt.2600.mbox:From: "Bill Smith" <momop@mvc.biglobe.ne.jp>
alt.2600.mbox:From: "yosinaga jackson" <purizou@geocities.co.jp>
alt.2600.mbox:From: "yosinaga jackson" <purizou@geocities.co.jp>
```

We do not have as many details within this data set as we did with the Giganews option. However, possessing the names, email addresses, and newsgroups provides a lot of value. Both the Giganews2.txt and UsenetHistorical2.txt files possess many duplicate entries wasting valuable space. You might consider the following command which combines both files into one file while removing all duplicate lines.

```
sort -u -f Giganews2.txt UsenetHistorical2.txt > UsenetFinal.txt
```

We now possess a single file, quite large in size, which possesses the names, email addresses, and interests of most users of the Usenet system over a thirty-year period. Now, let's discuss ways this can be used during investigations. Assume you are researching a target with my last name. When using Ripgrep, your command is as follows.

```
rg -aFiN bazzell UsenetFinal.txt
```

The result includes the following partial data.

```
microsoft.public.pocketpc,Steven Bazzell steveill@yahoo.com
sci.bio.microbiology,cbcWiW@UJOMHEH.EDU.TW Wayne A. Bazzell,M.P.S.E
sci.crypt,cbcWiW@UJOMHEH.EDU.TW Wayne A. Bazzell,M.P.S.E
sci.crypt,General Darcy J. Bazzell corporation@incidentally.mi.us
```

The first line identifies Steven Bazzell in the Usenet group of microsoft.public.pocketpc while using an email address of steveill@yahoo.com. You could search by names, email addresses, partial email addresses, domains, etc. I have successfully used my own Usenet archive in the following scenarios.

- When searching a unique target name, I have uncovered old email addresses which led me to otherwise unknown social network profiles.
- When searching an email address, I have identified various interests of the target, determined by the newgroups to which he or she has posted.
- When searching an email address, it serves as a great way to verify a valid account and establishes a minimum date of creation.
- When searching a domain, I often identify numerous email addresses used by the owner.
- When conducting background checks on targets over the age of 40, I often identify email addresses connected to questionable interests. While investigating a potential police officer, I located evidence he had previously posted images to a child pornography newsgroup. This was confirmed during the interview.

These collections possess over 43 million unique email addresses. You may be questioning the justification of the time it would take to create your own archive. While I encourage you to replicate the steps here as an educational opportunity, I also respect the difficulty involved. Therefore, I have made my own Usenet file available for download at the following URL.

https://mega.nz/file/mSJGGDYI#oNIeyaG2oIHcHQFfGeFuq3zxUp_cCgARVf6bQNqp9ls

The file contains only the name, email address, and newsgroup fields from both collections in order to keep the size minimal. I have removed all duplicates and cleaned the file formatting to exclude any unessential data. It is 12 GB compressed to 3 GB. I hope you find it to be useful.

We have only discussed a few databases stored within archive.org. I promise you there are many others containing sensitive details which would help greatly within your investigations. Conducting searches for any specific breached databases displayed on notification websites such as haveibeenpwned.com/PwnedWebsites should reveal interesting results.

Open Databases

The next time you hear about a "misconfigured server" which exposed millions of customer details, this is also likely a data leak. Our best tool to find this data is Shodan (shodan.io), and you will need to be logged in to a free or paid account to conduct these queries. I will focus only on open Elasticsearch databases for now, which are extremely easy to access. Our Shodan search is as follows.

product:elastic port:9200 [target data]

As a demonstration, I want to search for open Elasticsearch databases which contain an index titled "Customer". Think of an index as the title of a table or section of the database. The following search on Shodan produces over 200 results including an index titled "customer".

product:elastic port:9200 customer

The first result during writing was an open database with 401 GB of data. I have redacted the IP address and modified each address throughout this example. I will use a fictitious address of 34.80.1.1 throughout the entire demonstration. The following figure displays this result. Clicking the red square with arrow next to the redacted IP address connects to the database within your browser in a new tab. The second figure displays this result. This confirms that the database is online and open.

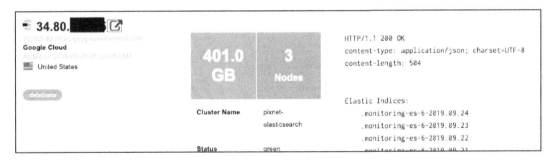

Next, we want to obtain a list of all indexes within this database. These titles are often indicative of the content. The following URL queries this data based on a target IP address of 34.80.1.1. The result can be seen in the following figure.

http://34.80.1.1:9200/_cat/indices?v

We now know there are several indexes which can be viewed. The first is titled "customer", but only contains a small amount of data (68 kb). Near the middle, we see an index titled "memberdisplayname20190903" which contains 124 MB of data including customer usernames. Some of these indexes contain email addresses and other sensitive data. Let's focus on the index titled "bank". We can view the content with the following URL.

http://34.80.1.1:9200/bank/_search?size=100

This combines the IP address (34.80.1.1), necessary port (9200), name of the index (bank), and instructions to display the first 100 records (/_search?size=100). If we wanted to view the maximum number of entries visible within the browser, we would query 10,000 records with the following URL.

http://34.80.1.1:9200/bank/_search?size=10000

The second figure displays actual redacted results from this query. It identifies the first name, last name, email address, gender, city, state, bank account number, and balance associated with a customer. The rest of the index contains the same information for additional customers.

health	status	index	uuid	pri	rep	docs.count	docs.deleted	store.size	pri.store.size
green	open	customer	xYPN7VCPQHuRdEfP5vEkvg	5	1	10	0	68.3kb	34.1kb
green	open	kkday	3kWWvvGSTOa1AXMVOJa-eg	5	1	3514	115	22.3mb	11.1mb
green	open	minhash2	7aEhgxDDQ-2nu-Vpjpsibg	5	1	135617	2855	1.1gb	593.3mb
green	open	.monitoring-kibana-6-2019.09.18	6aE7CmBBQV2Iqk-8PeVV9A	1	1	74164	0	21.5mb	10.7mb
green	open	memberdisplayname20190903	OARMG91LSP-rSOA49Pcc0g	1	1	220775	4567	124.6mb	62.3mb
green	open	.monitoring-kibana-6-2019.09.19	Yi7_DE_zTzaY7UCbIwVlWA	1	1	77753	0	22mb	10.9mb
green	open	streamtopic	KRzRxJ8eRd2Cpb5EG-tHXA	5	1	107379	771	211.4mb	105.7mb
green	open	articles20190114	5ZUb1CdWQE6jo6JQK2J7sA	10	1	10531578	3885123	45.6gb	22.8gb
green	open	.monitoring-kibana-6-2019.09.20	taiMN1rvT3qMNTULnpFvEw	1	1	77579	0	21.5mb	10.8mb
green	open	articles20190130	4ZCi8yaxQvWN3hj2TOOECQ	10	1	0	0	5kb	2.5kb
green	open	member20181029	_8fDS93vSm-6hEECcEaLuA	5	1	7293911	20	94.1gb	47gb
green	open	.monitoring-es-6-2019.09.19	nOMGgBlbQrSE79xru9KlOw	1	1	346888	3384	461.6mb	231.9mb
green	open	articles20181224	7iO-SW40TPiORKtyj3qkJA	10	1	23422119	141719	114.1gb	57.3gb
green	open	minhash5	t6B40-XeRcq3Vx0NPEVAeA	5	1	223639	0	1.5gb	778.3mb
green	open	test	Q9fEJj9nRs6H4oXNvekTmg	10	1	674654	220802	29.9gb	15gb
green	open	.monitoring-es-6-2019.09.20	1j4OGJUDSJuG7EfSuQp6qA	1	1	354940	3666	478.9mb	239.6mb
green	open	.monitoring-es-6-2019.09.23	KgZ_kQUEThG5Olai27Yc9Q	1	1	346850	3102	487.5mb	245.2mb
green	open	minhash4	G9ablmkIQRCjyPx32-fVIA	5	1	223639	3	1.5gb	811.5mb
green	open	articles20181214	vbVscTkfTiCI64mlmHj44w	10	1	22582851	0	103.2gb	51.3gb
green	open	.kibana	6zZoT6nwTieIp3OlmTCUTw	1	1	4	0	44.8kb	22.4kb
green	open	.monitoring-es-6-2019.09.18	-oWrFwD-RBixBG-m4V2Osw	1	1	347378	3384	453.3mb	225.3mb
green	open	minhash3	yWXB2EJXS4itId5GhT-BLA	5	1	223639	2304	1.6gb	834.9mb
green	open	.monitoring-es-6-2019.09.22	Qg7IefQUSf65DUG1bOcNQA	1	1	347452	2820	474.2mb	236.8mb
green	open	rainytest	Dlgkerx_Q0iO134yDeDePw	10	1	36	6	1.4mb	745.9kb
green	open	.monitoring-es-6-2019.09.24	Z9FjEfovRHe3sBCisb4Zog	1	1	224408	2820	347.4mb	185.2mb
green	open	.monitoring-es-6-2019.09.21	IqK2eVxwSHyX_mIzQLpkfg	1	1	346849	2365	472.5mb	235.6mb
green	open	.monitoring-kibana-6-2019.09.22	PzU8OoxKQJuMBurDPHmbmQ	1	1	77756	0	20.5mb	10.2mb
green	open	.monitoring-kibana-6-2019.09.24	o8yEB59SRZm7GbQjfCpDiw	1	1	50202	0	17.2mb	6.3mb

```
▼ 2:
    _index:          "bank"
    _type:           "_doc"
    _id:             "99"
    _score:          1
  ▼ _source:
      account_number:  99
      balance:         47159
      firstname:       ███████
      lastname:        "Heath"
      age:             39
      gender:          "F"
      address:         "██████ Place"
      employer:        "Zappix"
      email:           "████heath@zappix.com"
      city:            "Shaft"
      state:           "ND"
```

Open Databases Issues

There are many complications with acquisition of open Elasticsearch data. The first is the record limitation. Displaying results within a URL limits the results to 10,000 records. Modifying the URL as described previously presents all data possible within the browser. Saving this page stores all of the content for future queries. However, many of the data sets I find contain millions of records. A Python script which parses through all results and stores every record is most appropriate, and is explained in a moment.

Next are the legal considerations. Technically, this data is publicly available, open to anyone in the world. However, some believe the act of manipulating URLs in order to access content stored within a database exceeds the definition of OSINT. I do not agree, but you might. I believe most of this data should have been secured, and we should not be able to easily collect it. The same could be said for FTP servers, paste sites, online documents, and cloud-hosted files. I believe accessing open databases becomes a legal grey area once you decide to use the data. If you are collecting this content in order to sell it, extort the original owner, or publish it in any way, you are crossing the line and committing a crime. I remind you that the Computer Fraud and Abuse Act (CFAA) is extremely vague and can make most online activity illegal in the eyes of an aggressive prosecutor. Become familiar with the data access laws in your area and confirm that these techniques do not violate any laws or internal policies.

My final reminder and warning is that I am not an attorney. I am not advising that you conduct any of these methods on behalf of your own investigations. I am simply presenting techniques which have proven to be extremely valuable to many investigators. If you believe that accessing an open (public) Elasticsearch database is legal in your area, and does not violate any internal policies, it is time to parse and download all content.

Elasticsearch Crawler (github.com/AmIJesse/Elasticsearch-Crawler)

In early 2019, I was made aware of an open Elasticsearch database which exposed sensitive data associated with 57 million people. In most cases, these records contained personal information such as first name, last name, email address, home address, state, postal code, phone number, and IP address. These types of records are extremely helpful to me as an investigator. Connecting personal email addresses with real people is often the best lead of all online research. I had found the database on Shodan using the methods discussed here. Specifically, I searched for an index titled "Leads" and sifted through any results of substantial size. Once I had located the data, I was desperate to download the entire archive. With a browser limit of 10,000, I knew I would need the help of a Python script.

I reached out to my friend and colleague Jesse and explained my scenario. Within a few moments, he sent me a small Python script. This file is now a staple in my data leaks arsenal of tools. He has agreed to share it publicly, please use it responsibly. It can be installed within Linux with the following commands.

```
cd ~/Downloads/Programs
git clone https://github.com/AmIJesse/Elasticsearch-Crawler.git
cd Elasticsearch-Crawler
pip install nested-lookup
pip install release
```

You are now ready to download an entire Elasticsearch open database and specify which fields should be acquired. Note that you must open Terminal and navigate to your script in order to launch this utility. The following commands from within Terminal will launch the script.

```
cd ~/Downloads/Programs/Elasticsearch-Crawler
python crawl.py
```

This will present several user prompts to enter the target IP address, index name, port number, and fields to obtain. Let's walk through a real demonstration in order to understand the application.

I logged in to a free Shodan account and searched "product:elastic port:9200 leads" without the quotes. One hit was an Elasticsearch server in India. This database appeared to contain test data, so I will not redact any of the results. The IP address was 111.93.162.238 and the database was approximately 1 GB in size. Clicking the red square within the result on Shodan opened a new tab to the following address.

http://111.93.162.238:9200/

The brief response confirmed that the server was online. The URL discloses the IP address (111.93.162.238) and port (9200). This is the default port and is almost always the same. Now that I had the IP address, I launched a new browser tab and navigated to the following address.

http://111.93.162.238:9200/_cat/indices?v

This connected to the IP address (111.93.162.238) and port (9200), and then conducted a query to display all public indexes (/_cat/indices?v). The result included the following.

index	store.size
imobilestore	1.3mb
testcsv	190.7 kb
easyphix	1.8mb
index_test	7.2 kb
crazyparts	503.5 kb
valueparts	2.3mb
mobilemart	1.7mb
leads	280.8 kb

I usually look at both the names and the sizes. If I see an index titled "Customers", I know it usually contains people's information. If it is only 1 kb in size, I know it is too small to be of any use. When I see any index with multiple gigabytes of data, my curiosity kicks in and I want to see the contents. For this demonstration, let's focus on the index of our original search of "leads". I navigated to the following URL.

http://111.93.162.238:9200/leads/_search?size=100

This connects to the target IP address (111.93.162.238) and port (9200), loads the desired index (leads) and displays the first 100 results (/_search?size=100). This is usually sufficient to see enough target content, but this can be raised to 1000 or 10000 if desired. Below is a record.

```
"_index": "leads","_type": "leads",
"_id": "PXIhqmUBcHz5ZA2uOAe7",
"_source": {"id": "86",
"email": "test80@agencyinnovations.com",
"first_name": "test80","last_name": "test80",
"phone": "32569874",
"ip": "0.0.0.0",
"orgname": "Sales Arena",
"isDeleted": false,
"created_at": "2018-09-05 19:57:08",
"updated_at": "2018-09-05 19:57:08",
```

This is obviously test data, but assume it was a record containing a real person's name, email address, and phone number. Also assume there were over a million records within this index, which is quite common. We could save this page, but would be forced to save the undesired fields such as "tags" and "_source". Also, the data would be in a difficult format to search. This is where our new Python script is helpful. You have already launched the crawl.py script, and should have been presented with a prompt for the IP address of the target. The following displays each entry I submitted for this demonstration.

IP address: 111.93.162.238
Index name: leads
Port (Default is 9200): 9200
Field values to obtain (submit an empty line when finished):
Value: email
Value: first_name
Value: last_name
Value: phone
Value:

After being prompted for the IP address (111.93.162.238), it asked me for the target index name (leads) and port number (9200). It then prompted me to enter the first field I wanted to acquire (email). Since I entered a field, it then prompted for the next field (first_name). The tool will continue to ask for field names for as long as you provide them. Notice there is an empty line in the last "Value". This empty result tells the script you are finished, and it begins collecting the data. When finished, a text file will be saved in the same directory as your script. In this example, it was at ~/Downloads/Programs/Elasticsearch-Crawler/111.93.162.238-leads.txt. The title of the file was automatically created to reflect the IP address and name of the index. The following are the first three lines of this text file.

test65@agencyinnovations.com,test65,test65,987485746
test22@agencyinnovations.com,test22,test22,124958616
test69@agencyinnovations.com,test69,test69,2145968

If this were real data, you would see millions of people's email addresses, names, and telephone numbers. There are likely hundreds of legitimate databases on Shodan right now, just waiting to be found. The next time you see a news article about a security researcher who found an exposed database containing millions of sensitive records, it is very likely that Shodan and a similar script was used. If your downloaded file contains random text, you have likely encountered a patched version of Elasticsearch. At the time of this writing, Elasticsearch databases version 6.4.0 and newer were blocking the script. Anything older worked fine.

I predict we will see fewer open databases in the future. While we still hear about sensitive leaks every week, word is spreading and companies are locking down their data. This is a good thing for all of us. Until then, I will continue to search.

The JSON Dilemma

If you are lucky, you will always find a nicely organized CSV file with your new data, ready for "cutting" and storing. However, that is not always the case. Many times, you will encounter JSON data. At first, it may seem impossible to clean and minimize. The following is a partial example of JSON data extracted from a large file.

```
"status": 200,
"likelihood": 6,
"data": {
  "id": "qEnOZ5Oh0poWnQ1luFBfVw_0000",
  "full_name": "sean thorne",
  "first_name": "sean",
```

```
    "middle_initial": "f",
    "middle_name": "fong",
    "last_initial": "t",
    "last_name": "thorne",
    "gender": "male",
    "birth_year": 1990,
    "birth_date": null,
    "linkedin_url": "linkedin.com/in/seanthorne",
    "linkedin_username": "seanthorne",
    "linkedin_id": "145991517",
    "facebook_url": "facebook.com/deseanthorne",
    "facebook_username": "deseanthorne",
    "facebook_id": "1089351304",
    "twitter_url": "twitter.com/seanthorne5",
    "twitter_username": "seanthorne5",
    "work_email": "sean@peopledatalabs.com",
    "personal_emails": [],
    "mobile_phone": "+14155688415",
```

The full portion for this single entry would have filled four pages in this book. Now imagine that the data set included 100 million entries. That would be 400 million pages if you wanted to print the data. If you were to query this selected data with Ripgrep, it would either only present the line where something was found (without any other data), or the entire entry (several pages of compacted text). If I searched "sean@peopledatalabs.com" via Ripgrep, the result might be "work_email": "sean@peopledatalabs.com" if the data was separated with line breaks. We would not receive all of the other associated content. You could use a lot of sed commands to try and move each piece of data into one line for queries, but that would be time consuming and unnecessary.

When I encounter JSON data, I rely on **jq** (stedolan.github.io/jq/). Since we previously installed jq, we are now ready to launch it within Terminal (or Command Prompt). Assume we have a large file of JSON data, which contains the previous file structure, titled people.json. The following command would begin our extraction.

```
jq --raw-output
'"\(.data.first_name),\(.data.last_name),\(.data.gender),\(.data.birth_
year),\(.data.birth_date),\(.data.linkedin_username),\(.data.facebook_i
d),\(.data.twitter_username),\(
.data.work_email),\(.data.mobile_phone)"' people.json > people.txt
```

Let's dissect this:

jq	This command launches jq.
--raw-output	This outputs pure text without formatting.
""	This begins our string.
\(.data.first_name),	This extracts the first name field.
\(.data.last_name),	This extracts the last name field.
\(.data.gender),	This extracts the gender field.
\(.data.birth_year),	This extracts the birth year field.
\(.data.birth_date),	This extracts the birth date field.
\(.data.linkedin_username),	This extracts the linkedin username field.
\(.data.facebook_id),	This extracts the facebook field.
\(.data.twitter_username),	This extracts the twitter field.
\(.data.work_email),	This extracts the work email field.
\(.data.mobile_phone)	This extracts the phone field (no trailing comma).
""	This ends our string.

people.json	This identifies the input file.
>	This notifies of an output request.
people.txt	This identifies the new output file.

The result appears below.

```
sean,thorne,male,1990,null,seanthorne,1089351304,seanthorne5,sean@peopl
edatalabs.com,+14155688415
```

If you had a JSON file with 100 million entries, you might have several billion lines of unsearchable data. You would now have a single text file with the 100 million total entry lines, only containing your desired content. Notice in my command that I have "data" preceding each field request (\(.data.gender)). That is because those fields are under a section titled "data" within my JSON example on the previous page. If there was a section called "data" which contained a section called "people" which then contained a field called "gender", that field request would appear as follows.

```
\(.data.people.gender),
```

An entire chapter could be devoted to jq and its usage. If you find this tool valuable, I encourage you to visit the Github page for the project. It includes complete usage and tutorials. Now, let's test jq with some real data. The following pages access data leaks or previously public information.

People Data Labs Scrape (PDL)

In 2019, a security researcher claimed to have scraped an open database of over 1.2 billion PDL records including names, locations, and social network content. This data set is still floating around, and it is valuable. I know of someone who joined a channel called "Data stream" on Telegram and searched "people data labs". This person received a result of a torrent file called "PeopleDataLabs_416M.json.7z.torrent". They downloaded this file and opened it via Transmission, which downloaded an 11 GB compressed file. Extracting the file resulted in a new folder with a single file titled PeopleDataLabs_416M.json which contained 67 GB of data. Someone else had already parsed the JSON data to a single line for each entry, which appeared similar to the following.

{"a":"san francisco, california, united states","t":["14155688000"],"e":["sthorne@xxregon.edu","sean@peopledatalabs.com","sean@txxxentiq.co"],"liid":"**seanthorne**","linkedin":"https://www.linkedin.com/in/**seanthorne**","n":"sean thorne"}

This format could be sufficient for most readers, and no cleaning would be required. Since I try to eliminate any unnecessary data, I would consider the following commands, which will get rid of the brackets, quotes, and category identifiers.

```
sed -i "s/[\{]//gI" PeopleDataLabs_416M.json
sed -i "s/[\}]//gI" PeopleDataLabs_416M.json
sed -i "s/[\[]//gI" PeopleDataLabs_416M.json
sed -i "s/[\]]//gI" PeopleDataLabs_416M.json
sed -i "s/\"//gI" PeopleDataLabs_416M.json
sed -i "s/a\://gI" PeopleDataLabs_416M.json
sed -i "s/t\://gI" PeopleDataLabs_416M.json
sed -i "s/e\://gI" PeopleDataLabs_416M.json
sed -i "s/liid\://gI" PeopleDataLabs_416M.json
sed -i "s/linkedin\://gI" PeopleDataLabs_416M.json
sed -i "s/n\://gI" PeopleDataLabs_416M.json
```

Each command will take some time due to the size of the file. Each process on my MacBook Pro required ten minutes to complete. Notice the first four commands include brackets ([]) around the characters I want to remove ({}) and ([]). This is required with some special characters, especially any type of opening or closing bracket. I hope you see by now that many of these demonstrations are not necessarily to help you collect and clean data leaks, but more to teach you the commands which will be most helpful to overcome obstacles in your own data collection journey.

The result should be a 50 GB text file. The following Ripgrep command would search my last name through the data.

```
rg -aFiN bazzell PeopleDataLabs_416M.json
```

LinkedIn 2021 Scrape

In 2021, an unknown group released a huge data set which contained over 400 million user profiles from LinkedIn. Profiles are public, so the headline did not seem interesting at first. However, this data included over 140 million email addresses and numerous cellular numbers associated with the profiles. That caught my attention. It is suspected that the data was acquired by querying email addresses and cellular numbers from previous leaks through the official LinkedIn API in order to identify the associated profiles. Additional public data was then used to connect Facebook and Twitter accounts. The result was 1.4 TB of JSON files which contained the personal email addresses and cellular numbers of many LinkedIn users. I wanted it, but in a better format.

Currently, there is an active Torrent containing the entire data, which consists of 700 compressed files, each approximately 300 MB in size and titled similar to "part-00055.gz", for a total of approximately 200 GB. Once extracted, the data is 1.4 TB, and the files are titled similar to "part-00055" with no file extension. Searching "400M LinkedIn Torrent" on Google should begin your hunt, or searching the previous file name might lead you to a torrent. There is also a copy available on "NitroFlare", but the free download tier can be quite slow. Searching "Linkedin Scrapped Data 2021" should find it. I downloaded the Torrent in an afternoon. I then decompressed all the files.

Each file contains JSON entries which possess a lot of redundant data I do not want in my final copy, similar to the previous example. However, I do want the fields titled first_name, middle_name, last_name, gender, birth_date, linkedin_username, facebook_username, twitter_username, work_email, mobile_phone, location_name, phone_numbers, and emails. I placed all of the "part" files in my Downloads folder and executed the following from that path.

```
jq --raw-output '"\(.first_name),\(.middle_name),\(.last_name),
\(.gender),\(.birth_date),\(.linkedin_username),\(.facebook_username),\
(.twitter_username),\(.work_email),\(.mobile_phone),\(.location_name),\
(.phone_numbers),\(.emails)"' part* > LinkedIn.txt
```

This created a single file titled LinkedIn.txt, which only contained my desired data. It was 49.68 GB in size and possessed 400,101,052 entries. It contained a lot of entries containing "null" which offered no value, so I removed them with the following.

```
sed -i "s/null\,//gI" LinkedIn.txt
```

The final result was a single 37.46 GB file. I can query this data within a few seconds and only see valuable information. That is a big difference from querying the original 1.4 TB data, which took up to an hour per query and displayed 90% useless data. The following is a slightly modified and redacted (xxx) entry from the new file. It displays my target's first name, middle initial, last name, gender, date of birth, LinkedIn username, Facebook username, Twitter username, location, telephone number, and email address.

```
chelsea, a, jansen, female, 1982-0x-xx, chelsea-jansen-685axxx,
chelsea.
jansen.xxx, chelseaxxx, hartland, connecticut, +18608191xxx,
cjansen@xxx.org
```

I can now associate the name, email address, cellular number, Twitter account, Facebook account, or date of birth with any of the other details. I can query a name and often identify the email address behind it. I can query a Facebook username and possibly identify the true person or date of birth. When I find a target on LinkedIn, I can query the unique portion of the URL (`chelsea-jansen-685axxx`) and see all information from this leak, including a valid email address. While this content does not possess all data within every field, it has been quite beneficial to my investigations. Consider the following examples.

- I searched the LinkedIn profile "seitzjustin" through the data and received the user's full name, Twitter handle, location, and a new email address from a custom domain which I did not previously possess. Historical records of this domain identified a physical address and telephone number.
- While stranded after a canceled flight, I queried the LinkedIn username of the airline's CEO and identified a personal Gmail account and cellular number. I made direct contact requesting a solution.
- A client was receiving harassing messages via Twitter. The Twitter handle of the suspect was associated with a LinkedIn profile and a 33Mail email address. The subdomain of the email address was only assigned to this subject, and a query through additional breach data revealed online profiles associated with the true name.

I hope you can see the power of this type of data. Cleaning the set from 1.4 TB to 37 GB took some time and effort, but I now have a small file for my queries, which completes in less than 30 seconds from an external SSD. I placed this file in the "People" folder of my external drive, which is explained later.

IntelligenceX Scrape

In 2021, a disgruntled IntelX customer "scraped their scrapes". Today, the 80,000 copied documents, which were originally scraped from Pastebin before they terminated their free API, have been merged into one folder possessing sensitive data associated with 46 million email addresses. Many people have successfully downloaded the 1.6 GB compressed file titled "intelx_scraped, pass pompompurin.7z" from the popular Telegram channel called "LEAKS AGGREGATOR". Those who did reported that the file could be decompressed with a password of "pompompurin", but the compression program Keka was required for macOS users. The result was over 7 GB of text files. Let's make them easier to use. Navigate to the folder which stores the 87,813 files and conduct the following.

```
cat * > _IntelX.txt
```

I set you up for failure here. There are too many files for the Cat command. Instead, we must create a command which "finds" all of the files first, and then allows Cat to do its job.

```
find . -name '*' -exec cat {} \; > ~/Downloads/IntelX.txt
```

I instructed my machine to find every file in the directory (*), and then execute (exec) the Cat command, but save the result to a different folder (~/Downloads/IntelX.txt). The resulting file is the same size as the original files, but easier to work with. However, it is a mess of Pastebin scrapes which have no email addresses. I only want lines which include an email address, and no lines which do not include an email address. Therefore, the following command extracts any line which includes "@" and saves it to a new file.

```
cd ~/Downloads
awk '/@/' IntelX.txt > IntelX2.txt
```

The result is a 4.27 GB file. It still includes a lot of junk, but we can now sort for unique entries to remove any duplicates with the following.

```
LC_ALL=C sort -u -b -i -f -S 80% --parallel=8 IntelX2.txt > IntelX3.txt
```

This brought us down to 2.5 GB, which is manageable. Searching my last name with Ripgrep revealed hundreds of email addresses and credentials, as seen below (redacted).

```
sbazzell@sudde████████████12
svbazzell@aol.█████████████
tbazzell@atcdri██████████psqI
```

Telephone Number Leaks

Some of the leaks previously mentioned include telephone number details, but that type of content was not the main attribute of the data. On the contrary, there are several large leaks which focus exclusively on telephone numbers, and I find these very valuable. In fact, I query target telephone numbers almost as much as I search for email addresses. Many people possess numerous "burner" numbers which are not registered to them, and do not return any results within online searches. However, many of these people will rely on those numbers throughout various social networks and websites, causing them to appear within various leaks, breaches, and logs, which often identify the user. Let's walk through a few examples together.

There are dozens of large telephone number data sets, most of which include "cell" and "phone" within the file names. I searched "USA cell" within Telegram, and immediately received several results. The two visible in the following images appeared because I had previously joined the "LEAKS AGGREGATOR" and "Data stream" channels.

The 2.6 GB compressed file for the 183M USA Cell database was password protected. Downloading the image directly above the download link identified the password (t.me/HadesBreaches), which produced an 11.5 GB CSV file. The 3.1 GB USA Cell files produced a 19.82 GB CSV file. After closer examination, these files contained identical data, but the first option (183M USA CELL) did not contain quotation marks or other unnecessary characters. Therefore, I deleted the second set of data. A random (modified) entry appeared as follows.

MIKE,COLE,105 VALLEY DR,HOUSTON,TX,77042,7135910000,
MIKE.COLE@GMAIL.COM,AT&T MOBILITY,MALE

In this scenario, I now possess the names, physical addresses, and email addresses associated with 183 million cellular numbers in America. As a further value, I can see the service provider for each number. I can use Ripgrep to query through the data.

Facebook Telephone Number Leaks

In 2021, someone published the personal data of 533 million Facebook users, which included cellular telephone numbers associated with most of the accounts. The exposed data included account information from 106 countries, including over 32 million records on users in the US and 11 million on users in the UK. Most records included telephone numbers, Facebook IDs, full names, locations, and birthdates. As you may have guessed, the data is now widely available online. A quick search within the "Open Data" channel for "facebook dataset" on telegram revealed the files for each country, as seen in the following partial image.

Each country possessed its own file, and the "USA.7z" file was 669 MB compressed, which expanded to eight new text files totaling 3.28 GB. I combined all files into one with the following command.

```
cat USA* > Facebook-US.txt
```

A typical entry appeared as follows.

17244540000:9304000:Sara:Rose:female:Pittsburgh, Pennsylvania:Greensburg, ::::::

This displays the cellular telephone number, Facebook user ID, name, gender, and location of every victim. I did not see much value in cleaning this data further , so I left it as-is. Adding the Facebook ID to a URL navigates directly to each user. In this fake example, the page at https://facebook.com/9304000 opens the user's profile. I combined all country sets into one large file (82 GB) with the following command.

```
find . -name '*.txt' -exec cat > ~/Downloads/FB.txt {} \;
```

I am always skeptical of this type of data, so I conducted a quick test. I copied the telephone number in a random entry, such as the previous example, and searched the number within a reverse caller ID service (as explained in *OSINT Techniques, 10th Edition*). The result follows, which provided high confidence in the data.

"caller_name": "SARA ROSE",

Instagram Telephone Number Leaks

The previous Facebook leak was due to a poorly secured server. At one time, people could execute bulk queries of telephone numbers against the Facebook Application Programming Interface (API) and receive the profile IDs. Most of these holes have been plugged, but much data still flows freely. I have seen many Instagram telephone leaks which were likely obtained through the same technique. During this writing, I found two compressed files within the LEAKS AGGREGATOR Telegram channel.

The 86 MB file decompressed into five files totaling 288 MB containing 4,939,354 entries. The following is a modified example.

nast@charter.net,nicholas,ast,2013374000,@nast

This produces data which can be queried by email address, telephone number, or Instagram username. The "5 Million" file contained identical data with different file names. This is very common as people republish the data in order to appear as if they possess something special. Attempting to identify redundant data before you add it to your collection is important to reduce query times.

Searching "Instagram" or "IG" within your subscribed Telegram channels can produce valuable data for download. This is why it is so important to join as many data-related channels as possible. This widens the net. You will often identify breaches which have nothing to do with Instagram, yet still possess Instagram user data. During this writing, I received several search results of breached SQL files which contained entries for Instagram profile IDs as part of their data collection about their customers. SQL files are discussed later in the breaches chapter.

Telemetry (telemetryapp.io)

This service requires an account before searching, but allows five free queries per day. You can enter any term and identify Telegram rooms which contain your information. This will never be complete, but it may locate information about your target which could not be found otherwise.

Whois Information: Previously, I presented a small text file which possessed Whois information to be used to test your data manipulation skills. Whois data can display the historical registrations of domains in order to identify the owners, even if they currently use domain registration protection strategies. The easiest way to accumulate your own Whois data is through Telegram. As long as you are subscribed to the LEAKS AGGEGATOR channel, searching "whois" should display several gigabytes of compressed Whois content. If you have a BreachForums account, entire Whois databases are plentiful, but you must have credits to access them (never pay for credits). Some readers have located a thread there which only requires you to leave a comment in order to access the "Intelligence X (intelx.io) Leaked Data", which contains the entire 280GB collection of 62 million registration records. Others report that item "e6LEmohVwywg0z" on biteblob.com offers the data.

Summary

We have only begun the journey into leaked data. I have personally obtained, cleaned, stored, and queried tens of thousands of valuable data leaks as part of my online investigations. At least once a week, I identify my target's home address through leaked data after all online efforts have been exhausted. I have had countless suspects remove all of their details from people search websites in order to disappear, but they can never edit my own data collection. Aside from the data presented here, there are countless copies of other data sets floating around. It is now up to you to locate and clean the data. Later, we will use a script to help us quickly query all of the data leaks you locate.

CHAPTER FOURTY-ONE
DATA BREACHES

Now that you understand the basics of searching and modifying data, we should discuss the true value of this technique. Until now, we have only experimented with publicly-available data. The real power lies within the stolen databases that are now publicly available which I am about to discuss. There are usually two types of people that download these databases. The first are amateur criminals that use the data to illegally obtain account access to victims' accounts by supplying the usernames and passwords from one service into another service. As an example, if a criminal learns your username and password that you used on LinkedIn, he or she may try that same combination on Twitter. We will never do this, as it is illegal and unethical.

The second group of individuals who download this data are security researchers. Numerous private organizations authorize employees to collect this stolen information and use the data to make their own systems more secure. I personally know of many researchers who download this data, protect it from further distribution, and only use it in an ethical manner. This is the only acceptable use of this data. For those that still believe that we should not access stolen databases released to the public, consider one last argument. Tens of thousands of criminal hackers use this content to "dox" people every day. Doxing is the act of exposing personal information about a victim online. This is a very common tactic used against law enforcement officers when an event such as an officer-involved shooting happens. The government employees' passwords often get leaked on Pastebin or other similar sites. This stolen data is already out there, and it can never be secured. We should embrace the same techniques used against us when researching criminals. Enough warnings. Use your best judgment.

By now you may just want to know where to obtain these databases. The source websites which allow download of this stolen data get shut down often. However, the magic of internet archives can help us regain the data. The next exercise also involves archive.org. Specifically, data from LinkedIn. This version surfaced in 2017 and does not possess any passwords. It contains only LinkedIn user ID numbers and the associated email addresses. While this type of data was included within the original 20 GB LinkedIn breach, it was excluded from the popular password dumps which can be found online today. Since it does not contain passwords, it can be found on the Wayback Machine. At the time of this writing, the direct link to download the entire user ID database could be found at https://archive.org/details/LIUsers.7z.

Decompress this file to your Downloads folder. The text file contains the email addresses and user ID numbers extracted from the full LinkedIn breach. It is nothing more than each email address used to create a specific profile ID number. The following search within Terminal would display the results of a target email address, and the response is directly after the command.

```
rg -aFiN janewilson@microsoft.com linkedin_users.txt
```

1332567, janewilson@microsoft.com

You now know that your target's user ID number is 1332567. This data alone is not very helpful. Let's consider another perspective. Assume you find your target's LinkedIn profile page, and you want to know the email address used to create the account. Right-clicking on the profile allows the option to display the "Source Code" of the profile. Searching the term "member:" within this code presents numerous occurrences of that term. The occurrence toward the end should appear similar to "member:1288635". This tells you that the member ID for your target is 1288635. The following displays the email address associated with that number, with the results immediately below.

```
rg -aFiN 1288635 linkedin_users.txt
```

I have used this technique numerous times over the past several years. During one investigation, I located the LinkedIn profile of my target. I had previously found no email addresses connected to him. By looking at the source code of the LinkedIn profile, I could see his user ID. Searching that user ID within this LinkedIn data provided the personal email address used to create the account. That email address led to old passwords, which led to additional email addresses, as explained in a moment. Obtaining a confirmed personal email address can lead to numerous new investigation techniques. Note that member numbers only exist for accounts prior to 2015.

Credentials

Now that we are dipping our toes into the waters of "stolen" data, we should consider the big breaches. You have likely heard about LinkedIn, Dropbox, Myspace and Adobe being hacked. All of those breaches have been publicly released by various criminal organizations. At the time of this writing, most remaining sites which possessed this huge collection of stolen data had been shut down. However, the data lives on. Numerous "hacking" groups have collected tens of thousands of breached databases, both large and small, and combined them into credential lists. These lists contain only the email addresses and passwords of billions of accounts. They do not identify which breach each credential originated, but the data is extremely valuable for investigators. Before we analyze the content, we must obtain a full copy of the data. This is where things get tricky (again).

My attorney says I cannot HOST links to any of this content, which I understand. She also says that I cannot display any direct links to an identifiable breach, such as LinkedIn or Adobe. This would make me a target for a lawsuit, and seems like great advice. My only option is to "identify public resources which link to data without attribution of a specific originating source". In other words, I can tell you where you may find this "Combo List" content, but it is up to you to take action to obtain it. Let's connect our VPN; understand any employer policies which might prevent the following actions; and tiptoe into the world of stolen credentials.

COMB (Compilation Of Many Breaches)

In 2021, an unknown group of credential thieves created a huge collection of 3.2 billion credentials consisting only of email address and password combinations. This data set was titled "Compilation Of Many Breaches", otherwise known as "COMB". There have been numerous other combo lists released in previous years, such as Anti-Public, Exploit.in, and others. However, this set included a better search structure and ability to conduct queries within seconds. Some people may find that searching for "CompilationOfManyBreaches.7z" within Google might lead you to a copy. Others report that the following queries will display the torrent file for this data.

site:github.com "CompilationOfManyBreaches.7z"
site:github.com "1.4 billion"

At the time of this writing, the single result from this search possessed a torrent file which could be opened with a torrent software application such as Transmission. This program will download the 20 GB file to your computer. Depending on your internet connection, this entire download can take minutes, hours, or days to finish. If possessing user credentials violates your security clearance or organizational polices, do not proceed with this download.

Let's assume you now have a drive with the entire contents from COMB. The result is a 20 GB compressed file which contains all 3.2 billion credentials. The file itself is titled "CompilationOfManyBreaches.7z". If you chose to download this file, it must be decompressed. I prefer a utility such as 7-zip for Linux and Windows, or Keka for Mac. Upon decompression, you might be prompted for a password. A Twitter post located at https://twitter.com/BubbaMustafa/status/1370376039583657985 claims the required archive password is "+w/P3PRqQQoJ6g". Once decompressed, you should see a new folder titled "CompilationOfManyBreaches" which is 106 GB in size.

Assume you possess a folder called COMB within your external SSD which contains the data downloaded during this exercise. This folder should contain the three files and folder labeled "data". Within Terminal, navigate to that "COMB" folder. My Linux command for this was `cd "/media/$USER/DATA/COMB"`. macOS users would use `cd "/Volumes/DATA/COMB"`. In Linux, you could also find the external drive within the Files application, right-click, and choose "Open in Terminal". You should now be within your new data collection folder inside Terminal. We can conduct searches to start evaluating the benefit of this data. Since COMB includes a fast search option, we will start with it. However, we should make sure that our script is executable with the following command (on both macOS and Linux).

```
chmod +x query.sh
```

Execute the following command in Terminal from within the COMB folder.

```
bash ./query.sh michaelbazzell@gmail.com
```

This should result in no hits within a few seconds. Now try the following (notice the period in the email address).

```
bash ./query.sh michael.bazzell@gmail.com
```

The result should appear as follows.

michael.bazzell@gmail.com:password

This identifies a password "password". The first query failed because we did not include the "." within the search parameter. This tool can be fairly unforgiving and requires exact data. The following search provides any email address which begins with "michael.bazzell" with results which follow.

```
bash ./query.sh michael.bazzell
```

michael.bazzell@gmail.com:password
michael.bazzell@us.army.mil:redacted10
michael.bazzelle1970@yahoo.com:redacted201

This search tool is extremely fast. If you know the email address of your target, or at least the first portion of the address, searching through the native COMB query option is best. However, this presents limitations. You cannot use this tool to search a specific domain or password. For that we will once again rely on Ripgrep. The following queries will all assume that you have already opened Terminal and have navigated to the folder where your data is stored. The next search would attempt to identify a specific email address within all the files. Note that results were modified to protect the privacy of the individual. As a reminder, this command applies our parameters and identifies the target data to be searched. The result follows the command.

```
rg -aFiN mikewilson@microsoft.com
```

mikewilson@microsoft.com:bigbucks55

We now know that at some point a password of bigbucks55 was used in conjunction with an online account associated with our target email address. Would this password still work with any online accounts? Possibly, but we will never know. Attempting to log in to an account with this information is a crime. Instead, think about other ways that we could use this data offline. We know our target's work email account, but we may want his personal account. Since many people recycle the same password across multiple accounts, let's conduct a search for the password.

```
rg -aFiN bigbucks55
```
The results include accounts associated with our target, and some that are not. The more unique your target's password, the better quality of associated content you will receive. The following data was presented during my search. Notice the ways that data was displayed based on the search, and how any portion of the results were included. Since we specified our search parameters, we received results regardless of case.

bigbucks551@yahoo.com:towboat@1
bigbucks55@hotmail.co.uk:towboat@1
bigbucks55@hotmail.com:towboat@1
prizeunit@yahoo.com:bigbucks55
mike.wilson5@gmail.com:BigBucks55
mikewilson@microsoft.com:bigbucks55

This tells me that the last two results are very likely my target, since the names are similar and the passwords are almost identical. I can now assume that my target's personal email account is mike.wilson5@gmail.com. The first three accounts could be my target, but are probably not. This is likely just a coincidence. However, we can assume that the owner of one of those accounts is the owner of all three since the passwords are identical. The fourth response is a toss-up, but worth further investigation. We can also use this to query all credentials from a specific domain.

```
rg -aFiN @altonpolice.com
```

One of the results is quite embarrassing, as follows. I promise I have not used that password since the late 90's.

bazzell@altonpolice.com:mb01mb01mb

The tactic of searching leaked passwords and recovering associated accounts is by far the most successful database leaks strategy that I have applied to my investigations. In 2017, I was assisting a federal agency with a child pornography investigation where a suspect email address had been identified. This address was confirmed as being connected to the original person that had manufactured illegal videos of children being molested, but an alias name was used during creation. A search of this address through a breach compilation revealed a unique password associated with the account. Searching this password revealed only one additional email account, which was the personal Gmail account of the suspect (in his real name). The suspect used the same password for both accounts. The primary investigator made an arrest the next day after confirming the connection.

While some will say that we should never download leaked databases that contain personal login credentials, I disagree. There is great potential value in these data dumps that could solve cases on a grand scale, and make a huge impact on the prosecution of serious criminals.

I cannot overstate that this instruction is the very tip of the iceberg. There are tens of thousands of compromised databases online, and more being published every day. If you find "COMB" to be valuable, you may consider researching others. If you invest some time into seeking the sources of this data, you will quickly become overwhelmed at the mass amounts of content to properly obtain, clean, and store. I can only discuss the basics here. It is your job to proceed if you choose.

As a start, you may consider focusing on public credential leaks on Pastebin (pastebin.com). When you search an email address on Pastebin via Google, the results often include paste dumps. Clicking on these links will take you to the original paste document, which likely has many additional compromised credentials. A query of test@test.com on this site will likely present hundreds of data sets ready for download. Any time I see on HIBP that a new public leak has surfaced, I search for that specific data with a custom Google search. If I saw that Myspace has been exposed, I would use the following.

"myspace" ext:rar OR ext:zip OR ext:7z OR ext:txt OR ext:sql

There are many online database resources that will sell you the data. Please avoid these. First, you will likely get ripped off a few times before you find an "honest" seller. Second, you are giving money to criminals, and I don't like encouraging that behavior. Many researchers that I know possess over 100,000 databases which contain over four terabytes of total information, all found on public sites. A single query of this data can take a few minutes, even on a fast machine.

RaidForums Databases

In the previous chapter, I explained a method to open a torrent file which possessed voter registration data from several states. You may still have this torrent loaded into Transmission. If not, revisit that instruction to get it launched. Once opened, you should see 459 GB of databases which originally appeared on RaidForums. You should see data breaches from many familiar companies within this torrent, but I do not want to get sued by conducting demonstrations on them. Instead, I will focus on a few databases which were stolen from criminal marketplaces. I hope you see the irony. Criminals will also steal from other criminals.

I downloaded the databases associated with CrackingForum.com, CrackingItaly.com, and DemonForums.net. All three provide an online community which caters to criminal hackers. Let's jump into each.

The CrackingForum.com folder possesses a single text file which includes the email address and plain-text password of all 469,550 users of the site. This is the easiest data to consume, and the file is ready to be archived to your SSD. There is no cleaning to be done. If your email address target appears here, you know that suspect was a member of this hacking site, and you also see their password.

The CrackingItaly.com folder possesses a single text file which includes the member ID, full name, email address, hashed password, and IP address of all 18,132 users of the site. Again, no cleaning necessary here. This is a fairly minimal database. If your suspect email address appears here, you might learn their full name and an IP address which could identify their home internet provider (and approximate location). I will explain hashed passwords in a moment.

The DemonForums.net folder possesses a single SQL file which is not as straight-forward as the others. It is small enough that we can open it within a traditional text editor. The default option within Linux is fine with me. Apple macOS users might prefer the free version of BBEdit. When I open a SQL file, which is usually an exported backup of a database, I want to find the "Users" section. It is often toward the end of the file. In this scenario, searching "mybb_users" takes you straight to it. I then removed all of the data before this section and after, leaving only the 11,614 lines of user content. I then used my text editor's find and replace feature to remove all of the single quotes, and saved the file. This produced a 6.7 MB file which is quite small. I could have used the Cut command to extract only the desired columns of data, but that is overkill for such a small file. I can now query through usernames and email addresses of all 11,614 users of the service.

Only you can decide if you should proceed with downloading the remaining 450 GB of databases which were originally offered on RaidForums. If you do, many surprises await. Use the overall lessons throughout this guide to clean the data when needed and query the results. Many readers report that this torrent will only download 99% of the data. If that happens, archive as much of the content which is visible and move on.

Telegram Search

In the previous chapter, we relied on Telegram to find voter information. We will also rely heavily on Telegram to find stealer logs in the next chapter. Always check Telegram for breach data, as downloading from there is easier than various websites. Subscribing to channels such as "We Leak Database", "LEAKS AGGREGATOR", "DataLeak", "Open Leak", and "Leakbase Official" should present many breaches over the years. It also allows you to query the contents of these rooms with the general search field in Telegram. Anytime I hear about a new breach, searching the company's name within Telegram usually reveals some evidence. Let's conduct a few random demonstrations.

While writing this chapter, I saw a post on BreachForums.is discussing an offer of "USA / Payday Loans Database / 1 Million / 2020". As previously stated, I prefer to never earn, buy, or spend any "credits" on these types of sites. Instead, I searched the term "Payday" within Telegram. The following image displays the first result. Since I was subscribed to the "DataLeak" room, I received a search result which allowed me to download the file immediately, without spending any money or time to earn credits. In April of 2024, it appears this room was either voluntarily or forcefully shut down. This is very common on Telegram. When it happens, move on to the next lead.

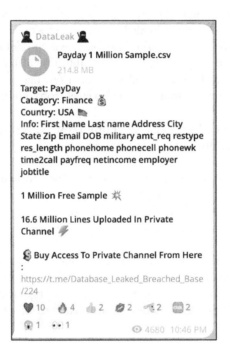

The next post on the BreachForums site was offering to sell a file called "+250 Million USA Huge Leak". The description of this data follows. Notice the total records size of 250,807,711.

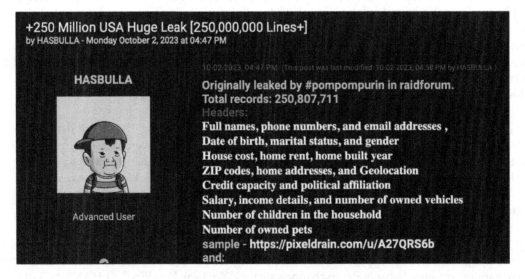

I conducted a search of "250 million" on Telegram, and received the following result since I was a member of the "Open Data" channel. The text file contained a torrent link, which I opened within my browser, which launched Transmission, and began downloading the data. Notice that the total record count matches the previous image of someone trying to sell the data. This is another room which many readers have reported as missing, but some readers have found success searching "250807711.7z" "torrent" within Google. Please remember that these examples are to serve as overall search methods, and not to provide data which will be archived forever. The next time you learn about data of interest, begin the hunt on Telegram.

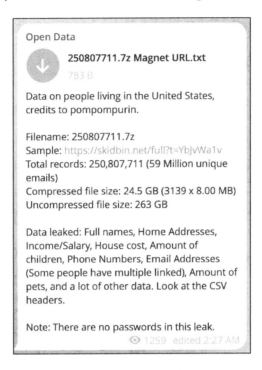

The next post on this page presented a file which contained the Fotolog breach data, as seen in the following image. A search of "Fotolog" on Telegram produced the result seen in the second image, offering this file for free.

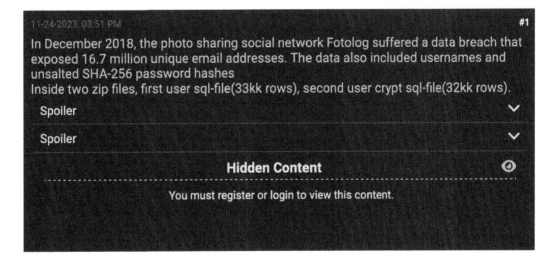

We could do this all day. The lessons are to join as many breach data channels as you can find, and search Telegram whenever you see something interesting being sold. You may find enough channels to keep you busy for weeks at the following URL.

https://github.com/fastfire/deepdarkCTI/blob/main/telegram.md

SQL Files

Some old-fashioned Google queries might find more data breaches and leaks than one can manage. Let's conduct a few examples with SQL files. SQL, often pronounced "sequel", is an acronym for Structured Query Language. It is a computer language used in programming and designed for managing data held in a relational database management system. In other words, most SQL files are databases of some sort. Many of the most popular database breaches were originally released as SQL files. WordPress backups, web forum exports, and other online maintenance files are also stored in this format. Searching for public SQL files can reveal surprising results. Let's search Google for SQL files with the following operators.

`ext:sql`: This returns thousands of results. While some are files with the extension of ".sql", most of the results are web pages ending with ".sql", and are not helpful. Let's modify the search as follows.

`ext:sql "create table"`: This returns 26,300 results which include the exact terms "create table". This is a standard statement within SQL files which specifies the names of tables within the database. This filters most of the website names from our search and displays only valid SQL files. Next, let's add to our search with the following modification.

`ext:sql "create table" "@gmail.com"`: This returns 5,160 results. Each is an SQL database with at least one entry of "@gmail.com" inside. This indicates that active email addresses are within the files, which is indicative of a true breach or leak. The following search should reveal data worth analyzing.

`ext:sql "create table" "@gmail.com" "'password'"`: This returns 3,060 results. Each is an SQL database with at least one entry of "gmail.com" inside and a table titled "password". Note the single quotes around password within double quotes. This tells Google to search specifically for 'password' and not the word alone. 3,060 results are overwhelming, and include a lot of test files stored on Github. Since many people use Gmail addresses as the administrator of test databases, we should add another email domain as follows.

`ext:sql "create table" "gmail.com" "'password'" "@yahoo.com" -site:github.com`

This reveals 67 results. Each are SQL files which contain at least one Gmail address, one Yahoo address, and a table titled password. Furthermore, all results from Github are removed. Most of these results will load as text files within your browser. However, some will be quite large and may crash your browser while loading. The following is a modified excerpt from an actual result, which I found by searching "@gmail.com" within the browser text.

```
(62,'RichardWilson','admin','richard@redactedemail.com','4d5e02c3f25128
6d8375040ea2b54e22','Administrator',0,1,25,'2008-05-28 07:07:08','2009-
04-02 13:08:07')
```

This is a very typical structure within SQL files. The following explains each piece.

```
62, (User ID)
'RichardWilson', (Name provided)
'admin', (Username)
'richard@redactedemail.com', (Email address)
'4d5e02c3f251286d8375040ea2b54e22', (Hashed password)
'Administrator', (Usertype)
0,1,25, (Variable internal codes)
'2008-05-28 07:07:08', (Registration date)
'2009-04-02 13:08:07', (Last visit date)
```

You could save the entire page as a .txt file (right-click > Save page as…) for your personal data archive. An alternative Google query for text files is as follows.

ext:txt "create table" "gmail.com" "'password'" "yahoo.com" -site:github.com

As I updated this section, I conducted a query of ".sql" in Telegram. Since I was subscribed to the "LEAKES AGGREGATOR" and "Leakbase Official" channels, I received hundreds of search results including recently breached SQL files. Most of these databases each possessed thousands of names, addresses, and often hashed passwords. You could spend weeks going through all of the data waiting to be plucked.

There may be a trove of sensitive information within these files, so use caution and always be responsible. Exercise good defense when browsing any of these sites or downloading any data. Trackers, viruses, and overall malicious software are always present in this environment. Using a macOS or Linux machine and a reputable VPN will provide serious protection from these threats. I search and store leaked and breached databases as a part of every investigation which I conduct.

I can say without hesitation that these strategies are more beneficial than any other online investigation technique of which I know. Some investigators within my circles possess several terabytes of this data from tens of thousands of breaches and leaks. Querying your own offline archive during your next investigation, and identifying unique data associated with your target, can be extremely rewarding. Again, I ask you to be responsible. Never use any credentials to access an account and never allow any data obtained to be further distributed. Use this public data, stolen by criminals, to investigate other criminals.

Hashes

Most websites store passwords in "hashed" form. This guards against the possibility that someone who gains unauthorized access to the database can retrieve the plain-text passwords of every user in the system. Hashing performs a one-way transformation on a password, turning the password into another string, called the hashed password. "One-way" means that it was practically impossible to go the other way and turn the hashed password back into the original password. This was true many years ago, but not so much today. There are several mathematically complex hashing algorithms that fulfill these needs. Some are very insecure and others are nearly impossible to crack. Let's look at a few examples.

Many older databases which have been breached possessed simple MD5 password hashes. The password of "password1234" is as follows as an MD5 hash. The Sha-1 hash of the same password, "password1234", is also as follows. Notice this is substantially longer, and a bit more secure. However, it will be quite easy for us to crack these passwords in just a moment. Below this example is the same password in Sha-256 and Sha-512 format. As you can see, these become increasingly complicated.

MD5: BDC87B9C894DA5168059E00EBFFB9077

SHA1: E6B6AFBD6D76BB5D2041542D7D2E3FAC5BB05593

SHA256: B9C950640E1B3740E98ACB93E669C65766F6670DD1609BA91FF41052BA48C6F3

SHA512: 8C7C9D16278AC60A19776F204F3109B1C2FC782FF8B671F42426A85CF72B 1021887DD9E4FEBE420DCD215BA499FF12E230DAF67AFFFDE8BF84BEFE867A8822C4

In regard to the various "older" breached databases which you are likely to find on the internet, you will most commonly see MD5 and SHA1 hashed passwords. Some of them possess a "salt". This is a small amount of data added to the hashing which makes cracking the password more difficult. If a breach does not possess the salt, the passwords are nearly impossible to crack. If the salt is present, it takes considerable additional resources in order to display the text password. The methods of "cracking" passwords exceed the scope of this book. Fortunately, we do not need the knowledge and computer horsepower to convert these hashes into valuable passwords. We simply need a third-party resource.

Hashes (hashes.org) attempted to reveal the plain-text of your submitted password hash. This was usually done in an effort to assist security professionals to evaluate the security provided by the relevant hash submitted. For us, it provided a new lead to follow. The database contained billions of cracked hashes available via web search and API. If I queried " BDC87B9C894DA5168059E00EBFFB9077" via the search page on the site, I was immediately presented with "password1234" as the password. Unfortunately, the service disappeared in late 2020. However, online archives exist. I consider the following technique to be advanced, and only suitable for those who have a need to reveal hashed passwords as part of their daily operations. The entire archive of hashes and passwords which previously existed on hashes.org is available as a torrent file. The following websites contain a "magnet" torrent link within them. Copying and pasting this link within your browser should launch your default torrent software and begin the 90 GB compressed download. Make sure you have room.

https://pastebin.com/pS5AQNV0
https://old.reddit.com/r/DataHoarder/comments/ohlcye/hashesorg_archives_of_all_cracked_hash_lists_up

Once complete, you should have a folder titled "HashesOrg Archive" with folders of "Hashlists" and "Leaks" inside it. These two folders contain thousands of compressed zip files. While you could issue commands via Terminal to decompress all files, I find it easier to simply select all files within a folder; right-click on them; and select to open with your desired decompression tool. Once you see the ".txt" versions of each file present, you might want to delete the original ".zip" files to free some space. Let's take a look inside the "Leaks" folder and open the file titled "20_casio-com_found_hash_algorithm_plain.txt". A partial excerpt follows.

MD5 00747af6279313863a0319070bdbfb80:168130
MD5 007be02e9bd7eb4402a15f377ad22e9e:zhangker46

The data tells us that this specific breach stored passwords in MD5 format. In this excerpt, we know that the MD5 hash of "00747af6279313863a0319070bdbfb80" reveals a password of "168130". We also know that a password of "zhangker46" was used within the Casio website at the time of the breach. Both of these pieces of data will be valuable to us. Let's conduct an investigation.

Your target has an email address of "badguy42@gmail.com". A query of this email address within the COMB data reveals a password of "verybad1234". However, this does not tell you which breach is associated with this address. Within Terminal, after navigating to the "HashesOrg Archive" folder, the following command is issued.

```
rg -aFiN verybad1234
```

The result appears similar to the following.

Leaks/713_forums-nodoubt-com_found_hash_algorithm_plain.txt.zip
MYSQL5 887b0eb63dbc543991567864efc0b05aad5a8ab2:verybad1234
We now have circumstantial evidence that a user on a web forum for the band No Doubt was using a password of "verybad1234" and the MYSQL5 hash of that password is "887b0eb63dbc543991567864efc0b05aad5a8ab2". Does this prove that "badguy42@gmail.com" was using this forum? No, but it is a solid lead. It could also be someone else using the same password. Since Hashes.org does not share the username or email address, we must continue the investigation with the OSINT methods previously explained. Is that email address associated with any conversations about the band? That would give me more confidence with the result. We should look at the typical way that one would use the Hashes.org data set. Assume that you have identified the following data within a breach, leak, or online website.

badguy42@gmail.com:14FDF540E39F0F154C8D0B3BD82ACE100B779DFA

Searching "14FDF540E39F0F154C8D0B3BD82ACE100B779DFA" through the hash identification website **TunnelsUp** (tunnelsup.com/hash-analyzer) reveals the following.

14FDF540E39F0F154C8D0B3BD82ACE100B779DFA - Hash Type: SHA1

We know this is a SHA1 hash which represents a password, and can execute the following.

```
rg -aFiN 14FDF540E39F0F154C8D0B3BD82ACE100B779DFA
```

The results appear below.

Leaks/706_forums-utorrent-com_found_hash_algorithm_plain.txt.zip
SHA1 14FDF540E39F0F154C8D0B3BD82ACE100B779DFA:stillverybad1234

Leaks/1182_prowrestlingfans-com_found_hash_algorithm_plain.txt.zip
SHA1 14FDF540E39F0F154C8D0B3BD82ACE100B779DFA:stillverybad1234

We now know that "badguy42@gmail.com" likely used a password of "stillverybad1234" at some point in time. We also know that someone using the password of "stillverybad1234" used that password on a uTorrent forum and a wrestling website, both of which suffered a breach. Are these all the same person? We cannot definitely conclude that. However, these are great leads. My next search would be the following.

```
rg -aFiN stillverybad1234
```

This may identify more data to be analyzed. However, this is all circumstantial. If a password is unique and complex, I have more confidence in the relationship to my suspect. If the password is "password1234" and appears on hundreds of sites, this has no value.

The **HashMob** (hashmob.net) community now offers a paid search service and free downloads of lists similar to those previously found at Hashes.org. Registration is not required to download "Found" lists from the "Official lists" menu. These files are very similar to the Hashes.org data, but updated often. I downloaded all 2,326 official (non-combo) hash lists with the following command.

```
wget --content-disposition -i
https://inteltechniques.com/data/hashlists.txt
```

WARNING: The result was 90 GB of data. A typical file was titled "330.3200.found", which identified the ID number of the breach (330) and the type of hash (3200-bcrypt). Each file contained numerous entries similar to the following.

00092f0f900824707b3508abc78aa6bb89f1e61bca81b0bcb01bb2efc6a1057:yanks2008

Everything to the left of the colon is the hash, and everything right of it is the password. Searching "330" (the ID of the breach) on the official HashMob website at **https://hashmob.net/api/v2/hashlist/official** reveals this is the hash list from a breach at Zildjian.ru.

Just like the tutorials within the Hashes.org section, this data allows us to search for either a hash or a password to identify if either is present within known breaches. It also allows us to query a hash in order to identify its plain-text password. After witnessing Hashes.org disappear, I prefer to possess my own archive of this free data. However, I also maintain a paid account with HashMob which allows real-time queries of hashes within their website, or via their API, which is much easier and immediately identifies passwords. If you need to query hashes often without downloading all the data, a paid account may be justified, and the results are updated daily. Next, let's take a closer look at some popular types of hashes.

MD5

Some older data breaches possess passwords hashed with MD5, an extremely insecure method. These hashes can be cracked very quickly. Below are two entries retrieved from various files.

174@gmail.com:482C811DA5D5B4BC6D497FFA98491E38
185@gmail.com:22F4182AAE2784FB3D1A432D44F07F46

Everything before the colon is the username or email address, and everything after is the MD5 hash. Searching these hashes in your Hashes.org data produces the following results. We now know that the first password is "password123" and the second is "reader12".

482c811da5d5b4bc6d497ffa98491e38:password123
22f4182aae2784fb3d1a432d44f07f46:reader12

MD5 + Salt (Vbulletin)

Some hashes will contain a "salt". This is usually a small piece of data after the hash, and both pieces are required to translate into plain-text. One of the most popular examples of this are the hundreds of Vbulletin online forums which have been infiltrated by various hacking groups. In the following examples, the salt is the final three characters after the last colon.

Aanas,menball@aol.com:9d9e3c372d054c0769bd93181240be36:tye
Traor,tranr@optusnet.com.au:9274583d060b3efb464115e65a8c1ead:vv#

Searching these hashes and salts through your Hashes.org data provides the following.

9d9e3c372d054c0769bd93181240be36:tye:eliza!%
9274583d060b3efb464115e65a8c1ead:vv#:runner

In the first example, you see the target password is "eliza!%". This proves that semi-complex passwords containing special characters are often dehashed and ready for conversion. This is where offline hashes stick out from the crowd. There are many online reverse-hashing tools, but most of them focus only on one format, such as MD5, and use minimal dictionaries to crack the hashes. Let's try one more demonstration.

SHA1

This format is slightly more secure than MD5, but still extremely easy to crack. The passwords obtained from the LinkedIn breach were all hashed in SHA1. Below are two examples.

174@gmail.com:403E35A2B0243D40400AF6BB358B5C546CDDD981
185@gmail.com:B1C4BBC4D7546529895CFABF8C1139CA7E486E18

The results from our offline hash collection follow. These two passwords are identical, but with different case. The first is all lowercase while the second contains uppercase. Notice that these create a completely different hash because of this. Keep this in mind when investigating passwords of your target.

403E35A2B0243D40400AF6BB358B5C546CDDD981:letmein!
B1C4BBC4D7546529895CFABF8C1139CA7E486E18:LetMeIn!

The golden days of data breaches from 2017 through 2019 are over. Sure, those databases are still floating around and very valuable, but recent breaches do not typically possess MD5 or SHA1 password hashes. We often see much more secure hashing algorithms such as BCRYPT or SHA512. Again, cracking these passwords with dedicated rigs exceeds the scope of this book. Searching "older" hashes can be time consuming, but the results can be extremely beneficial. It is quite a commitment to download hundreds of gigabytes of data for this purpose. Take time to think about your own needs.

Online Hash Search Resources

The following websites will convert MD5 and SHA1 hashes into passwords in some scenarios. The password must be within their limited system and should not be very complex. These are very limited, but may offer immediate data.

https://osint.sh/md5/
https://md5decrypt.net/en/Sha1/
https://www.md5online.org/md5-decrypt.html
https://www.dcode.fr/sha1-hash
https://md5decrypt.net/en/
https://md5hashing.net/hash/sha1

If you do not want to build, store, and maintain your own hash data set, I recommend **Name That Hash** and **Search That Hash** (github.com/HashPals/) over the online options. You can install it within your macOS or Linux machine (as long as you installed Pip, as previously explained) with the following steps.

```
sudo pip install -U search-that-hash
sudo pip install -U name-that-hash
```

Within Terminal, you can now execute the following to search a hash within multiple online converters.

```
sth --text "5f4dcc3b5aa765d61d8327deb882cf99"
```

The result appears as follows.

5f4dcc3b5aa765d61d8327deb882cf99
Text : password   Type : MD5

You can also search for only the type of hash with a command of `nth --text "5f4dcc3b5aa765d61d8327deb882cf99"`. The result appears as follows.

Most Likely MD5, HC: 0 JtR: raw-md5 Summary: Used for Linux Shadow files.

We now know that the hash value is a MD5 representation of the password "password". This process is included within the script titled "Breaches/Leaks Tool" included in the OSINT VM. I launch this application daily. When it cannot identify the password, I rely on my Hashes.org data set. If all of this is simply too complicated, we can always rely on more online services, as explained soon.

Hopefully, you now have a basic understanding of breaches, passwords, hashes, database files, and how all of it can work together to be a part of your online investigations. You might have a copy of the COMB data set which includes over a billion email addresses and associated passwords, but that was created for convenience. You may have encountered some hashes online and can reveal passwords hidden beneath, but those will be based on specific target queries. While the data discussed so far is easily assessable, new breaches might not be so easy to find and digest. Let's start over with two breach examples from data recently stolen.

As stated previously, I am not allowed to provide direct links to any breach data. However, I am allowed to discuss ways in which some people use OSINT to find this data. Let's take another look at Torrent search engines. If you were to search "Guron" on many Torrent sites, including The Pirate Bay, you would likely be presented a Torrent file which contains 241 GB of data titled "MyCloud". Expanding the data should reveal 1,315 files, each of which are a breached database obtained between 2016 and 2021. This is far from everything breached during that time, but it may serve as another introduction into this type of content. Warning: the **compressed** content is 241 GB, so expect the decompressed to reach a terabyte. I plucked two small random examples from this data set in order to explain the data within.

DogForum.sk: The file titled "Dump_public_dogforum.sk_2021.01.13.rar" is a 2.3 MB compressed file which decompresses to a 12.5 MB SQL database dump. This site's database was allegedly stolen on January 13, 2021. Opening the SQL file within a text editor reveals a table titled "phpbb3_users". The following displays only the ten most interesting fields for my investigations within this table.

```
CREATE TABLE `phpbb3_users` (
  `user_id` mediumint(8) unsigned NOT NULL AUTO_INCREMENT,
  `user_ip` varchar(40) COLLATE utf8_bin NOT NULL DEFAULT '',
  `user_regdate` int(11) unsigned NOT NULL DEFAULT '0',
  `username` varchar(255) COLLATE utf8_bin NOT NULL DEFAULT '',
  `user_password` varchar(40) COLLATE utf8_bin NOT NULL DEFAULT '',
  `user_passchg` int(11) unsigned NOT NULL DEFAULT '0',
  `user_email` varchar(100) COLLATE utf8_bin NOT NULL DEFAULT '',
  `user_birthday` varchar(10) COLLATE utf8_bin NOT NULL DEFAULT '',
  `user_lastvisit` int(11) unsigned NOT NULL DEFAULT '0',
  `user_timezone` decimal(5,2) NOT NULL DEFAULT '0.00',
```

A redacted example of one user entry is below (there are over 17,000 users).

(8419,'178.40.120.170',1275503507,'Ode','H9ftKyo59RKktw7Idj2TGaVweMH2ITG.',1350132160,'xxxxblac kjack@gmail.com',' 0- 0- 0',1371625109,+3,)
We can now assume the following about this user based on this data.

8419: The user number for this user on this forum.
178.40.120.170: The IP address of the user during registration.
1275503507: The UNIX time the user registered (June 2, 2010 18:31:47 GMT).
Ode: The username for this user.
H9ftKyo59RKktw7Idj2TGaVweMH2ITG.: The hashed password.
1350132160: The UNIX time the user last changed the password (October 13, 2012 12:42:40 GMT).
xxxxblackjack@gmail.com: The email address of the user.
0- 0- 0: The date of birth of the user (none was provided).
1371625109: The UNIX time of the user's last visit (June 19, 2013 06:58:29 GMT).
+3: The user's time zone (+3 GMT - Middle East).

Please take a moment to digest this example. This entry is only one of 17,000 within this single stolen breach. The Torrent mentioned possesses over 1,000 breaches, and there are tens of thousands of known breaches out there. There is the potential to collect this type of information from billions of accounts. I hope you see the possibilities for your own investigations. Every day, we digest dozens of breaches into our own system, which I will discuss later, and we see this type of result with almost every query we conduct. Sometimes, we receive this type of data from within several breaches associated with our single target email address. It is quite powerful. Let's conduct another example.

EscortReviews.com: The file "Dump_public_escortreviews.com_2021.01.27.rar" is a 51.7 MB compressed file which decompresses to a 223.3 MB SQL database dump. This site's database was allegedly stolen on January 27, 2021, and was publicly reported a month later. Opening the SQL file within a text editor reveals a table titled "user". The following displays only the most interesting fields for my investigations within this table.

```
CREATE TABLE `user` (
  `userid` int(10) unsigned NOT NULL AUTO_INCREMENT,
  `username` varchar(100) NOT NULL DEFAULT '',
  `password` char(32) NOT NULL DEFAULT '',
  `passworddate` date NOT NULL DEFAULT '0000-00-00',
  `email` char(100) NOT NULL DEFAULT '',
  `homepage` char(100) NOT NULL DEFAULT '',
  `joindate` int(10) unsigned NOT NULL DEFAULT '0',
  `lastvisit` int(10) unsigned NOT NULL DEFAULT '0',
  `birthday` char(10) NOT NULL DEFAULT '',
  `ipaddress` char(15) NOT NULL DEFAULT '',
```

A fictitious example of one user entry is below (there are over 470,000 users in this database).

(201,bobforfun,65184286F793B5E70ACA525E63DAE54F,2011-06-12,bob_love@ymail.com, bobforfun.com,1238309520,1307841316,06-02-1983,76.187.13.130,2)

We can now assume the following about this user based on this data.

201: The user number for this user on this forum.
Bobforfun: The username for this user on this forum.
65184286F793B5E70ACA525E63DAE54F: The hashed password for this account.
2011-06-12: The date the user last changed the password.
bob_love@ymail.com: The email address associated with this account.
bobforfun.com: The personal website associated with this account.
1238309520: The Unix time the user joined (March 29, 2009 at 06:52:00 GMT).
1307841316: The Unix time the user last accessed (June 12, 2011 at 01:15:16 GMT).
06-02-1983: The provided date of birth for this user.

76.187.13.130: The IP address of the user during registration.

This site was used heavily by escorts, pimps, and johns in order to promote prostitution. Anyone who conducts human trafficking investigations might benefit from this data on 470,000 registered members. The hash for this fictitious example is MD5. If you were to place that hash into our Search-That-Hash tool previously discussed, you would receive the following result.

65184286F793B5E70ACA525E63DAE54F
Most Likely
MD5, HC: 0 JtR: raw-md5 Summary: Used for Linux Shadow files.
Text : escorts

You would now know that this user was using a weak password of "escorts" for this site in 2011. These example files are fairly small, but there is still a lot of content inside them which is unnecessary. You could clean these files using the previous techniques, but that may be overkill for your needs. Since I collect terabytes of this data, I try to minimize every file as much as possible. Reconsider the "DogForum.sk" file from earlier. The following commands would extract only the columns we desire and remove the unnecessary tabs.

```
cut -d, -f1,6,7,8,10,11,13,15,16,29 dogforum.sk.sql > DogForum.txt
sed -i ''s/(ctrl-v-tab)//gI" DogForum-Cleaned.txt
```

This action shrank the 12.5 MB file to 2.4 MB and compressed each line to fit nicely within Terminal. That may not seem like much, but it can make quite a difference when dealing with thousands of files.

Archive.org Breach Data

Archive.org possesses a surprising number of data breach dumps. As one example, conduct a search on their site for "nulled.io" and click the "nulled.io_database_dump" page. It should present a download option for the entire 10 GB database from the Nulled hacking forum, as uploaded by "ntgrg". If you were to click on this profile, you would likely find other similar uploads. You could spend weeks on Archive.org identifying breach data.

Cit0day Collection

Next, let's take a look at an enormous data set and discuss the challenges of ingesting such content. This section will combine several techniques and commands which I have discussed throughout the previous chapters. In 2020, a criminal marketplace offering breached databases called Cit0day.in had allegedly been shut down by various government agencies. The same day the site displayed a seizure notification, the 23,618 hacked databases (containing 226 million credentials) from the site were provided for free download via a file sharing site. The government takedown of Cit0day was never proven, and most researchers speculate the seizure notice on the website was fake. However, the leaked data was real. Today, these files are still abundant on the internet for anyone to obtain.

If you were to search "cit0day", with a zero (0) instead of an "o", within the main Telegram search field, you would likely identify a channel called "cit0day collection in tg". Visiting this room should display thousands of these compressed breach data files within the channel. This room allows download of each of these individual hacked databases, or you can download the entire collection within three compressed files titled "Full Clouds Cit0day_2" near the end of the list. These files consisted of 9 GB of compressed data, which expanded to a single 9.1 GB compressed 7z file, which decompressed a folder titled "Cit0day_RF" containing 23,564 folders. From there, each folder possessed multiple files associated with a specific breached victim company. The data was 30 GB in size and consisted of 72,780 files. What a mess. Let's work through it together.

Some folders are easy. If you were to look at the contents of the folder titled "agekuda.net {8.882} [NOHASH] (Shopping)", you would see that only one file exists, titled "agekuda.net {8.882} [NOHASH].txt". This file possesses all 8,882 users of this site, and the contents appear similar to the following.

mge.com@ezweb.ne.jp:sundial
qbq@ezweb.ne.jp:apo11

All of the credentials within the file are plain-text passwords and there are no hashed passwords. This file is ready to be added to your collection. However, let's take a look at the folder titled "agenziaporto.it {6.405} [HASH+NOHASH] (Shopping)". It possesses the following five files.

NotFound.txt
Rejected.txt
Result.txt
Result(HEX).txt
www.agenziaporto.it {6.405} [HASH].txt

The "NotFound.txt" file contains all of the usernames and hashed passwords for this breach which were not dehashed into plain-text passwords. Everything within this file is redundant to the last "[HASH]" file, and this file is not needed. The "Rejected.txt" file is also redundant. The "Result.txt" file contains all of the hashed passwords from the final "[HASH]" file which were turned into plain-text passwords. This file has value, but the "Result(HEX).txt" file is not necessary for our needs. The final file titled "www.agenziaporto.it {6.405} [HASH].txt" contains the most important content. It contains the 6,404 usernames and hashed passwords from this breach.

If desired, you could simply copy these 23,618 folders into a directory called "Databases" within your SSD and query the data whenever needed. There is no shame in that, and you could move on to more data. However, I cannot stomach this. The amount of unnecessary data and redundant entries would bother me. It may not seem like much now, but when you have 200,000 breached databases which take several minutes to query, you may wish you had cleaned the data before archiving it. The first step I took was to open Terminal and navigate to the folder which stored all of this data. For me, the command was as follows.

```
cd ~/Downloads/Telegram\ Desktop/Cit0day_RF/Data/
```

Once there, I removed all files which included "Rejected.txt", "NotFound.txt", "Result(HEX).txt", "*not found*.txt", or "final" in the name. This eliminated much of the redundant data.

```
find . -iname 'Rejected.txt' -delete
find . -iname 'NotFound.txt' -delete
find . -iname 'Result(HEX).txt' -delete
find . -iname '*not found*.txt' -delete
find . -iname '*final*.txt' -delete
```

Below is the breakdown of the commands.

find	This tells Terminal to find something.
.	This tells Terminal to search everything below the current folder.
-iname	This tells Terminal to search for content without case sensitivity.
'*final*.txt'	This tells Terminal to find any text file with "final" in the name.
-delete	This tells Terminal to delete whatever matches our command.

Next, I wanted to combine all of the "decrypted", "result", and "no hash" files into one large file. These all contain redundant usernames which are already in the main file for each breach, but they also include plain-text passwords which could be valuable. The following commands combined all of the data and then deleted the unnecessary files. Notice that I removed the "i" from the "no hash" commands because I do not want to delete uppercase entries containing "NO HASH".

```
find . -iname '*result*' -exec cat {} \; > Pass1.txt
find . -iname '*decrypt*' -exec cat {} \; > Pass2.txt
find . -name '*no hash*' -exec cat {} \; > Pass3.txt
find . -iname '*result*' -delete
find . -iname '*decrypt*' -delete
find . -name '*no hash*' -delete
cat Pass1.txt Pass2.txt Pass3.txt > Cit0DayPass.txt
rm Pass1.txt Pass2.txt Pass3.txt
```

You would now have a file called Cit0dayPass.txt which contains several gigabytes of usernames and plain-text passwords from this collection. If desired, you could use the Sort command previously explained to remove duplicates from this file, as there are many. Since these usernames are already within the files we will deal with next, you do not need to know of which breach these entries originated. I will query this file in a moment. Finally, each folder should now be left with only one file which should be similar to one of the following naming structures.

3bbwifi.com {1.687} [HASH] [NOHASH].txt
agendadelasmujeres.com.ar {25.541} [HASH].txt

We could just save these to our Databases folder, but I want them cleaner. The following command renames every file to remove the unnecessary information within parentheses and brackets. We will need the Rename application, which can be installed with the commands.

macOS: `brew install rename`
Linux: `sudo apt install rename`

Once you know you have Rename installed, consider the following long command.

```
find . -type f -execdir rename
's/\{[^\}]+\}//g;s/<[^<]+>//g;s/\[[^\]]+\]//g;s/\([^\)]+\)//g' {} \;
```

This basically finds all files in all subdirectories and renames them to remove any parentheses and brackets, and all data between them. I use this command often when I download thousands of files with long unnecessary names. The previous files should now appear as follows.

3bbwifi.com .txt
agendadelasmujeres.com.ar .txt

This is much nicer, and I can now move all of these files into a single folder with the following commands. In this scenario, I am moving them to a folder called Databases within my SSD. If you named your SSD the same as mine, this should work for you too.

```
mkdir /Volumes/DATA/Databases/
find . -type f -name '*.txt' -execdir mv {} /Volumes/DATA/Databases/
\;
```

The result should be all 22,762 text files within the Databases folder on your SSD, with a total size of 20.37 GB (down from 30 GB). This also moved the Cit0daypass.txt file which we previously created. You may notice that many of the files possess a trailing space in the file name. If this bothers you, navigate to your new Databases folder and execute the following.

```
rename "s/ //g" *
```

Finally, let's conduct a query of a fictitious target.

```
rg -aFiN test9876@gmail.com
```

The results would appear as follows.

friuligol.it.txt
test9876@gmail.com:ef5381e56a457e62bf22976b5b4f4f8f

Cit0DayPass.txt
test9876@gmail.com:mypassword

This displays the presence of our target email address in the original breach (friuligol.it) with a hashed password, and the dehashed plain-text password (mypassword) from the file we previously created from the "results" and "decrypted" files. You would now possess this data in a format which is smaller, easier to digest, and faster to query. You can delete the entire "Cit0day_RF" folder once you know you have the necessary data on your SSD. If desired, you can conduct the following to see the total number of lines within all files combined.

```
find . -name '*.txt' | xargs wc -l
```

The result appears as follows.

50727432 total

We now know that the original report of 226 million credentials was likely based on all of that redundant data. A total of 50 million victims is more accurate. Journalists will often exaggerate the truth in order to get more clicks. Trust your own analysis. This is still not bad for a single data breach collection, which can be downloaded and cleaned in an hour. The following image displays a very small portion of this collection.

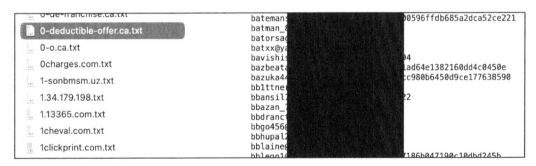

Password Commonality

If you encounter a password for your target, you may want to know if it was unique. As an example, I would assume my previous example of the password "escorts" is fairly common. I can confirm this through the Have I Been Pwned password site at haveibeenpwned.com/Passwords. The following figures display the result identifying 847 breaches containing that password (top). However, what if your target's password was "escorts!"? Surpassingly, there is only one reported breach which had this password, as seen in the second image.

Online Breach Search Resources

The following provides direct URL submission options for several breach data search websites. This will be vital for our Data Tool mentioned at the end of this chapter.

Email Address (test@test.com)

https://dehashed.com/search?query=test@test.com
https://intelx.io/?s=test@test.com
https://psbdmp.ws/api/search/test@test.com
https://check.cybernews.com/chk/?lang=en_US&e=test@test.com
https://portal.spycloud.com/endpoint/enriched-stats/test@test.com
https://cavalier.hudsonrock.com/api/json/v2/preview/search-by-login/osint-tools?email=test@test.com
https://api.proxynova.com/comb?highlight=1&query=test@test.com

Username (test)

https://dehashed.com/search?query=test
https://psbdmp.ws/api/search/test
https://api.proxynova.com/comb?highlight=1&query=test

Domain (inteltechniques.com)

https://dehashed.com/search?query=inteltechniques.com
https://psbdmp.ws/api/search/inteltechniques.com
https://intelx.io/?s=inteltechniques.com
https://www.hudsonrock.com/search?domain=inteltechniques.com
Telephone (6185551212)

https://dehashed.com/search?query=6185551212
https://psbdmp.ws/api/search/6185551212

IP Address (1.1.1.1)

https://dehashed.com/search?query=1.1.1.1
https://psbdmp.ws/api/search/1.1.1.1
https://intelx.io/?s=1.1.1.1

Name (Michael Bazzell)

https://dehashed.com/search?query=michael Bazzell
https://psbdmp.ws/api/search/Michael%20Bazzell

Password (password1234)

https://dehashed.com/search?query=password1234
https://psbdmp.ws/api/search/password1234
https://www.google.com/search?q=password1234
https://api.proxynova.com/comb?highlight=1&query=password1234

Hash (BDC87B9C894DA5168059E00EBFFB9077)

https://hash.ziggi.org/api/dehash.get?hash=BDC87B9C894DA5168059E00EBFFB9077&include_external_db
https://decrypt.tools/client-server/decrypt?type=md5&string=BDC87B9C894DA5168059E00EBFFB9077
https://md5.gromweb.com/?md5=BDC87B9C894DA5168059E00EBFFB9077
https://www.nitrxgen.net/md5db/BDC87B9C894DA5168059E00EBFFB9077
https://dehashed.com/search?query=BDC87B9C894DA5168059E00EBFFB9077
https://www.google.com/search?q=BDC87B9C894DA5168059E00EBFFB9077

Miscellaneous Sites

The following websites do not allow submission via URL, but a manual search may be beneficial. Please remember that all of these sites come and go quickly. By the time you read this, some of these services may have shut down. It is equally possible that new resources are waiting for your discovery.

HIBP: https://haveibeenpwned.com
LeakPeek: https://leakpeek.com
Beach Directory: https://breachdirectory.org
ProxyNova: https://proxynova.com/tools/comb/

H8Mail (github.com/khast3x/h8mail)

H8Mail attempts to combine many of the breach services we have explored into one utility. It should never take the place of a full manual review, but the embedded automation can be beneficial to an investigation. Conduct the following within Terminal.

```
sudo pip install -U h8mail
cd ~/Downloads
h8mail -g
sed -i 's/\;leak\-lookup\_pub/leak\-lookup\_pub/gI' h8mail_config.ini
```

Launching the following from the Downloads directory will produce minimal, if any, results.

```
h8mail -t bill@microsoft.com
```

Providing API keys from services such as Snusbase, Leak-Lookup, HaveIBeenPwned, Emailrep, Dehashed, and Hunterio will provide MANY more results, but these services can be quite expensive. If you rely on breach data every day; can afford premium services; and do not want to collect your own breach data; there may be value for you within this option. After you have obtained API keys from your desired services, open the Files application, enter the Downloads folder, and double-click the file named "h8mail_config.ini". You should see text similar to the following partial example. Add your API keys within the appropriate lines, similar to the entry for "leak-lookup pub", and remove any semicolons within lines you want to be used. If a semicolon is at the beginning of a line, that option is ignored. At the minimum, make sure the semicolon is removed from the "leak-lookup pub" line and execute another query. You should see new results. If you conducted the previous "sed" command, this should already be configured for you.

```
;hibp =
leak-lookup_pub = 1bf94ff907f68d511de9a610a6ff9263
;leak-lookup_priv =
;emailrep =
```

After this new configuration file modification, I executed a search for test@email.com. The result was a file which contained 172 results. The following partial view confirms that this address exists within breaches from TicketFly, TrueFire, and Tumblr. Eliminating this modification returned no results.

test@email.com,LEAKLOOKUP_PUB,ticketfly.com
test@email.com,LEAKLOOKUP_PUB,truefire.com
test@email.com,LEAKLOOKUP_PUB,tumblr.com

Sample Investigation

We have covered a lot so far within this chapter. Let's pause and conduct an investigation using this data. Assume that you possess the databases mentioned previously, especially "COMB". Your investigation identifies a suspect with an email address of johndoe1287@gmail.com. This appears to be a burner email account, as you find no evidence of it anywhere online. It was used to harass your client and likely created only for devious activity. Our first step is to query the address through all the databases you have acquired. Assume these are all stored on your external SSD, which is plugged into your host computer. Let's take each step slowly.

Open Terminal, type cd, then space, and drag and drop the external drive from your Files (Finder) application into Terminal. This makes sure you are in the correct path. My command appears similar to the following.

```
cd '/media/osint/DATA/'
```

I can now conduct a query within Terminal against all of my collected data. The following searches our target email address. Each query could take several minutes if you possess a lot of data and a slow drive.

```
rg -aFiN johndoe1287@gmail.com
```

This results in one entry as follows.

johndoe1287@gmail.com:H8teful0ne45

We now know that he used the password of H8teful0ne45 on a site. We should next conduct a search of that password to see if it is used anywhere else. The following query is appropriate.

```
rg -aFiN H8teful0ne45
```

This returned the following results.

johndoe1287@gmail.com:H8teful0ne45
johndoe@gmail.com:H8teful0ne45
johndoe1287@hotmail.com:H8teful0ne45

These addresses are likely controlled by our target since the passwords are the same and the addresses are similar. We now have new search options. However, this search only queries for this exact text password term. If you possess a database which has not been dehashed, your target password could be present within an MD5, SHA1, or other hash. Therefore, let's convert this password into the most commonly used hashes with the following websites, displaying the output below each.

https://passwordsgenerator.net/md5-hash-generator/
9EF0EC63E2E52320CB20E345DCBA8112

https://passwordsgenerator.net/sha1-hash-generator/
D15FB15C1BC88F4B7932FD29918D1E9E9BBE7CA5

https://passwordsgenerator.net/sha256-hash-generator/
37A790A268B9FE62B424BABFC3BCAB0646BFB24B93EC1619AAE7289E0D7086DB

We can now submit each of these throughout all of our data with the following three commands.

```
rg -aFiN 9EF0EC63E2E52320CB20E345DCBA8112
rg -aFiN D15FB15C1BC88F4B7932FD29918D1E9E9BBE7CA5
rg -aFiN
37A790A268B9FE62B424BABFC3BCAB0646BFB24B93EC1619AAE7289E0D7086DB
```

The first query returned the following result.

Leaks/1183_houstonastros-com_found_hash_algorithm_plain.txt.zip
SHA1 D15FB15C1BC88F4B7932FD29918D1E9E9BBE7CA5:H8teful0ne45

This tells us that a user with a password of "H8teful0ne45" was present on a breach about the Houston Astros. Is this the same person? It could be. It could also be a coincidence. The more unique a password is, the more confidence I have that it is the same individual. This definitely warrants further investigation. I might next try to locate the original breach data, which would likely include any email addresses associated with that password hash. All of these steps are designed to lead us to the next step. All of these results give me more confidence that these accounts are owned by the same person. The variant of the "hateful" password and presence of "johndoe" within the original email address and the new password convinces me we are on the right track. I would now target this new email address and replicate the searches mentioned within previous chapters. We should also check the online breach resources previously explained.

As previously stated, your biggest frustration may be the speed of each query. There is a lot to digest in this chapter. I want to state again that breach data has been the absolute biggest aid in my online investigations. I rely on it way more than Facebook, Twitter, and Instagram combined. In a future chapter, I will offer additional storage and query techniques which should assist with immediate access to your data.

IntelTechniques Breaches & Leaks Tool

This search tool combines most of the online search options mentioned throughout the chapter. The breach data resources are split into categories based on the target data (email, username, etc.). The last feature allows entry of found passwords and immediately generates an MD5, SHA1, and SHA256 hash for further research. Please visit **https://inteltechniques.com/tools/Breaches.html**.

CHAPTER FORTY-TWO
STEALER LOGS

I am absolutely fascinated by stealer log data. While I have always prioritized breach data as a vital part of my investigations, stealer log data presents a whole new world. This chapter offers two unique ways of acquiring stealer logs. The first is the manual process which collects more data, but requires a lot of effort. The second obtains only the most beneficial details with minimum effort, but misses some data you might find valuable. First, let's revisit the basics. This is my favorite chapter.

Stealer logs are created once a malicious virus has been installed to a computer (typically Windows). The victim may be tricked into installing a program after visiting a malicious website, or the virus could be included within an unauthorized application, such as pirated software. The virus sniffs through the computer to identify, extract, and collect any valuable data. These "logs" are then transferred from the host machine and distributed within shady online networks.

The most common stealer logs we would find in previous years were labeled as Raccoon Stealer, Redline Stealer, and Vidar Stealer. Today, every stealer log group rebrands the data they steal from other groups in order to present it as their own. There is no honor amongst thieves. The groups which offer data stolen via these programs are limitless. A new group pops up every week. Criminal marketplaces trade this data as a commodity. They use the stolen data to unlawfully access online accounts, steal cryptocurrency, make unauthorized purchases, and wreak havoc on innocent people's digital lives. Our systems ingest over one million logs every day which are being shared online.

Let's take a look at some real data. In the following example, I extracted a random log which was generated by the Redline Stealer and uploaded to a criminal marketplace. I redacted much of the content. First, let's understand the file structure. The following is a tree of a single log file for one victim.

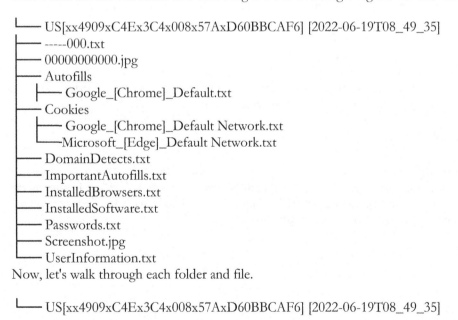

Now, let's walk through each folder and file.

└── US[xx4909xC4Ex3C4x008x57AxD60BBCAF6] [2022-06-19T08_49_35]

This top folder presents a two-letter abbreviation of the country of the victim (United States) followed by a unique Hardware Identifier (HWID) and the date and time of capture. The HWID is a security measure used by Microsoft upon the activation of Windows. This unique HWID is generated when the operating system is first installed. This will be vital in a moment. The date and time allow us to know the likely accuracy of the data.

├── -----000.txt

This is an information file about the thief. It often includes generic contact information, pricing for stolen data, and online communities associated with the product.

├── 00000000000.jpg

This is the logo of the Redline product.

├── Autofills
│   ├── Google_[Chrome]_Default.txt

This is where things get interesting. Your browser has likely asked you if you would like to store information which was entered into an online form. This could include your name, address, email, or other unique detail which gets entered into websites often. If you allow your browser to store this data, stealer logs easily collect it into their systems. The following is partial (redacted) data extracted from an actual victim. The original logs clearly displayed all data.

Name: email
Value: loxxx@gmail.com
===============
Name: username
Value: skxxxx22
===============
Name: lastname
Value: Loxxx
===============
Name: first-name-field
Value: Alixxx
===============
Name: address
Value: 20xx xxxx Lane
===============
Name: city
Value: Moxxx
===============
Name: phone
Value: 209-xxx-xxx
===============
Name: dob
Value: 10/xx/20xx
===============
Name: VIN
Value: kmhtcxxxxxxxxx
===============
Name: keyword
Value: 20xx Subaru xxxx
===============
Name: card-name
Value: Alixxx Loxxx
===============
Name: expiration-date
Value: 0x/2x

I now have the name, DOB, home address, email, cell, vehicle, and partial credit card details of the victim.

```
├── Cookies
│   ├── Google_[Chrome]_Default Network.txt
│   └──Microsoft_[Edge]_Default Network.txt
```

Your browser stores temporary internet files about your credentialed sessions. I may not have your password to your email account, but possessing the cookies from your browser could allow me to steal your credentialed session and replicate access to your account. The following details could be beneficial to a criminal (obviously redacted and abbreviated).

.paypal.com TRUE / FALSE 196941xxx cookie_check yes
.paypal.com TRUE / FALSE 168533xxx cookie_prefs P%3D1%2CF%3D1%2Ctype%3Dimplicit
.paypal.com TRUE / FALSE 196941xxx d_id 9ebfcxxxe8545ae9a39xxx2d228xxx116537xxx
.paypal.com TRUE / FALSE 1969xxxG8 KN2xxx0aJZzhbL_R4HkiO_kb5_yMTkUPrF-Ml6xxx
.paypal.com TRUE / FALSE 1685334379 X-PP-ADxxxYsNaAuNxxxHBuQ9dI
.paypal.com TRUE / FALSE 1716870381 _ga GA1.2.137xxx.165379xxx
.paypal.com TRUE / FALSE 1716912230 login_email lopxxxgmail.com
.paypal.com TRUE / FALSE 1969417578 rmuc KhGxxxmVv_x1Oo9gQ7axxxUk

```
├── DomainDetects.txt
```

This file offers immediate access to the priority domains which exist in the overall record. This allows criminals to quickly identify logs of interest.

PDD: [Amazon] amazon.com (2), [Games] steamcommunity.com (2)
CDD: [PayPal] paypal.com (40), [Amazon] amazon.com (14), [Games] battle.net (11), [Games] epicgames.com (1), [Games] steamcommunity.com (8)

```
├── ImportantAutofills.txt
```

This file parses data from the stored form fields which will be most beneficial to a criminal. The last two lines of my example suspect appear as follows. I also see full credit card details presented here often.

dob: 06/xx/xx
ssn: 248xx2xxx

```
├── InstalledBrowsers.txt
```

This file identifies all installed browsers and versions.

1) Name: Google Chrome, Path: C:\Program Files (x86)\Google\Chrome\Application\chrome.exe, Version: 102.0.5005.115
2) Name: Internet Explorer, Path: C:\Program Files\Internet Explorer\iexplore.exe, Version: 11.00.22000.1 (WinBuild.160101.0800)
3) Name: Microsoft Edge, Path: C:\Program Files (x86)\Microsoft\Edge\Application\msedge.exe, Version: 102.0.1245.44

```
├── InstalledSoftware.txt
```

This file presents all applications installed within the machine. While this may not be extremely valuable to a criminal, it is gold to an investigator. If my target possesses a stealer program, I get to monitor a lot of details about the person's computer usage. In the following example, I would know which VPN my target uses, hardware details, and preferred games. That could lead to quite a social engineering attack.

1) Adobe Acrobat Reader DC [22.001.20117]
2) Adobe Creative Cloud [5.5.0.617]
3) Adobe Genuine Service [7.7.0.35]
4) Adobe Photoshop 2021 [22.1.1.138]
5) Adobe Refresh Manager [1.8.0]
6) Epic Games Launcher [1.1.279.0]
7) ExpressVPN [7.7.12.4]
8) ExpressVPN [7.7.12.4]
9) Google Chrome [102.0.5005.115]
10) HP Audio Switch [1.0.179.0]
11) HP Connection Optimizer [2.0.17.0]
12) HP PC Hardware Diagnostics UEFI [7.6.2.0]
13) Intel(R) Chipset Device Software [10.1.18295.8201]
14) Launcher Prerequisites (x64) [1.0.0.0]
15) LOOT version 0.16.0 [0.16.0]
16) McAfee LiveSafe [16.0 R27]
38) Minecraft Launcher [1.0.0.0]
39) NVIDIA Texture Tools Exporter for Adobe Photoshop [2020.1.3]
40) Razer Synapse [3.7.0531.052416]
41) Red Dead Redemption 2 [1.0.1436.31]
42) Rockstar Games Launcher [1.0.59.842]
43) Rockstar Games Social Club [2.1.3.7]
44) Steam [2.10.91.91]
45) UE4 Prerequisites (x64) [1.0.14.0]

├── Passwords.txt

This file presents all of the passwords stored within all browsers. This is why it is so important to only use reputable password managers, and never the native browser password storage option. Below is one of 56 examples for this victim, redacted. The original file displays all passwords in plain-text.

URL: https://www.amazon.com/ap/signin
Username: xxxxxxx
Password: xxxxxxx

├── Screenshot.jpg

This is one of the most interesting pieces. It is a screen capture of the victim's machine at the time of infection. The following figure is an actual example (slightly redacted) which identifies the person's video interests, TikTok favorites, toolbar shortcuts, Google avatar (redacted), and an overall state of the computer at the time. This is quite invasive and can be a great lead in the investigation.

└── UserInformation.txt

The last file displays general details about the system, including the victim's IP address, hardware, location, and date. An example is below.

Build ID: REDLINEVIP
IP: 192.xx.xx.xx
FileLocation: C:\Windows\Microsoft.NET\Framework\v4.0.30319\InstallUtil.exe
UserName: xxx
Country: US
Zip Code: xxx
Location: xxx, Texas
HWID: 72xxxxxxxxxxxxxxxCAF6
Current Language: English (United States)
ScreenSize: {Width=1920, Height=1080}
TimeZone: (UTC-07:00) Mountain Time (US & Canada)
Operation System: Windows 10 Home x64
UAC: AllowAll
Process Elevation: False
Log date: 19.06.2022 8:49:35
Name: Intel(R) Core(TM) i7-10750H CPU @ 2.60GHz, 6 Cores
Name: NVIDIA GeForce RTX 2060, 4293918720 bytes
Name: Total of RAM, 12126.75 MB or 12715814912 bytes

You may be wondering why I get so excited about these logs when they expose sensitive details about innocent victims. I have two main reasons. First, it helps us defend our clients. We have had over a dozen clients who unknowingly installed a stealer virus. Our systems caught the infection within a few days and allowed us to contact the client to make notification. We have helped numerous organizations which had unknown infections within their network. Some of our staff calls this our "Pre-Crime Unit".

Next, it could be a priceless investigation tool. I have had numerous suspects within my own investigations who were victims of stealer logs. When this happens, I can see all of their email addresses, usernames, passwords, and computer information. This has revealed the true owner of many alias names and other deceitful tactics used by the suspect. If my target is the victim of stealer logs, my entire investigation is about to be wrapped up quickly. If I have the HWID, I can search through our troves of logger data to identify even more vital info about the suspect.

Because of this, we aggressively collect stealer log data every day. Some days we ingest over a terabyte of this data. The following Google queries might present interesting information, but most results lead to shady criminal marketplaces which require an account to see download links. Use extreme caution here, and I will present better options in a moment.

"stealer logs" "download"
"stealer logs" "Redline"

It is now time to dive into some very shady criminal communities. Ensure that your organization's policies allow this behavior; never publish or disseminate anything you find; understand any local, state, or federal laws which could disallow these actions; and always focus on the good usage of this data. Never attempt to log in to anyone's account and make sure your computer is well protected from online threats. The following is presented as an educational demonstration, and I take no liability for your own actions taken.

Full Stealer Logs via Telegram

Telegram is a cross-platform and cloud-based instant messaging service which provides group chat, optional end-to-end encrypted chats, VOIP calling, file sharing, and several other features. We installed it within a previous chapter and you may have already obtained some data from it. It has been scrutinized as a tool used by drug dealers, burglars, terrorists, child abusers, and many fringe groups. The software and services were developed, and are currently maintained, by a Russian company. I would never install this software on any personal or OSINT investigations machine. I only execute it on my dedicated leaks, breaches, logs, and ransomware desktop. Of any technique in this book, the following tutorial is the most likely to infect a machine with a virus. You have been warned.

However, I believe Telegram is quite possibly the best resource for Stealer Logs. Within seconds, you have access to terabytes of data without the need for links to third-party download providers which enforce slow download speeds for free accounts. We can download most of the data directly from Telegram servers at the full bandwidth of our internet connection. Let's start with a demonstration.

There are dozens of Telegram channels which offer free stealer logs in order to promote their paid services. I never recommend paying for any type of stolen data, but I will eagerly download and analyze any content they are sharing via their promotional channels. CRYPTON 2.0 is one of these services. If you were to search "CRYPTON 2.0" in Google, you will likely only see a few BreachForums posts offering logs, which have since been removed. However, if you were to navigate directly to the "CRYPTON 2.0" Telegram channel, you might find an overwhelming amount of free stealer logs. Next, we need to understand Telegram URLs. Telegram links might appear as the following fictious example, **which is not me**.

https://t.me/inteltechniques

If you navigate to a URL like this, your browser will likely prompt you to either choose an application or cancel the request to open an external program. If you have Telegram installed, you can select it and allow your browser to forward any channel links directly to Telegram Desktop. If you do not have Telegram installed, many channels will allow you to see a preview of the content. The URL for this browser-based preview would appear as follows.

https://t.me/s/inteltechniques

In these two examples, I had my name (inteltechniques) in the URL. You would replace inteltechniques with whatever channel you are seeking (channels start with "@"). However, searching a room name within the Telegram application is always the easiest route. Remember, I cannot provide any direct hyperlinks to any stolen data, but you should be able to adapt my following demonstrations in order to access a room such as "CRYPTON 2.0". If you were to find this channel through a URL, you would see a page within your browser similar to the following image to the left. Searching within Telegram should appear as the following image to the right.

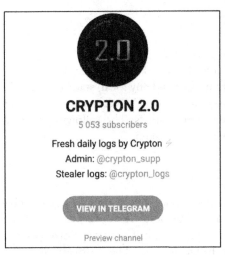

Clicking the "View In Telegram" option (URL) or room name (search result) should open this channel within Telegram and give you the opportunity to join. Notice this channel is promoting purchase of access to their logs collection, but also offering compressed samples for free. The following figure (left) displays how this would appear. In this image, clicking the downward arrow would download the 677 MB compressed archive of logs. Extracting the compressed file should result in a new folder which contains several (possibly thousands) of new folders. Each of these folders will possess a folder structure similar to that seen in the image to the right.

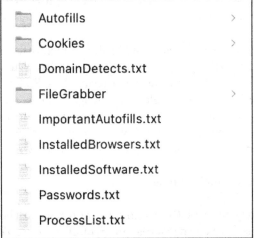

The "Autofills", "Cookies", "Passwords", and "Browsers" files contain the information as previously explained. The "FileGrabber" folder contains all documents stored within the default "Documents" and "Desktop" directories of the victim. These are typically full of Microsoft Word documents and PDFs. In this one sample file, we now have the passwords, documents, and other sensitive details of 1,101 victims. While this is scary and awful, it is also powerful as an investigative tool.

There are always dozens of active stealer logs channels, but you might prefer to only visit a room which attempts to combine free logs into one place. A channel called "Moon Cloud | Free Logs", which has a username of "Moon_Log" could be appropriate for you. At the time of this writing, it offered downloads of logs from DaisyCloud, LulzsecCloudLogs, Tiny Cloud, and dozens of others. There is easily over a terabyte of compressed logs in this channel alone, which presents the logs of hundreds of thousands of victims.

You could easily fill a 4 TB SSD with the logs you collect in one day. Some people save everything, but that can be a challenge. You could download as much as you can fit and then query the data with Ripgrep. However, what about the new 50 GB of compressed data which will be posted tomorrow? What about the next day?

Collecting and storing this data can be a full-time job. This is where I offer two paths to consider. You can continue to download the full logs and clean them, or rely on other people to do your dirty work. Let's understand both options, and start with the manual approach. Afterward, I present a much easier solution which collects less data.

Full Stealer Log Cleansing

Stealer logs are large. I estimate we now have over 40 TB of stealer log data. That is not only a lot of data to store, it can take a long time for Ripgrep to query. At my company, we place everything within a custom database, as explained later, but that is not feasible for most people. While writing this section, I downloaded over 25 compressed files which contained over 30 GB of data including over 37,000 victim logs. That was just as an afternoon demonstration. Imagine how quickly this would pile up if you do it every day. Because of this, I offer an option for those without the need for all of the data included within a typical log.

Most people find the email addresses, usernames, and passwords to be the most valuable part of this data. While the screen captures, documents, and cookies are beneficial, they take up the most space. If desired, you could just keep all of the password files and delete the rest. Some fellow data enthusiasts just cringed at that, but I want to be realistic. Searching through millions of files in order to locate the email addresses and passwords of a suspect may be overkill for some. Instead of saving the individual password files, let's merge them all into one file. Imagine you have thousands or millions of stealer log files decompressed within your Downloads folder. The following Terminal command would navigate to each "passwords.txt" file; extract all of the text data; and compile it into one file titled Passwords.txt. Make sure you are in the right folder within Terminal, which is usually your "Telegram Desktop" folder.

```
find . '*pass*.txt' -exec cat {} \; > ~/Downloads/Passwords.txt
```

We have a problem. Some stealer software titles the passwords file "Passwords.txt" with an uppercase "P". Therefore, the following command is better. It ignores the case of the file and would extract data from both "passwords.txt" and "Passwords.txt". We are using '*pass*' to pick up all files including "pass" anywhere in the name.

```
find . -iname '*pass*.txt' -exec cat {} \; > ~/Downloads/Passwords.txt
```

If desired, you could replicate this for " ImportantAutofills" files with the following.

```
find . -iname 'importantautofills.txt' -exec cat {} \; >
~/Downloads/ImportantAutofills.txt
```

I executed both commands against my test data, which produced a 200 MB Passwords.txt file and a 20 MB ImportantAutofills.txt file. These could be queried quite easily. If I had a terabyte of logs, my passwords file might be only 8 GB. While we keep all of the data we acquire, we also create an ever-growing Passwords.txt file which can be quickly queried for times we may not have immediate access to our entire database. If you were to execute the following command, the date would be appended to your new file, such as Passwords.2023-11-28.txt.

```
timestamp=$(date +%Y-%m-%d) && find . -iname '*pass*.txt' -exec cat {}
\; > ~/Downloads/Passwords.$timestamp.txt
```

The results within this large text file are split over several lines. This will require a variation of our Ripgrep command. As an example, the following text might be present within the file.

URL: https://www.amazon.com/ap/signin
Username: test123@gmail.com
Password: pass456

If we conduct a traditional Ripgrep search for "test123@gmail.com", the result would be as follows.

Username: test123@gmail.com

This is because Ripgrep only displays the line which possesses the data, and not the lines immediately before or after. The data within stealer logs typically splits the results over multiple lines. Therefore, if you want to query this type of data, I recommend the following Ripgrep command.

```
rg -aFiN -A2 -B2 test123@gmail.com
```
This conducts our typical Ripgrep query, but adds "-A" and "-B" followed by "2". This tells Ripgrep to display the two lines before and after each hit, which would appear as follows with our test data.

```
===================
URL: https://www.amazon.com/ap/signin
Username: test123@gmail.com
Password: pass456
===================
```

I suspect some readers are overwhelmed at the amount of data available for investigative use. I get it. I am overwhelmed every day. However, I believe that is part of the fun. If you need to keep screen captures of victim machines and any documents absorbed by the viruses, you will need to download, extract, and store entire stealer logs. Eventually, you will need a server with tens of terabytes of storage. That is what I do, but it is not necessary for most readers. This is where stealer log summaries enter the scene, and may be a more appropriate solution for you.

Stealer Log Summaries via Telegram

Now that there are so many stealer log channels on Telegram, we are seeing new rooms which only offer compressed text-only versions of stealer logs. These channels offer text file downloads of all URLs, usernames, and passwords recently posted within the full stealer logs which I just explained. There are benefits and disadvantages for each, so consider the following.

- Full stealer logs contain screen captures, cookies, and other documents which are not present within the stealer log summaries. This can identify priceless information about your target.
- Full stealer logs assign a folder to a specific victim. You can use this to associate multiple email addresses to a single user. Summaries combine all credentials into one big data dump.
- Stealer log summaries have already been cleaned for you. You simply need to download the text files, combine them, and sort for unique entries. You will only download the important data without the rest of the garbage. Instead of downloading a 1 GB compressed logs file, you can download a 10 MB summary of the credentials.

A typical entry within full stealer logs is as follows:

URL: https://www.amazon.com/ap/signin
Username: test123@gmail.com
Password: pass456

The same entry would appear as follows in a summary file.

https://www.amazon.com/ap/signin:test123@gmail.com: pass456
I will now assume you do not want to collect several terabytes of compressed files and parse through all of them simply to identify the credentials within stealer logs. Instead, we will download stealer log summaries. Much like

the previously mentioned channel of combined log sources called "Moon Cloud | Free Logs", we will focus on another channel called "Moon Cloud | Combo/txtbase" to download summaries.

There are two types of files in this room. The first are stealer log summaries, which tend to be at least 40 MB text files. The other are combo files from these summaries which tend to be less than 20 MB in size, often only a few kilobytes. The following image displays an example. The top file is only 151 KB and includes email addresses and passwords which were acquired from stealer logs. The second file contains 623 MB of URLs, email addresses, and passwords from stealer logs. For this section, we will focus on the latter.

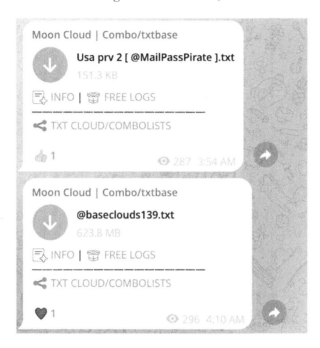

Let's start with the file seen in the previous image. After download, I can immediately access the data without decompression. The file is small enough I can open it within a text editor. The following is a redacted view of the first line.

kevinsaenxxxxient:kevinsaenxxxxientexx:https://www.netflix.com/ar/Login

This indicates that a person with that email address has been infected with a stealer virus; they stored their credentials directly to their web browser; they have a Netflix account; and the username and password combination is used to access that account. If you worked for Netflix, you could use this information to disable the account and prompt the user for a password reset. If you were a criminal, you would illegally use this to access free movies. Let's do another example.

Occasionally, a group will publish a huge collection of stealer log data as compressed files. The channel "Link Cloud" with a Telegram username of "@linkpass" is notorious for this. While writing this chapter, they posted 6.7 GB of compressed files which decompressed to 71.1 GB of text files containing stealer log summaries. Note the password required to decompress the data in the following image. All files should be decompressed before proceeding.

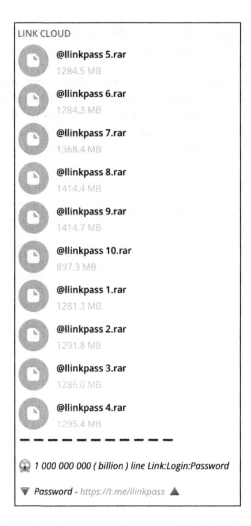

When combined with the posts from the other room, I possessed 76.5 GB of text data. This is quite a feat, and many might think the work is done. While you could offload all of these files onto a SSD for queries, you have two problems. First, many files will have the same file name but unique content. Therefore, saving all files downloaded over a year in one folder will be an issue. The bigger concern is duplicates. Since these groups steal log data from each other, that 76.5 GB of data most certainly contains redundant information. There is no justification to store duplicate entries.

Therefore, I will share my daily and weekly ritual with you. This method will download all available summaries every day; combine the daily haul into one file without any duplicates; then merge the data into your primary collection weekly, avoiding redundant data. While I hope you follow along and replicate my steps, I offer a script soon that will do all of the work on your behalf.

Daily Tasks

On today's date, I downloaded a total of 80 GB of decompressed text files containing stealer logs. That is higher than normal, but not completely out of the ordinary. I then executed the following commands within a single Terminal window, with an explanation of each. A replica of these will be used in our script.

The following creates a time stamp which we can use to name our file later. This is important so that we do not overwrite our collected data every day.

```
timestamp=$(date +%Y-%m-%d-%H-%M)
```

The following changes the active Terminal directory to the folder used by Telegram by default for downloads. Your folder may vary.

```
cd ~/Downloads/Telegram\ Desktop
```

The following command combines all text files into one file called Logs.csv.

```
cat *.txt > Logs.csv
```

The following commands delete all the original text files, then renames our working combined file to Logs.txt.

```
rm *.txt && mv Logs.csv Logs.txt
```

Next, we need to eliminate the duplicates with the following command.

```
LC_ALL=C sort -u -b -i -f -S 80% --parallel=8 Logs.txt > Logs-
$timestamp.txt
```

The result was only 57 GB of data within my new text file (down from 80 GB originally). Finally, the following commands remove our original Logs.txt file and moves our new file to our Downloads directory. This is to ensure that the next time we run this series of commands, we do not delete the file we just created.

```
rm Logs.txt && mv Logs-$timestamp.txt ~/Downloads/
```

Your daily task is complete and you would replicate these steps tomorrow with any new stealer log summaries posted to your joined Telegram channels.

Weekly Tasks

If you download the stealer log summaries every day or two and conduct these steps, you will soon have a substantial collection of stealer log data. I often find myself with a folder of files such as the following.

```
Logs-2023-11-25-09-39.txt
Logs-2023-11-26-09-48.txt
Logs-2023-11-27-09-19.txt
Logs-2023-11-28-08-41.txt
Logs-2023-11-29-09-00.txt
```

I can see from these file names that I tend to complete this process during the 9:00 hour. I try to collate these files every week or two in order to query them from my SSD. The following two commands merge all sorted logs files within the Downloads folder into a single file which should be free of any duplicates.

```
cd ~/Downloads && timestamp=$(date +%Y-%m-%d-%H-%M)
LC_ALL=C sort -u -b -i -f -m Logs* > Merged-$timestamp.txt
```

This creates our timestamp and takes any SORTED files in the current directory which begin with "Logs" and MERGES (-m) them into a single file. Finally, we can delete the original Logs files which are no longer needed with the following command.

```
rm Logs*
```

You can now move this merged file into your SSD. My SSD is labeled DATA and I have a folder at the root of the drive titled "Logs". The following command moves my new file to that folder if using macOS. The second command would move it if using Linux.

```
mv Merged* /Volumes/DATA/Logs
mv Merged* /media/$USER/DATA/Logs
```

You could collect these "Merged" files in your SSD and query them. There is no harm in that, as each file possess a unique name due to the timestamp. However, you will find the duplicates start piling up again. Several stealer logs will upload the same data every day from actively-infected computers. Therefore, I prefer to keep my primary stealer log collection free of redundancies.

Assume you now have a file similar to Merged-2023-11-23-09-11.txt (November 23, 2023) in your SSD Logs folder. It possesses all of the stealer log summaries which you collected over a week. It is now one week later, and you have seven new sorted Logs text files in your Downloads folder after conducting the "Daily Tasks" section previously mentioned. As also previously stated, you could merge them all and copy the new file to your SSD, but then we have redundancy issues. The following four macOS commands merges all of the sorted log files in your Downloads directory with your current primary merged file(s) in your SSD Logs folder to create a new file which possesses all of the data without any redundancies. The original files are deleted and this new file is copied to your SSD Logs folder.

```
cd ~/Downloads
LC_ALL=C sort -u -b -i -f -m Logs* /Volumes/DATA/Logs/* > Current.txt
rm Logs* /Volumes/DATA/Logs/*
mv Current.txt /Volumes/DATA/Logs/Current.txt
```

The following commands for Linux are slightly different.

```
cd ~/Downloads
LC_ALL=C sort -u -b -i -f -m Logs* /media/$USER/DATA/Logs/* >
Current.txt
rm Logs* /media/$USER/DATA/Logs/*
mv Current.txt /media/$USER/DATA/Logs/Current.txt
```

That was a lot. Let's summarize everything from the beginning. We collected a bunch of stealer log summaries from Telegram into the default Telegram downloads folder. After the daily downloads completed, we sorted all of the text files into a single file without any duplicates, and moved it to our Downloads folder. It appeared similar to Logs-2023-12-01-09-52.txt. We repeated this every day. Whenever these sorted files started to pile up, we merged them all into one file without any duplicates. We moved this file to our SSD for future queries. The next week, we repeated the process and had several new sorted Logs files in our Downloads directory. We executed a command to combine them with the file on our SSD to make a new primary logs collection file with no duplicates. We moved that to the SSD and eliminated the unnecessary files. You could repeat this every week (or month) as desired. Your "Current.txt" logs file will slowly grow without duplicates on your SSD.

Was it worth all the effort? Only you can decide. I currently possess a folder with 300 GB of unique stealer logs which I query almost every day. There are billions of credentials in there. It is priceless to me. At the time of this writing, the "Moon Cloud" and "Link Cloud" channels possessed many terabytes of stealer log summaries, in text format, dating back to August 2023 (with logs dating back to 2015). After downloading them all and removing duplicate entries, you should be able to replicate my entire 300 GB collection of most known stealer log credentials in one day. In fact, you will likely possess the exact same data as the numerous new companies selling stealer logs to organizations as a defense technique. Why pay for partial access when you can possess all of the data yourself?

In a moment, I will present a script which displays two sorting options. The first conducts your daily tasks for you while the second completes the weekly tasks. This script will also query all logs data. If you plan to only dabble in this type of data, these tutorials serve as an example to the threats and investigative benefits of stealer logs. The only way you could truly benefit from them within your own investigations is to download everything you find daily. That is quite a burden. I hired a full-time employee to do just that. He constantly acquires new leaks, breaches, logs, and ransomware, and then imports into our custom database for use by my staff. That comes with quite an expense, but we see results which justifies the activity.

Once you have built a massive collection of these logs, you can use Ripgrep to query them as previously mentioned. In 2021, I was investigating an unknown person harassing one of my clients. He was using a throwaway email address which seemed impossible to trace. It was not present within any breach data. However, it appeared within my stealer logs, which included a device name similar to Desktop-u3ty6. Searching that device identifier presented dozens of email addresses and passwords in use on that machine. This quickly revealed my suspect, a 15-year-old kid. Further investigation confirmed his computer became infected after downloading a pirated version of anti-virus software. The irony.

One week prior to writing this, I was investigating a financial account takeover attempt on behalf of a client. Someone switched her bank account to a "burner" email address. This criminal apparently possessed a stealer virus, because searching that email address immediately hit upon the entire logs for his computer. This included his "FileGrabber" folder which contained a recently modified resume. I was able to provide a full dossier on the suspect to my client, and the entire investigation took less than five minutes.

I suspect my attorney will scold me if I continue to provide more examples. Instead, I will leave you with a list of known Telegram stealer log rooms for you to conduct your own research. These include Base Cloud, Boosty, BradMax, Bugatti Cloud, CBank, Cloud Logs, Crypton, DB_Cloud, Eternal Logs, Expert Logs, Hub Head, HUBLOGS, Keeper Cloud, Link Cloud, Logs Arthouse, Logs Cloud, Luffich Cloud, Luxury Logs, Moon Cloud, NinjaByte, Observer Cloud, OneLogs, Redlogs Cloud, Ruban Cloud, Snatch Logs, Syxap's Cloud, Tor Logs, Wild Logs, and X-Cloud. This is only a sample, and there are many others which emerge and disappear daily. Start with Google.

I offer one final recommendation for Telegram: take advantage of the search field. As I wrote this, I noticed an announcement about a new breach at a cryptocurrency provider. Searching the name of the service within Telegram immediately presented numerous free download options. Follow as many breach-related channels in order to increase search results of interesting data.

You can also search sites such as BreachForums for logs, as a lot of members post direct download links which do not require purchased or earned credits. The following query would identify posts on BreachForums which may be helpful.

site:breachforums.is "Url-Log-Pass"
site:breachforums.is "mega.nz" "stealer log"

You may also have success with the following queries.

site:anonfiles.com "logs"
site:mediafire.com "logs"
Combo Files

If you were browsing the stealer logs offerings within the "Moon Cloud | Combo/txtbase" channel, you likely noticed a lot of smaller files which did not contain stealer log summaries. These are "Combo" files, which are typically the usernames and passwords extracted from the stealer log summaries. Most of the time, the content within these files is also available within the stealer log summaries, but that is not always the case. I have downloaded many combo files which contained data not present within any stealer logs. Consider the following screen captures.

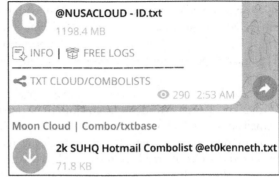

In the first image, the top file is only 1.6 MB while the lower is 310 MB. This is the first sign that the larger file contains stealer logs while the smaller possesses only usernames and passwords. In the second image, these are reversed. The top is a large stealer log summary while the bottom possesses only 2,000 Hotmail usernames with passwords. These channels will often extract credentials from stealer logs for a specific service (in this case Hotmail), and offer them to people who may want to target that service with illegal actions.

You may want to download all of these combo files for your own collection. I always recommend doing this after you have acquired and sorted the logs for the day. Otherwise, the combo files will get mixed into your logs. The process is the same. Download all of the desired combo files into an empty Telegram Downloads folder; remove duplicates; and move the result out of your Telegram directory. The following modified commands should work for macOS and Linux users. Note that the sort command is on two lines.

```
timestamp=$(date +%Y-%m-%d-%H-%M)
cd ~/Downloads/Telegram\ Desktop
cat *.txt > Combos.csv
rm *.txt && mv Combos.csv Combos.txt
LC_ALL=C sort -u -b -i -f -S 80% --parallel=8 Combos.txt > Combos-
$timestamp.txt
rm Combos.txt && mv Combos-$timestamp.txt ~/Downloads/
```

If you can only collect one type of data, I highly recommend logs over combos. Most combo files will display thousands of lines in the format of EMAIL:PASSWORD.

Mega.nz Issues

As you continue your journey into data collection, you will likely find several links on the popular file sharing website Mega (mega.nz). This service provides 50 GB of free storage, and is often used by criminals to store and share leaks, breaches, and logs. Download speeds are typically fantastic, but we have a new problem. Free users have a limited amount of bandwidth they are allotted within a 24-hour period. Even worse, those of us using a VPN, as highly recommended, are sharing IP addresses with people abusing Maga's free tiers. This often results in blocks from Mega encouraging us to purchase a paid plan. I cannot completely eliminate these hurdles, but I can make them much more tolerable. For this, I recommend Megatools, which can be installed with the following steps.

macOS: `brew install megatools`
Linux: Download and install from https://megatools.megous.com/builds/builds/
Windows: `choco install megatools`

Once installed, we can download a Mega link directly via terminal. A demonstration should explain the benefits of this method over a traditional web browser download. I opened Telegram and searched "mega.nz". I was presented a post which claimed to offer 63 GB of stealer logs hosted on Mega. I clicked the link and was immediately presented the following warning from Mega.

Limited available transfer quota

Your queued download exceeds the current transfer quota available for your IP address and could be interrupted before completion. Please consider subscribing to a MEGA Pro plan which will substantially raise your transfer quota.

⬤ Billed monthly   ◯ Billed yearly

I then opened Terminal; changed the directory to my Downloads folder; and entered `megatools dl` followed by the same Mega file URL. The download began immediately and it continuously disclosed the download speed and percent of completion. Whenever I encountered a bandwidth restriction, the Terminal command kept my place and retried to resume every couple of minutes. When that happened, I simply switched VPN servers and the download continued. This would not have helped with the browser download, as the session cookies monitor your overall usage, regardless of your IP address.

I use this method for every large Mega download I encounter. Not only does it bypass some of the restrictions, it is not prone to browser memory problems which can result in corrupted or incomplete downloads.

Criticism

I know what some readers are probably thinking. You may believe that sharing these types of details is irresponsible and will lead to further abuse of the victims of these attacks. I respect your opinion and understand your concern. I also believe that thinking is naive. The criminals who are going to abuse this data do not need a tutorial from me. If anything, they would laugh at my basic understanding and explanation of their world. I am sure they could teach me better ways of doing all of this. I do not believe anyone is going to buy this book and begin further abusing this type of data.

Hardware stores sell hammers; websites sell lock picks; and local stores sell guns. All of these can (and are) abused. That does not mean that they should be restricted from those who are responsible with the items. I would rather take the chance that one person will misuse this information if it helps a thousand people use it for good. The more analysts and researchers who understand and collect this data, the better we will all be. If we had enough large companies monitoring and acting upon this data, we may see it go away because it is no longer useful to the criminals. Ignoring these techniques allows the criminals to continue their games and win. If I was the CEO of PayPal, I would dedicate employees to this task; have them identify any presence of PayPal credentials; and disable them before they are abused. You could replace PayPal with any other financial institution in those statements.

There are books about detailed computer hacking, malware creation, and various "black hat" lessons. They are used by security researchers, penetration testers, and other professionals who are tasked with responding to bad situations. My hope is that this book can help those who can use this data for good (defense and offense). I would have loved to have all of this when I was investigating cyber-crime for the FBI, but they probably would not have allowed me to use it. We can either pretend there is not a problem or we can take action to stop some of this mess. We can either allow criminals to have all of the power with this data or we can use it against them. I have witnessed countless examples of criminals accidentally infecting their own machines and exposing their own data.

CHAPTER FOURTY-THREE
RANSOMWARE

If you thought I was pushing the boundaries of ethical data acquisition, the following might make you uncomfortable. You have likely heard about ransomware infection. It is the illegal activity by criminals which steals data from a company, encrypts all of their files, and demands a ransom to gain access to the unusable data remaining on their own servers. When companies began creating better backups which eliminated the need to pay the ransom, the criminals took a new route. If the victims do not pay, all of their data is uploaded to the internet via Tor websites for anyone to download. This generates terabytes of private documents, email messages, databases, and every other imaginable digital file. Is this OSINT data? I don't think so. However, an investigator working on behalf of a victim company should know where to find this information.

Most sites which announce and distribute ransomware will require the Tor Browser. However, we will also retrieve recent data posted within clear-source options such as Telegram. Let's start with a demonstration using the Tor browser. The first step is to identify the current URLs for the various ransomware groups. I present the following resource, which should be all you need to identify your targets.

https://github.com/fastfire/deepdarkCTI/blob/main/ransomware_gang.md

This collection does not require access to the Tor network, but many of the sites included will. This site attempts to provide a current status of various criminal groups; direct links to otherwise hidden sites offering data; and identify sites which have gone offline. The following figure displays a current partial view of this service.

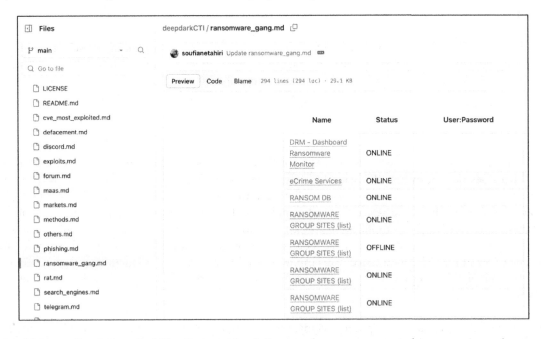

You should have already installed Tor Browser by following the steps presented in a previous chapter. If you did not, navigate to https://www.torproject.org/download/ and install the Tor Browser for your operating system. You should then be able to copy any links from the previous Github page and paste them into Tor Browser to see the content. Any website ending in ".onion" will require the Tor Browser.

I copied the Everest link to navigate to the official Everest ransomware distribution page. I then saw dozens of victims listed within their page. I will not identify any victims throughout this chapter, and will focus only on the data and type of organization. I clicked on the first victim, which was a non-profit health care organization which was hit with ransomware in October 2022. The page offered three links hosted at gofile.io, each approximately 30 GB compressed. The following figure displays one of the download options. Notice we can see the number of successful downloads. This could be vital if you are investigating this breach on behalf of the company. This confirms people are actively downloading the stolen data from this group.

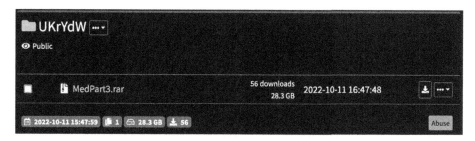

If you were to download these files, you would have 120 GB of data which was stolen during the breach. Most of the data is of no use to an online investigator. We intentionally destroy anything which contains intellectual property or internal housekeeping affairs. The breach provided over 37,000 medical documents including patient records. This breach also included many copies of driver's licenses (front and back), insurance cards, and other forms of identification. This data is quite invasive and you may feel uncomfortable accessing any of it. I completely understand. We digest it into our system in order to make immediate notifications to any of our clients which are present within the breach. We only use this data for defensive practices, and mark all medical data to be ignored when staff conducts OSINT queries into the data.

Recently, we took in a large ransomware data set which included scans of the front and back of thousands of customers' driver's licenses. Our systems analyze all images, documents, and PDFs, and extract any text content via Optical Character Recognition (OCR). This allows us to query or monitor our clients' details, which can notify us when their identification cards or financial data is present online. This process has weaknesses, especially when scanned images are of poor quality. The text must be properly identified in order to receive any alerts about client data.

We also started scanning all documents for any type of barcode, including QR codes and license barcodes. This has paid off greatly, and this recent breach turned out to be quite beneficial. Our automated barcode scanning element immediately identified the text details of all customers, which allows us to query by name, address, DOB, DL, etc. The following figure (left) displays a redacted back of a scanned DL from this recent breach.

The figure (right) displays the (redacted) automated text conversion of that barcode, which allows us to ingest text data into our overall breach database for easy access. The first lesson here is that barcode analysis of entire data sets can reveal much more data about the victims within the breach. In this example, our systems ingested the images; performed OCR on all text; scanned the barcodes; populated all text data within our database; and alerted us that a client's driver's license was within the breach, all without any manual effort from us.

The second lesson is to never allow companies to scan your identification. It will never be stored securely and will be leaked during the next attack. The barcode on the back of a passport card only includes the passport number, and may be much safer whenever required to hand over ID. My driver's license possesses a vinyl sticker on the back which contains a new barcode. Scanning it reveals a stern text message about consumer rights. I have yet to allow anyone to scan it though.

The Everest site has terabytes of data published for anyone to see. Add that to the other dozens of groups and you have more data than you likely want to store. We typically eliminate large files such as PDFs and Office documents once our system has ingested the text from the data. Let's conduct another example on the clear web and look at some pure text data which would be much easier to analyze.

In October of 2022, I reviewed a Telegram channel called "baseleak". This channel was offering a 1 GB download of recently stolen medical data in text format. The first figure displays the original post. However, there was no instant download option. Please note I have redacted these posts in order to protect the identity of the victim organization. This group adds a layer of complexity in order to retrieve and analyze the information. I had to copy the text on the last line, as visible in the second figure. I then had to click "@MotokoBot" to load the view seen in the third figure), where I had to paste this text. The password to access the file was present in the comments of the post, as seen in the fourth figure. This finally unlocked the link, which is visible in the fifth figure, which connected me to the download site Mega, as seen in the final figure. The entire process took only a couple of minutes.

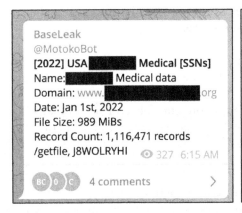
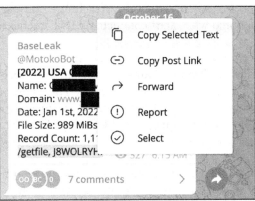

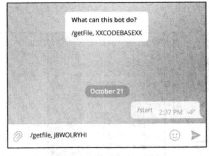

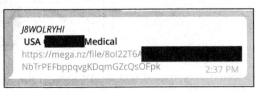

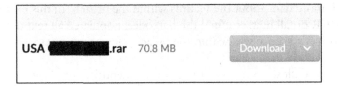

The 70 MB compressed file extracted to an almost 1 GB CSV file titled "data.csv". It contained the following 92 fields of data.

Master Patient ID, Name, Sex, Date of Birth, DOB Approximate, Age, AgeInDays, AgeText, PrematureDays, GestationalAge, BSA, Ideal Body Weight, Height, Weight, HeightMod, WeightMod, SSN, BMI, Brand Preference, Safety Caps, Race, Language, Religion, Pregnant, Breast Feeding, Smoker, Address 1, Address 2, City, State, ZIP, Last Room, Last Hospital#, Last Admit Date, Last Discharge Date, Last Visit #, AllergyList, DiagnosisList, PhoneNumber, AssigningAuthority, Visit #, Medical Record #, Hospital #, Room #, CurrentOrPreviousRoom, Room, Prev Room #, Admit Date, Discharge Date, PlannedDischargeDate, PCU, Facility Code, Service Type, Service Type Description, CommentsTextID, Physician Code, Physician, Unverified Orders, CrCl, AdminRecord, Diet Code, Diet Description, Clinical Service, PassStart, PassStop, Encounter Number, AccountNumber, AllowLateCharges, AccountNumberAssignAuth, MedicalRecordNumAssignAuth, HospitalNumberAssignAuth, InternalCommentsTextID, InternalCommentsText, CommentsText, org_int_id, loc_lvl_3_id, loc_lvl_4_id, loc_lvl_5_id, pcu_int_id, pat_grp_int_id, psn_int_id, Patient Type Group, SerumCreatinine, PatientCategory, VisitActive, out_prt_lc, pat_cat_cd, vst_sta_cd, visit_status_code, PatientInBed, Complaint, FinancialClass

That is a lot of invasive and sensitive content. We avoid possessing explicit medical data, such as medical conditions or patient data. However, we do collect and store names, DOBs, SSNs, addresses, and phone numbers in order to make proper notifications to our clients. Therefore, I executed the following command to extract only the fields important to me (and my clients), as previously explained.

```
cut -d, -f1,2,3,4,6,17,27,31 data.csv > data-cleaned.txt
```

This minimized my CSV to a 228 MB txt file. I noticed there were many duplicate entries, so I executed the following, also as previously explained.

```
LC_ALL=C sort -u -b -i -f data-cleaned.txt > Data-Final.txt
```

I then noticed a lot of extra spaces within the lines, so I executed the following to replace every two spaces with only a single space.

```
sed -i 's/  / /gI' Data-Final.txt
```

This resulted in a 31 MB text file with 375,000 unique entries. A redacted example of the text follows.

Master Patient ID, Name, Sex, Date of Birth, Age, SSN, Address 1, ZIP
00xx3, PRESTON, JAxx, F, 1982-xx-xx, 459xxxxxx,47xx Rxxxxx RD, ROxx, TX, 77xxx

This file contains extremely sensitive stolen information about 375,000 people. If any of our clients are within this data, we will receive an alert and can make notification. I hope you now see why it is so important to protect any breach data which you acquire. While it is publicly available content, you must ensure that you do not leak it further. This is why we never store any breach data within the cloud. It is all stored on a physical server in our office, and access is tightly controlled. We also monitor all activity for abuse.

Telegram Ransomware Search

Monitoring every ransomware group within their dedicated Tor websites is exhausting. Fortunately, we have an easier option. I highly recommend joining a Telegram channel called RansomWatcher. This channel monitors all of the active ransomware groups and posts a notification when a victim has been infected. The following image represents only a fraction of the victims posted the day I wrote this section. This channel does not possess or offer any sensitive data.

```
Group:Snatch

Victim:Museum Für Naturkunde

Discovered:2023-11-30 11:49:50.357378      5:29 AM

Group:Snatch

Victim:Tyson Foods

Discovered:2023-11-30 11:49:50.998497      5:29 AM

Group:Donutleaks

Victim:Albert, Righter & Tittmann Architechts, Inc.

Discovered:2023-11-30 11:50:01.820972      5:29 AM

Group:Donutleaks

Victim:Carriereindustrial.Com

Discovered:2023-11-30 11:50:02.989838      5:29 AM

Group:Donutleaks

Victim:Sidockgroup. Published

Discovered:2023-11-30 11:50:03.848498      5:29 AM

Group:Donutleaks

Victim:Who Is MONTY? ;)

Discovered:2023-11-30 11:50:04.610201      5:29 AM
```

I can now search the name of any company within this channel to see if they appear in any known ransomware attack. If anything is present, I can research the group responsible for the attack on the previous GitHub page. I can then navigate to the group's Tor page and see if any data has been published from the attack. Another alternative to this type of monitoring is https://ransomwatch.telemetry.ltd.

If your employer tasks you with the investigation of content stolen from your organization, I want you to know what to do. I want you to locate, obtain, and analyze the exact same data which criminals are abusing. We can no longer keep our heads in the sand and hope no one notices the leakage of sensitive data. We must think like the criminals and attack from their mindset.

If you are an online investigator who can responsibly benefit from this type of data, I want you to know what to do with the content you find. I also want you to protect the data and make sure you cause no further harm. Every day, this type of data assists me with positive identification of the true identity of stalkers, harassers, scammers, and other unsavory people. We can either allow this data to be solely used by criminals to make our lives more difficult, or we can use it as a tool to expose those criminals which would otherwise remain hidden.

CHAPTER FOURTY-FOUR
QUERIES, SCRIPTS, DATABASES, & BACKUPS

This brings us to the elephant in the room. How does someone new to breach data collection organize and query all of it? The obvious optimal solution is to create a database and then identify any fields which should be indexed when importing each breach. Elasticsearch would work well for this. However, maintaining an internal database would be a full-time job and database maintenance far exceeds the scope of this book. I believe large databases are overkill for most individual data collectors. Where does that leave us? I have simpler options.

While I was writing this section, I put my feet in the shoes of a reader new to this type of data collection. I pretended I did not have access to our investigations server and grabbed a couple of terabytes of data similar to that which has been previously discussed here. Conducting the Ripgrep queries discussed throughout the guide worked fine, but they were dreadfully slow across 2 TB of data. I needed to isolate the scope of each query to eliminate unnecessary search time.

I decided to create a script which would manually query the data in the most efficient way possible, absent a structured database. First, I categorized all files in order to limit the data for each query. I then placed everything on my SanDisk 4 TB Extreme Portable SSD (amzn.to/3GO0cP2). The drive was labeled "DATA" and possessed the following folders at the root of the drive. After each folder name, I include a brief description of the content within parentheses.

COMB	(The COMB user:pass database previously explained)
Combos	(Additional user:pass files)
Databases	(Breached databases containing SQL, txt, csv, and other formats)
Hashes	(The Hashes.org and HashMob data sets)
International	(International data which may not apply to every daily investigation)
Logs	(Stealer logs acquired using the previously-explained techniques)
People	(Various people search database leaks and breaches)
Ransomware	(Any ransomware content including txt, pdf, csv, and other data)
Voter	(All voter data acquired during the previous tutorials)
Whois	(All Whois data acquired during the previous tutorials)

You can either manually create these folders on your own drive, or copy and paste the following commands to replicate the structure on your own drive labeled "DATA" on your macOS machine. It is vital that your drive possesses this internal name for all of this to work.

```
mkdir /Volumes/DATA/COMB/
mkdir /Volumes/DATA/Combos/
mkdir /Volumes/DATA/Databases/
mkdir /Volumes/DATA/Hashes/
mkdir /Volumes/DATA/International/
mkdir /Volumes/DATA/Logs/
mkdir /Volumes/DATA/People/
mkdir /Volumes/DATA/Ransomware/
mkdir /Volumes/DATA/Voter/
mkdir /Volumes/DATA/Whois/
```

Linux users would conduct the following.

```
mkdir /media/$USER/DATA/COMB/
mkdir /media/$USER/DATA/Combos/
```

```
mkdir /media/$USER/DATA/Databases/
mkdir /media/$USER/DATA/Hashes/
mkdir /media/$USER/DATA/International/
mkdir /media/$USER/DATA/Logs/
mkdir /media/$USER/DATA/People/
mkdir /media/$USER/DATA/Ransomware/
mkdir /media/$USER/DATA/Voter/
mkdir /media/$USER/DATA/Whois/
```

You now have some structure for your data. You can place the files you obtain in the folder most appropriate for that type of data. Once my data was split into these folders, I created a script to query all of it. The entire text from the macOS script is presented here soon. However, let's download and prepare it with the following commands.

macOS Users:

```
cd /Applications
curl -O https://inteltechniques.com/data/DataTool
chmod +x DataTool
```

Linux Users:

```
cd /home/
sudo curl -O  https://inteltechniques.com/data/DataTool.sh
sudo curl -O https://inteltechniques.com/data/DataTool.desktop
sudo chmod +x DataTool.sh
sudo mv DataTool.desktop /usr/share/applications/
```

This will present an executable script within the Applications folder (macOS) or the Show Applications menu (Linux) called "DataTool". Clicking the file launches the script and presents the following menu. Make sure you have installed all necessary software from the previous chapters. The following images display the menu, an information notice, and query window.

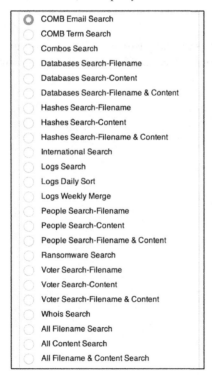

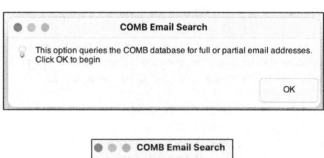

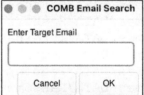

The following six pages presents the entire macOS script, which is almost identical to the Linux option previously downloaded.

```
opt1="COMB Email Search"
opt2="COMB Term Search"
opt3="Combos Search"
opt4="Databases Search-Filename"
opt5="Databases Search-Content"
opt6="Databases Search-Filename & Content"
opt7="Hashes Search-Filename"
opt8="Hashes Search-Content"
opt9="Hashes Search-Filename & Content"
opt10="International Search"
opt11="Logs Search"
opt12="Logs Daily Sort"
opt13="Logs Weekly Merge"
opt14="People Search-Filename"
opt15="People Search-Content"
opt16="People Search-Filename & Content"
opt17="Ransomware Search"
opt18="Voter Search-Filename"
opt19="Voter Search-Content"
opt20="Voter Search-Filename & Content"
opt21="Whois Search"
opt22="All Filename Search"
opt23="All Content Search"
opt24="All Filename & Content Search"


menu=$(zenity --list --title "Data Tool" --radiolist --column "" --column "" TRUE "$opt1" FALSE "$opt2"
FALSE "$opt3" FALSE "$opt4" FALSE "$opt5" FALSE "$opt6" FALSE "$opt7" FALSE "$opt8" FALSE
"$opt9" FALSE "$opt10" FALSE "$opt11" FALSE "$opt12" FALSE "$opt13" FALSE "$opt14" FALSE
"$opt15" FALSE "$opt16" FALSE "$opt17" FALSE "$opt18" FALSE "$opt19" FALSE "$opt20" FALSE
"$opt21" FALSE "$opt22" FALSE "$opt23" FALSE "$opt24" --height=700 --width=300)


case $menu in


$opt1 )
zenity --info --text="This option queries the COMB database for full or partial email addresses. Click "OK" to
begin" --title="COMB Email Search"
data=$(zenity --entry --title "COMB Email Search" --text "Enter Target Email")
cd /Volumes/DATA/COMB
bash ./query.sh $data
echo
echo "Press Enter to return to menu"
read data
exec /Applications/DataTool
;;


$opt2 )
zenity --info --text="This option queries the COMB database for any term. Click "OK" to begin" --
title="COMB Term Search"
data=$(zenity --entry --title "COMB Term Search" --text "Enter Target Data")
cd /Volumes/DATA/COMB
```

```
rg -aFiN $data
echo
echo "Press Enter to return to menu"
read data
exec /Applications/DataTool
;;

$opt3 )
zenity --info --text="This option queries combo files for any term. Click "OK" to begin" --title="COMB
Term Search"
data=$(zenity --entry --title "Combos Search" --text "Enter Target Data")
cd /Volumes/DATA/Combos
rg -aFiN $data
echo
echo "Press Enter to return to menu"
read data
exec /Applications/DataTool
;;

$opt4 )
zenity --info --text="This option queries all file names in the Databases folder. It is used to identify the exact
file name to be searched next. Click "OK" to begin" --title="Databases Search-Filename"
data=$(zenity --entry --title "Databases Search-Filename" --text "Enter Partial Filename")
cd /Volumes/DATA/Databases
find . | grep -i $data
echo
echo "Select and copy any file path and press Enter to return to menu"
read data
exec /Applications/DataTool
;;

$opt5 )
zenity --info --text="This option queries all Databases for any term. Click "OK" to begin" --title="Databases
Search-Content"
data=$(zenity --entry --title "Databases Search-Content" --text "Enter Target Data")
cd /Volumes/DATA/Databases
rg -aFiN $data
echo
echo "Press Enter to return to menu"
read data
exec /Applications/DataTool
;;

$opt6 )
zenity --info --text="This option queries only a specific Database file for any term. Click "OK" to begin" --
title="Databases Search-Filename & Content"
data1=$(zenity --entry --title "Databases Search-Filename & Content" --text "Enter File Path")
data2=$(zenity --entry --title "Databases Search-Filename & Content" --text "Enter Target Data")
cd /Volumes/DATA/Databases
rg -aFiN $data2 $data1
echo
echo "Press Enter to return to menu"
read data
```

```
exec /Applications/DataTool
;;

$opt7 )
zenity --info --text="This option queries all file names in the Hashes folder. It is used to identify the exact file
name to be searched next. Click "OK" to begin" --title="Hashes Search-Filename"
data=$(zenity --entry --title "Hashes Search-Filename" --text "Enter Partial Filename")
cd /Volumes/DATA/Hashes
find . | grep -i $data
echo
echo "Select and copy any file path and press Enter to return to menu"
read data
exec /Applications/DataTool
;;

$opt8 )
zenity --info --text="This option queries all Hashes for any term. Click "OK" to begin" --title="Hashes
Search-Content"
data=$(zenity --entry --title "Hashes Search-Content" --text "Enter Target Data")
cd /Volumes/DATA/Hashes
rg -aFiN $data
echo
echo "Press Enter to return to menu"
read data
exec /Applications/DataTool
;;

$opt9 )
zenity --info --text="This option queries only a specific Hashes file for any term. Click "OK" to begin" --
title="Hashes Search-Filename & Content"
data1=$(zenity --entry --title "Hashes Search-Filename & Content" --text "Enter File Path")
data2=$(zenity --entry --title "Hashes Search-Filename & Content" --text "Enter Target Data")
cd /Volumes/DATA/Hashes
rg -aFiN $data2 $data1
echo
echo "Press Enter to return to menu"
read data
exec /Applications/DataTool
;;

$opt10 )
zenity --info --text="This option queries International files for any term. Click "OK" to begin" --
title="International Term Search"
data=$(zenity --entry --title "International Search" --text "Enter Target Data")
cd /Volumes/DATA/International
rg -aFiN $data
echo
echo "Press Enter to return to menu"
read data
exec /Applications/DataTool
;;

$opt11 )
```

```
zenity --info --text="This option queries Logs files for any term. Click "OK" to begin" --title="Logs Search"
data=$(zenity --entry --title "Logs Search" --text "Enter Target Data")
cd /Volumes/DATA/Logs
rg -aFiN $data
echo
echo "Press Enter to return to menu"
read data
exec /Applications/DataTool
;;


$opt12 )
zenity --info --text="This option combines all log files within the Telegram download folder and sorts for
unique entries. Click "OK" to begin" --title="Logs Daily Sort"
timestamp=$(date +%Y-%m-%d-%H-%M)
cd ~/Downloads/Telegram\ Desktop
cat *.txt > Logs.csv
rm *.txt
mv Logs.csv Logs.txt
LC_ALL=C sort -u -b -i -f -S 80% --parallel=8 Logs.txt > Logs-Sorted-$timestamp.txt
rm Logs.txt
mv Logs-Sorted-$timestamp.txt ~/Downloads/
echo
echo "Press Enter to return to menu"
read data
exec /Applications/DataTool
;;


$opt13 )
zenity --info --text="This option merges all sorted Logs files within the Downloads folder with the primary
collection on the SSD. Click "OK" to begin" --title="Logs Weekly Merge"
cd ~/Downloads
LC_ALL=C sort -u -b -i -f -m Logs* /Volumes/DATA/Logs/* > Current.txt
rm Logs* /Volumes/DATA/Logs/*
mv Current.txt /Volumes/DATA/Logs/Current.txt
echo
echo "Press Enter to return to menu"
read data
exec /Applications/DataTool
;;


$opt14 )
zenity --info --text="This option queries all file names in the People folder. It is used to identify the exact file
name to be searched next. Click "OK" to begin" --title="People Search-Filename"
data=$(zenity --entry --title "People Search-Filename" --text "Enter Partial Filename")
cd /Volumes/DATA/People
find . | grep -i $data
echo
echo "Select and copy any file path and press Enter to return to menu"
read data
exec /Applications/DataTool
;;


$opt15 )
```

```
zenity --info --text="This option queries all People data for any term. Click "OK" to begin" --title="People
Search-Content"
data=$(zenity --entry --title "People Search-Content" --text "Enter Target Data")
cd /Volumes/DATA/People
rg -aFiN $data
echo
echo "Press Enter to return to menu"
read data
exec /Applications/DataTool
;;

$opt16 )
zenity --info --text="This option queries only a specific People file for any term. Click "OK" to begin" --
title="People Search-Filename & Content"
data1=$(zenity --entry --title "People Search-Filename & Content" --text "Enter File Path")
data2=$(zenity --entry --title "People Search-Filename & Content" --text "Enter Target Data")
cd /Volumes/DATA/People
rg -aFiN $data2 $data1
echo
echo "Press Enter to return to menu"
read data
exec /Applications/DataTool
;;

$opt17 )
zenity --info --text="This option queries all Ransomware data for any term. Click "OK" to begin" --
title="Ransomware Search"
data=$(zenity --entry --title "Ransomware Search" --text "Enter Target Data")
cd /Volumes/DATA/Ransomware
rg -aFiN $data
echo
echo "Press Enter to return to menu"
read data
exec /Applications/DataTool
;;

$opt18 )
zenity --info --text="This option queries all file names in the Voter folder. It is used to identify the exact file
name to be searched next. Click "OK" to begin" --title="Voter Search-Filename"
data=$(zenity --entry --title "Voter Search-Filename" --text "Enter Target Data")
cd /Volumes/DATA/Voter
find . | grep -i $data
echo
echo "Select and copy any file path and press Enter to return to menu"
read data
exec /Applications/DataTool
;;

$opt19 )
zenity --info --text="This option queries all Voter data for any term. Click "OK" to begin" --title="Voter
Search-Content"
data=$(zenity --entry --title "Voter Search-Content" --text "Enter Target Data")
cd /Volumes/DATA/Voter
```

```
rg -aFiN $data
echo
echo "Press Enter to return to menu"
read data
exec /Applications/DataTool
;;

$opt20 )
zenity --info --text="This option queries only a specific Voter file for any term. Click "OK" to begin" --
title="Voter Search-Filename & Content"
data1=$(zenity --entry --title "Voter Search-Filename & Content" --text "Enter File Path")
data2=$(zenity --entry --title "Voter Search-Filename & Content" --text "Enter Target Data")
cd /Volumes/DATA/Voter
rg -aFiN $data2 $data1
echo
echo "Press Enter to return to menu"
read data
exec /Applications/DataTool
;;

$opt21 )
zenity --info --text="This option queries all Whois data for any term. Click "OK" to begin" --title="Whois
Search"
data=$(zenity --entry --title "Whois Search" --text "Enter Target Data")
cd /Volumes/DATA/Whois
rg -aFiN $data
echo
echo "Press Enter to return to menu"
read data
exec /Applications/DataTool
;;

$opt22 )
zenity --info --text="This option queries all file names. It is used to identify the exact file name to be searched
next. Click "OK" to begin" --title="All Filename Search"
data=$(zenity --entry --title "All Filename Search" --text "Enter Partial Filename")
cd /Volumes/Data/
find . | grep -i $data
echo
echo "Select and copy any file path and press Enter to return to menu"
read data
exec /Applications/DataTool
;;

$opt23 )
zenity --info --text="This option queries all data for any term. Click "OK" to begin" --title="All Content
Search"
data=$(zenity --entry --title "All Content Search" --text "Enter Target Data")
cd /Volumes/Data/
rg -aFiN $data
echo
echo "Press Enter to return to menu"
read data
```

```
exec /Applications/DataTool
;;

$opt24 )
zenity --info --text="This option queries only a specific file for any term. Click "OK" to begin" --title="All
Filename & Content Search"
data1=$(zenity --entry --title "All Filename & Content Search" --text "Enter File Path")
data2=$(zenity --entry --title "All Filename & Content Search" --text "Enter Target Data")
cd /Volumes/Data/
rg -aFiN $data2 $data1
echo
echo "Press Enter to return to menu"
read data
exec /Applications/DataTool
;;
esac
```

Let's break down the sections. The following identifies the text file as a bash script.

```
#!/bin/bash
```

The following begins our menu entries as they will appear on launch.

```
opt1="COMB Email Search"
```

The following builds the menu content and size, and selects the first option as default.

```
menu=$(zenity --list --title "Data Tool" --radiolist --column "" --column "" TRUE "$opt1" FALSE "$opt2"
FALSE "$opt3" ... FALSE "$opt24" --height=700 --width=300)
```

The following begins our set of function options.

```
case $menu in
```

The following presents the first menu option.

```
$opt1 )
```

The following presents an informational dialogue to the user.

```
zenity --info --text="This option queries the COMB database for full or partial email addresses. Click "OK" to
begin" --title="COMB Email Search"
```

The following presents a menu to collect a piece of data to query.

```
data=$(zenity --entry --title "COMB Email Search" --text "Enter Target Email")
```

The following changes our target directory to the desired folder on the SSD.

```
cd /Volumes/DATA/COMB
```

The following executes a command and enters the collected target query data.

```
bash ./query.sh $data
```

The following presents instructions to return to the menu when finished.

```
echo "Press Enter to return to menu"
```

The following returns to the main menu in macOS.

```
exec /Applications/macos
```

The following represents the end of a function and then the end of the script.

```
;; esac
```

Next, let's walk through each query option within this menu.

COMB Email Search: This option prompts the user for an email address and then queries the COMB data set using the included database. Make sure the three files and "Data" folder are directly in the COMB folder at the root of the SSD. Results should appear almost immediately. While this will also accept username queries, password searching will fail.

COMB Term Search: This option prompts the user for any term and queries the same COMB data, but uses Ripgrep. The results will take more time, but you can query any portion of the data, including passwords or partial content.

Combos Search: This option prompts the user for any term and queries all data within the Combos folder with Ripgrep. The speed of results will depend on the amount of data within this folder.

Databases Search-Filename: This option prompts the user for any term and searches all filenames (not content) within the Databases folder. This identifies files of interest which can be specified in order to decrease query time. You would copy the entire path of any result of interest. If I searched "LinkedIn" and received a full path of "/Volumes/DATA/Databases/LinkedIn2022.txt", I would copy that entire path and paste it into the upcoming menu option to isolate my search results only to that file.

Databases Search-Content: This option prompts the user for any term and queries all data within the Databases folder with Ripgrep. The speed of results will depend on the amount of data within this folder. If you have thousands of files in this folder, you may want to focus on the next option.

Databases Search-Filename & Content: This option prompts the user for both the file path (identified in a previous search) and any term for a specific query. In this scenario, you would paste the "/Volumes/DATA/Databases/LinkedIn2022.txt" result from a previous query; submit it; then provide any term which should be queried within that file. This drastically reduced search time when otherwise searching a folder with thousands of large files.

Hashes Search-Filename: This option prompts the user for any term and searches all filenames (not content) within the Hashes folder. This identifies files of interest which can be specified in order to decrease query time. You would copy the entire path of any result of interest. If I searched "LinkedIn" and received a full path of "/Volumes/DATA/Hashes/LinkedIn2022.txt", I would copy that entire path and paste it into the upcoming menu option to isolate my search results only to that file.

Hashes Search-Content: This option prompts the user for any term and queries all data within the Hashes folder with Ripgrep. The speed of results will depend on the amount of data within this folder. If you have thousands of files in this folder, you may want to focus on the next option.

Hashes Search-Filename & Content: This option prompts the user for both the file path (identified in a previous search) and any term for a specific query. In this scenario, you would paste the "/Volumes/DATA/Hashes/LinkedIn2022.txt" result from a previous query; submit it; then provide any term which should be queried within that file. This drastically reduced search time when otherwise searching a folder with thousands of large files.

International Search: This option prompts the user for any term and queries all data within the International folder with Ripgrep. The speed of results will depend on the amount of data within this folder.

Logs Search: This option prompts the user for any term and queries all data within the Logs folder with Ripgrep. The speed of results will depend on the amount of data within this folder.

Logs Daily Sort: This option conducts all of the steps within the "Daily Tasks" section of the Stealer Logs chapter. You only need to make sure that all of your decompressed log files are in the default Telegram Desktop folder within Downloads.

Logs Weekly Merge: This option conducts all of the steps within the "Weekly Tasks" section of the Stealer Logs chapter. Your final result should be a new "Current.txt" file within the Logs folder of your SSD, free of any duplicate entries.

People Search-Filename: This option prompts the user for any term and searches all filenames (not content) within the People folder. This identifies files of interest which can be specified in order to decrease query time. You would copy the entire path of any result of interest. If I searched "Experian" and received a full path of "/Volumes/DATA/People/Experian2015.txt", I would copy that entire path and paste it into the upcoming menu option to isolate my search results only to that file.

People Search-Content: This option prompts the user for any term and queries all data within the People folder with Ripgrep. The speed of results will depend on the amount of data within this folder. If you have thousands of files in this folder, you may want to focus on the next option.

People Search-Filename & Content: This option prompts the user for both the file path (identified in a previous search) and any term for a specific query. In this scenario, you would paste the "/Volumes/DATA/People/Experian2015.txt" result from a previous query; submit it; then provide any term which should be queried within that file. This drastically reduced search time when otherwise searching a folder with thousands of large files.

Ransomware Search: This option prompts the user for any term and queries all data within the Ransomware folder with Ripgrep. The speed of results will depend on the amount of data within this folder.

Voter Search-Filename: This option prompts the user for any term and searches all filenames (not content) within the Voter folder. This identifies files of interest which can be specified in order to decrease query time. You would copy the entire path of any result of interest. If I searched "Florida" and received a full path of "/Volumes/DATA/Voter/Florida2022.txt", I would copy that entire path and paste it into the upcoming menu option to isolate my search results only to that file.

Voter Search-Content: This option prompts the user for any term and queries all data within the Voter folder with Ripgrep. The speed of results will depend on the amount of data within this folder. If you have thousands of files in this folder, you may want to focus on the next option.

Voter Search-Filename & Content: This option prompts the user for both the file path (identified in a previous search) and any term for a specific query. In this scenario, you would paste the "/Volumes/DATA/Voter/Florida2022.txt" result from a previous query; submit it; then provide any term which should be queried within that file. This drastically reduced search time when otherwise searching a folder with thousands of large files.

Whois Search: This option prompts the user for any term and queries all data within the Whois folder with Ripgrep. The speed of results will depend on the amount of data within this folder.

All Filename Search: This option prompts the user for any term and searches all filenames (not content) within the entire SSD. This identifies files of interest which can be specified in order to decrease query time. You would copy the entire path of any result of interest. If I searched "Facebook" and received a full path of "/Volumes/DATA/People/Facebook2022.txt", I would copy that entire path and paste it into the upcoming menu option to isolate my search results only to that file.

All Content Search: This option prompts the user for any term and queries all data within the entire SSD with Ripgrep. The speed of results will depend on the amount of data within this folder. If you have thousands of files in this folder, you may want to focus on the next option.

All Filename & Content Search: This option prompts the user for both the file path (identified in a previous search) and any term for a specific query. In this scenario, you would paste the "/Volumes/DATA/People/Facebook2022.txt" result from a previous query; submit it; then provide any term which should be queried within that file. This drastically reduced search time when otherwise searching a folder with thousands of large files.

Having all of these options reduces your query time, and gives you greater control over the data included. Instead of waiting for Ripgrep to search through 3 TB of data, you can focus on either one folder or one specific file. Once you master this technique, your search results should return quickly.

Notifications

Every time you select an option within this menu, you will be greeted with an informational notice identifying the steps which are about to take place. I believe these are important until they become a nuisance. If you are sick of these notices, you can simply remove every line which begins with "zenity --info" from your script. If that seems too tedious, you can complete the entire process with the following commands for each macOS and Linux, respectively.

```
sed -i "s/zenity \-\-info/\#\#zenity \-\-info/gI"
/Applications/DataTool
```

```
sudo sed -i "s/zenity \-\-info/\#\#zenity \-\-info/gI"
/home/DataTool.sh
```

Internal Storage

If you plan to host all of your breach data within your internal drive for the fastest queries possible, you only need to change the paths within the script. As an example, each path on the script typically begins by changing the directory to the SSD as follows.

```
cd /Volumes/DATA/
```

If you wanted to host your breach data within a directory labeled "Breaches" within your Documents folder, you would change every instance of this to the following. Make sure to maintain any subfolders such as COMB or Voter exactly as they appear in the script. You only want to change the part of the path from the SSD to internal. This is completely optional, and only appropriate for those with huge internal drives.

```
cd ~/Documents/Breaches/
```

Zenity

While writing this chapter, I was often annoyed with the way macOS implements Zenity into its system. Zenity is the software which presents selectable menus for our script. The Linux version is much smoother and more functional. I intentionally used the default macOS version of Zenity in order to keep everything similar. However, I currently use a different version of Zenity on my macOS device. If you are a macOS user, and are also annoyed at the fluidity of the menu for this script, you can change to an alternative version with the following commands.

```
brew uninstall zenity && brew install ncruces/tap/zenity
```

If you dislike the alternative version worse than the official option, you can reverse this change with the following commands.

```
brew uninstall zenity && brew install zenity
```

Qgrep

Until this point, we have been using Ripgrep to query our files. This is much faster than traditional Grep queries, but it can still take a long time to sort through a large amount of data. The speed of your drive will determine if this takes minutes or hours. Creating a proper database from scratch can quickly exceed the scope of this book, but we do have one easy option if we want to create simple databases which can be queried in a fraction of the time it would take Ripgrep. This is not a magic bullet, as it has some caveats, but it can be a game-changer for querying folders with thousands of files in seconds. You have already installed Qgrep in an earlier chapter, so you should be ready to go. We must first navigate to the folder where we installed the program. The following should apply to macOS and Linux users who followed my guide.

```
cd ~/Documents/Qgrep
```

We can now launch Qgrep and create a new entry called "Voter", which will create a database with all content in the Voter folder on our SSD, with the following commands for macOS and Linux.

```
./qgrep init Voter /Volumes/DATA/Voter/
./qgrep init Voter /media/$USER/DATA/Voter/
```

This created a configuration file within a hidden folder titled ".qgrep" in our Home folder. However, this file contains no voter data. It only has the settings for our new database. You should be prompted to update this database, as it does not have any data in it yet. The following command should complete the process.

```
./qgrep update Voter
```

You should receive a result similar to the following in a couple of minutes.

```
[100%] 42 files, 34228 Mb in, 10926 Mb out
+42 files; 68454/68454 chunks updated in 165.80 sec
```

This tells us that we now have a database of all Voter information which is ready to query with the following command.

```
./qgrep search Voter i bazzell
```

Let's break this down.

./qgrep This is the command to run the application.
search   This tells the program we want to search data.
Voter   This identifies the database we want to search.
i   This informs Qgrep to run without case sensitivity.
bazzell   This is the term we want to query.

This process completed in a few seconds, and produced all lines within any files inside the Voter folder on our SSD which matched the search term. The same query with Ripgrep would have taken much longer. You may be wondering why we are not building these simple databases for all of our data. Well, there are issues.

- Every database you create requires additional storage of approximately 1/3 of the total data indexed on your host drive. This can add up quickly, and may introduce undesired redundancies. If you have 3 TB of data, you would need 1 TB of internal storage for the indexed database.
- The update process can only tolerate files which are less than the size of your available RAM. If every file you are indexing is less than 32 GB on a machine with 32 GB of RAM, you might be OK. The moment your stealer logs file (or any other large data set) crosses that line, Qgrep will crash.
- Every time you add any files to a folder indexed by Qgrep, you must update the program in order to receive search results for all data. This can become a nuisance if you add data often, however, it is quite fast.

By default, Qgrep stores the databases it creates on your internal drive in a hidden directory called ".qgrep" in your home folder. If you are able to view hidden files, you can navigate to this folder to see the contents. If you cannot see it, you must conduct the following to enable hidden file view.

macOS: Press the "Command" + "Shift" + "." (period) keys at the same time.
Linux: Open Files and enable "Show Hidden Files" in the upper-right menu.

You should now see the contents of the .qgrep folder. Mine appeared as follows.

Voter.cfg
Voter.qgd
Voter.qgf

My Voter folder on my SSD had 36 GB of data, and the Voter.qsd file was 12 GB. This matches with our 1/3 rule. If you decide to use Qgrep for most of your data, I would consider moving the databases to your SSD and execute the queries from there. Let's conduct a thorough demonstration of all options to determine the best query speed for you.

My initial query of the Qgrep Voter database from my internal drive took 8 seconds. A second query was only 2 seconds. This is because Qgrep had stored much of my data within RAM. That is very fast for querying 36 GB of original data. Every query I conducted within this Terminal session consistently took 2 seconds to complete. A Ripgrep search of this same data took 39 seconds. That is a substantial difference.

Next, let's move our Qgrep database to our external SSD. I created a new folder at the root of the SSD titled .qgrep. I moved the three Voter files from my internal drive to this external SSD. I made sure the files no longer existed internally with the following commands.
```
cd ~/Documents/Qgrep
./qgrep search Voter i bazzell
```

This resulted in an error since the files are no longer present in the place where Qgrep thinks they should be. Instead, I must specify the location of this Voter database with the following command.

```
./qgrep search /Volumes/DATA/.qgrep/Voter.cfg i bazzell
```

This specified the path to our configuration file which is now stored on our SSD. This query took 19 seconds, over twice as long as the initial query when the database was on our internal drive, but still half the time as Ripgrep. Additional queries were slightly faster, but did not make a huge difference.

Whenever I update any files within my Voter folder, I must execute the following to also update the Qgrep database since I moved the files.

```
cd ~/Documents/Qgrep
./qgrep update /Volumes/DATA/.qgrep/Voter.cfg
```

Overall, you must decide what is most important to you. Consider the following.

- If speed is your ultimate priority; you need to query specific data often; and you have the extra internal disk space, then default Qgrep is a great solution for you.
- If speed is a priority; you need to query specific data often; you do not have the extra internal disk space; and you do have extra SSD space, then Qgrep with databases stored on your SSD is a great solution for you.
- If simplicity is your priority and you can tolerate longer query times, then strict text files is better for you.

I do a mix of both. Over 90% of my queries utilize the standard script previously presented. That works fine for most needs. However, I have built a few Qgrep databases. One is for a folder of text files identifying the owners of cellular telephone numbers obtained from a huge data leak from a caller ID database provider. This folder has over 300 GB of text files, none of which are over 32 GB in size. Any time I identify new leaks or breaches which contain phone owner info, I put them in this folder on my SSD. I have created a Qgrep database using the previous commands, and update the database whenever needed. When I conduct a Qgrep query on this data, Qgrep is using a compressed version of that data which exists on my internal drive (now with 100 GB of extra data). The results take only a few seconds to arrive and my SSD does not need to be connected to my machine. I conduct the following any time I need to search a number from my internal drive database.

```
cd ~/Documents/Qgrep
./qgrep search Phone i 6185551212
```

SQLite

After the initial publication of this guide, several readers requested a tutorial for creation and maintenance of a traditional database. I have always resisted this because I am not a database expert, and I even hired someone to handle our extensive in-house database needs. However, I respect that a proper database can be the most appropriate tool when handling large amounts of data. I want to preface this section by stating that we will only dive into the basics of database creation using only one of many options, but you might see the value with a brief tutorial. I believe the best database software for a beginner is SQLite. You may already have this software of your machine, but let's make sure with the following commands.

macOS: `brew install sqlite`
Linux: `sudo apt update && sudo apt install sqlite3 -y`

SQLite is also available for Windows, and the following commands should work the same way as within macOS and Linux. Since my demonstration involves stealer log data, I will refrain from any specific Windows commands due to the high risk of virus infection. The following commands navigate to the Documents folder and creates our first SQLite database called "Logs.db" within that folder.

```
cd ~/Documents && sqlite3 Logs.db "PRAGMA journal_mode = OFF;PRAGMA
cache_size = -64000;PRAGMA synchronous = 0;"
```

You should now see "sqlite>" within your Terminal, which confirms we are working within our new database. Let's create a table called "Logs" and a single column called "log" with the following command. This command instructs SQLite to make sure no duplicates ever appear within this database. Make sure you see "sqlite>" on your Terminal line, as these commands will do nothing if pasted directly into a standard Terminal session. The following should be copied and pasted in its entirety.

```
CREATE TABLE Logs(log TEXT PRIMARY KEY,UNIQUE(log)) WITHOUT ROWID;;
```

We now have an empty database. I like to enter the following two commands which are likely already set by default, but they make sure that data headers are off (for stealer logs) and that the mode is set to list any entries one line at a time.

```
.headers off
.mode list
```

The next command creates a data separator as a character which we should never encounter within our data. This is because we only want to import one line of stealer log content into our only column, and not have things sporadically split into additional columns which may be ignored by our database. Since this demonstration will involve stealer logs which are typically separated by a colon (:), we do not want SQLite trying to split the lines by colon, which would be common with a CSV file. This could create a huge mess when the database encounters lines which begin with "https:" or include a colon, comma, pipe, or other character within a password. The following command is a way to cheat and tell SQLite to avoid a separating character when importing data.

```
.separator "\a"
```

We are now ready to import data. Assume you have a stealer log text file titled "logs.txt" within a folder called "Logs" on your SSD. The following SQLite command imports this file into our Logs table. Since this table only has one column and we have no valid separator set, this should just import each line directly into the column.

```
.import /Volumes/DATA/Logs/logs.txt Logs
```

Depending on the size of the file, this process can take seconds or several minutes. You might see several lines which display "INSERT failed: UNIQUE constraint failed: Logs.log". This is a great error to see. It informs you that SQLite detected an entry which you already possessed and ignored the duplicate. This unique designation does two things. It prevents duplicates, but it also creates an index of your data. This provides faster search queries, but with some caveats which are discussed in a moment. We can now see our progress with the following.

```
.databases
```
- This displays your database location details.
```
.table
```
- This displays the table details.
```
.indexes
```
- This displays the name of any indexes.
```
SELECT COUNT(*) FROM Logs;
```
- This displays the total rows of a database.

During this writing, I imported 25 GB of stealer log text files into my new database, which took about ten minutes. Since the data was imported and then indexed for unique entries, the database was 30 GB in size. That is larger than the data itself, but that is the nature of indexed data. If you are following my tutorial, this database is stored within the Documents folder of your internal drive, so be aware of internal storage requirements. This database file can be created or moved anywhere desired, and you would only need to navigate to that directory to open it. Finally, we can query our data. The following SQLite command queries the "log" column within the "Logs" table for any entry which includes "inteltechniques" within the line.

```
SELECT log FROM Logs WHERE log LIKE '%inteltechniques%';
```

My query of the 25 GB of original data (30 GB database) took over fifteen minutes to complete from the internal drive, and the results appeared within the Terminal in real time. That seems very slow for an indexed query. This is because the previous command did not actually take advantage of the index at all because we used a wildcard (%) at the beginning and end of the query. We can use the following command to see what will happen behind the scenes for our first query without searching any data.

```
EXPLAIN QUERY PLAN SELECT log FROM Logs WHERE log LIKE
'%inteltechniques%';
```
The result should be similar to "--SCAN Logs". This tells us that SQLite will go through each line, one at a time, and display any results. Let's try again with the following command which tells us the search plan for a query for any line BEGINNING with "https://inteltechniques".

```
EXPLAIN   QUERY   PLAN   SELECT   log   FROM   Logs   WHERE   log   GLOB
'https://inteltechniques*';
```

The result should be similar to the following.

```
--SEARCH Logs USING COVERING INDEX sqlite_autoindex_Logs_1 (log>? AND
log<?)
```

This confirms that our fast index will be used instead of scanning all of the data one line at a time. This is because we are specifying the first part of the line and not using a wildcard. Now, let's execute the actual query with the following. Note that "*" is a wildcard to replace "%" from our previous query.

```
SELECT log FROM Logs WHERE log GLOB 'https://inteltechniques*';
```

This query was much faster and completed within one second. It displayed every line in my stealer logs which BEGINS with "https://inteltechniques". If you know exactly how your target data begins, such as a URL, this index can be the fastest option. If you are searching data which may appear randomly within a line, as will be most common for our queries, the index will not assist with the speed of your search. However, it still assists with making sure duplicate data is never imported into your database.

You may be wondering why we do not separate each field of the URL into multiple columns for better indexing. Unfortunately, all of the stealer logs we acquire will have various formats. Some will appear similar to URL:LOGIN:PASS while others will be LOGIN:PASS:URL. Some will use semicolons, pipes, or other separators. Many will be formatted as USER@PASS:URL. **There is no standard**. Therefore, creating a properly separated and fully indexed database will take a lot of time, and will never be perfect. You could create multiple columns with unique indexing and import all data with a separator, but I think you will be displeased with the size of your database and the errors encountered due to poor formatting of the data. This would also delete duplicate email addresses for various sites. This is why my demonstration only focuses on a single column of data. You may be able to justify the extra effort, but the exact steps to configure your own perfectly-indexed custom database exceed our scope. While testing this data, I downloaded new stealer log files from Telegram. I conducted the "Daily Task" as previously explained, and then opened my database and imported the "new" data with the following single command.

```
sqlite3 Logs.db "PRAGMA journal_mode = OFF;PRAGMA cache_size = -
64000;PRAGMA synchronous = 0;" ".headers off" ".mode list" ".separator
\a" ".import ~/Downloads/Logs/logs.txt Logs
```

I immediately observed that most of this data was already present within my SQLite database. Since I configured this column to only accept unique data, I never need to "sort" for unique entries. Every time I import data, only the unique entries are added. In my experience, importing unique entries into SQLite is more accurate than sorting for unique entries with the Sort command. Once your database becomes substantially larger than the content, you may want to optimize the data with the VACUUM command. This will attempt to optimize and shrink the size of the database. While working within your SQLite database in Terminal, execute the following command.

```
VACUUM;
```

Note that you must have at least the size of your database available as free space. Results will vary. My 30 GB test database only reduced to 29 GB, but it was fairly new. A 250 GB database that has seen hundreds of imports might benefit more. You can always export a current copy of the text data with the following SQLite command from the folder of your database. This can be valuable if you are using SQLite to import non-duplicate stealer logs in order to keep the data to a minimum, but also want a non-database backup of the data. I can state from experience that databases eventually become corrupt. Having a backup of the database is great, but having a text-only backup of the raw data is even better. If you rely on SQLite databases, make sure you have updated and archived data.

```
sqlite3 -header -csv Logs.db "select * from Logs;" > ~/Desktop/Logs.csv
```

For most readers, I think Qgrep and SQLite are overkill. If you have a specific data folder which you query many times every day and you can no longer stomach the wait times, then you should test these strategies. For those who conduct an occasional daily query, the previous search script is a much simpler solution. If you need to query terms which could appear anywhere within your data, Qgrep is faster than Ripgrep, and Ripgrep is faster than SQLite. If your query appears at the beginning of an entry, SQLite is fastest, followed by Qgrep then Ripgrep. If your priority is to eliminate redundant data, SQLite is the best daily solution. Remember that Qgrep will only ingest files which are smaller than the available RAM, but SQLite should be able to import any size. If you want to create a Qgrep database out of a 100 GB Stealer Logs file, you will need to use the Split command to create multiple smaller files. You could then search the entire data set in seconds, but could no longer merge these smaller files with new data to eliminate duplicates with the Sort Merge feature.

If you collect stealer logs every day and you want an easier way to import them into your collection without duplicate entries, a SQLite database is great. You may find that the space required to store an indexed database is too much more than that required for the original data alone. Ripgrep may be better for your needs. Only you can decide which route is best for your data. I prefer the simplicity and speed of Qgrep with the immediate delivery of keyword queries, but respect the ability to remove duplicates while importing into SQLite. We have only briefly discussed SQLite databases. Tweaking your configuration, indexing, compression, and queries can open even more doors. If this is of interest to you, I highly recommend researching SQLite further.

Duplicate Files

If you collect enough breach data, you will likely find many duplicate files with different names. This could be due to poor file naming or deliberate trickery in order to distribute inaccurate data. Regardless, I find it beneficial to eliminate duplicate files frequently. The following commands install fdupes.

macOS: `brew install fdupes`
Linux: `sudo apt-get install fdupes`

The next command launches fdupes, scans recursive files within the Downloads directory, and prompts you to select which duplicate file to keep.

```
fdupes -r -d ~/Downloads
```

I placed two identical files with different names in the same directory, the following was the result. Entering "1" would keep the first file, while "2" would preserve the second.

```
Set 1 of 1:
  1 [ ] /Users/mbp/Downloads/1/Real Breach.txt
  2 [ ] /Users/mbp/Downloads/1/Fake Breach.txt
( Preserve files [1 - 2, all, help] ):
```

Backups

You have worked hard to collect, clean, and organize your data. However, storage devices crash all of the time without warning. I would be devastated if I lost my collection. Therefore, a good backup system should be in place. You should have already installed FreeFileSync, and we can use it to easily copy our data.

Until now, we have been copying our data to an external SSD labeled DATA. You should now insert your backup drive, and make sure it is labeled BACKUP. In the previous hardware chapter, I recommended a cheap 4 TB external USB drive with a small spinning disk inside. Since this is only used as a backup of our data, speed is not a priority.
Follow the previous tutorials to encrypt this new external backup drive, then conduct your first backup within FreeFileSync.

- Close any pop-up windows and click "Browse" in the left "Drag & drop" area.
- Select your root folder of your SSD in the left menu.
- Click the "Open" button and click "Browse" in the right "Drag & drop" area.
- Select your root folder of your backup drive in the right menu.
- Click the right arrow icon next to the green cog wheel near "Synchronize".
- Change the option to "Mirror".

The mirror option makes sure that the data on the SSD is always an exact replica of the content on your backup drive. If your drives match the labeling of mine, yours should look similar to the image below. You could save this configuration with the "Save as" icon, naming it "Data Backup".

Next, click "Compare" and allow the analysis. You may receive warnings that FreeFileSync is trying to access folders, but this is acceptable for this purpose. You may also receive a warning about an area which is inaccessible to the program. I click "Ignore All" when this happens. Once complete, you should see a summary of all files which will be synchronized. Clicking the "Synchronize" button begins the backup process, which can take some time on the first run.

The next time you need to back up your data, you would connect your drives; unlock the encryption by entering the passwords; open FreeFileSync; and select the "Compare" button again. This time, you should only be presented the files which have been modified since the last backup. Then, the synchronization process should be much faster. I do this weekly.

You now have ONE backup. To some, that is plenty. To me, that is risky. What if my house explodes with both drives inside? What if I accidently erase data from my DATA drive, and then synchronize that to my BACKUP drive? Most computer professionals will tell you that you need three copies of any important data, and I agree. This is why I keep one off-site backup in addition to the previous backup we just made. I have another external USB drive which has a replica of all data stored at another trusted home. When I visit monthly, I take my laptop and SSD in order to update the second backup drive off-site. It might not always be up-to-date, but the majority of my data collection is present in the case of catastrophe.

Putting It All Together

I am simplifying the explanation of these steps, but you have everything you need to conduct your own research into its capabilities. Possessing an efficient way to query your data will increase the likelihood that you will take advantage of these techniques. During my testing, I could use the script to query the entire COMB data within a few seconds; display file names from thousands of breaches immediately; or focus my queries within generic data types or specific files in less than a minute, all from an external drive. Consider the following typical usage.

- **Internal Investigations**: This one is obvious. This type of data can be crucial to investigations. It can immediately uncover real and alias information. Every day, breach data reveals the true person behind a burner account due to sloppy OPSEC.
- **Client Vetting**: We take our clients' privacy very seriously. We would never use a third-party system to properly verify the identity of a potential client. Instead, we use our own in-house system to make sure we know who we are dealing with. At least twice, a potential client's record in our system revealed suspicious activity related to criminal prosecution, identifying the reason they were asking about anonymous relocation services (we never assist in those situations).
- **Client Exposure**: We have many clients who keep us on a retainer. Part of that service is an initial analysis of exposed information, and a constant monitoring for any new details. Every week, we reach out to clients to let them know of a new breach, ransomware attack, or password log which may impact them or their company. Just a few months ago, I was able to alert a close friend that his daughter's full name, address, DOB, SSN, and banking details were being passed around a criminal marketplace focused on identity theft. We received the internal alert within two days of the initial exposure.

Breach data is nothing new to investigators. I have explained how we ingest typical text-based breach data since the 7th edition of *OSINT Techiques*. The new world of daily ransomware dumps and stealer logs changes everything. We are collecting this data in masses never seen before. We often bring in over 2 terabytes of new stolen content weekly, which we parse down to an average of 50 GB of useful data for the week. Our current collection is over 40 TB. We focus mostly on text and private documents, and try to eliminate all public docs, company materials, and anything else which does not have an immediate impact on an individual.

The following figure displays a heavily redacted screen capture of my company's internal investigation portal, which was created specifically for our needs by a database expert. In this example, I searched only the email address of my target. Since this address appears within multiple breaches, it connects me to her real name (from the MGM and LinkedIn breaches). From there, the system cross-references that name to her driver's license. This license was scanned by a mortgage company, which was later hit with a ransomware attack, which resulted in all of their data being published on an onion site. Our system scanned the characters within the scanned image but also the barcode, as explained in the previous text. Now that our system has enough true data about our target, it can cross-reference everything within our collection of breach data, including ransomware dumps, Tor content, and stealer logs. From there it determines her home address, which is cross-referenced with people search data, historic Whois data, vehicle data, and numerous public APIs. The result is an immediate view of all available public, private, and stolen data. Our team relies heavily on this portal, and each query takes approximately 5-10 seconds. It cross-references any data we have until all options have been exhausted, as encouraged throughout this book.

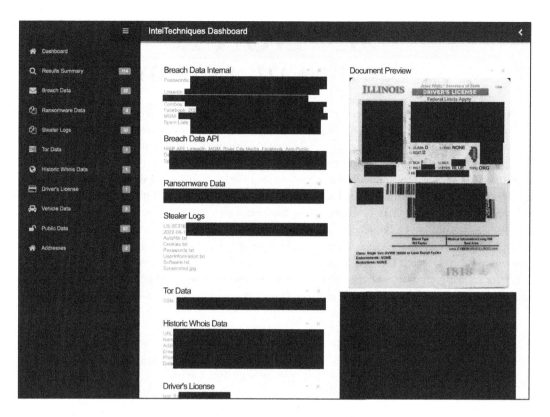

I want to close this chapter with some final warnings and reminders. Forgive me if this seems redundant, but we can all use another mention of the risks and concerns. Leaks, breaches, logs, and ransomware always consist of data which was either stolen or never meant to become publicly available. It is abused every day by professional and amateur criminals. Many readers will be disgusted by these chapters and upset that I share details on the acquisition of this content. When collected and used properly, I believe it can be beneficial to both investigators and those who monitor this activity from a defense perspective.

We are only beginning the journey into data collection. I hope I have sparked your interest for this type of investigation technique, and I challenge you to see what else you can find. If you are an early adopter of this guide, you should have all of the basics to get started. As time passes, I hope to continuously update these pages with new techniques, data sources, and other ideas. When this document should need updated, all modifications are completely free. If you purchased this PDF through my website, you will be notified via email when revisions can be downloaded. If you downloaded an unauthorized copy from a piracy website, please consider purchasing a legitimate copy. Your $20 purchase supports the research which goes into creating and updating these guides. Finally, if you find anything which needs updated or corrected, please email us at books@inteltechniques.com. My staff cannot respond to emails directly, but they will monitor them for any changes which we need to apply to the next version of this guide.

SECTION IV
OSINT METHODOLOGY

In the late 90's, I was tasked to investigate a computer-related crime involving inappropriate online contact from a registered sex offender to children in his neighborhood. The internet was new to most people; AOL dial-up connections were common; and there was very little monitoring or enforcement in place. I contacted the subject at his home and conducted an interview. He admitted to inappropriate behavior and showed me the evidence on his computer. I had no forensic imaging machine or acquisition methods. I didn't even have a digital camera. I had my notepad and pen. Months later, I testified about the illegal activity this suspect conducted with local children. I verbally explained what I observed on his computer without any digital evidence. It was a very different time, and would never be acceptable today. Current prosecution would require forensic acquisition, detailed logs, and pictorial proof of every step. This is a good thing, but presents a higher demand toward your own documentation and overall OSINT methodology. Without digital evidence, the computer crime or online incident you are investigating never happened. Without proper training and policies, your evidence may never be considered. Without confidence in your work, you may not be taken seriously.

We can no longer ignore discussions about workflow, documentation, and other formalities of our investigations. It is also time that we tackle the ethics surrounding online investigations. These are not easy conversations, and many people will have their own opinions. I do not claim to have all of the answers. I only have my own experiences and lessons learned from many mistakes.

I rely heavily on assistance from my friend and colleague Jason Edison throughout this entire section. Jason is a 25-year veteran of a major U.S. police department where he serves as the investigative lead for the agency's Digital Crimes Unit. He has trained thousands of students in the public and private sectors on various topics related to open source intelligence and cyber-crime investigations. In fact, he is an official IntelTechniques OSINT instructor who travels the world presenting my methods. He also maintains the IntelTechniques online video training courses at IntelTechniques.net. Most of the content in this section is directly from him. I maintain the first-person usage of "I" throughout the section. It is a collective "I" from both of us.

Jason and I do not agree on everything presented here. This is why you see alternative tools and methods which may contradict each other. This is a good thing. We need as many thoughts and opinions as possible in order to present ideas applicable to many situations. As an example, I try not to use Microsoft or Google products unless absolutely necessary. I have forced myself to use Linux whenever possible, and avoid closed-sourced tools which "call home". Jason prefers Microsoft OneNote, which is extremely robust. His need for an ideal note-taking solution outweighs my paranoia of metadata collection by Microsoft. He prefers Chrome while I insist on Firefox. Neither of us are right or wrong. We simply have strong preferences. We only hope to present numerous options which may help you choose the best methods for your own investigations. Only you can decide what is most appropriate for your daily workload.

It is now time to take a breath and get back to basics. You may have been overwhelmed with the techniques discussed throughout the previous sections. You may wonder how you will present your findings, create a report, and defend your right to access public information from the internet. This section tackles these issues. Throughout this section, we present numerous document templates and workflow diagrams. All of these are available to you via digital download at the following URL.

https://inteltechniques.com/osintbook11

Enter a username of **"osint11"** and password of **"bk3t7"** (without quotes) if required.

CHAPTER FORTY-FIVE
METHODOLOGY & WORKFLOW

An often overlooked component of open source intelligence gathering is the importance of establishing an efficient and repeatable workflow. You need to be thoughtful and deliberate in how you proceed on an investigation rather than wading in haphazardly. As an instructor, one of the most common stumbling blocks with which I see new practitioners struggle is putting the tools into action in a fashion that results in a professional looking work product. This section provides a step by step walkthrough of the entire investigative process, from receiving an OSINT assignment all the way to submitting a professional case report.

This chapter assumes you have already completed the steps laid out in the previous sections of this book. You will need familiarity with each of those tools and techniques if you wish to take full advantage of the recommended workflow. If you have an existing investigative process, there will likely be pieces shared here that can be folded into your current procedures. The examples used here were chosen purely for demonstration purposes and not due to any association with ongoing criminal investigations.

Receiving the OSINT Mission

The first step in most investigations is what we in law enforcement refer to as "intake". This is the process of receiving a mission assignment from a supervisor or fielding a request for investigative support from another internal unit or outside agency. For those in the private sector, this might be accepting a contract investigation from a client or conducting a security assessment as part of your normal duties. The following are examples of OSINT requests that we receive on a regular basis:

- **Threat Assessments (Individuals):** Online threats to carry out an act that we wish to prevent. Who is this person? Where are they? What is their capability and true intent?
- **Threat Assessments (Events):** Monitor intelligence prior to and during a significant event that impacts the organization or region of responsibility. Who is involved? What are their intentions? What is the scale of impact on available resources?
- **Target Profiles (Individuals):** Uncover the target's entire online presence, including email addresses, home addresses, friends, hobbies, etc., often referred to as "due diligence" investigations.
- **Target Profiles (Organizations):** Uncover an organization's online footprint and/or entire technological infrastructure. This can be a business, criminal enterprise, or group of individuals organized to pursue a shared goal.
- **Subscriber Identification/Account Attribution:** Identify the person associated with a domain, IP address, or account. Who runs a malicious website? Which child predator has traffic through this IP?
- **Vulnerability Assessments:** This is a defensive assessment where we will map out the sensitive data exposures and operational security weaknesses for an individual or organization.

The following recommendations can be applied to any of these common investigative scenarios. More than anything else, the key to success is staying organized and having a repeatable process.

Triage

Triage is the practice of assessing a situation or mission to calculate an approach that is likely to result in the best possible outcome. A common mistake that is made when working OSINT investigations is to rush to action with no clear plan or direction. You should take time at the beginning of a mission to ensure you are following a productive path to relevant answers. Depending on the urgency of the situation, this step could be 30 seconds or 30 minutes. The important thing is to make a plan of attack and move forward with purpose rather than just bush-whacking your way through the internet. Here are some of the key considerations during the triage phase.

Be certain of the mission objectives. If you ask a professional analyst to describe the first step they take in any assessment, they will tell you that it is to identify the question. This of course could be multiple questions, but the important thing is that you articulate the investigative goals. This can be a verbal or written confirmation, depending on your situation, but written is preferred should the other party later misremember the conversation.

The first benefit of articulating the questions is establishing a clear set of expectations with the person asking you to do the work. This could be a supervisor, contract client, colleague, or victim of a crime. Do not overthink it. An example could be: "To be clear, you want to know the real name and physical addresses associated with the person in control of the email account of ramit@iwillteachyoutoberich.com, and we have two hours to accomplish this. Is this correct?"

Include in your verification any specific identifiers (email addresses, names, phone numbers, IP addresses, etc.) that were originally provided by the requestor. It gives them a chance to catch any typos or miscommunications. They may have given you the email address of the victim rather than the suspect. Those types of mix-ups occur frequently and can waste a lot of valuable investigative time and resources if not caught and corrected early on. That quick clarification also defines the primary goals for our investigations, similar to the following.

- Find the legal name of the real person associated with ramit@iwillteachyoutoberich.com.
- Find any home and/or work addresses for ramit@iwillteachyoutoberich.com.

When it comes time to write your investigative report, these questions should be clearly addressed in the summary of key findings. Taking the time to articulate and clarify mission goals up front lays the groundwork for your final work product. You should also ask questions regarding the source of any initial leads or other intelligence on your target. Why do we believe that email address belongs to our suspect? How was that lead obtained and how certain are we that it is correct? Information is not intelligence until it has context. Consider asking additional questions up front to establish any available context for the target. Do we know anything about their location, profession, known associates, or culture? Once you get to the research phase of the investigation, you will have a far easier time locating pages, accounts, and identifiers related to your target if you start learning about his or her day to day life. Never assume that the person tasking you with this work has given you all available information. Ask questions and be persistent.

Legal Service & Preservation Letters

If you work in support of law enforcement, you should consider if there is likely to be a legal request made to any known social media platforms. For example, if a Gmail address was involved in a crime, you might want to issue a preservation letter to Google requesting that they retain any data related to the specified address. The preservation letter is issued in anticipation of a future subpoena or search warrant for account data, such as subscriber information. If you are unsure of whom to contact at a particular provider in order to submit this request, a good starting point is the ISP list at https://www.search.org/resources/isp-list/.

Deconfliction

Not all investigations involve infiltration into criminal organizations. However, when they do, you may want to check with colleagues in other agencies to make sure you are not stepping on any ongoing investigations. This could also save you time should you locate an investigator who has already laid groundwork into the online communities in question. We always want to be respectful of another professional's work and collaborate whenever operationally appropriate. In the past, I have concluded long-term investigations only to find out later that other teams were running operations in that criminal community at the same time. While reviewing the case, we found that we had wasted time working to gain reputation with users who, unbeknownst to us, were other undercover investigators. This is not only a waste of time and focus, but can complicate the individual cases where they overlap. Ask the person for whom you are doing the work if anyone else is working on the case. You would be surprised how often two branches of the same agency are unknowingly pursuing a common target.

Note-Taking

The triage stage is the appropriate time to begin your note-taking. I will discuss specific tools in the next chapter, but at its core you will need a paper scratch pad and digital notebook, such as Microsoft OneNote. A paper notepad allows for quickly noting key details without having to move out of your browser during searches. This is even more crucial if you are on a laptop or otherwise have limited screen real estate with which to work. Your digital note-taking application is for pasting content as you copy it from your browser. Keep in mind using Microsoft products allows them to collect user information, so make sure that this is within the operational security requirements of your organization. At the top of your legal pad, list out the details you are seeking and any initial investigative steps. This does not need to be comprehensive or detailed. We are simply establishing some first steps by clarifying our mission goals and known leads.

In your digital notebook, create a new section and title it logically based on the date of request, incident type, or case number if there is one. For example, "OSINT Request Jan_10_2025" or "Robbery 25-486544". Any emails or other written correspondence received leading into the case should be copied into your digital notebook. Finally, before moving on, ask yourself if OSINT is the right tool for the job. I have made the mistake of investing hours into online searches, only to realize later that a two-minute phone call would have likely given me the same information. Do not make the mistake of overlooking traditional investigative resources. Would a phone call to a postal inspector identify the occupants of a residence quicker than an online search? The strongest investigators are ones who think outside the box while also using every tool in it.

Knoll Your Tools

Now that you have established a plan and a clear understanding of the mission goals, you need to prepare your workspace for the investigation. "Knolling" is the process of organizing your resources so they are ready to go and easily accessible once you start the actual work. Think of how a surgeon's instruments are sanitized and laid out in an organized fashion. The time spent preparing up front will result in a more efficient overall operation while also reducing the chances of unnecessary mishaps. If you followed the instructions and recommendations in previous chapters, you should already have a custom Linux VM. It should be patched and preloaded with your preferred OSINT applications. Additional recommended preparations prior to the search phase include the following.

- Verify your VPN connection and consider connecting to a VPN server in your targets region
- Start you OSINT Virtual Machine and if necessary run any updates
- Open and have ready your notepad, digital notebook, and/or investigation template
- Load your investigative browser and log into any covert accounts, such as social media platforms
- Open the OSINT tools dashboard https://inteltechniques.com/tools/ (consider pinning that tab)
- Create an investigative directory and any desired sub-directories on your workstation or external drive

Your knolling is complete. You have a virtual machine preloaded with the most useful OSINT tools, and you are on a secure and private connection. We are prepared to search quickly, collect pertinent content, store it logically, and track our progress within our notes.

Closed-Source & Premium Data

You should now be ready with all your tools and note-taking resources. Begin the research phase of the investigation by querying your target against any in-house, premium, or proprietary data sources. This includes any of the following.

- Commercial aggregators such as Accurint (LexisNexis), TLO, Clear, and others.
- Premium products such as BeenVerified, Intelius, Spokeo, Pipl, and WhitepagesPro.

- Government and LE databases such as Department of Licensing, Criminal Records, Department of Corrections, and Agency Records Management Systems (if available to you).

Whereas using purely open-source tools typically requires visiting dozens of sites in order to find just a few leads, paid services often quickly provide a list of possible addresses, associates, and accounts. If you have services like LexisNexis or Clear available, use them early for easy additional leads on your target. These services obtain much of their data from credit histories and utilities. Therefore, they tend to be good sources for residential address history, land-line phone numbers, employers, roommates, and family members. They tend to work very poorly with email addresses, usernames, and social media accounts.

This is also when you should run any premium people-search services such as Pipl, Spokeo, or BeenVerified. These types of services range from $15-$300 a month depending on the subscription tier, but tend to offer a much richer, immediate return on queries than their free counterparts. However, they will push you to spend more money for "premium" data about your target. Many investigators kickstart the early stages of their open source investigations using one of these cheap premium aggregators, but keep in mind everything you get from paid people search sites is available for free elsewhere (although with considerably more time and effort).

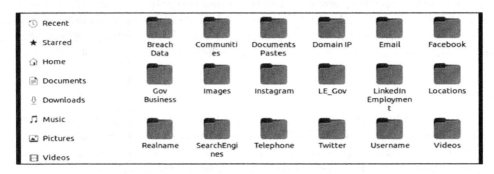

Figure 45.01: A logically structured case directory.

For those on the government or law enforcement side of the house, internal agency records systems, department of licensing requests, and criminal history queries can be very powerful additions to your early digging. An advantage that government investigators have is that many of these systems will provide access to a photo of the target, which can be used to verify or rule out possible social media accounts. These records also typically include recent associates, phone numbers, and residential addresses. Even if the subject did not use their own address during a previous contact with government agents, they likely used one where they can receive mail, such as a relative's house. Most people are not trained to think on their feet and will use familiar data when cornered with hard questions.

Any promising identifiers from your premium or government searches should be added to your case notes, and generated reports should be dropped into your digital notebook as pdfs. Photos can be copied and pasted into your digital notes or dropped into your designated directory within the shared folder on your desktop. This reflects our workflow going forward. Any valuable page, image, or identifier is noted, and a corresponding pdf or image capture is placed either in our digital notebook or investigative folder.

Open-Source Research & Collection

Once you have exhausted your in-house and paid data resources, it is time to dive into your OSINT tools and resources. This tends to be the most involved stage of research due to the large number of sites that you will check for your target's information. Tab management is critical in staying organized. If you have not already done so, add the **OneTab** (one-tab.com) extension to Chrome and Firefox within your VM.

- In your VM, open your custom OSINT tools and use the tool category that corresponds to your known identifiers, such as the email and search engine tools.

- Perform any additional queries on sites not included in your custom toolset. For example, a colleague may have very recently recommended a new email search site. If that resource provides good results, consider adding it to your custom toolset.

At this point, you should be in your VM looking at several open tabs in your browser. These tabs represent the results from the Google and custom tools queries which you have executed. The rule going forward is to deal with each tab completely, and intentionally keep or discard it before moving on to the next. A common misstep is to start clicking on leads that look interesting prior to completely reviewing the page on which you are currently visiting. Therefore, tab discipline should be in the forefront of your mind as you parse through your first batch of search results. Consider the following.

- Review the first tab of Google results, looking for anything that stands out as a likely valid lead on your target. For any results that look promising, right-click the link and choose "Open link in new tab".
- Continue to scroll through the first page of Google results and when you get to the image results, right-click on it and choose "Open link in new tab". If Google does not include an "Images for…" section in the first page of results, you may need to select "Images" from the tabs at the top of the page. The image results are always worth reviewing as you can quickly scan the page for potential profile images or other photos of your target.
- Once you are satisfied that you have fully reviewed the first page of Google results and have opened any promising leads in their own tabs, you can move on to the next tab.
- As you start to do more OSINT work, small efficiencies compound to save a lot of time in the overall investigation. Learning keyboard commands for frequently used browser actions will be very beneficial. In this case, you can press "Ctrl" + "tab" (Windows) or "command" + "tab" (Mac) to move to the next tab to the right. Holding down "Shift" with the previous key combinations will cycle through tabs in the opposite direction, from right to left.

This system of exhausting leads on the current page before moving on to other tabs is crucial in ensuring that you do not overlook potential intelligence or lose your way by moving too quickly from lead to lead. That is called "rabbit holing" and it is one of the most common mistakes made by new investigators. You also need to be disciplined about closing any tabs that are false positives or otherwise present no fruitful results. This will help to control browser clutter and reduce the load on your workstation resources.

As you move through your tabbed results methodically, you may come upon a page of results which is a jackpot of links to potential target data. This is a good problem to have, but a problem nonetheless. The same rules apply, but with one additional recommendation, which is that any lead that warrants its own full set of queries should be opened in a new window rather than a new tab. Consider the following example.

- You have located a social media account containing several strong leads which require their own full set of queries using Google and your custom OSINT tools.
- The Twitter usernames need to be queried through the Twitter tools and the email addresses through the email tools. Think of each of these as a new path that needs to be followed independently.
- Any strong leads should be represented in your notes. Write down any account identifiers on your notepad, and for each create a new page in your digital notebook. Figure 45.02 displays the documentation in OneNote.
- Much like a family tree forks into new branches which create even more branches, following online leads often presents new leads. Browser tabs and windows can help you categorize and isolate all leads, providing a sense of structure to your investigation.

This OneNote digital notebook is logically structured to organize intelligence leads as they are uncovered. The notebook title on the top left reflects the case number and name of the target organization. I should mention that this example was chosen arbitrarily, and the group depicted is not likely criminal in nature. I have tabbed sections for the target individual and the organization. I also have a tab which contains fresh copies of my

OSINT templates should I need them. The visible section represents a "real-name" investigation into my primary target. On the right, I have added pages that reflect each strong lead, which was created for each account identifier. This ensures that every new investigative path I open has a place to paste relevant data, while also making it easier to visualize my leads as a whole. The following explains some of the options present in Figure 45.02.

- The Scratch Page is for quickly pasting links and reminders for items which I want to have quick access or revisit later.
- The Request Details page is where I paste the details of the investigative request along with any other important details gleaned during triage.
- The various Premium/Government Data resource pages contain pasted reports or snippets from closed-source, in-house, and paid services.

Strong leads are given a new browser window and their own page in my digital notebook. The list of pages can also be used as a checklist or "to-do" list. Once you have fully exhausted that lead, you can add a "+" symbol or any other desired character to the title to indicate that it is complete.

Tab Management

When you reach the last open tab in your current search, look back and make certain that any open tabs are pages that have useful data. Prior to moving on to a new window and path of inquiry, you should preserve your list of tabs. This is where your tab manager can be beneficial. OneTab's primary purpose is its ability to quickly collapse all tabs into an exportable list of URLs. These bookmarks can then be pasted into your notes or shared with a colleague who can import them into their own OneNote instance. Once you are finished working with any set of tabs, conduct the following.

- Right-click anywhere in the window, select the blue OneTab icon, and click "Send all tabs to OneTab".
- You will now be looking at the OneTab manager, which was explained in Chapter Three. The list of bookmarks for the tabs you just collapsed will be at the top of the list.
- Click in front of the number of tabs to add a title, such as "Google Target Name". Logical naming is the cornerstone of staying organized and making your work searchable. Eventually this set of bookmarks will get pushed farther down the page as you add newer tab sets. To find it again, press "Ctrl" + "F" (Windows) or "command" + "F" (Mac) to conduct a keyword search for the custom title you added.

The list of tabs is saved locally in your VM within your browser extension data, but you will want it in your notes for easy access. Click on "Export/Import URLs" on the top right of the page. Figure 45.03 displays an example. The export page is missing titles, but each set is separated by a space and the URLs are in the same order as the lists on the OneTab management page. Consider the following steps.

- Left-click and drag your mouse to highlight your set of URLs. Press "Ctrl" + "C" (Windows) or "command" + "C" (Mac) to copy the list.
- Move to your digital notebook, select the appropriate page, and press "Ctrl" + "V" (Windows) or "command" + "V" (Mac) to paste the list into your notes.

Although OneTab is the tab manager I recommend for most people, if you require online sync or advanced features, some other tab extensions are Toby, Tabs-Outliner, Workona, and Graphitabs. As discussed earlier in this book, extensions always come with a security cost, so use them sparingly and only when the added functionality is mission critical.

Context Menu Queries

Speed and efficiency are key if you are conducting OSINT at the professional level. Context search extensions, such as **ContextSearch** (github.com/ssborbis/ContextSearch-web-ext), allow you to query a keyword or link just by right-clicking on it. These extensions come with a predefined set of search options, such as Google reverse image, and allow you to also add your own custom queries.

Queries are customized via the options menu by adding structured URLs to the existing list of popular search engines. To add your own custom search strings, conduct the following.

- Left-click on the "ContextSearch" extension in your toolbar and then click the gear icon to go to settings.
- Select the "Search Engines" tab and click the "Add" button.
- Type in a name for your new search and click "OK".
- In the template field, paste the URL query for the search you want to execute. These can be some of the same queries that you have added to your custom OSINT toolset. At the end of the URL add {SEARCHTERMS}.

Context-based search capabilities complement, but do not replace your custom toolset. They offer speed and convenience, but lack the full level of control and customizability that you have with your own tools.

Figure 45.02: Structuring digital notes in OneNote.

Figure 45.03: The OneTab management page.

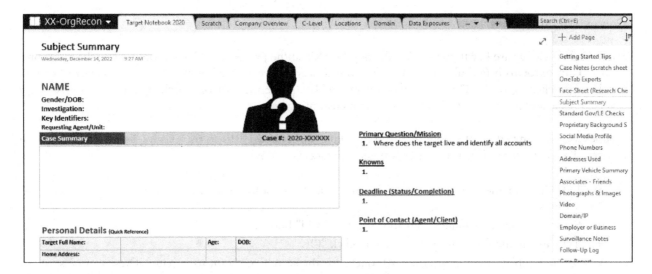

Figure 45.04: An OSINT case template in OneNote.

Capture and Collection

You should now have a reliable, repeatable process for working through your OSINT queries and capturing results in your paper and digital notes. The final piece of the research phase is capture and collection. This is made up of the steps involved in preserving content for evidentiary or reporting purposes. There are three approaches to collection depending on the tools you have available.

Manual Capture

Manual capture includes any technique that is user-initiated and results in capturing a single file or multiple files within a single page. These are often browser-based tools such as JavaScript or extensions. Here are the steps to integrating manual capture into your workflow.

- Create a case folder in your VM shared directory named logically for your case.
- Open that case folder and create a new folder matching the corresponding category from your toolset. If I am working on an email address, this will be titled "Email Addresses".
- Open that directory and create a folder titled appropriately for the identifier you are querying. If an email address is the target, the folder may be titled similar to "ramit@iwillteachyoutoberich.com".
- Repeat this for any other strong leads, such as Twitter usernames, names, domains, etc.
- Now you have a logically structured set of folders to store any saved digital content.
- As you work through your set of tabs specifically for that lead, capture any pages that support your findings and save those to this folder.
- Any time you save an image or video related to that lead, also save it to this directory using any of the tools referenced earlier in the book.
- Any time you save a specific image or video, you should also save a screen capture of the page from where you obtained it. This shows visually how that image or video was laid out on the page. The capture of the entire page is saved to the same folder where you placed the image or video it references.

If you followed the prior steps for tab management, these subfolders should match up with any strong leads that you have opened in their own windows. At the conclusion of your investigation, the digital evidence is nicely organized by its corresponding identifier and tools.

Passive Capture

The best example of a passive capture tool is Hunchly. It records pages loaded in Chrome at the source code level, as well as any images on those pages. It provides a wide safety net, but you should be more intentional in taking advantage of its capture capabilities. The following steps assume you have Hunchly and Chrome installed in your custom OSINT VM. If you are not a Hunchly user, you may skip this section and move on to scripted capture.

- Create a new Hunchly case named the same as your investigative notebook and your digital directory.
- Click the Hunchly extension icon on the top right of your Chrome browser and make sure it is set to capture and that it is set to the correct case name.
- Proceed with your research in Chrome as described in the previous sections. Any time you find an image that is key to your case, right-click it, select the Hunchly entry on the context menu, and choose "Add Caption to Image". Provide a logical caption and click "Save".
- Hunchly can later generate a forensically sound report containing all tagged images.

Scripted Capture

Scripted capture is made up of the manually activated programs that collect or "mine" digital content on our behalf. A good example of this is using Instaloader to rip all of the photos from a specified Instagram account. These types of tools were covered earlier in the book, and there are only a few things to keep in mind on how they fit in our workflow, as explained below.

- For scripts that prompt you for a save location, you should use the same system that was described for manual capture: a series of logical nested folders.
- Some scripts will store collected data in a default directory, such as Downloads or Documents. In these cases, complete the collection and then manually move the files over to your case directory. When reasonable, move rather than copy files to limit clutter and abandoned case data.
- Add a line to your notes indicating which script was used, what it was directed to collect, and the date and time. Unlike Hunchly, most of these tools do not annotate or generate a log of their actions.
- If you are collecting digital evidence for use in court, you should consider also conducting a manual capture of any crucial items. The problem with scripts is that you may not be able to explain how they work in court. A manual save is easy to explain confidently to a jury when the time comes to testify.

Multimedia and Link Analysis

Whether you are working your case independently or have the support of a dedicated team, the research phase will include some level of multimedia analysis. This is the process of examining the visual and metadata characteristics of recovered images and video. Visual examination is exactly what it sounds like. View each image or clip at the highest resolution possible and methodically examine media for any intelligence that was unintentionally included in the frame. You are looking for things like business signage in the background of your target's profile photo. Identify anything that narrows down who or where they might be, and include this in your case notes. This process can be very time consuming, but it remains one of the best methods of locating an elusive target who has otherwise covered their online tracks.

Link analysis is the process of using charts and diagrams to illustrate how information and entities are connected. These can be people, locations, websites, phone numbers, or any other identifiers you see associated with online accounts. Figure 45.05 displays a link analysis showing connections between specific people and domains. You will see specific examples of link analysis tools in the following chapter. Not all cases require a link chart, but you should consider its value when faced with complex organizations or anytime your case might benefit from a visualization of how entities or accounts are connected.

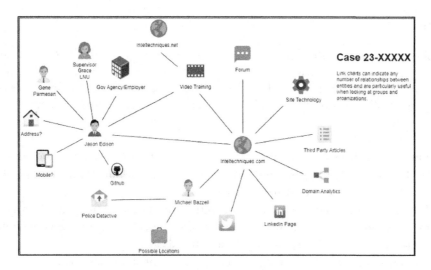

Figure 45.05: A link analysis example with Draw.io.

Once your research is complete, you will need to prepare your report. Several of the steps in this workflow were in preparation for the reporting phase. If you have followed along diligently, your efforts will be rewarded by painless report creation. Chapter Thirty-Five is dedicated to taking all of the intelligence that you have collected and using it to build a professional case report.

Submission and Cleanup

It is not unusual to move from one investigation to another very quickly. Just as we took time to properly set up our research, we also need to appropriately close out our work before moving on to the next task. The following may be beneficial.

- Transfer any handwritten notes to either your digital notes or final report. If you prefer, you can scan the notes as a pdf using your scan enabled printer or scanning straight to OneNote. Any paper notes or printouts are then either filed in a secure location and in compliance with your agency's policies or they are shredded.
- Do not leave case assets scattered about or they will get mixed in with future case work. Your investigative directories should be archived in accordance with your agency's evidence submission and retention policies. Some teams retain copies of these "working files" on network attached storage or optical discs. If the subject should resurface, as criminals tend to do, having historical notes from previous incidents can be a huge time saver.
- If appropriate, export a copy of the VM that you used for the case. Then return to a clean snapshot or clone as described in earlier sections of this book. Consider preparing fresh accounts for the next investigation and find replacements for broken tools.

20 Minutes vs. 20 Days

Some major case investigations take place over a series of days or even months, while critical incidents may require you to give a threat assessment in 20-30 minutes. Your workflow will remain the same for each situation, but the time spent on each step will obviously be reduced. When you reduce the "time-to-solve" drastically, there will be compromises made to the quality of work and operational-security. A common scenario where I use a streamlined workflow is a threat assessment, such as a person threatening suicide in an online chatroom. Consider the following threat assessment steps and workflow charts on the following pages.

- **Triage:** Verbally clarify the known identifiers and expected intelligence, such as: "User D1ckTraC on 4chan is threatening to kill himself in a post. We want to know who he really is, where he lives, and whether he is likely to carry out the threat".

- **Knoll Your Tools:** Grab your legal pad and a pen. Ideally you will have a fresh instance of your OSINT VM ready to use. If you do not have this prepared ahead of time, use "utility" social media accounts. Utility social media accounts are those on hand for assessments where speed is essential and cross-contamination is a reasonable concession. Fresh accounts are always preferable.

- **Collaboration:** If you are collaborating with a team on a platform such as OneNote, create a page for each user to paste key findings so that you do not confuse one another. Keep in mind that OneNote in a browser syncs almost instantly, whereas several users on OneNote desktop will have syncing issues. Assign one person to keep track of everyone's progress and build out the big picture.

- **Premium/Government Resources:** Run your target through any commercial aggregators and government databases. These checks should run very quickly and return basic data with minimal effort.

- **OSINT:** Begin with Google searches such as: site:4chan.org "username". Then query your target's known identifiers through your custom OSINT tools.

- Only open very promising links in new tabs and visually scan each page quickly for words or images that jump out at you. The images results can be especially useful on time sensitive assessments because your brain can process them exponentially faster than text.

- For anything useful, make a note on your legal pad and leave the corresponding tab open.

- Be prepared to give a briefing at the deadline, even if it is just a situational report similar to "we've located and preserved the original posting, there's a history of similar suicidal threats from that user, but we do not know who or where he/she is yet".

- Take care of any additional collection, analysis, and reporting once the crisis has passed. At that point you will fall back into the normal workflow and documentation steps.

Target Flowcharts

I have conducted numerous OSINT training programs over the past few years. Regardless of the audience, I receive the question "Is there a standard process or workflow for each type of OSINT target?" at every event. My short answer was always "no". I had always looked at each investigation as unique. The type of investigation dictated the avenues and routes that would lead me to valuable intelligence. There was no cheat-sheet that could be used for every scenario. While I still believe there is no complete template-based solution for this type of work, I now admit that some standards can be developed. This section will display my attempt at creating workflows that can quickly assist with direction and guidance when you possess a specific piece of information. These documents are presented in six views based on the information being searched: Email, Username, Real Name, Telephone Number, Domain Name, and Location.

Each example will try to show the standard path that I would take when provided the chosen type of data. The goal with my investigations is to get to the next topic. For example, if I am given an email address, my goal is to find any usernames and real names. When I have a username, my goal is to find any social networks and verify an email address. When I have a real name, the goal is to find email addresses, usernames, and a telephone number. When I have a telephone number, my goal is to verify the name and identify a physical address and relatives. When I have a domain name, my goal is to locate a real name and physical address. The cycle continues after each new piece of information is discovered.

Download all flowcharts at **https://inteltechniques.com/data/osintbook11/flowcharts.zip**. This file includes full-size image exports of each flowchart and the original Draw.io file which can be modified. I no longer visually present the files in this book in order to save space. I believe that all of these will always be a work in progress. As everything else in OSINT changes, these will too. I used the free open-source application Draw.io (draw.io) to create each of these. I installed the desktop application, but you could also use their free browser-based solution to open and modify the documents to fit your own investigations.

CHAPTER FOURTY-SIX
DOCUMENTATION & REPORTING

Once you have completed your research, you will need to compile your intelligence into a professional report. Using the correct tools and techniques for documentation throughout your investigation will make generating your final report a relatively painless process.

Investigative Note-Taking

Like any form of research, note-taking is essential when conducting a professional OSINT investigation. As mentioned in the previous chapter, I prefer to take my notes in both paper and digital formats. The paper scratchpad is for quick identifiers, reminders, and at times a rough diagram. The digital notes are for pasting copied text, images, video, or other files. My hand-written notes tend to be unstructured, whereas collecting digital content often benefits from a pre-structured destination. The following are my recommendations for solid digital notebook applications for OSINT work, along with some of their respective pros and cons.

Standard Notes (standardnotes.org)

Standard Notes is the best privacy focused note-taking application with AES-256 encryption and has a very clear privacy policy. It has open-source versions for Mac, Windows, IOS, Android, Linux, and web browsers making it a great fit for OSINT work. You can use Standard Notes completely offline, but if you choose to make an account even the free tier supports sync and end-to-end encryption. The premium version adds advanced features such as multi-factor authentication, automated backups to your own cloud service of choice, and some aesthetic options, such as themes.

OneNote (onenote.com/download)

OneNote is the power option for digital note-taking at the price of a privacy compromise, but it is worth mentioning because many of us work for organizations that use Microsoft Office as their enterprise office platform. I recommend installing the standalone version of OneNote unless your agency requires use of the cloud-based Office 365 ecosystem. Creating a fresh Microsoft account will prevent the installation from cross contaminating your other MS Office projects. Microsoft will offer to provide you with a new Outlook.com address, but a Proton Mail address would be the better choice for most people.

The desktop version of OneNote is supported on Mac, IOS, Android, and most major browsers, but each will require authentication with the account you used for installation. Microsoft, like other major platforms, forces you to sync to their ecosystem whenever possible. Similar to Standard Notes, OneNote stores data in a hierarchical structure of pages, sections, and notebooks. From an organizational perspective, it functions exactly like an old-school case binder of paper reports and printouts. I can create a new notebook titled "CopperThieves" with tabbed sections for each suspect. Each section is then broken down into my desired pages: Bio, Facebook, Twitter, Vehicles, Employment, etc. These pages can be populated from scratch, or I can preload them with my case templates or a simple spreadsheet.

What makes OneNote possibly worth the privacy compromise is its ability to ingest just about any type of digital file as an attachment. I can drag a pdf report from the Department of Licensing and drop it on the "Vehicles" page of a target and OneNote will ask if I want it added as a printout or file. The printout option adds a human readable image of the file, while the file option embeds the pdf file itself. Double-clicking on that pdf file after import would open it in a browser window or pdf reader of choice.

You may organize your digital notebook to suit your investigation, although I typically use the section tabs to separate out case targets and then each page of a section represents a major investigative lead (username, email address, employer, etc.). I can also export entire notebooks by clicking on "File" and then "Export". Notebooks can be exported in a proprietary format, whereas sections and pages may also be exported as pdfs, docs, and several other file formats. This is convenient should you want to export sections from your digital notes to include in your report appendix. Although OneNote can be used in an online capacity via browser from any operating-system, implementation on Mac and Linux is clunky at best. For MacOS users you may have better luck with a OneNote clone called Outline (outline.app/mac). Linux users have the option of a project called P3X (github.com/patrikx3/onenote) which will allow you to create edit OneNote files in your browser.

CherryTree (giuspen.com/cherrytree)

CherryTree is my note-taking application of choice for Linux. It ticks all the boxes we like such as being open-source and offline. What separates it from other Linux options is its ability to support both hierarchical notes and some limited support for storing images, tables, and other filetypes. The following steps will install CherryTree to your Linux Original VM.

- Open a terminal window by clicking on the shortcut in your Dock.
- Type the following into terminal: `sudo apt install -y cherrytree`
- Press enter and you will see CherryTree and all dependencies installed.

Open CherryTree from the Applications menu and add to your favorites, if desired. CherryTree has vast functionality, but the core feature of which we want to take advantage is the hierarchical node structure. Think of Nodes as notebook sections and SubNodes as pages within those sections. On the left side of the CherryTree window is the "node tree", which shows everything in your current notebook. To add a new section, click on "Tree" in the top toolbar and then "Add Node". Give your node a logical name such as "Facebook" and select "OK". To add a page or "SubNode" to that section, right-click on the node and select "Add SubNode". Name it appropriately and click "OK". Most of the functions we care about can be completed via the "Tree" menu in the toolbar or by using the right-click context menu.

CherryTree is not without its downsides. It is not nearly as user-friendly as OneNote when it comes to drag and drop and its support for inserting non-text filetypes is inconsistent. However, it is a hierarchical digital notebook within our Linux VM and one with much greater privacy than we could ever obtain using a Microsoft or other closed-source office application. There is a windows installer available as well, although I recommend using the Linux version in your VM whenever possible. A CherryTree template is included in the files download page.

Joplin (joplinapp.org)

Joplin is a free and open source note taking application which is supported on iOS, Android, Mac, Linux, and Windows. Joplin is a great option for anyone wanting a simple digital notebook with an intuitive structure of notebooks and pages. Markdown format is supported for notes as well as the ability to create notes in a "to-do" format which adds a checkbox to the title in the navigation panel. Notebooks may be exported in markdown or HTML formats, with pdf export as an additional option for individual note pages. Although fairly simple by design, Joplin does support modern features such as search, tagging, plugins and small quality of life features such as dark mode. Joplin supports optional notebook sharing and synchronization via various cloud services such as OneDrive, S3, and their own premium Joplin Cloud service. The privacy-minded can take advantage of their self-hosting support with NextCloud or a Joplin server. If you choose to utilize any of the syncing options, make sure to enable end-to-end encryption and set a strong master passphrase at "Tools" > "Options" > "Encryption". Joplin clients for each operating system are available for download at https://joplinapp.org/help/install/.

Obsidian (obsidian.md)

Obsidian offers the simplicity of a basic text editor but also supports some limited graphical capabilities such as mind maps and ingesting images. The graph functionality allows you to create a rudimentary link chart showing connections and relationships between various notes. Obsidian also has a very active community and plugin ecosystem. The free version is fully featured with a paid tier for those intending to use the application for commercial purposes. Obsidian is available for all three major desktop platforms as well as mobile (https://obsidian.md/download).

Cryptpad (cryptpad.fr)

Cryptpad is a privacy respecting online office suite with support for online collaboration. While it lacks the more advanced features of something like the Microsoft Office ecosystem, it is very simple to use, and it does not collect and sell your data. Your documents are encrypted by default on the Cryptpad servers. There are built in comment and chat features for real-time collaboration on shared documents. As a guest you can create, store, and share documents for up to 90 days. Setting up a free account requires only a username/password and will net you an additional 1 GB of persistent online drive space for storing and sharing your documents. The team at Cryptpad is not collecting your contact information, which is great for privacy, but they cannot reset passwords, so store your credentials appropriately. There is also a premium tier which includes more storage and faster support should you require either. As with any online service, we recommend maintaining a local backup of any files stored on the Cryptpad servers.

Advanced Text Editors: You may want to consider adding Interactive Development Environments (IDEs) to your arsenal of documentation tools. These are applications built for programmers and web developers for writing and testing their code. While full IDEs can be very complex, there are a handful of "light" IDEs or advanced text-editors which fit well into your workflow. The editors handle basic note-taking quite well. They also provide additional capabilities such as built-in terminals and mark-down support, which is exactly what we need when customizing your OSINT tools as previously explained. There are significant efficiency gains to be had when using a tool that supports note-taking, running scripts, and editing code all within a single interface. While many readers will continue to rely on office suites from major publishers to prepare your final reports, these light IDEs are capable of handling much of your investigative workflow.

VSCode (code.visualstudio.com)

VSCode is very close to being a fully functional IDE and it has a huge following in the programming and web development communities due to its extensive catalogue of available extensions. Extensions are plugins which add additional features and customizations such as interface themes. While the source code is open, the application itself is a proprietary free Microsoft product and its primary weakness is the standard telemetry and data collection that accompanies most Microsoft products. Therefore, VSCode is a good option for someone already working in a Microsoft enterprise environment. In addition to simple text capabilities, VSCode supports mark-down. This makes it a good tool for both notes and also for working on your custom tool files. It has a very responsive interface and does not bog down when dealing with large files. It has arguably the largest collection of extensions of any editor in its class and it supports running code should you want to customize some scripts. The standard install includes a terminal so you can run CMD, PowerShell, or bash from within the application. VSCode is available for macOS, Windows, and Linux. Following installation, immediately review all settings and disable telemetry. You can accomplish this by selecting "File" > "Preferences" > "Settings" or "Code" > "Preferences" > "Settings". Using the search box, submit a query for "telemetry" and uncheck "Telemetry: Enable Telemetry setting". Now search for "@tag:usesOnlineServices" and review the settings which make calls to online services such as those querying for extension updates. Disabling these will reduce your exposure to Microsoft but may limit some functionality such as automatic updates and notifications.

VSCodium (vscodium.com)

VSCodium is an open-source clone built from the VSCode source. It removes the Microsoft data collection in exchange for a slightly more complicated configuration process. VSCodium offers most of VSCode's capabilities. If you are not already using Office or other Microsoft products, this is the best choice for you. Although the bulk of data sharing is disabled by default, it is recommended that you review all application settings and look for any which use "online services". There is no substitute for reviewing configuration settings yourself. VSCodium presents a slightly less polished user experience. Some extensions require additional installation steps and there is a much smaller community from which to draw support. VSCodium is available on macOS, Windows, and Linux using the package managers which were previously explained.

Anatomy of an OSINT Report: Although some investigators choose to write their reports as they go, I prefer to use handwritten and digital notes to complete the formal report at the conclusion of the investigation. I have created a series of templates in Microsoft Word and Adobe Acrobat, each of which are available in the digital files download, which provide a polished documentation framework for the most common mission scenarios. Although they vary in format, each contains a common structure including face-sheet, narrative, analysis, and appendix.

Face-Sheet: The face-sheet is typically one or two pages and is the most important piece of any report. It is meant to quickly convey the most important intelligence. The mark of a good face-sheet is that a boss or client can glance at it and instantly know the case name/number, who collected the intelligence, investigative timeframe, primary subject identifiers, and a concise set of key findings. The key findings can be in bullet or paragraph format, but should be no more than a half of one page. If you choose to include a table of contents for the report, it is often placed under the case title and prior to key findings. Figure 46.01 (upper-left) displays an example of a simple face-sheet while Figure 46.01 (upper-right) displays a full report version.

Narrative: The narrative follows the face-sheet and it tells the story. This is your opportunity to describe the path you took to reach your key findings. I like to organize my narrative in either chronological order or match the order of findings as listed on the face-sheet. I always prefer to tell a story in the order in which things occurred. This can be vital if your report will later be used as part of your courtroom testimony. Write in the first person and as concisely as possible, just as you would for any written statement for a police report or other legal document. Write just enough to provide context and a clear understanding for each piece of discovered intelligence. This section can be a couple of paragraphs to several pages, depending on the complexity of the case. The narrative should address any discoveries that impact the investigative findings. It is important to acknowledge any exculpatory evidence and ensure that it is represented in your reporting. This is especially true for those working in the criminal justice and government sectors. Likewise, if your report takes the form of an intelligence briefing, your audience may expect confidence levels associated with your conclusions. Use terms such as "unsubstantiated", "likely", or "highly likely", rather than expressing the chances in percentages. Consider adding a section describing the best-practices used during the online investigation. Key points to be made here are compartmentalization from other casework; thoroughness of research; software and services used; and a brief statement of training and qualifications. Think of this section as demonstrating why your work should be trusted. Figure 46.01 (lower-right) displays a partial example of a report narrative.

Link Analysis & Timelines: Not all reports will contain an analysis section, but this is where I present graphical components that support understanding of the preceding narrative. These include timelines of key events and link charts mapping out relationships between individuals, groups, locations, and internet sites. In my organization, this type of specialized work is often handled by civilian analysts who are proficient in software such as Maltego or I2 Analyst's Notebook. I provide them with a copy of my face-sheet, narrative, and a hand drawn map of the case entities and corresponding relationships. They use these to construct a more professional, visually appealing, and understandable graphical representation of the criminal organization or series of events. Not every investigation warrants this level of investment and not every investigator has these resources available, but they are a nice touch on major cases. When I do not have analyst resources available, I leverage one of the following free and user-friendly link visualization tools.

Draw.io (www.diagrams.net/integrations.html)
Gephi (gephi.org)
MindMup (mindmup.com)
NWU (knightlab.northwestern.edu/projects)

Open Source Investigative Profile

Agency/Org Name
Section or Analyst Name

Date Completed:

```
┌─────────────┐
│  Subject    │
│  Photo      │
└─────────────┘
```

Summary of Findings

Subject ID

Name:	DOB:
Address:	Phone #1:
	Phone #2:
Employer:	SS#:
Vehicle #1:	Associate:
Vehicle #2:	Other:

Alternate Identities and Associations

Email #1:	Email #2:
Email #3:	Email #4:
Username:	Username #2:
Facebook:	FB #:
Twitter:	Blog:
Instagram:	Forum:
Other:	Domain:

Photos/Video

	Description	Source
☐Photos		
☐Video		

Attachments

☐ Excel/CSV Spreadsheets   ☐ Link Analysis Report
☐ Digital Media (Optical Disc)   ☐ TLO/Clear/Accurint Report
☐ Photographs   ☐ DOL/GOV ID
☐ DOC/Criminal History   ☐ Other: _____

Case # 2020-XXXXXX

Subject Name

R/G/DOB
Phone Number(s):
Last Known Address:

```
┌──────────┐
│ AGENCY   │
│ LOGO     │
└──────────┘
```

Requested By:	Report Prepared By:
Unit:	Approved By:
Date:	Date:
	Date:

Investigative Summary

❗ Clear and concise synopsis of the case findings. Information critical to understanding can be included as bullet points or short paragraphs. Detailed evidence will be included in subsequent sections of the report.

[Intelligence detailed in this report was collected from publicly available sources on the internet and in compliance with agency policy as well as local and federal law.]

[Finding 1]

[Finding 2]

[Finding 3]

[Finding 4]

[Finding 5]

Subject Profile

❗ Add target details such as personal identifiers and account names/numbers. Retitle and/or delete cells as needed.

Target Full Name:		Age:	DOB:
Home Address:			
Mailing Address:			
Telephone:		Telephone:	
Target Email:			
Target Usernames:			
Target Social Network Profiles			
Facebook:		Twitter:	

LOGO HERE

Event Name
Section or Analyst Name

Threat Assessment - Event

Event/Assessment Details

Event ID

Event Site:	Date(s):
Location:	Official #:
	Official @
Security Contact:	Contact #:
Incident Command:	Contact #:

Hashtag, Users, Sites

Hashtag:	Site:
Hashtag:	Site:
@User:	Site:
@User:	Site:
@User:	Site:
@User:	Site:

Groups/Individuals of Interest

Description	Details

Intel Feeds

Video Feeds	Maps

Case Narrative

❗ Intelligence detailed in this report was collected from publi
and in compliance with agency policy as well

Training & Qualifications – Jason Edison is a 20-year veteran of the Sp
as the investigative lead in the departments Digital Crimes Section. He
online investigations and digital forensics training. He has conducted l
served as an expert witness regarding digital evidence.

On 11/14/2019 Detective Johansen with the Homicide Unit requested
possible witness to a shooting death that occurred at 4200 N Jackson S
Johansen provided me with a tip sheet wherein an anonymous caller pu
"@Jakijumpjorp66" had posted photos of the shooting as it took place
the anonymous complainant.

I researched user "@Jakijumpjorp66" using a fresh Chrome browser w
These best practices ensure that the online research is free from cross
conducted keyword searches of the username against the site Twitter.c
Yahoo, Duckduckgo, and Exalead. Google returned a result that show
intersection in question. I browsed to the corresponding page on twitt
(https://twitter.com/Jakijumpjorp66/media) and preserved a copy of
Chrome browser (see appendix item 3.46). The photo depicted a man
for "Tom's Waterbed Warehouse." I saved a digital copy of the photo
it in the digital media archive which is included in the optical media att

---

Figure 46.01: Document templates available at https://inteltechniques.com/osintbook11.

I formerly used the free, stripped-down version of Maltego called CaseFile for my link charts. I have since moved on to better open-source options that are far less resource intensive and less of a privacy concern. Remember, when working in our VM, we are borrowing resources from our host machines, so we need to use lightweight applications whenever possible. I prefer Draw.io for most investigations. It is most commonly used online as a browser-based diagram solution. When you browse to the site it will prompt you to create a new diagram, but first click on "Change Storage". Select "Device" and check "Remember this setting" to establish that we will be saving our work locally rather than with Google or Microsoft. Once you select either a blank diagram or one of the many templates, you will be ready to start building a link chart representing your investigative diagram. Before moving on, consider a more private option by installing the offline desktop application, which is available for MacOS, Windows, and Linux (https://github.com/jgraph/drawio-desktop/releases).

Once the application is installed and running, choose to create a new diagram, and a window will open offering you several templates. Some of the options in the network category work well for OSINT, or you can start with a blank project. Draw.io is very intuitive, allowing you to select icons on the left and drag them into your chart. Any linear icons (lines or arrows) are connectors and can be used to represent relationships between entities on the diagram. Double-clicking on text will allow you to edit the labels. The toolbar at the top and the right-click context menu offer many additional options for editing or adding components to the link chart. Save and export options are in the "File" menu. Draw.io supports export in the most common filetypes such as pdf, docx, png, and html. When you first install Draw.io the default settings will present charts which appear a bit outdated due to the art style of the standard icons. Changing the following settings can fix this.

- Click "Extras" at the top and select one of the additional themes. I use the lighter options, as seen in Figure 46.02, for anything being printed, but I find that dark works well visually.
- At the bottom of the "Shapes" panel on the left, click "+More Shapes...".
- Browse through and check any sets that look useful and click "Apply". One I always include is "Web Icons" under "Other". The "Web Icons" and "Web Logos" work very well for OSINT charts and the icon styles tend to be more modern than the default selections included in the offered templates.
- There is also a + button in your toolbar that will allow you to import your own images into the chart or even draw shapes freehand.

Timelines and Event Maps

Draw.io is very flexible and you could use it to create timelines or event maps. However, I like to have multiple options for any task. The following descriptions are of two other applications for dedicated timeline and mapping tools.

Event Viewpoint (eventviewpoint.com)

Event Viewpoint is a free, closed-source, browser-based timeline and mapping application. It will allow you to create events made up of a location, designated span of time/date, and event notes. You may add images and view your case as a list, timeline, or geographical map. An example is seen in Figure 46.03. You will need to sign up for a free account using a non-attributable email address. I never use these types of browser-based applications to work with sensitive data.

Time Graphics (time.graphics)

Time Graphics is a premium browser-based timeline tool and you will need to make an account using a valid email address. Only premium users can save privatized projects and remove watermarks. The interface is driven by an intuitive right-click context menu and will allow you to add events, pictures, video, and notes. Figure 46.04 shows an example. You can export your project in several formats including pdf, docx, and json.

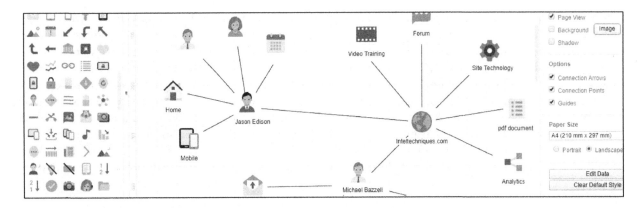

Figure 46.02: The Draw.io light theme.

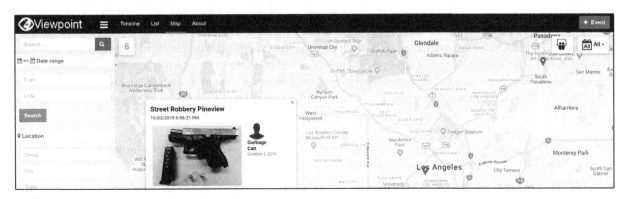

Figure 46.03: The Event Viewpoint timeline and mapping application.

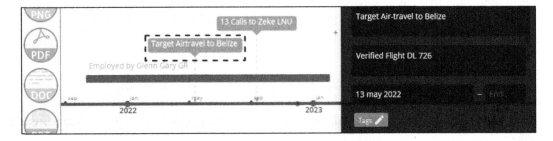

Figure 46.04: The Time Graphics application.

Appendix

The appendix of a report is made up of all the supporting documentation and media captured during the investigation. This will be screen capture files, still frames from YouTube evidence, spreadsheets of social media contacts, and any other digital evidence that can be displayed in a document format. These are working copies only, with the digital originals preserved on external media or other format approved by your agency's digital evidence policy. Many of your tools are going to generate pdf files which you will then need to include in your report appendix. If you have Adobe Acrobat Pro you can easily combine the working copies of your pdfs into a single document for easier distribution. The free versions of Acrobat do not support combining or conversion of multiple documents. I prefer a privacy respecting open-source option that does not require an account with Adobe, such as the following.

PDFsam Basic (pdfsam.org/pdf-merge)

PDFsam Basic is a free and open-source application for merging multiple pdf files. It is available for Linux, Mac, and Windows, but the Linux version is the perfect fit for our investigative VM. Installation in Ubuntu Linux is straightforward, as follows.

- In your Linux VM navigate to pdfsam.org/download-pdfsam-basic/.
- Click on "Deb package for Debian based Linux distributions" to download the app.
- Right-click the file and choose "Open with Software Install".
- Click the "Install" button.

This installation provides a new icon in the Applications menu. Opening the application presents a user-friendly menu with many options. To consolidate PDF files, select "Merge" in the left menu, then "Add" to select the desired files, and then "Run". A new combined pdf document will be created in the same directory as the source documents. PDFsam Basic has many more features that will allow you to manipulate your pdf documents, such as removing or rotating a single page within a long document. There are additional customizations available in the settings menu, such as changing the default directory to that of your case file. The premium versions of PDFsam are closed source, and primarily adds support for alternate filetypes.

Sourcing & Annotation

It is important that in our documentation we include annotation indicating the source of each piece of intelligence. The following are some of the most common methods for adding sourcing to reports:

- **Footnotes** – This is one of the most common methods of including sources in documentation. It has the added benefits of looking professional and also being intuitive.
- **Tables** – Tables make for easy organization and association between specific identifiers (accounts, usernames, etc.). If your report includes ratings, such as seriousness of data exposure or confidence levels, you may wish to color code cells and include a color key.
- **Embedded Links** – Embedding the links in the listed identifier is an option but is often not ideal because you lose that link if you print out a hard copy of the report.
- **Combination** – Footnotes can be included in tabled entries or the links to the source may be listed in the table directly depending on formatting preferences. Including embedded links in your tables along with footnotes or full URLs is an option that some choose. Just ensure with embedded links that you are not directing your client to any questionable sites that could expose them to threats or an adversary.
- **Appendices** – Your report appendix may include full captures, lists of sources, or both. Keep in mind that even if you include sources in your appendix, you may want to include them in the profiles portion of your report as well for convenience. If your client has to hunt through the appendix any time, they wish to see an exact source, they may find the report cumbersome to digest and make use of.
- **File Attachments/Supplemental Documentation** – Larger captures of raw pages, images, or videos may be provided in a zip file or other archive. This should be in addition to proper sourcing in the report, not in place of. Many clients will not be interested in digging through the raw data and we want the archive of captures to be a bonus, but at the same time we do not want them to have to dig though the raw data to find the source URLs.

Quality and Diversity of Sources

In addition to how we memorialize and present our sources, we need to also bear in mind the value of the sources themselves. We often say in our line of work that information does not become intelligence until it has context. Sourcing our findings adds context while also providing an avenue for further validation/verification. The sources may also lend to the level of confidence we have in our findings. Just how likely a certain assumption or belief is to be true. Whenever possible we should include multiple diverse sources for each data point in our report. For example, if we find our target's address on a people search engine such as truepeoplesearch.com, that alone would be a fairly low confidence finding as people search engines are notorious for inaccuracies and false positives. However, if we locate and properly source the address from a county tax parcel database, that will increase the confidence level and overall value of that particular finding.

Hunchly (hunch.ly)

Hunchly was mentioned in prior chapters and is one of the only paid OSINT tools I use daily. If you are a Hunchly user, the report builder can be used to create your appendix even if you are not planning to use Hunchly to prepare the entire report. The first step is to set aside the evidentiary copy of your recovered data. This is accomplished by clicking on "Export" and then "Export Case". This will organize the raw data into an archive which can then be transferred to optical or other storage media. We may want a visual representation of this data included in the appendix of our report, which can be accomplished by using the report builder option to export pertinent captures to a consolidated PDF. The primary advantage of using Hunchly to generate your appendix is that it will add the capture date, hash, and URLs to each preserved page and image. This is beneficial when using the appendix as a hard-copy visual reference for the full evidentiary case export.

Document Sanitization

Although I prefer to submit paper reports with an attached optical disc of supporting digital evidence, you may be constrained to the documentation procedures defined by your organization. If your agency uses any of the full-feature proprietary products such as Word or Acrobat, there is going to be metadata included in the digital version of your report that could unnecessarily expose your account details. While we would never want to remove metadata from evidentiary documents, removing hidden author data from your investigative report prior to submission is a recognized best practice.

To accomplish this in Microsoft Office products select "File" > "Info" > "Check for Issues" > "Inspect Document". This will open the inspector window with a list of possible metadata. Check all boxes and click "Inspect". This will execute a scan and any concerns will display a red exclamation point. Typically, these will be in the "Properties" or "Header, Footers, and Watermarks" sections. I often want to keep footnotes and do not remove this section. However, next to "Properties" click "Remove all". This will delete most of the metadata such as the username of the author. This is by no means a complete cleanse, but is an easy way to remove low hanging fruit. To perform a similar metadata removal in Adobe Acrobat, click on "Tools" and under "Protect & Standardize", click "Protect". A new set of options will show up just below the top toolbar. Click "Removed Hidden Information" and a window will open listing the types of removable metadata. You should uncheck boxes next to any items that you do not want removed. When you click "Remove", anything with a check mark will be deleted permanently from your document.

It should be noted that removing metadata can potentially break formatting or corrupt the entire file; therefore, it is wise to create a backup copy prior to metadata removal. You can also use third-party scripts and tools to clean documents, such as the Metadata Anonymization Toolkit (https://github.com/jubalh/MAT) for Linux. I find that these tools are more prone to breaking documents created in Microsoft and Adobe products. Thus, for those types of documents, I use the built-in removal tools described above. Keep in mind an old, but still very effective, method for removing metadata from non-evidentiary documents is using a scanner. Just print your report and scan the paper report back to a digital format using a scanner. The new document will have metadata based on the scanner/copy machine rather than your own accounts or workstation. If this scanner is an enterprise grade copier, it likely saves this data temporarily to a hard-drive and you would never want to use this technique with sensitive documents.

Case Archiving & Cleanup

Upon completing a report, I collect my analog and digital case work and archive it for future use. The length of retention of these notes, virtual machines, screen captures, and reports are dependent on the policies of my organization or the expectations of the client for contracted work. When appropriate I keep handwritten notes for six months and digital documentation for at least three years. Should the case be later adjudicated, I have the documentation available. It is also not uncommon to have a current target resurface in a future investigation; in which case those digital notes will give you a head start on that new case. A final warning for users of OneNote or other digital notebooks. The search capabilities built into OneNote are very useful when querying subjects for any previous work your team has completed. However, hoarding data long-term can leave you with an awful mess if you do not have a system for archiving old cases. I have an archive notebook for each year and within it sections broken down by month. Any completed cases get moved to the archive, and at the end of each month I review any remaining sections to assess their status. Then, at the end of each year, I go through all my notebooks to tidy up any loose ends and consider purging any archived notebooks that have gone untouched for longer than three years. Another approach is to export older notebooks and save them to optical discs or other long-term storage. In your own agency, please ensure that you implement an organization system that works for your workflow and one that is also compliant with retention/audit policies.

Large-Scale Continuous Investigations

Many of my investigations span weeks or months. Most are extremely sensitive and must possess complete isolation from any other investigations. This goes beyond a clean virtual machine. They demand management of dedicated Facebook, Twitter, email, and other accounts, which can become difficult when providers detect my behavior as suspicious. In these scenarios, I assign a dedicated mobile device and cellular data account to each investigation. This may sound ridiculous and expensive, but we can provide this extreme layer of protection at minimal cost. My process is as follows, and only applies to investigations which cannot afford to be compromised by case-contamination or suspended accounts.

First, I need an unlocked mobile device. This will never be used outside of the investigation or for any personal use. I usually buy refurbished Android devices at local cell phone repair shops for $20 each. These are generic, low-powered, and overall undesired units which have very little value. You may also find similar new phones in grocery stores, pawn shops, or online through eBay or Amazon. I then purchase Mint Mobile SIM cards from either Amazon or mintmobile.com. These are $2.00 each, but include a $5.00 credit for service and a one-week free trial. Three months of service is $15 per month ($45 total), and T-Mobile is the data provider. I purchase the phones and service with prepaid gift cards or Privacy.com virtual cards.

I insert the SIM into the device; download the Mint Mobile application over Wi-Fi; register an account under an alias name; and start my trial. Since this is prepaid service, there are no verifications or credit checks. I choose a local telephone number issued by Mint Mobile which can be used for the countless verification text hurdles I am likely to face over the course of the investigation. When Facebook demands a real cellular number, I give this out freely. When Gmail blocks my account as suspicious, I can unlock it with a verification text. I no longer dread the suspension notices typically received when relying on VOIP numbers, VPN connections, and burner email accounts. This cellular number is my ticket out of most negative situations.

I can also place applications on the device when an emulator is not appropriate. As an example, Snapchat and Tinder usually block Genymotion and other virtual Android environments. With this device, I can install the native apps, launch a GPS spoofer, and conduct my investigation without roadblocks. My device appears "real" and I bypass scrutiny from the providers.

At the end of the investigation, I remove the SIM and place it and the phone in a sealable plastic bag with holes punched for use in a binder. These can be found in any office supply store. The phone and SIM are part of the investigation. The service will expire on its own and I have a clean digital trail. If necessary, I can provide the device and account details as part of discovery in court. I have no concerns if an expert witness wants to clone the machine for their own analysis. If the number should become exposed in a data breach, it is not a problem. It will never be used again. If you plan to replicate this technique, I advise preparing now. You do not want to be shopping for a device and waiting for delivery of a SIM card while you should be investigating your target.

CHAPTER FORTY-SEVEN
POLICY, ETHICS, & DEVELOPMENT

There is much controversy over the use of social media and personal data for investigative purposes. Therefore, it is critical that your organization has a clear and concise technical investigations policy in place. This should be a one or two-page document and it must include at a minimum a training standard, an approval process, and an appropriate use policy. Avoid using language tied to specific technologies or platforms, as those will change rapidly over time. In-house council may request language pertaining to Facebook or another specific third-party platform. They may recommend building policy around specific tools or technologies. It is our responsibility to demonstrate how the rapid changes in technology will make such a policy ineffective and almost immediately irrelevant. Moreover, limitations imposed by overly specific regulations will likely confine us to difficult options.

Responsible investigative policy should focus on the appropriate use of techniques and technologies. Review and borrow heavily from the mission statement and boilerplate language that your organization already applies to traditional investigative procedures. Any existing policy relating to training, equipment, enforcement, supervision, or chain of custody will have language that will fold easily into the framework of your online investigations policy. I believe that for most agencies an online investigations policy should be no longer than two pages. The framework for an appropriately non-specific policy typically includes the following sections: Definitions, Appropriate Use, Approval Process, Training, Retention/Audit, Approved Forms, Revision History, and Appendix. We have a sample boiler plate policy included with our digital templates referenced in the previous chapter and downloadable at https://inteltechniques.com/osintbook11/.

For smaller teams or organizations lacking an official policy structure, an alternative format could be a set of standard operating procedures (SOPs). The content will be essentially the same, but less formal in structure. Take the previous policy example, delete the definitions and headings, and paste the remaining content into your agency's memorandum template. Then, have it approved by a commander or manager higher in rank than the front-line supervisor. The important thing is to have some type of documented standard for these types of investigations. Eventually a controversial incident or high-profile case will expose your team to scrutiny and a well-structured policy will go a long way to demonstrating transparency and professionalism.

If your organization requires language around "interaction", such as "friending", make this as non-specific as possible. Some agencies also restrict the use of covert social media accounts, which will extremely limit the effectiveness of your OSINT work. You have to educate management and legal advisors on the importance of covert accounts in building actionable intelligence. Decades of case law supports the use of "undercover" operations for traditional investigations and online investigations should be treated no differently.

I am not an attorney and the best path is always to solicit advice from legal counsel that is familiar with the local, state, and federal laws affecting your jurisdiction. Common sense goes a long way and I always ask myself if there is any way a target could argue a reasonable expectation of privacy. Additionally, being good stewards of privacy is important when building trust with our communities. We never want to portray any hint of recklessness during intelligence gathering. Practice good documentation during the process in order to build favorable case law and maintain as many of our tools as possible.

Child Sexual Abuse Material (CSAM) Policy

In the course of our investigative work, there are times where we might locate content that is, by its very nature, illegal. If we are investigating crimes such as child exploitation, this might be intentional and we likely have a procedure in place. Those outside law enforcement may unintentionally stumble into digital contraband and find themselves unprepared to deal with the ramifications. Although there is a range of digital contraband which could potentially fall into this category, the most critical issue to address in your process and policy is Child Sexual Abuse Material (CSAM). Within the open source intelligence community, specifically the crowd-sourced programs investigating missing or exploited persons, we see an increase of investigators locating material with a reporting requirement. I am not an attorney. I recommend investigators within the U.S. becoming familiar with **Title 18 Part 1 Chapter 110 Section of 2258A** of the U.S. legal code. First, let's address what you should do if you stumble onto content which you feel may be CSAM, or otherwise require reporting responsibility. The following are recommendations for those who do not already have a policy.

1) Do not capture it: Creating copies of CSAM can result in further harm to the victims depicted in the images and, unless you are operating under special legal authority (such as law enforcement), the mere possession of exploitation images on your workstation could constitute a crime, regardless of your intent.

2) Notify a supervisor: Due diligence is essential in these incidents. One of your first actions should be notifying a superior and starting a paper trail to show that the incident was all handled above board.

3) Report the incident to law enforcement: Reporting requirements will vary between jurisdictions, but ethical responsibilities for reporting are universal. Reporting the incident to authorities further solidifies the paper trail and demonstrates due diligence on behalf of your organization.

4) Report the incident to NCMEC: Report the content to the National Center for Missing & Exploited Children (missingkids.org/gethelpnow/cybertipline). Memorialize this reporting in your notes and consider saving a screenshot of your submission.

5) Report it to the involved platform: The timing and appropriateness of this will depend on the platform and your investigation. If the platform itself is potentially involved in the criminal activity, we do not want to tip our hand. Also, if you are working with law enforcement, ensure that they are ready to disclose the case prior to any third party notifications.

6) Document the incident: Create a concise record to memorialize encountering the contraband material. If you are uncertain what to document, consider including the date, time, investigator, supervisor, URLs, and description of the contents. Again, do not include any exploitation images or videos in your documentation, just descriptions.

7) Wellness: Even for seasoned investigators, exposure to CSAM or other materials depicting victimization can be very disturbing. There can be lasting personal emotional impacts if not properly addressed. It is entirely appropriate to speak with a professional counselor or other support personnel following an exposure to images, video, and even secondhand accounts of inhumane acts.

The largest pitfalls in properly handling this material are in the reporting. Again, we do not create copies of the photos or videos unless we are trained to do so. We want to document enough information to direct authorities to intervene, and yet we want to be certain that we are not making things worse for the victim(s). I believe that every full time OSINT team should have a procedure for handling CSAM and for those who wish to translate this into policy, we have sample language included in our policy template within the book portal on our website at https://inteltechniques.com/osintbook11.

Once you have a policy drafted it is wise to have it reviewed by your in-house council or other legal advisory body. Remember to provide training for employees on both the policy and procedures. A baseline of awareness will save you a fair amount of stress when an incident involving CSAM occurs during an investigation or intelligence operation.

If you are a student or non-professional OSINT practitioner, consider starting a conversation with your instructors and peers about the proper handling of illicit materials. If you join a crowd-sourced or charity event related to crimes against children, please ask the organizers for direction and education regarding appropriate procedures for responding to occurrences of CSAM or other digital contraband. As with most other aspects of online investigations, the key is having a plan and showing that a reasonable level of due diligence was applied.

Ethics

Privacy is certainly the cornerstone of ethical considerations related to open source intelligence gathering, but I will also be discussing issues of intent and deception. Privacy is a broad issue and will pertain to almost every portion of our case. Deception becomes pertinent when we engage in active covert measures such as undercover accounts or "friending" targets. We each value privacy in our own lives and we should always be as mindful as possible in regard to the data we collect during our investigations. Early in an investigation, you should clarify the scope of engagement. How deep are you going to dig and what is the appropriate balance of intrusion? Here are two scenarios from the law enforcement world that represent opposing ends of the spectrum.

Scenario #1: I receive a report of online threats against a public official and am asked to make an assessment and if necessary, identify the owner of the account. I locate the account and posts in question and immediately see that although they are mean spirited, the comments do not articulate a true intended threat. A common example of this is similar to, "I hope you get cancer". It is a terrible thing to say, but there is no threat implied. At this point, I can report back to my boss that there is no threat. If necessary, I can show her a screenshot of the post. I have accomplished the mission and there is no justification to dig into the details of that person's life.

Scenario #2: We receive a tip from an internet service provider that a specific IP address is pushing traffic containing a large amount of child pornography. I investigate the IP address and find that it is a listed Tor exit node. That means the person operating the router at the associated residence or business is allowing people on Tor to funnel their internet traffic through their device. Now I know there is a fair chance that the person at that residence is not directly involved in the child pornography and may be unaware of its presence. I do not stop my investigation. I dig up every piece of public data that I can on the people controlling that router.

My decision to press forward on the second scenario is based on the seriousness of the crime. For a situation like crimes against children, you need to exhaust all reasonable means up until there is a certainty that the persons of interest bear no public threat. I am still obeying all laws, but it is far more reasonable for me to sort through the entirety of someone's public data if failing to do so might cause extraordinary harm to someone. The seriousness of the crime being investigated justifies a far broader scope of investigation and level of intrusion.

While some data on the internet is clearly public, there is questionable data that is publicly accessible and legally obtained, despite the owner intending it to be private. An example of this might be an Elasticsearch database that was improperly configured. If we can access it via a browser and providing no credentials, we should be in good legal standing. However, we are taking advantage of a mistake on behalf of the owner rather than something being intentionally shared. My feeling on these types of data sets is that our intentions make all the difference in deciding if it is appropriate to use them.

In the workflow section, we talked about identifying your mission goals at the beginning of any OSINT engagement. Establish the reason why you are collecting intelligence on this target. This not only helps you to get organized in your approach, but also raises the question of intent. It might be that I am following orders or fielding a request from a colleague. The target might be related to a person of interest on a larger investigation. They might even be a future employee going through a background investigation. All of these are typical and reasonable business purposes for exercising our intelligence gathering skills. Whether doing work for the public or private sectors, receiving your assignment in writing is a wise move in establishing a record of the initial request and its justification.

Deception is any behavior that misleads another person to believe something that is not true. This seems wrong when taken at face value, but there are occasions when deception is ethical and warranted. Take for example using social engineering to get your home address removed from a site run by a data-mining company. You are doing no harm to others, but you are most certainly using deception to accomplish your goal. The two most common forms of deception in open source intelligence are the use of covert accounts and the practice of infiltration or "friending" target individuals or groups. Let's look at each of these and their ethical considerations.

Covert Accounts: The use of covert accounts violates the "terms of service" of most social media platforms and online services. However, covert accounts are critical to successful queries into social media platforms, and not authenticating with these services would hamper the effectiveness of our work. If we have articulated the reasonable justification for the use of these accounts and stayed within the confines of our investigation, this deception will not be invasive to the other users. We are one of many anonymous accounts.

Infiltration: Infiltration, such as "friending" individuals or joining social media groups, is far more invasive than merely using covert accounts to run queries. When you join a group, you are, to a small degree, changing the dynamics of that group. Infiltration has its place in an ethically conducted OSINT investigation. Joining a criminal forum to gain the confidence of, and to deanonymize, child predators is a case where the greater good significantly outweighs the level of intrusion. Regardless of the mission, I make certain that I am able to articulate my justification before interacting with targets online.

Finally, I believe that we have an ethical responsibility to engage in ongoing training in both OSINT and privacy. Lack of familiarity with both technique and legal requirements leads to mistakes. Sloppy casework does a disservice to us all. We owe it to the people we serve our best efforts and discretion in making sure that we uncover the truth and bring it to light. A big piece of protecting our tradecraft is showing that we wield our tools and talents with restraint and thoughtfulness.

Professional Development

One of the most common inquiries I receive is regarding the establishment of a career in open source intelligence. This often comes from individuals in the private sector who are new to online investigations and those in the public sector looking to move into OSINT as a specialization. Although some concepts are universal, let's look at each of these scenarios. I will share some considerations for your new career.

Formal Education

If you look at practitioners in the open source intelligence field, you will find a wide variety of educational backgrounds. While there are universities that offer degrees and programs specific to analysis, intelligence, or investigations, I do not think you need to necessarily have that specific educational background. Many successful colleagues have degrees completely unrelated to this line of work, and many more have received their education from the military or other organizations which provide internal training. Some employers will require a degree or a certain number of years of secondary education, but these prerequisites tend to be arbitrary. Many will accept work experience in place of educational requirements.

Some of the most important skills in this line of work can be non-specific to our field. The ability to organize information and communicate well, both verbally and in written form, are indispensable. There are very few assignments or contracts which do not involve generating some type of written report. You can be the best researcher and investigator in the world. However, being unable to package and present your findings in an understandable and professional fashion will prevent you from successful employment.

Experience

Experience is arguably the most valuable resume item and yet it is probably the most difficult qualification to gain. Many new analysts and investigators run into the chicken-and-the-egg issue. Most employers are only looking to hire experienced professionals, but it is difficult to gain experience until you are employed. I have seen colleagues and students successfully build experience in the following ways.

- **Military Service:** Many colleagues received their initial intelligence training and experience in the military. Military service may also provide opportunities for language studies and exposure to other cultures, both of which are very valuable in our field.

- **Law Enforcement/Gov**: Many LE and government agencies have units or entire branches which provide intelligence operations, investigations, or other OSINT products on a daily basis. The downside to this approach is that you may need to provide many years of service prior to being eligible for placement into one of these specialized teams.
- **Private Sector:** Although the intelligence units in larger firms are looking for specific experience and educational backgrounds, there are other departments, such as loss prevention, which can be a foot in the door. The requirements tend to be lower but still include opportunities to use investigative skillsets.
- **Create a Program**: If you already work at an organization which does not have an OSINT function but could benefit from one, you might consider writing a proposal for adding that capability. Put together a demonstration for management and make sure to include success stories using OSINT.
- **Volunteer:** Find a person, team, or organization that does this type of work and volunteer to assist them whenever possible. If you can pass a background check, and you are able to work for free, unpaid internships are fantastic opportunities which can lead to full-time employment.

Early in your career, expect to do a lot of work that is outside of your area of interest. If you expect to be paid well to do interesting tasks, but you have little work experience, you are probably going to be disappointed. I have worked many assignments and roles which had very little to do with the intelligence field but were invaluable experiences. Be gracious, patient, eager to learn, and those disinteresting entry-level positions and internships will turn into something resembling a gratifying career.

OSINT Specific Training

Learning and honing any skill takes time. The length of time depends on your level of focus and interest, but this can be greatly influenced by the quality of learning materials. I believe that someone who is motivated can learn just about anything on a near-zero budget if they are willing to devote time, attention, and dedication. Materials such as paid courses, and even this book, simply do the research for you and accelerate the learning process. Therefore, a good learning strategy takes advantage of the resources you have available.

For those with a tight budget, you should expect to do a lot of research and self-learning. However, there are many benefits to this. Autodidactic learning is the process of figuring out something or solving a problem on your own. Conducting your own problem solving can make you a stronger investigator. Performing investigations and gathering intelligence are often exercises in problem solving. When we are given all the answers, we do not strengthen those important areas of our brains. The beauty of open source intelligence is that it builds upon itself. We are learning to get better at conducting online research, which is a skillset that we can use to locate new techniques for improving our online research. This book, a browser, and determination can get you quite far towards building your own solid skillset.

Where do live courses, bootcamps, and other premium training programs come in? If you or your employer have a healthy budget for training, and you have less time to spend doing your own research, premium training may be worth the investment. For most people, live, hands-on training is the fastest way to learn something new or to improve existing skills. Live courses tend to be quite expensive. The area between live training and self-study is where online video training resides. It affords the opportunity to watch concepts and tactics demonstrated, but often lacks the hands-on labs common to live sessions. You can do a lot with a book and determination. Having a dedicated instructor and more materials just gets you there quicker.

IntelTechniques provides a variety of training tools, including this book which is affordable for almost anyone. For those who want to accelerate their learning curve, there is online video training at **IntelTechniques.net**. If you are looking for hands on instruction, we also offer live training sessions. Regardless of your budget and goals, make sure to do your research before settling on a training program. There are dozens of OSINT "experts" claiming to have the best courses and techniques. Use the research techniques in this book to get a peek at previously released content or to find communities where people are discussing the courses and instructors. Identify your goals, do your research, and execute the work to get where you want to be.

CONCLUSION

I hope the techniques presented here have sparked your interest in finding new avenues of research and investigations. With patience and diligent effort, this book will be a helpful reference guide to assist in performing more accurate and efficient searches of open source intelligence.

Permanently documenting these techniques on paper ~~may~~ will provide outdated content. Technology changes quickly and methods must adapt to keep up. Ten years from now, this book may be an amusing piece about how we once managed our online data. To keep up to date with the changes in various OSINT strategies, please subscribe to my blog at *IntelTechniques.com*; or monitor my Twitter (X) account at *IntelTechniques*. The chances are good that as you read this, new content has been posted about the very topic you are researching.

Since the original publication of the printed edition, we have created an official digital PDF version which is an exact replica of this eleventh edition. It is designed for those who prefer a digital experience and want the ability to easily copy text or print a specific page. We respect that a digital version is much easier to access at all times than a 590-page book, and the full-color screen captures appear nicer than those in the monochrome prints. More details can be found at **https://inteltechniques.com/book1.html**.

I am often asked my opinion about the future of OSINT. In short, YOU are the future, not artificial intelligence or online services. Occasionally, I am asked to advise intelligence collection companies during the creation of a new "all-in-one" OSINT solution. I decline these requests because the easy solutions are usually short-lived. Constant changes in technology, and automated data collection restrictions, make these commercial products less powerful over time. I do not believe these can ever replace your analytical brain. The truly valuable and powerful OSINT techniques are going to require manual work from an individual investigator. Your OSINT analysis skills cannot be replaced by a machine. Please go do good things with these methods, and never allow a program to become more beneficial than you.

With this book, I am passing the torch. YOU are now the search tool. As you find new resources and modify your files, let the community know over Twitter or other networks. When you configure a new Linux application in your custom virtual machine, tell us how you did it. When an online OSINT service disappears, I am eager to hear how you resolve the issue. I am truly excited to see how we all adapt to the impending OSINT changes sure to come.

Finally, remember that each of these investigation techniques could be used against you. When you find your own information exposed, take action to protect yourself. Personal defense against OSINT is as important as offense. If you would like to stay updated on these topics, please consider my other series, *Extreme Privacy*.

Thank you for reading. ~MB & JE

A special **THANK YOU** to our editors. You make us appear smarter than we are. This book would be a mess without your input and guidance. We owe you all more credit than we can possibly give within this closing thought.

Index

Made in the USA
Monee, IL
24 July 2025

21822461R00326